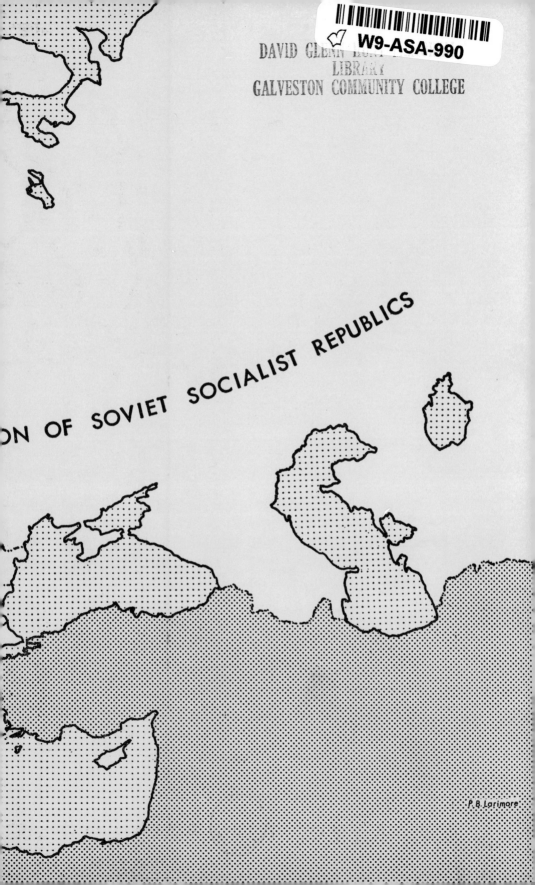

ON OF SOVIET SOCIALIST REPUBLICS

P. B. Larimore

The History Makers

The History Makers

The Press of Europe
From Its Beginnings through 1965

Kenneth E. Olson

louisiana state university press
baton rouge, 1966

Contents

v

vi *Contents*

The Neglected Makers of History

It is curious that so many European historians, in tracing the story of their own nations—even in dealing with their cultural development—have credited novelists, dramatists, poets, and essayists but have said so little about the press. They have done this despite the fact that newspapers have not only recorded their history year by year but have helped make it. In western Europe the press has played a vital role in winning independence for their peoples and in gaining for them the liberties they enjoy today. Even dictators such as Napoleon, Mussolini, and Hitler made newspapers the principal instrument for enchaining the peoples they conquered, while at the same time underground papers stirred the populace to hope and to resist till finally their conquerors were overthrown. In eastern Europe a Communist press, though better than it was a decade ago, still manipulates the news and has often kept people in ignorance during periods of crisis.

It is understandable that earlier historians might neglect their press, for in the long history of European journalism, newspapers and newspapermen have often been held in low repute. Many early newspaper proprietors were at least part-time blackmailers. Some were not above accepting bribes and throwing the support of their papers to the political leader or party which would pay most. They have often been accused of lack of courage by later critics who did not realize that death by firing squad, guillotine, burning at the stake, or garroting or sentences to the galleys or prison were the prices exacted for any criticism of government. Even in the nineteenth century Bismarck of Germany had no regard for the press. He called those papers which followed his orders his "Reptile press," for they crawled on their bellies. He bribed, thundered, and drove out those who opposed him. He professed no regard for public opinion; yet he used the German press as did no other statesman of his time to intrigue for his own advantage.

Older historians looked askance at the newspapers as a research source. Yet, as the late Dr. Frank L. Mott has pointed out, all leading contemporary workers in social, economic, and political history have found newspaper files an invaluable source. Many have found the files of the New York *Times* and the London *Times* indispensable tools, but in every western European country there are outstanding papers which are equally valuable as recorders of the history of their countries.

Despite the attempts of governments to control and use the press, in every period there have been press heroes—men who risked their lives and often gave them to provide information their people should have, or those who ventured to criticize rulers who encroached on the rights of citizens. Johan Palm in Germany was hauled out of his printing shop and shot by a French firing squad for having circulated a paper attacking the Napoleonic regime and the German princes who cooperated with it, and in so doing having started the flood of underground papers in his country; Eero Erkko of Finland bravely opposed the Russification of his people; and Harmsworth of England dared to be the most hated man in his country in order to turn the tide of battle in World War I.

Late in 1963 an old friend, Dr. Oskar Pollak of Vienna, died peacefully. That he should have done so is surprising, for during most of the thirties and early forties he was one of the most hunted men in Europe. Two years after he became editor of *Arbeiter Zeitung*, Hitler took power in Germany. Knowing there were many pro-Germans in Austria, Pollak fought Naziism. The next year an Austrian Fascist, Engelbert Dollfuss, took control in his own country. Pollak would have been the last to call himself a political theorist, but he sensed that the range of political theories is much like a horseshoe: its base, the theories of democracy and freedom; its two prongs, the extreme right and the extreme left, not far apart. So he now fought Dollfuss as he had already fought Hitler, and he became a marked man. After his newspaper was banned, he had to go underground for five years, fighting as he could to get his pleas to the people. When in 1938 Hitler took over Austria, the Nazis really set out to get Pollak. He escaped to Czechoslovakia and smuggled into Vienna a miniature edition of *Arbeiter Zeitung*. They tracked him there and he fled to Paris. When Paris fell to the Germans he managed to get to London. Once the war was over, Pollak returned to Vienna to publish his paper again; but now part of Vienna was in the Russian zone and he started right in to fight Russian oppression. So angry were Austrians with the Russians that they bought any papers which attacked them, and Pollak's paper soon led all others in circulation. Twice the Russians tried to get rid of him, but he persisted till in 1955 his nation at last won its freedom. To a casual acquaintance Pollak could have passed for a mild university professor; one could not guess the iron in his soul nor the courage in his heart. He could have been a professor, but he preferred to spend his life fighting for freedom.

The record of these heroic journalists and newspapers does not gainsay the fact that in every country there were also great literary figures, political leaders, statesmen, and prestigious social and economic thinkers who, through their books and pamphlets, enunciated their theories for the improvement of their society. Yet too often what they wrote was over the heads of the people and reached only the literati, whereas newspapers, speaking the people's language as did Cobbett's in England, reached many more.

This, then, is the history of the press of the twenty-four nations of Europe, east and west, the part it has played in the political, economic, and cultural development of their peoples, and also the story of the men who have made this press.

Whether we like it or not, almost all that the citizens of any nation know about public affairs is what they get from their newspapers, radio, television, or magazines. It is by these agencies of information that public opinion is made today, and the policies of nations may well be decided by the character of information habitually provided which marshals public opinion to permit a government to act. The inhabitants of some countries today are being taught to hate and fear the United States because when a dictatorial government has a tough program to put over on its own people, it helps to have an outside enemy against whom to stir up hate in order to rally the people and achieve the economic goals of the government.

Governments have always been concerned with the agencies which shape public opinion. The absolute monarchies which governed much of western Europe well into the nineteenth century closely controlled the press. Early editors found it safe to print only news bulletins from other countries and seldom published anything of their own domestic news. Rulers might tax their people into poverty or plunge their nations into war to satisfy their own ambitions; yet no voice of opposition was ever permitted. The press could print only such domestic news as the government thought it good for the people to know. For long periods only literary criticism was safe. As far as foreign affairs were concerned, rulers had no regard for the wishes of the people; communications were so slow that the public learned of events only long after they had happened. The 1815 Congress of Vienna could proceed with its bartering of territories and populations without regard for the people concerned, knowing that they would not learn of their fate for months and then could do nothing. The web of world life was then too loosely woven to bind nations together in any contemporaneous outlook on world affairs.

Later in the nineteenth century the nations of the western world gradually began to win their freedoms. The flame that had been lighted by the American and the French Revolutions and their declarations of the rights of man spread to other countries. It was not until after 1848, however, that in many European nations the people, urged on by their press, rose in revolt and won constitutions with parliaments to put checkreins on their monarchs. And, interestingly, the rights of a free and unfettered press were among the first reforms demanded. In France when Louis XVI had to summon the Estates General to consider the country's financial plight, among the first demands made by the three estates in their *Cahiers de Grievances* were freedom of speech and press.

In the latter half of the nineteenth century there came tremendous improvements in communications—the telegraph, cable, telephone, wireless telegraphy, radio, and later airplanes. Under their impact there was an almost literal contraction of the globe, and news from far away places became available almost as soon as it happened. People began to understand how events elsewhere might affect their lives. When diplomats met at Versailles after World War I, they had to redraw the map of Europe while constantly gauging the fears and feelings of people in every country affected. In little more than a hundred years after the Congress of Vienna a revolution had taken place in opinion-forming. Many more improvements in communications came in the twentieth century. The newest miracle, a communications satellite in outer space, enabled inhabitants of the West to occupy grandstand seats at the 1964 Tokyo Olympics.

But obstacles to the free flow of news had also arisen. In Russia a Communist regime had created a new kind of press, completely a servant of the state, manipulating the news to suit the masters of the proletariat. Dictators rose in Italy and Germany who took control of all means of news communication to keep themselves in power. In some other western states international tensions caused governments to take control of their news agencies. Even after freedoms had been restored following World War II, governments contrived to control news by withholding information.

In the United States, as free as any, newspapers have had to wage a continual battle for the people's right to know. One high Washington, D.C., official has even contended that the government has the right to manage the news. Under the Johnson administration the position of the press in the United States has deteriorated, for the President has proved most tight-lipped, not understanding that the press has the obligation to report to the people as much of the truth as it can find, not merely what one party or politician wishes. His walking news conferences have produced little news. His infrequent press conferences have been held only when he could stage-manage the event and put over his own ideas. He simply has not understood that a democracy cannot be operated in the dark.

It behooves every intelligent citizen, therefore, to understand the sources of the news which comes to him, for there is a certain amount of poison in the world's news stream. What is the character of the news agencies which distribute the news of events in their own countries? What are newspapers like in these European countries; how well do they inform their own people; and why do they react to political developments as they do? How well have they been able to achieve financial independence so that they can be politically independent?

Newspapers are different in every country. Scandinavians, Englishmen, and Americans would not, as a steady diet, like the papers of their European continental neighbors. Americans may be surprised to learn that most Europeans do not like American newspapers and protest that they are too big, too full of trashy features and advertising, making it difficult to find the news. Each people has developed newspapers which suit its interests. The kind of papers we have today in France, Germany, Italy, Greece, or any other of the twenty-four nations in western and eastern Europe can only be explained against the backdrop of the historical, political, economic, and cultural development of the people in each nation. This book is that explanation.

The world's newspaper press is a tremendous complex. Swelled by papers rising in new nations, some 40,000 exist today. This number will grow as the literacy and economy of new nations rise. UNESCO's 1964 edition of World Communications lists 7,454 daily papers. But its compilations were made in 1960–62. Since then increased production costs and competition have caused mergers and disappearances in some countries, but numbers have increased in others till in 1964 there were 7,556 dailies.* The daily papers in the twenty-four nations of western and eastern Europe considered in this study represent 28 per cent of the total number and 57 per cent of the world's total daily circulation. Hence they represent a most important segment of the world's press.

In many countries newspapers are as tightly controlled today as

---

* In each chapter final newspaper statistics must be given as reported at the end of 1964, for 1965 figures will not be available until 1966 yearbooks appear giving figures as they stood on December 31, 1965.

were those under Mussolini and Hitler, and the incursions on the press are never ending. In late 1963 Nehru, in the name of freedom, asked for legislation to permit his government to control the press. Newspaper publishers in Pakistan were ordered on the pain of prison or fines to print all government releases and to publish no proceedings of the legislature without official approval. In the Middle East, in the rest of Africa, in Asia and Latin America every new dictator quickly moves to control the press, often under the same trappings of "freedom." It must be admitted that some papers have been excitable and sometimes violent. It takes time for journalists to learn that there are two faces to the golden coin of freedom. One side represents liberty; but to merit that freedom, the other side represents at least accuracy in reporting facts.

The degree of penetration of press information depends upon important variables. In England, for long, most of the masses could not read. But it took only a generation after the passage of the 1870 Education Act till the new mass of literates wrought a revolution in the British press, and today more Englishmen buy papers every day in proportion to their population than do people in any other country in the world. In many European nations literacy is so high that every family takes one or more papers a day, permitting an unusual concentration of papers within their borders. Many other countries of the world, however, have a literacy rate so low that newspapers can reach only the upper crust of the intelligentsia. Furthermore, limited railroad lines and roads, for distribution of papers over vast distances, may limit dailies to the capital cities and permit only weeklies in provincial cities. Economics is also a limiting factor. In countries where there are few retail stores and most merchandise is sold in bazaars or markets, there can be no retail advertising and, because of low purchasing power, only a limited amount of general advertising and classified. Any country with an average per capita income of less than $300 a year is considered undeveloped, yet there are nations where this per capita income is only $80 a year. Hence, few can buy newspapers, even if they could read them.

In most of the western European nations which we shall discuss, these variables are not factors. Literacy is very high; their economies have been booming; advertising and circulation income have increased until the papers are financially independent and can keep their readers fully informed. In eastern Europe the picture is less clear. There are serious economic problems, and there is little advertising. Many newspapers may have to be supported by various devices of state subsidy, and they are concerned not so much with the distribution of news as with propaganda. We need, therefore, to understand the nature of this Communist press.

The world press, a giant in its extent, holding together cultural and nationalistic groups, is today having to report and interpret a constant succession of world crises. And what it does is so extremely important. The press of any nation can rouse its people into terrible, unthinking anger. On the other hand, it can ease tensions and promote understanding. It can shake people from complacency, or it can lull them into thoughtless and dangerous sleep as did the press of France prior to World War II.

There have been many journalists who have argued that if the press of the world were free to tell the truth and if the press of every nation were economically viable enough to stand on its own feet, this world press might be a great agency for peace and understanding between peoples. But in the present stage of world press development this can be only a hope for the future. In the press of the western European nations, which we shall discuss, this could be true now, but in that of eastern Europe it is too often an instrument for promoting misunderstanding.

The author has had so much help from European editors, publishers, and working newspapermen, university professors, museum directors, librarians, USIA men, International Press Institute friends, and American correspondents that this book is dedicated to these many friends who have helped bring it together. Grateful acknowledgment is also made to foreign journalists who have read and made valuable suggestions on the chapters submitted to them and also to European embassies and consular offices in the United States as well as the information offices of many European nations which have supplied much valuable material.

The author also acknowledges a special debt to his wife, Mildred, an ex-newspaperwoman who has edited the entire manuscript; to Mrs. Mildred Arnold, his secretary, who has done much of the typing; and to Dean I. W. Cole of the Medill School of Journalism at Northwestern University who has offered not only encouragement but also every facility and much clerical assistance in the final preparation of the manuscript.

The History Makers

Part 1

The History Makers
of Northern Europe

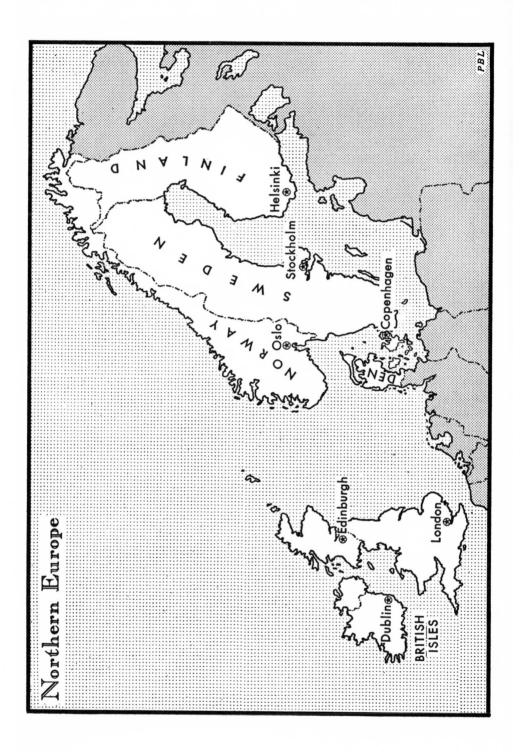

Northern Europe

FINLAND

Helsinki ⊕

SWEDEN

Stockholm ⊕

NORWAY

Oslo ⊕

Copenhagen ⊕

DEN

Edinburgh ⊕

London ⊕

Dublin ⊕

BRITISH
ISLES

PBL

Oldest Battlers for Freedom

The Press of the British Isles

John Wilkes was a libertine and a heavy drinker. But in the 1770's he was the idol of American colonists, for he dared defy King George. In that day British papers still could print nothing about parliamentary proceedings. The king and his ministers ran the country and felt that the less people knew what was going on, the better. But Wilkes, who put out a little weekly, *The North Briton*, fought this system. He had great wit, and the public loved his gibes and his calculated insolence. London powers at first let him alone, for he was "way up country" and could cause little trouble; they did not realize that the *Briton* was eagerly read by Britishers whenever they could get a copy. Wilkes was soon a public idol. When, however, he rashly criticized a speech by the king, he was arrested for "infamous seditious libel." He was acquitted, though, and even collected damages for false arrest. "Wilkes and Liberty" became a popular cry. Wilkes was only one of a long line of British newsmen who represent the oldest tradition of freedom fighters in Europe. Yet it was not until the time of the American Civil War that the British press really became free.

Nevertheless, London had made itself one of the great news and communications centers of the world; and the remarkable British people, living in an area roughly equivalent to the combined size of Illinois, Indiana, and Ohio, had won so dominant a place in world affairs that they ruled a worldwide empire. Today Britain no longer has an empire; but her press, which serves the thickly populated islands of 54,200,000 persons, is still one of the most important and interesting in Europe. The very compactness of the Isles enables London to dominate British journalism, as no American city can dominate in the United States; several of Britain's dailies run into millions of circulation. It has some of the best papers in the world and also some of the most sensational, for when papers are interested only in making money they tend to appeal to the lowest common denominators of reader interest, as their handling of the Profumo–Christine Keeler–Dr. Ward story in 1963 shows.

Printing Had to Precede Newspapers

Printing was slow in coming because England was for so long an agricultural nation. True, small manufacturing towns had developed, but they were peopled largely by artisans and merchants. The growth of larger cities, which had meant a quickening of culture on the Continent, came slowly in England. In 1450, when Paris had 300,000 population, London had only 40,000. Furthermore, rulers had dissipated the country's energies in wars abroad and at home. It was not until Edward IV became undisputed king in 1461 that conditions became favorable for cultural growth.

William Caxton, a wealthy merchant who had established a press at Bruges in Belgium, moved it to England in 1476 and set it up near Westminster Abbey, a quarter century after the first presses were used on the Continent. Unlike continental printers, who produced mainly religious and classical works, Caxton printed the best of good recent English literature, including the works of Chaucer and Lydgate. But the rulers who followed Edward gave printing little encouragement. To supervise the press, royal patents were issued to a limited number, the first to William Fagues in 1504. Under Henry VII, Henry VIII, and Queen Mary, the power of the crown to regulate printing was confirmed. Queen Elizabeth's Star Chamber ordinances set severe penalties for unauthorized printing. There are records of printers who were hanged, beheaded, tortured, branded, who had their ears cut off, or who were hounded out of the country for their temerity.

Forerunners of the Press

First came the broadsheets describing a crime, catastrophe, battle, or important death, carrying no political news, dealing only in trivialities, designed for entertainment alone, and therefore escaping official censure. Hawkers sold them on the streets. There were also educated intelligencers, news-letter-writers for statesmen and wealthy clients. Occasionally small pamphlets of foreign news were available from the Continent. From free Holland came the first newssheets printed in English; and from 1620 onward, with the outbreak of the Thirty Years War, these Dutch *corontos* had a ready, though surreptitious, sale in England.

The first *coronto* to be published in England in July, 1621, is believed to have been issued by Thomas Archer, who was arrested for his enterprise. Three months later Nicholas Bourne brought out a little newssheet without title, merely a headline which read "Coronto or Newes from Italy, Hungarie, Spaine and France, 1621." Only five issues have survived, indicating no regular publication, for Bourne evidently brought it out only when foreign events warranted. Next came the newsbooks of eight to forty-two pages, the first issued by Nathaniel Butter, Bourne, and Archer on August 2, 1622, headed "Weekley Newes from Italy, Germanie, Hungarie, Bohemia, Palatinate, France and the Low Countries." The list of countries varied from issue to issue, but the first step toward regular publication had been taken. From the founding of the first printing press, 146 years had elapsed till the establishment of a regular news publication. Other newsbooks appeared, all a rough blend of fact, conjecture, and sensationalism finding safety in avoiding any domestic news and confining themselves to foreign intelligence.

This first press soon suffered eclipse, for although English nobles had won the Magna Carta from King John at Runnymede and Tudor kings had generally observed the people's rights as represented by their Parliament, Charles I, who came to the throne in 1625, was a firm believer in the divine right of kings. He precipitated a contest of wills between himself and Parliament which finally led him to dissolve the latter for eleven years. He supressed all *corontos*, but the pressure of the people and parliamentarians forced him to relent. In 1638 Butter and Bourne were given the exclusive right to print foreign news and were able to revive their *coronto*.

Events were moving toward a climax in the contest between king and Parliament. In 1641, to demolish the machinery of absolutism, Parliament abolished the Star Chamber and other arbitrary courts and, to lay before the people its side of the controversy, permitted the publication of journals of its proceedings called Diurnals, the first English periodicals to deal with domestic news. Samuel Peck's *A Perfect Diurnal* was most important. To present the king's side, Sir John Birkenhead in 1643 brought out *Mercurius Aulicus*. Altogether some two hundred periodicals were involved in this controversy. In time some carried not only parliamentary proceedings but also political and military events. When Parliament caused the execution of two of the king's favorites, the king tried to arrest five leading members of the House of Commons. Now there was no turning back; in 1642 England was plunged into a civil war between the Cavaliers and the Roundheads. The latter found an able leader in Oliver Cromwell, a Parliament member and an astute general, whose compact army of "God-fearing men" in three years defeated the king's forces and imprisoned Charles.

The battle against royal autocracy and its suppression of civil liberties brought the desire for other freedoms. Journalistic heroes such as William Walwyn, Henry Robinson, and Richard Overton, the Tom Paine of his day, argued for press liberty. John Milton in 1644 had published his famed *Areopagitica*, best known of the great pleas for press freedom, in which he declared, "Though all the winds of doctrine were let loose to play upon the earth, so truth be in the field, we do injuriously by licensing and prohibiting to misdoubt her strength. Let her and falsehood grapple; whoever knew Truth put to the worst in a free and open encounter? Give me liberty to know and to utter and to argue freely according to conscience, above all liberties."

But Freedom Was Still Far Away

After the House of Commons had tried and executed the king, it proclaimed England a Commonwealth without a king or upper house. Cromwell, as Lord Protector, ruled without Parliament, as despotically as any king. Although he brought order at home, suppressed revolts in Ireland and Scotland, fought a successful war against the Dutch, and made England secure abroad, he was as impatient with the press as Charles. A drastically repressive act inflicted heavy penalties on printers of unauthorized publications. Licensed newsbooks were suppressed; and in their stead Cromwell authorized an official one, *Mercurius Politicus*. In 1665 there was added *Publick Intelligencer*, the two together making a semiweekly.

After Cromwell's death came the Stuart Restoration under Charles II. Again the control of printing became a royal privilege. Roger L'Estrange, a former Royalist cavalryman, was made king's licenser; and Henry Muddiman was given the right to publish newsbooks. He took over the two official court organs. But L'Estrange suppressed Muddiman's two newsbooks and brought out his own *Publick Intelligencer* in 1663. Both houses of Parliament meanwhile had issued orders against publication of their proceedings, which ruled out any diurnals. In this period of repression England went back forty years to written newsletters as the favorite method of distributing foreign and domestic news.

The year 1665 brought an interesting development. The king and his court, to escape the black plague in London, had fled to Oxford. There Charles found himself annoyed without any news. He feared to bring L'Estrange's paper lest it carry the plague, so he called in Henry Muddiman who brought out the semiweekly *Oxford Gazette*, a single sheet printed on both sides. Although it was chiefly a court gazette, it did carry some foreign news. Macaulay said at the time that it contained nothing but what the Secretary of State wished the nation to know. Earlier publications had been better papers, but now for the first time people began to speak of this single sheet as a "newspaper." When the court moved back to London, the paper became the *London Gazette*, which continues today as the official court register.

England became alarmed over the king's attempt to bring in Catholicism by force and in 1679 returned a Parliament which not only put an end to threatened absolutism but refused to renew the 1662 act regulating printing. The next three years saw the birth of some twenty papers, most important of which was Benjamin Harris' *Domestick Intelligencer or News from Both City and Country to Prevent False Reports*. All imitated the gazette format.

James II, who succeeded to the throne in 1685, proved even more pro-Catholic. His heir was his daughter Mary, wife of William II of Orange. On Parliament's plea, William came with 16,000 men, swelled by a popular rising named the "Glorious Revolution" which sent James into exile in France. Parliament then enacted a Bill of Rights which paved the way for a liberal constitution. The press benefited when in 1695 Parliament allowed the "Regulation of Printing and Licensing" act to expire. Censorship was gone and papers began taking sides in the rivalry between the Whigs and Tories. New faces in London included the *London Post* and the *English Courant*, and now provincial cities began to have papers—*The Edinburgh Gazette* in 1699, *The Worcester Journal* in 1690, and *The Norwich Post* in 1701.

England's First Daily

With the new freedoms, the time was propitious for press expansion, but the reading public was limited and advertisements few. Deficiencies were made up by subsidy as the Tories and Whigs, alternating in power, resorted to bribery for newspaper support. Yet papers did provide a wider range of news and became increasingly popular until on March 11, 1702, Elizabeth Mallet brought out the *Daily Courant* as England's first daily, filled with translations of foreign items from Dutch and French papers.

She was soon in financial trouble but was saved by a fellow printer, Samuel Buckley, who took over the paper and set a new standard in foreign news coverage. He was the first English journalist to show a real jealousy for facts; and he printed news as news without comment, to keep out of trouble. His circulation grew; his paper attracted advertising; soon he was putting out four to six pages. He made money and was able to continue for thirty years.

The next important development was the rise of the periodical. Daniel Defoe, best known as the author of *Robinson Crusoe*, the first serial story run in an English paper, was the leader. After an earlier career as a soldier and business man, he began writing pamphlets and commentaries on public affairs for several journals. He was imprisoned for his daring but after his release in 1704 began his *Review*, the first approach to an English magazine. Written entirely by Defoe in a popular style representing better writing than had appeared before, it presented more constructive criticism, not only of political, social, and moral topics but often of the lighter aspects of English life. Defoe is generally considered the father of the English editorial. *The Review* attracted many readers and continued for nine years.

The greatest influence on journalistic style came from Joseph Addison and Richard Steele, who became important figures in English literature. *The Tatler*, started in 1709, was not a newspaper, though it did carry a few short foreign news items. The bulk of its content consisted of essays on topics discussed in coffee houses, on literature, on the fads and foibles of the day; it also carried letters from contributors, real and fictitious. *The Tatler* was discontinued in 1711 after which the two brought out *The Spectator*, as a daily, the second in England. It was an instant success. While essentially moralists, Addison and Steele blended instruction with wit; hence readers found in *The Spectator*, wise and satirical comment on the follies as well as the civilized interests of the day.

The Taxes on Knowledge

Other newspapers and periodicals were springing up, but in 1712 the press suffered a sharp setback. Parliament, jealous of the increasing popularity of the press and looking for a way "to suppress its libels," imposed a tax on each sheet and on each advertisement. This forced papers to raise their prices, which was what the authorities desired. It also dried up advertising. Many papers had to close, but the people's appetite for news could not be denied and after a time circulations rose again. These taxes were doubled in 1757 and were to remain a serious handicap to the press till the middle of the nineteenth century.

By 1763 when George III (against whom Americans were to fight their revolution) had come to the throne, newspapers were beginning to be a little better off. Under England's first responsible prime minister, Sir Robert Walpole, the country had enjoyed twenty years of peace and prosperity. Then, under Sir William Pitt, who took the reins in 1757, England won from France her great possessions in North America and was confirmed in her position in India. The Industrial Revolution, now beginning to take hold, found expanded markets in the colonies; workers were attracted to cities, and they represented buying power which advertising could reach.

Henry Woodfall's *Public Advertiser*, started in 1730, had been the first to carry a larger volume of advertising. Under his son Henry Sampson Woodfall, the paper won distinction with its "Letters to Junius," whose slashing attacks on King George brought Woodfall's arrest for seditious libel. But the jury refused to convict, and the Junius letters continued. This sturdy independence was new in English journalism, and *The Advertiser* came to be considered England's foremost paper. Its advertising income enabled it to provide more news coverage and more cultural material. Other papers followed its formula and, as advertising increased, newspapers got out of the hands of printers and into those of groups of proprietors. With new stability papers now moved forward.

Wilkes, Perry, and Stuart

The Press still lacked the fundamental right to print news of government, for Parliament permitted no reporting of its proceedings. The illiberal policies of government caused great discontent in England and the colonies. It was now that John Wilkes led the fight through his *North Briton*. On his acquittal from the charge of seditious libel Boston raised the flag on Liberty Tree and the South Carolina Assembly voted 1,500 pounds to pay his debts so that he could get started again. Wilkes continued his attacks and won tacit removal of the ban on reporting parliamentary proceedings.

Among the important papers in this period was *The Morning Chronicle*, started in 1769, which under James Perry achieved real stature. He sent shorthand reporters in shifts to take down parliamentary debates verbatim; he introduced new literary features and engaged such writers as Charles Lamb, William Hazlitt, and Samuel Taylor Coleridge. He employed foreign correspondents instead of copying continental papers and went to Paris himself to report the French Revolution. His innovations raised *The Chronicle* to front rank and demonstrated that editorial excellence could make newspapering profitable.

Another important journal was *The Morning Post*, founded in 1772. Its able editor, Daniel Stuart, soon made it a dangerous rival of the *Chronicle*. Assisted by great writers such as Robert Southey and William Wordsworth and good coverage of the French Revolution, the *Post* became a top-ranking paper and by 1803 had passed the *Chronicle* in circulation.

The Coming of the Times

Meanwhile a new and formidable rival, *The Daily Universal Register*, had been started by John Walter in 1785. In 1788 it became the

London *Times*. There were already eight morning papers in London, but Walter felt he could find readers for a paper which was "a register of the times, a faithful recorder of all species of intelligence and independent of any party." He provided better governmental reporting than his rivals and more complete foreign news. His Paris correspondents scored high with reports of the terrors of 1792–93 and the execution of Louis XVI and Marie Antoinette. For the first ten years Walter had financial problems, had to accept government subsidies, and derived additional income from a form of common journalistic blackmail—accepting fees for suppression of paragraphs which might embarrass the subjects approached.

When John Walter II took over the paper in 1803, it began to show signs of responsibility. He set himself against corruption and succeeded in producing sufficient income from sales and advertising to make his paper independent. He named Thomas Barnes, a great liberal, as editor and gave him more freedom than was enjoyed by other editors. Barnes developed *The Times* into a powerful independent journal far ahead of its contemporaries in circulation and influence. *The Times* was known as "The Thunderer," and Barnes became one of the most powerful men in England, responsible for many reforms. With the help of Walter and his foreign editor, Henry Crabb Robinson, he greatly expanded foreign coverage. People learned to turn to *The Times* to see what it had to say on any subject. By 1841 it had reached a circulation of 30,000, far ahead of any competitors.

Cobbett, Voice of Reform

Most English papers were written for the upper classes; there was nothing for the common people until William Cobbett started his *Political Register* in 1802. For thirty years it was to be the most disturbing paper in England. It had become apparent that there was great need for governmental and social reform. Parliament had become a council of wealthy landlords and nobles. They dominated Parliament through a system of rotten boroughs, owned by the privileged, whereas many growing industrial cities had no representatives at all. The English criminal law was barbarous, with 250 offenses punishable by death; conditions in prisons were horrible. The introduction of steam-driven machinery in factories had made possible large scale use of child labor, and the conditions of adult workers were almost as wretched.

Cobbett preached the need for reform. He attacked public men, regardless of party. No journalist of his time equalled the blunt simplicity of his appeal to the masses, for he talked to them in their own language and tried to teach them to fight for their rights. He served time in prison, was exiled for two years, but always returned to the attack. As an editorial writer he rivaled Barnes; and, although he lacked the ability to produce the all-round type of newspaper *The Times* represented, he rendered undeniable service to the cause of the people and reform.

Press Wins Economic Freedom

Cobbett was not alone. The rising spirit of liberalism brought the passage of the Reform Bill of 1832 which did away with the rotten borough system and by some widening of the franchise brought more power to the rising middle class. Then in 1833 Parliament reduced the hours of child labor and abolished slavery in the colonies. And now, as Queen Victoria ascended the throne in 1837, England entered on a long period of change, peace, and prosperity. In 1867 the franchise was extended to double the number of voters, and it was doubled again in 1884. Criminal procedure was revised and new measures were enacted to protect factory workers. A significant change had come in 1870 with the enactment of the Public School Law, making attendance compulsory to the age of twelve. Up to 1843 a third of the men and half of the women were illiterate. Now a new generation was to be brought up which would add to the newspaper reading public.

The new Parliament of 1832 brought a changed attitude toward the press. Reformers saw that if the press could be freed of "the taxes on knowledge," cheaper papers would be possible and public opinion would have a greater opportunity for expression. Bulwer-Lytton, a press champion, pointed out that in England only one person in thirty-six bought a newspaper, whereas in Pennsylvania every fourth person did, for the simple reason that Pennsylvania papers could be bought by anyone. The first step toward economic liberation came in 1833 when the advertisement tax and the stamp tax on each copy were reduced. Some papers were able to lower their price from seven to five pence per copy, but this was still too high. Except for *The Times*, other London dailies ranged in circulation from 2,500 to 6,000. Agitation continued; time after time resolutions in Commons were beaten down in the House of Lords, but ultimately in 1853 the tax on advertisements was removed. Then in 1855 the newspaper stamp tax was discontinued after a bitter battle. It was not until 1861 that the tax on every sheet of newsprint was ended and the last of the taxes on knowledge removed through the maneuvering of William E. Gladstone, Chancellor of the Exchequer, who found a way to give effect to the bill by detouring the House of Lords. Newspapers were, at last, economically free and the time was ripe for press expansion.

Many new papers came into existence. By 1870 there were 1,490 publications, including 99 dailies and 626 magazines. There were dailies in all the big provincial cities. The now famous Manchester *Guardian*, a weekly since 1821, became a daily. Soon there appeared the Edinburgh *Scotsman*, Glasgow *Herald*, Birmingham *Post*, and many others.

Birth of the Penny Press

Lowered costs enabled papers to reduce sales prices and ushered in the development of the more popular penny press, such as had come in the United States thirty years earlier. *The Daily Telegraph*, started in 1855 as a two-penny paper, came into the hands of Joseph Levy, who made it London's first penny paper. His son, Edward Levy Lawson, really made the paper by widening its interests, giving it a more human appeal, enlisting brilliant men for its staff, and breaking tradition by providing better headline display. It became the favorite middle class popular paper of the metropolis. By 1875 it boasted a circulation of 190,000.

A formidable rival was *The Standard*, made a popular morning paper in 1857, directing its appeal to the less prosperous. By 1871 it had a 140,000 circulation. The old *Daily News*, whose first editor had been Charles Dickens, also dropped to a penny in 1861. It became the organ of the Liberal party, a leadership it was to exercise for fifty years. It earned an excellent reputation for its foreign correspondence and its literary reviews, and by 1871 it was selling 90,000 copies. A number of provincial dailies also became penny papers.

This new competition hurt the old stalwarts. The *Morning Chronicle* had had to close in 1863, the *Morning Herald* in 1869. *The Times*, refusing to lower its quality, had only dropped to three pence; and although people recognized its excellence, its circulation dropped. But under John Delane, its editor, and John Walter II, both of whom refused to compromise with the new popular journalism, the paper moved ahead. The coverage of the Crimean War (1853–56) by William Howard Russell was an outstanding feat and raised the circulation of *The Times* to 70,000. Its independence in criticizing the conduct of the war, its public services, and its zeal in helping Florence Nightingale raise funds for the care of the wounded earned the respect of all England. Yet by 1871 its circulation was down to 61,000. Of the old guard in London only *The Times*, the *Morning Advertiser*, and the *Morning Post* remained. One new paper which was to be heard from later, *The Daily Chronicle*, had been founded by Edward Lloyd in 1877. It acquired importance as a left-wing liberal paper.

Now came the new half-penny evening papers which attained great success. Outstanding was Frederick Greenwood's *Pall Mall Gazette*, founded in 1863. Under aggressive editors such as John Morley, J. L. Garvin, and W. T. Stead, it forged ahead. It was Stead who became the leader in this new journalism through his formula of putting the reader into the news by reporting divorce and other sensational stories. Sunday-only journals, which were to become a feature of English journalism, began to take hold. Lloyd's *News of the World*, Reynold's *Weekly Newspaper*, and the *Weekly Dispatch* were the first. Though they catered to the working class, it was for long considered not respectable to read a Sunday paper with its emphasis on crime and scandal. Not until after the turn of the century, when *The Observer* and the *Sunday Times* were remodeled into well-informed and responsible papers did Sunday readers spread through all classes.

News Agencies Develop

A great step forward came with the development of news agencies. At first provincial papers had had to await the arrival of London papers before they could give their readers outside news. The coming of the telegraph encouraged many to open London offices from which short wire dispatches could be sent, enabling provincials to print this news hours ahead of the arrival of London papers. But it was not till they organized a cooperative news gathering organization, Press Association Ltd., that provincial papers could provide better foreign and domestic news.

This development was speeded by the establishment of Reuters News Agency. Julius Reuter, who had worked with Havas and Wolffe on the Continent, opened an office in London in 1851, at first to provide only commercial intelligence; after 1858, foreign news as well. He was rebuffed by *The Times*, but the *Morning Advertiser* subscribed and other papers followed. Press Association also contracted for this service; thus all papers were able to expand their news coverage considerably at modest cost. As Reuters extended its service all over the world, the level of foreign news coverage in English dailies was raised. Two other agencies, Central News started in 1870 and Exchange Telegraph in 1872, added to this development.

Adapting to New Times

Despite improved news service and the public service of responsible papers, many were in poor financial condition by the end of the century. A new generation had grown up since the 1870 School Act. They could read and they wanted information; but the dailies of the day bored them, for they were heavy and verbose, filled with overdoses of politics. Long political speeches were reported down to the last cough of the speaker. Stories were headed with only discreet labels and had never a subhead. They looked dull, gray, and forbidding. Leading articles were long and took half an hour to read. The new readers could not find their way through a gray forest of solid columns and had neither the time nor the inclination to wander through them. They wanted news of sports and women's activities, interspersed with human interest stories. They could take politics only if it was made interesting. The old dailies following the nineteenth century formula were losing out.

There were men who sensed that something had to be done to get the papers read. The *Pall Mall Gazette* and the *Star* had pointed the way. A real innovator, George Newnes, brought out a sixteen-page weekly in 1881 called *TitBits* that was full of harmless little human interest stories, amusing anecdotes, and unusual bits of information similar to "fillers" in modern papers. With promotions such as free insurance against railway accidents and organized hunts for "buried treasure" for which clues were provided in *TitBits'* stories, its circulation zoomed to 700,000. Newnes' success brought imitators, the most successful being Alfred Harmsworth. While working on *Ladies Pictorial*, Harmsworth had observed the success of the *Answers to Correspondents* column, and in 1888 he began publishing *Answers* to intrigue a public thirsting for information on all manner of subjects. The first year was disappointing. Something more was needed. He offered a "pound a week for life" to the reader who guessed closest the total gold and silver in the Bank of England on a given date. A pound a week was then standard pay for working people; this was independence—everybody's dream. *Answers* soon was selling a million papers a week. Harmsworth was joined by his brothers, and together they brought out several other small periodicals. His enterprises began making great profits. He now had the wherewithal, and he began to get a glimmering of a newspaper which might reach a mass audience.

Harmsworth launched Britain's first mass paper in 1895 when he acquired the almost moribund London *Evening News* for 25,000 pounds. But it was a new kind of paper he envisioned, one that would give readers news which interested them. He gave them news in shorter stories, simply told and made clear with pictures and maps. His leader articles (principal editorials) were brief and easily understood, for they were on what he called "talking points"—what the British people were talking about that day. One day it might be a speech by a statesman, on another the Derby, or a murder trial or a rumor of war. Readers were made to feel a part of big things, and the great descriptive writers he employed made people visualize the events reported. As

McNair Wilson described it: "The London crowds hurrying home one evening found themselves transported to Windsor castle, as hosts to the young German emperor visiting Queen Victoria. They tasted a little of the flavor of royalty on a ceremonial occasion but to get it down to their level they were made to feel that the Kaiser had just come to visit his Granny as they might have done in their own families." With better headline display Harmsworth made his paper look attractive and stimulating. It caught on quickly and, since it appealed to women as well as men, the great shops and stores began to compete for advertising space. It was to go on to earn the largest evening circulation in the world.

Harmsworth saw that a national morning paper might offer greater opportunity and in 1896 launched *The Daily Mail* at a half-penny, cheaper than other morning papers. Because it was a morning journal, he felt it had to be more conservative than his *News*, even to retaining front page advertisements. He set out to provide all the news other morning papers gave but in more concise and interesting form. It was designed to appeal to everyone but, particularly, to the middle and working class men and women. He gave them foreign news, home news, sports, reports from the law and police courts, and something else—a daily magazine page with cookery, fashions, household problems, serial stories, and heart advice. People liked the fact that everything was arranged for easy reading with bright heads which told at a glance what each story was about. The first year's circulation averaged 200,000; but Harmsworth realized he had to give his readers more than others did, and with great enterprise he dispatched correspondents to all parts of the world to send back graphic firsthand accounts of the presidential election in the United States, the Turko-Grecian war, the installation of Lord Curzon as Viceroy of India, and the South African war. By 1900 his circulation was near a million.

Harmsworth's success stimulated others. Arthur Pearson, who had first worked for Newnes, then had made a fortune publishing a competitor to *TitBits*, brought out *The Daily Express* in 1900. It, too, was a half-penny paper appealing to the masses at their breakfast tables with "sunshine news and a smile." Pearson broke the old morning tradition of front page advertisments and instead provided a bright front page of news. *The Express* also won a large following. By 1904 *The Daily News* and *The Daily Chronicle* had also become half-penny papers with front news pages. All went in for picture display. The new style brought with it the pursuit of sensational news, and the exploitation of murders and trials began to be the feature of some papers.

Harmsworth, meanwhile, had established a plant at Manchester to provide simultaneous publication of the *Daily Mail* in order for it to reach quickly all parts of the country, thus adding to its circulation. In 1903 he founded the *Daily Mirror*, written by women for women; but it lost him 100,000 pounds before he turned it into a half-penny illustrated daily, England's first picture tabloid, which quickly achieved large circulation.

Harmsworth Buys The Times

This great institution had lost circulation till it was down to 38,000, which meant serious advertising losses. Then, during 1887, it made the mistake of printing articles in which it said the Irish leader Charles Stewart Parnell had signed a letter apologizing for his earlier disavowal of sympathy with the dynamite outrages of the Phoenix Park murders. Parnell had, in fact, been prostrated by the news of the murders and had said publicly that no act had so stained the name of Ireland. When the letter was proved to be a forgery, the moral standing of *The Times* was seriously hurt. C. F. Moberly Bell, general manager, no longer could pay creditors, and a court of chancery ordered the sale of the paper. Several persons, including Pearson, attempted to gain control; but when Moberly approached Harmsworth, the latter quickly put up the required 320,000 pounds. To Harmsworth this acquisition in 1908 was the fulfillment of a dream, but to many British this produced a shock such as the people of the United States might have felt had Hearst bought the New York *Times*.

Harmsworth had great respect for *The Times*, and he recognized the enormous competence of its staff of educated men. John Walter III remained chairman. George Buckle stayed as editor, and Harmsworth was only "Mr. X." When Buckle died, George Geoffrey Dawson, extremely capable, took over. While preserving the integrity of *The Times*, he worked with Harmsworth to make it more attractive and easier to read. Great new presses and other equipment were installed. But news was Harmsworth's great interest, and with Dawson's help the home news service was tremendously improved. To bring the paper within the reach of more people, he reduced the price from three pence to one pence. Far from ruining *The Times*, he not only saved it from extinction but brought about its renaissance. In a year after the outbreak of World War I its circulation had risen to 318,000.

The Years Before World War I

The era which had come to an end with the death of Queen Victoria in 1901 had been a brilliant one, but signs of international strife had appeared in many parts of the world and most embarrassingly in the

South African Boer War. Now tension came closer as Kaiser Wilhelm began arming. Newspapers voiced their fears that Germany was increasing her navy to invade England and insisted that, since Britain's whole life depended on her security, she could not afford to get behind in the naval race. Under King Edward VII and Prime Minister Herbert Asquith, Britain began a great new naval building program. The House of Lords' opposition to the budget led, in 1910, to its reform, making it only a deliberative body without any power over financial legislation. Thereafter, old age pensions, accident and unemployment insurance were adopted. The Liberals also passed the Irish Home Rule bill against violent opposition from the province of Ulster. King Edward was succeeded by George V in 1911 and now growing international tension led to the forming of the Triple Entente of Britain, France, and Russia to counter the Triple Alliance of Germany, Austria, and Italy. In this period the Harmsworth papers strongly supported the government's armament and diplomatic program.

Changes were taking place in the press. The ability of London papers to cover the country led to the demise of many provincial morning papers and the development instead of provincial evening papers which could hold their own against London. *The Times*, *Telegraph*, and *Morning Post* were still the quality London papers; *The Daily Chronicle* had some of its best years under Sir Robert Donald. A new paper, *The Daily Herald*, organ of the Labor party, was launched in 1912. Greatest casualties took place in the London evening field where the ranks were reduced from eight to three. But the "populars" led by *The Daily Mail* and *Express* were forging ahead. *The Mirror*, too, grew rapidly and was joined in the pictorial field by *The Daily Sketch* in 1909. Most important change in the Sunday field came in 1908 when Harmsworth bought the *Sunday Observer* and, with J. L. Garvin as editor, revitalized it into a new type of Sunday journal for the serious reader. Harmsworth later sold it to Lord Astor but Garvin remained editor and soon had raised its circulation to 200,000.

The Press in World War I

In the weeks before the war broke, newspapers were more concerned over a possible civil war in Ireland than with a continental war. Up to the end many were hopeful that England would not need to be involved in a European conflict. But once Germany invaded Belgium, which England was pledged to defend, the whole nation and its press rallied back of the government.

Military censorship had been imposed, but most disturbing to the press was the fact that war correspondents were barred from the front and could write only vague military communiques which glossed over the truth. Harmsworth had won the enmity of General H. H. Kitchener, supreme commander, when he published the story of the retreat from Mons. For this he was labeled as "the enemy of the army." The public and most papers were confident "Kitchener would see it through." The year 1914 had been Germany's year, but now Britons felt the tide should turn. Yet, Sir John French was skeptical. When he was ordered to attack at Neuve Chapelle with ammunition left from the Boer War, he secretly appealed to Harmsworth and asked him to send a reporter who could get news past the rigid controls Kitchener had surrounding information about the war effort. Colonel A'Court Repington, military correspondent of *The Times*, was smuggled to the front. Repington told the story of the artillery attack which failed to demolish barbed wire, trenches, and machine gun nests and left British soldiers to advance against murderous fire which mowed them down. On May 21, 1915, Harmsworth attacked Kitchener in *The Daily Mail* for having ordered the wrong kind of shells, the same kind used in the Boer War, which were useless in trench warfare and which had caused the death of thousands of British soldiers through inadequate preparation for their advance.

This attack on the most popular man in the country brought violent reaction. *The Mail* was burned in the Stock Exchange; libraries and clubs banned it; circulation fell; advertisers cancelled. But Harmsworth persisted. He appealed to fathers and mothers of British soldiers who had been killed, pointing out that their sons might be alive if the artillery had been supplied with better shells. He refused to print government advertisements for volunteers and urged the conscription of younger men so that England might have sufficient manpower for fighting on many fronts. Generals might command armies but Harmsworth talked to millions, and gradually people began to feel he was right. Before long conscription was adopted, the Asquith government was defeated, and Lloyd George became prime minister. It was he who forced the unification of the French and British war efforts under Marshal Foch which, with the aid of American forces, brought the final defeat of Germany in 1918.

The war produced some famous war correspondents, including Phillips Gibbs, Perry Robinson, Beach Thomas, Percival Phillips, and Herbert Russell, who were all later knighted. Lloyd George honored proprietors with lordships. Thus Harmsworth became Lord Northcliffe; his brother Harold, Lord Rothermere; Max Aitken of the *Express*, Lord Beaverbrook; and Lawson of the *Telegraph*, Lord

Burnham. Whereas earlier journalists had often been despised, these great figures now won recognition for their service or their political and economic power.

Press Changes

During the early twentieth century, however, a new trend in the British press had evolved which placed less emphasis on news. Max Aitken, a new figure in British journalism, had come from Canada with a fortune made in engineering a cement trust. He had entered British politics and won a seat in Commons. In 1913 he acquired a large interest in *The Daily Express* after Arthur Pearson became blind. Aitken knew little about newspapering, but after the war he took an active interest. He and his editor saw eye-to-eye on a formula of 90 per cent entertainment and 10 per cent news. By catering to low, mass intelligence they built the *Express* to the largest circulation in England.

Lord Northcliffe died in 1922; and in the estate settlement Lord Rothermere got control of *The Daily Mail*, the *Evening News*, and the *Sunday Dispatch*. He already had *The Mirror* and dailies in Glasgow and Leeds. A new force in British journalism had come in with the Berry brothers, William and James, later titled as Lord Camrose and Lord Kelmsley. They started with *The Advertising World*. In 1915 they acquired *The Sunday Times* and gave England another Sunday paper of distinction. Now they bought from the Northcliffe estate the great magazine and trade publication complex known as the Amalgamated Press.

The trend toward consolidation was setting in; and by acquiring chains of provincial papers, in addition to London papers, great press groups such as Rothermere, Beaverbrook, Berry, Cadbury, and Hulten were beginning to take shape.

Postwar Problems

Britain faced serious economic and budgetary problems after the war, but by the mid-twenties conditions had improved. The war had brought new dominion status to the colonies. Civil war in Ireland produced a new Irish Free State and a separate Ulster dominion. The people of India were becoming dissatisfied with anything less than independence. Britain had early recognized the new Russian government, but her hostility to communism led her to follow an anti-Russian policy. These were momentous news years; and while better papers kept their readers informed, the populars did less well. Postwar reaction had brought changes in reader interests, and mass paper proprietors began to feel that their readers took no interest in politics or foreign affairs unless presented with the sensation of a murder trial. Significant stories were drastically cut, leading articles shrank to twenty lines, and the columns were filled with human interest, crime, sex, fashions, cooking, sports, and entertainment—all with exaggerated display.

Although advertising income increased sharply in the late twenties and circulations zoomed with expensive promotions, the world depression which hit Britain in 1930 caused a quick decline in foreign trade and much unemployment, and forced England off the gold standard. Advertising dropped and all papers had to cut the size of their editions. It was not until 1936 that conditions returned to normal. This period also saw changes in newspaper ownership. The Berry brothers acquired the Hulten provincial papers and the London *Sunday Chronicle*. Then in 1927 they bought the *Daily Telegraph* and surprised Fleet Street by showing that there was a much larger public for a serious journal than had been believed. Next they bought the *Morning Post* and combined it with the *Telegraph* and by the late thirties had a circulation of 750,000. The Odhams Press, owning many periodicals, acquired a 51 per cent interest in Labor's *Daily Herald* in 1929 and quickly boosted its circulation from a few hundred thousand to 1,500,000. Then in 1930 England got her first Communist paper, *The Daily Worker*.

The Press and Events Leading to World War II

Hitler had come to power in Germany in 1933 and crisis mounted on crisis as he withdrew Germany from the League of Nations; started building a fleet, an army, and an air force; sent his troops into the Rhineland; and made a mockery of the Versailles Treaty. New tensions came with Mussolini's war on Ethiopia, Hitler's and the Duce's cooperation in the Spanish Civil War, and the forming of the Rome-Berlin Axis. Hitler insisted that he had no thought of attacking France or England, that he was only seeking to keep Germany from being overrun. This the English people desperately wished to believe. When the government, nevertheless, speeded up armament, the Labor Party and its *Herald* fought defense budgets and conscription right to the very eve of the war. *The Times, The Telegraph-Post, Daily Mail,* and other responsible papers kept their readers informed of what was happening on the Continent; but the more sensational populars, sensing the pacifist mood of the masses, gave scant information on these momentous events and filled their columns with human interest and entertainment.

Winston Churchill, who dared to warn of Germany's intent, was regarded as a dangerous warmonger. Even after Hitler had taken Austria and Neville Chamberlain had returned from Munich, after capitulating to Hitler, many papers bannered the prime minister's claim that "We have Won Peace in our Time." *The Telegraph* was the strongest voice against appeasement but as late as July, 1939, *The Express* proclaimed, "There will be no European War involving Britain this year or next." However, Britain had guaranteed aid to Poland, if attacked; and on September 3, 1939, after the Germans had loosed their blitz on Warsaw, Britain declared war.

Covering the War

Once the die was cast the British people closed ranks. There was a job to be done and all rallied back of Churchill, who had become prime minister. Soldiers, seamen, and airmen proved their mettle in terrible battle. At home people lived through what Churchill called "their finest hour" under concentrated German air attacks intended to soften up England for invasion. But the Germans could not cow the British, and the RAF destroyed so many German planes that by the spring of 1941 Britain was seriously bombing Germany.

This time military chiefs realized the importance of keeping their people and the world informed. Correspondents were allowed on the front with the fighting men and given facilities for speeding their dispatches home. Never was a war covered as was this one. Fighting fronts spread from Norway, Denmark, the Low Countries, and France, to the miracle of Dunkirk, the German conquest of the Balkans, and the battles leading to the surrender of Axis forces in Africa. The bitter invasion of Italy, the liberation of France, then the climax of the Normandy landings led to the invasion of Germany and the surrender of the Nazis in ruined Berlin. In the Far East there followed the reconquest of the great areas taken by Japan till finally the bombing of Hiroshima and Nagasaki brought the quick surrender. Allied newsmen covered every front except the Russian, where only battle reporters for *Red Star* were permitted. Scores of correspondents were killed or wounded.

On the home front papers were irked by the ineptness, slowness, and multiplicity of military censors through which a story had to go and by the stupidity of certain regulations—for example, when Bristol was subjected to one of the worst bombings of the war and no paper was permitted to name the city. The Bristol *Mirror* next morning had to act as if none of the city's 400,000 people knew what had happened and could only headline, "Big Night Raid on West Town."

For a year after September, 1940, Fleet Street newspaper plants suffered heavy bombing damage. *The Evening Standard* and the *Daily Herald* were among the first hit. *The Times* was seriously damaged by direct hits. *The Daily Sketch, Telegraph*, the old *Daily News* building, and the *News of the World* plant were set on fire. In most cases alternate arrangements had been made in advance. When the author visited *The Times* plant in 1945, he saw press, composing rooms, and editorial offices in subbasements far underground. In other cases undamaged papers printed editions for those hit. Usually continuous production was delayed only a few hours. In the provinces as plants were hit in Coventry, Belfast, Cardiff, Yorkshire, and other cities, neighbors undertook their printing as well as their own. Because Britain was cut off from her normal newsprint supply, dailies that wished to keep their present circulation were reduced to four pages. Only *The Times* and *Telegraph* elected to cut off a fourth of their circulation in order to have six pages for better news coverage; even the populars eased their human interest formula to tell the story of the war adequately if not fully. Again, because of rationing, papers could no longer placard their heads on news posters and had to use their front pages for news instead of advertising. *The Daily Mirror* was threatened with suspension and severely castigated by other papers for fomenting opposition to successful prosecution of the war. *The Daily Worker*, the communist organ, was suppressed for nineteen months for its subversive activities.

Despite their war difficulties most papers managed to carry on financially. The general manager of *The News Chronicle* explained to the author that the reduced size of the paper had cut costs, that even with the loss of many younger men to armed services those left could still get out smaller papers. Thus payrolls were lower, and all papers abandoned their previous costly circulation promotions. Furthermore, with limited space, old advertising rates were gone and everything was sold at higher special position rates. There were casualties, however, among weeklies; and some magazines and periodicals were either suspended or amalgamated. For all dailies, circulations had risen from 19,000,000 in 1938 to 25,000,000 by the end of the war.

The Aftermath

When the war was over the people wanted a new deal, despite their veneration of Churchill. Labor won a smashing victory in 1945, and *The Herald* became important as the voice of the Clement Atlee government as it nationalized the Bank of England, communications services, coal mines, and railroads. In three years old-age pensions and free medical and hospital services had been put into effect. Conservative papers tried to apply the brakes; but the wealthy owners of the populars, while themselves conservative, sensed the postwar mood of the masses and supported what their readers wanted.

Unfavorable trade balances forced the Labor government to an austerity program of continued food, clothing, and newsprint rationing. But the European recovery program, backed by billions in American aid, brought a rapid comeback. Although papers were not entirely freed from newsprint restrictions until 1957, circulations were not limited and boomed, particularly those of the populars.

Government Examines the Press

The press became the subject of a parliamentary inquiry in 1947 when the National Union of Journalists, disturbed over monopolistic tendencies in the control of papers, urged an inquiry to see what could be done to further free expression of opinion. A Royal Commission returned its report in 1949. It found that "the present degree of concentration in ownerships . . . is not as great as to prejudice free expression of opinion and accurate presentation of news." It asserted that the press was free of corruption and that there was negligible evidence of advertising influence, but admitted that the failure of the press to meet the requirements of society was attributable to the fact that an industry, which lived by the sale of its product, had to give the public what it would buy and that the tendency to lower standards to gain advantage over competitors was not always resisted. Some sober newsmen felt it was a whitewash, but Sir George Waters of *The Scotsman* pointed out that the commission's criticisms showed signs of ill health in British journalism.

Acting on the commission's recommendation that a General Council of the Press be established to safeguard freedom by encouraging the growth of responsibility, this council has made annual reports citing papers for irresponsibility, sensation, and inaccuracy. Some continental observers have felt that these citations were mere slaps on the wrist, yet the council's reprimands have been by no means ineffective. Even the censured papers print its reports, and most journalists take note of them. There has been a growing awareness of the need for a satisfactory code of professional conduct. It is significant that in its 1963 report the council scored the handling of the Profumo—Ward—Keeler story and particularly condemned *The News of the World* for paying 23,000 pounds to print Christine Keeler's sordid confessions. "By exploiting vice and sex for commercial reward," said the report, "*The News of the World* has done a disservice both to public welfare and the press." What disturbed sober English journalists was that the populars were becoming more sensational in their efforts to gain readers. As Britain gave up her colonies and relinquished her international role, the populars gave less space to significant news and placed more emphasis on crime, sex, human interest, and entertainment.

The trend toward consolidation continued with the emergence of two new press lords. Roy Thompson, a Canadian publisher, invaded Britain to buy the London *Sunday Times, The Sunday Graphic*, the Manchester *Empire News*, and thirteen of Kelmsley's provincial dailies. Then Cecil Harmsworth King, nephew of Lord Northcliffe, with a talent for money-making, took over the *Daily Mirror, The Sunday Pictorial*, and a great group of trade publications.

The Country Moves Ahead

The Conservatives again came into power in 1951 with Churchill as prime minister; he resigned in 1955 and was succeeded by Anthony Eden. The latter did not survive the Suez crisis and gave way to Harold Macmillan. Now with a more stable government, Britain was launched on her greatest boom. Wages had gone up till working men had more spending power than ever before, and with an enormous increase in installment buying, advertising increased. New buildings rose everywhere; new steel and glass skyscrapers changed the face of London. Nevertheless, the late fifties and early sixties were difficult for newspapers. Circulations rose to an all-time high during the Suez crisis and the Soviet suppression of the Hungarian revolt. But increased production costs forced all the populars to raise their prices to 2½ pence. Readers decided that instead of buying two or three papers a day they would get along with their favorite, and circulations were hard hit. The advent of commercial television also hurt, as big advertisers shifted large expenditures to this new medium. Curiously, while all the big populars lost circulation, the quality *Times, Guardian*, and *Telegraph* gained. In the Sunday field the *Times* and *Observer* rose while the lurid papers showed losses of near 20 per cent.

These were serious conditions, for British papers had long depended on circulation for half of their income. October, 1960, brought a tragic episode when three large circulation papers died in a week. It started when Roy Thompson closed his Manchester *Sunday Empire News*, for even with a 2,000,000 circulation, it was losing money. A seven-weeks' strike of mechanical workers forced the sale of the final liberal *News Chronicle* with over 1,000,000 circulation to the *Daily Mail*. This really shocked Fleet Street, and the closure of its evening companion, *The Star*, reduced London's evening press to two, *The Evening News* and *The Evening Standard*, both circulating largely in a fifty-mile radius of London, both centering on sports, racing, and entertainment, with little significant news. Continued economic problems and the rising costs of production caused further losses in both the provincial evening and morning fields. A special Royal Commission to investigate press problems put the blame on printing craft unions for bleeding papers to death through appalling inefficiency and waste, featherbedding, enforced overemployment, insistence on archaic methods which entailed excessive costs, and unwarranted wage demands despite the fact that these unions enjoyed the highest wage scale in British industry. The dominance of London morning papers through their ability to cover the country dealt provincial morning papers a blow. The big chains absorbed some; many had to suspend. In 1921 there had been seventy-one provincial morning dailies; in 1964 only twenty-six were left. The dominance of the "London mornings" is indicated by the fact that in 1964, of a total morning circulation of 18,423,447, the London papers had 16,234,165 and four big populars had 81.3 per cent of that. Nevertheless, a number of provincial morning papers including the *Birmingham Post*, Darlington's *Northern Echo*, Glasgow *Daily Record*, Belfast *Telegram*, Dublin's *Irish Independent*, and the Yorkshire *Post* are influential papers, strong in their territories; and the Manchester *Guardian* has gained such national independence that it has moved its base of operations to London.

Fleet Street received another shock in September, 1964, when King, despairing of reviving *The Daily Herald* in spite of the vast sums poured in, closed it. It was succeeded almost at once by *The Sun*, put out by the old *Herald* staff but with new techniques of display and a new approach on content, the first British paper conceived on the results of market research. It started well with a curiosity circulation of 3,000,000 but quickly slumped and by November, 1965, was down to 1,300,000. Though it was losing money, by the end of the year King had not yet decided what to do with it.

The provincial papers represent largely an evening press. They number seventy, and with great attention to local and regional news they carry weight in their areas. Five with circulations of between 200,000 and 450,000, including the Glasgow *Evening Citizen*, Liverpool *Echo and Evening Express*, Newcastle *Evening Telegraph*, Manchester *Evening News and Chronicle* and Sheffield *Star*, are important papers. Not counting three small London dailies devoted to sports, retailing, and advertising, the British Isles in 1964 had 109 regular daily papers with a total circulation of 28,049,837 as compared with 123 dailies with 22,700,000 in 1961. Thus, while there has been a loss of fourteen dailies, the resulting combinations have shown an increase in circulation. By geographic distribution, England has seventy-three, Scotland twelve, North Ireland three, South Ireland seven, Wales four, and the small islands three.

The Sunday press is still a phenomenon. It consists of fifteen papers, eight in London, two each in Glasgow and Dublin, and one each in Birmingham, Newcastle, and Plymouth. Yet they have a total circulation of 27,466,730, almost equal to all morning and evening dailies together. These are not Sunday editions of regular dailies but separate operations. Visitors to London frequently think *The Sunday Times* is a Sunday edition of *The Times*, but they have no connection. *The Sunday Times* is part of the Thompson Press, a quality paper which provides serious treatment of the news and excellent backgrounding and has attained a circulation of 1,240,239. The circulation leader, despite a loss of over 2,000,000, is still the *Sunday News of the World* with 6,224,174. Britain also has some 1200 country and suburban weeklies.

One striking fact about the British press is the monopoly situation which prevails in the seventy-one cities where newspapers are published. In fifty cities there is but one local daily, and in thirteen others both morning and evening papers are owned by the same publishing company. It has been charged that this deprives people in these sixty-three cities of a choice of different political opinions, but this situation is more apparent than real because of the availability of national morning and Sunday papers of political diversity. This monopoly situation is due to economic competition which has forced consolidations and the sale of papers to newspaper chains. Of the 109 regular dailies almost half are owned by chains. Some are small, involving only two or three towns; four are tremendous.

When Cecil Harmsworth King in 1961 won control of Odhams Press, it gave him virtual monopoly in mass magazines, an overwhelming position in trade publications, plus ownership of *The Daily Herald* and one of the largest Sunday papers, *The People*—altogether one of the largest magazine and newspaper publishing groups in the world with 252 magazines and newspapers. The star of his empire is *The Mirror* with 5,000,000 circulation which he says "provides light entertainment to millions laced with what instruction the traffic might bear."

Even more important from the newspaper standpoint is the Thompson chain which owns not only *The Sunday Times*, two other Sunday papers, and fifteen provincial dailies, but sixty-five papers in six other countries from Canada to Africa. Then there is the Rothermere group which has the *Daily Mail*, *The Daily Sketch*, and the London *Evening*

News plus fifteen provincial dailies. Important from the standpoint of circulation is the Beaverbrook group, whose founder died in 1964 but was succeeded by his son as the new Lord Beaverbrook to carry on the same policies. It has the London *Daily Express, The Sunday Express,* the London *Evening Standard,* and the Glasgow *Evening Citizen.* Interesting also is the Westminster group, founded by Quakers who after making fortunes in breweries and chocolate decided to use them for the good of the country and founded this chain of nine good provincial dailies, all operating under considerable local autonomy. Altogether chain newspapers account for 76 per cent of the total daily circulation. Another interesting fact is that of the morning nationals, so important in Britain, the class papers (*The Times, Telegraph, Guardian*), with 1,871,069 circulation, represent only 11.5 per cent of the total compared to 16,102,879 for the populars.

Why This Distribution?

Why do 88.5 per cent of the people who buy morning nationals vote day by day for the sensation, news triviality, human interest, entertainment fare of the populars? In explanation it might be pointed out that up to World War II, 90 per cent of the people had only an elementary school education, the last years of which were in trade schools. While secondary schools have been expanded, and more are added each year, the great majority of people have not had a secondary school education; also, while Britain has some of the best universities in the world, and the opportunity for higher education has been broadened and democratized, the percentage of university graduates is small. In the 1963–64 school year Britain had only 130,000 students in universities. Thus the great masses choose daily the papers which give them a minimum of hard news and provide instead a heavy diet of sensation, human interest, and entertainment. It is true the populars have often capitalized on crusades, many trivial, some worthwhile. As Rebecca West pointed out in "The Vassal Affair," it was the populars which stirred the nation to a recognition of security dangers beginning with the Burgess–MacLean case. On the other hand it may be true, as some critics assert, that when the populars have had any influence on public opinion it has been when they supported their readers' preconceived notions of how a given issue might affect them personally. Sir Gerald Barry, long editor of one of England's outstanding reviews, delivered one of the most scathing criticisms of all when he said: "The populars exert a myopic influence, inculcating false notions of life, false sets of values—values which invite the reader to think of Hollywood as more important than H-Bombs—or rather never to think at all."

The Wilson Labor government won by a narrow margin in 1964. Although supported by this same mass audience, Wilson talked darkly of controlling the press by curbing the immense advertising expenditures. He began an ambitious program of nationalizing steel, reforming taxation, and increasing social benefits; but when Britain's economy sagged seriously, he had to impose import surcharges and increase taxes. Surcharges on newsprint forced many papers to raise their sales prices, but increased income soon improved newspaper finances.

Britain faced a crisis in November, 1965, when white Rhodesia declared her independence. Supported by Conservatives and Liberals, Wilson inflicted severe economic sanctions. It was soon clear, however, that Rhodesia, despite the economic squeeze, would make good her bid for independence. Wilson had not dared send troops for fear of bringing Conservative opposition. When, because of deaths, his majority in Parliament was reduced to one, Conservative papers began to hope that Wilson's austerity program might cause the fall of the Labor government. Moreover, in an attempt to hold the votes of the nine Labor M.P.'s, in his year-end statement of policy he did not mention nationalization of steel and warned against wage increases. The Conservative *Daily Mail* headlined this report, "The Day They Buried Socialism."

The British are the world's most insatiable newspaper readers. UNESCO in its 1964 "World Communications" reported that they buy 50.6 copies per 100 persons compared with 46.2 for the Swedes, 38.4 for Norwegians, and 35.8 for Finns.

News Agencies Play Large Role

British papers are well provided with news agencies to supplement their own news-gathering efforts. Most important is Press Association, cooperatively owned by the provincial dailies, with some 1,750 full- and part-time correspondents covering news from all over the British Isles and furnishing also a comprehensive daily report on parliamentary proceedings and news from other London government offices. Then there is Exchange Telegraph Company Ltd. (Extel) which provides not only national and foreign news but complete reports on fast breaking financial and sports developments through some 1000 full- and part-time correspondents.

While the Associated Press and United Press International do serve a number of British papers with foreign news, by far the greatest number are served by Reuters, now cooperatively owned by Press Association, the London Newspaper Proprietors Association, the Australian Associated Press, and the New Zealand Press Association. With its independence and integrity guaranteed by a trust arrangement,

Reuters operates one of the world's largest news-gathering agencies serving papers directly in 110 countries and many others indirectly through the forty-five agencies with which it has exchange agreements. In addition, many British dailies and Sunday papers have their own correspondents in the major capitals of the world. There are usually from fifty to sixty British correspondents in Washington, D.C., and New York.

What Britain Owes Its Press

It must be recognized that Parliament and the British press are the two institutions to which the British people owe their freedoms. For long years despotic rulers and the House of Lords held the press in chains. It was not until 1770 that newspapermen won the right to publish parlimentary proceedings. For almost another century Parliament kept the press in economic fetters with its taxes on knowledge. Once free, the press brought reforms in Britain's rotten electoral system, won the franchise for masses who had not been able to vote, brought about changes in criminal procedure, and fought for measures to protect factory workers and provide wider educational opportunities.

A little more than 150 years ago Macaulay spoke of the press as having become "an estate of the Realm." It has only been a hundred years since the British press won its freedom. In that century it has won many worthwhile changes for its people. The British press today has its problems but the press of no nation is perfect. Britain's press will change, for its public is changing; and in another generation, as a higher level of education permeates, today's press will have to evolve just as it had to at the end of the nineteenth century when Harmsworth found the papers of that day were not meeting the needs of the public. And though newspapermen were at first reluctant to accept the censures of the Press Council, these are slowly but surely proving a healthy influence and awakening an awareness of the need for a higher standard of professional responsibility.

REPRESENTATIVE NEWSPAPERS

British newspapers vary widely in appearance and news presentation, depending upon their character. *The Times, Telegraph, Express, Daily Mail, Guardian,* and many fine provincial papers appear in full-size pages. *The Mirror* and *The Daily Sketch* are picture tabloids. Here are thumbnail sketches of some representative papers:

The Times. One of the oldest and most respected, with a circulation of 256,123. Stays with old tradition of a front page cover of classified. Its real front page is the center spread. Content is departmentalized starting with sports, home news, government and parliamentary news, overseas news, to the main news page in the center, opposite which is the editorial and letters page. Next is a cultural page and one of law and court reports, followed by six pages of finance and business. It appeals to the intelligentsia and government and business leaders. Rich in advertising for it goes to the quarter million most important breakfast tables. Independent Conservative and one of the most influential papers in Britain.

The Telegraph. Circulation 1,343,247. A quality paper which looks more like an American paper with a good front newspage. Considered by many as providing the most news. More popular than *The Times,* with Family Forum pages carrying well-illustrated women's features, several pages of sports, but with excellent foreign and national news coverage and good background articles and columns. It, too, is heavy with advertising for it caters to higher incomes. Generally regarded as the quasi-official voice of the Conservative party.

The Daily Mail. Circulation 2,423,424. Most newsworthy of the populars. Aggressive display; stories in capsule form; short, easy-to-read editorials; even heads are "folksy." Top national and foreign stories followed by pages of local and home news with plenty of crime, sensation, and well-illustrated pages of features to titillate the mass reader. Filled with advertising. Conservative with strong imperialist orientation.

The Manchester *Guardian.* Circulation 271,739. From a provincial serving prosperous north England it has made itself a national paper; strong liberal views of national and foreign affairs; often quoted. Thorough coverage of foreign and home news. More attractive in display than either *Times* or *Telegraph.* Strong on background articles, cultural affairs. Has been growing in popularity with those who wish to keep informed.

The Daily Express. Circulation 4,329,128. Much more aggressive in display than *Mail.* Front page plays top national and foreign news from Beaverbrook outlook but always has a good crime story and many short-short stories. Then follow pages profusely illustrated featuring crime, sex, human interest. There are women's pages, popular columnists, guides to London's night life, much sports, featuring racing news and betting tips. Politically independent, conservative but reflecting the prejudices of its empire-conscious owner. Critical of U.N.; fought Britain's entry in Common Market; criticizes U.S.

The Daily Mirror. Circulation 4,951,488. England's largest. A sensational picture tabloid—raucous journalism at its loudest. "Terror in the City," "The Kiss-and-Run Gunman," "Persian Delight—Belly Dancing," "Was Johnny Killed to Cover up Lovers' Secret?" plus plenty of cheesecake pictures, comic strips, entertainment features. Has some widely read columnists, particularly the vitriolic "Cassandra." Weak on significant news, but it makes money. Usually pro-Labor.

The Daily Worker. A poor sheet of few pages. Follows religiously the Moscow line. Official organ of British Communist party. Makes a pretense of being a national paper but it has only 61,256 circulation and has made this same claim year after year.

The Newspapers of Sweden

Lars Johan Hierta was disgusted with the spinelessness of Swedish papers which had for so long been held down by royal autocrats that they seldom dared take a stand on anything. He started *Aftonbladet* (Evening News) in 1830 with a new idea. Inspired by the liberalism sweeping Europe, in courageous editorials he championed humanitarian and economic reforms. For ten years he fought and was suppressed, fought on and was suppressed. But under the law, permission to publish a new paper could not be refused another person. Each time he was stopped, he got dummy editors to publish his paper under slightly changed titles such as *Nya* (New) *Aftonbladet, Tredje* (Third) *Aftonbladet,* and *Fjarde* (Fourth) *Aftonbladet,* until he made a laughing stock of the government's policy and after a decade forced a more liberal attitude toward the press. Hierta was but one of the great figures who made this press an invincible power in the nation.

Sweden, with an advanced civilization, is the fourth largest country in Europe. Her area is comparable to that of Minnesota, Iowa, and Missouri combined. She supports some excellent newspapers; and although her 7,600,000 people represent only a seventh of the United Kingdom's population, she has as many daily papers as England, Scotland, Wales, and Ireland together. It is a beautiful land of plains, forests, and 96,000 lakes; and though it reaches above the Arctic Circle, the climate is tempered by the Gulf Stream. Five-sixths of her people live in the southern half; in the north they are more thinly spread. Hence Stockholm cannot dominate its country as does London, and Sweden has many strong provincial papers.

Precursors of the Press and Its Beginnings

In 1483, seven years after William Caxton had set up the first press in England, Sweden had her first printed book; but it took 150 years for a newspaper press to emerge. This was the time of great warrior

kings. Gustav Vasa who, after defeating Denmark and winning independence for Sweden came to power as Gustav I, relied upon handwritten newsletters for his intelligence from the Continent. The first
printed *flygblad* (flysheet) appeared in 1673 and dealt with the coming
of a comet. Others followed, all dealing with mysteries and unnatural
phenomena; but in 1598 there was printed in Stockholm the first
newssheet with real news. Catering to public interest in foreign news,
such sheets increased in the next twenty-five years.

Then in 1624, three years after Bourne, Butter, and Archer had
brought out England's first weekly, there appeared at Stregnes *Hermes
Gothicus*, a forty-page news journal carrying news from Sweden,
Italy, Spain, France, Germany, England, Norway, Denmark, Holland,
Russia, and Turkey. Only one copy is in existence. If that copy were
one of a regular series, it may have been Sweden's first newspaper. Ten
years later there appeared in Stockholm *Aviso* (News), which many
consider Sweden's first. It reported events of the Thirty Years War, as
well as other foreign happenings. Sometimes it was guilty of reporting
rumor as when it created a sensation with a story that the Pope was
about to abdicate in order to marry.

Sweden's intervention in the Thirty Years War under Gustavus II
Adolphus raised her to the status of a great power. At home the king
reorganized his government, drew plans for a postal system which later
was to facilitate the distribution of newspapers, and established a
Council of State, a parliament, and law courts. His death in the battle
of Lutzen, brought to the throne his daughter, Christina, but the reins
of government were held by a great statesman, Axel Oxenstierna.
During his regency Swedish armies swept as far south as Prague, and in
the Peace of Westphalia Sweden was confirmed in her control of the
Baltic and part of northern Germany.

It was in 1645 that Sweden's oldest existing paper was established.
Postmaster General Johan Beijer under royal initiative brought out
Ordinarie Posttijdender. He was given access to the government's
news correspondence and to foreign newspapers received; but he had
to maintain his own correspondents in Germany, France, Holland, and
Italy. This paper was distributed to postmasters in Sweden, Finland,
and the Swedish provinces across the Baltic where news could be read
to the public. As an official paper it carried nothing which might
adversely affect the king or the government. During the rest of the
seventeenth century this journal was Sweden's only paper, later called
Posttidningen, a closely censored organ until 1791, when the Swedish
Academy took it over and gave it a more cultural role. It now became
known as *Post och Inrikes Tidningar*, which is its title today as a
government gazette.

Karl X, who succeeded Christina, added to Swedish territory by taking from Denmark the valuable southern province of Skåne, giving his country her natural boundary to the tip of the peninsula. He also inaugurated social and economic reforms necessary to Sweden's stability. His successor Karl XI was of a different stripe. He broke the power of the nobility and of the *Riksdag* (parliament) and established royal despotism. *Posttidningen* now became only an organ for royal decrees. Underground newssheets began to appear to inform the people of their monarch's disastrous wars against Russia, Denmark, Saxony, and Poland—wars which lost Sweden her entire empire except Finland and reduced the nation to poverty. His successor, Karl XII, was no better and in further unsuccessful wars brought ruin to the country. On his death the *Riksdag* voted to end the absolute power of the monarch and drew up the new constitution of 1719.

The half century following has been called the Era of Liberty, a period of cultural development, scientific progress, the beginnings of industrial life, and economic recovery. A second privileged paper, the *Stockholm Gazette* published by Peter Momma, appeared in 1742. Both it and *Posttidningen* gradually improved, printing more foreign and domestic news.

Unprivileged papers, unable to publish political news or comment, turned literary. First of this character was *Then Swänska Argus* (1732), edited by Olof von Dalin, one of the literary figures of the day. His journal with its essays and literary criticisms resembled the *Tatler* and *Spectator* in England. *Den Swänska Mercurius*, published by C. C. Gjorwell, was both literary and scientific. Then in 1775 came the first independent political weekly, *En Ärlig Swensk* (An Honorable Swede). Its publisher, Nicolas von Oelreich, was the official censor, but he believed in greater freedom; when the king tried to augment his own power, Oelreich, with the support of *Riksdag* members, used his weekly to plead the cause of liberty and enlightenment. His paper was followed by others in the capital and the provinces. The first provincial paper, *Göteborgs Wekolista*, was founded in 1749; then *Carlscrona Wekoblad* in 1754, and *Norrköpings Wekotidningar* in 1758. The latter still survives as *Norrköpings Tidningar-Östergötland's Dagblad*.

A First Taste of Freedom

The year 1766 was an important landmark for the Swedish press as censorship was abolished and the press made free. This brought an increasing number of papers, among them the first daily, *Dagligt Allehanda* (Daily General News). Peter Momma, who had been publishing the weekly *Stockholm Gazette*, began in 1769 to put out a daily supplement which his son William developed into a regular daily. The latter, a man of enterprise, began providing more news, not only Swedish news but foreign news lifted from German papers. Readers liked getting reports daily instead of waiting for *Posttidningen*. Circulation grew and soon began to attract advertising. Momma developed another source of income by charging space rates for contributed articles, and men who wished to voice their opinions found it cheaper to pay Momma than to get out pamphlets. Hence his columns were soon lively with political discussion. To increase interest he began running serial stories thus introducing the *feulleton*, which fifty years later was to prove so popular in France. To swell sales he employed vendors to cry his latest news and so initiated street sales. By many promotional devices and by developing a piquant, newsy style, he made his paper the most widely distributed in Sweden. It survived till 1944. Another important publisher of this period was Johan Rosen whose *Hwad Nytt? Hwad Nytt?* (What News? What News?) appeared in Göteborg.

The furious disagreements involved in the *Riksdag* battles between the Hat Party and the commoners of the Cap Party brought a flood of political publications often violently vituperative. When these conflicts brought the *Riksdag* to complete ineffectiveness and the country to near anarchy, the new king, Gustav III, by a coup forced the adoption of a new constitution in 1772 to put an end to party strife and strengthen the monarchy. The king's advisers, stung by criticism of the government and what they felt were abuses of press freedom, tried to persuade the king to restrict this liberty; but the king contended that the advantages of a free press outweighed its disadvantages and that it was important for the king, through an uninhibited press, to learn the true thoughts of the people. As newspaper criticism mounted, he finally yielded however, and rescinded the free press laws. Thus Sweden's first press freedom lasted only six years. The king extended his power and during the rest of his reign and that of his successor, Gustav IV, the press remained fettered.

War with Russia Brings Change

Gustav IV was dethroned in 1809 after a costly war with Russia brought the loss of Finland, which had been united to Sweden for six hundred years. His despotism, moreover, had alienated the people. The revolt led by the army was inspired by liberals who had caught the spark of freedom from the French Revolution. The new constitution guaranteed citizens protection of their rights against any attempt by the sovereign to subvert them, established parliamentary government, and vested control of finances in the *Riksdag*. Press freedom was made explicit by a clause which guaranteed every Swede, without obstacles being put in his way by public power, the right to publish writings, and provided that he could be prosecuted in a lawful court only if his contents had transgressed a definite law.

Royal tyranny was now ended, and Sweden entered a new and happier era. A Danish uncle of the deposed king held the throne briefly; then in 1800 the Swedes elected Marshal Bernadotte, one of Napoleon's generals, to occupy the throne as Charles XIV. To the Swedes he was known as Karl Johan and they came to love him. He had been chosen because the Swedes wanted a ruler with Napoleon's blessing, hoping that the French emperor might help them regain Finland. But Karl Johan, a wary realist, set himself against all schemes for the reconquest of Finland, "that testament of wars and misfortunes," rebuffed Napoleon's attempt to involve Sweden in war with England, sought peaceful relations with Russia, and turned westward, seeking union with Norway. A brief war with Denmark forced her to cede Norway, and the two nations were united in 1814 as free and independent realms under one king. Peace had come at last, and Karl Johan set his nation to building up its internal economy, its foreign trade, and its cultural and material well-being.

Birth of the Modern Press

In spite of their new freedom, Swedish papers, because they had been held down so long, did not take advantage of the opportunity to exercise political leadership. It was not till the 1830's that a modern press began to emerge. The leader was Lars Johan Hierta who in 1830, when the penny press was being born in the United States founded *Aftonbladet*, which was to revolutionize Swedish journalism. He adopted a new format and makeup for a newsier-looking, more interesting appearance and arranged for speedier publication of much more news, both foreign and domestic. It is, however, as father of the Swedish editorial that he is best known. Hierta, a strong liberal, conducted an indefatigable campaign for needed reforms and, despite frequent suppressions, gained circulation and influence till the Swedish poet Esaias Tegner complained that *Aftonbladet* had "become the bible of the Swedes." Meanwhile *Dagligt Allehanda*, which as more of an advertising paper had survived the years of repression, became a political journal and fought alongside Hierta. In Göteborg the *Handels och Sjöfarts Tidning*, founded in 1832 as a commercial and shipping paper, also took its place as a liberal organ. It was inevitable that this triumvirate should come into conflict with the government. While the king and his ministers were somewhat liberal, they were sensitive to criticism and began using an old statute which provided that papers which libeled the government might be withdrawn from circulation. It was Hierta whose title substitutions showed how to defeat this. Swedish press historians credit Hierta's ten-year fight against press infringement with winning newspaper political freedom.

When Karl Johan died in 1844, Sweden had had thirty years of peace and was committed to the neutrality which has kept her at peace for 150 years. Sweden had rebuilt and grown strong. Her farm areas had been increased and the great holdings of nobles broken up to give land to small farmers; with improved methods the nation became self-sufficient in food. Schools had been established in every village, and by encouraging higher education and scholarship, Sweden enjoyed a golden age in literature. Under Oscar I, Karl XV, and Oscar II (who followed Karl Johan) this progress continued. Railroads were built in the fifties, industrialization began in the sixties and with the introduction of steam sawmills the timber industry grew apace. The great orefields in the north began to be worked, and industrial cities grew around them. Sweden's foreign trade, particularly with England, expanded rapidly.

The Press Expands

This growing material prosperity gave the press new impetus, and in the forty-year period after 1840, many of Sweden's modern newspapers were born. In Malmö, Bernhard August Cronholm founded the well-edited, conservative *Snällposten* (Express Post), which in 1872 merged with its rival to become today's *Sydsvenska Dagbladet-Snällposten*, one of Sweden's outstanding papers. Meanwhile Otto Gumalius had started *Nerikes Allehanda*, and Johan Staaf had founded *Sundsvalls Tidning* to give powerful stimulus to the development of the press outside the capital. By 1850 there were fifty-eight provincial papers.

In 1864 Rudolph Wall founded in Stockholm *Dagens Nyheter* (Daily News), which is today Sweden's largest morning daily. Thirty years earlier Day, Bennett, and Greeley had won success in the United States by bringing out newsier papers, keyed to the common man and priced so that everyone could buy them. Wall saw the place for such a paper in Sweden. With the introduction of modern reporting methods, with the presentation of much more news with a more popular treatment, by journalistic enterprise which spread its appeal to all classes, and at a lower price, *Dagens Nyheter* gained considerable circulation and acquired influence as a strong liberal leader.

A succession of bad harvests in the 1880's brought Sweden's farmers to a desperate plight. Led first by the more adventurous, who saw in America a land of opportunity, more than a million followed till Sweden lost a fourth of her population to the United States. But industry began to step into the place of agriculture as the principal means of livelihood, and the 1890's saw the dawn of a great industrial age for Sweden. She became the world's largest timber and wood products exporter. Her iron, steel machinery, and chemical industries became world famous. Abundant water power stimulated this expansion. Her growing merchant fleet began carrying goods to all parts of the world.

The swelling ranks of industrial labor brought the first trade union in 1881, and in 1885 August Palm started *Social Demokraten* on a shoestring as labor's first weekly. Later Hjalmar Branting, a great newspaperman, took it over, made it a daily in 1890, and built it into such a powerful organ of the labor movement that in 1920 labor carried the national elections and Branting became prime minister.

With growing prosperity daily papers now began to appear in most of the larger provincial cities. In the capital there appeared in 1884 *Svenska Dagbladet* as a conservative voice. In 1897 it proclaimed itself primarily a cultural organ and immediately began to attract leading writers as its contributors. With the turn of the century under the editorship of C. G. Tengwall the paper was enlarged, made more newsworthy, given more interesting makeup, and dressed up with more illustrations than any other Swedish paper. It is today the leading conservative journal. Sweden had now become a stable, democratic, parliamentary state; and the press played an increasingly necessary role in keeping the electorate informed so that democracy might function. In 1905, in peaceful negotiations, Norway was given her independence.

Technical improvements in composing machines, stereotyping, and presses paved the way for larger and better publications, and after 1900 Swedish papers began to look modern. But greater plant investments now made newspaper publishing a big business enterprise. No longer was it possible for an aggressive journalist with a cause to start a paper with $20, as August Palm had done with his *Social Demokraten*. The social democratic press now had to have the widespread support of labor. The agrarian press found its support in broadly spread joint-stock companies. The liberal and conservative papers came to be owned by family partnerships, corporations, or wealthy individuals. Growing industrial and commercial activity gave a strong impetus to advertising, and many papers achieved a sound financial footing. Steady increases in population and literacy enabled larger dailies to double their circulations in each decade.

War, Postwar Difficulties, and Change

The outbreak of World War I brought grave problems. Sweden early declared her neutrality, but belligerents fought desperately all around her. The Allied blockade and German submarines took heavy toll of her merchant fleet. Her imports were detained by both sides, which caused a good deal of suffering. Foods of all kinds were scarce and high-priced. Meat and milk had to be reserved for children and invalids. All this had its effect on the press. At first circulations had risen because of interest in war news; but as people grew poorer, circulations declined. Advertising losses forced all papers to reduce their size. Pictures became fewer and smaller.

It took a while for Sweden to come back. There was serious depression after the war; unemployment and extensive strikes were of paramount concern. As normal trade with neighboring countries was restored, industry began to revive; and Sweden and its press began to move forward. By 1928 there were 328 newspapers, of which 100 were dailies. Advertising forged ahead till most dailies were getting 50 per cent of their income from this source. The larger dailies experienced marked increases in circulation; and by the thirties, instead of their prewar four to eight pages, they were appearing with twenty or more and giving their readers much more complete news coverage. The hardships and dissatisfactions of the war years brought far-reaching electoral reforms which enfranchised women and brought universal suffrage. This tripled the number of voters and increased the political awareness of readers. A democratic wave swept the Social Democrats into power in 1920. They proceeded to nationalize railroads and telephones and to adopt extensive social insurance, health, welfare, and old-age pension systems.

In the thirties Sweden had one of the highest living standards in Europe. Heightened political interest brought a sharp orientation of the press between the Conservative, Center or Agrarian, Liberal, Socialist, and Communist parties. In these cleavages there were almost no neutrals. The press was greatly divided on Sweden's entry into the League of Nations, but once she had joined, most papers supported cooperation with the League. Because of lack of faith in the League's strength, however, the press also advocated no letdown in Sweden's own defenses.

World War II Restrictions

Although Sweden was not involved in World War II, her life was dominated by it. With Russia in Finland and Germany occupying

Norway and Denmark, Sweden's position was precarious. Blockaded by both sides, her economy was hard hit. Twice Hitler set dates for the invasion of Sweden. In 1940 she could not have withstood him; but in 1941 she could have made an invasion exceedingly costly, and Hitler, by this time involved in war with Russia, decided against the gamble. Sweden's only hope lay in neutrality even though her sympathies were with Norway, Denmark, and the western Allies; and she gave unprecedented aid to her neighbors.

Fortunately, Sweden and her press suffered little war damage and total daily circulations soon went up 25 per cent. But the war brought other problems. At the outbreak of hostilities Sweden's press had been legally free for 127 years, and its liberty had come to be regarded as an indispensable component of Swedish democracy. Because Swedish editors were outspoken, the German ambassador in Stockholm insisted that Germany would hold Sweden responsible for what appeared in the press. The government countered that under the constitution the press was free and the government not responsible for press criticism. The German foreign office replied that it did not care what was in the constitution, that unless the anti-German press was curbed, economic and military reprisals might be necessary.

Under this pressure an obscure clause in the 1812 press law was revived, permitting the Minister of Justice to confiscate single issues for printing insulting attacks against a foreign power. Altogether 318 confiscations took place, 284 at the behest of the Axis and Russia. These were, however, mere tokens for by the time the German ambassador had read an article and protested, most of the editions would have been distributed to subscribers or sold at newsstands. The Germans declared this to be mere lip service and demanded further controls. Informed by Swedish Intelligence that a date had been set for the invasion of Sweden, the government after a furious debate finally passed the censorship amendment of 1941 which provided that only in the event or threat of war could prepublication scrutiny be put into effect by a three-fourths vote of the *Riksdag*, and it could not be carried out until general mobilization had been ordered.

Yet Sweden's papers, realizing the precarious position of their country, maintained a voluntary censorship, printing the military communiques of both sides, trying not to antagonize either one. The government information board issued "suggestions" rather than instructions. This did not prevent more courageous editors, notably Torgny Segerstedt of Göteborg's *Handels och Sjöfarts Tidning*, from bitterly attacking Hitlerism; hence, his paper suffered numerous confiscations. So strong was the reaction to this humiliating amendment that it was erased in 1945, and in 1949 a new press law was enacted forbidding censorship even in war time.

Postwar Changes

War's end saw Sweden's economy almost as sick as that of her Scandinavian neighbors, for Germany's collapse and the financial crippling of England lost Sweden her best customers. Postwar inflation added to her woes. But because her industry had not been wrecked, recovery set in as rigid export and import regulations corrected unfavorable trade balances. Newspapers felt these restrictions in the reduction of their newsprint supply, which was done so that more might be available for export. With a very small amount of Marshall Aid, Sweden stepped up her production and by 1950 was well on the way to a sound economy, to again give adequate base for a stable press. Once again it moved ahead, marked first by the advent of new provincial dailies converted from triweeklies. In Stockholm the Social Democrats brought out a new evening paper, *Afton Tidningen*, to counteract the influence of the pro-German *Aftonbladet*. The demise of the 175-year-old *Nya Dagligt Allehanda* in 1944 offered *Dagens Nyheter* an opportunity to publish an evening companion, *Expressen*, which took hold quickly. *Dagens Nyheter*, *Göteborgs-Posten*, and *Stockholms-Tidningen* were the circulation leaders. By 1950 Sweden counted 239 papers, of which 131 were dailies; but triweeklies in twelve other cities published on alternate days gave Sweden, in effect, 143 daily papers, a tremendous number for so small a populaton.

In the next few years rising costs and intense competition forced the same consolidations as took place in other countries—sometimes by merger, more often by the death of weaker papers—till by 1957 forty-one papers had disappeared, mostly in the provinces. In the capital, too, changes were taking place. Stockholm in 1950 had had eleven dailies. Two had such serious declines in circulation that they gave up daily publication. Then Torsten Krueger was forced to sell his two papers, *Stockholms-Tidningen* and *Aftonbladet*, which had been in trouble partly because of his alleged pro-Germanism and partly because of financial difficulties in the debacle of the financial empire of his brother Ivan Krueger. In the scandal that followed, Torsten Krueger was imprisoned for seven years for fraud. On his release he repurchased his papers, partly as an investment but more to carry on his fight against the courts and prove his innocence. By 1955 he was losing $400,000 a year, and in 1956 he sold them to the Socialists. Because of competition the latter were forced to merge their two evening papers and to discontinue their *Morgontidningen*, reducing the number of Stockholm dailies to seven.

Sweden's Press Today

As a result of these changes Sweden in 1964 counted 222 newspapers, 107 of them dailies, with a total circulation of 3,904,011, of which the six remaining Stockholm dailies get 37.4 per cent. With so many dailies for a population of only 7,581,000, 68 per cent have under 30,000 circulation, many only 1,000 to 5,000. There are only six with more than 100,000. Even so, one may wonder how this small nation can have so many dailies. The answer lies partly in the fact that Swedes are voracious newspaper readers and buy 46.2 copies per 100 persons, second only to Britain, and partly in the earlier political history of the press when every party tried to be represented in as many cities as possible, a situation which no longer exists.

In 1964 the Social Democrats, who had been in power for thirty-two years, again won the election but not a parliamentary majority. Tage Erlander, premier since 1946, continued to hold office. By careful management his party had brought national prosperity, provided labor its highest wages in history, and developed the most comprehensive welfare program in Europe. By joining the European Free Trade Area Sweden had greatly expanded her markets for Swedish products, not only in EFTA countries but with Common Market nations as well. In 1962, however, industrial production fell, and precautionary measures against an excess of imports over exports caused unemployment and industrial unrest. This recession had been overcome by 1964 although there were now inflationary dangers. Khrushchev visited Sweden prior to the election; and, interestingly, the attempt of Swedish Communists to question the Soviet refusal to permit Esthonians, Latvians, and Lithuanians to join their relatives in Sweden caused Moscow to cancel its subsidies to the three Communist dailies, forcing them to become weeklies.

Swedes classify their papers as national, provincial, and local. Only *Dagens Nyheter*, *Stockholms-Tidningen*, *Svenska Dagbladet*, *Expressen*, and *Aftonbladet* in the capital and Göteborg's *Handels och Sjöfarts Tidning* are counted as *rikspress* or national papers. Eighty per cent of all dailies appear in the morning. Evening papers have their circulation confined largely to the city and its environs except on Sunday when they circulate more widely. The *rikspress* provides not only excellent coverage of national and foreign news but also, because they emanate from the cultural centers of the nation, a good deal of literary and other cultural material. Sweden's geography and great distances make provincial papers important. The larger ones are very good, with strong emphasis on world and national news, fine coverage of regional news, and a powerful influence in the areas they serve. The local press is made up of 115 weeklies, biweeklies, and triweeklies providing much more local news.

There is a curious imbalance between party organ circulations and votes; thus the Social Democrats with only 23.5 per cent of the daily circulation got 52 per cent of the vote in the 1964 election while the Liberals and Conservatives, which together have 68 per cent of the circulation, got only 33 per cent of the vote. However the Liberal and Conservative papers are so well off financially that they can be independent politically, back the best candidates regardless of party, and place major emphasis on news. This has forced some Socialist papers to improve their news coverage, for Swedes prefer papers which provide the most news.

The Liberal and Conservative papers are independently owned by individuals or publishing firms. *Dagens Nyheter* and *Expressen* are held by the Bonnier family, which also publishes some of the larger magazines and owns one of the biggest book publishing firms. Some Agrarian papers are owned by the party, some by the Farmers Union. The Social Democratic papers are owned by the party and the Trade Union Federation. About half of these are self-supporting; the others have their deficits made up through a press tax on all union members. Most Swedish dailies are economically independent, and their volume of advertising makes them look like American papers. The larger papers derive 60–70 per cent of their income from advertising; even the smaller ones are likely to get 50–60 per cent of their income from this source. Most circulation is home delivered and provides a steady backlog of income. All the better papers differentiate clearly between news and comment. News is presented fairly and objectively and opinion is reserved for editorial columns. One thing that characterizes this press is the sense of responsibility on the part of proprietors to the people. The Swedes hold their heads high, for they are never pawns of the state; even the king is their servant. The press, as a result, is constantly on the alert to safeguard and promote the interests of the people.

Sweden's News Agency

While Sweden is a constitutional monarchy, it is also one of the most successful democracies. Her people take a keen interest in national and foreign affairs; and they are kept well informed by a press, radio, and television system which is free and responsible and an integral part of the successful functioning of this democracy. Both press and electronic media are served by *Tidningarnas Telegrambyra* (T.T.). An earlier agency had been founded in 1857 by A. E. E. Fitch, a Dane who was associated with Erik Ritzaus, founder of the Danish news agency bearing his name. This earlier agency went through several periods of private ownership till, in 1921, T.T. was set up under the ownership of the Swedish press itself. It is a cooperative agency, operating much like the Associated Press. It serves all dailies and handles the news broadcasts for the Swedish Broadcasting Corporation. Subscribing papers funnel their news to the main office in Stockholm. A Stockholm Reporting Service covers the news of the capital.

T.T.'s foreign department relies mainly on Reuters but also has exchange agreements with the agencies of other Nordic nations and special correspondents in capitals around the world. Some larger papers also use the services of the Associated Press or United Press International. The three Communist papers of course use TASS, but with the exception of these three, the coverage of world news in the Swedish papers is full and fair. The Swedish people are by tradition and conviction strongly pro-western.

Press Self-Control

One thing that strikes any student of the Swedish press is its responsibility and self-regulation. All papers belong to the *Svenska Tidningsutgivareföreningen* (Swedish Newspaper Publishers Association), founded in 1898, which deals with common business problems including the purchase of newsprint. Editorial workers belong to *Svenska Journalistsforbundet* (The Swedish Union of Journalists), founded in 1901, which has, in conjunction with the employers association, worked out scaled contracts for wages, hours, conditions of work, and pensions. But it is more than a labor union, for over the years it has worked for the improvement of the profession and publishes a professional journal, *Journalisten*. Another organization is *Publicistklubben*, founded in 1874 to promote good relations between members of the press regardless of party politics, but, more important, to act as a watchdog over the relations of the press with the public.

As a result of this cooperation between publishers and unions Sweden has had none of the crippling newspaper strikes which have so often beset American cities. There has not been a newspaper strike since 1937 when publishers and graphic arts workers agreed on a peace pact in recognition of the obligation of both sides to keep presses rolling so that the people of Sweden might be fully informed day-by-day. When disagreements occur they are at once referred to a court headed by the chairman of Sweden's Arbitration Court with two members representing the parties to the dispute. For twenty-seven years this court has settled all disputes fairly and amicably.

As another result of cooperation the Swedish press has since 1916 been governed by a Fair Practices Commission or court of honor.

There have been many such courts set up around the world since World War II, some not very effective; but the one in Sweden has really seemed to function. The press has adopted a Code of Ethics which this court enforces. Beyond the laws defining abuses of press freedom which are criminal, the court of honor calls to account papers which publish information which is incorrect or, because it is incomplete, is injurious and subjects the individual to unnecessary suffering. As a consequence Swedish papers have developed a high sense of the rights of privacy. Court convictions of minors may be reported but, out of consideration for the family, names are not used. The same holds for suicides; but when an important person is involved, the death is reported with no intimation of suicide. Any person or company may complain to this court if he deposits an expense fee of 40 kroner, and great care is taken to assure a fair hearing for both the individual and the paper. Decisions are made public, and also an annual report is published. Sweden's newspapers as a whole represent a high journalistic level, and they are held in respect by both the people and the government.

Three-fourths of Swedish daily papers are in a financially sound position but some twenty-five papers, mostly Social Democratic, have had to be subsidized by their parties. All are "second papers" in their cities. The government press commission proposed a $5,000,000 yearly state contribution because of its concern over the monopoly situation enjoyed by some larger dailies. This brought a heated debate in Parliament, which finally defeated the proposal.

The Character of Swedish Papers

In appearance and content Swedish papers are much like those in America. A few, such as *Svenska Dagbladet* in Stockholm and some provincials, devote pages one and two to advertising, in which case, page three is then like the usual page one. Front pages are display windows playing the top news of the day, world, national, and local. Good clean typography makes these papers easily readable. Seldom is there a banner head; instead there is horizontal display, with two-, three-, and four-column heads. American visitors are always impressed by the number of pictures. Inside display advertising is pyramided just as in American papers. All except the tabloid afternoon papers are standard-sized. Larger Stockholm papers run from fifty to sixty pages, stronger provincials eighteen to thirty, and smaller dailies eight to sixteen.

Papers are carefully departmentalized, for Swedes like them that way. The editorial page is usually page two, followed by a good cultural page, then pages of foreign and national wire news. Next come pages of local and provincial news and features. Provincial papers run departments devoted to news of nearby cities. Then comes a family page of light features and humorous columns followed by a woman's page with fashions, menus, and household hints. There is no society page, except for a half page of *familjenytt*, which briefly lists engagements, weddings, and deaths. The most important feature on this page is the Birthday Column, paying tribute to leading citizens on their birthdays. Succeeding pages carry theater, music, radio, TV, then sports, for the Swedes are very sportsminded, followed by the business and financial pages. Next come solid pages of classified advertising broken by a few comic strips and often a serial story. The back pages hold late wire and local news and sometimes good local or provincial feature stories. Syndicated columnists are not used. Instead staff members develop excellent, well-illustrated feature articles; and leading economists, political scientists, and government officials write *kroniks* or background articles.

Stockholm evening papers are a phenomenon in Sweden's otherwise staid journalism. Tabloid or semitabloid in size, with main headlines in red and a more popular news treatment, they were first considered shocking but have now taken hold and developed sizable circulations. They run heavy on picture display, including pinup girls, theater, film, and sports personalities. While at first news coverage of world and national affairs was presented in abbreviated form, they have come, in time, to provide a very broad coverage and considerable backgrounding. There are of course many light features, much sports and entertainment news, and many comic strips. Stockholm's *Expressen* has today the largest circulation in the country.

Swedish Press's Contribution to the Nation

As one looks back over the story of the Swedish press, one cannot but be aware of the role this press has played in the history of its nation. It fought long against royal despotism and inspired the revolt of 1809 which ended royal tyranny and gave the country a democratic constitution guaranteeing Swedes protection of their rights against any attempts of the monarch to subvert them. Through the years its press heroes have been history makers who have played a vital role in keeping the electorate informed so that their democracy might function. After World War I the press demanded sweeping reforms which brought universal suffrage and extensive social insurance. It fostered a stable economy which has brought Sweden the highest living standards in Europe. Today with unusual responsibility it continues to serve as a guardian of the peoples' rights and their best interests.

Dagens Nyheter (Stockholm)—Probably Sweden's best national newspaper. With its many news services and correspondents it provides wide news coverage and fine backgrounding. Though it is a Liberal paper, members of other parties buy it all over the country. Has more than doubled its prewar circulation and in 1964 had 377,200 daily and 471,800 Sunday. Earlier its appeal was to the intellectuals and middle class, but its circulation has spread among all classes. Although it generally supports the Liberal party, it is completely independent and often takes issue with its party leaders. Is pro-western.

Expressen (Stockholm)—the popular evening companion of *Dagens Nyheter*. The capital's first shocker, Sweden's most surprising postwar success. A picture tabloid, but with good coverage of late foreign and national news, much theater, sports and entertainment news. Has forged into first place with 451,300 circulation daily and 478,600 Sunday.

Svenska Dagbladet—Stockholm's leading voice of Conservative party and one of best and most respected papers in the capital. Reaches a quality circulation of the educated and upper income classes; heavy with advertising. Rich in cultural material but provides excellent news coverage with its many services and foreign correspondents. Fewer entertainment features, for its main emphasis is news and culture. Supports Swedish neutrality but also military preparedness. Pro-western; circulation, 150,584, Sunday 155,673.

Stockholms Tidningen—Strongest voice of Social Democratic party. Has fought for many social reforms and extensive social welfare programs. Is proneutrality, anti-Soviet, and friendly to West. An attractive, well-madeup and illustrated paper. Circulation 156,900 daily, 247,000 Sunday.

Aftonbladet—Afternoon companion of *Stockholms Tidningen* now in third place with 288,900 circulation daily and 300,200 Sunday. Hierta, father of Sweden's press freedom who founded this paper, might be disturbed if he could see it now as a picture tabloid devoting much space to sports, light features, and entertainment. Anti-Communist and pro-western.

Göteborgs Posten—Strongest of provincial papers. Conservative in appearance; provides good coverage of foreign and national news and intensive coverage of west coast news. One of Sweden's most profitable newspaper enterprises. Liberal in internal policy, pro-western, circulation 248,700 daily, 266,900 Sunday.

Handels och Sjöfarts Tidning (Göteborg)—One of Sweden's most famous papers because of its courage during World War II. Starting as a commercial and shipping paper, it has made itself a good general paper. Changed to morning publication in 1947 and modernized its appearance. Strongly Liberal, opposed Socialist neutrality policy, and advocated adherence to Atlantic Pact. Circulation 60,500.

Sydsvenska Dagbladet-Snällposten (Malmö)—A strong Conservative, attractive, and lively newspaper. Good coverage of world and national news but intensive coverage of south Sweden. Because of importance of agriculture to this region, pays much attention to farm problems. Good cultural section. Vigorously anti-Communist and pro-western. Circulation 92,727 daily, 139,816 Sunday.

Skånska Dagbladet (Malmö)—Important because it is the leading voice of Agrarian party. Known as farmers' paper in southern Sweden. Good coverage of south Sweden and Sweden's third largest city. Circulation 41,100.

Nya Wermlands Tidningen (Karlstad)—One of best papers of west central Sweden with separate departments for surrounding provinces. Circulation 74,900.

Vestmanlands Läns Tidning (Vasterås)—Serving an industrial area northwest of Stockholm. An excellent example of a good small daily edited by Anders Yngve Pers, whose editorial column is frequently quoted. Pers is one of Sweden's foremost press historians and a member of the court of honor of the Swedish press. Circulation 44,200.

Denmark's Healthy Press

Denmark, smallest of the Scandinavian nations and a favorite of tourists, is known as "the land of newspaper reading," for she has a remarkable density of papers, including two of the best in Europe. Her 4,600,000 people are highly literate, well-informed, and progressive. They live in an area equivalent to that of the states of Massachusetts, Connecticut, and Rhode Island—but with half their population. Yet Denmark has almost as many papers as these three states have together. This nation is a democratic constitutional monarchy, but until a little over one hundred years ago the Danes were governed by an autocratic, absolute monarchy which long delayed the development of her press.

Denmark is nearly surrounded by water; her archipelago embraces five hundred islands. The largest, Zealand, is most populous, for here at the capital, Copenhagen and its environs, live a fourth of her people. Her sea and soil have been her two great resources; hence, Denmark has long depended on foreign trade. This, coupled with the fact that she is surrounded by larger nations, has meant that her people have taken a keen interest in world affairs.

The historical development of this country has had an important effect on the character of its press. Denmark was once a great power, sitting astride the bridge between the Scandinavian peninsula and the great trade routes on the Continent. To control these routes, Danes first conquered what are now the Netherlands and northern Germany. Then Danish Vikings took eastern England. Under Canute the Great, in the eleventh century, they ruled a great maritime empire. After Canute's death this fell apart, but Danish kings reached eastward to control much of the Baltic. After 1389 Denmark ruled Sweden and Norway until her defeat in the Napoleonic wars reduced her to a minor power.

The Rise of the Danish Press

First precursors of the Danish press were flysheets appearing as early as 1542, handwritten in German, and chronicling a single, marvelous occurrence or unnatural phenomenon. Kings, nobles, and city magistrates, however, found it useful to subscribe to handwritten newsletters from correspondents in foreign cities. Establishment of a postal system by Christian IV paved the way for wider distribution of newssheets within Denmark, and in 1634 the first royal *Avisprivilegium* (Privileged Newspaper License) was granted to two German book printers whose irregular publication, printed in German, lifted small items from continental papers.

The second license went to Peder Morsing, the book printer of the University of Copenhagen, and permitted him to distribute by royal mail his *Ny Affiser*, the first sheet to be printed in Danish. The rulers, however, did not encourage the development of regular newspapers, and it was 57 years after the first weekly had appeared in Germany before Denmark had a regularly appearing publication. Frederick III wished to give éclat to his realm and its intellectual life by establishing a state paper and entrusted the publication of *Den Danske Mercurius* in 1666 to Anders Bording, who has sometimes been called the father of Danish journalism. It was only a monthly and was a peculiar journal, for it was written entirely in Bording's original German verse, extolling the king and his family, carrying his communications, and incorporating small news of visiting diplomats and some foreign items. Yet it was all Denmark had for some years, and it appeared regularly till 1675. In 1672 Daniel Pauli started the first paper in Danish prose. By the end of the century there were several weekly and monthly publications.

First Newspapers of Merit

After the seventeenth-century conflicts had ended with serious losses to Denmark, peace came at last; for a century and a quarter the nation enjoyed a period of reconstruction and intellectual uplift. The first steps toward popular education came with the establishment of elementary schools. Danes speak of the eighteenth century as the Age of Enlightenment. Interest in literature and science grew, and public interest in news of their own land and from foreign countries increased the demand for newspapers. Although news from Stockholm, Berlin, or Amsterdam might be a week old, that from Paris or Vienna two weeks late, or from Madrid, Rome, or St. Petersburg a month delayed, on the day the news appeared Danes felt themselves citizens of the world.

The first journalist who met this need was Joachim Wielandt, the university printer who in 1720 obtained a royal privilege to bring out his *Ekstraordinaire Relationer* (Extraordinary Information). He filled his paper with news from many foreign countries as well as from Denmark and for the first time raised the level of the Danish press to that of contemporary papers in Germany and Holland. He was also the first to develop advertising for his paper. He, far more than Bording, deserves to be called the father of the Danish press.

After Wielandt's death his newspaper privilege was acquired by Ernst Heinrich Berling, a German printer who had come to Copenhagen and set himself up as a printer and book publisher. Now with a newspaper privilege he brought out in 1749 *Kobenhavnske Danske Post Tidender* (Copenhagen Danish Postal News). His first issue was little more than a sixteen-page pamphlet, the first three pages devoted to a poem lauding the king, the next three to news from foreign capitals, and the remaining ten to advertising. But Berling began giving his readers more foreign news besides giving big play to Copenhagen's local affairs, and the paper grew. For 150 years it enjoyed a special position as the voice of government; but some sixty years ago it became an independent paper, and as *Berlingske Tidende* it not only enjoys the prestige of being Denmark's oldest paper but also that of being one of the best in Europe. Meanwhile, the first paper in the provinces, *Ugentlige Provincial Notis Lister* (Weekly Provincial Notices) had appeared in Odense in 1735. It was followed by *Aalborg Stiftstidende* in 1764, the second oldest paper today.

Freedom and Reaction

To prevent attacks on royalty and religion the University had for many years exercised an official press censorship. But in 1770 Denmark became one of the first European nations to be given press freedom. Johann Friederick Struensee, a German physician to the king, had become his confidant; and as the king's dissipations eventually rendered him completely incompetent, Struensee became his trusted minister, empowered to issue decrees in the king's name. A disciple of Voltaire and Rousseau, he wanted to make Denmark an enlightened monarchy. One of his first moves was to try to break up the power of the great landowners and to free the peasants from villeinage. Then he ended censorship of all publications, for, in his decree, he said: "It is our firm conviction that it is just as harmful to the search for truth, as it is a hindrance to the discovery of inherited delusions and bias, when honest patriots are deterred from writing freely according to their insight and convictions in attacking abuses."

But the press freedom he had granted also gave his opponents, among the nobility and great landlords who felt their own interests threatened, the opportunity to attack him; and Struensee was vulnerable for he had made the mistake of becoming the queen's lover. When these papers printed scandalous accounts of his amours, they brought about his downfall. He was arrested and executed in 1772.

The Conservative ministry which took power ushered in a period of complete reaction. Freedom of the press, which had lasted only two years, was abolished, strict censorship was imposed, and for twelve years the press had to operate under the harsh curbs of a new penal code. But the more enlightened Bernstorff ministry, which took over in 1784, realized that if Denmark was to increase her farm production and her foreign trade she must free the peasants from semislavery, give them their own plots of land, and also adopt a free trade policy. To put these reforms into effect, the government needed the support of public opinion and thus restored a considerable measure of freedom to the press. The country's economy boomed, and the press expanded and enjoyed some good years.

Crown Prince Frederick who, at his majority, had assumed the right to rule as regent in view of his father's imbecility, was so fearful that the revolutionary movement which had swept royalty from power in France might do the same in Denmark that by a 1799 decree he ended press freedom. Severe penalties of imprisonment, banishment, and even death were provided for attacks on the government or any advocacy of change in government. Rigid censorship was restored. Thus the Danish press, which had enjoyed two short periods of freedom, was now set back so severely that it was to take another fifty years for it to achieve real liberty. By 1800 it had been reduced to ten papers with a total circulation under 10,000.

Denmark was allied with Napoleon in his wars; and his final defeat left her with crippling losses, the surrender of Norway to Sweden, the destruction of her entire fleet, and bankruptcy. Thereafter her policy had to be one of keeping out of conflict. There was much reconstruction to be done; but her poverty permitted only one reform, the creation of a greatly expanded schools system which was not only to give the press a broader base in the years to come, but also to provide the peasants the education they needed to fight for their rights. There came an intellectual awakening in the first half of the nineteenth century in which the press cooperated by becoming literary publications, for cultural content was the only avenue of safety under the government's rigorous repression.

Revolution Brings Freedom

Denmark's absolute monarchy still fought every movement for further freedom; but after the July, 1830, revolution in Paris, the Danish movement toward democracy was not to be stopped. In 1834 the people won consultative provincial Diets. In that year the first liberal paper, *Faedrelandet* (Fatherland), appeared. Because of its greater emphasis on news, it soon developed a strong following and for a decade was the leading opinion-molder; but its daring brought it into frequent conflict with authorities. Denmark had acquired her first daily in 1831 when Berling's paper changed to daily publication. The 1848 revolutions which swept Europe spurred the Danes to march on the Royal Palace to demand a free constitution. The king was persuaded to accept the status of a constitutional monarch and on June 5, 1849, signed a new constitution based on the French declaration of human rights, which placed power in a bicameral *Rigsdag* elected by the people. Thus, at long last, the Danish press was liberated. Clause 91 stated: "Everyone has a right to publish his ideas in print but with responsibility before the law. Censorship and other preventive measures may never be introduced again."

This new freedom and the political controversies brought an increase in the number of papers and a political division between them. The large landowners, the substantial burghers, and the professional gentry formed the backbone of the Conservative party, whose strongest voice was *Berlingske Tidende*. Its M. L. Nathansen steered it on a course of level-headed discussion of public issues. The Liberal party had two powerful voices in *Faedrelandet* under Carl Ploug and its new *Dagbladet* founded in 1851 under Carl Billie. Quarrels with Prussia over the border provinces of Holstein and Schlesvig led to a war with Prussia and Austria in which Denmark was badly defeated in 1864 and gave up these provinces. Since the Liberals had backed the war they were blamed for the debacle and lost power. The party disintegrated, and many joined the Conservatives.

New parties were now arising. The postwar period saw a rapid development of agriculture, and its new prosperity ushered in the Agrarian party which set out to develop press voices. By 1876 it had nineteen papers in the provinces and more were to come till there was soon a *Venstre* or Left paper to oppose the Right paper in most towns. But the party needed a voice in the capital and founded *Morgenbladet*. Its brilliant editor, Viggo Horup, wielded an ironic pen which made him his party's leading spokesman. He made a sharp break with literary romanticism and set out to educate his readers to a realistic understanding of the problems of the day.

Meanwhile industrial expansion was producing a large working class. Labor unions grew, and in 1871 Louis Pios brought out the weekly *Socialisten*, later renamed *Social Demokraten*. Emil Winblad, editor after 1881, changed it from a labor union organ to a real daily newspaper, championing the rights of labor. By 1906 this party had 31 papers. The last quarter of the nineteenth century saw a great struggle between the Conservatives, who controlled the upper house, and the *Venstre*, who dominated the lower house. The former favored a strong defense policy and an end to social reforms. The latter insisted Denmark had no business with warlike preparations against larger powers and urged attention to domestic problems. When this struggle grew so bitter that it seemed parliamentary government might break down, many Liberals made peace with the Right. The rest broke away to form the new Radical (Reform) party to fight for a liberalized constitution, further social reforms, and reduced defense budgets. To gain a voice in the capital, they established *Politiken* in 1884 and Viggo Horup became its editor. Under his leadership it attracted the most talented journalists, and Horup came to be considered the leader of public opinion in Copenhagen. By 1915 the Radical party had twenty-three dailies with nineteen affiliated editions for smaller towns. In the 1913 election the Radicals came into power and in 1915 brought about the adoption of a more liberal constitution.

Thus there developed a four-party system under which each party sought to have papers in as many localities as possible. Many principal towns had four dailies, one for each party. Whereas in 1850 Denmark had had only eight dailies, by 1901 she had 206 and by 1925 she was to have 273—at the time when Britain had but 131 and France 151. The nineteenth century Danish press was overwhelmingly political; and great editors dominated it with their editorial thunderings.

Modernization of the Press

As the twentieth century opened, members of the press began to sense that the old formula no longer met readers' needs. In England and the United States editors had discovered that readers were more interested in news than in polemics, and some editors had had great success in playing up human interest in the news. Henrik Cavling, who became editor of *Politiken* in 1905, took the lead in this modernization. As Denmark's foremost foreign correspondent he had traveled widely and developed a large following because he tried to let his readers see the human side of the statesmen he interviewed and of the little people in the countries he visited. Thus when he came to *Politiken*, he determined to bring the world home to the Danes in a way they could understand. At the same time Vilhelm Lassen on *Aalborg Amtstidende* led another revolt away from the oratorical style of political writers to simpler language which every reader could comprehend.

Cavling wrought a startling revolution when he changed the form of his paper from a long blanket sheet, whose front page, except for the leader article, was filled with small advertising, to a shorter paper, more easily handled, with a front news page using arresting heads and picture display. He recognized that the Greco-Turkish War, the Boer War, the Spanish-American War, and the Russo-Japanese War had whetted the public's appetite for more world news; and he put out a paper with a principal emphasis on news, evaluated from the standpoint of the reader's interests rather than party needs. Editorials were moved inside, shortened, and given a broader appeal. Not only were horizons widened by correspondence from many parts of the world, but better coverage was provided for provincial and local news. More space was given to sports, and special departments were created for women readers.

Politiken's success was immediate. *Berlingske Tidende*, under Christian Gulmann, *Social Demokraten*, and even some provincial papers joined in developing this new type of journalism.

War and Postwar Depression Affect Press

World War I completed the revolution, for the public's great interest in the news forced the last conservative holdouts to the new journalism. Denmark cooperated with the other Scandinavian nations in maintaining neutrality and for a time prospered till Germany's submarine warfare and the British blockade not only caused heavy shipping losses but seriously hampered Danish foreign trade. Despite war anxieties a revised constitution was put into effect introducing full suffrage for men and women in elections to both houses of the *Rigsdag*, thus doing away with the privileged suffrage of the wealthier classes.

Denmark moved hopefully into the period of peace following the war, but the early twenties were difficult. Many factories had had to close; unemployment, added to inflated prices, caused hardships for workers. There were crippling strikes; labor unions grew in strength; and in 1924 the first Labor government came into power. With but one interruption it remained in control till 1940. The nation's economy gradually improved; agricultural exports grew and industry expanded till by 1930 almost as many people were engaged in industry as in farming.

These were good years, and the press grew in vigor with the general prosperity. The war and the years following had brought a great increase in circulations. Where in 1901 total daily circulations had been only 516,000, by 1925 they had risen to 1,154,000, which meant that every home had its daily paper and that the newspaper was as necessary as bread. The result of the increased business was a marked rise in advertising. All this had not produced impressive circulation figures for any paper. *Politiken* rose to 68,000; *Berlingske Tidende* to 47,000. But for many, figures were around 10,000; and most smaller ones had under 5,000 because when 273 dailies divided available circulation there could not be a large amount for any one.

The great depression of the early thirties brought disaster. England, to satisfy her dominions, had to reduce drastically her food imports from Denmark. The latter had no recourse but to turn to her other big customer, Germany, an act which placed her increasingly under Nazi economic dictatorship. And when England concluded her naval treaty with Germany in 1935, practically relinquishing the Baltic, Denmark was virtually under Nazi guns.

This soon had its effect on the press. Outwardly there was complete freedom; newspapers in all shades of opinion came out regularly. Any paper could attack the government and nothing happened as long as papers held to Danish affairs. But the Foreign Office had to ask papers not to print anything prejudicial to the country's interests in its relations with Germany. When Nazis began holding air maneuvers over Denmark and fleet maneuvers around her coasts, papers were persuaded to use discreet forbearance. Some editors continued to tell the truth of what was going on in Germany despite the protests of the German Foreign Office, but most papers accepted a voluntary censorship. The press as a whole did not keep its readers informed and left them unprepared for the catastrophe of 1940.

Germany Strikes

Denmark had been marked by Nazi strategists as a source of food for Germany in the event of war and as a base for her naval and air operations. On April 9, 1940, Germany invaded Denmark "to protect her from England." Danish troops fought desperately against overwhelming power but in a day it was all over. The Danish government insisted, however, that jurisdiction over its citizens should be in Danish hands and that every German demand must go through the Danish Foreign Office. Germany's need for food and her announced desire to make Denmark a model protectorate may have dictated accession to Danish demands; at any rate, it saved the Danish government and spared the press from direct censorship.

But censorship there was. True, no German officers sat in newsrooms, as in Norway, yet the Danish Foreign Office hand was firm. Danish editors showed their independence by refusing to print German propaganda articles. They printed German war communiques alongside Allied communiques. Some editors tried to circumvent censorship by printing forbidden news. This was quickly halted, for the Danish government in its critical situation could not speak openly nor permit the press to do so. Hostility to the Germans was so great that the seeming collaboration of the press caused it to lose the people's confidence. Crowds cheered when Minister Kaufman in Washington declared himself not bound by the coerced Danish government, and permitted the United States temporary bases in Greenland.

The Germans tried to silence certain newspapers by blowing up their plants. In fact, five provincial papers had their plants utterly wrecked by bombs. The saboteurs were never in uniform; thus the Germans could blame the bombings on Danes. But the people were not deceived. *Berlingske Tidende* learned that its plant was marked for sabotage and fortified it with sand bags and armed guards. They thought if they could hold off the attackers till they could call for help, German troops would have to protect them to keep up the pretense that the saboteurs were Danes. The assault took place one night, but guards and staff members, hastily armed with rifles, drove off the bombers.

Rise of the Underground Press

The real press of Denmark during the occupation was the illegal press. First flysheets appeared shortly after invasion, but the government and its police stopped their distribution. In 1941 patriotic leaders organized rings of young people for the distribution of information, first through hand written sheets and later through stenciled or printed ones. By the end of the year underground papers were appearing regularly with large circulations. Actual distribution figures meant nothing, for the papers were passed from hand to hand until they fell apart. By 1942 the trickle of illegal information had become a flood, not only in Copenhagen but in all the provinces. Each party had its own paper. They gave the people news they could not get from the regular press—of German defeats and local German terrorism—thus spurring the people to resistance. Many of the men working on regular newspapers secretly wrote for or edited underground sheets. *Berlingske Tidende*, while putting out its regular edition under censorship, also printed an underground paper. Later one of its staff members was found to have been a Nazi collaborator, but even he had not informed on his paper.

Resistance grew as German oppression became worse; and in 1943 large-scale sabotage, widespread strikes, guerrilla warfare by an underground army, and the scuttling of the Danish fleet moved events to a climax. The Danish government, in alarm, violently denounced people who would bring their country into open conflict with the German army. But there was no stopping these patriotic papers. In August, 1943, the Germans brought in additional troops, took over all the regular papers, and instituted a reign of terror to put an end to the resistance papers. Many printers and writers were caught by the Gestapo, but there were always others ready to take the places of those executed or imprisoned. More and more newspaper men deserted their jobs on daytime papers and went underground, risking imprisonment, torture, and death to serve their country.

In all, 552 illegal papers appeared during the occupation, and they were the instruments through which the Freedom Council roused the people to stand against the enemy. As this resistance press brought news of German setbacks in Russia, North Africa, and Italy, sabotage and guerrilla activity grew like a hurricane. On May 4, 1945, when word came that Germans were capitulating in Holland and northwestern Germany, Denmark's underground army rose, fought its way to occupy all important points, imprisoned Germans, and interned Danish Nazi collaborators. Liberation was complete, and the people rushed into the streets to embrace each other—a mass of joy-intoxicated citizens.

Because Denmark had not suffered any lengthy military action, her industrial plants and her farms were intact. She had, however, lost much of her shipping; her railroads were wrecked; and the Germans had robbed her of more than $2,000,000,000. Yet the Danes went to work with enthusiasm and made a rapid recovery. By 1947 Denmark was considered one of the bright spots of Europe.

The Postwar Press

When liberation came, the old, regular papers which had published during the occupation had some explaining to do. Some had to remove editors too closely identified with the Germans; but once the people understood that their old papers were now free to publish as before, they went back to them. A few resistance papers emerged as regular dailies; in Copenhagen only *Information* and *Land og Folk* continue today. Though the war had caused the demise of some papers, by 1950 there were again 132. Now increased production and newsprint costs caused some casualties, but by 1954 there were 118 major dailies or *huvudblad*. Yet under Denmark's *aflaeger* system a single provincial paper might put out separate editions for neighboring towns, each under its own title, though it has only a page for local news and advertising. Thus in addition to the 118 *huvudblad* there were 103 *aflaeger*, a total of 221 daily titles. Most of the larger provincial towns had three or four dailies representing different parties. With this system covering the countryside intensively, there was little need for weeklies except in capital suburbs. When Danes speak of their weekly press they refer to their weekly and monthly illustrated news reviews, women's, farm and family interest magazines.

Denmark in 1953 adopted a new constitution providing for a uni-cameral parliament (*folketing*). Moving closer to the English system, they made provision for votes of "no confidence" which might unseat a single minister or the whole cabinet. To guard against one-party dictatorship, one-third of the *Folketing* might call a plebiscite on any question. The Social Democrats remained in power but often had to govern in coalition with the Radicals. For a time an excess of imports over exports endangered reserves, but by 1957 import restrictions and higher duties gave Denmark again an export balance. Industrial production had risen from an index of 100 in 1955 to 125 in 1960. In 1962 Denmark reached peak economic activity, but there was serious inflation. Jens Otto Krag, an economist who became prime minister in 1963, put through Draconian measures to curb the trend: purchase taxes were raised and the bank rate was increased. But inflation continued. In 1965 newspapers found themselves in financial difficulties, and all those except the Social Democratic ones began vigorous opposition.

This increased prosperity did not result in any press expansion, for Danish newspapers encountered the same problems in the late fifties and sixties as did the press in other countries. Continuing cost increases and forced amalgamations produced stronger regional papers but put many small dailies out of business and very much reduced the number of *aflaegers*. The old four-paper system based on party lines began to pass. By the end of 1964 there were only seventy dailies left, ten in Copenhagen and sixty in provincial cities, many of the latter dominating a considerable area. They were financially independent and tended to be politically independent as well.

Morning papers dominate the Copenhagen field, but most provincial dailies publish in the evening. Two new popular tabloid noon papers in the capital, *B.T.* and *Ekstrabladet*, have shown surprising growth and, by utilizing air transport in order to be on sale everywhere, have gained ground in the provinces. Unlike Norwegians, the Danes like their expanded Sunday papers with strong emphasis on features and entertainment. Five Copenhagen papers and twelve of the larger provincials put out Sunday editions, and these have larger circulations than weekday editions, totaling 1,286,331.

Copenhagen is the publishing center of Denmark, and its dailies have 44 per cent of the total daily circulation of 1,664,618. This represents a distribution of 36.3 copies per 100 persons, one of the highest ratios in Europe. This capital press is led by *Berlingske Tidende and Politiken,* the two largest papers in the country which also represent the two great publishing houses dominating Copenhagen. The former publishes not only *Berlingske Tidende, B.T., Berlingske Aftenavis,* and a provincial paper at Kolding, but other periodicals as well, and is a prominent book-publishing house. The latter publishes *Politiken,* its popular *Ekstrabladet,* plus periodicals and books. Not far behind *Politiken* is the new revitalized and popularized version of *Social Demokraten,* now called *Aktuelt.*

Largest of the provincial dailies is *Jyllands Posten* at Aarhus, the capital of Jutland. Other leading provincial papers are *Aarhus Stiftstidende, Aalborg Stiftstidende, Fyens Stiftstidende* at Odense, and *Vestkusten* at Esbjerg, all holding strong positions in their territories. With seventy dailies to divide among 1,500,000 families, circulations cannot be large. Only four papers sell more than 100,000 copies, all in Copenhagen; a third of the provincial dailies sell less than 10,000.

Effects of Financial Independence

Danish dailies today are financially healthy, for advertising is well-developed. They look very much like American dailies in their volume of display and classified advertising. Larger papers get from 50 to 60 per cent of their income from this source, and even the smaller ones get from 30 to 40 per cent. Most dailies are owned privately or by local joint-stock companies. The Social Democratic papers are owned by the Trade Union and the party organization, and it is possible that some of their smaller papers have deficits made up from profits on larger papers. It is certain, however, that the little eight page tabloid *Land og Folk* with only 7,800 circulation and almost no advertising could not exist without Communist party subsidy.

Although amalgamations have resulted in the domination of their areas by single papers, which has meant they must serve all readers regardless of party, and although there is still a certain tradition of political affiliation, in 1964 fourteen papers labeled themselves independent or nonpolitical. Most of the rest do not claim to be tied to any party but assert instead that they are of Liberal, Conservative, Radical-Liberal, or Social Democratic appeal.

Actually, there has been a marked weakening of political emphasis as the whole stress has turned to news and information. No longer is it true that every daily city has three to four party dailies. Outside the capital there are only three of the larger provincial cities where this is true. Provincial readers may subscribe to one of the national papers from Copenhagen, but they are also loyal to their local or regional paper. It is this newspaper-mindedness which accounts for the fact that most families read two papers daily. Even though radio and television are available, the people consider their newspapers the major and preferred source of information. News and opinion are carefully separated, and regardless of the political tendency shown in the editorial column, the news is handled objectively, for Danish papers feel their obligation is to provide a well-balanced and comprehensive picture of what is going on in their country and in the world.

Americans traveling in Denmark are always amazed to see the fat papers displayed on newsstands. Today many provincial papers issue twenty- to twenty-four-page editions while the big Copenhagen papers print up to forty-eight pages weekdays and often more than eighty on Sundays.

As in other Scandinavian countries, the news-editorial departments are sharply divided from the business departments, and the editor is king pin—sovereign over all that goes into the paper. This press is well-organized; the Danish Newspaper Federation includes both editors and publishers and speaks for the press of the whole country. Unlike some European countries, where the advertiser never knows what he is buying, the Danes have their *Danske Reklame Forenings Oplagskontrol*, which functions as does the Audit Bureau of Circulation in the United States. The working press has its Journalists *Forening* and Journalists *Forbundet*, both of which devote themselves to the economic and professional advancement of their members.

News Agencies

Denmark's dailies are well-supplied with provincial, national, and world news. Their agency, known as Ritzaus, was founded in 1866 by E. N. Ritzaus, who had worked with Reuter on the Continent. A family enterprise till 1947, it then became the property of the Danish daily press, operating as a cooperative agency. In 1948 it was joined by *Berlingske Tidende* and *Politiken*, which had held off because of their own extensive system of correspondents. This not only bettered the financial position of Ritzaus but permitted it to improve its service. The main office is in Copenhagen with suboffices in larger provincial cities. It has correspondents on its member papers all over the country and foreign correspondents as well. The news of Denmark is gathered and exchanged with Reuters, the Norwegian, Swedish, Finnish, Dutch, Belgian, and Swiss agencies for their national and world news. In addition to Ritzaus a number of dailies use either Associated Press or United Press International services. Some of the larger dailies also have foreign correspondents of their own.

Characteristics of Danish Papers

These dailies are as newsy and striking in appearance as those in America, except they seldom employ banners but use a horizontal display that is lively and attractive. Often they carry more pictures and arresting displays than do American papers. There are no dead-looking pages, for every inside page is as carefully made up as the first. Most papers pyramid their advertising for the first half of their pages and keep these fairly open to draw the reader into the paper; then the last half may have solid pages of advertising.

A typical Copenhagen morning daily starts with a front page display window, playing top stories, foreign, national, or local. Then follow jumps interspersed with comic strips, a section for women, a page or two of local news, and a family page. This last is not like an American society page. Although it carries weddings, engagements, anniversaries, birthdays, and brief announcements of meetings, it provides also family features and local personals. Now come sports and a roundup of news from provincial cities. Next are pages providing a heavy coverage of wire news followed by the editorial page featuring one or two editorials, the daily *kronik* by some well-known authority, and background-of-the-news articles. Succeeding pages carry cultural news and local and provincial, well-illustrated feature articles which take the place of syndicated features provided in American papers. These are followed by the business and financial pages. The rest of the paper will be almost solid with advertising, broken up here and there with comic strips and panels. The back page is something special, for this is the fun page with local columns in a light vein often illustrated with humorous cartoons. Here the reader also finds his theater and film columns, radio and television programs. The Danes are a fun-loving people, and they enjoy humor in their papers.

Copenhagen's big morning papers represent a serious press with good coverage of national and foreign news, but they pay less attention to local happenings than do the noon and evening Copenhagen papers and the provincial dailies. These noon and evening papers are more popular and sensational, with bolder headline and picture display. Their pages are filled with features, women's departments, expanded sports, film and entertainment news, more comic strips, even bridge and lonely hearts columns. They never go to press without pinup girl pictures. Danes are less squeamish when it comes to crime news than their Norwegian and Swedish neighbors and will play a good local crime story. But since the adoption of the new 1960 rules, Danish newspapers have cut down on sensational details and are careful about handling stories involving minors. The provincial evening dailies are much more serious, give a good coverage of national and foreign news in condensed form, and strong coverage to local and regional news.

Denmark has a good press and, with the single exception of *Land og Folk*, it is pro-democratic and pro-western. Most Danish journalists are well-paid and respected. No one has to write against the dictates of his conscience, for every Danish writer is free to report the news as he sees it. Like their American contemporaries, Danish reporters and editors complain about secrecy in the government which prevents them from keeping their readers fully informed. Denmark represents a healthy area in the world's journalism.

REPRESENTATIVE PAPERS

Berlingske Tidende (Copenhagen)—Denmark's oldest paper and one of the best in Europe with 175,060 daily circulation and 332,394 on Sunday. Considered one of the most independent. No party affiliation but has Conservative leanings. Appeals to middle and upper middle class. Provides outstanding coverage of national and foreign news; also carries many popular features. Its newspaper and publishing plant occupies a city block; its sumptuous editorial offices would be the envy of most American newspaper men.

Politiken (Copenhagen)—Second largest with 139,522 daily circulation and 243,101 on Sunday. Very influential, well-written, well-informed. Danes value it for its exclusives from its large corps of foreign and provincial correspondents. More liberal than its chief rival and backs social reforms. Editorially, has often backed Radical Liberals but is essentially independent. Strongly pro-western and anti-Communist.

Aktuelt (Copenhagen)—The former *Social Demokraten*, changed in 1959 to broaden its appeal. Circulation 101,495 daily and 67,449 on Sunday. Now under new formula, provides more national and world news than before, but in its usual sixteen pages has to condense this. Carries much labor news as it caters to this audience. Bids for popularity with many features. Backs Social Democrats; generally pro-western and urges trade with Soviet Union.

Information (Copenhagen)—One of the wartime resistance papers. An elite-oriented paper, hard-hitting in its editorials, proud of its independence of party or economic interest. An attractive, compact little daily; within its few pages it provides good news coverage. Strongly pro-western and anti-Communist. Circulation 21,760.

Jyllands Posten (Aarhus)—Largest provincial daily with 63,789 daily circulation and 144,950 on Sunday. Published in Aarhus, an important industrial port. Dominates its area with a quality that makes it considered a national paper. Attractive and well-edited. Independent with Conservative leanings. Most pro-western and influential of provincial dailies.

A Heritage of Freedom

Norway's Vigorous Press

Norway is a stronghold of press freedom; its people and its press have always fought for their liberties. Their geography and history have helped determine the character of the press. This long, lean land, 1,000 miles in length, stretches from well above the Arctic Circle to the latitude of Labrador. It is extremely rugged, covered by mountains, a land of great distances. From Oslo to northern Norway is as far as from Oslo to Rome. It embraces little more territory than Wisconsin and Illinois together, yet its population of 3,681,000 supports more than twice as many dailies as does Wisconsin. In the long Arctic reaches people are thinly spread; 76 per cent live in the lower third of the country where newspapers are most numerous. The struggle for life has produced a tough-minded people who have built a progressive democracy. It was the first to give women the right to vote; its program of social services is well-advanced. The nation that gave the world Ibsen, Grieg, Nansen, Amundsen, Ole Bull, Björnson, Hamsun, and Vigeland is proud of her cultural traditions. There are no illiterates in Norway, and this has made for a wide and discriminating reader audience with an avidity for knowledge that accounts for the density of newspapers and other publications.

To understand this press, one must consider the background of the people. The original Finno-Ugrians were overrun around 1700 B.C. by a Teutonic invasion from what is now Sweden. For long centuries each district or *fylke* was ruled by its own feudal lord till in 873 A.D. Harald Haarfager (Fair Hair) united the country and established the first national assembly. For the previous seventy-seven years Norwegian, Swedish, and Danish Vikings or sea warriors had been raiding and conquering parts of England, Ireland, Scotland, Germany, France, Spain, and Russia. Norwegian Vikings under Leif, son of Eric, sailed west to discover and settle Greenland and Iceland and then discovered the New World long before Columbus's time. Dr. H. Ingstad's discovery in 1963 of the ruins of the original Vineland settlement attests that Leif's colony was on the coast of Newfoundland about 1000 A.D.

For the next three hundred years Norway's history was one of internal and external wars until in 1397 Denmark, Sweden, and Norway were joined in the Union of Kalmar. For Norway this meant her reduction in the following more than four hundred years to little more than a neglected Danish province.

Press Origins

First precursors of the press were handwritten newssheets called *Cedula Novitatis* and later *Tidende*, edited for groups of subscribers. They described political events, battles, or catastrophes, mostly from abroad; occasionally they included local items. The earliest example of these, in the state archives in Oslo, is dated 1326; in the Munich collections others are dated from 1524 to 1625.

Because Denmark completely neglected her northern province, Norway did not get a printing press till 1644 when one was imported from Copenhagen. This was almost 200 years after presses had appeared elsewhere on the Continent. Now occasional printed newssheets appeared. The oldest carried the long title "Summarized Description of Events in the County of Akershus in this Current Year of 1644." Then in 1660 came a paper known as *Postmesterblad* (Posmaster's Paper), edited by the postmaster at Christiania (Oslo) for subscribers in other parts of the country. It was supposed to be issued every three months, but there is no evidence that it achieved this regularity. The only two extant copies are in the Royal Library in Copenhagen dated 1711 and 1718.

Norway had to wait for longer than a century after her first printing press for her first own regular weekly newspaper, *Norske Intelligens Sedeler* (Norwegian Intelligence Leaves), which appeared in Christiania in 1763. From the time Queen Margaret had engineered the Union of Kalmar for the benefit of her son, King Eirik, the Danes had controlled Norway. Danish officials governed the provinces, bleeding the people for their own enrichment, treating peasants as little more than slaves. Popular revolts were quickly put down. Kings, called Christian or Frederick, alternated, but few even visited Norway. Norwegian pleas for a university of their own were denied, and anything as dangerous as a Norwegian press was not encouraged. One reactionary prime minister, Ole Hoeg Gulberg, expressed the Danish attitude when he wrote, "No Norwegian exists. We are all citizens of Denmark. Do not write for the despicable Christiania 'raisoners.' "

Nevertheless, the first paper at Christiania was followed by a second at Bergen in 1765 and in 1767 came the *Trondheim Addressavisen*. The first two did not live long, but the third survives today as Norway's oldest newspaper. It developed out of an advertising office set up by a printer, Jens Christensen Windon, in 1739. Then in 1767 Martinus Lind Nissen obtained a royal privileged license to enlarge this "want-ad sheet" by adding news with the explicit reservation that he must not deal with public measures or politics. It was a small four-page sheet appearing on Fridays, and thirty years later it still had a circulation of only 500. Outside of local personals its content had to be literary. But after the turn of the century it began to grow. In 1839 it became a triweekly and since 1862 has been a daily. It will celebrate its two hundredth anniversary shortly.

A Short Breath of Freedom

Although autocratic Danish rulers had maintained strict licensing and censorship, a change came in 1770. King Christian VII, so debauched that he had become incompetent, had made his personal physician, Johann Friederick Struensee, his confidential advisor and in time gave him absolute power to issue edicts in his name. Struensee, a strong liberal, removed all censorship, giving Norwegians an opportunity to express their national feeling. A flood of pamphlets, newspapers, and periodicals appeared picturing Norway as a stepchild, possessing rich possibilities for development, but a martyr to Danish selfishness. This press freedom, however, gave Danish nobility and high officials the same opportunity to attack Struensee, and by disclosing his illicit love affair with the Queen they ruined him. He was executed in 1772. Thus ended the attempt to establish an enlightened despotism in Denmark and Norway and ushered in a strongly reactionary government which ended all press freedom.

Danes Cede Norway to Sweden

Continental events brought an eclipse to Denmark's power. She had been allied with Napoleon; and when the British blockade cut Denmark off from Norway, the latter became almost independent and her papers free to discuss any question. There were now seven political papers which grew more vigorous in championing national independence. Napoleon's final defeat and the surrender of Denmark forced the Danes to accept the Peace of Kiel under which they ceded Norway to Sweden. One Christiania paper, *Tiden*, greeted this news with an "extra of joy"; but the others raised a storm of protest contending that, while the Danish king might renounce his right to the Norwegian crown, it was contrary to international law to dispose of an entire nation without the consent of its people. Led by Count Wedel Jarlsberg, Judge Christian Magnus Felsen, and Professor George Sverdrup, a national assembly met at Eidsvold and on May 17, 1814, declared Norway's independence. It adopted a constitution placing the power in a people's parliament and denying the king any veto power of dissolution. Section 100 of this constitution said: "There shall be liberty of the press. Everyone shall be at liberty to speak his mind freely regarding the administration of the state or any other subject whatsoever."

But the great powers would not relinquish their plan for the union of Sweden and Norway, which was intended to compensate Sweden for her loss of Finland. Charles XIV, the first of the Swedish Bernadotte kings, invaded Norway to enforce his claim; but after two weeks he opened negotiations by proposing an alliance under the Swedish king, with the Eidsvold constitution remaining as Norway's fundamental law and permitting Norway to have her own government and parliament. This was approved by the Norwegian *Storthing*. Norway had her first daily in 1819 when *Morgenbladet* appeared in Christiania.

The early years of the new union brought poverty and depression to Norway. The fortunes of even the wealthiest had been wrecked during the long period of war and blockade; hence there was no capital available. Crop failures caused great suffering. Trade with England and Denmark declined, and many factories had to close. Gradually, with help from Sweden, an industrial and commercial revival began. By the 1830's the outlook was brightening; by the forties improvement was marked.

The Press Fights King

When, however, the Swedish king began developing absolutist tendencies, the press took as its task the defense of the constitution and the championing of Norway's rights within the union. The king, frustrated by the slowness of the *Storthing* in passing legislation he wanted, proposed amendments which would increase his power. The press fought these with determination. But soon there developed a division in its ranks as the nobility and privileged class urged amendments to strengthen upper-class control in parliament. With the literary figure J. S. Welhaven as their champion, they formed the Intelligence party, posing as the representatives of refinement and culture, and brought out in 1815 *Den Constitutionele* as a daily. The more liberal group, representing the *Bönde* or peasant class, small and large landowners, and the common people, formed the Patriot party, most jealous of Norway's independence. Their first great champion was

Henrick Wergeland, the leading literary figure of the day who, through his articles and poems, roused his people to safeguard their democratic freedoms and who fought for the rights of the farmer and common people. The Patriots brought out in 1831 *Folkebladet* edited by P. P. Flor. These two were the first party papers in Norway.

The July, 1830, Revolution in France had stimulated political consciousness and brought further press development. Now the provincial press began to expand. On the death of Charles XIV in 1844 Oscar I took the throne. He improved relations between the two peoples through governmental reforms, helped Norway build roads and her first railway, and developed trade and shipping till Norway had one-fourth of the world's merchant marine. The press shared this growing prosperity, and by 1849 Norway had forty newspapers.

Press Develops in Controversy

The political battles of the next thirty years gave increasing impetus to press growth as the country was split between the Conservatives and the Liberals. Outside these were the tenant farmers, farm laborers, and the growing number of industrial workers who were still unenfranchised. Their first great supporter was Marcus Thrane who in 1848 began advocating what to the other parties was radical socialism. As editor of *Drammens Adresse,* he demanded a better deal for those still denied the ballot. The startled owners of his paper dismissed him, but he proceeded to organize *arbeider foreninger* (labor societies) all over Norway. When his overenthusiastic followers among farm laborers began appropriating land from their bosses and cutting down trees, the government reacted quickly and arrested 149 labor leaders. Thrane himself was sentenced to four years in prison and after his release came to Chicago to edit *Norske Amerikanaren.*

Efforts to make the *Storthing* a more permanent power in the life of the nation, to admit members of the Cabinet to parliament, as under the British system, and to extend suffrage led to vehement election campaigns. Eventually Norway won true parliamentary government. In this political debate the press took an increasingly important part, and by 1885 Norway had 133 newspapers and 87 magazines and other journals.

This period saw the birth of many of Norway's leading papers of today. *Aftenposten,* the foremost daily in 1965, was begun by Christian Schibsted in 1860. His son Amandus took over the editorship in 1889. Up to this time Norwegian papers had placed their chief emphasis on leading articles. But young Schibsted sensed that readers might be more interested in news than in political polemics, so he began emphasizing local news coverage. To combat *Aftenposten,* the well-established *Morgenbladet,* charging 24 kroner per year, brought out its own afternoon edition. Schibsted countered by providing a morning edition at no increase over his 10 kroner price. By expertly organized local and governmental reportage, by correspondence from many Norwegian cities and abroad, Schibsted brought *Aftenposten* to a circulation of 14,500 while *Morgenbladet* stood at 10,000.

Morgenbladet had its great editor, too, in Nils Vogt, an educated man from an important family. When he elected journalism as a career it was a startling innovation which brought new prestige to the profession. He was a hard taskmaster and edited most of the copy himself; his red and blue pencils tore out everything vulgar, banal, inaccurate, or not up to the literary tone he had set for his paper. He made it of such high quality that literary critics of the day, when they wished to compliment an author, would write that the work was good enough to have appeared in *Morgenbladet.* He was a one-man school of journalism, and many able men graduated from his paper. It was his goal to raise journalistic standards, and he was the first president of *Norsk Press Forbund,* Norway's first professional organization, founded in 1910. After the turn of the century he became the strongest proponent of the dissolution of the union with Sweden and an advocate of Norwegian independence.

Dagbladet, which was to become the chief organ of the Liberal party, was founded in Christiania in 1868 as was *Verdens Gang,* whose great editor from 1878 onward was O. Thommasen, one of the most respected and hated of his day by his conservative opponents. He made his paper a new power in Norwegian journalism, for he was completely independent and fought for what he thought was good for Norway, irrespective of the Liberal party line. His paper was one of the most widely circulated in his time, and by 1884 it had outdistanced *Dagbladet,* reaching a circulation of 14,000. In the provinces two outstanding papers of today, *Bergens Tidende* and *Stavanger Aftenbladet,* were begun in 1863 and 1883, respectively.

A new force emerged with the growth of labor unions in the seventies and eighties. In 1884 the United Norwegian Labor Union was formed, which brought out the first labor paper, *Vårt Arbeide.* As Labor gathered strength this paper changed its title to *Social Demokraten* to support the Norwegian Labor party, organized in 1887. In 1923 this was to become *Arbeiderbladet,* the leading Labor organ today.

Norway Wins Independence

Oscar II had come to the throne in 1872 and, as a gesture of goodwill, proposed that cabinet ministers be admitted to the *Storthing.*

When the proposal was to be accompanied by amendments giving him the right to dissolve parliament, the Liberal press fought him till he was compelled to ask John Sverdrup, the great Liberal reform leader, to form the first Liberal ministry in 1884. It proceeded to work out and establish important reforms, including universal suffrage for men, a jury system in criminal trials, the reorganization of the school system, and social legislation for control of child labor in factories, protection for women workers, and accident insurance.

The following years were marked by tremendous debates in the press over the conduct of Norway's foreign affairs. Her foreign commerce was twice that of Sweden yet Sweden controlled the whole consular service, placing consuls where Norway had little trade but providing none where Norway had her largest business. The Liberal party and its papers protested that Norway must have her own foreign minister and her own consular service. When the king refused and the Swedish *Riksdag* became hostile, there was danger of an open rupture. But the Swedish king was a man of peace, and a widespread peace movement in his country turned the tide. Sweden agreed to a dissolution of the union provided the Norwegian people signified this desire in a plebiscite. This they proceeded to vote almost unanimously on August 13, 1905. At last Norway was independent. There were many who wanted a republic, but the supporters of a limited monarchy won out. Rather than choose another Bernadotte, they conferred the crown on Prince Charles of Denmark. On November 25 the king, who took the name of Haakon VII, and his Queen Maud, the daughter of Edward VII of England, entered the Norwegian capital.

The Press Strides Forward

The final achievement of independence gave great encouragement to the Norwegian people, and the press began to progress rapidly. The spread of education had fostered literacy, and increased industrialization brought growing prosperity. The press took a lively part in the discussion of issues facing the nation—the controversies over labor and social welfare legislation. Whereas in 1902 there had been 462 newspapers and other publications, by 1913 the number had grown to 679. The outbreak of World War I caused a temporary panic but, since Norway was neutral, she soon began to reap great profits by supplying the belligerents. All sorts of commercial and industrial enterprises were begun; wages and salaries rose. But the necessity of keeping the nation on a war footing to protect itself from any invasion was costly and when Germany launched her unrestricted submarine warfare to cut off Norway's trade with England, Norway lost almost half her tonnage.

There was a postwar depression, but soon the nation was on the road to recovery, and the next fifteen years were a period of economic progress. One of the things that gave Norwegians satisfaction was the changing of the name of their capital to Oslo. This had been its original name under Harald Haarfager as early as 1048 but during their Danish captivity it has been renamed Christiania, in honor of Christian IV. Following a succession of coalition governments of the Conservatives and Liberals, the Labor party, in 1935, won a decisive victory. This party had earlier flirted with Moscow but in 1923 it had severed all connections with Communism. An extreme left wing group, had, however, formed a Communist party. Under the Labor party a broad public health program, extensive adult education, old-age pensions, and unemployment insurance were adopted. The years between the two wars saw a greater development of the press than ever before, and by 1940 Norway had 300 newspapers and 1200 other publications.

The Press in World War II

Norwegians through the thirties were aware of the dangers of Hitlerism, and they hated the small Nazi party headed by Vidkun Quisling. At the outbreak of World War II they declared their neutrality but, remembering the previous war, began arming. What they did not know was that Quisling had warned Hitler that the western Allies were planning to occupy bases in Norway, and that he had advocated German invasion. When the Germans struck in the early morning of April 9, 1940, the Norwegians were caught by surprise. Before they could muster sufficient defense the Germans had taken the seaport towns of Narvik, Trondheim, Bergen, Stavanger, Christiansand, and Oslo. When Norwegian newspaper men in these cities reported for work, they found their papers had been taken over by the enemy.

The editor of *Aftenposten*, for instance, had put his paper to bed the afternoon before without any inkling of danger. He was awakened by storm troopers beating on his door. His family tearfully saw him taken away. He was marched to his newspaper where he found his former elevator operator sitting in his chair in a German officer's uniform. This man announced that he was now in charge of the paper and that, since it was the largest in Norway, it would continue under German direction. The same thing happened on other papers. Soon German press officers arrived by plane to take over radio, newspapers, and the news agency, *Norske Telegrambyra*. Editors in Oslo were called to the Grand Hotel and assured that no censorship was intended but that the Germans merely wished to orient and help them. It was explained that all political and military stories had to be approved by the Germans, that German communiques must be printed word for word, that all criticism of German measures was forbidden, that makeup must be restrained so as not to alarm the people, and that only such telegraphic news as was provided by the German-controlled *Norske Telegram-byra* could be used. Such was the freedom granted a press which had long been completely free.

Every loyal Norwegian newspaper man had to face the question of whether to flee to Sweden. Many were so closely watched they had to remain and hope thereby to serve their country by getting some true reports through censorship to the people. In the North, behind the fighting lines, loyal papers were still publishing. From Ålesund, Bodö, Hamar, Lillehammer, Svolvaern, and Sunmore, papers printed the news of Norway's fighting forces, communications from the king, and appeals to Norway's sons to join the loyal forces. From the occupied area young men disappeared to enlist. They fought valiantly; but after the Allies had had to withdraw their help, the situation became hopeless. The king and his staff were evacuated to London. Many of the fighting men were imprisoned, while many escaped to continue as underground fighters.

In the occupied area Norwegian editors were handcuffed by daily directives; but often by double-talk they contrived to let the people read between the lines. They printed Nazi press directives in such a way that people would know how they were controlled. If the Germans were furious, the Norwegians said that they had assumed such important orders should be published. In innocently worded want ads they tucked forbidden information. The more audacious were thrown into concentration camps. One newspaperman after another went underground. Now the Germans ushered in their tough period. More and more editors were arrested and replaced by "quislings." Paper after paper was closed. *Arbeiderbladet*, the principal organ of the Labor party, was suppressed and its plant, the most modern in Norway, was taken over by Quisling's paper, ironically called *Fritt Folk*, which set the pace with its vicious lies and attacks on patriotic Norwegians and the Allies.

But a new free press sprang up from the underground and published its first paper in May, 1940. Despite purges, arrests, and executions some three hundred of these papers were published in Norway during the occupation with an average weekly circulation of 231,907. Nearly all were single sheets mimeographed on both sides; a few were printed. They came to mean so much to Norwegians that the people risked their lives, and sometimes lost them, to get a forbidden copy. News was gathered by secret radios from the Norwegian government in exile in London, from Sweden, and from underground receivers and senders all over Norway. Producers worked in attics, basements, and secret shacks; and each man knew only the next link in his chain so that, if he were captured and tortured, his chain could not be destroyed. The year 1942 was particularly hard, for the Germans set out definitely to destroy the underground press. Sometimes entire news organizations were rounded up and shot. It might take weeks to reorganize, but there were always new heroes and heroines to take the vacant places. In all there is record of sixty-nine who were executed, but more than 3,000 others received long sentences or were sent to concentration camps in Germany and Norway. Burgitt Hallen, an underground editor, said, "They succeeded in torturing and killing our people but they never could kill the truth—their worst and most powerful enemy." And this underground press was the unifying force which kept the Norwegian people firm during the long days and nights of Nazi occupation.

Postwar Problems

During the war Norway's greatest contribution to the war effort was made by her merchant fleet, which the British said was worth a million soldiers. As the war moved to its final crisis, the Germans began a scorched earth program in the north; but on May 7, 1945, German forces had to surrender. Forty thousand underground fighters came out of hiding and took control. King Haakon returned on June 7.

The Labor party won the 1945 election only to face grave problems of food, clothing, and housing shortages. Industrial production had been halved, farm production crippled. But with help from the United States, England, Sweden, and Denmark a recovery began. What to do with some 40,000 "quislings" was a problem. All were given a fair trial; Quisling himself and top Norwegian Nazis were executed; many others were imprisoned. All "quisling" newspapermen were banned from ever again working in journalism.

When liberation came Norway's newspapermen who were still alive reported back to their old papers. Some of the papers had had their plants destroyed. Others, now impoverished, found it impossible to continue. Where in 1940 Norway had had 300 newspapers, by 1949 there were only 214, of which 89 were dailies. Circulations soared, for people were hungry for free news. By 1949 daily circulations were double those of 1939, and selling 1,500,000 papers represented one copy for every two Norwegians. The weekly press and magazines and other periodicals added 2,351,000 more. Probably no other country, at this time, had as many publications in proportion to its population as Norway.

King Haakon died in 1957 and was succeeded by his son Olav V. Norway continued to stand boldly for cooperation with the west. There was frequent friction with the Soviet Union over its espionage, and the Communist vote declined steadily till in 1961 the party lost its last seat in parliament. The government and the people worked vigorously to improve the economy, and by 1961 it was burgeoning. In 1964 Norway was buoyant with a marked advance in production and foreign trade. The Labor party, which has been in power for twenty-nine years except for a brief twenty-three-day interregnum in 1963, had continued its leadership of the country under Premier Einar Gerhardsen. However, in the September, 1965, election a coalition of nonsocialist parties—Conservative, Liberal, Center (Agrarian), and Christian Peoples—unseated Gerhardsen and the Labor party. Coalition candidates had accused that party of mismanagement of state-owned industries and failure to solve the nation's housing and inflation problems. The attack was successful, for it persuaded voters that it was time for a change.

In view of Norway's booming economy, one might have expected an expansion of the press; but increased production costs and heightened competition have forced a reduction in numbers. In 1964 Norway had 84 dailies with a total circulation of 1,559,847, which meant a sale of 42.3 copies per 100 persons—the third largest ratio of reader interest in Europe. The weekly press, publishing from one to four times a week, has been reduced to 82 with a total circulation of 400,000. Nevertheless, 166 papers are still a large number for so small a country.

Why This Large Number?

Norwegians support so many newspapers because they are literate and highly news-oriented. Recent surveys have shown that even though radio and television are available, the people place their main reliance for information and opinion on the press. Norwegians also take politics seriously; hence there has been a tendency for the six major parties to have voices in as many cities as possible. The spread of Norway's small population over 2,000 miles of fjord-indented coastline has isolated many communities. Therefore, the Oslo press has not been able to dominate the country, and a strong provincial press has developed. Before the last war many small towns had their own weeklies; but, as strong provincial papers were able to spread their news coverage and circulation over a wider area, the number of small weeklies was reduced. Of necessity the daily and weekly press have had to play complementary yet distinctive roles, for since so many people are dependent on their nearest available daily, weekly, or triweekly, Norway's weekly press has not been able to confine itself to local news. Instead, papers have to contribute their part to the total information picture by providing some national and foreign news as well.

Nevertheless, there is a multiplicity of papers in many cities and towns because of the political division of the press. Oslo, with a 484,000 population, has 10 dailies; Bergen with 115,689 and Stavanger with 52,600 each have four dailies, and Christiansand with 28,000 has three. Many smaller cities have two or three, and there are only 17 one-daily towns. This multiplicity has, of course, meant smaller circulations. More than half the dailies sell under 10,000 copies, more than three-fourths under 20,000. There is only one paper with a circulation larger than 100,000.

Norwegian newspapers today are not as totally concerned with politics as they were in the nineteenth century. The better ones pay more attention to news coverage, yet most have political leanings. Only ten dailies and thirty-four weeklies label themselves independent and nonpolitical. The Conservative and Liberal parties with thirty-six papers have the strongest press support, but Labor with twenty-six dailies continued till 1965 to draw the largest number of votes.

Most Papers Are Economically Sound

Editorial support of a party does not usually mean party subsidy, for most Norwegian papers are self-supporting. The larger ones are solid and profitable businesses. It took some time after the war for advertising to come back, but today many papers are getting two-thirds of their income from advertising and one-third from subscriptions. In some smaller cities this may not be true and subsidy may be necessary. There are no chains of papers in Norway. The closest approach is Labor's *Arbeidernes Presskontor* and *Arbeidernes Samvirke AS*, which manage the Labor papers, economically and technically, and which may distribute profits from larger papers to make up deficits on a few small ones. Certainly the one Communist daily could not survive without party support. But on the whole Norway's newspaper economics is sound. Most papers are owned by individuals or family corporations.

One peculiarity American visitors are quick to note is that there are no Sunday papers, for they have been forbidden by law for many years. As a result, dailies are limited to six days a week, but a number of the larger ones issue expanded Saturday editions carrying much more feature and cultural material.

Both daily and weekly papers are well served by *Norske Tele-grambyra* (NTB), established in 1876 by A. E. E. Fitch, who founded the Swedish *Tidningarnas Telegrambyra*. It must be remembered that Norway was then a joint kingdom with Sweden. NTB was a private enterprise till 1918 when it was taken over by the Norwegian press and reorganized as a cooperative undertaking with its shares owned exclusively by Norwegian papers. Income is derived from subscription fees paid by papers according to their circulation and from fixed fees paid by Norwegian radio and television. The agency has 125 correspondents in Norway and 25 stringers abroad; but when big news breaks, its own special correspondents are sent out. NTB has contractual arrangements with the leading European agencies, but places its chief reliance on Reuters. News of the capital is covered by the home office staff in Oslo. Both Associated Press and United Press International have offices in Oslo and provide service directly to some of the larger papers. Many papers use at least two services, including those of other Nordic agencies, but all take NTB. About two-thirds of NTB's daily output is domestic news, one-third foreign news. A daily picture service, distributed by an extensive telephoto network, is also provided by NTB.

What Are Norwegian Papers Like?

In appearance Norwegian papers seem as newsy as American papers, and their typography and makeup are good. There are seldom any big black banner heads, for most circulation is by subscription and papers do not need to sell themselves with banners. Instead they achieve an interesting horizontal makeup with two-, three-, and four-column spreadheads, broken by compelling news pictures. Most papers are standard-sized.

Front pages are display windows for the best stories—foreign, national, or local. Significant news is covered thoroughly, and spot news is supported by good backgrounding. Every paper has its daily *kronik* written by well-known authorities on historical, economic, social, and political questions. There is less local news than in American papers, though there is usually one local page. Newswriting style, in the European tradition, is strictly chronological without any summarizing lead. Papers carry little crime news, and even when a major crime occurs, it is covered briefly without any lurid details. There are no accounts of divorces and no sensational sex stories, although there is no law against printing them. Norwegian editors consider this type of story in bad taste, and they have a high regard for the rights of privacy. There are many good news pictures, but anything approaching the cheesecake variety is rare. Norwegians love sports and these are given good coverage: larger papers carry up to four pages.

There are no society pages as such. Announcements of engagements and weddings are listed briefly, as are meetings of various organizations. Like those in Sweden, Norwegian papers run columns of congratulations to leading citizens on their birthdays. These papers carry much art, music, literary, and other cultural material. There are no advice to the lovelorn or health columns, and gossip columns would not be tolerated. Some of the larger papers carry two to four comic strips and occasionally comic panels. Instead of syndicated articles, staff members develop homegrown features dealing with the local scene or with life and institutions in other parts of Norway. It must not be thought, however, that the Norwegian press is dour and stern. Local columnists write in a light vein, often dealing humorously with events in their communities. Many papers carry movie, radio, television, and bridge columns, crossword puzzles and daily serial stories. The contents of these pages are conveniently spread out on almost ad-free pages in the first half of the paper and on the back page. Advertising is concentrated in the last few inside pages. There is always a definite editorial page, usually with one long leader article; the rest of the page is filled with background articles.

In the years directly after World War II, because of newsprint rationing, many dailies were limited to four pages; even the larger ones seldom more than eight. But today the larger papers run twenty-four to thirty pages and even the smaller ones have eight to ten. Oslo is the great publishing center, and its ten dailies represent 40 per cent of the total daily circulation. It is mainly a morning press. The views of all political parties are represented, but Oslo papers devote more news and editorial attention to international affairs than do the rest of the press. By contrast the provincial dailies appear mainly in the evening.

A Responsible Press

Norway's press is free and democratic. Its people are provided with the facts on every issue and in every shade of opinion. The watchword of this press is "freedom with responsibility." The Norwegian Press Association has established clearly defined directives for good press practice. Papers are cautioned to strive tirelessly to provide correct and factual information, to exercise extreme care with information which might damage the good name or reputation of individuals, to avoid mentioning suicide except in connection with crimes of grave character, and to use caution in police and court reporting. This organization has, furthermore, set up a court of honor to which any person can appeal if he feels he has been maligned by inaccurate facts. This court has won great respect, and no Norwegian journalist wants to risk being condemned by it for unethical or unprofessional conduct. Norwegian newspapers have acquired the status of social institutions, and editors are respected figures in their areas.

Norway has no special press law, for its constitution has firmly established the basic principles of freedom of information and the liberty of the press. Newspapers are subject to the same laws that apply to any citizen regarding false and defamatory accusation, libel, slander, subversive activities, or blasphemy. There are also special rules which give an attacked person the right to answer accusations in the paper which printed them. But the press is also protected in its right to shield news sources.

Norway's press is, on the whole, a good press, a bit more sober and staid perhaps than that in many other countries; but this is part of its sense of responsibility. It is free to attack the government or any minister of a governmental department and serves as a watchdog over the rights of the people. While many Norwegians read religiously the paper representing their party viewpoint, they read other papers as well. If they did not, Norway could not support 166 newspapers. As a result the people are well informed: they know much more about what transpires in the United States than Americans know about what goes on in Norway. The presentation of this news is fair and friendly, for, with the exception of the one small Communist paper *Friheten,* this press is pro-democratic and pro-western.

REPRESENTATIVE PAPERS

Addresseavisen (Trondheim)—Norway's oldest paper, founded in 1767. Largest paper in major port city. Wields considerable influence in north-central Norway. Conservative; strongly pro-western. Circulation 67,405.

Aftenposten (Oslo)—Norway's largest with a 174,934 circulation mornings, 148,191 evenings, and 194,809 on Saturday. Has reached this position by providing better news and picture coverage than any other daily. Has network of correspondents all over Norway and abroad. Heavy on advertising; most profitable newspaper enterprise; Conservative but not a party organ. Pro-western; favors Nordic cooperation.

Arbeiderbladet (Oslo)—Third largest in capital with 66,879 daily circulation and 80,246 Saturdays. Chief organ of Labor party. Well made-up, fairly strong on foreign and national news, but strong on Labor news and party policies. Consistently anti-Communist but has favored friendly relations with Soviet Union. Its back page is one of the best background-of-news pages in Norway.

Bergens Tidende (Bergen)—Largest paper in Norway's second largest city and chief shipping center with circulation of 72,755. Considerable influence on west coast. Anti-Communist and friendly to U.S. Though privately owned, is one of chief spokesmen for Liberal party. Well-edited; rich in cultural material. Looks more conservative than Oslo papers.

Dagbladet (Oslo)—Second largest in Norway with 92,346 daily circulation and 130,401 Saturdays. An afternoon "boulevard paper," more popular than other Oslo papers. Fairly good coverage of foreign and national news, but digested; strong on sports; has many local columnists. Many of its staff are well-known authors. Appeals to intellectuals; gives good space to back-grounding. Pro-western; Norwegians call it "radical liberal."

Morgenposten (Oslo)—Fourth largest in capital with a circulation of 40,460. More popular than other morning papers. Carries women's fashions, many features and entertainment news. Independent of party, but tends to be conservative on domestic issues. Friendly to U.S. and anti-Communist.

Nationen (Oslo)—Official organ of Agrarian party. Circulation 23,403. Champions cause of farmers; carries considerable cultural material; smaller than other Oslo papers. Nationalist, strongly pro-western.

Stavanger Aftenblad—An evening paper, important in southwest Norway. Liberal in politics, it has a highly literary quality. Circulation 40,115. Carries much prestige, is often called Norway's "Manchester Guardian."

Verdens Gang (Oslo)—The most independent paper in the capital with circulation of 33,706; but its influence is not to be measured by circulation, for it has long been one of the strong voices of Norwegian journalism. Speaks out for whatever it thinks is right regardless of party. Influential among intellectuals and leaders.

The Brave but Careful Finnish Press

To Americans, the thought of Finland evokes memories of her great athletes, of Jean Sibelius, her beloved composer, of her integrity as the only European nation to pay her World War I debts, and of her courage as she fought a valiant if futile war with Russia in which she had every American's sympathy. Today she rests under Soviet pressure, but of all the nations on Russia's western border, she alone has managed to stay outside the Iron Curtain.

One of Europe's northernmost countries, Finland is about the size of Minnesota and Iowa together but has a population of only 4,575,000. Ninety per cent of the people speak a language akin to Esthonian, the rest Swedish. They are highly literate and provide a wide audience for newspapers. One-third of the nation is above the Arctic Circle. Communications in the southern two-thirds permit distribution of Helsinki papers far north, but beyond the last railhead this is difficult.

Press Began in Swedish Regime

Finno-Ugrian tribes migrated from the south shores of the Finnish Gulf in the first century and in time established trade relations with the Swedes. In 1157 they joined the Swedish kingdom and later became Christianized. For 600 years their history is that of Sweden, and Finns were equally native Swedes before the law and shared in the upbuilding of their common institutions. The first book printed in Finnish, a prayer book, was produced by a Stockholm printer in 1544. After a period in which only religious works were produced, some Swedish *flygblad* or newssheets were appearing at irregular intervals by the end of the sixteenth century. Not until in the half century of freedom after 1718 could the first regular newspaper appear. A small Swedish weekly, *Abo Tidningar* (Abo News), was brought out in 1770 by a patriotic society at what is now Turku. A second paper, the first in Finnish, appeared in 1776 when a clergyman Antti Liselius brought out his *Suomenkieliset Viikkosomat* (Finnish Language Weekly News) in 1771. But Gustavus III reestablished a royal autocracy in 1772 and during his reign and that of his successor, Gustavus IV, strict authoritarian control prevented any further growth of the press.

Tsar Alexander I of Russia defeated Gustavus IV in 1809 and took Finland from Sweden. He began his reign over his new Finnish subjects in a spirit of liberalism and made Finland an autonomous constitutional grand duchy, though constitutional government in Russia itself was still decades away. Four new weeklies were established; and when the capital was moved from Abo to Helsingfors (now Helsinki), an official paper *Allmana Tidning* (General News) was started in 1820. In the same year A. T. Arvidson launched *Abo Morgenblad*, historically important because it was the first paper which dared speak out for Finnish nationalism. It was banned after nine months and its editor exiled. In 1824 *Abo Underrattelser* (Abo News), the oldest existing paper in Finland, was born. But there was still no real freedom such as had come to the press of Sweden, for Alexander became increasingly reactionary. While thirteen papers had been started in the 1820's, only three lasted more than a few months.

Repression Brings Literary Phase

Nicholas I, who became tsar in 1825, was a rigid absolutist who tried to freeze every free thought which might disturb the order of things entrusted by God to his personal care. Censorship became more and more oppressive. The *Turun Viikisonomia* (Turku Weekly News) managed to survive till 1831 by restricting itself to literary sketches and historical essays; such others as survived had to follow the same formula. Yet they did contribute to both the cultural development of the people and the growth of modern literary Finnish, and promoted a love of the fatherland. By 1840 Finland had thirteen papers with a total circulation of less than 6,000.

Yet the 1840's saw the birth of a new period in Finnish journalism when J. V. Snellman founded *Saima* in 1844, the first paper which dared deal with problems of public interest. The importance of schools, railways, a more enlightened tariff policy, and the development of industry all were grist for his mill; and he dealt with them so objectively that he escaped serious censorship. *Saima* became Finland's leading paper until 1846 when it was suppressed. Snellman soon brought out a monthly cultural journal which, while seemingly literary, still carried his message and continued to prove that the usual plaint of Finnish journalists, "We write what we can, not what we would," was too often a blind. He ushered in a period in which thoughtful leader articles replaced the writings of romanticist litera-teurs. Nicholas gradually tightened the reins of tyranny, dismissed the Finnish Diet, and brought political life to a standstill. His involvement in the Crimean War, however, brought the Finns some respite and again papers dared raise their heads. Among the newcomers was *Suometar Finlandia*, a nationalist paper founded in 1851. It was the forerunner of *Uusi Suomi*, one of Finland's leading papers today.

A Brief Respite, then Repression

The reform-minded Alexander II, who became tsar in 1855, brought greater liberty. The Finnish Diet, which had not met for many years, was permitted to convene regularly and proceeded to enact much needed changes. A national primary school system was established, Finnish was made an official language, and press laws were liberalized. Political parties appeared and the press, expanding in numbers and influence, began to play an important role in national affairs. A number of Finland's dailies of today began as weeklies and semiweeklies in the last thirty-five years of the nineteenth century. Up to 1870 Swedish-language papers with their appeal to the upper and middle classes had been most numerous while the Finnish papers had been read by the common people. But by 1886 there were fifty-one Finnish to forty-four Swedish papers. Among the important papers founded in this period was *Hufvudstadsbladet*, started in 1862 as the organ of the Swedish party. It is still one of the leading Helsinki papers.

After Tsar Alexander's assassination in 1881, Alexander III launched a period of complete reaction. Thus, at a time when the press in other Nordic countries was beginning to flower, that in Finland suffered a severe setback. Fearful of revolution, Alexander tried to suppress all liberal organizations and so muzzled the press that in Russia there were no papers left except the rose-colored affairs in Moscow and Petro-grad. In Finland, papers led a precarious existence. Nevertheless, in 1889 Eero Erkko and a group of young liberals brought out *Päivälehti* (Daily News). These young Finns, dissatisfied with the Finnish papers of that day, wanted a more progressive paper that would "let fresh winds blow through open windows into the stuffy social and political conditions"; and they soon made it Finland's most important paper. Papers representing labor groups also appeared, the most significant of which was *Tvomies* (Worker), founded in 1895 in Helsinki.

Conditions worsened after Nicholas II came to the throne with his intent to defend autocracy unswervingly and began his program of

total Russification of Finland. He made the Russian language obliga-
tory and foisted Russian officials with dictatorial powers on the Finns.
Scores of papers were suppressed. Heavy fines and tightened censorship helped silence any press opposition, but underground papers kept
alive the flames of Finnish nationalism and fought Russian policy. As
an example of press difficulties in this period, *Päivälehti*, which tried to
champion Finnish freedom, was suspended eleven times and finally
closed in 1902. Its editor Erkko was banished on twenty-four hours
notice and fled to Brooklyn, where he became editor of a Finnish
paper. After the revolution of 1905, when he returned to Helsinki, he
was arrested and held in prison under sentence of death until eventually released in 1918. His son Eljas, however, had brought out in 1904
Helsingin Sanomat (Helsinki Mail), with a strong emphasis on news,
which was destined to become Finland's largest daily.

The Yoke Is Lifted

Russia's crushing defeat in the Russo-Japanese war had brought the
1905 revolution into Russia itself. The Finns called a general strike
which in six days forced the Russians to capitulate and to restore the
status quo prior to 1899. The Finnish Diet now assembled and rescinded all the autocratic decrees of Nicholas which had violated the
Finnish constitution. Savoring this new breath of freedom, the press
expanded so rapidly that by 1910 Finland had 128 newspapers, and a
number of former weeklies had become dailies. A new Farmers party
was formed; and its organ *Ilkka*, founded in 1906 and named after a
peasant hero, is still one of the leading voices of this party.

This era of peace, freedom, and internal progress lasted only two
years, for in 1908 Nicholas began his second period of Russification.
The Finnist Diet was again dismissed and the press severely censored.
By 1916 there were only a score of papers left in Finland. The Russian
people had themselves won a constitution and a parliament, the Duma,
but its rule of Finland was as oppressive as that of the tsar. For nine
years the Finns suffered. Then came World War I which proved
catastrophic for Russia and brought the 1917 revolution that deposed
Nicholas. Again Finnish papers stirred the fires of nationalism and on
December 7, 1917, the Finns declared their independence.

Before this could become an actuality, the Finns under General Karl
Mannerheim had to fight a six-months war against Russian Red Guards
and Finnish Reds who sought to establish a soviet-styled republic in
Finland. Mannerheim's forces could not do it alone and called for help,
to which only the Germans responded. This left Finland at the end of
the war an ally of the Germans. Yet by mid-1919 Finland, after the

defeat of Germany, was able to declare herself an independent republic. The constitution established a government responsible to the people under universal suffrage with a unicameral parliament. The rights of free speech, free assembly, and free press became a solid part of the new republican order. Within a year the prewar twenty-three papers had grown to thirty-nine.

The Postwar Press

The press now began to take on distinguishing characteristics. As free political voices they could advocate their policies without fear, and each policy represented a different approach to postwar problems. It became wholly a party press in which the newspapers of a faction formulated the party position on everything, from foreign policy to education, temperance, and other domestic issues. While, according to Finnish writers, this represented "the power and deep emotion of the press," it also led to partisanship in news presentation. At the same time it became a matter of national honor that no paper could accept subsidy from any donor or even from its own party.

In the two decades after independence, Finland experienced tremendous economic growth. Her national income doubled an the standard of living increased 50 per cent. Advertising developed as an important source of newspaper income, and circulations expanded. Many papers derived additional income from commercial, periodical, and book printing. Thus a great change had taken place in the financial underpinnings of the press. Prior to World War I no man entered the newspaper business to make money, but only to influence public opinion, even at the risk of his own funds. Now by the end of 1930 most papers were self-supporting. By 1931 there were 201 papers, 48 of them dailies, 176 in the Finnish language and 23 in Swedish. The press became more modern; papers began to carry larger headlines, better display, and many more pictures and to give increasing space to news. Because of their political character most papers devoted considerable space to editorials and backgrounding articles interpreting the news according to the party viewpoint.

The multiplicity of parties made it necessary for Finland to be governed by coalitions, usually of the Social Democrats, the National Progressives, and the Agrarians. The Communists sometimes made trouble, and in 1930 the party was outlawed as treasonable and its papers suppressed. In foreign policy Finland sought peaceful relations with her neighbors and close cooperation with the League of Nations and other Scandinavian countries. Finland and Russia were always suspicious of each other, but the Finns did sign a nonaggression pact with the Soviet Union. Regardless of their differences on domestic issues, the Finnish press strongly supported this foreign policy.

Until 1939 Finland was a healthy nation and a successful democracy. She had no rigid class society; no first families or aristocracy dominated. Educational advance was not blocked by any caste system. Every Finn was the equal of his countrymen, and sons of farmers and laborers could rise to some of the highest posts in the land.

Disaster Strikes

The outbreak of World War II brought catastrophe. The Finns did everything to avoid conflict with the Soviet Union. But after the German conquest of Poland, Stalin demanded, for Russian protection, the cession of strategic islands in the Gulf of Finland, part of the Karelian Isthmus, and the ice-free Petsamo port in the far north. The Finns were willing to make some concessions but not enough to satisfy Stalin, and in November, 1939, the Red army attacked. For three months the Finns made an amazing stand against the Russians. World opinion condemned Russia and the League of Nations expelled her. But superior Russian forces eventually overwhelmed the Finns; in the 1940 peace, Finland was despoiled of 10 per cent of her territory, including the whole Karelian peninsula, and 14 per cent of her economic resources.

When the war broke out, the Diet gave the government power to limit certain constitutional rights. Censorship, which the Finnish press had not known for twenty years, was imposed. It was a confusing censorship, for the military wanted nothing released while the government, sensing the need of winning world sympathy, wanted to get its story out.

Hitler's invasion of Russia enabled the Finns to recapture some of the territory taken from them; but as world war spread and Germany's eventual defeat became apparent, the question of how to get out of the war became the overwhelming problem. At war with Russia, the Finns were reckoned a co-belligerent with Germany. The Allies repeatedly advised the Finns to stop fighting; but when the Russians again attacked them in June, 1944, it seemed to them they had no alternative. The press urged the armies to stand and fight lest Finland lose her independence and be annexed by Russia. They fought on till September, 1944, when Finland was forced to cede the areas the Russians had forcibly annexed in 1940, to lease to them the Porkkala base, ten miles from Helsinki, and to pay $300,000,000 in goods as reparations in eight annual payments, a staggering burden for a little nation of 4,000,000 persons.

The Nation and Its Press Fight Their Way Back

The years that followed were hard. War losses had amounted to $788,000,000, and now there had to be added heavy reparations. The loss of life and the disruption of business, industry, and agriculture had brought the country to its economic depths. Food and fuel were desperately short. Besides, there were 450,000 Karelian refugees to be fed and housed. Yet the stubborn Finns in two years had paid off 30 per cent of their reparations debt. Russian insistence on payments in ships and machinery forced the development of industries that were to have great future potential.

For newspapers the immediate postwar effect was a drastic decline in advertising. Papers became smaller and thinner. The papers in the war-torn Karelian peninsula had all been forced to close. Now others in Finland proper had to give up. Strict rationing of newsprint was imposed in 1946, and all newspapers had to cut their size so that Finland might have more pulp and newsprint for export. Some forty magazines had to stop publication, for no paper was allowed for entertainment. But by mid-century the Finns had delivered 75 per cent of their war indemnity, and their rapidly expanding industry had more goods available for export. Things began to improve. Paper rationing was removed in 1949, and circulations expanded rapidly. Finnish newspapermen explain that in the postwar years many consumer goods were unobtainable and newspapers, magazines, and books were almost the only things the people could buy freely. Now as more consumer goods became available and people again had money to spend, advertising began to improve till by the end of 1950 the total advertising bill of the nation was back to three-fourths of the prewar level and the better papers were getting 40 per cent of their income from this source. By this time Finland had 167 newspapers of which 61 were dailies, 56 biweeklies and triweeklies, and 50 rural weeklies.

Showdown with Communists

While Finland was coming back economically, she was under great political strain. Bound by Russian exactions implemented by Communists in her own government, Finland was for three years subjected to a "new order." Although Communists had won only a fourth of the seats in parliament in 1945, Russian pressure forced the appointment of four Communists to important ministerial posts, including the Ministry of Interior, which controlled police. By staging arrests and mysterious disappearances, the police tried to intimidate the people. Personal liberty became limited, free speech curtailed, freedom of assembly restricted, and the formerly unhampered press enchained by censorship. In 1946 when tension rose against the government's pro-Russian policy, the premier warned that unless papers "took a correct attitude" they might be banned.

In February, 1948, things moved to a showdown when Stalin demanded a treaty of friendship and mutual assistance against Germany. One by one, the Soviet Union had taken over the other states on its borders. Finland alone had not joined the ranks. By force of will and skillful negotiating, coupled with world reaction against the Soviet coup in Czechoslovakia, she won a pact which left the country free and committed only to a friendship agreement. Having won that victory, Finns began to show their independence by freeing army officers they had been forced to arrest and by bringing the Communist minister of interior, Yijo Leino, to trial and forcing his resignation. In the July, 1948, elections Finnish voters routed the Communists. Russian press and radio lashed out at the new premier, Karl Fagerholm. Communist controlled labor unions in 1949 called strikes to cripple Finland's industries. Now the whole Communist purpose was in the open. The Federation of Trade Unions expelled the Communists, and Social Democrats won control of twenty-five of the thirty-three unions while workers generally refused to follow Communist orders. The strike was a failure and the crisis was over. From then on Communist papers began to decline.

Finnish newspapers had courageously debated the issues in this crisis and had been instrumental in winning this victory. These stirring events had increased readership till total circulation for papers issued three times a week or more had risen to 1,500,000, a remarkable figure for a nation of 4,000,000. The press was still strongly political in character but was giving better coverage to foreign and local news. National and economic issues were most animatedly debated. Some strong papers were now emerging. Largest was *Helsingin Sanomat* (Helsinki Mail), which by a strong emphasis on both foreign and domestic news and with an independent liberal policy had built a circulation of 180,000, largest in Finland. Other strong Helsinki papers included the Swedish moderate, *Hufvudstadsbladet* (Capital Daily); the principal labor paper, *Suomen Socialidemokratti;* and *Ilta-Sanomat,* evening companion of *Helsingin Sanomat.* Strong provincial papers too were developing, representing the Conservative, Social Democratic and Agrarian parties.

Pressures from the Bear

The Finns moved cautiously toward greater independence, but economically they were still beholden to the Russians. They could not accept Marshall Aid, but they did accept a $50,000,000 loan from the United States, which helped. Almost a tenth of total production still had to go to pay Russian reparations. For the first half of the fifties economic problems and their political repercussions kept governments in turmoil. Uneasy coalitions, usually of Agrarians, Social Democrats, and the Swedish party, succeeded each other, sometimes two or three times a year. Arbitrary Russian demands caused governments to fall as the Soviet Union put particular pressure on the Social Democrats who, they claimed, were working against good relations between the two countries. On September 19, 1952, Finland paid off the last of the $300,000,000 reparations. This left more of her production for export, but her industry had been so geared to the Russian market that she remained tied to her neighbor as before. Finland had to seek new markets, yet under her labor government, wages had gone so high that Finnish products were dear in other countries. This was accentuated in 1953 when the world market for wood products slumped, bringing unemployment and another government crisis.

The year 1955 saw an upturn as Finland began to find new markets in Britain and Germany, and industrial production stepped up markedly. New land settlement schemes enabled more small farmers to acquire acreage, and Finland made herself self-sufficient in food so that rationing could be removed. Russia surprised Finland by returning the Porkkala naval base in exchange for a twenty year extension of the treaty of friendship. This relieved the Finns, for Porkkala dominated military approaches to Helsinki.

Yet the Russian press assailed Finland's attempt to negotiate for admission to EFTA (European Free Trade Area). Finland, by giving Russia a "most favored nation" clause in her trade treaty, was permitted to continue negotiations and in 1961 finally won an associate membership in EFTA. This not only brought increased trade with these seven nations but also with common market countries as well. Economic conditions improved, but again Russia caused the fall of a socialist-dominated government, making it clear that she would tolerate only a pro-leftist Agrarian regime. Then in 1961 the U.S.S.R. demanded consultations on joint defense measures in view of the threat from West Germany. President Urho Kalera Kekkonen succeeded in getting Khrushchev to waive this requirement with assurances of Finland's neutrality. But it remained clear that Finland must continue to live with the Russian bear looking over her shoulder.

All this had its effect on the press. While under law newspapers were completely free in the western sense, their realistic editors and publishers were careful not to offend their powerful neighbor. The Finns were making a desperate effort, despite great provocations, to keep peace with Russia, and the press, so closely interwoven with the political life of the country, felt a special responsibility in not provoking Soviet anger. Having been invaded twenty-five times in 700 years and periodically beaten up by the Russians, Finland had no wish to precipitate another attack.

The people apparently supported Kekkonen's policy of neutrality and coexistence with the U.S.S.R., for in 1962 he was reelected for a six-year term—but not until after the attorney general, Olavi Honka, supported by Conservatives, Socialists, and Liberals, had been compelled to withdraw under Russian pressure. The year 1963 saw the end of the industrial peace and prosperity which Finland had enjoyed for two years, for massive strikes crippled railroads, industrial production, and foreign trade. These developments, plus increasing unemployment, brought on political crises which caused the fall of two successive coalition governments. The strikes were settled by peaceful negotiation in 1964, and the economy moved forward again.

Finland's Press Today

In 1964 Finland counted 208 newspapers of which 66, published from four to seven times a week, were listed as dailies. In addition there were 142 nondailies, including 48 weeklies published officially by their municipalities to supply news in remote areas. In spite of economic setbacks, readership continued to grow till daily circulations had risen to 1,667,176, representing 37 copies for every 100 persons, a readership ratio just slightly behind Norway and Switzerland and far ahead of most other European nations. Most dailies are located in the more populous southern half of the country, though there is a good small daily at Rovaniemi right under the Arctic Circle. Like the Danes, the Finns enjoy their four Sunday papers, three in Helsinki and one in Turku. Almost every Finnish home subscribes to a daily in addition to its local paper and receives one or more periodicals per week. This press is bilingual, for Swedish is the second language. Seven dailies and 183 periodicals appear in that language and 131 periodicals are bilingual, Finnish-Swedish.

Helsinki is the chief publishing center not only for newspapers but for magazines, other periodicals, and books. There are ten dailies in this city of 477,062. Several are truly national in scope and are distributed throughout the country. Helsinki daily circulation amounts to 37.1 per cent of the national total. Important provincial press centers are Tampere, the inland industrial center with a population of 133,406 and three dailies; Turku, the important southern port city of 130,844 with five dailies; and Oulu, the largest city on the northwest coast, with

63,707 persons and three dailies also. With such a concentration of dailies, circulations do not run high. A third of all daily papers sell less than 10,000 copies and only one more than 100,000. That exception is *Helsingin Sanomat* with 260,596.

The reason for this large number of papers goes back to the days when political parties sought to have voices in as many cities as possible. This is changing, for in 1964, twenty-nine of the sixty-six dailies listed themselves as independent or neutral. Of those parties with supporting papers the Agrarians led with fourteen. The Conservatives were next with eleven, followed by the Social Democrats with seven. The Communist Peoples Democratic party has only five small papers. Interestingly, the independents have 39.2 per cent of the total daily circulation. By placing their stress on news coverage, they are gaining subscribers faster than any of the party papers.

The independents are generally self-supporting, as are the stronger party papers, with advertising and circulation providing almost equal amounts of revenue. *Helsingin Sanomat*, with the largest circulation, has little need for advertising solicitors, for its problem is reserving enough space for news. It averages nearly 60 per cent of its income from advertising. Many of the smaller party papers have a more limited advertising revenue and, although they have additional income from job printing, may have to rely on party subsidy. This is especially true of the Communist papers.

One fortunate circumstance for Finnish papers is that while there is extensive distribution of radio and television sets, these media are supported by license fees on each set and for a long time carried no commercials. Recently, however, a private company providing commercials has been permitted to share some TV time with the state-operated, noncommercial programs; but competition with newspapers is still not serious.

Circulation is also on a stable basis for almost all of it is by subscription—very little from newsstand sale. There is a Finnish Audit Bureau of Circulation to certify circulation figures. Except in Helsinki where department stores are prominent, there is not the amount of retail advertising found in American or Swedish papers, and none of the large ads are for supermarkets. Cooperatives dominate this field and do not advertise; they rely rather on the purchases of their members who share the dividends. Most of the display advertising is by manufacturers of household appliances, automobiles, medical products, cosmetics, coffee, and tobacco. There is little liquor advertising for liquor is a state monopoly. One finds much classified advertising and a surprising amount of *kuolleita* or family death notices. In a forty-page

Sunday edition, *Helsingin Sanomat* is likely to run sixteen pages of classified ads.

What Finnish Papers Are Like

American visitors are quick to note that Finnish papers appear larger than those at home, for their pages are made up in seven wide columns. This is made necessary by the long words in the language which are given additional meanings by adding more syllables. Words of twenty to twenty-four letters, which would give headaches to American headline writers, are common in Finnish heads. Single-column heads are not possible, therefore a horizontal makeup of two-, three-, and four-column heads is necessary. The larger papers are attractive and open in their appearance with good picture display. Some of the smaller papers have poorer typography and look less interesting. Because paper and pulp are Finland's most important products, her papers were not limited by as severe rationing after the war as were those in other European countries, yet sharp price increases in newsprint have tended to keep the number of pages down. Nevertheless, Helsinki papers range from twenty to twenty-four pages except for *Helsingin Sanomat* which runs from thirty to forty. The larger provincial papers have ten to twenty pages, smaller dailies six, and weeklies often four.

The front news page usually carries the top foreign and national news and several striking news pictures. Then follows the editorial page with backgrounding articles. In succeeding pages there is good coverage of wire news and fair coverage of local. Sensation and divorce are not reported, and crime is covered briefly. There is no society page as such: engagements and weddings are given only a few brief lines, and meetings of social organizations and clubs are not reported. Many papers, however, follow the Scandinavian custom of congratulating local citizens on their birthdays; the larger papers often have women's pages devoted entirely to fashions. Considerable space is, however, given to sports; there may be two pages of this in even the eight-page dailies. On the lighter side, some papers provide comic strips, bridge columns, and crossword puzzles. Emphasis is placed on local and provincial features, often well-illustrated. Music, art, literature, and education are also given much space.

In the non-Communist papers editorials about the Soviet Union are written in a responsible, measured tone. They may criticize Russia but this must be done in such an objective way that it will not antagonize. They have been told to be moderate in treating East-West disputes, and none feel at ease in discussing them. One self-made rule, which will seem strange to Americans, who never have any hesitancy in assailing their leaders, is that Finnish newspapers never attack their president. Many papers carry "Press Voices" quoting selected editorials from other papers to provide their readers with differing viewpoints. The Communist papers follow the Moscow line slavishly but sometimes get caught short when there are sudden shifts in Moscow policy, as there was when Khrushchev was ousted in 1964. Because of their position, Finns are vitally concerned with news of the cold war and world news in general.

The dailies and some of the triweeklies and biweeklies are served by *Finska Notis Byran*, the cooperative news agency owned by the capital and provincial papers. FNB gathers the news of Finland through its cooperative members and a network of correspondents. It gets its outside news from Reuters, Swedish TT, Norwegian NTB, and French AFP. TASS, with a bureau in Helsinki, serves the Communist papers. Several of the larger papers subscribe to UPI and have their own foreign correspondents.

Under Finland's constitution and laws there is no censorship. Yet it is considered an offense to endanger Finland's relations with her neighbors. In practice this has come to mean mainly the U.S.S.R. But even without any precensorship, some Finnish editors complain that the government sometimes imposes a news blackout on subjects affecting relations with Russia and that these restrictions, on information the public ought to have, distort the news and are equivalent to censorship. In 1965, after the fining of a woman reporter for her refusal to answer questions in court which involved her professional secrecy, journalists rose in protest and called on the minister of justice to provide a measure as soon as possible to safeguard the journalist's right to protect his sources. In February, 1965, Finland suffered the loss through death, of Eljas Erkko, who distinguished himself as a commander in the 1918 war of liberation, later became Foreign Minister, but as editor of *Helsingin Sanomat* made it the largest and best in his country.

Later in the year the government, because of the financial difficulties of Agrarian, Social Democratic and Communist party papers, proposed a $3,120,000 state subsidy for thirty-three such papers. After violent debate Parliament rejected the proposal.

Journalists and Their Nation

Journalists in Finland occupy a position of prestige and command the respect of their readers. They are organized in *Suomin Sonamalehtimiesten Litto* (Finnish Union of Journalists), which acts both as a professional society and as a journalists' union in negotiating wages, hours, and working conditions. Interestingly, membership includes all professional journalists, editors, and subordinates, and some publishers.

The story of Finland's journalists has been a chronicle of courage. Through a particularly difficult history this press has helped shape the course of events in its nation. Despite the fact that it was held down for so long by autocratic Swedish kings and Russian tsars, its brave journalists, though their papers might last only a few months, had the courage to speak out for Finnish nationalism till in 1919 Finland was able to declare her independence. Even in the catastrophe which befell Finland in World War II, the press kept urging the people to fight lest their *suomi* (homeland) be completely subjugated by the Russians. And after the war it helped lead the country to recovery and played a major role in upsetting the Communist "new order" and in routing it completely in 1948. The Finns have an old word, *sisu*, mystic and untranslatable, but roughly it means "guts." It denotes the Finn's ability to pay his debts, to hold his own against his enemies, and to maintain his independence whatever the odds. Precarious as this independence may often have been, the Finns still have it; and their press, although it must tread warily, is looked upon as the guardian of their *sisu*.

REPRESENTATIVE PAPERS

Helsingin Sanomat—Finland's largest and most outstanding independent paper with 260,596 daily circulation and 278,630 on Sunday. Only one-third of its circulation is in the capital; the rest spreads all over the country as a national paper. Has built its reader following and advertising dominance by providing for many years the best and most complete news coverage. Originally catering to the upper class, it has spread its appeal to all levels. When Eljas Erkko, Finland's greatest journalist, died in 1964, his son Aatos became head of his family's great publishing empire.

Ilta Sanomat (Evening Mail)—Tabloid afternoon companion of *Sanomat* with a circulation of 62,063. More popular than its morning companion with greater coverage of sports and entertainment, more pictures, comics, and features but with high standards.

Uusi Suomi (New Finland)—Second largest with 88,589 circulation mornings and 94,828 Sunday. A national paper with subscribers far north into Lapland. Long the chief Conservative organ. Bulk of its readers are businessmen, civil servants, professional people, and more prosperous farmers. A big, newsy, well-illustrated paper, well-supported by advertising. Led in development of color printing.

Aamulehti (Morning Post)—Published at Tampere. Third largest paper with 89,435 circulation daily and 90,154 Sunday. The outstanding provincial paper. Strongly Conservative.

Huvudstadsbladet (Capital Daily)—Circulation 67,785 daily and 71,372 Sunday. Leading Swedish organ. Typographically one of most attractive. Provides good foreign and national coverage and much news of Sweden.

Turun Sanomat (Turku Mail)—Largest in Finland's great shipbuilding center with 79,905 circulation daily and 77,029 Sunday. Strongly independent but liberal in sentiment.

Savon Sanomat (Savonian Mail)—Published at Kupio. Leading voice of Agrarian party, now largest in parliament. Circulation 55,151.

Suomen Socialdemokraatti—Official organ of Social Democratic party. Was more important when it spoke for the government in power, but with splits in its ranks circulation has fallen to 35,584. Success in 1964 municipal elections indicated a comeback of this party.

Kansan Uutiset (Peoples Voice)—Leading organ of the Communists, has moved from Kupio to capital. Circulation 58,515. Strongly anti-U.S. and anti-west. Follows Moscow line religiously.

Part 2

The History Makers
of Middle Europe

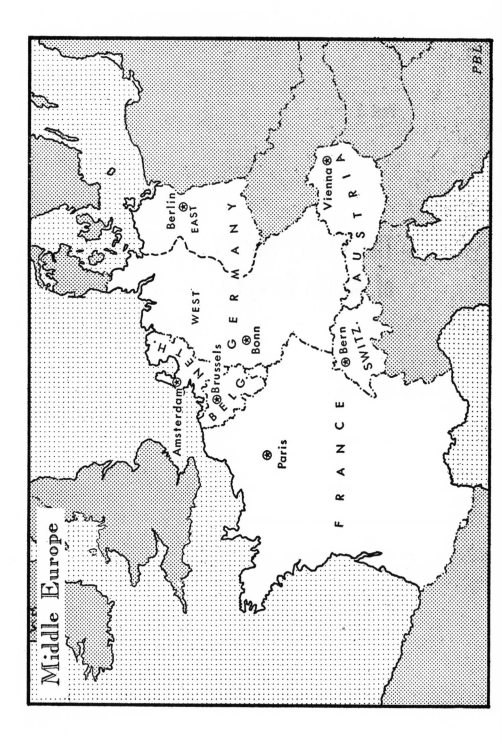

Middle Europe

The Turbulent Story of the German Press

Germany is not only the probable birthplace of printing but the cradle of European journalism. Her press is the oldest on the Continent, and in its 350 years it has experienced more turmoil than any other in Europe. For the last century and a half all the great international wars have been fought on German soil; and after her defeat in two world wars this land has become a divided nation with the western part of her press free and vigorous, the eastern part in slavery.

Most of her people are descendants of Germanic tribes who swept into western Europe in tidal waves of immigration. They fought the Romans; they fought each other, till finally in 771 under Charlemagne the Franks brought all tribes under one rule. Originally pagan, they were converted to Christianity by missionary monks and priests. In the disorganized centuries when barbarian kings had been unable to keep their realms in order, it had fallen to the Church to assume the powers it had enjoyed under the Romans. When Charlemagne restored Leo III to his papal throne in Rome the grateful pope crowned him ruler of the Holy Roman Empire, which Charlemagne proceeded to extend by fifty-four wars in forty-three years till it embraced much of continental Europe. But by the mid-fifteenth century this empire was disintegrating as the people of Spain, Portugal, France, England, Denmark, Hungary, Poland, and Burgundy set up their own independent nations. Yet Emperor Frederick III spent his energies trying to impose his domination on Europe in costly wars fatal to the German people who were hopelessly divided into some three hundred sovereignties from small city states to kingdoms.

Printing Gives Wings to Knowledge

Nevertheless, this was the period when the German Renaissance was born, fostered by the universities. There was great activity in unearthing old manuscript rolls and books scattered during barbarian invasions. These were laboriously copied by hand. But in time copyists could no longer keep up with the demand, and men set out to find a quicker way to produce books. Seven European cities claim to be the birthplace of printing. In Germany it was Johann Gutenberg who first perfected his process so that he could begin work on his forty-two-line *Bible* in 1450. Gutenberg, Fust, Schoeffer, the Bechtermuntz brothers, and others made Mainz the first center of printing; but, after Adolphus of Nassau sacked Mainz, they scattered, taking their new art with them. Presses were soon established in Cologne, Augsburg, Nuremberg, and Strassburg. The chief interest at first was in the production of classics, the *Bible*, and other religious works. By 1500 there had been published 291 editions of Cicero, 95 of Virgil, 57 of Horace, and 91 of the Latin *Bible*. The invention of printing gave wings to learning and caused the darkness of centuries to recede.

More than 160 years were to elapse before the emergence of the first German papers, but precursors early made their appearance. The earliest known handwritten newssheet was put out in 1603 by a Leipzig bookmaker who issued a *Zeitung* on the funeral of Emperor Frederick. The first known printed newssheet appeared in 1505 when Erhard Oeglin at Augsburg printed *Copia oder Neuen Zeitung aus Preisel Landt*, telling of the discovery of Brazil. This initiated printed newssheets giving news of rulers, battles, peace treaties, plagues, and often human interest stories of murders, executions, and trials. Records of these run into the thousands, but all appeared only on the occasion of special events.

These newssheets soon lent themselves to greater purpose. Evils of the Church and state were crying for redress. The mercenary shamelessness of the popes, their extortionate taxes, their worldly priests, their attempts to keep the people in ignorance caused widespread discontent. Then the weak internal administration owing to the emperor's long absences, the difficulty of getting justice, the oppression by nobles who lived in luxury while keeping their people in menial servitude—all were building fire under the cauldron of unhappiness. Now flysheets and pamphlets became important in influencing public opinion. Martin Luther and other reformers used them; so did their opponents. Authorities were often disturbed by this inflammatory journalism, and printers were imprisoned and sometimes executed. For

Aviſa
Relation oder Zeitung.

Was ſich begeben vnd

zugetragen hat / in Deutſch: vnd Welſch-
land/Spannien/Niederlandt/ Engellandt/ Franck-
reich/Vngern / Oſterreich / Schweden / Polen/
vnnd in allen Provintzen/ in Oſt: vnnd
Weſt Indien etc.

So alhie den 15. Januarij angelangt.

Gedruckt im Jahr/ 1609.

Frontispiece of *Avisa Relation oder Zeitung*, published at Strassburg in 1609.
This weekly was the world's first regular newspaper.

Auß Antorff von 2. Jenner/ Anno 1609.

Vß Holland hat man/das die General Staaden auff antrieb des Printz von Brannien die Frantzösische vnd Engelländische Gesandten beschlossen / die Treueß noch für 6. Wochen zu prolongirn/ vnd mit jhrem Gegentheil noch für einest/ vnd für das letzte mahl des Anstandts halben in Tractation zu tretten / zu welchem End dann beyderseits deputierte auff 10. diß zu Brettau erscheinen werden / vnd wehren die Staaden zu frieden / den Anstandt auff folgende Conditiones einzugehen / nemblich / das der König in Spa: die soveranitet auff die vnirte Provintzien gantz vnd gar quittiren solle / vnd das die Holl: vnd Seeländer die freye Naviga-tion auff die Indien/ wie bißhero behalten möge/ auch den Römischen Catholischen keine öffentliche Vbung der Religion in gedachten Pro-vintzien zuzulassen/was darauff erfolgt/ gibt die Zeit/ vnd ist man eheſt des Ertzhertzogs Beichtvater wieder auß Spannien gewertig / vnnd melden Brieff von dar/das selbiger König noch zum Krieg gegen den Holländern geneiget / so hat der Ertzhertzog die Besatzung im Gra-bandt vnd Flandern gesterckt/ so ein böses anzeigen des Friedens/ son-derlich weil die Staaden gewisse Auiso / das jhr Maytt: in Spannien viel Volcks werben / deßgleichen in Italia 6000. Neapolitaner nach Niederlandt durch Schweitz zusenden / verordnet / also thun sie sich auch mit Kriegsvolck versehen / beneben wieder ein Armada auff die Indien von neuwen zu rüsten.

Auß Cöllen von 4. Jenner.

Auß Ambsterdam hat man/das ein zeithero allda grosse Sturm-windt auch ein grewlich Wetter mit Donner vnd Plitzen gewesen / so in der See grossen Schaden gethan / vnd ein Schiff mit etlich 100. Kisten Zucker / vnd viel 1000. Realen den Portugessern gehörig / zu grund gangen.

Sonsten hat man zu Brüssel publicirt/ das alle die jenigen / so dem gefangenen Kauffman Henrich Hanitzen schuldig seyn / bey ver-luſt Leib vnd Gut sich anmelden / vnd solche Schulden zu erkennen geben sollen.

A ij   Auß

First page of 1609 issue of the historic *Avisa Relation oder Zeitung.*

a century the German states were torn by religious wars culminating in their involvement in the Thirty Years War in 1618.

The First Newspapers

It was shortly before this that Johann Carolus at Strassburg brought out the first regular newspaper, *Avisa Relation oder Zeitung*. Earliest extant issues at the University of Heidelberg are dated 1609. Because of censorship it gave most space to brief bulletins of foreign news. Its thirty-seventh issue reported from Venice Galileo's invention of the telescope. Issues of another weekly, *Avis Relation oder Zeitung*, likewise dated 1609 at Augsburg, have also been brought together. These two weeklies, so far as is known, are the oldest regularly published newspapers in the world. Frankfurt had its first weekly in 1615, Berlin in 1617, Magdeburg in 1626, and Munich in 1628. They were small folios of four to eight pages bringing brief bulletins from other nations. These weeklies could be better controlled than irregularly appearing flysheets, and authorities quickly devised a system of licensing them, usually to their trusted postmasters. Censorship was strict; many of these sheets were short-lived, having to bow to official *Postzeitungen*.

The Thirty Years War, arraying Protestant German states aided by Swedes, Danes, and French against the pro-Catholic German states aided by Austria, Hungary, and Spain, involved much of Europe. At first hunger for war news gave great stimulus to the press, but in the end the ravages of war dealt it serious blows. The two hundred principalities left after the Peace of Westphalia were almost ruined, their population reduced from 30,000,000 to 20,000,000, their intellectual life stifled. Many towns were completely deserted. In a number of states journalism was set back to mere flysheets. The British Museum has 14,902 of these published from 1640 to 1661.

Revived Press Is Hobbled

Wars continued in the last half of the seventeenth century, yet some German princes undertook the reconstruction of their principalities, the resumption of education, and even the encouragement of newspapers. Soon papers were appearing in a number of cities, some twice weekly; and in 1660 came the first daily, *Neue Einlaufende Nachrichten von Krieg und Welthandeln*, published by Timotheus Ritsch, a bookseller. Later he changed the title to *Leipziger Zeitung*.

Prussia, in particular, made rapid strides and emerged as the strongest German state. But Frederick William permitted papers no freedom, and a force which might have helped rouse the people to unified effort was restricted to reporting his victories. Frederick the Great (1740–80), who almost trebled Prussian territory, likewise kept the press in restraint; but it is doubtful if the papers of any German state could have exerted any influence, for they were poor papers. Hence, journalists came to be considered wretched persons and the public turned to Dutch papers, the freest in Europe, which the German princes permitted to enter rather than grant their own papers any freedom.

As a result intellectual leaders turned to *zeitschriften* (magazines) to restore German cultural and political life. The first were founded by university professors. Most important were the *Patrioten* which drew outstanding men together to raise cultural and moral standards. From 1716 to 1761 a total of 178 magazine titles appeared, some of important influence. Meanwhile newspapers encountered new competition from the official *Intelligenz Blätter*, advertising sheets started by the Prussian king in 1727 to turn advertising revenue to the profit of the state. Regular newspapers were prohibited from carrying advertising if they wished to retain their licenses. Many papers were reduced to penury. Nevertheless, several papers destined to become important voices in German journalism were founded, including Marcus Dumont's *Kölnische Zeitung*, Christian Voss' *Vossische Zeitung*, and the *Hamburgische Unparteiische Correspondent*, which tried to give more reliable news coverage and more space to public affairs than to literary subjects. But a handful of better papers were the only glimmers of light in the surrounding darkness of German journalism.

Press Dares to Rouse Patriotism

Although journalism may have been in low estate, the latter part of the eighteenth century saw a brilliant literary period represented by men such as Goethe, Schiller, Johann von Herder, and Gotthold Lessing. The latter was a regular contributor to *Vossische Zeitung*.

The American Revolution against British rule and the mounting resentment against royal tyranny in France were reflected in Germany in the founding of several papers which ventured to deal with public affairs, notably Martin Weiland's *Der Teusche Merkur* and Christian Schubart's *Deutsche Chronik*. Schubart tried to rouse German patriotism and boldly attacked the policies of German princes. For this he spent ten years in prison. Not long after the French Revolution, in 1798, there appeared in Tubingen the first daily of real merit founded by the bookseller Johann Cotta. His *Allgemeine Zeitung* sought to be a trustworthy historical record and tried to interpret current events through thinkers, statesmen, and the best writers. Heinrich Heine was for several years his brilliant Paris correspondent. But Cotta got into trouble with authorities and had to move to Stuttgart, then to Ulm and later to Augsburg; yet his paper achieved the reputation of being the best in Germany and even won European fame.

Napoleon and the Press

The French Revolution had been hailed with great enthusiasm in Germany, and indeed Napoleon's invasion of the German states in 1803 had been greeted by German papers as deliverance from their feudal lords. But German journalists soon found they had a sterner master. Once he had amalgamated many of the smaller states into the Confederation of the Rhine and had absorbed the rest into his empire, Napoleon repressed all existing papers and replaced them with his own, all echoes of the official Paris press. The Germans, however, benefited from better order, greater justice, and civil rights they had not known before. But when in 1809 the Corsican launched his war against Austria, his demands became intolerable. His excessive levies of men for cannon fodder, his unwarranted exactions of money to support his armies, and his cruelties antagonized most Germans.

Press hero of the period was Johann Palm, an Augsburg printer, who circulated a clandestine sheet, *"Germany in her Deep Humiliation,"* attacking the Napoleonic regime and the German princes who cooperated. Palm was executed by a French firing squad, but his example spurred suppressed German papers to appear as underground sheets. This press had a common aim and German patriotism caught fire. After Napoleon's disastrous retreat from Moscow and his defeat at Leipzig, Germans rose and helped drive the French across the Rhine. For the first time German papers had exerted real leadership. Outstanding among those which appeared was *Rheinische Merkur*, published by Joseph Goerres, best German journalist of his day, whose influence led Napoleon to call *Merkur* the "fifth great power."

Authoritarianism Returns

Press freedom which came with liberation was, however, short-lived. The 1815 Congress of Vienna did not bring the united Germany for which patriots had hoped. Instead Prince Clemens von Metternich of Austria formed the Deutscher Bund, a loose federation of thirty-nine states dominated by Austria. German princes were given autonomy in internal affairs and were united only in mutual defense and the suppression of internal progress for many years. The old absolutists were back in the saddle.

In Prussia, where German nationalism had found most fertile soil, more benevolent rulers had abolished serfdom and feudal privileges, instituted land reform, and developed a public educational system. In other states the thousands of young men who had fought for liberation in 1813–15 kept up their agitation for union and freedom. University students were particularly alarming in their activities; and when a Russian agent was assassinated by a student, every reigning prince imagined his own life in danger. Metternich's Congress of Ministers at Karlsbad took drastic measures against revolution, abolished press freedom, wiped out student societies, and placed universities under strict control. A savage police system not only hounded newspapers out of existence but also so suppressed civil rights that there were few areas where people had as much liberty as one hundred years before.

The press dared to show its face again after the Paris revolution of 1830. Everywhere in the German states the cry rose for the fulfillment of the promises of the war of liberation, a new constitution, liberty of the press, a return of civil liberties, and improved trade facilities between states. But the old governments were too strong. Again liberation died aborning, and protest once more had to find its voice in underground sheets.

The Revolution of 1848

When, however, the *Kölnische Zeitung* on February 28, 1848, issued an extra announcing the revolution in Paris and the proclamation of the Second Republic, the unrest in Germany could no longer be held down. Soon the whole country was in an uproar. Newspapers, flysheets, and pamphlets fanned the outrages of thirty years and the aspirations for political freedom. The growing outcry forced authorities to give way. Frederick William of Prussia took the lead in summoning an assembly to draw up a new constitution for Prussia. Other leaders forced the summoning of a national assembly at Frankfurt to draft a constitution for a united Germany. As a first step this assembly permitted the states to lift censorship. The *Vossische Zeitung* in an "extra of joy" proclaimed, "The Press is Free."

There came a quick development of parties. The *Deutsche Zeitung* at Mannheim was the leading voice of the Liberals. To counter these ideas a Prussian nobleman, Baron Otto von Bismarck, founded at Berlin *Neue Prussische Zeitung*. Growing industrialization had brought a labor class, and the first Socialist paper, *Rheinische Zeitung für Politik, Handel und Gewerbe*, appeared in 1848 with Karl Marx as editor. There were other parties and each had to have its organs. Thus 1848 was the birth year of the political party press.

But the Frankfurt Assembly, through fears and jealousies, was impotent. Revolts in other states than Prussia were put down; by mid-1849 armed resistance was at an end and the authoritarians were again in control. Socialist and radical newspapers were suppressed as "dangerous to the state"; all others had to be cautious. Yet in every state there were intelligent men who resisted reaction by every legal means. Furthermore, increasing literacy, the growing courage of the press, the extension of railroads, and improved trade relations were all agencies of progress. And Prussia, with its new constitution, emerged as the one German state in a position to head the movement for national unity.

Bismarck Unites German States

William I succeeded to the Prussian throne in 1861 and ushered in a new epoch when he called Baron von Bismarck to head his government. As a university student Bismarck had been a rake and a cynical liberal, but with age he had become converted into a stalwart defender of religion and a roaring reactionary. He had helped organize the Conservative party, dedicated to protecting the interests of the Junker class, the church, and the army and to building a powerful Prussia as a nucleus of a German nation. Now he started plotting how to eliminate Austria from her commanding position in the Deutscher Bund. With diabolic cleverness he persuaded Austria to join in a war with Denmark over Schleswig-Holstein in 1864. This was quickly won; the Danes were compelled to cede these provinces to Prussia and Austria, but Bismarck left the division of the spoils dangling.

Except for two conservative papers the rest of the press had bitterly opposed Bismarck's policy of governing in defiance of the elected assembly. When he demanded appropriations for the army, which were refused, he took the money anyway. After his victory over Denmark, criticism moderated; but when he precipitated a quarrel with Austria over the division of Schleswig-Holstein, press hostility reached a climax. After he declared war on powerful Austria, he was denounced as a man who was about to ruin his country. But when he vanquished Austria in the Seven Weeks War of 1866, his political opponents could not resist celebrating his victory which, at one stroke, had produced a unified Germany of 30,000,000 under Prussian leadership. Now Bismarck recognized the advantage of the support from Liberals and made peace with the assembly. Then he was ready for his next step. He knew that a quarrel with France would be the best means of kindling German nationalism in Bavaria, Wurtemburg, and other states south of the Main, so he provoked Emperor Napoleon III into a declaration of war. Immediately the south German states rallied to the side of Prussia. The Franco-Prussian War of 1870 resulted in a crushing defeat for France and the joining of the last German states to the new German empire which now became a power in Europe. The King was crowned Emperor and Bismarck, made a prince, became the first Imperial Chancellor.

Iron Chancellor Shapes the Press

For Bismarck, to govern meant to command. Like Caesar he believed that one man should think for the whole people. To mold them he set about molding the press. He had small regard for journalists and professed no concern for public opinion, yet no statesman of his century used the press more unscrupulously for his own advantage. In truth, public opinion hardly existed at the birth of the new empire. In schism and controversy the German people had grown from infancy to manhood. From the centrifugal congeries of their separate state interests they had, by Bismarck's policy of "blood and iron," been brought to national unity almost overnight. They lacked singleness of purpose and understanding of their epochal achievement. They had little conception of the fact that now, as a European power, their relations with neighboring powers were among their most pressing problems. The political party press developed rapidly, supporting a dozen or more parties. But German readers selected the papers which agreed with their own views. Hence in national and foreign affairs the result was often a chaos of opinion. Bismarck in his driving purpose felt that the press, instead of dividing the people, should support and explain his program.

In the early period of mild liberalism the press had been freed of previous censorship but the Press Law of 1874, while guaranteeing press freedom, provided that every paper must furnish the censor a copy of each issue. This might be suppressed if it contained "provocation to treason, incitement to violence, offense to the sovereign or encouraged resistance to the government." The penal code made it easy to hale an editor into court, and Bismarck used this often against papers which indulged in "Bismarck badgering." Even though the courts were fair, editors and writers could never escape the chilling consciousness that they wrote under a threat.

Then came the Law of 1878 which suspended any paper advocating Socialist or Communist views. This exterminated a whole section of the press. But Bismarck was not content with preventing papers from publishing opinions he opposed; they must also defend what he said or did. He had a ready tool in Dr. Bernhard Wolff's Telegrafische Buro, founded in 1849, which Bismarck now made the semi-official voice of the Foreign Office. It distributed to papers such foreign and national

news as the government desired and submitted all questionable material
to the Foreign Office.

The Ministry of Interior and the Imperial Home Office then organized a press bureau which supplied hundreds of small local *kreisblätter*,
articles expounding government policy. The Foreign Office press
bureau at Wilhelmstrasse also played one correspondent against another
by handing out exclusives which made one seem exceptionally well-
informed so that he would print Bismarck's test balloons. His famous
apothegm that "the German government had to pay for window panes
smashed by the press" gave German papers a reputation for irresponsibility, but it was Bismarck who inspired the test balloons. Then, if they
brought the wrong reaction, he denied authorship and blamed the
press. Bismarck called journalists his "quill cattle" and said "decent
people do not write for me." He called those papers which faithfully
followed his orders his "reptile press"—they crawled on their bellies.
But Bismarck realized the importance of the press, used it, and bent it
to his will till it became the most well-drilled and controlled in Europe.

Popular Press Develops

Yet, under Bismarck, Germany strode forward economically and
her press expanded. With every party needing voices, every town of
1,000 people had two papers and cities had several. Local advertising
did not develop, but with Germany's increasing industrial and commercial activity, general advertising grew. The large number of papers,
however, kept circulations small; and for some years most German
papers were poor.

In the eighties there developed a popular press seeking more readers
by providing more news, features, and serials, and by being neutral in
politics. Most successful was Berlin's *Der Lokal Anzeiger*, started in
1883 by August Scherl, who after some years in the United States
returned to found a paper more along American lines. Berliners liked
its newsiness, and it soon had a circulation of 100,000, largest in
Germany. Others followed—they became known as the *anzeiger* or
advertising press; but none had the characteristics of the sensational
populars developing in the United States, for the German press remained essentially staid.

Because for centuries Germany had been a loose aggregation of
separate states, regionalism was long a characteristic of this press.
Unlike England and France where national papers developed in London and Paris, there were no national papers till near the end of the
century when *Kölnische Zeitung* and *Frankfurter Zeitung* began to
achieve national circulation. It was not till after Bismarck had central-

ized national life in Berlin that the *Berliner Tageblatt* succeeded in achieving the importance of these two western papers. There were now a number of strong papers which had such financial independence that they were conscious of the fact that, in their relations with authorities, the advantage was no longer all on one side. By 1894 Germany had 3,337 papers. Each larger city had several dailies: Berlin had 45, Leipzig 18, Munich 12, Hamburg 11.

The Kaiser Takes Over

The accession of William II to the throne in 1888 marked a turning point. A strong believer in his own abilities, he did not relish being overshadowed by the chancellor and dismissed Bismarck in 1890. He started acquiring colonies and disturbed the English by developing German sea power. The first twenty-five years of his reign, however, were peaceful as, curbed by his advisors, he turned his attention to development of internal prosperity and foreign trade.

Believing implicitly in the divine right of kings, he considered himself a vice-regent of God, surrounded by a special grandeur; and when the growing independence of the press brought increasing criticism, there were frequent prosecutions for *lèse majesté*. But many of his journalistic opponents were sufficiently embittered to hazard insults. To draw a cartoon so cleverly or to hurl an epithet so deftly that everyone knew at whom it was aimed, and yet leave no ground for prosecution, was considered a feather in the cap of a journal. When caught, papers had "responsible editors" who cheerfully went to jail for three months at good pay. The emperor's growing fear of revolution made him particularly bitter toward the now reborn Socialistic press, and there were few Socialist editors who did not serve one or more terms in prison. Attempted direction of the press continued under Bismarck's successors, Prince Chlodwig Hohenlohe and Prince Bernhard von Bülow, but it was less blatant, characterized rather by psychological treatment of individual journalists. The entire daily press depended on the economical service of Wolff's, which supplied carefully screened news. As a result public opinion did not develop the power achieved in other countries. One critic of the period said, "The press was more a valet than a counselor of government." There were critics, but no thunderer like the London *Times* to keep a checkrein on government.

Solid substantial papers were developing, however; larger ones with sixteen to twenty pages, dignified and ponderous, printed in German Gothic type, difficult to read, the great majority were party papers giving greatest play to leader articles. By 1912 there were 4,036 dailies and some 3,000 weekly and monthly publications. *Kölnische Zeitung* and *Frankfurter Zeitung* sought to rival the London *Times* in breadth of news coverage, but although they might take issue with the government on national questions, seldom did they take an independent stand on foreign policy. Both were national papers, but neither had circulations of more than 75,000. *Der Lokal Anzeiger*, called the Daily Mail of Germany, had grown to 300,000 but kept so neutral in politics that it had little influence.

Press Decries Drift Toward War

Meanwhile Germany had outdistanced France and was rivaling Britain in industrial power. With her powerful navy, industry, and geographic position, she was inspiring fear and envy. Desire for economic power had gone hand in hand with increasing military preparedness and higher taxes. There was much press criticism of the government and widespread attacks on Germany's policy of committing herself to underwrite "Austria's suicidal policy in the Balkans." As military preparations mounted, Socialist papers and many others decried these steps and government brinkmanship which might precipitate war. Europe was now divided into two great camps—Germany, Austria-Hungary, and Italy on one side, Britain, France, and Russia on the other. Both sides faced each other warily. The assassination of the Austrian crown prince at Sarajevo and Austria's ultimatum to Serbia precipitated World War I.

The press was divided in its immediate reactions. Some blamed Serbia; others Austria. The Austrian ultimatum was a shock. *Vossische Zeitung* and *Frankfurter Zeitung* pointed out that Serbia could not accept Austrian demands without surrender of her sovereignty. The Socialist press led by *Vorwärts* was vehement in its protestations that Austria was leading Europe into war. But the bulk of German opinion, led by the Conservative *Kreuz Zeitung* and *Berliner Tageblatt* held that because of the assassination and the incitement of Serbian propaganda against Austria, the latter had no alternative but to bring a showdown. When news began to filter out that Russia was preparing to mobilize for aid to her Slavic neighbor, there came a press clamor that Germany must mobilize at once lest she be caught unprepared if Russia invaded. Yet there was less war spirit in Germany than in Austria.

Once the die was cast, however, the entire press, as indeed the whole people, united behind the government in "Germany's war of defense against Russia, England, and France." Even Socialist papers supported the government's request for war credits. The invasion of Belgium was justified as a military necessity, and French and British charges of atrocities were branded as base fabrications.

War's Effect on the Press

The German plan had been to knock out France by a quick and massive encircling drive through Belgium to Paris and then turn and attack Russia to avoid having to fight a two-front war. Newspapers rejoiced as German armies drove to within eighteen miles of Paris. Circulations soared as people eagerly read the war news. But at the Marne the Germans were thrown back by the French and British. On the eastern front the German victory at Tannenberg was offset by a Russian drive deep into Austria. By mid-October, 1914, the combatants on the western front were stretched from Flanders to Switzerland, locked in a trench warfare. It became clear that the war would go on for a long time. The press spurred the people to make the sacrifices that were necessary. By March, 1915, Maximilian Harden, editor of *Zunkunst*, was pleading that the government not conceal defeats which were being kept from the papers.

Now the war began seriously to affect newspapers. The calling up of class after class of reservists depleted newspaper staffs; many lost half their employees. In the first year, 905 papers had to suspend operations. Then as industry shifted to all out war production, advertising was cut drastically. Obituaries for fallen soldiers soon took the largest ad space. Newsprint, copper, and zinc were cut off by the British blockade. Pictures became fewer and smaller; all papers had to cut their size. By the end of the second year, a fifth of all smaller papers had disappeared. Not only for selfish reasons, but because the blockade was seriously affecting food supplies, papers began calling for relentless undersea warfare.

Newspapers suffered increasing censorship. The military gave them only what items they wanted printed. Papers willingly submitted to military censorship for the safety of their country, but they protested wrathfully when all criticism of domestic questions was forbidden. The outspoken *Vorwärts* had its issues confiscated many times. The *Berliner Tageblatt* was suspended three times for criticizing the conduct of the war. *Kölnische Zeitung* and *Frankfurter Zeitung* were denied circulation outside the country for taking too strong an attitude on the food supply. The war-party papers of the Conservatives and National Liberals, however, condemned the pacifists, and urged vigorous prosecution of the war.

Collapse of Germany

As the war dragged on, popular discontent rose. The press became more outspoken; and in the *Reichstag* the Socialists, the Center party

Catholics, and other democratic parties began urging a negotiated peace and demanding reform of the rationing system and extension of suffrage. The overthrow of the tsarist government in Russia had a profound effect in Germany. Growing death lists and news of German defeats could not be kept dark. The government promised reforms to counteract Allied claims that in fighting Germany they were fighting for democracy against autocracy. But events were moving too rapidly. The entry of the United States into the war reinforced the Allied push; Ludendorf's last desperate drive toward Paris failed; fresh American troops broke through the Hindenburg line; by August, 1918, the Germans were in full retreat. The refusal of President Woodrow Wilson to deal with the Kaiser brought widespread strikes, mutinies, and revolts throughout the country till William II had to abdicate.

For a time Germany was on the verge of a Communist revolution. A Red republic had been set up in Bavaria; and a quickly established Red press, fed by funds and propaganda from Communist Russia, preached violence as the only way of creating a new order. Responsible German papers fought this and urged the establishment of a democratic republic. The urgings of the sober papers for sanity won. By May, 1919, the Red republic of Bavaria had fallen, revolts had been put down, and a new Weimar republic had been established under the presidency of Socialist Frederick Ebert.

Under the Weimar Republic

The new republic was, however, born to trouble. Peace treaty terms which imposed heavy reparations and cost Germany an eighth of her area, all her colonies, her armament, and her merchant marine shocked Germans. Old Conservative papers bitterly attacked Ebert's government for accepting a treaty which "plunged Germany into an abyss." There were monarchist attempts to overthrow the regime, Communist uprisings, and in 1923 the Munich Putsch of a new movement led by Adolph Hitler. Yet the republic survived and proceeded to give to the people a modern democratic government and to the press the freest period German journalism had enjoyed.

The economic disorganization of the country, with the difficulty of meeting huge reparations payments brought a financial crisis. The ill-advised resort to printing paper money caused a precipitous fall of the mark till by autumn, 1923, it was quoted as four trillion to the dollar. Drastic devaluation bankrupted many. A number of old family newspapers had to sell to industrialists. Out of this debacle Alfred Hugenberg developed the most powerful communications empire in Europe. Headed by four Berlin dailies it included a chain of provincials,

Telegrafen Union—a press association serving 1,600 papers—a big syndicate service, and UFA, which produced 75 per cent of German films. All of the papers he acquired became Nationalist organs. Political dissension brought many parties ranging from the Nationalist and Nazis on the extreme right through the liberal parties in the center to the Socialists and Communists on the left. As all had to have their voices, the press developed into a classic example of the "group press," each group appealing to a limited audience. Hence circulations were small, advertising revenue meager. Many papers had to be supported by parties, politicians, or industrialists.

President Ebert died in 1925 and was succeeded by Field Marshal Paul von Hindenburg, the military hero who Germans hoped would lead them out of their troubles. The Dawes Plan for graduated reparations payments, plus foreign loans, restored confidence and brought an industrial advance. The last years of the twenties saw better times: most people had jobs, and there was plenty of food and beer. Hitler and his rabid nationalism were forgotten. Until the Beer Hall Putsch, Hitler had been riding on a wave of national despair, supported by the army. Now, in the calm of good times and international cooperation, Hitler found himself deserted by his big friends, who further advised cooperation with the Republic. In the 1928 election Nazi representation in the *Reichstag* fell to thirteen, and by 1929 Nazi party membership totalled only 178,000.

The world depression hit Germany severely. There were 2,000,000 unemployed by early 1930; and the number rose to 6,000,000 in 1933. There were riots in the streets, chaos in the cities. The economic catastrophe gave Hitler his opportunity. To the people in their misery, Nazi promises to restore order by a national dictatorship, to remove Jewish competition, to repudiate war debts, and to seek a return of lost colonies were infinitely appealing. In the 1930 election, while the Socialists won 143 *Reichstag* seats, the Nazis won 107.

The Nazis Move In

The battle for public opinion intensified. Hitler had started with only *Völkischer Beobachter* at Munich. Others under flamboyant titles such as *Die Faust* (The Fist), *Die Flamme* (The Flame), and Joseph Goebbels' *Der Angriff* (The Attack) had been started—all provocative, vicious examples of gutter journalism. Then Hugenberg, to combat the Young Reparations Plan, enlisted the Nazis with their network of local branches and rabble-rousing orators. Big money flowed into the Nazi war chest and more papers were started. Furthermore, the large rightist papers and Hugenberg's press agency now gave Hitler's movement respectable publicity. Nazi chiefs, whom many

Germans had considered gangsters, now moved into the limelight of the front page with advance publicity of their meetings. Nazi membership doubled. As the depression deepened, Hitler became the incarnation of German desperation and bitterness. By 1932 the Nazis had 120 papers, all exploiting the economic crisis and attacking reparations, the Jews, and Chancellor Heinrich Brüning, whom they reviled as the "Hunger Chancellor." Leagued with the 49 Nazis dailies were 32 Nationalist party and 17 Peoples party dailies, but these 98 had more circulation than the 603 Center party papers. In between were a number of *partielose* (nonparty) papers. On the Left were 135 Socialist and a few Communist dailies. In 1932 Germany had 3,262 dailies, twice as many as the United States, which had double Germany's population. Except for the rabid, sensational Nazi papers, the rest were still sober and serious, presenting news briefly, giving emphasis to articles interpreting the news according to the party viewpoint. Yet all had freedom; the organs of twenty parties could express themselves as they wished.

Frontal attacks of the Nazis against the republic finally forced Brüning to invoke Article 48 of the constitution which permitted the curbing of press freedom when public order was seriously threatened. Several Nazi papers were closed down for short periods when they were too violent. *Völkischer Beobachter* and *Angriff* were suspended several times. Mounting unemployment and distress made Germans reckless. In the 1932 election Nazis doubled their representation. Hitler demanded sole power but Hindenburg refused till, after a Nationalist government had made no progress, a coalition was worked out with Hitler as chancellor and Franz von Papen as vice-chancellor. Hitler took power on January 30, 1933, and to give himself a working majority in the *Reichstag* called for an election. The bitter campaign was climaxed by the burning of the *Reichstag* building by Nazi plotters, for which the Communists were blamed. Hindenburg was persuaded to issue decrees on February 28, 1933, restricting freedom of speech, press, and assembly. The Socialist and Communist parties were outlawed and their papers, led by Socialist *Vorwärts* and Communist *Rote Fahne*, suppressed. The country was flooded with rumors of the danger of a Communist coup. The Nazi and Nationalist parties won a majority of *Reichstag* seats, for the German people were now ready for a strong hand. Even the Center party voted to grant Hitler emergency powers so that he could govern by decree.

Nazis Take Over the Press

To Nazis this was merely a beginning, for they were only a militant minority and they had to make their ideology accepted by the whole people. Joseph Goebbels was made minister of propaganda and public enlightenment. Since the press was the great instrument for educating the public, the state had to secure it with relentless vigor and place it in the service of the nation. Nazis had already confiscated Communist and Socialist newspapers; now others began to feel the bridle. Party watchers sat in newspaper offices to see that nothing critical appeared. Then, as a quicker means, papers were suspended as "dangerous to public order." Suspension would then be withdrawn if the paper replaced its editor or changed its policy. Some papers were squeezed into selling to the Nazis; many were persuaded to conform; all lost their right of free expression.

Now Goebbels took control not only of press and radio but of films, theater, music, literature, and advertising by setting up seven chambers embracing every German cultural worker. The president of any chamber could forbid anyone from working at his profession or assess staggering fines for any violations of his orders. Max Amman, Hitler's old sergeant-major who had been manager of *Völkischer Beobachter*, headed the press chamber; and he turned with relish to molding the press. The profession of journalism, as it existed in other countries, was abolished and journalists became public officials responsible to district *kultur* wardens and to Goebbels. Only those who were Aryans to the second generation could be registered on the professional roster; this banned many Jewish journalists. Ullstein and Mosse, the two great Berlin publishing firms which had put out fine liberal papers, were among the first to be suppressed. From then on any paper not sufficiently enthusiastic about Nazism was quickly brought to heel. Proprietors were told they were marked for suppression and offered the choice of accepting a fraction of the paper's worth or losing everything by confiscation. The initial clean-up lasted until April, 1934, when 1,284 papers had been closed and 327 others had ceased voluntarily. There were still a few nominally independent papers like *Kölnische Zeitung, Frankfurter Zeitung, Hamburger Fremdenblatt,* and *Berliner Tageblatt,* so respected abroad that Nazis hesitated to suppress them; but they were so persecuted by bans and suspensions that they led a harried life.

To control all news, Goebbels amalgamated Wolff's and Telegrafen Union into the new *Deutsches Nachrichten Buro* (DNB). Through it the news could be marshaled as the Nazis wanted it, daily instructions could be sent concerning the line to be taken on world and national affairs, the stories to be given top play, the size of type to be used in heads, even the wording of derogatory catchphrases. The press became a disciplined orchestra obeying every move of Goebbels' baton. It could be made to scream as with one voice at any enemy Hitler wished to attack, and the crescendo of hate could be turned on or off as he wished. Having taken over all means of communication, the Nazis now had the German people in a mental strait-jacket.

The Nazis had plausible arguments when they contended that there were too many newspapers, that many were not good papers, that they had split people into warring segments instead of uniting them to meet Germany's problems, that they were too often standard bearers of parties fighting about the state but actually working against its best interests. Many found these arguments reasonable; but, having given up their basic right of freedom of information, they woke to find out that they had been regimented into giving up freedom of education, freedom of religion, and all their civic rights as well.

Now with complete control of all communications, the Nazis proceeded to whip up enthusiasm for the new order. Then they moved to make Germany strong through rearmament and the enrolling of both employers and employees in a labor front working to help Germany regain its rightful place in the sun. They built up hate against the Allies who had dictated the "injustices of Versailles" and against smaller nations which stood in Germany's way. Whatever qualms Germans may have had were dispelled by rising employment, the creation of an air force and army, the occupation of the Rhineland, and the success of Hitler's foreign policy which, in bloodless victories, brought the return of the Saar, the *anschluss* with Austria, and the dismemberment of Czechoslovakia. Then the hymns of hate were turned against the Poles who, it was alleged, were committing "intolerable wrongs against the East Germans." Hitler and Goebbels played the tunes of "Injustices to Germany," "Encirclement by the Allies," "Blood Calls to Blood," and "Home to the Reich" day after day from 1933 to 1939. They relentlessly sealed off the German people from any outside information. Foreign newspapers, magazines, and movies were banned and it was made a criminal offense to listen to foreign shortwave broadcasts. Constantly pounded by Nazi propaganda and unable to hear or read anything to the contrary, many Germans in time began to believe.

Through the thirties the screws were tightened on the press. The Anzeiger papers, neutral but important because of their mass appeal, were forced to sell to the Nazis. A new Nazi publishing corporation, Vera Verlag, bought up, for a fraction of their worth, papers marked for extinction. The *Hamburger Fremdenblatt* was expropriated because the publisher was "not politically reliable." Hugenberg, who had helped Hitler to power, lost all his papers, his news and feature agencies, and UFA pictures. In 1935 Amman struck another blow by banning all papers that accepted subsidies from vocational and religious bodies. This silenced the Catholic press. Then in 1936 he decreed that every press member must furnish proof of his Aryan ancestry to the year 1800. This purged most of the remaining Jews. By 1939 Germany had only 2,200 papers left, but the Nazis papers had a 13,200,000 circulation compared to 6,600,000 for all the allegedly independent papers, which also were shackled.

The Press in World War II

By August 23, 1939, after having signed a nonaggression pact with Russia, Hitler was ready. On August 29 he demanded that a Polish emissary be sent to Berlin with full powers to cede Danzig and the Polish Corridor to Germany. No emissary was sent; and on September 1, without declaration of war, German troops and planes attacked Poland. The Second World War had begun. In three weeks Polish resistance had collapsed, and Germany and Russia divided Poland between them. Britain, France, Australia, New Zealand, South Africa, India, and Canada had promptly declared war on Germany, but for six months there was a *sitzkreig* with little land fighting as both sides squared away. But England and France had imposed their naval blockade, and German submarines and surface raiders had struck at Allied ships.

In early April, 1940, the Nazis quickly took Denmark and Norway; in May they loosed their blitzkreig in which panzer divisions rapidly engulfed Belgium and Holland and bottled up the British at Dunkirk, from which an impromptu fleet evacuated 338,999 British, French, and Belgians. Now panzer divisions fanned out across France while dive bombers visited terror on French towns and parachutists leap-frogged their way forward. Paris surrendered June 14, and on June 22 the French signed Nazi terms of surrender. Since Italy had finally come into the war as an ally of Germany, Hitler now controlled much of western Europe.

Strict military censorship had been imposed in Germany. In the first year the victory theme was the ace card in Nazi propaganda, and the people were kept at a fever pitch of pride with the succession of victories which marked the conquest of western Europe. They became convinced that they were on the march; and many were now ready to ride the Nazi bandwagon toward the day when Germans, as the master race, would rule Europe and enjoy "the greatest prosperity man had ever known," as Hitler had promised. But the war had served as a pretext for closing down 550 additional papers.

Hitler now turned on his one remaining enemy. Directions for Operation Sea Lion were signed July 16, and Goering's Luftwaffe began preparing the way. He had twice as many planes as the British, but the latter had technical superiority and a new weapon, radar. For two months England suffered massive terror raids, but British pilots outfought the Germans and destroyed more than half their planes. By early August they were counterattacking German industrial cities. Hitler ordered that Sea Lion be postponed indefinitely.

Instead Hitler turned eastward. He forced Hungary, Rumania, and Slovakia to join the Axis. Yugoslav patriots refused to pay the tribute Hitler demanded and revolted. Russia now threw off her last pretense of cooperation with Germany and went to the aid of the Yugoslavs. Meanwhile, Mussolini had run into trouble in his invasion of Greece, and Hitler had to go to his aid. Yugoslavia and Greece were invaded, and by June 18 all the Balkans had been conquered. Then German armies attacked the Soviet border. At first the assault went well; and by the time Germans reached Stalingrad, they had conquered a third of the population and industry of Russia. But there the Russians held, and the tide began to turn.

The Japanese attack on Pearl Harbor had brought the United States into the war in December, 1941; and by November, 1942, Anglo-American operations under General Dwight D. Eisenhower in North Africa had begun. In seven months German and Italian forces in Africa were defeated, and whole armies surrendered. This now became the base for an attack on "the soft underbelly of the Axis." Landings were made in Sicily. Mussolini fell from power, and Italy was knocked out of the war; but the Germans fought stubbornly as British and Americans slugged their way north. At the same time the Russians steadily pushed the Germans back and by the spring of 1944 Soviet troops stood on the borders of Esthonia and Latvia and crossed into Poland and Rumania. In the west, Normandy landing forces began driving Germans to their final defeat.

The Last Days

The illusion of victory still had to be kept up at home. Now the German people began to hear of "strategic withdrawals," "shortening lines," "disengaging the enemy according to plan." The capture of most of the Sixth Army under General Friedrich Paulus before Stalingrad brought a morale crisis. Hitler now declared total war. Amman closed another 950 papers. Some of Germany's fine old papers, including the *Frankfurter Zeitung*, disappeared. The Nazis could still keep their people in ignorance. Defeats were minimized; Africa was a long way off; Sicily, once called an impregnable stronghold, was written off as an unimportant outpost. Yet growing death lists, hardships, and food scarcity could not be kept dark. Newspapers became smaller. Increasing discontent with Hitler's intuitive conduct of the war spread to the general staff and an attempt was made on Hitler's life. Immediate purges and more newspaper closings followed till there remained but 977 papers. Of 25,000,000 circulation the Nazi papers now had 82.5 per cent.

It must not be thought that all Germans climbed on the Nazi bandwagon. There were resistance groups in Germany just as there were in other Nazi-dominated countries. Professors, jurists, ex-journalists, noblemen, high army officers, union leaders, and people from many walks of life worked in underground cells. There is record of at least four other attempts to remove Hitler, all of which miscarried.

In the last days of the war the number of papers was reduced as allied airmen, visiting destruction on German cities, bombed out many plants. Little newsprint was now available. In the final days, what newspapers were left were scarcely more than one-sheet handbills. From the east and west conquering armies were closing in. Cornered in Berlin, Hitler and Goebbels committed suicide. Where a few weeks before some 17,000,000 copies of newssheets had been published, suddenly there were none.

The First Postwar Period

Allied armies had to communicate their regulations to the conquered people. Orders could be posted, but as soon as possible there had to be newspapers. Mobile press units advanced with the armies, and psychological warfare branches sent teams of German-speaking newsmen and printers. From under the rubble they dug out newspaper plants and started presses. In the west they began in Luxembourg and moved on to Aachen and Cologne. Small newssheets were dropped over enemy lines to break morale. The first postwar newspaper, *Aachener Nachrichten*, appeared as a weekly January 24, 1945, four months before German surrender. As armies advanced, all German newspapers and radio stations were closed. Actually there was little left; what plants had not been hit by bombing were often wrecked by Nazi press leaders as they fled.

Out of this chaos the Allies started building an ersatz press, hoping that in time the Allied graft would bear native fruit in a reborn German press. Even before V-E Day an American team was rolling out 620,000 copies of the *Frankfurter Presse* in the old *Frankfurter Zeitung* plant. Soon there were seven weekly newspapers in the American zone with a circulation of 3,139,500, trying to tell the people what had happened and what was then taking place. Most important was *Die Neue Zeitung*, started in Munich in October, 1945, first as a semi-weekly, then as a daily printed simultaneously in six different cities. Its purpose was to set an example, through the objectivity of its reporting and its separation of fact from opinion, and to give Germans information which had been kept from them by the Nazis. It became popular and at its height had 1,600,000 circulation. The British military government also started papers in its zone, most important of which was *Die Welt;* and in their zone the Russians set up papers headed by *Die Täglische Rundschau.*

The Licensed Press

These papers, however, were still an alien product to the people. It was felt that they could best be reeducated if Germans spoke to Germans. A licensing system was established, but no license was given to any man who had worked as a journalist under the Nazis. Even the *Frankfurter Zeitung* and the *Kölnische Zeitung*, which had published under the Nazis, could not resume publication. The problem was to find competent and reliable men; many who might have been dependable either had died or been so broken in concentration camps that they no longer could work. But men were found; sometimes they had not been newspaper men but had had some experience in printing or publishing.

American press officers, feeling that the old party papers had been a weakness of the prewar press, did not grant licenses to political groups but to carefully screened groups of individuals. The French did likewise at first, but later gave licenses to party groups. The British licensed one paper for each of the larger parties in each important city. The Russians did the same but gave preference to Communists they brought with them and also to Germans who, as exiles in Russia or as prisoners of war, had been "reeducated" and prepared for their tasks as journalists. By the end of 1946 the Americans had licensed forty-four papers, the British forty-two, the French twenty-two, the Russians seventy-one. Because of the struggle for public opinion in Berlin, divided as it was between four powers, all provided daily papers so that Berlin had eleven with a circulation of 4,000,000. The emergence of licensed papers caused most military government papers to disappear.

Germans who had been suspicious of military government papers now greeted their own with enthusiasm, and whole editions were sold out quickly. Many papers, starting with a press run of 50,000, soon grew to 200,000 or 300,000. The scarcity of newsprint, which resulted in the licensing of only one paper for a wide area, caused a new pattern to emerge with fewer but stronger papers. The closing of DNB had left the country without any press agency. Now the licensed papers in each zone were encouraged to set up their own. Prepublication censorship, to make sure Nazi ideas were not promoted, was found unnecessary and quickly dropped in western zones. Only one license revocation occurred—when a German de-Nazification court found one man had been an active Nazi. There were a few short suspensions for unwarranted criticism of Allied powers, but on the whole the record of the new press was good. In the Russian zone it was different. Here any paper which showed independence of the Moscow line was harried by newsprint cuts, suspensions, and removal of its editors. In the end the Russians achieved in their zone a press closely following the pattern of the Berlin Communist papers.

Steps to Rehabilitate Germany

Allied efforts with the press were only one part of the rehabilitation program, for Germany had to be helped to support itself. Anyone who was in Germany after V-E Day will recall the devastation: seven million soldiers and civilians had been killed in the war; cities were a shambles; large areas were piles of rubble; women and children had to haul debris out of basements to get a roof over their heads. Many of the industrial plants had been bombed, and the Russians, French, and British took away remaining machinery as reparations. Despair ruled this people, and hard work represented the only way to salvation. By incredibly hard labor and sacrifice, helped by massive aid from the United States, the Germans built new factories and began making their farms once more produce food.

By the end of 1946 it became apparent that the four zones would progress faster economically if they worked together. British and Americans, in particular, found themselves drawn together in opposition to the economic policies of the Russians. Flooding of the country with Russian "occupation money" had depreciated the mark, and inflation had set in. Early in 1947 the American and British zones were fused into a bi-zone which the French and Russians were invited to join. The French did later, but the Russians refused to join or to have anything to do with the proposed currency reform. In January, 1948, they began setting up a blockade of all traffic between the western zones and Berlin. By April it was complete, and the Allies had to start supplying their sectors by the celebrated airlift.

Since priority was given to food and fuel, Berlin papers faced a crisis. Paper stocks were pooled, and papers had to operate on short rations. The Berlin press played such an important role in the battle for public opinion that newsprint was eventually flown in, but all western papers had to cut their size and press runs. Not until Americans had flown sixty super-fortresses across the Atlantic and the Allies had set up a counter-blockade against Russian traffic out of Berlin was the Russian blockade lifted in May, 1949.

In June, 1948, a six-power conference representing the United States, Britain, France, Belgium, the Netherlands, and Luxembourg agreed to the creation of a federal state out of the western zones of Germany. In the same month the long projected currency reform was put through. A new Deutschmark replaced the old Reichsmark which gave western Germany a solid currency. It marked an economic turning point and had immediate effects: production rose, consumer goods began to appear in shops, and for the first time since the war Germans had money which was worth working for and which could buy the things they needed. Soon industrial production was back to three-fourths of its 1936 level.

For newspapers there were immediate problems. Instead of buying newsprint for 260 cheap Reichsmarks a ton they now had to pay 460 dear Deutschmarks. Readers, too, found it harder to get the new marks, and circulations fell off. All papers went through a period of financial stringency, but with sharp economies they carried on. Soon the revival of business brought a new revenue from advertising such as they had not had before because, prior to currency reform, there had been little advertising except for small classified. Now that manufacturers and merchants had goods to sell, more advertising appeared; and the new revenue helped them get back on their feet. Newsprint controls were also lifted, and with the continued revival some weeklies were now able to come out twice or even three or four times a week.

Licensing Is Removed

By this time the western Allies felt that their licensees were sincere in their efforts to develop a democratic press. They were producing good papers with more objective news and using their freedom wisely to help rehabilitate their people. They were also showing political independence by criticizing governmental arbitrariness on federal, state, and local levels. It came to be realized that licensed papers could never have the full confidence of the people and furthermore that only through turning them loose in free competition could they learn to stand on their own feet and provide an independent force for German democracy. In addition, licensing was not consistent with the kind of democracy the Allies were trying to foster nor with their own traditions of press freedom.

But first the Allies insisted that the separate states pass laws to guarantee press freedom, to prohibit censorship, and to prevent government control of the news. Such laws were passed, and press freedom was also guaranteed in the new federal constitution being drafted at Bonn. In the American zone the removal of licensing began in June, 1949, and was made effective in all western zones in September. Immediately many new papers appeared. In all West Germany some 2,000 new papers, magazines, and periodicals emerged.

The old licensed papers had attempted to cater to local interests by publishing side or sectional editions with more regional news for towns in their areas. Now there appeared many small local papers under the flag, "independent home papers." Some were sponsored by political leaders. Socialists and Communists started several. Most disturbing was the emergence of some pro-Nazi journals. Many of the new publications were not good papers. They were small, poor sheets full of boiler plate and with little local news. Furthermore, many of the new publishers had not reckoned with the change that had taken place in German readers. Prewar editorial formulae no longer suited. True, many went back to the papers they or their fathers had read before the war; but they soon returned to papers they had learned to like which gave them more objective news and eschewed long political dissertations which they now suspected. To be sure, the flood of new papers with lower subscription and advertising rates created terrific competition for a time; but the formerly licensed papers met this by expanding their content, increasing their frequency, improving their news coverage, and adding special departments for women, young people, farmers, and refugees. Most of these survived. In the American zone a 1950 report showed that not one formerly licensed paper had died; and that while they represented only a sixth of the papers, they still had three-fourths of the circulation.

In the British and French zones, where political party papers had been licensed, new publishers, sensing that the public might have grown tired of purely political sheets, exploited this by launching new nonparty papers emphasizing news rather than party propaganda; and these won such success that they displaced some of the older party papers. Many other new papers failed quickly, for, launched on borrowed money at high interest rates, they did not achieve the circulation they expected and soon gave up. Some became local editions of larger regional papers. But a considerable number did succeed, and the newspaper situation resolved itself into a pattern of two or more large circulation papers in each major city with side editions for smaller towns around them and, for the rural areas, many small independent community papers. Soon the distinction between the old licensed and the new unlicensed papers disappeared in the minds of German readers.

Most notable of the effects of license removal was the increase in dailies. Whereas in 1949 there had been no dailies outside Berlin, by 1951 there were 950. But of this number only 351 were *selbstandige* or main dailies; the others were side editions for surrounding towns requiring only a change in masthead and the make-over of a page for local news. In 1954 when German press directories claimed 1,276 dailies, UNESCO reduced this to 670 main editions and 605 side editions.

New News Agencies Appear

Another important result of the new press situation was the emergence of a fresh news agency to serve the entire West German Republic. In the fall of 1949 the separate former agencies in the British, American, and French zones merged to form *Deutsches Presse Agentur* (DPA), a cooperative agency owned by newspapers, some magazines, and radio stations. Headquarters were set up in Hamburg, and bureaus located in many cities gathered all domestic news. Correspondents were maintained in foreign capitals, and the agency also exchanged news with a number of European agencies. Thus it soon provided a very complete foreign and domestic news report. Then it added a cultural service, special sports and financial wires, wirephoto for its larger clients, and a daily mail picture service for smaller dailies. It set as its goal quick, comprehensive, and nonpartisan service; and its objective and honest reporting earned approval.

In the Russian zone *Allgemeiner Deutscher Nachrichten* (ADN), which had been established early in 1946, was reorganized as an alleged cooperative, owned and financed by East German papers. Its main office was in Berlin, its director a Soviet citizen. Any text sent out by the government was put on the wire without editing. ADN obtained its foreign news from TASS. Just as DNB served the Nazis, so ADN now served its Communist masters to set the pattern of news presentation for the entire East German press. While at first a pretense had been made of permitting the publication of non-Communist party papers, these soon lost their independence and found themselves as closely controlled as any Communist party paper. The Berlin press, headed by *Neues Deutschland*, the organ of the Central Committee of the Communist party, the *Pravda* of East Germany, and *Berliner*

Zeitung, the organ of the government, set the pattern for other dailies and weeklies in East Germany.

Germany Moves Forward

The next ten years were momentous ones for West Germany. Hard work on the part of the people, the wise leadership of Konrad Adenauer who had been made Chancellor in 1949, substantial aid from Marshall funds, and Germany's entrance into the steel and coal community set the nation on the road to recovery. By 1955 her industrial production index was up to 210 as compared with 100 in 1938. The West German mark represented one of the most stable currencies in Europe. The Federal Republic signed an agreement for its participation in the European Defense Community. This brought such sharp reaction from the Soviet Union that it killed all hopes for reunification with East Germany. Continuing difficulty with Communists led to the banning of the Communist party and its papers. In 1955, ten years after the end of the war, the Federal Republic became a fully sovereign state; all allied controls were removed, and West Germany was admitted to NATO. Adenauer and his Christian Democratic party had won a sweeping victory in 1953, and they won by a landslide in 1957.

West Germany had joined the European Common Market, embracing also France, Italy, and the Benelux nations; and under the astute guidance of her economics minister, Ludwig Erhard, she had by the early sixties become the most prosperous nation in Europe. These were troubled years, however, as the Soviet Union pressed its demands for West Germany's withdrawal from NATO; for making Berlin a demilitarized free city, terminating the four-power rule which would have given East Germans complete control over access to the city; and for confederation of the two cities on Communist terms, concluding with Khrushchev's threat to sign a separate treaty with East Germany. But West Germany stood firm. There were continual interferences with transportation between Berlin and West Germany, culminating in the erection of the wall between East and West Berlin and the sealing off of the entire 824-mile frontier to prevent any further defections, for over 3,000,000 had fled the Soviet zone since 1945. Reunification still remained a dream of West Germans, but most recognized that this could not be accomplished without war. Yet West Germany remained the most prosperous and viable democracy in Europe.

Changes Come to German Press

One might presume that this burgeoning economy would have brought a considerable press expansion. This did not happen for several reasons. West Germany had achieved a tremendous concentration of newspapers; but wages, which had tripled in a decade, and increased costs of newsprint and production forced changes. The advent of commercial television advertising also cut into newspaper revenue. Furthermore, Germany's boom had begun to slow in 1962. Her gross national product had fallen because of a shorter work week and because wages had increased so much faster than productivity. This made prices of German products higher, increased the cost-of-living index, and caused her export market to decline. All these factors did not encourage press expansion. Instead there were newspaper mergers; and as stronger papers developed regional editions, smaller local dailies united in rings to cut down costs by sharing editorial features and by central printing. As a result the 1963 report to *Editor and Publisher's International Yearbook* showed only 324 *hauptzeitungen* or main dailies and 590 side editions for a total of 914 titles, a considerable drop from the 1,500 claimed in the fifties.

In 1964 increased production costs and advertising competition from radio and television brought a further concentration, heralded first by mergers of large dailies in Düsseldorf and Cologne and the absorption by larger regional dailies of many small local papers which were then handled as side editions. Thus the report for the 1965 *Editor and Publisher Yearbook* showed only 143 main dailies. The Bundesverban Deutscher Zeitungs Verlager (official statistical organization for the German press) insists that there are 616 *hauptzeitungen* and 759 *nebenausgaben* (side editions) but explains that special conditions in Germany make it impossible to conform to UNESCO's requirement that only those papers publishing four times or more a week be counted as dailies. Many German papers which print editions two to three times a week must assume an informational character simliar to that of dailies because of the needs of their readers. These papers, with their many side editions, account for the extraordinary number of dailies and side editions. The 1965 report of 143 German dailies may not be complete because it is possible that some papers failed to return their questionnaires. But even if the total should not exceed 175 or 200, it would still be a remarkable number for a country which could be contained in the single state of Texas. By comparison, France has only 112 regular dailies, and Great Britain only 110. Yet the German dailies that survive are sound, modern editions which provide an effective medium for advertisers. While there had been a decline in total daily circulations, by 1964 they were up to 17,388,000, which represented 30.7 copies per 100 persons. In addition to dailies there are 51 tri-weeklies, 36 biweeklies, and 133 weeklies.

One weakness of the press under the Weimar Republic was its multiplicity of political party organs. Today there is almost a two-party system with the Christian Democrats and Socialists getting the overwhelming number of votes. Most surprising is the fact that today 85 per cent of Germany's dailies label themselves as independent and another 7.7 per cent list no political affiliation. Only seventeen admit political leanings, and their circulations are small compared to the independents. A majority of the dailies are information papers emphasizing news, but this does not mean that they may not support or oppose editorially the policies advocated by parties.

By 1961 resentment had grown against Adenauer's rule, and Germans realized that he could not govern indefinitely. In the 1961 election the Christian Democrats had to form a coalition with the Free Democrats in order to be elected, but they joined only on Adenauer's agreement to retire before his four-year term expired. Hence in 1963 he was succeeded by Ludwig Erhard, the architect of the miracle of West Germany's recovery. Adenauer had, however, won recognition as one of Germany's greatest statesmen, a man who had become chancellor at the age of seventy-three—when most men's careers are over—yet in fourteen years he had brought his nation out of defeat and chaos, had restored its national dignity, and had given it a political continuity it had not had since World War I.

Although the West German economy suffered a setback in 1963, its growth increased in 1964. But Erhard's position deteriorated. First came the revolt of farmers against his price-fixing; then came worsening relations with France and added difficulties with the Soviet Union, climaxed by a week-long traffic barricade when the German parliament met in West Berlin. Socialist gains in the local elections of 1964 brought claims that they would carry the 1965 elections. Yet, when elections were held in September, 1965, Erhard's party won 47.6 per cent of the vote as compared to 39.3 for the Socialists. Now Erhard took a stronger stand, insisting that West Germany be on the "first team" of the Western Alliance with access to nuclear weapons under U.S. leadership, a condition which President Lyndon B. Johnson confirmed was already in effect. Erhard also made it clear that he disagrees with practically everything De Gaulle wants to do in Europe.

One interesting change is that the German press no longer has a central point from which it can exercise national influence. Before 1945 Berlin was the focal point, but today a divided Berlin, cut off from the rest of the country, no longer has this influence. Hamburg has become the principal printing center, and its *Die Welt* has national influence, though its 245,000 circulation reaches only a small part of

Germany's 56,000,000 people. West Germany has some fine news-papers although their influence is largely regional.

For a long time the large number of dailies limited circulations. But today there are only eleven with circulations under 20,000. By contrast Germany has more large dailies than most other European countries, for there are thirty-six with circulations over 100,000. Largest are *Bild Zeitung* (Hamburg) with 3,829,944, *Westdeutsche Allgemeine* at Essen with 417,959, *BZ* in Berlin with 322,607, *Hamburger Abendblatt* with 314,173 and *Rheinische Post* at Düsseldorf with 268,318. Close behind is *Frankfurter Allgemeine* with 243, 816, which many consider the most respected paper of really national influence.

Bild Zeitung was the pacemaker in a new crop of illustrated papers which appeared for a time. It is not an actual newspaper, for its aim is not so much to inform as to entertain. It started as a picture tabloid with no text item longer than thirty-five lines. Postwar Germans after hard years welcomed something lighter. They soon dubbed it their "blood and bosom" journalism. At first they bought it surreptitiously, tucking it into one of their respectable papers, and it was cheap at ten pfennigs. But its flashy makeup, its concentrated way of presenting material with sequences of pictures and text, and its appeal to the emotions caught on all over the country. It is part of the empire of Axel Springer, Germany's biggest press lord who has, however, used his profits to put out excellent papers in *Die Welt*, *Abendzeitung*, and *Welt am Sontag*. He is also associated with Verlag Ullstein, famed prewar Jewish publishers, in two of the largest Berlin dailies, *Morgenpost* and *BZ*.

Is the West German Press Free?

After its long history of government manipulation prior to 1920, its brief period of freedom under the Weimar Republic, and then its complete domination under the Nazis, the West German press tech-nically has about the same liberties as those enjoyed by newspapers in other western countries. True, the old Bismarckian press law of 1874 was still on the books but it was generally conceded to be outdated. Liberty of the press and freedom from censorship is guaranteed in the constitution, but it also provides that those laws are limited for the protection of youth and the inviolability of personal honor and that whoever abuses the freedom of expression to attack the free demo-cratic order forfeits his rights. Protection for youth was provided by the "dirt and trash" law which forbade the sale of obscene matter to young people, but then the government introduced laws curbing the press by forbidding criticism of heads of foreign states and protecting the honor of officials, which would have been tantamount to silencing criticism of government leaders.

This attempt was foiled by the protest of the entire press. But when the minister of defense began arresting newsmen for treason for printing information touching on defense, despite the fact that this was in the public interest, newspapers again rose in protest. Most notable was the 1962 *Spiegel* case in which a publisher and three of his staff members were arrested and imprisoned for revealing that a report of recent NATO maneuvers had been critical of the performance of West German forces. This set off a storm from the whole press, brought the release of the men, and forced the resignation of the defense minister.

Newsmen in Germany, as in Britain and the United States, have been arrested for refusing to divulge the sources of their information, but on April 1, 1965, the parliament of the state of Hamburg became the fifth to pass a new press law which invalidates the old 1874 law and recognizes the public role of the press and its right of refusal to give the sources of its information. Similar laws have also been passed by all but three other German states.

West German journalists have been apprehensive of governmental attempts against the press because their country has no long tradition of press freedom; they feel that the newspapers therefore have an obligation to keep the public alert and enlightened on all matters affecting the people and their government. They are convinced that derelictions of the press cannot be dealt with by censorship or restrictions which deprive the people of their right to know but by self-control from the press itself. To that end they established their *Presserat* or court of honor to safeguard press freedom by insuring its fairness and responsibility. It has only the power of publicity and reprimand against erring publications, but its citing of irresponsible papers has had a healthy, educative effect. It has also won the respect of government, and all legislative proposals affecting the press are now referred to the *Presserat*. In cases of protests from foreign governments, these are passed on to this body for discussion and settlement.

The West German press has shown significant independence also in fearlessly criticizing both national and local governments. Adenauer never did enjoy the luxury of unswerving support, for although most papers respected what he had done for West Germany, they opposed his policies aimed at too great domination of political life. The Social Democratically-inclined papers bitterly fought his rearmament program. Press treatment of such issues as reunification and relations with the Soviet Union or the reporting of alleged corruption in high places do not suggest any bridling of the press.

A Look at West German Papers

In the days following the removal of licensing, many small four-page *kopfblätter*, local home papers with a cursory coverage of local items and filled with matted news and feature matter, existed; but these have long disappeared. The few smaller dailies under 20,000 circulation today provide a well-balanced news coverage and generally average about ten pages. The big city papers are excellent information journals averaging twenty pages or more and up to sixty pages in their weekend editions. To British, Scandinavian, and American readers, German papers look conservative; but Germans like them that way and to them they are more interesting than ever before. Papers are made up in four or five wide columns broken up by spread heads in modest type sizes. Most carry few pictures except on sports and cultural pages. A few, however, like *Münchner Merkur, Kölner Stadt Zeitung, Die Welt,* and *Hamburger Abendblatt,* have broken with old traditions and provide really interesting and attractive headline display and many good news and feature pictures. Stronger papers give 50 per cent of their space to advertising—most of it national—classified display, and small want ads. Some local retail advertising has begun to appear.

A typical midweek sixteen-page edition of *Frankfurter Allgemeine* gives three front page columns to top national and foreign stories and two to leading articles. Then follow three pages of more wire news interspersed with some advertising, the daily serial story, editorials clipped from other German or foreign papers, radio and TV programs. Now come four pages of news from all over Germany, local news and sports, and considerable advertising. The second section opens with a page of special background-of-the-news articles followed by three solid pages of advertising, three pages of financial and business news, and a back page of cultural news and criticism. It is a solid substantial paper providing a wide coverage of news carefully departmentalized. Germans speak of it as the successor to the famed prewar *Frankfurter Zeitung.*

The West German press has made tremendous strides since the war, and there are some excellent papers with extensive and reliable domestic and foreign news coverage. Most separate fact from opinion. The overwhelming majority are independent, and even those which back a political party are independent of party support. Newspapers are generally fair and objective. This is a far cry from the very partisan group press which existed before the Nazis took over. This press has played a great role in making its nation an important and respected factor in European affairs, and it remains a solid press serving its people well.

Frankfurter Allgemeine—243,816 circulation daily, 283,194 Saturday. National appeal. One of West Germany's most prominent and most widely quoted papers. Very well-informed on foreign and national affairs. Conservative but independent. Was strong supporter of Adenauer.

Berliner Morgenpost—Strongest daily in West Berlin with 216,741 circulation daily, 366,837 Sunday. Although most of the circulation is in Berlin, the paper goes all over the Federal Republic. Owned by Ullstein-Springer organization. Strongly anti-Communist. Independent but has generally backed Christian Democrats.

Die Welt (Hamburg)—National in appeal with 245,761 circulation daily, 271,008 Saturday. Good coverage of foreign and national news. Springer's best paper. Independent, it tends to be neutral in politics.

Hamburger Abendblatt—Springer's most popular evening paper with 314,173 circulation weekdays and 381,868 Saturdays. Most successful evening paper in Germany. Much local news and even a full page of comics and other popular features. Independent.

Bild Zeitung (Hamburg)—Circulation 3,829,944. Springer's greatest money-maker. A tabloid picture paper, has strictly mass appeal, with its sensation and its uncoventional makeup.

Westfaelische Rundschau (Dortmund)—Circulation 218,945. One of the most influential Socialist party supporters. A well-informed paper, but tends to follow Socialist line closely in editorials and play of news.

Rheinische Post (Düsseldorf)—268,000 circulation. Most influential in the North Rhine–Westphalia area. Generally has supported the Christian Democratic Union.

Süddeutsche Zeitung (Munich)—Circulation 197,199. Probably most influential in South Germany, particularly Bavaria, but read in many other parts of Federal Republic. A good newspaper, independent but liberal. Generally pro-west but has been critical of some aspects of U.S. foreign policy.

The Press of East Germany

The situation here is far different from that in West Germany, for the Communists have found it easier to control information by limiting newspapers. The 17,000,000 East Germans have only thirty-four dailies, a considerable drop from 1957. East Berlin has eight; Dresden, Halle, and Rostock each have three; Leipzig, Potsdam, Schwerin, and Weimar have two; other cities have only one. No West Berlin or other western papers are permitted to enter.

This press is organized on the same hierarchical plan as is that in the Soviet Union with *Neues Deutschland*, the *Pravda* of this satellite state, leading with a claimed 800,000 circulation. Statistics are given only for a few of the larger papers, and these round-numbered reports have not varied for years; hence their accuracy is doubtful. With so many millions of East Germans having defected to the West it is questionable whether East Germans, except the party faithful, give their papers much readership.

Despite claims to the contrary, the entire press is controlled by the Social Unity party (SED), the arm of the Communist government. A pretense is made that some papers are published by the Liberal-Democratic, National Democratic, and Christian Democratic parties, but they are captive organizations, and their papers are strictly kept in line by *Pressamt*, the official press control bureau. Every bit of news, every argument in all papers bears an official character. The role of the press in East Germany was made clear by this announcement: "Our newspapers are not being published to entertain people or to make money for profit but to make political propaganda. They are political institutions which for purposes of efficiency bear the character of newspapers."

The *Sächsisches Tageblatt* at Dresden, a supposedly Liberal Democratic paper, on July 10, 1957, outlined its duty: "The task of the non-Communist press . . . is to win fellow fighters for our (i.e. Communist) struggle against anti-pacifist militarism in Western Germany and for the upbuilding of a peaceful and happy socialist future for our country."

A content analysis of representative East German papers shows that 60 per cent of their space is given to political and economic ideology, descriptions of the achievements of socialism, deficiencies demanding better performance, drives for greater production, and appeals for loyalty. Considerable space is given to cultural material but a relatively small amount to local news and sports. Foreign news is gleaned from TASS and ADN to unmask the weaknesses of capitalism and its "atom bomb diplomacy" and "dollar imperialism." Foreign stories are often held up for days till "cleared" by the government. *Neues Deutschland* is a well-madeup paper running ten to twelve pages; most others run only eight pages and look dull by comparison with those on the other side of the Wall. This press is rigidly controlled by Communist press chiefs.

The Berlin Wall was breached three times in 1964 so that East and West Berliners might visit relatives on the other side. In October East Germany offered elderly persons a chance to join relatives in the western sector, but this meant only shunting the burden for the support of these unproductive people to West Germany. At the same time it was announced that 10,000 political prisoners would be released. This proved pure blackmail, for West Germany had to pay ransom in food and consumer goods for those released in 1965. The Wall was breached again on Easter Sunday in 1965, but this time no East Germans were allowed to cross for fear they might stay. Otto Grotewohl, longtime premier, died in September, 1964, and was succeeded by Willi Stoph; Walter Ulbricht remains as head of the Communist party and dictator of all East Germans.

The Newspapers of Belgium

It was the morning of May 15, 1940. General Alexander von Falkenhausen, the Nazi governor of conquered Belgium, stretched contentedly as he woke and saw the sun streaming in through the lovely colored windows of the medieval building he had commandeered for himself. Things had gone well. The old Schlieffen plan involving a wide sweep through Belgium to permit a quick attack on France had worked perfectly this time. It had been just four days since Germany had launched her blitzkrieg, and here they were in Brussels already. This would be a good place to make his headquarters. The lightning thrust of panzer divisions under Rundstedt, Bock, and Leeb had quickly knifed through Belgium's small army. True, it had been necessary to shoot some foolish people who resisted as they entered the city; but today Brussels would be quiet, though perhaps sullen. There would be no troubles like the ones his uncle, Baron Ludwig von Falkenhausen, had had in 1914.

He pulled open the windows and looked out over the beautiful Grand Place at the fifteenth century Hotel de Ville, the Maison du Roi, and the famed old Guild Houses. This would be all right. He went to the door of his room to call his orderly. What was this? Here at his feet lay a paper whose masthead he recognized—the same *La Libre Belgique* which had been his uncle's greatest headache in World War I. And under it an editorial calling on the people to resist till victory came again. But what infuriated him was that it gave its address as "Commandatura," headquarters of the occupation army; its editor as "Peter Pan"; and the price, "Free since the Boche have already wrecked Belgium."

Determined to stamp out this troublesome sheet he issued orders to confiscate all copies that could be found and to start a search for the culprits. He fixed penalties far more severe than those in the last war. For mere possession of a copy the penalty was from one to twelve years of solitary confinement; for distribution the punishment was death. But he had not reckoned on the Belgian spirit. Soon *La Libre Belgique* was appearing daily; and other resistance papers began to spring up, not only in Brussels but in other cities as well. For this was the work of Belgian newspapermen, as stubbornly independent and courageous as any in Europe.

This press is young, yet old; young in that a real press did not emerge till after 1830 when the present kingdom was established; old, because this country gave birth to one of the earliest newspapers in Europe.

Belgium is a small country, little larger than Maryland, yet one of the most densely populated in Europe with over 9,000,000 people, three times the number in Maryland. To the west and north of the capital, Brussels, lies the Flanders plain where people speak Flemish, akin to Dutch. To the south and east are the rolling downs rising to the Ardennes where the people speak French or its Walloon dialect. Hence this press is bilingual.

Early trade routes between the north and south of Europe crossed Belgium. One power after the other coveted her ocean gateways and the rich trading centers which grew around them. For centuries Belgium was a perpetual battleground. Her first conquerors had been the Romans; then came the Franks, Teutons, Burgundians, and Spaniards. Cruel Spanish repression brought a fifty-year revolt till Phillip II of Spain tried a new method by marrying his daughter Isabella to Archduke Albert of Belgium.

Birth of Belgium's Press

Albert and Isabella, who began their reign in 1598 after bringing the war of exhaustion against the Dutch provinces to an end, began a course of peace and reconstruction, rebuilding churches, and encouraging elementary and higher education. There followed a renaissance in art and literature. The Flemish school of painting led by Rubens, Van Dyck, David Teniers, and Jacob Jordaens became famous. During this period Belgium's first newspaper was born. In 1605 Abraham Verhoeven, an Antwerp printer, was given the first *privilegium* to publish, for the princes, accounts of victories, sieges, and other news of lands governed by their majesties. Verhoeven's *Nieuwe Tijdinghen* for some years was only an occasional flysheet, but incomplete files in the Royal Library at Brussels indicate that in 1617 it was appearing regularly.

Its life was short, for after Albert's death in 1621, the Belgian provinces reverted to Spain; and for the next 92 years Spanish armies occupied the land. No journals could be published without their authorization. Yet Brussels had its first paper in *Courier Veritable*, founded by Jean Monnart in 1649, and Ghent had its first in *Ghent-sche Post-Tijdinghen*. These early papers could carry only such news items as censors permitted and no political comment. Such expressions occurred only in clandestine sheets *circulent sous le manteau*.

In the eighteenth century, Belgium, after the War of the Spanish Succession, became the property of Austria, which wisely granted Belgians considerable autonomy and assisted in their economic development. But Austrian rulers were as suspicious of Belgian journalists as they were of their own, and such publications as were permitted had to confine themselves to culture. Belgium's first literary journal, *Le Littérateur Belgique*, founded in Brussels in 1755 by E. A. Essarts, was suppressed in five months. The first daily, issued in 1777 under the curious title, *La Feuille Sans Titre* (The Sheet without a Title), while seeking safety in literary discussion, was also short-lived.

In the revolution of 1789 Belgians drove out the Austrians; but in the Treaty of the Hague the great powers restored Belgium to Austria, and the revolution was quickly put down. The new Austrian rule was of short duration, for the French Revolutionary armies invaded Belgium and annexed it to France. For fifteen years Belgium was treated as a conquered province. The few papers allowed had to project Napoleon's propaganda. Nothing could be published without the approval of the French censor.

Under Dutch Rule

After the fall of Napoleon in 1814, the Congress of Vienna rearranged the map of Europe to prevent any new French menace. Belgium and Holland were united as a neutral buffer state to act as a barrier to France. Thus the Belgians, without being consulted, were handed over to William I, king of Holland. Despite the fact that there were 3,500,000 Belgians to 2,000,000 Dutch, the latter controlled the country. Belgian editors attacked Dutch rule, but they were hunted down one by one and imprisoned for sedition.

Following Napoleon's Waterloo defeat, King William imposed a new constitution which gave the state monopoly in all educational matters and suppressed church schools, thus infuriating Catholic Belgians. Freedom of the press was rescinded and special tribunals were created to punish "crimes of the press." This was too much for the sons of patriots who had fought the tyrannies of Spain, Austria, and France. Catholic papers and Liberals led by Louis de Potter in his *Courrier des Pays Bas* defied the tribunals and denounced the king.

De Potter was captured and imprisoned. But *Le Mathieu Laensberg*, *Le Belge*, *L'Observateur*, *Den Vaterlander*, and others took up the cry for independence. The king countered by founding his own paper, *Le National*, at Brussels, edited by Florentine Libry, Count de Bagnano, an unscrupulous opportunist who soon came to be hated by all Belgians. From his prison De Potter smuggled out patriotic appeals which were printed in many papers. In spite of a rigorous persecution of journalists all Belgian papers, both Liberal and Catholic, kept up the agitation for independence. Too late the Dutch tried to make concessions; these were condemned as insufficient by Belgian papers which demanded more profound reforms including liberty of the press, freedom of education, ministerial responsibility, trial by jury, and relief from oppressive taxes.

Freedom at Last

On the evening of August 25, 1830, the Brussels opera company performed Auber's *La Muette de Portici*. When the hero sang the famous air appealing for revolt and liberty, the audience rushed into the streets, sacked the house of Van Maanen, the king's unpopular minister of justice, and wrecked the offices and presses of the hated *Le National*. The revolt spread; other chief towns confined Dutch garrisons in their forts. The king sent an army of 12,000 to attack Brussels, but after four days the Dutch were forced to retreat. All other towns expelled Dutch troops and placed themselves under the authority of the provisional government.

On October 4, 1830, this government declared Belgium an independent state and convened a national assembly which proclaimed a new constitution, providing for a constitutional monarchy, equality of all Belgians before the law, and freedom of worship, association, and education. It declared: "The press is free; censorship may never be reestablished and no surety bond may be exacted from writers, editors or printers. In matters concerning the press, closed hearings may be held only with unanimous consent. Jury trial is required in all criminal cases and in all hearings of political and press offenses."

Thus the Belgian press at last won its freedom and a constitutional guarantee against the kind of star chamber courts which had suppressed it in the past.

The Rise of a New Press

To give the public full news of debates in the national congress, the government brought out *L'Union Belge*, later named *Le Moniteur Belge*, as an official state organ. Many independent papers also came into being. *L'Emancipation* and *L'Indépendant* had been born in Brussels with the start of the revolution; *Le Courrier des Pays Bas* and *Le Mathieu Laensberg*, which had played such an important role in the prerevolutionary period now changed their names to *Courrier Belge* and *Politique*. In the provinces there were soon papers representing every shade of opinion. Circulations were small, often only 500 to 1,500; but copies were passed from one person to another and helped immeasurably in forming opinion in the early days of the new state. By 1840 twenty-eight dailies, nineteen triweeklies, fourteen semiweeklies, and ten weeklies had appeared. Some of these, with insufficient financing, had to close. In 1850 M. Ulysse Capitain, author of a study of newspapers of this period, wrote: "The newspaper has taken an important part in the formation of public opinion; the people have come to regard the press as the counsellor of the country, the defender of the constitutional liberties which it has given them. The liberal institutions which the constitution and our organic laws have provided are considered as a victory of the press."

To satisfy the great powers, Belgium had elected Prince Leopold of Saxe-Coburg-Gotha as King Leopold I. Even King William of Holland had in 1839 acknowledged adherence to the Treaty of London which recognized Belgium as a perpetually neutral kingdom under the guarantee of the five great powers.

The first two decades of the new freedom were, however, a period of great economic difficulty. Separated from Holland, Belgium found her seaborne trade through Antwerp cut off. Leopold proved to be an able king and encouraged progressive industrialization; but with Dutch, French, and Spanish markets closed and English competition formidable there came a glut in Belgium's factories. Many men were thrown out of work. For the press this meant that few could buy newspapers, and advertising dried up. In 1850 one editor complained that the circulation of all Brussels and provincial papers did not exceed 45,000, or one subscriber for each one hundred inhabitants.

In the 1850's, however, Belgium removed some of her own protective tariffs, made favorable commerical treaties with neighboring countries, and improved her economy. The abolition of the stamp tax on newspapers enabled publishers to cut their prices and increase circulation. Growing prosperity also brought more advertising. This permitted better news service, particularly on foreign news. *L'Indépendance Belge* was the first to have a foreign correspondent in Paris to report the 1848 French Revolution, and as revolts spread through Europe all Belgian papers of any importance sent correspondents wherever big news was breaking.

Political Press Develops

During the first ten years after the revolution the press buried its differences and supported the Liberal Catholic coalition government. But soon sharp divisions began to appear, particularly between Liberal and Catholic papers. The cleavages were largely religious. The Liberals respected religion but combatted its interference in civil life, demanding that the state, not the Church, should control education. The Catholic papers insisted that since the majority of Belgians were Catholic, the Church should supervise education, poor relief, and other social measures. The coalition government fell in 1847; and thereafter the Liberal and Catholic parties alternated in power till 1856 when the Liberals, with one brief interlude, remained in control until 1884.

Each party now felt it had to have voices in as many cities as possible. King Leopold II had come to the throne in 1865, and his forty-four-year reign meant to the Belgians what the Victorian age signified to England. This was a period of great material progress in agriculture, industry, and foreign trade. The press also shared in this prosperity, and by 1880 Belgium had 77 dailies and 244 weeklies and semiweeklies. The outstanding paper was still *L'Indépendance Belge*, which enjoyed an international reputation for its news coverage and cosmopolitan character and whose volume of advertising made it the most prosperous paper in the country.

The first Belgian equivalent of a penny paper had come in 1869 when De Busschere in Ghent brought out his *Het Volksblad*, later changed to *De Gentenaar*, which still exists today. To compete, some of the other papers lowered their prices; and this started a revolution in the press, for to exist such papers needed larger circulations. This meant that, in order to reach a wider circle of readers, they must place more emphasis on news than on political opinion.

The period from 1885 to 1914 was one of significant expansion. Large-scale industry tended to replace small businesses and in turn caused a great increase in the number of industrial workers. The press thus far was still mainly for the upper and middle classes. The masses of common people were still disenfranchised because of heavy property qualifications. Only 100,000 out of 4,000,000 had the right to vote. Workers and peasant cooperatives as well as Socialist clubs had begun in the seventies to agitate for the electoral franchise so that they might get from parliament the sweeping reforms they demanded. The first Socialist paper of any influence was *La Voix de l'Ouvrier* (The Voice of the Worker), founded in 1879 by Cesar de Paepe and Louis

Bertrand. It was succeeded in 1894 by E. Anseele's *Vooruit* (Progress), published in Ghent, and in 1885 by Bertrand's *Le Peuple*, printed in Brussels. Both are today leading voices of the Labor party in Belgium.

The new Labor voices took up the cry against the insufferable hardships of the masses and, supported by strike after strike, forced a constitutional revision in 1892 which increased the number of voters tenfold. Meanwhile a section of the Catholic party, while declaring its fidelity to the Church, demanded more social justice and formed the Christian Democratic party. Thus there were now four major parties, and the press became more than ever politically partisan with its organs hammering each other.

As the lower classes won a share in public affairs, the language question came to the fore. French had been established after the revolution as the official language, yet Flemish remained the tongue of the working people in the western part of the country. A Flemish literary revival gave impetus to a demand for language equality, and in 1898 Flemish was made equal to French before the law. By 1904, though there were still sixty-five dailies printed in French, there were twenty written in Flemish.

The Quiet before the Storm

The general prosperity of this period gave rise to new papers which are important today. In 1885 Victor Jourdain founded *Le Patriote*, which lives today as the famous *La Libre Belgique*. In 1886 Julius Hoste founded in Brussels *Het Laatste Nieuws* (The Latest News), which was destined to be the first Flemish mass circulation paper, largest in Belgium today. Next year Emile Rossel brought out *Le Soir* (The Evening) as the first politically neutral paper, which today is second largest in circulation. In Antwerp *De Gazet van Antwerpen* was born in 1891 and in 1894 *Volksgazet*, which are the leading papers in this city. In 1905 the radical progressive wing of the Liberals brought out *La Dernière Heure* (The Latest Hour), today a significant figure in Belgian journalism.

Leopold II, seeking new markets for expanding industry, had by adroit diplomacy persuaded the great powers to approve the establishment of the Kingdom of Congo which, in 1908, he made a Belgian colony, thus adding a territory eighty times the size of the home country. This brought not only expanded markets but wealth in ivory, rubber, and minerals. Leopold was also concerned with Belgium's defenses, for even at the beginning of the twentieth century it was possible to visualize the mounting tensions between the two great blocs of powers which were to face each other in 1914 and to sense the danger that neutral Belgium might encounter between the two. The Catholic party and its press fought increased military expenditures; but before his death the king, aided by the Liberal press, obtained funds to strengthen border fortifications and provide a larger army through military conscription. Albert I succeeded to the throne in 1909, and although heightened international tensions forced greater consideration of military defense, the first five years of his reign were increasingly prosperous. Belgium's commerce grew until it ranked fifth among the nations of the world. The country and its press dreamed only of economic expansion.

Disaster Strikes

Germany, fearing a two-front war against France in the west and Russia in the east, decided to take advantage of slow Russian mobilization by launching a massive attack on France. By driving to Paris through Luxembourg and Belgium, of whose neutrality Germany was herself a guarantor, the Kaiser could thus eliminate the western threat. He declared war on France on August 3, 1914, and the next day invaded Belgium.

Even though Belgium had built strong border forts, she had an army of only 150,000. It fought heroically but had no chance against five great German armies. By November the country had been occupied, and it remained under German occupation through the four years of the war. As the enemy penetrated the country, newspapers closed their doors and announced that no Belgian paper worthy of the name would reappear till liberty was restored. In Brussels the whole press closed on August 20 when General Sixtus von Arnim's army entered the capital. Papers moved to Le Havre, Paris, Amsterdam, Leyden, the Hague, and to London. From exile, despite financial difficulty, they tried to tell Belgium's story to the world and to sustain the courage of the people.

Within occupied Belgium, Germans took over vacated newspaper plants and brought out their own papers. Most hated was *Le Bruxellois*. Only five Belgian papers succumbed to German bribes and resumed publication under German censorship. Their names were forever dishonored. Through their own organs and the few traitorous Belgian papers, the Germans sought to create despair by spreading false news and announcing their victories loudly and daily. They tried to excite animosity against England and to sow dissension between Flemings and Walloons.

To counteract this poisonous propaganda, a clandestine press sprang up. Victor Jourdain, editor of the prewar *Le Patriote*, brought out early in 1915 *La Libre Belgique*, which became the most famous of the underground papers. It was followed by others such as *Patrie, La Vérité, L'Âme Belge, De Vlaamsche*, and *Le Flambeau*. Newspapermen, clergymen, teachers who had gone underground, secretly wrote and edited them. Loyal printers and stencilists risked their lives to produce them. Scores of patriots took over at night to distribute them. Each copy, passed from hand to hand, reached many more. These papers blasted German lies, debunked the continual claims of victory, inspired underground resistance and sabotage, and sought to keep alive the hope of eventual liberation and victory. German efforts to stamp out this press never succeeded, for there were always others to step into the places of those arrested.

Between the Wars

At the peace conference Belgium's former status as a neutral buffer was removed, and she was given full freedom in the conduct of her foreign affairs. Popular King Albert returned to rebuild his country, much of whose industry had been wrecked by the Germans. Railroads had to be rebuilt, and a million refugees, returned from other countries, had to be cared for. There was much unemployment, but after 1926 industry began to recover, and the last years of the twenties were good years.

Most of the prewar papers had resumed publication soon after the armistice, and their reappearance was greeted with joy by a people who for fifty months had missed their free and independent press. Though newspapers were in serious financial difficulties in the first postwar years, in the late twenties they began to forge ahead, modernize their plants, and improve their news service. By 1930 there were a number of substantial dailies with circulations of 100,000 to 200,000 or more.

Belgium, depending on her foreign trade, was hit hard by the world depression. By 1934 more than a fourth of her industrial workers were unemployed. Léon Degrelle's Rexist movement made headway and won twenty-one seats in parliament, but it soon became clear that the Rexists were as totalitarian as the Nazis and that Degrelle was but a tool of Hitler. A great majority of the papers joined in exposing Degrelle, and in the election of 1939 the Rexists lost seventeen of their twenty-one seats. Germany's reoccupation of the Rhineland sent a wave of apprehension through Belgium as editors realized that their collective security within the League of Nations was ending. As he sought to immunize his nation from attack, Leopold III, who had succeeded his father, on the latter's death in 1934, announced that his country would reshape its foreign policy and shun all military alliances. Belgium, however, rapidly rearmed and strengthened her border forts.

The Press Goes Underground Again

Belgium clung to her tenuous neutrality for eight months after World War II began; but on May 10, 1940, Germany struck without warning and in eleven days reached the English channel, trapping the whole Belgian army. Leopold ordered his troops to capitulate. This action was branded as illegal by Premier Hubert Pierlot and his parliament, meeting in Paris, who voted to dethrone the king.

Again all Belgian papers closed down when the Germans invaded. Paul Jourdain, Victor Jourdain's son who for twenty-two years had carried on in his father's footsteps, destroyed the press of *La Libre Belgique* rather than let it be used by the enemy or his collaborators. He was compelled to flee for his life to Morocco, but other resistance leaders continued to publish *La Libre Belgique* in its old tradition regularly through the war. Some papers moved to Ostend and Paris, but the German conquest of both Holland and France made continued publication impossible. Journalists who escaped to England began publishing, with the cooperation of the government in exile, two weeklies for distribution among the refugees in England. Numerous copies of the weeklies were also parachuted by the British to the people in occupied Belgium. Other journalists helped organize *Radio Belgique* and *Radio Belgie* to broadcast "The Voice of Belgium" to the people under occupation.

Within Belgium *La Libre Belgique* was the first of the courageous underground papers to appear, and it was quickly followed by others. By 1942 there were fifty or more with a combined circulation of 100,000, but each copy was read by many times that number. In all, more than three hundred resistance newspapers appeared during the occupation. Among those which played a significant part were *La Voix des Belges, Front, Libération, Vrij,* and *Front Flammand.* But the Socialist organ *Le Peuple* and the Communist *Drapeau Rouge* were most persistent. There were clandestine papers for every group—farmers, doctors, lawyers, teachers, workers, students—providing news the Germans tried to conceal—of German defeats, the destruction of German cities by Allied bombers, of German cruelties. They gave instructions for slowdowns and sabotage, and a regular feature was the blacklisting of collaborators. Although people listened to forbidden London broadcasts, the clandestine press, which shared their suffering and brought them news from their own battle front, was something they lived with. Camille Joset, president of the National Council of Resistance, characterized this press as "the brightest jewel in the crown of resistance."

Hundreds of Gestapo agents hunted the courageous men and women who produced these papers. Many were arrested and executed, but these voices could not be stilled for long. The Germans, too, had their papers. Some, like *Brusseler Zeitung*, were run by Germans. In other cases Belgian collaborators were installed in vacated plants to publish papers under their former titles. Thus *Le Soir*, Brussels' largest prewar daily, was continued as the principal Nazi mouthpiece. This collaborationist press was especially hated and more than one editor was slain by outraged patriots. Ridicule of this press was one of the most effective devices of the resistance papers. German communiques, Nazi military heroes, and the occupation authority were frequent butts of the underground writers. When *Brusseler Zeitung* proclaimed, "Every family should sacrifice at least one son for the Cause," *La Libre Belgique* responded, "Agreed; let the Schicklegruber [Hitler] family set an example.

When on June 6, 1944, Belgian secret radio brought the news of the Normandy landing the resistance press brought the glad news of coming deliverance to every part of the land. People were given instructions as to the part they were to play; underground guerrilla forces were rallied to widespread revolt. On September 2 the American 1st Army crossed into Belgium; on September 4 the British freed Brussels; and on September 7 the Belgian government in exile returned to the capital.

The Postwar Press

Immediately after liberation the twenty-one dailies published by the Germans and their collaborators disappeared. *La Libre Belgique, Het Laatste Nieuws, La Dernière Heure, La Nation, Belge, Gazet van Antwerpen, Matin*, and other prewar stalwarts were soon publishing in their old plants. Strange to say, *Le Soir*, which had been taken over by the Germans, was able to resume publication without loss of prestige. Now that underground newspapermen could report back to their old papers, many of the clandestine papers disappeared while a few emerged as new dailies, more as weeklies. A few of the older papers had become casualties of the war and did not resume publication.

Publishing a paper in the first year of liberation was a problem, for the Germans had pillaged the country; business and industry had to start from scratch; there was little advertising; and newsprint was so scarce that six months after the liberation the larger Brussels and Antwerp papers were still putting out single sheets printed on both sides. Yet the people were so famished for news that the circulations of most papers soon exceeded prewar figures, even with many losses from the newspaper ranks. Whereas in 1939 Belgium had had 65 dailies and 425 weeklies, by the end of 1945 she had but 56 dailies and 165 weeklies.

The first postwar years were marked by exceptional political instability. The cabinet of "London men" soon had to give way to one composed of men who had remained in Belgium during the occupation. Public opinion and the press were so divided on the return of King Leopold III that seven governments fell in three years till in 1947 Paul Henry Spaak succeeded in forming a coalition of Christian Socialists and Socialists. Yet the country carried on a course of reconstruction that brought industrial production to 99 per cent of the 1936–39 level. This should have improved the position of newspapers, but greatly increased costs had forced them to raise sales prices and advertising rates. Circulation losses resulted, and some of the new dailies founded after liberation went under or changed to a weekly basis.

The next few years saw Belgium profiting from increased trade growing out of her association with the Benelux economic community and the European coal and steel community. Meanwhile the long constitutional dispute over King Leopold's return had seemed ended by the 1950 plebiscite in which 57.6 per cent voted for his reinstatement. But when the Christian Socialists, then in power, attempted to effect the restoration, the Socialists ordered new resistance, strikes, and a march of protest to Brussels. To avoid strife the king transferred his powers to his son Prince Baudoin who became Belgium's fifth king on July 17, 1951. The settlement of this thorny question did not, however, change the political disputativeness of the press.

After her bitter experience in two wars Belgium sought to protect herself through collective security. She became a strong supporter of NATO and the Western European Union. There was considerable support in the press for giving up some measure of national sovereignty to facilitate the formation of a United States of Europe. The whole orientation of Belgium and her press became decidedly pro-western. Although Belgium had made a cultural exchange agreement with the Soviet Union, she promptly canceled this after the Soviet suppression of Hungary in 1956.

When the world recession came in 1957–58, the government had to inaugurate an austerity program involving cuts in social welfare benefits which provoked major strikes. This situation was aggravated when

Belgium was forced to grant independence to the Congo in 1960. It meant major economic losses in addition to the financial burden of bringing home the many Belgians who fled tribal violence. But the Common Market, which Belgium had joined, began to effect such a remarkable recovery that the shadows which had hung so darkly in the postwar years were all but forgotten. It brought a great boom to the country. Brussels not only buzzed with activity as the capital of the European Economic Community but, with an expanded market, Belgium's production and her foreign trade grew apace. Advertising increased; and although newspapers now had to share advertising budgets with radio, television, and other media, the press got the major portion of these expenditures and prospered. Belgium's economy continued to expand in 1964; but since 1961, wages had risen three times as fast as prices, and the possibility of inflation became a major concern.

The Press Today

In 1964 Belgium counted fifty-two dailies; two of these were sports papers and one was a financial paper, hence there were only forty-nine regular daily newspapers. Brussels, with a metropolitan population of 1,439,536, is the journalistic capital with thirteen dailies and 55 per cent of the total daily circulation of the country. Belgium is so small that her six major papers, headed by the independent *Le Soir* and the liberal *Het Laatste Nieuws* at Brussels, both selling more than 300,000 copies, are truly national newspapers. Liege, the great industrial and mining center to the east, serving an area with a population of 1,603,526, is second with four dailies, of which *La Meuse* is most important.

Antwerp, the large port city serving a province of 1,443,355, is third with seven dailies, of which *Gazet van Antwerpen* and *Volksgazet* are also national in influence. Then comes ancient Ghent, the capital of eastern Flanders, with 158,000 inhabitants. It also has four dailies, and its *Het Volk* is one of the notable papers of the country. Although 50 per cent of the dailies are small, ranging in circulation from 7,000 to 25,000, Belgium has nine which reach from 100,000 to more than 300,000 persons. Because of the dominance of the big city papers, there are only 32 nondailies. Some cities of 25,000 to 50,000 are without any daily papers; but, because each party needs voices, such cities may have two or more semi- or triweeklies representing different parties. If these papers appear on alternate days, the cities in effect have the equivalent of daily papers. This weekly press concerns itself more with local news, but this does not mean that it may not express sharp political differences on national questions.

The Belgian press is still strongly political. There are a few dailies like *Le Soir* in Brussels and *La Meuse* in Liege which have been very successful as independents, but most support one party or the other and represent an opinion rather than an information press, with the leading article likely to be the front page feature. The Christian Socialists are the conservatives, upholding the position of the Church in national life and supporting commercial and industrial interests. Their leading voices are *La Libre Belgique* and *Het Nieuws van der Dag* in Brussels, *Gazet van Antwerpen* and *Het Volk* in Ghent. The Liberal party, in the center, favors free enterprise, less governmental control and more social reforms. Its leading papers include *Het Laatste Nieuws* and *La Dernière Heure* in Brussels and *La Nouvelle Gazette* in Charleroi. The Socialists, left of center, are strongly backed by trade union groups and favor a moderate socialist program. Their strongest papers are *Le Peuple* in Brussels, *Volksgazet* in Antwerp and *Vooruit* in Ghent. The Communist party has lost much of its following since the end of the war. It has but one small daily, *Le Drapeau Rouge*, which claims a 25,000 circulation, as it has for years, and probably has much less. Yet despite the political character of this press few papers are official party organs.

In the sixties Belgian papers have overcome their postwar newsprint difficulties, and larger papers run eighteen to twenty pages weekdays and up to forty on Sunday. Smaller papers have eight to ten pages. Advertising, too, has greatly increased with Belgium's boom till Belgian papers are carrying more advertising than French papers but nowhere near the amount found in Scandinavian papers. There is little retail; some manufacturers' ads and much classified, set in solid pages at the back, are frequently printed in half-columns to conserve space. A large paper like *Le Soir* may give 40 per cent of its space to advertising weekdays, 50 per cent or more on Sundays; but many others run only 20 to 30 per cent. The smaller party papers have even less advertising revenue, and it is likely that some must be subsidized by their parties. This is certainly true of the Communist daily. Nevertheless, most Belgian papers have enough circulation and advertising income to be independent of outside subsidy. The reader interest of the Belgian public is indicated by a total daily circulation of 3,186,703, which represents 34 copies per 100 persons, a ratio exceeded only by Britain, the Nordic nations, and Switzerland. The geographical and linguistic distribution of dailies is well-balanced; twenty-eight are published in French, eighteen in Flemish, and one in German. The majority are privately owned.

In 1965 Belgium and her press ran into trouble. To halt inflation, the government put through an economic restraint program, but popular resentment over rising prices and increased taxes brought the fall of this government. The new regime was so dominated by French-speaking Walloons that it embittered the Flemish people in the north and caused a grave split in the unity of the press. In addition, De Gaulle's paralyzing of the Common Market instigated a business decline. When 1965 press figures are available, it is possible that some smaller dailies will have closed and that circulation will have declined.

What Belgian Papers Are Like

What kind of press has emerged from these centuries of war and foreign invasions? On the whole it is a serious and often a belligerently independent press. Belgian journalists have lost their freedoms so often that they are alert to any incursions on their rights and demand the privilege of speaking their minds freely on any issue. While the press of other small nations, prior to World War II, yielded to government pressure in the handling of foreign news, the papers of Belgium spoke out boldly for the rights of man and respect for international treaties, right up to the eve of German attack. Belgian newsmen, moreover, are very jealous of their rights as professional journalists. The arrest by Belgian police of an alleged foreign agent, who described himself as a journalist, gave point to the demand of their newspaper associations that they be given legal status in their profession, for while remaining ardent champions of press freedom, they have also believed that freedom should not be confused with license and that unless they took steps to set up a barrier against abuses, their press freedom might be endangered. In 1962 the Belgian cabinet approved the text of a bill presented by the prime minister and the minister of justice, limiting the title of "journalist" to working newspapermen on Belgian papers or news media, over twenty-one with at least two years of experience, and providing fines for the unauthorized use of this title.

This concern over journalistic ethics is evidenced by the shock felt by Belgian journalists who have visited the United States at the display given to crime and sensation in American papers. They too carry crime news but in short paragraphs in a "city briefs" column on an inside page. Similarly they are surprised at the space given in American papers to local news, for they take care of this in columns of briefs, headed "Nos Echoes" or "Dans la Ville." They consider foreign and national news of overriding importance.

Front page display is given to the most important national and international stories and the leading article, and the first few inside pages contain wide open display of wire news, parliamentary debates, and serious articles on important news developments. Local and regional news is dealt with briefly. Newspapers carry a number of pictures although their picture coverage and display does not approach that of the Scandinavian papers. True to their cultural tradition, they are likely to devote one or two pages to literature, art, music, theater, and education. Then come the more popular pages. Belgians are greatly interested in sports, and larger dailies give this four to six pages. Women's departments, radio-TV programs are followed by financial and business pages. Interspersed with the advertising which fills the last few pages are serial stories, comic strips, crossword puzzles. News display is generally modest and conservative, for Belgian editors feel that their readers' interest in news is so high that they do not need to shout with banner heads.

Sources of Wire News

The preoccupation of Belgian papers with foreign news is understandable, for this people, so often overrun by warlike neighbors, has developed a deep interest in world affairs. Prior to World War I they were dependent on the old French news agency, Havas, which they suspected was unreliable. Hence in 1920 they organized their own *Agence Belga*, a joint stock corporation, in which shares are owned not only by newspapers but by banks and industrial firms. *Belga* has correspondents on all Belgian dailies as well as in London, Paris, Rome, and other foreign capitals. It exchanges news with the Dutch, Swiss, and Scandinavian agencies. Most of its foreign news, however, comes from Reuters and French AFP. It distributes about 50,000 words a day in French and Flemish, about half of it foreign news. Daily papers pay according to their circulation.

Some of the larger papers also join Associated Press or subscribe to United Press International; some have their own correspondents in important capitals. Despite its political character, the Belgian press performs a key function in keeping its readers informed; and most papers carefully separate fact from opinion.

REPRESENTATIVE PAPERS

Het Laatste Nieuws (Brussels)—Largest Belgian daily with 310,000 circulation; national paper for Flemish speaking Belgians. Lively, interesting, attractive with good news coverage. Especially good on sports. Liberal and pro-western.

Le Soir (Brussels)—Belgium's outstanding independent information paper. Belgians call it their New York *Times*. Its 301,285 circulation goes throughout the country; excellent coverage of foreign and national news. Publishes six editions a day, carries heavy volume of advertising; better off financially than any other. Pro-western.

Het Volk (Ghent)—Third largest in country with 218,270 circulation. Conservative in sympathy, but places main emphasis on news; a national paper in Flanders.

La Meuse (Liege)—A strongly independent paper with emphasis on news rather than politics. One of the largest outside capital with a circulation of 198,000. Heavy with advertising, strongly pro-western and anti-Communist.

La Libre Belgique (Brussels)—Conservative in both politics and appearance, it is a well-informed paper with circulation of 170,000. Appeals to businessmen, industrial workers, and middle class. Carries good volume of advertising. Strong friend of U.S. and anti-Communist.

Gazet van Antwerpen (Antwerp)—Conservative in politics; provides excellent news coverage. Attractive, interesting paper with circulation of 155,600. Well-supported by advertising. Pro-western, anti-Communist.

Le Peuple (Brussels)—Leading organ of Socialist party, circulation 80,360. Usually averages eight pages, as a popular afternoon paper. Heavy on sports and entertainment but after front page display of leader articles and political stories, gives good foreign coverage inside. Much attention to social welfare, trade unions, and party affairs. Pro-western, anti-Communist.

The Newspapers of Holland

Jan Thorbecke was not a newspaper man. He was a professor at the University of Leyden and the staunch liberal leader of the 1840's who became one of Holland's great press champions. King William I, and William II who succeeded him in 1840, were autocratic rulers. The Dutch people, experiencing hard times, burdened with heavy taxes and a cumbersome illiberal constitution which vested too much power in the king, started an agitation for reform led by Thorbecke. He realized the value of the press in rousing liberal opinion and with the aid of some of the best newspapermen in the country launched *Nieuwe Rotterdamse Courant* as a weekly in 1843. It became a daily next year and grew to be one of Holland's best newspapers. Other newspapers joined the movement for reform; the ferment grew, and popular outbreaks in the country forced the king to yield. The Liberals came into power in 1848 with Thorbecke as premier. He proved to be one of the most eminent statesmen in his country's history. A new, more democratic constitution was adopted which guaranteed press freedom. It was he who in this critical period made it possible for the press to use its power in the service of the nation.

Because Dutch traders rubbed shoulders with men from many climes and creeds, they learned to live and let live. Holland early became a haven for political and religious refugees. The Puritans of East Anglia were so harried in England that they sought and found ten years of refuge in Leyden until they migrated to establish the first colony in New England.

Printing came to Holland early. In 1473 Gerardus Leept and Nicholas Ketalaer were producing Holland's first dated and signed books at Utrecht. By the end of the fifteenth century Dutch cities had become important printing centers. Although political pamphleteers did make use of the press to spread their ideas, 150 years were to elapse before the first precursors of the press appeared.

The Dutch have long been sturdy fighters for independence. Hapsburg Emperor Maximilian married Mary of Burgundy in 1477 and thus gained contol of realms which included the present Holland and Belgium. His grandson Charles V succeeded him in 1519 to rule over more of Europe than anyone since Charlemagne. Born and brought up in Holland, he was sympathetic with his Dutch subjects who had conquered their unproductive environment by reclaiming lands from the sea and who, by their maritime enterprise, had built a far-flung foreign trade and developed considerable port and manufacturing cities such as Haarlem, Leyden, Amsterdam, and Rotterdam. But Charles' successor, Phillip II of Spain, was of different stripe and used the Spanish Inquisition to try to stamp out the heresy of Holland's predominantly Lutheran and Calvinist beliefs. Led by Prince William of Orange and aided by a rebel fleet of corsairs called "The Sea Beggars," the Dutch revolted. A desperate struggle went on for eighty years, but by 1605 Spanish troops had been driven out. The Dutch would accept nothing less than unconditional independence. A truce in 1609 ended the fighting, and the young republic entered a period of peace and prosperity.

The Dutch Corontos

First precursors of the press were handwritten newsletters known as *corontos*. In time printed *corontos* appeared, and in 1618 two began regular publication, marking the birth of the Dutch press. Earliest known copies of *Courante uyt Italien, Duytslandt* in the Royal Library at Stockholm are dated November, 1618, at Amsterdam. Issues of 1619 and 1620 indicate that Ioris Veseler was printer and Caspar van Hilten, couranteur. This was to continue as a weekly for forty years. The other pioneer was Broer Jansz who published at Amsterdam starting in June 1619 *Tidninghen uyt Verscheyde Quartieren* (News from Different Places). At first these papers were small single sheets printed on both sides; after 1620 the news of the Thirty Years War forced expansion to seven or eight printed pages. By 1626 papers were also appearing regularly in Arnhem, Delft, and Leyden. These papers showed considerable enterprise in gathering news from correspondents along the main postal routes of Europe and also from foreign newspapers. Most space was given to news of the war, but there was also domestic news of ships returning to Holland and tales of sea monsters and miracles, sensational accidents and executions. By 1624 all regular papers were carrying advertisements.

The Dutch Republic meanwhile had experienced a tremendous material upswing. Towns hummed with industry; skilled artisans flocked to this little country till it became the leading industrial nation of Europe in that day; Dutch traders and their ships found their way all over the world. By 1661 the Dutch had deprived the Portuguese of their East India possessions and had a monopoly on Far Eastern trade. They even founded New Amsterdam, on what is now Manhattan Island, and operated it as a prosperous venture for four decades. This was also a golden age for Dutch literature, science, and art. Great intellectuals, including Hugo Grotius, Simon Stevin, Christian Huygens, Spinoza, and Jan Swammerdam were among the mental giants of the day. Rembrandt, Frans Hals, Jan Vermeer, Jacob Van Ruysdael, and Jan Steen were some of the painters who gave this era its chief glory. Each Dutch town was ambitious to see its Latin school excel all others. The general level of education was probably higher than that in most parts of France and England. Though the University of Leyden remained foremost, each province had its university and spared no funds to attract the leading scholars on the Continent who, in turn, drew students from all over Europe.

The Press Expands

This prosperity and intellectual awakening had its reflection in the press. Newspapers now appeared in many Dutch cities, and biweeklies and triweeklies appearing on alternate days gave some cities the effect of having dailies. Thus Amsterdam had ten papers appearing on different days so that readers had papers available every day but Sunday. Growing literacy swelled circulations, and advertising grew. By the 1650's Dutch papers had a greater variety and volume of advertising than the papers of England, France, Germany, and Sweden were to have for some years. The Thirty Years War had resulted in the United Provinces again being declared free and independent. In this period, war and foreign news made up the great part of newspaper content, well-departmentalized for the convenience of readers. The oldest paper in the Netherlands today, now known as *Nieuwe Haarlemsche Courant* was born in 1656 as *Weckelycke Courant van Europa*. The comparative freedom accorded the press in Holland at this time, when newspapers in all other European countries were strictly controlled, made this country the haven for political refugees. From Amsterdam, Leyden, Rotterdam, The Hague, and Utrecht came clandestine papers which were smuggled across the border into France.

Eighteenth Century Restrictions

Toward the end of the seventeenth century Dutch prosperity began to decline. The English and French, turning to the pursuits of peace, began to compete with the Dutch in world trade. Industry too was hit as other nations began to manufacture goods which the Dutch had previously made for them and sought to exclude Dutch products by high protective tariffs. Dutch commerce dwindled and the government, to recoup its losses, imposed taxes on home products. Taxes were also levied on newspapers in 1674, doubled in 1690, and increased again in 1750. As the tax was assessed according to the paper's size, newspapers had to reduce their pages and even resort to printing in the margins to keep dimensions as small as possible. Municipal authorities also made the right to print subject to official permission. While precensorship was not imposed, the heavy fines, which might be levied for printing any news the authorities did not deem prudent, led papers to become silent on national and local issues. Through the last years of the seventeenth and most of the eighteenth century the press, under sharp supervision, lost much of its previous independence and declined in the quantity of its news coverage.

In resisting British shipping restrictions against trade with the American colonists, the Dutch became involved in a war with England in 1780 which was to bring about the final ruination of the Dutch Republic. At war's end in 1784, the country became torn by party battles led, on the right, by the Orange party urging the unification of the country under Stadtholder William V, and opposed by the Patriot party which sought to abolish privilege and to establish the sovereignty of the people. Attempts to control the press broke down as each party sought to sway public opinion. Papers which had not dared venture opinions for years now launched violent atttacks against their political enemies. In the summer of 1778 both sides mustered forces and a civil war threatened, but Frederick William II of Prussia, whose sister had married William, intervened with his army and speedily restored William to a dominant position in the state. Patriot leaders fled to France and Belgium and press trials became the order of the day as the Orange party sought to still opposition voices. Many papers disappeared.

The French Impose Controls

The power of Stadtholder William and the Orange party was short-lived for in 1792 France, having overrun and annexed the Belgian provinces, declared war on the Dutch. By 1795 General Pichgru, aided by Patriot party leaders, who hailed the French as deliverers, had conquered all of Holland and a new Batavian Republic was set up. Although freedom of expression was decreed and the words "liberty" and "equality" were emblazoned everywhere, representatives of the

French government ruled with despotic authority and shackled the press. When Napoleon came to power in France, he incorporated Holland into the French republic; he allowed no paper any freedom, for he declared, "If I allowed a free press I would not be in power for another three months."

Intolerable French tyranny, ruinous taxation, and the impoverishment of the country united all the people, regardless of party, in a determination to expel the French, to establish a free constitution, and to bring back to the throne a representative of the House of Orange, which had brought them their first independence back in 1581. When the tide turned against Napoleon after his disaster in Russia, the Dutch joined the Allies in attacking him. Once the French were expelled, William of Nassau, heir to the Orange line, was called to the throne in 1813 as William I, King of the Netherlands. At the Congress of Vienna in 1815 the great powers united the Dutch, Belgians, and Luxembourgers to form the Kingdom of United Netherlands.

The Press after Independence

The new 1815 constitution provided for a limited constitutional monarchy, guaranteed justice for all and freedom of religion. Liberty of the press was recognized as "a useful means to promote knowledge and information." A free press without any preventive censure was guaranteed. But legal phrases alone do not make for liberty. Old habits of repression and old fears of suppression persisted. While the Dutch people and the press had greeted the accession of William with joy and generally supported the regime, any whisper in the newspapers of a desire for more democracy was frowned upon by the government. In the Belgian provinces where the press fought the Dutch rule imposed upon them, special press tribunals soon destroyed all freedom. The government became increasingly dictatorial and the people began to yearn for the democratic freedoms they had had under their earlier republic and for the free newspapers they had enjoyed then. When William II came to the throne in 1840 and proved as autocratic as his predecessor, a strong liberal movement arose. It was then that Jan Thorbecke, the political science professor, crystallized the discontent by enlisting courageous journalists to demand reform and to campaign for a new constitution till in 1848 the Liberals swept into power.

The new constitution established a liberal parliamentary system in which the complete control of public finance and of colonial administration was in the hands of parliament and provided direct elections, freedom of assembly, speech, and press. Despite this new freedom the press could not develop because of the stamp tax which ran as high as ten cents a copy on larger papers. This not only held down the size of newspapers and limited their news presentation, but made subscription rates so high they were out of reach of most people. It kept circulations small; hence newspapers were less attractive to advertisers. How ruinous this tax was is evidenced by the fact that in 1868, in addition to the official government paper, *Nederlandsche Stats Courant,* there were only ten other papers.

Modern Dutch Press Is Born

Twenty years of press agitation finally brought the repeal of this tax in 1869. Now many new papers appeared. Those which started as weeklies or semiweeklies soon became dailies. With the tax eliminated papers could bring their subscription rates within the reach of masses and circulations grew rapidly. Newspapers again became valuable advertising media and soon were on a sounder financial footing. And as they increased in number and influence, they began to take on the ideological and political character which was to become typical of the Dutch press. In his serious concern with religion and politics, every Hollander began to look on his newspaper as his mentor—the source of his information, his ideas, and his judgments.

As the old Liberal party, the first reform party, in time came to represent the conservative viewpoint which maintained that the freedom and prosperity of industrial and commercial leaders would automatically extend itself to the lower classes, the Progressive Liberals who favored social reform, universal suffrage, and compulsory education broke away. So did the more radical Liberal Democrats who favored government ownership of public services. Their great opponents were the religious parties. The Catholics, who split with the Liberals over secular education for Catholic children, became another Conservative party. The Protestant parties opposed the godlessness of the French revolutionary theories and the politico-sociol reforms advocated by the Liberals. Then with the rise of big industry there developed a new industrial proletariat who lived in pauperism and worked under bad conditions and who, to get justice, organized the Social Democratic Labor party in 1897.

All these parties had to have their voices, and out of this development many of the leading Netherlands papers of today were born in the last thirty years of the nineteenth century. The old Liberal party had had its *Algemeen Handelsblad,* founded in 1831, and *Nieuwe Rotterdamse Courant,* founded in 1843. Now in 1868 they added *Het Vaderland* at The Hague. The Progressive Liberals established *Haagsch Dagblad* in 1885; the Protestants founded *De Standaard* at

Amsterdam in 1872. The Catholics, who had *De Tijd* at Amsterdam and *De Gelderlander* at Nijmegen, in 1868 founded *De Maasbode* at Rotterdam and in 1887 *De Volkskrant* at Amsterdam. The Socialists at first had had only weekly papers; in 1900 they established *Het Volk* at Amsterdam as a daily. It was to be their leading party voice.

But a new trend was appearing in the establishment of politically independent papers—the placing of a greater emphasis on straight news rather than political interpretation. Among the most important born in this period were *Haagsche Courant* in 1883, *Haarlems Dagblad* in 1883, and *De Telegraaf* at Amsterdam in 1893. The latter, with its very complete coverage of wire news and its more popular treatment, quickly attracted a large circulation and became known as the Daily Mail of Holland.

In the years of peace, following the settlement of her problems with Belgium in 1830, Holland had gradually recovered her economic well-being. Industry, agriculture, and world trade expanded. This prosperity continued under Queen Wilhelmina, who came to the throne in 1898. These improved conditions were reflected in a vigorous press that grew till by 1898 there were sixty-two dailies and a considerable number of weeklies.

The First World War did not touch Holland directly since she remained neutral. Her army was mobilized to protect her borders, and for four years she was an armed camp. She gave refuge to great numbers of Belgian refugees and several Belgian papers that were published in exile at The Hague, Amsterdam, Leyden, and Maastricht. Her own press carried on, trying to walk the tightrope of neutrality, without censorship, but restricted by the army from touching any defense matters. War news filled the papers, and as a direct result international news came to assume greater importance in the Dutch press.

Between the Wars

The redrawing of the map of Europe at the end of the war brought financial difficulties to Holland for she was cut off from some of her former markets. Dutch export industries also began to suffer from increased competition from other nations. For a time there was serious unemployment and unrest. Immense housing projects and the reclamation of the Zuider Zee brought some relief. Then new industries such as rayons, radios, electrical appliances, and chemicals developed new markets till Rotterdam came to be the fifth largest port in the world in tonnage cleared. Prosperity did return in the late twenties but not to the prewar level.

Holland's newspapers, however, had forged ahead till by 1930 this little country of 9,000,000 had seventy-eight daily papers which had become fatter and carried more news, advertising, and pictures. Constitutional revisions of 1917 and 1922 had brought proportional representation based on universal suffrage. This not only greatly augmented the number of voters but increased circulations, for now the whole people had become politically conscious and the press became more party-minded than ever before. Even the thirty-two neutral papers took strong political or religious stands in their editorials. Very few were official party papers, but all the other financially independent papers tried to provide political leadership. In the election of 1933 fifty-four parties entered candidates. Although the major parties were most strongly represented among the dailies, the minority groups found voice in weekly political organs. Two new parties, which disturbed Hollanders, had emerged. A Communist party had arisen, but it never gained many adherents, for even at its high point after four depression years it had only four seats in parliament. A Nazi party appeared in 1931, but its advocacy of authoritarianism antagonized most people.

The entire press was much concerned during the thirties with threatening international developments, and foreign news became of paramount importance. To provide better coverage, the four small existing news agencies were combined in 1934 into the Algemeen Nederlands Persbureau (ANP—Netherlands General Press Agency), which in two years was providing an expanded and accelerated service to all dailies simultaneously by telex. On domestic news, this press would have seemed to Americans a straitlaced, very respectable old lady, showing an almost puritanical estimate of the kind of news that was fit to print. It never indulged in gossip or slander, it never glorified criminals; it had a high regard for the rights of privacy.

The three leading papers were *De Telegraaf* and *Algemeen Handelsblad* in Amsterdam and *Nieuwe Rotterdamse Courant*, all politically independent. The chief party papers were Socialist *Het Volk*, the Protestant *De Standaard* and the Catholic *De Maasbode*. The black sheep was *Nationale Dagblad* published by Dutch Nazis. Except for the smaller party sheets, papers carried enough advertising to be financially independent.

Under German Occupation

Holland declared her neutrality when World War II broke but mobilized her army against invasion. During the eight months of *sitzkrieg* it became increasingly evident that Germany would strike. On May 10, 1940, German panzer divisions invaded, quickly overrunning the northern provinces; but Dutch forces held on the eastern front till German paratroopers leapfrogged behind them. On May 13 the Netherlands government moved to London. Next day the Germans issued an ultimatum that, unless resistance ceased, Holland's principal cities would be bombed out of existence. Before the ultimatum expired, Rotterdam was subjected to a murderous attack which destroyed the entire center of the city. Dutch forces capitulated that afternoon.

On May 15 German occupation forces took over the press and silenced Catholic and Communist papers. At first others were permitted to resume publication "without censorship," but they soon found they could publish only what the Germans wanted them to print. Unable to stomach the kind of material they were forced to give out, many ceased publication. If they could be found, Dutch editors who would not collaborate were packed off to concentration camps. Many had already gone underground. When it became evident that Dutch journalists would not cooperate, the Germans took over the press completely. Citing newsprint shortage as an excuse, they liquidated most newspapers and periodicals. That left many cities with only a single small newssheet put out by Germans or Dutch Nazis. To give their press some semblance of respectability the Germans took over *Het Volk*, *Telegraaf*, *Handelsblad*, and *Nieuwe Rotterdamse Courant* and made them their principal propaganda sheets. Dutch Nazis also brought out new publications like the anti-Semitic *Misthoorn* (Foghorn), spouting its venom and hate. The Dutch quisling, Mussert, published his *Volk en Vaderland* and *Volk en Evangelie*.

Hollanders lost all faith in the papers and no longer read them except for ration information. But they trusted their twice daily broadcasts of Radio Orange in London. As the Germans confiscated all radio sets they could discover, those who managed to hold on to hidden shortwave radios would type up broadcast bulletins and pass them on to others. Underground newssheets began to appear; but as more and more Dutch journalists went into hiding, regular resistance papers began to emerge. Among the more important were *Vrij Nederland*, *Trouw* (Faith), *Het Parool* (Password), *De Orangekrant* (Orange Journal), *De Waarheid* (Truth). The Allies dropped from planes *The Flying Dutchman*.

Most underground papers appeared weekly and all regularly except when the Gestapo caught up with them. Captured editors and writers were executed or sent to concentration camps. Distribution was as hazardous in Holland as in other occupied countries. Circulations were not large, but papers were passed along by a news-hungry people who risked arrest and punishment for even possessing a copy. These underground papers debunked Nazi lies and gave news of the fighting on other fronts to gainsay Nazi claims of continual victory. They warned of Nazi tricks, told of atrocities, exposed collaborators. They urged resistance and carried instructions to underground groups. As the mass deportations of Dutch workers to Germany began, the papers urged men to join the underground forces rather than accept slavery. When the Allies started their invasion of the Continent, the underground press roused the people to impede German defense by every kind of sabotage and armed attack. Allied forces crossed Dutch frontiers September 4, 1944; and on May 4, 1945, the German army in the Netherlands capitulated. The government in exile returned to The Hague, and the wartime cabinet was replaced by one including many resistance leaders.

The Postwar Press

Holland had been severely damaged. There had been great losses through bombing, and in the last months the Germans had broken dikes and deliberately flooded one-tenth of Holland. Industry too had been hard hit for the Germans had shipped out much of its machinery. The first postwar years were a period of economic stringency. As a result the press had great difficulty. Many newspaper plants had been damaged, and the Germans had carried off most of their equipment. Readers everywhere were poor; there was little advertising.

All papers which had operated under the Nazis were closed down. The resistance papers, whose names Dutch readers dared mention only in whispers during the occupation, now filled newsstands. Gradually old prewar friends, suppressed by the Nazis, reappeared; and even some which had been taken over by Nazis were cleared after their former owners appeared and all collaborators were purged. But former resistance papers took the lead. *Het Vrije Volk* of the Labor party (formerly *Het Volk*) drew the largest circulation. *Trouw*, Conservative Christian, and *Het Parool* were close behind. Plant shortages were solved by cooperation with one another. In Amsterdam three papers, with circulations from 151,000 to 266,000, were printed for a time in the plant of the old *De Telegraaf*. Newsprint was scarce, and for a year all papers were limited to two pages daily. Not till 1950 could the larger dailies put out eight to ten pages. The postwar press also suffered from the loss of many able prewar editors; furthermore many resistance papers did not realize that the editorial formula of an underground paper no longer served the needs of readers in peacetime. Those who expanded their news service went ahead; others failed before growing competition. Yet with so many resistance and political groups trying to put out papers, Holland had more than before the war. In 1948 there were 81 dailies and 270 nondailies appearing from one to three times a week. But the Dutch people, eager for news after the years of occupation, bought more and more papers. Whereas before the war a circulation of 100,000 was exceptional, by 1947 Amsterdam had five papers ranging from 150,000 to 330,000; and total daily circulation had risen from 1,952,000 in 1939 to 2,840,000 in 1948.

By dint of hard work and sacrifice the Dutch overcame their first starvation days. Flooded areas were drained, dikes repaired, and the land planted. Everywhere agricultural production increased till by 1948 most food rationing had been removed. Industry too moved forward, and with Holland's participation in Benelux and the coal and steel community, real progress was made. Advertising revived and by 1950 many papers were again deriving half of their income from this source.

Economic Boom Brings Growth

The upsurge in the economy, started in 1955, continued and expanded. With her Benelux partners, Belgium and Luxembourg, Holland joined the Common Market which became operative in 1958. With a much wider market her industry and agriculture boosted their production and export till by 1963 the Netherlands was enjoying the greatest prosperity she had ever known. In 1964 the economy continued strong, but slowed from previous years as measures were taken to combat inflation. Despite these good years the Netherlands had but 67 main dailies in 1964, a drop from 101 in the previous year. Competition and increased production costs had forced mergers and the closing of some uneconomic operations. Eleven of these main dailies have twenty local side editions for smaller towns in their areas so that actually there are eighty-seven different daily titles, though the circulations of these side editions are included with that of the parent dailies.

The press divides itself into three categories. First there is the national press of eight dailies: six in Amsterdam, one in Rotterdam, and one in The Hague. The Amsterdam nationals are headed by *Het Vrije Volk* which, with 308,675, has the largest circulation in the country, followed by *De Telegraaf*, *De Volkskrant*, *Het Parool*, *Trouw*, and *De Courant Nieuws van der Dag*. The national in Rotterdam is *Algemeen Dagblad*, and that in The Hague (which shares with Amsterdam the honor of being the capital) is *De Haagsche Courant*. These eight, while divided evenly between morning and evening fields, can quickly cover the entire country; and all have circulations of more than 100,000. Together they have 41 per cent of the total daily circulation. In the second category are fifty-nine regional dailies with twenty local side editions. Third are 278 weeklies and triweeklies. Although the number of dailies has declined, their circulations have held up fairly well and in 1964 totaled 3,349,095. This figure indicates that for a population of 12,041,000 there is a distribution of 27.8 copies per 100 persons, an index of readership which ranks eighth among the nations of western Europe.

Amsterdam, the leading port city and official capital with 868,437 population, is the journalistic capital with ten dailies. Rotterdam with 730,963 people has eight, The Hague four. Utrecht, the railroad center, has three as has ancient Leyden, university and manufacturing center. Most smaller cities have become one-newspaper towns owing to the diminution in numbers of newspapers; but some cities of 16,000 to 80,000 which in the United States would have only one daily, still have two or three. The Netherlands, which could be contained in the narrow neck of northern Illinois, is one of the most densely populated nations in Europe; and, for the size of the country, sixty-seven main dailies are still a considerable concentration of daily papers.

There are no Sunday papers, for Netherlanders, with their strong religious scruples, have never countenanced commercial papers on their Sabbath day. And because no Hollander likes to read his paper in a hurry before going to work but prefers to peruse it carefully at night in the family circle, most dailies are published in the evening. Unlike the situation in some other countries where most papers are distributed on newsstands, Dutch papers have 95 per cent of their circulations going out to regular subscribers, for every Netherlander sticks to his paper because it sticks with him, gives him the information he wants, and serves as his guide and mentor.

Dutch newspapers appear to have undergone an amazing change in that 58 per cent now proclaim themselves as independent or neutral, or at least Independent Progressive or Independent Liberal. Actually, most papers support one party or the other, as was evidenced in the 1963 election when the Catholic party won fifty seats, the Labor party forty-three, the Liberals sixteen, with the rest split among seven other parties, a sharp setback for the Socialists. And yet in contrast to other west European countries where information papers command the largest circulations, in Holland it is *Het Vrije Volk*, organ of the Socialist party, which enjoys this position. Its news of foreign, national, and local affairs is reported as objectively as in any information

paper; but any story with political implications is likely to be interpreted from the party standpoint and supported by leader articles. In a
country which is 40 per cent Catholic and 37.6 Dutch Reformed and
other Protestant denominations, it is not surprising to find that the
Catholic party leads with nineteen dailies.

Greater consumer spending power has brought more advertising till
most larger dailies get 50 per cent or more of their revenue from this
source, even smaller dailies 30 to 35 per cent. Unlike newspapers of
other continental countries which run most heavily to classified, Dutch
papers carry more display. Department and other retail stores advertise
but in smaller space than do stores in America. Advertising is not
pyramided but is concentrated on solid pages alternating with news
pages.

In 1965 newspapers made much in stories and feature articles of the
turn of the tide in Holland's battle with the North Sea. The Zuider
Zee project, nearing completion, had reclaimed half a million fertile
acres; and the more dramatic project in the Rhine and Maas river deltas
promised to keep the sea from ever again causing the floods and deaths
which occurred in 1953.

The press also became involved in the parliamentary debate over
whether to allow Crown Princess Beatrix to marry a German diplomat,
Claus von Amsberg, who at 17 had been drafted into Hitler's army.
Earlier opposition changed; and parliament approved the match, 132–9,
in November.

Faced with the threat of inflation, the Dutch government was forced
to apply precautionary economic strictures. This, plus De Gaulle's crippling of the Common Market, brought increasing economic difficulties
for the press.

How Dutch Papers Are Put Together

The pattern of Dutch newspaper makeup varies; but the front page
is generally a newsy looking display of the top foreign, national, and
sports stories. Some play the leading article at the top of columns one
and two, but others lead an inside page with it. Often page two carries
news from all over Holland including local news, briefly reported.
Because of the great interest in politics, often a page is given to
parliamentary debates. Then follow two pages of wire news, mostly
foreign, and a page of background and interpretative articles. Now
comes a two-page spread of cultural material followed by a double-
page spread for sports. There are no society pages, for social events are
briefly covered among local stories. Instead there are illustrated news
feature pages which carry none of the syndicated items common in
American papers; they have their own homegrown features, even

occasional women's fashion articles. Local personal columns are popular. Toward the back will be a page or two of financial, business, and shipping news. Some carry a few comic strips; most run a serial story. On the whole it is a sober and serious press, for Netherlanders want significant news. Despite this seriousness, Dutch papers are not dull looking. Headline display in the larger journals is attractive, and pages are broken up with good pictures. Display in smaller provincial papers is often more modest. Pages are of standard length but about three inches broader and usually set in seven wide columns. Larger papers run sixteen to twenty-five pages, smaller ones eight to ten.

Because this small country is surrounded by other nations and its life is so easily affected by what happens in the rest of the world, Dutch papers try to keep their readers informed of the important developments abroad and at home. They are well served by their own cooperative ANP which has its main office in The Hague and sub-offices in Amsterdam, Rotterdam, and Utrecht. Its six hundred correspondents in Holland collect the news of all the Netherlands, and it has exchange agreements with Reuters, AFP, and the Swedish, Norwegian, Danish, Belgian, and Swiss agencies. *De Waarheid* of course takes TASS. ANP service is distributed by teleprinter network. About a third of its daily budget is foreign news, the rest domestic, including sports, financial, and economic news. It also supplies a daily picture service to its clients. Every Dutch daily uses ANP; some of the larger papers also use AP or UPI, and a number have correspondents in foreign capitals.

Freedom of Expression

Dutch newspapers, the news agency, radio, and television are free. Yet the sobriety of the press has always hedged this freedom with a sense of responsibility. There is no illiteracy, hence Dutch papers have learned to cater to a well-educated public which regards news, politics, and religion as of great importance. These papers are solid and well-informed. Political differences do not permit the press to be called impartial, but it is honest; and with the single exception of the Communist *De Waarheid*, it is pro-western. This does not prevent these independent Dutch editors from taking issue with the United States whenever they think its policy is wrong.

REPRESENTATIVE PAPERS

Het Vrije Volk (Amsterdam)—Largest in Holland with 308,675 circulation. Puts out thirty regional editions to cover whole country. Official organ of Labor party but provides good news coverage. Usually friendly to U.S., but sometimes suspicious of its policies in Europe. Anti-Communist and distrustful of Soviet Union.

De Telegraaf (Amsterdam)—Came back after being seized by Nazis; has become second largest with 281,240 circulation by making itself a good information paper. More popular than party organs. Has one of best sport sections. Friendly to U.S. and anti-Communist.

De Volkskrant (Amsterdam)—Chief Catholic paper with 162,500 circulation. Conservative in politics, well-edited, newsy, and interesting. Since Catholics have had strongest representation in postwar governments, has supported government policies. Pro-western but has urged avoiding open break with U.S.S.R.

Het Parool (Amsterdam)—One of the underground papers that has become one of Holland's important dailies with 162,400 circulation. Lists itself as Independent, but leans to Labor. Less doctrinaire than *Het Vrije Volk* and can be critical of government.

Trouw (Amsterdam)—Another underground paper which made a postwar success, with circulation of 110,930. A national paper among Protestant groups. One of most attractive and interesting looking papers in Holland. Conservative in politics; bitterly opposed to Communists.

De Haagsche Courant (The Hague)—The leading paper at the seat of government with circulation of 120,928. Independent, nonpolitical; a good information paper.

Nieuwe Rotterdamse Courant (Rotterdam)—Though it has a circulation of only 56,147, it is considered one of Holland's best dailies because of its exceptional coverage and backgrounding of international news through the efforts of its own foreign correspondents and its editors, A. Stempels and Maarten Rooy, two of Holland's outstanding journalists.

Algemeen Handelsblad (Amsterdam)—Holland's oldest daily and an outstanding Liberal paper with a circulation of 63,200. Somewhat "circusy" in makeup, but it provides excellent coverage of foreign and national news; lively features and good pictures.

The Newspapers of France

France was for centuries one of the world's great powers, but royal absolutism kept her press from developing. In the last 135 years, however, newspapers have often been a vital influence in this nation's history; and journalists have frequently been presidents and premiers. Since Liberation in 1944 a new press has arisen to replace the discredited prewar and collaborationist wartime journalism.

France was already a formidable power when in 1471 the Sorbonne invited three German printers to set up a press. The art spread quickly to other cities but was confined to religious works and books for scholars.

Earliest news dispensers were the troubadours who in the thirteenth and fourteenth centuries traveled the country singing their ballads and reciting their tales of news and rumors. Then came the letter writers for statesmen, bankers, and wealthy merchants who developed networks of agents in European capitals to report important government and business developments. After the establishment of the royal post in 1464 some letter writers were putting out veritable gazettes. Postmasters began issuing small letter services as they picked up news from other postmasters, postillions, and passengers. Printers too began looking at news as a source of extra revenue, for their books were high-priced and had a limited clientele. But authorities exercised such strict surveillance that printers were often imprisoned and dispossessed of their presses; hence, they found safety in tales of volcanic eruptions, comets, floods, princely marriages, royal funerals, assassinations and executions described in gory detail, and in reports of battles; but these *papiers nouvelles* were published only at irregular intervals at times of exceptional events.

The First Regular Publications

Under the wise rule of Henry IV, France was set on the road to recovery after three decades of wars. It was during his reign in 1605 that *Mercure de France* appeared as the first regular publication, issued annually to recount the principal events of the year in France and neighboring countries. When Henry was assassinated, his widow, Marie de'Medici, came to power as regent for his son. She did not know how to govern, dissipated the treasury Henry IV had left, and let her country be torn apart in quarrels between rival factions. France deteriorated badly till Marie brought in Armand de Richelieu as her advisor and elevated him to a cardinalate. For eighteen years he was the real ruler, dedicated to making the monarch supreme in France and France supreme in Europe. To influence public opinion he took control of *Mercure de France* and with the aid of his confidant, Father Joseph, supervised it till the latter's death in 1638.

In 1631 Jean Martin and Louis Vendosme started the first weekly, *Nouvelles Ordinaires de Divers Endroits*. It lasted only five months, for Theophraste Renaudot, the king's physician and commissioner of the poor, had started a want ad bureau, putting out a sheet of small advertisements, and persuaded his patron Richelieu to give him a royal exclusive privilege to expand his sheet into a weekly paper dedicated to the needs of the monarch. This put his rivals out of business. A man of enterprise, he built a good news organization and in his *Gazette* presented dispatches from many cities in Europe; but it was only a propaganda sheet and told its readers only what Richelieu wanted them to know. For 157 years it was the one official paper permitted to print political news and comment.

A Clandestine Press Develops

Through wars and diplomacy Richelieu made France great, but he quintupled the national debt and by a vicious tax system impoverished the people. In anger and despair his opponents began circulating underground sheets attacking the regime. When Richelieu died in 1642, bonfires were lighted in celebration. He was succeeded by his disciple Jules Mazarin, who for nineteen years ruled as advisor to Anne of Austria, regent for her infant son Louis XIV. The condition of the people grew steadily worse, and now there were numerous *relations*, not newspapers, attacking one person or question. They were often slanderous and venomous, but they were read by many to learn what the official *Gazette* did not disclose.

At Mazarin's death in 1661 the young king Louis XIV, then nineteen, took the reins in his own hands. He considered himself a "Lieutenant of God" and tolerated freedom only for himself. To give himself a temple he built the palace at Versailles where he created the most glittering court in Europe, the playground for his parasite nobility. To sate his thirst for glory, he plunged France into war after war, but the territories he won were dearly bought with the blood and impoverishment of the people. Yet he continued till his death to lead his country ever deeper into ruin. This brought a growing clandestine press attacking the king and baring court scandals. Printers and writers were hunted down and given punishments such as branding, imprisonment, life sentences to the galleys, strangulation, or burning at the stake. Those caught, disappeared, though some escaped to neighboring countries to publish papers that were smuggled into France. In Holland, particularly, this exiled press flourished. Holland's own papers, the freest in Europe, were also smuggled in and helped stimulate the desire for liberty.

Prelude to Revolution

The new king, Louis XV, who after a twenty-eight-year regency took power in 1743, proved to be a bored debauchee. He ruled till 1774, so apathetic to the welfare of his subjects that he permitted his mistresses the real power. The clandestine press became more bold, assailing the regime, Madame du Barry, and Madame Pompadour, thus building the first fires of the revolution. Louis XVI who next came to the throne was weak, vacillating, sometimes stupid, and dominated by his frivolous queen, Marie Antoinette. Her extravagance, her dismissal of Robert Turgot, who was bringing about financial reforms, led the people to call her Madame Deficit. Clandestine papers now attacked the basis of government itself, discussed the reciprocal obligations of sovereign and people, and urged a constitution. This discussion spread throughout the country by word of mouth, even among the illiterate. As clamor rose the government had to ameliorate its press restrictions. The old *Gazette* had been glamorized into *Gazette de France* and made a daily in 1772, but no one paid attention to this vapid journal. One misanthrope of the period said it was "good only for toilet paper." The first real daily, *Le Journal de Paris*, was born in 1777. When Louis XVI was compelled to summon the Estates General on May 4, 1789, to consider the regime's financial problems, the three estates—nobles, clergy, and commoners—demanded among other reforms freedom of speech and press. Jacques Brissot and the Comte de Mirabeau, two responsible revolutionary leaders, did not wait and on May 6 announced the publication of their papers, *Le Patriote* and *Les États Généreaux.*

Press Flowers under Assembly

The nobles, to preserve their privileges, insisted on voting by separate estates and refused the demand of the commoners who wanted a general session to secure voting by individuals. The third estate thereupon proclaimed itself the National Assembly, which was joined by the clergy and lesser nobles. When the king brought in troops, the whole city rose and stormed the Bastille on July 14. The king had to yield; and the first step of the revolution had been accomplished, for the Assembly now had all the rights and the power, too. At once new radical papers appeared led by *Ami du Peuple*, edited by Jean Paul Marat, a physician who had become the fiery leader of the downtrodden. Others defended the monarchy but urged its reform; still others called for death to all revolutionaries.

Then on August 26, 1780, the Assembly adopted the Declaration of the Rights of Man, which not only affirmed that all men were born free and equal but as to the press declared: "No one shall be disturbed on account of his opinions providing they do not derange public order. The free communication of ideas is one of the precious rights of man and every citizen can freely speak, write and print, subject to responsibility for the abuse of that freedom in cases determined by law."

Immediately there came a great flowering of the press. Paris alone had 150 papers, and every important provincial city had its own. In four years 435 were founded but many of the poor papers quickly succumbed. There were, however, good papers like Brissot's *Le Patriote Français*, Prudhomme's *Les Revolutions de Paris*, which by fair and impartial reporting reached an extraordinary circulation of 200,000, and Sabatier's *Le Journal Politique National*, featuring brilliant analyses of Assembly debates and decrees.

But revolutionary leaders fell out among themselves. The more moderate Girondists who had led the first stage of the revolution were attacked by the more radical Jacobins for delaying the revolution; and the Assembly was indicted for not carrying out practical reforms quickly enough. The Assembly had accomplished much in three years; but because of the economic disruption following the revolution, it had become harder for the worker to earn his bread. It dawned on the common people that the new constitution with its tax qualifications had denied most of them the right to vote; and after the Assembly had led France into a disastrous war with Prussia and Austria, the belief arose that this was due to treasonable dealings of the king and the conservatives. The popular uprising of August 10, 1792, led by the radicals, swept out the old leadership and ushered in a reign of terror in which the king and queen, thousands of the old nobility, royalist and conservative, were guillotined. Then the Commune of Paris decreed that all poisoners of public opinion, the editors of promonarchist papers, should be arrested. Most were guillotined, and in five weeks all voices of opposition were stilled.

Now a duel to the death developed between the Girondists and Jacobins. The latter, led my Maximilien Robespierre, inaugurated a second reign of terror in which many Girondist editors and thousands of other alleged enemies of the revolution were guillotined. Even Jacobin editors who, sickened by the bloodshed, tried to halt it, were killed. When Robespierre himself became a threat to the National Convention he was similarly executed. In all some 20,000 died in these terrors.

Reaction against the Jacobins was so severe that many people favored a restoration of the monarchy. To forestall this the Convention drew up a new constitution which vested power in a Directory of five. By the end of 1795 the revolution was dead. The new regime began with assurances of press freedom, but two years of attacks was all the government could take. Then it struck again with the suspension of many papers and decreed the death penalty for anyone advocating the dissolution of the Directory. In a month all opposition had vanished.

The Press under Napoleon

Napoleon returned from victories in Italy, Germany, and Egypt and in 1799 deposed the Directory and substituted a Consulate of three with himself as First Consul. Journalists who had hailed his coming as a saviour of the revolution soon found their leader could brook no opposition. Fifty-nine of the seventy-two papers which had appeared at the birth of the Consulate were suspended. The thirteen others continued under draconian regimentation. Napoleon kept peace for a time, consolidated the gains of the revolution, settled financial problems, and through his Code Napoleon provided a modern legal system. So popular was his work that a plebiscite approved his proclamation as Emperor in 1804.

The empire of which he dreamed, however, was not one of France and her colonies alone. In brilliant campaigns he made Italy, Germany, Holland, Poland, and Spain his vassals and forced Austria and Prussia into alliance. His wars justified, in his mind, strict discipline at home. Journalists also had to be his soldiers, thundering against his enemies and indulging only in adulation of himself. Then in 1811 he made all papers the property of the empire without any indemnity for the proprietors. Thereafter there were only four official papers in Paris, *Le Moniteur, Journal de L'Empire, Gazette de France* and *Le Quotidien*. In the provinces there was only one paper for each department under the strict authority of the prefect.

When Napoleon at last overreached himself by his attack on Russia, followed by his retreat from Moscow, the result was a disaster of such proportions that the nations allied against him took Paris and exiled Napoleon to Elba. Though he escaped and rallied his old army, an Anglo-Prussian army crushed him at Waterloo and ended the Napoleonic era.

The Press Under the First Restoration

The restoration of the Bourbons seemed the only avenue to peace and order, and the current pretender was installed as Louis XVIII. He won favor with a new constitution establishing parliamentary government and promising press liberty, but he soon instituted such rigorous repression that most opposition papers were silenced.

The king died in 1824 and was succeeded by Charles X, a fanatical emigré who had learned nothing from the revolution and imposed such an authoritarian rule that the people rose in 1830 and drove him into exile. Now a limited monarchy was proclaimed under Louis Phillipe. He tried at first to be a benevolent monarch and even abolished censorship. New papers appeared everywhere, but the growing ferment between monarchists and republicans led the government to reimpose censorship and enforce severe press laws.

Despite these restrictions this period gave birth to an innovation in French journalism, Emile Girardin's *La Presse*. At 80 francs per year few could subscribe to papers. Girardin reasoned that at a lower price he could get larger circulation and attract more advertising. He launched his paper in 1836 as a nonpolitical daily at a price of 40 francs. Eschewing all political comment and devoting his paper to the small news of Paris, its entertainment and life, he escaped the attentions of the censor and soon had a circulation of 7,000, more than the combined circulations of several leading political papers.

Louis Phillipe's government worsened, and the people resented the fact that only 200,000 could vote. Opposition papers pleaded for more democracy, but the king listened only to his capitalistic bourgeois supporters who were chiefly interested in getting rich. The government grew increasingly corrupt; and when the king stopped a demonstration intended to impress him with the need for reform, the people rose in 1848 and forced him to abdicate.

The bourgeois, still in control, called for the election of a president and Assembly for the Second Republic. Louis Napoleon Bonaparte, nephew of Napoleon I, was overwhelmingly elected. He started by conciliating the people; and when the Assembly passed a law restricting suffrage, he repudiated it and assumed temporary dictatorship. In a year, posing as champion of the people, he assumed the title of

Napoleon III, Emperor of the French. Before long he was an absolute dictator and now had to control the press. A new 1852 law restored royal authorization, strict censorship, warnings, and suspensions, and imposed a stamp tax on each copy. The press withered; most provincial papers disappeared. In Paris only twelve remained, four of which were taken over by the government; the rest were forced to abandon any political comment. Again a clandestine press arose, the most important paper being Victor Hugo's *Chatiments*, preaching a return of power to the people.

Curiously, there now emerged one of the great figures of French journalism, Hippolyte Villemessant, who in 1854 started a little daily, *Figaro*, today one of the leading Paris papers. Small in format, light, satirical, amusing, seemingly concerned more with the theater and literature, it escaped the attention of authorities who were more occupied with the *grande presse* whose political comment might be dangerous. But Villemessant ushered in a new journalism, concerned with the people and their interests. He introduced local reporting, personality interviews, news briefly told and departmentalized. Each morning he published news that had happened the night before, told with a new freshness. In his whimsy he shot arrows at everyone and his readers loved it. He touched on political matters only by allusion and his readers laughed with him. This was the piquant boulevardier to perfection. *Figaro* was an instant success though its circulation was limited to the people of society, the theater, cafes, and boulevards. It did not reach the masses.

La Presse à un Sou

Moise Millaud took the next step with his *La Petite Presse* founded in 1863. By cutting his price to a sou, he placed his paper within the reach of the common people not only in Paris but in the provinces. It was like the birth of the penny press in the United States thirty years before. Millaud realized that the masses were not interested in heavy political discussion and that by avoiding it he could escape the stamp tax. Instead, every day he gave the little people brief government releases plus much local Paris news, bulletins from the provinces and abroad, theatrical reviews, court news, and a serial story. But the big circulation on which he had counted did not materialize, so he turned to humorous court reporting, murder trials, sensation of every kind to give his readers what René Mazadier called a "punch in the stomach" in each issue. In the "Affaire Tropman," the story of a criminal who had murdered a father, mother, and six children, he gave columns each day to the horrible details. In three days his circulation soared to

400,000; by the time the sixth body had been found it had reached 470,000. Millaud's method was a spectacular financial success. Soon there were several representatives of *la presse à un sou*—all sensational at first, but who gradually tempered their news treatment and laid the foundations for the popular journalism of a later day.

The first years of the emperor's reign had gone well. He had built roads, railroads, and a magnificent boulevard system for Paris and, by policies favorable to business, had brought increasing prosperity. But his misadventure in trying to set up an overseas empire in Mexico with Maximilian of Austria on the throne went badly. When Maximilian was shot and French troops were forced to withdraw, public opinion at home turned against him. To retrieve his fortunes, he involved France in the War of 1870 with Prussia. France was badly defeated, the emperor himself captured. Two days later his government was overthrown and the Third Republic proclaimed. But it took five years for the republic to be made a reality—years of civil wars and attempts to restore the monarchy. Provisional governments which followed each other kept the press in restraint. A new constitution was eventually adopted but it was not till 1881 that the press was granted full liberty.

Freedom and Progress

In 250 years the French press had known but a few short periods of liberty. Now at last it was really free. In the thirty-three years of peace which followed, France advanced in prosperity, agriculture and industry made great progress, and Paris grew to rival London as a European banking center. In this period the press expanded. The development of public education had spread literacy through all classes, and the intensity of national political life created a great new body of readers. Railroads which now fanned out from the capital enabled the larger Paris papers to achieve national circulations. By 1895 Paris had 81 dailies and the provinces 333.

The most interesting advance was the development of *journaux d'information* which devoted themselves more to news than political argument. To widen their appeal they added many popular features. *Le Petit Parisien* by 1910 had reached 1,500,000 circulation; *Le Matin* and *Le Journal* were pushing 1,000,000. These three plus *Le Petit Journal* and *Echo de Paris* were the big five.

Because of its long political struggle the press remained essentially partisan, and journals of opinion made up the great majority. Newspapers tended to devote themselves to political rather than commercial ends. Every important political figure had his organ; industrialists with axes to grind had theirs; each party had to have one. Straight news in most papers became subordinate to interpretation. Journalists selected such news facts as fitted in with their thesis, discussed them, and came to a conclusion. French readers, too, wanted the news presented to fit their own political viewpoints. Hence, while the discussion of national and international events bulked large, readers were given comparatively little straight news.

Newspapers had few pages; every line counted; everything had to be written concisely. Yet fine writing, lucidity, and sparkling style were stressed. Newspapers were literary productions, and this factor had influence in the fields of literature, art, music, and drama. News items served but as springboards for excellently written interpretative articles by featured experts on foreign, national, social, and economic questions. Such was the character of the press which developed in this period.

But newspaper economics was the determining factor in the moral character of this press. Advertising did not develop in France as it had in England, Holland, and the Scandinavian countries. What little there was consisted mostly of *petites annonces* (classified) and a small amount of national. Despite handsome circulations, at 15 centimes per copy, there was seldom enough revenue from sales and advertising to meet the costs of production. Hence papers had to find other sources to make ends meet. Many were subsidized by parties or special interests. Publicity was sold to those who wished it. A politician paid for good publicity at so much a line. Favorable reviews in art, music, and literary sections were sold the same way. Foreign governments bought favorable publicity for their policies. Bismarck, in his diaries, boasted of the sums paid to win a friendly French press; and the Communists in 1917 released official tsarist documents disclosing the large sums paid to Havas, Paris and provincial papers, from 1905 to 1917. Thus, while papers in other countries, through their development of advertising, had achieved both financial and political independence, most French papers were beholden to someone.

The Insidious Controls of Havas

Havas News Agency, the oldest in Europe, had been founded in 1835 by Charles Havas, who had made a fortune dealing in commercial licenses under Napoleon. Starting with a pigeon-post, he had, with the coming of the telegraph, expanded his news network all over Europe and had made exchange agreements with Reuters in England and Wolff's in Germany. Havas became one of the big three who dominated news communication in Europe. But Havas also had the ability to snuggle close to government. Balzac commented that Havas had seen many governments and had served them all with equal fidelity. Most Paris papers used Havas' service, but many provincial papers could not afford it until the agency offered them an abbreviated daily French and foreign wire in exchange for free space on pages three and four which he then sold to advertising clients. Most accepted, and in time Havas came to control a large part of the advertising in French papers. With its quasi-monopoly on both news and advertising, it had most dailies under its thumb, for to alienate Havas might mean the loss of advertising. Havas was paid by French governments to provide news that would support their policies and to conceal any that was adverse. It was also paid by foreign governments to provide news which would give them a favorable press in France and in southern European countries where Havas had newspaper clients.

The Press in World War I

During all these prosperous years France, like other European powers, had become involved in power politics. By 1900 the old balance of power had come out of adjustment. Germany had become a great new force, outdistancing France in industrial power and competing and intriguing against her in world markets. From the beginning of the century Germany, France, Britain, Austria-Hungary, Russia, and Italy were competing for power, security, and economic advantage; and all were arming frantically in the belief that their national security depended on their naval and military preparedness.

The nationalistic aspirations of the Serbs, smarting under Austro-Hungarian rule, touched a match to the explosive international situation with the assassination of the Austrian crown prince. Austria's belligerent ultimatum and Russia's threat to come to the aid of her Slav brothers precipitated events. By August 4, 1914, France, Britain, and Russia were at war against Germany and Austria-Hungary; the holocaust which was soon to engulf all Europe had begun.

The Germans struck quickly through Belgium, driving to within fourteen miles of Paris. There the French and British held and began driving the Germans back in the first Battle of the Marne. Soon the fighting settled down into four years of cruel trench warfare, in which the northern departments of France saw the most destructive warfare the world had seen to that point. Naturally the whole press in this area disappeared.

Back of the fighting front, the war brought great hardships. There was tremendous disruption of economic life as France fought for survival. Advertising dried up; scarcity of transportation curtailed distribution; readers and staff members were drained off to the front. All papers had to curtail their size because of newsprint rationing, and many had to close. With the declaration of war a law governing "indiscretions of the press" was promulgated providing imprisonment or heavy fines for offenses. Newspapers demanded military censorship so that they might know what could be published without running afoul of the law. But this military censorship soon became political censorship as ministers found they could use it to still any criticism of themselves. Georges Clemenceau first opened fire. After his *L'Homme Libre* had been suspended for eight days, he brought it out as *L'Homme Enchaîne* and kept up the fight. Yet suppressions and punishments went on till Clemenceau became premier in November, 1917. That was the year of great discouragement in France, and a defeatist peace propaganda was started in the army and behind the front. There were some French papers, subsidized by Germany, which supported this but the great majority fought it. Clemenceau, however, provided the strong government needed, swept out traitorous ministers, and with British collaboration provided a unity of command under Marshal Ferdinand Foch.

Through much of the war the press had to assume the role assigned to it by the government—softening the bad news and shouting the good to keep up morale. However, most papers with courage continued to denounce inefficiency in the cabinet, maladministration in internal affairs, the conduct of the war, and leniency in dealing with disloyalty in high places. The press also contributed to the final victory, which came after the last German drive on Paris had been stopped and the unified forces of the French, British, and Americans, in a seven-months sustained drive under Foch, drove the Germans to their final capitulation.

Recovery after the War

After the terrible battering of four years of war and the death and disablement of one out of every four French fighters, the people responded hopefully. After all, France had won; she now was the leading continental power; she had gained Alsace-Lorraine with its industrial assets, and German reparations were to pay for the war. But impoverished Germany was unable to meet all her reparations, and France had to undertake her own reconstruction. Despite a succession of governments, progress was achieved, and by 1928 France was on a firmer economic basis.

The press recovered slowly. Censorship was gone, but newspaper buyers were poor. Newsprint was scarce and high-priced; newspapers stayed small. Labor, caught by postwar inflation, struck for higher wages. In 1921 Paris papers had to combine to put out a single joint paper, *La Presse de Paris*. Once the strike was settled, the press began to move ahead. For a time it lost some of its political character, partly because the people had to bend to common tasks but more because of the importance of international developents affecting France. More space came to be given to foreign news, and for larger papers foreign correspondents became a necessity. Skilled interpreters of international affairs now brought distinction and high readership. While the *feuilleton* and cultural departments kept their places, more space was given to sports and local news. To gain readers some papers began playing crime and sensation, and a few of the more extreme in their makeup came to "outcircus" anything in the United States.

Rising costs of production and costly strikes, often Communist-inspired, made publication increasingly difficult. The long-ingrained shopping habits of French housewives and their extreme suspicion of advertisements kept retail advertising small. Although manufacturers' advertising increased and industry developed, most advertising was still classified. There were also too many papers to divide what was available, and even with larger circulations few papers had enough revenue to meet all their costs.

Moral Deterioration Sets In

There were a few independent papers, but the press as a whole became more and more corrupt. The sensational, jingoistic *Le Matin* started a violent campaign against Leopold II of Belgium which ceased when the Belgian Congo colony bought at a high price the shares of the Congo railroad owned by Maurice Bunau Varilla, the publisher. It tried to blackmail the Greek and Spanish governments into allocating sums in return for "the hospitality of its pages." Lacking adequate financial support, many other papers had to look for "angels." Munitions combines, steel, mines, railroads, oil, coal, chemical corporations, and banks either acquired interests in papers or subsidized them. François Coty (perfumes) bought *Figaro*, and Jean Hennesey (cognac) took over *Le Quotidien* and made it a National Socialist organ.

Hitler had come to power in 1933; and monied interests supported through the papers they dominated a policy of accommodation to Hitler, hoping this would enable them to retain their industrial and financial empires. Nazi money began to flow in to support the propaganda that Hitler had only the most peaceful intentions toward France, that his successive coups had but removed sources of friction, that there was no need to spend money on the French army for there would never be a war between Germany and France. Again *Le Matin* became a principal mouthpiece of this propaganda. New weeklies began to appear, outwardly published by Frenchmen but actually run by Germans. The French government too used secret funds to persuade papers to follow the government line on foreign affairs. And Havas, now controlling over 80 per cent of all newspaper advertising and getting 36,000,000 francs a year from the government, served it by releasing news as the government wanted it presented and, by its advertising control, made sure that public opinion was shaped as the government desired.

As a result there was no real public opinion in France. What took its place was manufactured by a press tied to a government which could panic public opinion in any direction. What was more insidious was corruption from many foreign governments. During the Ethiopian War *The Manchester Guardian* published an enlightening list of sums paid by Italy to influence the French press, and *Le Matin* was at the top of the list. Edouard Daladier, French premier, said in 1936 that four-fifths of French newspapers lived on subsidy.

But not all newspapers were venal. *Paris Soir*, founded in 1920, the best of the information papers, fought against government press control to the very end; *Le Petit Parisien* also remained clean; and *Figaro*, once it had escaped the hand of Coty, became one of the best papers in France. In the provinces, too, the standards of the better papers were far higher than those in Paris.

The world depression hit France hard in 1932 and brought riots in the streets and political chaos till a Popular Front of Radicals, Socialists, and Communists took over, headed by Léon Blum, a Socialist and a distinguished intellectual. In rapid-fire moves Blum nationalized munitions, reorganized coal, gave workers a forty-hour week, put through measures to aid farmers, and formed a firm alliance with Britain. Concerned over press venality, he proposed reforms which would have broken the Havas monopoly and instituted rigid controls of subsidies and strict regulation of advertising. Under Daladier, who returned to power in 1939, a series of fourteen laws was put through restricting the press from printing anything harmful to national or army morale and establishing a Commission on Information with control over press, radio, and cinema to keep out foreign propaganda.

In 1939 France had some 1,900 papers of which 233 were dailies, 40 of them in Paris; these dailies had two-thirds of the total daily circulation. Three Paris morning papers had over 1,000,000, and *Paris Soir* with 2,000,000 was the largest on the Continent.

Yet the sad truth was that for twenty years the press as a whole had not served its people well. Government leaders had often kept the people in the dark to play politics, and papers which cooperated had lulled the people into a false sense of security. The many parties, with their special pleadings, kept the nation confused and divided. The Communists and Socialists with their pacifist campaigns for disarmament and collaboration with Russia were as much to blame as the monied interests who hoped to retain their holdings by cooperating with Hitler and who played that tune through the papers they controlled. Instead of uniting the French people against the dangers surrounding them, the press had so divided public opinion that there was no strength to stand against any enemy.

The Press under the Nazis

Although war had been declared on September 3, 1939, there was little action during the *sitzkreig* until Hitler loosed his panzer divisions in May, 1940. They quickly took Holland and Belgium, then swept across France. By June 14 Paris had fallen, and on June 22 the French signed their surrender.

When German legions rumbled into Paris, their propaganda and press sections came with them. For the first five days only German radio, broadcast in French, could be heard. But on June 18 *Le Matin* was on kiosks. Bunau Varilla who had been taking German cash was now ready to collaborate. He was the only Paris publisher who did not evacuate his staff to the provinces. At *Paris Soir* Joseph Schleisse, its former elevator operator, now in the uniform of a German officer, took over. Fifth columnists were recruited and on June 9 *Paris Soir* was also on the newsstands. Readers eagerly seized copies, but as soon as they began to read they understood. Soon *Le Petit Parisien, Paris Midi, L'Action Française, L'Intransigeant*, and *Le Temps*, now christened *Le Nouveau Temps*, appeared—all under German direction with staffs of collaborators.

Under surrender terms the Germans occupied the north of the country, and here a number of papers were started, all controlled by strict military law. The publication of any anti-German news was forbidden. Listening to non-German broadcasts was made a treasonable offense. In the southern half a totalitarian state under Marshal Henri Petain was set up at Vichy. Here strict press control, including previous authorization and a devastating censorship was imposed. Any political comment or criticism of the Petain government or the Germans was impossible. The Vichy government supported its own official press, spewing propaganda against the Allies and counseling cooperation with the Germans. Chief organ was *Le Moniteur* at Clermont-Ferrand directed by Pierre Laval, Petain's right hand man, who made unregulated profits from Vichy government printing. Havas, too, was taken over when Laval created FIO (French Information Office), which appropriated what remained of the agency. A complicated financial reorganization brought it under German control. Thus Havas fell a victim to the totalitarianism it had helped to create.

A New Press Is Born

Loyal French newspapermen refused to collaborate. Papers evacuated from Paris tried to carry on at Bordeaux, Grenoble, Lyon, and other cities with some show of independence by printing British communiques as well as the Vichy handouts they had to carry. One after the other was suppressed, the editors imprisoned. Soon all ceased and went underground.

In the dark hour of defeat a clandestine press was born. Three days after surrender a little one-page sheet, *Victoire*, appeared in Paris. It lived only a few days; but others emerged, not only in Paris but in the north and in the Vichy south. First in the north was *Conseils à l'Occupe*, a typewritten sheet passed from hand to hand. In Paris *Pantagruel* published bravely till its whole staff was shot. Others took its place. People eagerly sought news from these underground sheets, even though mere possession might mean dire punishment. The official collaborationist press had little influence. As *Paroles Françaises* said, "Let no one be fooled. Apart from the journals of resistance there is no longer a French press. The official press is morally dead; the disgust of the people has killed it." At first resistance papers were produced by local or regional groups making a common cause in encouraging readers to believe in eventual victory, in baring German lies, in enlisting men for the underground Maquis army and spurring patriots to sabotage.

At first these local papers gave little outside news, leaving that to British and Algiers radio. Instead they told the story in their own area—of German cruelties, of the murder of local patriots, of the executions of informers, of the local girls who walked out with Germans, of the names of employers in the area who tried to blackmail their workers by threatening them with deportation to Germany, of their own local resistance efforts, of successful night battles between Maquis and Germans. Here is an example of their reporting:

Clermont-Ferrand—Our comrade ———— was arrested at 16:30 October 26. He was brought to the morgue at two o'clock next afternoon. His face was swollen beyond recognition. He bore marks of strangulation; all his fingernails had been torn out. He had two bullet holes in his temple. His murderers are known. They will not be tortured. They will be shot down like dogs.

It was truly an uncensored press printed at risk of death, perhaps the most honest press France had had in years. Starting as small handwritten or stenciled sheets, they grew into printed papers. Getting newsprint was difficult, but the Germans had frozen prices at a low point and wholesalers were willing to sell at blackmarket prices without asking questions. Money came from sympathizers in France or was parachuted in from General Charles de Gaulle's headquarters in London. Presses hidden in barns, basements, shacks, and churches had to be small so they could be moved frequently when the Gestapo got close. Salesmen, mothers with baby carriages, peddlers, even children aided in distribution. First recipients passed them on to others. Often a line at the bottom of page one read: "Do not save this paper; do not destroy it; make it circulate." Many newspapermen were executed, yet most papers managed to maintain fairly regular publication. Among the important ones were *France Tireur, Résistance, Front National, Défense de la France, Parisien Libéré.*

In time the more important resistance groups combined their local sheets into larger regional papers. Thus the De Gaullist movement combined its papers into *Combat* with a number of regional editions, avoiding political appeals to left or right, trying to unite the people into one national resistance movement. The Socialists put out seven regional editions of *Populaire* encouraging resistance among workers. The Communists published *L'Humanité* and the Conservatives had their *L'Aurore,* both of whose regional editions gained wide distribution. These larger four-page papers carried more news. Although they might lead with appeals and denunciations, page two would be given to regional news of resistance forces or German atrocities. Page three, which ran through all editions, gave news from all fighting fronts to gainsay German claims of victories, while page four was given to national news of France and attacks on the Vichy government. It was a fighting journalism, and it played a tremendous role in uniting the people in resistance. When the Allies finally made their Normandy landing, this press almost as with one voice bannered their front pages, "To Arms, Citizens, This is the Final Battle." By September 15 General Eisenhower's six armies had driven the Wehrmacht out of all but a small section of eastern France. Allied blows from east and west precipitated the German collapse and on May 8, 1945, the war was over.

Post-Liberation Problems

The French Provisional government in Algiers had made plans to set up a free press once France was liberated and had condemned to death all collaborationist papers. But the proposed press law set up government controls which underground journalists in France resented; and when a new news agency, to be subsidized by the government, was proposed, they remembered with distaste the old Havas and its subservience to government.

The newsmen of the resistance went ahead with their own plans. Their National Federation of Resistance Papers proscribed all collaborationist papers; only those which had voluntarily ceased publication during the war or had been born as underground papers were allowed to continue. All newspaper plants were allocated to different members of the Federation. In Paris in some cases as many as four papers were assigned to the same plant, publishing mornings and evenings. Staffs were organized and the underground printers' union rounded up linotype operators and pressmen. Weeks before liberation everyone knew where he was to go. Five days before the Germans officially surrendered Paris, the first liberation papers appeared; and by the day of surrender nineteen dailies and many weeklies were on sale in Paris alone. There was a tremendous upsurge of publishing all over France.

Each resistance group, each party had its papers. Because of a newsprint shortage, all were limited to single tabloid sheets printed on both sides. At first all were given enough for 180,000 sheets daily, but soon the demand for some fell off while others could not print enough. The Ministry of Information therefore adjusted allocations giving some enough for 300,000 papers daily while cutting others to 50,000. French newspapermen were determined to build a new kind of press, economically free to obviate prewar corruption. Thus the price of all papers was set at two francs, many times the prewar price to enable papers to meet production costs without need for subsidy and to pay adequate salaries and wages so staff members would not be tempted by bribery. Since there were not enough resistance papers to replace all suspended ones, papers were licensed for cities and departments, left without any. The French press took on an entirely new face. Many of the old familiar titles were obliterated; most had new names and in many cases took a different political orientation. In view of the leftwing character of the first postwar government, it is not surprising that *L'Humanité* and *Populaire* led all others in newspaper sales and that Communist papers represented 26.8 per cent of the total circulation, Socialist papers 21 per cent, while information papers, moderate and rightist journals had much less.

The Battle of the Bulge worsened the newsprint situation, for transportation was essential for military needs. By the end of 1944 newspapers were almost forced to shut down. In Bordeaux two rival papers had to print on opposite sides of a single sheet, often with editorials attacking each other. When strict rationing continued, even after V-E Day, the press charged the government with restricting paper for political purposes; and all Paris papers issued a manifesto declaring that a free people must have a free press and threatening a strike in protest. The government found more newsprint and made enough available so that papers might have four full-sized pages or eight tabloid pages daily. Censorship was galling; and when papers were suspended for running blank spaces in which they printed, "No Censorship Exists," the whole press threatened to close down. Finally in September, 1945, censorship was lifted.

There were other problems. Collaborationists had to be tried. A number were executed, including Pierre Laval. Others were sentenced to prison with national degradation for life. What to do about printing plants that former underground papers had taken over was another problem. Many had expected that the use of these would be gratuitous since former owners would probably be convicted and deprived of their properties; but some could prove they were not responsible, that the Germans had taken over their plants, or that they had evacuated them, tried publishing in the free zone for a time, and then had gone underground to produce a clandestine paper. Some were acquitted, others partially cleared. The government set up *Société Nationale d'Enterprises de Presse* (SNEP) to hold titles and collect rents, pending adjudication. Then, allegedly to protect resistance papers, the Socialists and Communists enacted the 1946 Law of Defere, which expropriated all plants in question with compensation at a fraction of their worth, and spread annual payments over a period of fifty years, which meant that the rightful owners would not be paid off till the year 2000. It was not until the Leftists lost their power in government and were succeeded by the more conservative Radicals that a law was passed doing away with licensing. This was interpreted as superceding the Law of Defere; but it was not till late in 1947, under the Schumann Ministry representing the MRP, that restitution of plants of former owners began to take place.

Economic Difficulties Bring Adjustments

The falling value of the franc and the rising cost of living caused strikes, the most serious in early 1947 when all Paris papers had to close for twenty-three days. Provincial papers were similarly affected as strikers demanded a 25 per cent pay increase. Papers were finally permitted to double their price to grant a 17 per cent increase. These strikes resulted in the survival of the fittest: many small papers died and the principal loser was the resistance press. Although these papers had been excellent weapons during the war, they tended to lose their purpose as the war receded. They lost to those whose journalistic competence enabled them to appeal to more readers. Paris had thirty-two dailies when the strikes began; only twenty-two survived. In all France 25 per cent of the resistance papers disappeared. Now with the demand for more news, information papers again came to the fore.

Costs continued to rise, and although sales prices were increased step by step from four to six francs to eight and then in 1950 to ten, there was still not enough revenue. In the first postwar years there had not been enough consumer goods to advertise. But under the stimulus of Marshall Aid, industry and agriculture made a remarkable recovery, and by 1950 some of the larger papers were getting 25 to 30 per cent of their revenue from advertising. In 1950 France had 167 dailies and 731 nondailies. But Paris was reduced to ten morning and five evening papers, a 53 per cent drop from 1945. This was an inevitable and perhaps fortunate development, for none of America's larger metropolitan cities could support thirty-two dailies and neither could Paris. An improvement came in 1950 when papers were finally freed from size limitations; many cut down on politics and devoted their increased space to more news and features.

Another interesting postwar change was the growing importance of provincial dailies. Before the war Paris dailies had circulated all over the country. During the war those Paris papers which appeared openly were collaborationist, and provincial readers wanted none of them. After the war the people's loyalty to their nearest resistance paper remained when it became a regular daily. And Paris papers, in their straitened circumstances, could not make a bid for provincial circulation with extensive coverage of their news, whereas the local dailies, sometimes with as many as twenty editions, could give intensive coverage of the news of their areas. For a time some of the morning dailies in major provincial cities exceeded the circulations of Paris papers.

And Then Came Great Changes

The fifties and sixties saw tremendous political and material changes. From October, 1949, to May 28, 1959, France had fifteen successive governments, some lasting only a few days, none as long as a year. Although these governments had negotiated the Common Market treaty, initiated a program of industrial expansion, and brought inflation under control, political instability had brought the Fourth Republic almost to the point of disintegration. And when an army revolt in Algeria threatened to bring civil war to France itself, the president appealed to Charles de Gaulle, the man who had stood alone when

France had fallen and headed Free France. He demanded full powers to meet the crisis and on June 2, 1958, was granted them by an impotent National Assembly. At once he took measures to restore calm and to lay the foundations for a new regime which was to emerge as the Fifth Republic. The new constitution giving him almost supreme power and making parliament but a rubber stamp was approved by a landslide in a national plebiscite. Currency reform was completed, political deadwood pruned away, and young vigorous planners brought in to push economic growth. Fourteen French African possessions were soon made independent states. Then by 1962 De Gaulle had brought the seven-year Algerian war to an end, granted independence to Algeria, and smashed the OAS (secret army organization) terrorists. Now under a completely managed economy and with the great benefits accruing under the Common Market, France was launched on the greatest boom in her history.

By 1963, however, inflation, reflected in the rising wages and a deterioration of the balance of trade, was seriously affecting the French economy; and deflationary measures, limiting credit and money supply, were put into effect. Politically, De Gaulle launched an anti-American program, first recognizing Red China. Then he began trying to squeeze the United States out of Europe by insisting that Europe should rely on neither the United States nor the Soviet Union but should itself constitute a third force in which France would hold the principal position. He strongly attacked the American policy in Viet Nam and tried to embarrass the dollar position; but this came to naught, for the economy of the United States and its dollar proved stronger than his own.

The French boom should have given great impetus to the press. There was more advertising for cars, appliances, and other manufactured products as well as growing retail. Some of the better papers were for the first time getting 50 per cent or more of their revenue from advertising, but many others which had declined in circulation did not share this prosperity. Although France's population had risen by 4,000,000 in ten years, daily circulations had not kept up. The 15,000,000 circulation just after the war when a news-hungry people bought every paper they could lay their hands on could not continue. By 1962 the total daily figure had dropped to 9,810,000; and in 1964, despite a 200,000 gain in population, circulations had risen to only 10,380,000. The number of dailies had dropped from 167 in 1950 to 113, and it must be remembered that 2 of these were sports dailies and 2 were Paris editions of the New York *Herald Tribune* and the New York *Times*, which left but 109 regular French dailies. Of the 1964 total daily circulation, the 98 provincial papers had 6,699,186, while Paris papers had 3,681,159.

Reason for Decline

French newspaper researchers were understandably disturbed by the fact that in Britain and the United States, where there had also been reductions in the number of dailies in the same period, total circulations nevertheless had grown steadily. Henri Calvet came to the conclusion that the French press had perhaps "lost its radiance"; yet he was reluctant to believe the French public was dissatisfied with the press as a whole, for it was superior to that of previous periods with improved reporting, better commentaries on foreign affairs, more interesting appearance, and greater accuracy and speed in presenting the news.

Other factors played their part. For one thing the French people, as have other west Europeans, became dissatisfied with political papers. *L'Humanité*, the Communist mouthpiece, which once had 600,000 circulation, had dropped in 1964 to 147,164; and its companion, *Libération*, because of financial difficulties, had had to close December 28, 1964. The old Socialist *Populaire*, which earlier had sold more than 400,000 copies, had to give up daily publication; and *L'Aube*, MRP organ, had to suspend publication. This lack of interest in party propaganda has been accelerated by developments under the Fifth Republic in which one party, the Gaullist, holds complete control. Those papers which have increased their circulations have tended to become independent information journals. While there are still strongly political papers like *L'Aurore*, staunchly De Gaullist, and *La Croix*, far right, balanced by *L'Humanité*, far left, party politics today has found its chief battleground in weekly opinion papers such as *L'Express, Canard Enchaîné, Candide*, and *France Observateur*. A 1963 survey disclosed, however, that only one Frenchman out of twenty bought a political weekly.

Even the big information papers have lost some circulation owing to steady price increases. After devaluation of the franc in 1962, the price per copy went to 30 francs. Each price increase brought a circulation drop of 3 to 4 per cent; some papers regained their publics but not all. Still more important factors were radio and television. The latter, as it grew in popularity, took people away from newspapers with its news bulletins, filmed reports of important events, music, plays, and glamor. Some French critics also felt that the more sensational Paris papers in their attempts to gain readers with sex, crime, and noisier makeup had "lowered the image of the whole press." On the other hand one postwar paper, *Le Monde*, had done much to raise the tone of the information press. Completely independent, providing serious backgrounding, it has made itself a "must" for those who wish to be informed not only in France but in many foreign capitals. *Le Monde* has become the most quoted paper in France and has grown steadily.

Paris is still the journalistic capital with its sixteen regular daily newspapers and many periodicals and magazines of all kinds; but whereas before the war there were five dailies with circulations of 1,000,000 or more, there is now only one—*France Soir.*

Although some Paris papers do reach all parts of the country, the development of strong papers in larger provincial cities has been the significant feature of recent years. In the provinces, too, there has been a diminution in numbers as small dailies have given way to bigger, multiple-edition regional papers, fanning out to give not only intensive coverage of the areas they serve but also well-balanced information on national and foreign news. Thirteen major provincial dailies, with near-monopolistic dominance of their areas, have more than 50 per cent of the entire provincial circulation and almost as much as the sixteen regular daily newspapers of Paris. Among the largest are *Ouest France* at Rennes, the third largest in France, with 549,575 circulation, *La Voix du Nord* at Lille with 367,929, and *Le Progrès* at Lyon with 368,014. There are still many small dailies, a fourth of them under 25,000 circulation and many of these under 5,000, yet the economy of the press is on a sounder footing than when there were 167 dailies.

Most of the major provincial papers are published in the morning as are the majority of those in Paris. There is only a handful of Sunday papers, for Sunday is a French family holiday. There are, however, several large Saturday evening weeklies.

Agence France Presse *Survives Its Problems*

Very important to the daily press is its new cooperative, *Agence France Presse* (AFP), now one of the five great world news gathering agencies serving papers in forty-four countries. During the war loyal Havas men in London had started *Agence Française Indépendante,* and other French newsmen in Algiers had established *Agence France Afrique.* After liberation the De Gaullist Consultative Assembly created AFP to be subsidized by the government until newspapers could get back on their feet. But in their straitened circumstances, even by 1949, newspapers were able to pay only a third of their service costs. Newspapers became more and more restive as their agency remained a semigovernmental one with its executives removed from time to time if they showed any resistance to the government. Finally on January

10, 1957, AFP was given its independence. Government subsidies were withdrawn; instead the government bought AFP service for its world-wide system of embassies and consular offices. Fees from client daily papers and radio and television stations were raised 30 per cent to make AFP operations viable. Government control was removed and placed under a council of fifteen, eight from the press, two from AFP, three from Radio-Television Française, and three from the government. This greatly increased the agency's prestige in the international news world. It rapidly gained clients in many countries and became com-mercially profitable and economically independent.

How Free Is the French Press?

French newspapers still operate under the 1881 law which granted press freedom but permitted censorship in times of crisis. Many new bans have been added over the years, and to maintain respect, a French editor must prove his innocence when accused of acting in bad faith. Beginning with the war in Indo-China and extending all through the seven-year Algerian War, a new measure was added allowing prefects to confiscate an entire edition when the news or comment of a paper was considered dangerous to internal or external security. It is true that one of De Gaulle's first moves after taking office in 1958 was to remove the precensorship imposed by Pierre Plimflin's government. But precensorship was soon ordered in Algeria, and papers from France were seized when they arrived in Algeria if they contained anything reflecting on the army. In 1959 and 1960 seventy-three seizures were made in Algeria and thirty-one in continental France. When in 1960 the International Red Cross made its report on condi-tions in Algerian internment camps, including charges made by in-ternees of tortures perpetrated by the army, *Le Monde, L'Humanité, L'Express,* and *France Conservateur,* which printed these charges, promptly had their editions confiscated. Thus while there has been no precensorship within France under the Fifth Republic, there has been postcensorship.

President de Gaulle has no love for reporters or newspapers; he says the press is neither truthful nor objective. But French newspapermen told this author that any news story, article, or commentary critical of the regime is likely to be considered "not objective." Hence the president has not felt it necessary to give the press full access to government information, preferring to use the state-owned Radio-Television to convey his messages to the people. One French editorial writer in an International Press Institute Report wrote:

As far as the press is concerned, France is now an authoritarian country. The press is despised by the government; its representatives are received—when they are received at all—with a haughty attitude and are told nothing. But, in fact, it is the public which suffers. How can the French people react if the press does not furnish them with the elements necessary to form their judgments? Freedom of the press is the sign of a democratic state, just as the substitution of official statements of information or propaganda is an attribute of an authoritarian state.

It was hoped that after the Algerian War had ended, confiscations would cease. But although they greatly declined there were occasional seizures through 1963, in 1964, and into 1965; publishers and editors were given jail sentences or fines for articles considered insulting to De Gaulle or reflecting on the government. As an example of denial of access, the science correspondent for *Le Monde* was banned from investigating the information sources of all scientific organizations for a story on atomic explosions in the Sahara, despite the fact that the details had already been reported by an American news agency. While Premier Georges Pompideau declared a policy of easier access, French newspapermen still protest against undue government interference with the press and continued difficulties in getting information on political facts and government decisions because of the attitude of mistrust on the part of authorities. The government also regulates sales prices, freight rate discounts, newsprint rates, and the distribution of advertising space for nationalized industries. Withdrawal of the latter might be a blow to a paper.

It is difficult to assess the degree of press freedom in France. On the one hand it is possible to buy both Communist and extreme right-wing papers on any newsstand. It is also true that there has been some recent amelioration in the government attitude toward the press. Yet under a one-party system, exceedingly sensitive to criticism, it is still hard for papers to inform the people about their government and what it is doing—though they have every right to know.

Late in 1965 Charles de Gaulle, as expected, won another seven-year term as president in a run-off election against Francois Mitterand, the Socialist-Radical-Communist candidate. After getting only 44 per cent of the vote in the December 5 election, De Gaulle won 55 per cent of the votes cast on December 19. But Jean Lecanuet, middle-of-the-road candidate who had run third on December 5, advised his followers not to vote either for De Gaulle or Mitterand but to abstain, and 4,500,000 followed his advice. Thus, De Gaulle won with only 45 per cent of the total electorate while 55 per cent showed their hostility toward him. During the campaign the controlled De Gaullist press supported him, but the rightist, centrist, and of course leftist papers opposed him while the independent *Le Monde* heaped scorn on his policies.

Now that he has the power, he probably will not be deterred from his efforts to wreck NATO, to intensify his antagonism to the United States, to force its withdrawal of troops from Europe, and to accelerate his attacks on American policy in Viet Nam. He may, however, have to reconsider withdrawing from the Common Market, for this would give the French economy a severe wrench and impose great hardship on French farmers. Even if he should withdraw, his West European neighbors have shown no readiness to follow him and are prepared to go ahead with or without De Gaulle and France.

French Papers Have a Character of Their Own

The press of any country reflects the tastes and interests of its readers; and, since French citizens are such individualists, it is natural to have a wide variety of newspapers. As William Stoneman of the Chicago *Daily News* has pointed out, "There is a paper for everybody from far left to far right, there are papers for those who want to be informed and spicy papers for those who just want the news in a pleasant package."

While the judgment of French editors about what is news is much like that of American editors, their handling of the news is different. There are no summary leads. The emphasis is on personalized writing, for the average reader is more interested in the writers' impressions of an event than in an ordered series of happenings. French reporters enjoy considerable latitude in writing a story, whether it be of a crime or a governmental development; and a large percentage of the content appears in the form of interpretive stories. Similarly, few papers have an editorial page, for the opinion function is delegated to staff experts or contributors who in signed articles express their own opinions. These contributors are often distinguished men of letters, respected authorities on foreign or national affairs, political scientists, historians, or economists. They develop strong followings, as do columnists in the United States; but they are not syndicated, for each paper has its own.

The great majority of the dailies are information papers. Few, except party organs, adopt a hard political line. For a relatively flourishing paper to do so might cause its readers to melt away, for so many Frenchmen are disillusioned with parties; less than 4 per cent belong to a party. This does not mean that papers do not criticize the government and its policies through their own opinion writers. The independent *Le Monde* never shirks comment on political matters;

rather it speaks in a straightforward, though reserved, manner. As for the rest of their content French papers carry sports, financial and stock-market reports, fashions, amusements, book, theater, and literary reviews as well as comic strips. They also carry good fiction in serial form and nonfiction including memoirs to a greater extent than is done in the United States.

Most French papers are standard-sized but run to fewer pages than do those in other countries. Generally they publish eight to ten pages although the larger information papers may run from sixteen to twenty-four. In an attempt to bolster declining circulations, *France Soir* and even the conservative *L'Aurore* have copied the sensational *Le Parisien Libéré* in presenting screaming front pages made up entirely of black heads and pictures with only direction lines to indicate where the stories are to be found inside.

The front page of a more typical information paper will play, in the top half, the heads for the major foreign, national, local, and sports stories with direction lines to their texts and below one or two signed opinion articles. This will be followed by a second page of local crime, accidents, provincial news, births, deaths, and other local briefs. Pages three and four are likely to be devoted to foreign news with the daily *roman* or serial story at the bottom of one. Page five is often a background-of-the-news page; then come three solid pages of advertising. Page nine would then be given to political, social, and economic news including a brief listing of stock market reports. This might be followed by another page of advertising and another of foreign news. Page twelve is then the sports page, thirteen a feature page, fourteen a woman's and cultural page. Now there follows an amusement page, including radio and TV programs; the back page contains late wire news. Everything is well organized so the reader can find what he wants. There are no dull pages; the reader is never bored, for French writers are well-informed, literate, and forceful and the news is interestingly presented. Although radio and television have become popular, most Frenchmen realize that these media are governmentally owned and operated; and the readers depend on their newspapers to give them as much of the straight facts as possible.

The French press is much improved over its pre-World War II character; there is none of the corruption which existed then. French newspapermen today are literate and well-informed, and their papers give readers a much more thorough and realistic picture of France and the world. Except for the few party organs, most papers are more objective and place their emphasis on news rather than opinion. They deserve better readership than they have; but because of the factors already cited, which have changed the reader habits of French people, newspapers sell only 21.2 copies per 100 persons, a ratio lower than that in nine other northern and middle European nations.

REPRESENTATIVE NEWSPAPERS

France Soir (Paris)—Largest mass circulation paper with 1,109,852. An afternoon paper started by dynamic Pierre Lazareff who spent war years in exile working on New York *Mirror*. Came back to try *Mirror* formula in Paris. As others outpaced it in sensation, it changed to formula of more news and features and complete impartiality in politics. Carries practically no opinion but provides good news coverage plus plenty of popular features, much sports, and a full page of comics.

Le Figaro (Paris)—Dean of French dailies. Became daily in 1866. Fled Paris when Germans came in, published for a time in free zone; hence, permitted to reappear after Liberation. A postwar success under able Pierre Brisson. Circulation 393,337. One of the best information papers in France; most influential, particularly with the upper middle class. Excellent foreign coverage and backgrounding.

Le Parisien Libéré—Second largest, a sensational mass-appeal paper with right-wing inclinations. Provides little real news, mostly crime, sex, and other sensation. Yet 733,236 pick it up daily for entertainment and vicarious thrills.

L'Aurore (Paris)—Born as a resistance paper, today fourth largest in capital with 368,763. Won out over others by making itself a good information paper. Rightist and strong supporter of De Gaulle.

Le Monde (Paris)—Founded in 1944 by six resistance editors from different parties who felt France should have a London *Times* type of paper to replace the discredited *Le Temps*. An afternoon semitabloid, the most serious paper in France, more interested in the meaning of the news than spot developments. Has 188,723 circulation.

L'Humanité (Paris)—Official voice of French Communist party. Well-madeup and illustrated but more sensational than it used to be. Selects its news to play up the glories of communism and the depravities of capitalism. Exalts U.S.S.R. even at expense of French nationalism. Continually crusading against U.S. imperialism. Had 147,164 circulation in 1964.

La Croix (Paris)—An afternoon daily with 112,489 circulation, the leading voice of the Catholic party. Provides general news coverage, shows little religious bias. Is far right politically and a strong supporter of De Gaulle.

Ouest France (Rennes)—Largest of French provincial papers, published at Rennes with 574,804. Distributes fifty-two editions through twelve departments. Dominates its area through intensive local and regional news coverage. But also provides good national and foreign coverage.

La Voix du Nord (Lille)—Another of the postwar successes, a strong provincial regional with 367,929 circulation. Dominates a large area in northern France.

The Cautious Austrian Press

Lovely little Austria, which attracts so many tourists and music lovers, does not, because of the serenity and *gemütlichkeit* of her people, reveal her tragic history. Not until one talks with her newspapermen does he become aware of her peculiar position between West and East, which has enforced on her press a special character.

Austria first appeared in history when she was conquered by the Romans in 15–14 B.C. Her Danube River became a boundary of the empire and Vindobona (now Vienna) an important fortified town. Germanic and Slavic tribes overran her till she was eventually conquered by the Frankish kings and under Charlemagne made part of the Holy Roman Empire. The Magyars, who swept over the land in the eighth century, were not driven back till 955, and it was not till 976 that the true birth of Austria was marked. For 270 years she grew in power. The Hapsburgs began their rule of the Austrian provinces in 1273, but the emperors dissipated their energies and those of their people in wars to hold the empire together. For the people the later middle ages were times of wretchedness and oppression.

Press Origins

The revival of learning sponsored by the Hapsburgs brought some extension of elementary education and cathedral schools of higher education leading to the founding of the University of Vienna in 1385. Handwritten newsletters were the initial precursors of the press. In 1480 a German printer set up the first press in Vienna to produce religious works. Other presses came, and in time printers found it profitable to issue single newssheets on special events. The first such *relation* describing the funeral of Frederick III appeared in 1493. For the next hundred years Austrian journalism consisted only of newssheets dealing with miracles, catastrophes, executions, coronations, and the wars with the Turks. Martin Luther's Reformation brought more *relationen* reflecting bitter controversy as Catholic rulers persecuted Protestant printers. Every publication had to be approved by authorities, and burning at the stake was prescribed for violators. From 1600 on a system of licensing limited to a few trusted families was introduced. Improvements in posts permitted weekly arrival of mail, and 1620 saw the first regular publication, *Ordinari Zeitung*. Three more *Ordinari Zeitungen* are known to have been published between 1620 and 1660, all strictly censored. They contained mostly news from abroad and court announcements. But *relationen* still appeared at times of special events. The big news of the period was the Thirty Years War during which Germany and Austria were ravaged and Austrian journalism suffered a sharp setback. In the end, because of censorship and the preference of the court for Italian, there remained only one weekly, printed in Italian. For native Austrians journalism went back to the handwritten newssheets of the previous century which alone could evade censorship.

Austria's First Daily

The Hapsburgs, step by step and war by war, had added to their holdings till Leopold I ruled much of the Danubian basin. Shortly after these victories had been confirmed by the Peace of 1699, the Ghelan family in 1703 launched in Vienna a twice-a-week paper called *Post-tagliche Mercurius*, which in 1714 became the first daily. Ten years later it was made the official organ of the government. As *Wiener Zeitung* it still exists as the official voice of the coalition governing Austria today.

Hapsburg rulers were absolute autocrats opposed to any press freedom. Hence, there arose in the reign of Maria Theresa weekly papers of a new type modeled after the English *Tatler* and *Spectator*, devoted to improving the morals of the people. They brought in their wake others concerned with literature, theater, and music, the safest subjects under an authoritarian regime.

A Brief Breath of Freedom

Joseph II, who came to the throne in 1780, was an enlightened ruler who put through many long needed reforms. He abolished serfdom and capital punishment, extended freedom of religion, removed discriminations against Jews, even nationalized the church and made it subservient to the state rather than the Pope. For the press his reign was a milestone, for in 1781 he abolished censorship and established press freedom. A number of new dailies appeared, but so long had the press been under the hard heel of censorship that it was hesitant to use its new liberty. Instead of assuming leadership in supporting worthwhile reforms, papers printed only such foreign news as might please the government and filled their columns with items of low entertainment and amusement. Joseph may have been disappointed with this press for in 1789 he imposed a tax per page as a means of holding down the number of "useless papers." Press freedom lasted only nine years. When Joseph died in 1790 his brother Leopold II, who succeeded him, renounced Joseph's more provocative reforms; and, since he feared his subjects might emulate the French Revolution, he reestablished censorship, particularly of news from France. As a brother of Marie Antoinette he joined with Frederick William of Prussia in declaring that the reestablishment of the monarchy and order in France was the concern of all European rulers.

Press Control Is Intensified

His son Francis II became Holy Roman Emperor in 1792 and was immediately involved in war with Napoleon. French Revolutionary armies took from him Belgium, the left bank of the Rhine, and part of his Italian states. It became apparent that the end of the Holy Roman Empire was near; and after 1806 he ruled only as Emperor of Austria, giving some semblance of unity to his dominions in Germany, Bohemia, Hungary, and Italy. At home he did nothing for education, nothing about reforms. His dread of revolutionary ideas led him to apply to freedom of thought a harsh prohibitive system. Censorship was intensified; political news was prohibited; the newspaper page tax was increased, making smaller papers necessary and putting many out of business. Those which survived were prohibited from being read in coffee houses to prevent any discussion of political affairs. Opponents of the regime had to go back to the clandestine publications of an earlier day.

Austrian armies, allied with England and Russia against Napoleon, were twice terribly defeated, and Austria lost valuable territory and millions of her subjects. During the Napoleonic occupation the Austrian press saw little change from its previous enslavement except that it now took orders from the French. *Wiener Zeitung* became the official organ of the French occupiers, and such other papers as were permitted had to be faithful copies of the Paris press. Once peace was signed, Francis II, now ruler of a much weakened state and almost ruined financially, named Prince Clemens von Metternich as his first minister. When Napoleon launched his war against Russia, Austria had to accept the position of a subordinate ally, but she did not take part in the expedition to Moscow. This war was unpopular with Austrians and, after Napoleon's disaster in Russia, Austria allied herself with the powers fighting Napoleon. Her great general, Schwartzenberg, as allied commander in chief, defeated Napoleon at Leipzig and led the campaign through France, capturing Paris. No Austrian fought at Waterloo, after Napoleon's escape from Elba, but as the result of Metternich's skillful playing of one power against the other, Austria came out of the Congress of Vienna with most of her former possessions intact except for Belgium and Holland. What is more, Metternich defeated the unification of the German states and instead created a Confederation of these states with Austria as its leader.

Metternich Muzzles Press

The Austrian press, which had assailed Napoleon and had been promised freedom after victory, never saw this promise fulfilled. Metternich was the leader of all the reactionaries who fought any tendencies toward liberalism or constitutional government. The assassination of a tsarist agent by a student in Germany provided the excuse for calling a Confederation Congress which passed the Karlsbad Resolutions muzzling the universities and the press in all Confederation states in order to suppress any revolutionary talk. Thereafter the Austrian press withered. The official *Wiener Zeitung* and a new government paper, *Oesterreichischer Beobachter,* were the only real newspapers left. Such other papers as appeared were reduced to insignificant sheets printing innocuous news and comment on literature, art, music, and fashion.

The discontent of the people of Europe with authoritarian rule had been mounting. The success of the 1848 revolution in France encouraged Metternich's opponents in Germany, Austria, and Italy; and on March 13 Vienna rose in revolt. Metternich fled to England, the parliament was summoned, censorship abolished, and a new liberal press law enacted. After 228 years of autocratic suppression, freedom had finally come to the Austrian press; and in a short time 206 papers, 90 of them dailies, appeared. The *Oesterreichischer Beobachter* was shut down forever and the *Wiener Zeitung* was taken over by the revolutionaries.

Most important of the new papers was *Die Presse,* founded in 1848 by August Zang. Inspired by the success of Emile Girardin with his *La Presse* in Paris, Zang too brought out a paper priced within the reach of the masses. He eschewed political comment but provided much news from at home and abroad. His growing circulation attracted advertisers till he broke the advertising monopoly of the *Wiener Zeitung.* It was Austria's best newspaper for years and did not falter until 1896.

Army Crushes 1848 Revolt

Metternich's fall had triggered revolts in Hungary, Bohemia, Italy, and Germany. But the separate states could not agree; and the Austrian army, still loyal to the emperor, vanquished one after the other, swept out their republican governments, and restored the former despotic rulers. Vienna was the revolutionary center where a convention was drafting a new constitution. These armies converged on the capital and by October 31 forced its capitulation, after which Prince Alfred Windischgrätz entered the city and took his terrible revenge. Among the many shot were the editors of "radical" newspapers. The revolution of 1848 was over.

A new absolutist government headed by Prince Schwartzenberg was set up and a harsh police system installed. Liberty of the press in everything concerning public affairs was stifled. Political life ceased and a period of intellectual torpor set in. For a time all papers except *Wiener Zeitung* were suppressed. Then in 1849 a new press law was proclaimed, requiring heavy deposits as a surety of good behavior from every publisher, instituting prepublication censorship of every issue, and establishing a warning system under which a first dereliction might bring only a reprimand but a second might bring punishment of the responsible persons or even suppression of the paper. An advertising tax was also imposed. Nevertheless, by carefully obeying orders, some of the better papers managed to survive. The ninety dailies of the revolution had by 1850 shrunk to twenty. For the next decade the Austrian press remained in chains.

In this period the new emperor Francis Joseph antagonised England, France, and Russia, and in a war with France and Italy, he was soundly defeated. The financial crisis which followed forced Francis to come to terms with his subjects. Provincial diets were revived, but he was still far from letting his people take a hand in government. He distrusted the press and in 1857 introduced a new stamp tax which seriously curtailed circulations. But the people were still unsatisfied; the Hungarians wanted nothing less than their constitution of 1848; the people of Austria, Germany, and other sections demanded constitutional rights. Step by step the emperor was forced to constitutionalism. Amendments to the press act were put into effect which eased restrictions against political news and comment, and this return to political journalism gave the press new vigor. The new press law of 1862 abolished censorship and ended the warning system and consequent punishments. This brought a sharp upturn, and by the end of 1862 there were 345 dailies, weeklies, and magazines, of which 109 were political.

Dual Monarchy Is Established

In 1866 Bismarck, who had become the strong man of Prussia, found an excuse in the haggling over settlement of the Schleswig-Holstein War to attack Austria and decisively defeated her in a three-weeks war. Austria now found she had lost what influence she had had in the German and Italian states, her army was demoralized, her finances ruined, and she was face to face with her discontented Slav and Magyar minorities. Since Hungary possessed too highly developed a national life to enter a centralized monarchy, a dual system, the Austro–Hungarian Empire, was established in 1869. Vienna was made the capital of the western provinces plus Bohemia, Galicia, and Dalmatia. Budapest became the capital of the eastern provinces including Hungary, Croatia, Slavonia, Transylvania, and Serbia. Both parts were given constitutional governments, parliaments of their own, and full control of internal affairs. Only defense and foreign affairs were left as the function of the empire.

The western part was given a liberal constitution recognizing the equality of all citizens, personal, religious, and political liberty. Non-Germans were assured their rights to their own language and schools. Freedom of press was reaffirmed, but in execution this was often nullified in Bohemia where Czech papers were harried when they grew too violent in behalf of their rights. In the eastern part a new liberal constitution was also adopted; but harsh laws were imposed on Rumanians, Serbians, and Slovaks. Though Magyar publications were freed from censorship, press laws enabled the government to hold in check the "incendiary publications" of Slavic minorities. Editors and political leaders of these minorities were often haled into court.

The years following 1869 were given to keeping the peace. Count Julius Andrássy, the great Hungarian leader who had become foreign minister of the empire in 1871, realized that friendship must be maintained with the new German empire which Bismarck had forged in 1870 and that Russia must be kept from going to war with Turkey, to protect the Slavs under the rule of the Porte. When the Russo-Turkish War of 1877–78 broke out anyway, he kept his country neutral despite the fire-eating Francis Joseph and his generals. At the Congress of Berlin, while Bulgaria was dismembered, both Turkey and Austria were given another generation of existence, not because of the strength of either, but because of British resolution, Russian weakness, and Bismarck's determination to avoid a general war.

These settlements made it possible for Austria-Hungry to enjoy the last quarter of the century in peace, stability, and growing prosperity. Compulsory education, introduced in 1869, meant a growing literacy to provide a broader base for press expansion. Increasing industrialization developed a middle and a labor class, out of which new parties came into existence, a fact which also contributed to press development.

More extensive news coverage was made possible by the development of a national news agency, started in 1855 under private ownership but taken over by the government in 1860 and operated as *Kaiserlich-Königliche Telegram Korrespondenz Buro* (known generally as K.K.K.). It exchanged news it gathered from Austria, Hungary, and the Balkans for world news dispatches from Reuters, Havas, and Wolff. For smaller dailies the agency provided most nonlocal news; but larger papers, while using it, relied more on their own foreign correspondents.

The Press Expands

The last quarter of the century cradled Austria's political party press. Foremost among the political groups was the Christian Socialist party, rising as a Roman Catholic movement among the middle and upper classes, later attracting farmers and businessmen. It was the forerunner of the Peoples party (*Volkspartie*), one of the two largest in Austria today. In the 1890's this party had six dailies with circulations of about 10,000 each. Most important was *Das Vaterland*, mouthpiece of the aristocracy, high clergy, and conservative elements. In 1893 the party brought out a more liberal paper, *Die Reichspost*, which soon became the leader and the mouthpiece of the government whenever this party was in power.

Second was the Social Democratic party, drawing its support first among industrial workers but later spreading its appeal to liberal elements in the whole population and developing strength equal to the Christian Socialists'. Its important papers included *Die Volkstribune*, *Der Strom*, and *Kampf*, followed in 1889 by *Arbeiter Zeitung*, today the leading voice of this party.

The German Nationals formed the third party, advocating closer cooperation with the new German empire. Its most important paper was *Deutsches Volksblatt*, established in 1888 as a radical anti-Semitic paper, but it deserted this line after 1898 to move closer to the Christian Socialist camp. While these were the leading Vienna party papers, the capitals of the provinces each had three or more papers representing different parties.

But the great papers of the period were not party organs. Foremost was *Die Neue Freie Presse*, founded in 1864 when the two chief editors of the old *Die Presse*, Theodor Friedlander and Michael

Ettienne, walked out with the best part of the *Die Presse* staff to start a new paper. They made it the best Austria had seen, with extensive foreign and national news, able commentary and backgrounding, thorough first class correspondents and leader writers. Its *feuilletons*, too, reached a new high through contributions of noted writers such as Speidel, Hofmannsthal, Herzl, Spitzer, Sweig, and Polgar. It set the pace for a cultural revival which was one of the marked contributions of the nonparty press in the period from 1900 to 1914 and became the leading paper of the empire, recognized as one of the best in Europe. In internal affairs its influence was strong. One Austrian high official said: "It is nearly impossible to govern against *Die Neue Freie Presse*." From a 30,000 circulation in 1900, it went to more than 100,000 in the next decade.

Second was *Neues Wiener Tagblatt*, founded in 1865; but it did not get the wind in its sails until it was taken over in 1872 by the Styermuhl Paper factory interests, who poured money into it to compete with *Neue Freie Presse*. It provided good news coverage and excellent cultural pages but remained a paper for the Viennese rather than the empire. Yet it outdistanced its competitor in circulation and became the advertising leader of the country.

The maverick among all papers was *Die Illustrierte Kronen Zeitung*, founded by Gustav Davis at the end of the century as a popular mass picture paper. It specialized in city news, particularly court reports of disreputable affairs, with direct quotations in Viennese slang. It promoted its circulations with prize contests and rose to 300,000, an incredible figure for Austrian journalism.

The new century opened peaceably. Austria enjoyed a breathing space in foreign affairs as Russia became involved in a disastrous war with Japan. Trouble came nearer home when Serbia broke away from Hapsburg control. Austria annexed Bosnia and Herzegovina to cut Serbia off from her Slav neighbors. The rabid anti-Austrian attacks in the Serbian press increased Austria's enmity, but she could do nothing when the Slav states in the Balkan wars of 1912 not only drove Turkey out of Europe but annexed the conquered territories. Serbia emerged as a leader of the south Slav peoples.

World War I Affects Press

By 1914 Austria-Hungary was almost forgotten by the great powers. But the assassination of Crown Prince Francis Ferdinand by a student in Sarajevo in Bosnia catapulted Austria into the limelight of international concern. Austria was sure Serbia was back of the assassination and sent her an ultimatum. The reply was conciliatory but Austria declared war. In so doing, she precipitated World War I, for in a few days Germany, Russia, France, and England had become belligerents.

The first effect on the press was a great increase in circulation as readers bought out every edition. The papers were filled with war news, and at first it was all victory. Under the war emergency the government became a military dictatorship, and its strict censorship kept papers from telling all that was happening. But major defeats could not be hidden as the Serbians drove back the invading Austrian army and the main Austrian army was defeated by the Russians in Galicia. In Italy, too, the Austrians failed, and the Germans had to bolster their line. By the end of 1915 Austria had become a mere satellite of Germany.

At first some papers tried to blame defeats on Germany's failure to assist her ally, but this excuse disappeared as Austria realized her complete dependence on Germany. The drain of war costs and loss of export trade brought a financial crisis. Newspapers loyally supported government drives for subscriptions to war loans. Food became so scarce that a near famine developed. The shortage of newsprint affected all papers, and they had to cut down on page sizes and editions. Younger newspapermen, too, were being drained off to the front, leaving older men to put out the papers.

Discontent was growing in the empire's Hungarian, Bohemian, and Slav territories as these peoples began demanding their independence. In 1918, after the failure of Ludendorf's last drive on Paris, the tide turned rapidly against the Germans; and at the end of September Germany and Austria appealed to President Wilson for an armistice. In October Austria suffered her last great defeat on the Italian front and lost 500,000 prisoners. She surrendered on November 3. The new Czech republic had already been proclaimed as had the new Yugoslav and Hungarian states. The Austro–Hungarian Empire was no more. Everything was stripped away by the peace settlement but the German provinces in Austria and a small strip on the Hungarian border. In all, 43,000,000 of the empire's former citizens were lost, and Austria was left with only 7,000,000 in an area of but 32,000 square miles.

Postwar Problems

Revolutionary disturbances in Vienna and news of the German revolution forced the postwar state council to make Austria a democratic republic. The first elections brought a coalition government headed by the Socialists. Establishment of a Soviet republic in Hungary made Communism the great threat. But Socialists staked everything on resistance to Bolshevism, and by mid-1919 Communism had been checked.

Austrian papers first reacted to peace settlements with consternation and resentment. The desperate food, fuel, financial, and unemployment situation led Socialist papers to favor union with Germany; but Christian Socialists were opposed and the Allies would have none of it. In their despair several provinces tried to claim complete independence, and the government had to make wide concessions to federalism. This tended to make provincial papers of importance. The great prewar paper, *Die Neue Freie Presse,* which had previously covered the empire and Europe, now lost much of its circulation and faced great financial difficulties. Even *Neues Wiener Tagblatt,* in the face of Austria's extreme poverty, found its advertising income greatly reduced.

Industry was almost at a standstill and workers were hard hit. Even the large middle class was reduced to pauperism. Vienna, robbed of her agricultural hinterland, was like a head without a body. People scoured the countryside, trying to hawk anything portable for a loaf of bread or a pint of milk. The government attempted to care for its thousands of refugees and to support its unemployed on doles but also resorted to printing money which only aggravated its problems. The 1920 election turned against the Social Democrats and the Christian Socialists took power. Internal strife dominated the country for the next decade. While the ruling party was strong among farmers, business people, the former imperial class, army officers, and bureaucrats, the Social Democrats had an unshakable majority among workers. The urban middle class, hostile to both workers and farmers, became rightist German Nationalists, and the Christian Socialists had to make a coalition with them. The German party under the leadership of Prince Ernst von Stahremberg developed a private army, the *Heimwehr,* while the Social Democrats formed their *Schutzbund;* and there were continuous clashes between the two.

The press reflected these differences. By the mid-twenties Vienna had twenty-five dailies taking violent sides in the nation's controversies. Provincial dailies showed the same partisanship, and each provincial capital had several. Most circulations were small; the exceptions were the popular tabloids. To reach the masses the Social Democrats in 1928 established *Das Kleine Blatt,* and in 1929 the Christian Socialists brought out *Das Kleine Volksblatt.*

Meanwhile the ruling coalition had begun rehabilitation. Ignatz Seipel, a Catholic priest, was made chancellor in 1922 and obtained a substantial loan from the League of Nations; a new national bank was organized and the currency stabilized. Retrenchments were put into effect, and some 80,000 former empire bureaucrats were pensioned off. Taxes were increased, foreign capital began to be attracted, and some factory wheels started turning again. By 1924 the budget was balanced and a feeling of stability had set in.

Government Moves to Control Press

But Seipel found working under a republic too slow. In 1927 in clashes between *Heimwehr* and *Schutzbund* fighters, an old man and a child were killed. When those arrested were acquitted, there were mass demonstrations in Vienna. Seipel ordered the police to fire on the crowds and eighty-four were killed. Social Democrats answered with a general strike which was quickly put down. Christian Socialists now began an offensive against the Social Democrats and their papers. In 1929, when constitutional amendments were adopted enabling Seipel to govern by decree, the end of Austrian democracy was in sight. The government now moved to control the news. The former imperial news agency was renamed *Amtliche Nachrichtenstelle*, and through it the government could see that only the right news went to the papers. Radio, too, was under the control of the government.

The world depression hit Austria harder than many other countries. The Creditanstalt, largest Austrian bank, collapsed; trade and industry stagnated. When Austria tried to improve her trade through a customs union with Germany, France blocked it. Seipel deepened the crisis by resigning and as conditions grew worse the people began listening to extremists. In the 1932 elections the Christian Socialists, headed by Engelbert Dollfuss, won with the support of the Nazis. Soon Dollfuss dismissed parliament and began governing by decree. By 1933 Hitler's propaganda began flooding Austria; and the people responded eagerly, for many had long wanted union with Germany. Dollfuss, regarding Social Democrats as his chief enemy, began to persecute them in earnest. They fought back, but in February, 1934, after a four-day revolution, they were defeated; their party was declared illegal and driven underground.

All Social Democratic papers were closed. Oskar Pollak, editor of *Arbeiter Zeitung*, who had fought Engelbert Dollfuss with great courage, had to flee to Czechoslovakia. But no authoritarian regime can continue without complete control of the press. Licensing was reintroduced, and papers began to have entire issues confiscated if their handling of the news seemed out of line. Once suspect, they had to submit to precensorship, and they might have their postal rates raised or their street sales prohibited or be worried out of existence. Those which continued to publish did so under a tight government bridle. The leading dailies were now the official *Wiener Zeitung, Reichspost,* and the new extreme rightist *Wiener Neueste Nachrichten.*

Dollfuss, fearing German Nazism might endanger his own dictatorship now decided on an independent course. The Austrian Nazi party was dissolved, Nazi leaders in the government dismissed, and even *Wiener Neueste Nachrichten* curbed. Austria's Nazis tried a take-over and murdered Dollfuss, but quick government action ended this revolt; what had been planned as another Hitler bloodless victory misfired. Kurt von Schusnig, who succeeded Dollfuss, continued the dictatorship and after October, 1935, with Prince Stahremberg as his right-hand man, Austria became a hard police state.

Nevertheless, illegal papers managed to come out. From Brunn in Czechoslovakia Pollak contrived to smuggle in a miniature *Arbeiter Zeitung*. The Communists too had their *Rote Fahne*, and other dissident groups often flooded Vienna with leaflets. Schusnig tried to hold out against Hitler; but when he called for a plebiscite to decide on Austria's "independence," Hitler dared wait no longer. German troops invaded and on March 13, 1938, Hitler proclaimed the union of Austria and Germany.

Hitler Takes Over the Press

Hitler's "coordination" of Austria was rapid and thorough. Austria's press was liquidated, and from 1938 to 1945 Austrians had no papers of their own. Papers appearing under their old titles were now put out by Nazis. *Die Reichspost* was a principal organ. Hitler's *Volkischer Beobachter* flew in a Vienna edition. The famed old *Neue Freie Presse* and *Neues Wiener Tagblatt* were now consolidated into another Nazi mouthpiece. The four popular tabloids were merged into one *Kleine Kriegs Zeitung*, and the old pro-Nazi *Neueste Nachrichten* earned a berth in the hierarchy as the leading Nazi evening paper. The Austrian news agency was incorporated into the German agency, DNB, and all radio stations were made part of the German broadcasting network. Austrian papers were completely regimented and could tell the people only what the Germans wanted them to know.

Underground papers were, however, produced and distributed at the risk of life, for the Nazis proceeded to rout out dissidents with violence. Jews, Socialists, Freemasons, and old Hapsburg legitimatists bore the brunt of this persecution. Papers and plants owned by Jews were confiscated. By July 1938 some 7,000 Jews had committed suicide to escape Nazi cruelties. In addition to the appalling number of Jews killed by storm troopers, some 40,000 were sent to Dachau and Buchenwald from where their families received bills for the cremation of their loved ones. In this Jewish liquidation the Nazis dealt Austria and its press a severe blow, for Jewish intellectuals had been in the forefront of the cultural heyday in the prewar Austrian press and numbered some of its most talented journalists. The hell of the Nazi years will be long remembered by the Austrian newspapermen who lived through them. As the war became more difficult newsprint shortage curtailed the size and number of Nazi publications. Toward the end some papers were only single sheets.

Under Four-Power Occupation

Austrians fought in German armies, but since Austria was now part of Germany she was practically a forgotten country. By 1943, however, the Allies decided to work for a free, democratic Austria with her prewar boundaries; hence, in the peace negotiations after German defeat, Austria was treated as a liberated country. A great part of the land was liberated by the Red army by late April, 1945. A provisional government headed by Dr. Karl Renner, a Social Democrat, was set up with Socialists, Christian Socialists, and Communists in almost equal number. Thus the second Austrian Republic was born.

The expected early signing of the peace treaty was delayed for ten years, partly by the Allied deadlock on what should be done with Germany, but more by Russian insistence on collecting reparations. They requisitioned oil refineries, river transport, factories, farm equipment, livestock, even food and clothing. The country was divided into four Allied occupation zones, the largest one Russian, including most of Vienna; a smaller center of this city was put under four-power occupation. An Allied Control Council representing Britain, France, the United States, and Russia exercised joint administration of the country.

Austria was hardly free and independent although the first election returned a national assembly of moderates, with only four Communists. The new republic faced grave problems, for the food situation was desperate. Even with Allied aid this was still one of the worst fed countries in Europe. Housing was short; in Vienna alone 100,000 apartments had been destroyed, and there were hundreds of thousands of displaced persons to care for. For every fifteen Austrians there was one Russian soldier to be fed. Thirty-five per cent of the national budget had to go for occupation costs. All these factors left the Austrians completely frustrated.

A New Press Is Born

Since all Nazi publications had been closed, occupying forces started providing papers in German to give the people the news they had been denied and to channel military government proclamations. In the

American Zone, for example, when the psychological warfare branch of the Anglo-American 15th army entered Linz, it took over available printing plants and had *Oberösterreichischer Nachrichten* rolling by June 8, 1945, as a two-page paper selling for two cents. Its sales had to be held to 200,000 because of paper shortage. In their Vienna zone they launched the evening *Kurier* with heavy emphasis on straight news; soon it completely overshadowed its Communist competitor, *Der Abend.* In the British Vienna zone *Weltpresse* gained popularity, and in the Russian Vienna zone *Österreichische Volkstimme* appeared.

In October, 1945, when the four powers agreed to issue Austrians licenses to publish their own papers and to permit party papers, a number of nonparty organs were allowed to begin operating. But only six party papers were licensed in Vienna and three in each province. In Vienna Oskar Pollak, who had been in exile in London, reestablished the famed Socialist *Arbeiter Zeitung.* The Peoples party, successor to the old Christian Socialists, had *Das Kleine Volksblatt* and *Neue Wiener Tageszeitung.* The Communists had *Volkstimme* and *Der Abend.* A new coalition organ representing the two major parties in power was named *Neues Österreich.* One of the renowned old titles, *Die Presse,* was revived as a serious independent paper. Occupation army papers continued, and the Soviet forces added *Österreichische Zeitung.* Vienna had eleven dailies; and *Arbeiter Zeitung* led all others with 287,000 circulation, followed by *Kleine Volksblatt* with 190,000, *Kurier* with 187,000, and *Weltpresse* with 150,000.

In the provinces, despite the appearance of party organs, independent information papers quickly came to the fore. Thus in Linz *Oberösterreichischer Nachrichten* by 1947 had a sales total of 200,000 compared to 40,000 for its nearest rival. Its able editor, Hans Behrman, stood above parties and fought for what he thought was good for the country. In Salzburg, likewise, the *Salzburger Nachrichten* made itself one of the most independent papers in Austria and with 100,000 circulation, far outdistanced its political rivals.

In 1948 there were thirty-three dailies, eleven in Vienna and twenty-two in the provinces. Total circulations were 2,275,000, more than one copy per family. Because of paper shortages most papers had only four pages weekdays, eight to ten on weekends.

Occupation Press Problems

While the British and Americans took over their own occupation costs and removed censorship in their zones, the Russians remained as oppressive as ever. Not only did they maintain censorship but confiscated issues from other areas when distributors crossed into their zone. Russian kidnappings, looting, acts of violence, interference with the transport of goods from one part of Austria to the other, imposition of new taxes to pay occupation costs (of which the Russians took 70 per cent), and exorbitant demands for two-thirds of Austria's oil output for fifty years and 30 per cent of her depleted rolling stock, so embittered the people that they eagerly bought any paper which criticized the Russians. Oskar Pollak in his *Arbeiter Zeitung* was Russia's particular gadfly, and his circulation zoomed. Massive aid from UNRRA (United Nations Relief and Rehabilitation Administration) and the United States under the Marshall Plan helped restore the economy till by 1950 industrial production had risen to 109 per cent of the 1937 figure. Austrians came to feel that the western allies were sincerely trying to be of help and that only the Russians were exploiting them.

The death of Stalin brought changes. Soviet zonal frontier controls were lifted, censorship was ended, and Russians agreed to pay their own occupation costs. Then on May 15, 1955, the peace treaty was finally signed, providing for a sovereign and democratic Austria with her 1938 frontiers. She pledged herself to perpetual neutrality, and by October all occupation troops had been withdrawn.

In May, 1965, when Austria celebrated the tenth anniversary of her freedom, highest honors were accorded to Leopold Figli who, as premier from 1945 to 1953 and then as foreign minister, had been most responsible for persuading the Russians to agree to Austria's independence.

Independence at Last

Now Austria was free and on her own for the first time in eighteen years. There were enthusiastic celebrations all over the country. But the years of darkness had forged a new kind of Austria. Once she had known greatness as a major European power; now her people were content with their much smaller place in the sun, recognizing it merely as their home to which they were attached by a deep patriotism born out of years of repression, hardship, and sacrifice. And the years of struggle for survival had impressed upon them a deeper appreciation of what their liberties meant. In the last ten years Austria had literally built strength through opposition to the Communist threat.

The new state headed by Theodor Korner, Socialist, as president and Julius Raab, Peoples party, as chancellor started out on a constantly improving economy. Although American aid had ceased, foreign trade had grown till Austria was a creditor nation. Income from tourism set new records; industry expanded. The two leading parties,

In 1915 British newspaper publisher Alfred Harmsworth dared attack Kitchener's conduct of the war. His *Daily Mail* was burned, banned, took circulation and advertising losses, but turned the tide of the war.

Powerful Labor editor Hjalmar Branting, who was thric
premier of Sweden after World War I.

Torgny Segerstedt, whose Göteborg
paper suffered many confiscations for
its courageous attacks on Hitler.

C. G. Tengwall made his conservative *Svenska
Dagbladet* one of the most newsworthy in
Sweden.

Through his *Aftonbladet*, Lars Hierta set
the Swedish press on the path to becoming
an invincible power in his country.

Paul Usteri, dauntless fighter for reform and press freedom. He was an early editor of *Neue Zürcher Zeitung*.

When the Nazis took over Austria, Oskar Pollak, courageous editor of *Arbeiter Zeitung*, had to flee for his life.

Manuel de Fraga Iribane, Spanish Minister of Information, who has brought a breath of freedom to his country's press.

George Vlachos founded *Kathimerini* and made it one of the largest and best papers in Greece.

Count Camillo Cavour, *Risorgiment*
editor and a prime figure in the unif
cation of Italy.

Pierre Brisson made *Figaro* one of France's most influential newspapers and a great postwar success.

Luigi Albertini made *Corriere della Sera*
one of the best newspapers in Europe
until he was forced out by Mussolini.

Victor Jourdain, whose underground paper *L*
Libre Belgique was a leader of Belgian resistanc
in World War I.

Christian Gulmann, who transformed *Berlingske Tidende* with great news coverage and a literary touch.

In *Politiken*, Henrik Cavling developed Denmark's first approach to modernization of its press.

Eljas Erkko, freedom fighter and diplomat, made *Helsingin Sanomat* the best newspaper in Finland.

Viggo Horup, brilliant editor of the reform-minded *Politiken*, became a leader of Danish public opinion.

LA LIBRE BELGIQUE

CHAGRIN D'AMOUR

Front page of *La Libre Belgique*, showing German commandant with heap of arrest warrants for staff men of this paper which he never was able to stop.

NOUVELLES ORDINAIRES DE divers endroicts, du 17. Juillet 1631.

Num. 27.

Front page of *Nouvelles Ordinaires*, first weekly newspaper in France, brought out in 1631 by Jean Martin and Luis Vendosme.

Pravda on the day Khrushchev surrendered to Kennedy on Cuba so quickly that the front page was still full of anti-U.S. diatribes and it did not get to "Peace and Justice" until page two.

Historic front page of Hitler's *Völkischer Beobachter*, calling for vote to support his "New Reich" and listing his program, including war on the Socialists and Communists.

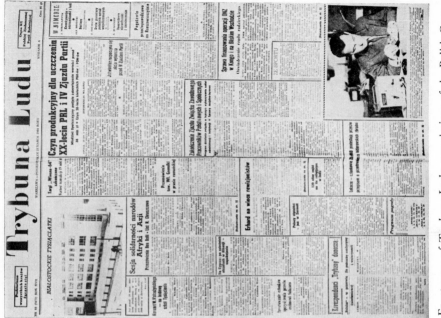

Front page of *Trybuna Ludu*, mouthpiece of the Polish Communist government.

Front page of *Borba*, chief voice of the Communist party of Yugoslavia.

which in earlier years had fought each other bitterly, decided to govern in coalition to prevent their former prewar antagonism and instability.

There were also changes in the press. The Red papers had gone with the withdrawal of Russian troops. *Weltpresse* disappeared after 1957. Fritz Molden, director of *Die Presse*, started *Express* in 1957 as a popular picture paper to balance his more serious journal. The old *Illustrierte Kronen Zeitung* had been revived in 1949 and quickly drew readers. *Kurier*, acquired from American occupation forces by a Viennese industrialist, was made an independent paper, devoting itself to good news coverage; and it quickly outgained all others in circulation. One great improvement was the development of a new press agency, *Österreichische Presse Agentur*, as an independent cooperative, owned by the newspapers, and receiving its income from assessments against papers according to their circulations. It developed exchange agreements with thirteen foreign agencies but obtained the bulk of its world news from Reuters, France-Presse, and Associated Press; and it put out a straight, impartial news service.

The coalition continued to rule, but understanding between the two parties deteriorated. Raab resigned as chancellor and in 1961 was succeeded by Alfons Gorbach of the Peoples party. Inflation brought strikes from workers who won wage increases, thus adding to living costs and the price of Austrian goods abroad. By 1963 Austria had a trade deficit which inspired Socialist charges of mismanagement. The great argument came over the European Economic Community, more often called the Common Market. Austria had joined EFTA, but much more of her trade was with EEC, and the Peoples party favored joining the latter. The Socialists fought that proposal on the ground that the supranational implications of the Common Market might endanger Austrian neutrality. Party papers became more shrill. The people grew impatient with this party fight, and the independent papers showed great strength in rallying the people against the coalition and its monopoly and misuse of power.

By February, 1964, relations between the two major parties had worn so thin that Gorbach resigned and was succeeded by Joseph Klaus. While he was chairman of the Peoples party, Klaus proved to be a different type of leader, intent on giving Austria's provinces the same kind of rights as are enjoyed by American states. The 1955 peace treaty granting Austrian independence had forbidden any overt preference for either the east or the west, hence his open declaration of friendship for the United States showed courage. He entered into negotiations with the Common Market despite Russian opposition.

The press, however, has to maintain caution. Vienna is but thirty miles in one direction and forty miles in another from Hungary and Czechoslovakia. Because of Austria's geographical position between the West to which it strongly leans and the hostile and suspicious East, the press sometimes must walk on egg shells. It may evidence brisk internal disagreement, but this must always stay within the bounds of preserving national unity. Newspapers played a significant part in opposing the extension of Communism in Austria, but they must be wary in order not to antagonize the eastern neighbors. Austria's prosperity expanded in 1964; and although there was a gap between exports and imports, this was more than made up by increased tourist receipts.

Notwithstanding this economic improvement, total daily circulations, which had declined to a low of 1,226,000 in 1957, had in 1964 moved up to only 1,517,000. For a population of 7,172,000 this represented a distribution of but 21.1 copies per 100 persons, the lowest index of reader interest in all the nations of northern and middle Europe. This may be due to the fact that the government coalition, dominated as it is by two almost equally strong parties determined to avoid disagreement or dissension, has led many readers to conclude that there is not much use in getting excited about matters which they can do little to affect. Thus, Austrians have become indifferent to their press. It is interesting also that the ownership of radio sets has risen to 2,040,240 and television sets to 397,000. Together these two media have more than 900,000 more outlets than all the daily papers, which may indicate that they have become more important providers of news and entertainment.

In late 1965 the two coalition parties split over defense spending. Socialists attacked the Peoples party defense minister for using his entire budget to buy thirty-six Oerlikon antiaircraft guns with a maximum range of 12,000 feet—over which even a Piper Cub could fly. Socialist papers maintained that the cost of one Oerlikon would have paid for many badly needed workers' apartments. This split may bring a heated campaign in the next election, give impetus to the press, and rouse the people from their former apathy toward it.

The Press Today

Austria in 1964 reported twenty-nine dailies, ten in Vienna and nineteen in the provinces. In addition there were 154 nondaily papers, most of them weeklies serving smaller towns. The fact that most dailies do not publish on Monday has permitted the development of the "Monday only" papers which look like dailies but have livelier makeup and provide some general news in brief, while devoting much of their content to weekend sports, features, and entertainment. Largest of these are *Welt am Montag*, published in Vienna with branches in other cities and having a circulation of 170,000, *Wiener Montag* with 150,000, and *Grazer Montag* with 49,000.

In its report for UNESCO's 1964 edition of World Communications, Austria claimed thirty-eight dailies, but twelve are branch editions of the *hauptzeitungen* (head papers) with a page or so of local news, the rest the same as the parent papers. Of the twenty-six dailies, fourteen are party papers, eleven are independent, and one is a government gazette. With the exceptions of the excellent *Salzburger Nachrichten* and *Oberoesterreichische Nachrichten* at Linz, the papers outside the capital are apt to be provincial.

Yet a number of Vienna newspaper men agree that there are too many papers and that the press is too political. They point out that Vienna, with a population of 1,634,000, is too small to support ten dailies. They also speak of the declining circulation of party papers. Thus *Arbeiter Zeitung*, which once led all others with 246,000, was down in 1964 to 108,500; *Das Kleine Volksblatt*, of the Peoples party, which had boasted 193,000, had fallen to 113,000; and *Volkstimme*, the Communist organ, formerly with 105,000 circulation, was down to a claimed 40,000, probably much less.

By contrast independent papers have done much better. *Kurier*, devoting itself to good news coverage, leads all Austrian dailies with 273,000 daily and 324,000 Sundays. The popular boulevard-type *Express*, also independent, is second with 250,000. A similar development has taken place in the provinces. For the whole country the eleven independent papers had in 1964 a total circulation of 1,008,300 as compared with 432,500 for the fourteen party papers.

An indication of the power of the independents came in the summer of 1964 when, disgusted over poor radio programing and the overuse of radio time for political propaganda by the major parties controlling Austrian Broadcasting Ltd., forty-four daily and weekly papers, all independents, joined in a campaign calling on readers to send in forms asking a plebiscite, as provided in the constitution, to permit a direct vote of the people on the radio problem on which the coalition had failed to take action. Seven times as many forms poured in as were needed to ensure the plebiscite. Some Vienna observers saw in this unexpected success the possibility that the independents who have promised to help the people free themselves of the present party machinery may come to represent an important third force in the life of the nation.

One adverse factor for the press is that it has not shared the prosperity resulting from Austria's boom because it has not developed advertising. There is little retail advertising; rather most of it is classified or the advertisements of Austrian and foreign manufacturers. No single paper covers the whole country though it is smaller than Maryland. Many dailies carry little advertising in the fore part of the week but make up for it in their big weekend editions, for advertisers feel that this is the one time when readers have leisure to go through the paper. With the exception of the larger independents, most papers have to rely on circulation for more than 75 per cent of their income and on advertising for 25 per cent or less. Party papers with their declining circulations might have been in a precarious position except for their party subsidies. But some independents also have had help from industries or businessmen.

When one looks at other western European nations, one is struck by the fact that Austria, in proportion to her population, has fewer daily papers and lower total daily circulation than most other nations, despite the fact that her literacy rate is 98 per cent. One has only to drop into any coffee shop or *bierstube* to find part of the answer, for here Austrians, over their coffee or beer, can read a number of papers. A recent survey showed that 85 per cent of Austrian adults do read their dailies regularly, many two or three a day, but they give their papers only a half hour; thirty minutes divided between two or three papers means quick skimming. In this survey Austrians rated human interest stories first and editorials lowest.

What Are Austrian Papers Like?

Americans would find Austrian papers quite different from their own. None have standard-sized pages; most are semitabloid, made up in four or five wide columns. *Volksblatt* and *Kronen Zeitung* are really diminutive tabloids. Larger papers run twelve to sixteen pages daily, more on weekends. In makeup they range all the way from the flashy *Express* with its red and black heads to the very attractive *Die Presse* with its neat Bodoni heads. Most are well-illustrated; several carry daily picture pages. Content is well-departmentalized, starting with the top foreign and national news, followed by more wire news, local and regional news, feature and cultural pages, business and sports items. Seldom are there editorials as such. Party papers get their opinion across by presenting the news from their viewpoint, more often through special articles analyzing a particular development, sometimes through *kroniks* contributed by recognized writers and authorities. Only a few papers carry comic strips, but almost all present a daily serial story. Weekend editions carry much more cultural material, articles backgrounding the news, and feature matter.

The Austrian press in its long history has had only short periods of liberty. It did not get its present freedom till 1955, yet it is still possible for issues to be confiscated for attacking government ministers or policies. Even though it must be cautious in its relations with its eastern neighbors, the press is often courageously anti-Communist. When asked about this, one Austrian editor said: "Oh yes, we know that if the Red army should march into Austria we would probably be the first to be hung from the lampposts, but after the Russian occupation we know what Red rule would do to our liberties; hence we must keep our people continuously alert to the dangers of Communism."

REPRESENTATIVE PAPERS

Kurier—Largest circulation, independent, good coverage of foreign, Austrian, and Viennese news, sports, cultural material. Acquired by Dr. Ludwig Polster from U.S. occupation forces. From three ruined family mills he built an industrial empire. Made fortune out of Cosmopol, leading film company. Found his greatest challenge in *Kurier*. Circulation 273,000.

Arbeiter Zeitung—Socialist organ and a good paper. Frequently excellent background articles. Strongly anti-Communist; pro-western but sometimes critical of U.S. Recently shaken up to make it more popular. Circulation 108,500.

Das Kleine Volksblatt—Diminutive-sized morning tabloid. Peoples party organ, appeals to conservative classes and many farmers. Circulation 113,000.

Neues Oesterreich—A good factual paper; strong on national news, economics; special appeal to women; independent of any party. Circulation 62,000.

Die Presse—Independent, best-informed on international news through able corps of foreign correspondents. Less concerned with local news; strong on financial and business news. Appeals primarily to intellectuals, businessmen, and upper middle classes. Circulation 52,300.

Salzburger Nachrichten—Best of provincial papers and one of best in country. Independent politically and financially. Covers provincial news well but provides excellent foreign coverage and backgrounding of international and Austrian questions. Circulation 37,000.

The Newspapers of Switzerland

Beautiful Switzerland, which each year lures thousands of tourists, is one of Europe's oldest newspaper lands. Mountains constitute 70 per cent of its area; and they have shaped the character of the people and the press, for the Swiss are as ruggedly independent as their peaks. Mountains furthermore divide the country into hundreds of compartments, each with its own papers. Hence this nation of 6,030,000 has a remarkable number of papers for its size. Its press is unusual, too, because it is so multilingual. Most of the people living in the east and center, closest to Germany and Austria, speak a form of German known as "Schweizer Deutsch"; the inhabitants of the western cantons nearest France use French; and those in the southern cantons, toward the Italian border, speak Italian. Over in the eastern Alps live descendants of the Rhaeto-Romans where older people still speak Romansh, an old Romance language akin to Latin.

The Swiss first appear in history as the Helvetii, whom Julius Caesar conquered in 58 B.C., and who for two hundred years were under Roman rule. But their frontier position made them among the first to be overrun by barbarians—the Allamanni, Ostrogoths, Burgundians, and finally the Franks who ruled them for three hundred years till they became a part of the Holy Roman Empire under Charlemagne. After his death feudal lords ruled sections of the country until the Hapsburgs became dominant. In time some of the larger cities and forest cantons won charters of freedom under the empire, but when the Hapsburgs encroached on their liberties these intrepid mountaineers began a rebellion which lasted two hundred years till eventually in the Peace of Basle in 1499 the practical independence of the Swiss Federation was recognized.

First Printers and Flysheets

Toward the end of this fight for independence, the printing press first arrived in Switzerland when Berthold Ruppel, who had worked with Gutenberg, set up the first Swiss press at the University of Basle in 1463. By 1483 there were presses operating in Geneva and Lausanne and soon in other Swiss cities. Their first products were religious and classical works, but in time they began issuing pamphlets and news-sheets. There had been handwritten newsletters before this. The Central Library at Zurich has a collection of some 900 printed news-sheets which appeared between 1560 and 1587, without regularity. Like the flysheets in other countries, they often dealt with battles, crimes, marvels of the world, abnormalities in nature, and sensations calculated to appeal to the public.

The sixteenth century opened with Switzerland considered a power in Europe because of her military prowess. Other states sought alliances to obtain help from Swiss mercenary troops. A loose federation developed into a strong federal government. Industry grew and increased trade brought wealth. The University of Basle gained renown throughout Europe; art, drama, and literature began to flourish. Life was good except for two things. First, there was strong reaction against the Church, dominated by a corrupt clergy, which had brought moral decay in contrast with new Swiss views of living. Second, there was growing resentment over the oppression of the peasants and the domination of the government by a wealthy class of mercenary officers who had benefited greatly from foreign pay.

The first great leader of the Swiss reformation was Ulrich Zwingli, a Catholic priest who began preaching a gospel of Christ and salvation by faith rather than ritual. He attacked the Papacy, the Mass, fasts, monastic orders, the priesthood, indulgences, and penances. He also assailed other social ills such as the hire of mercenaries. Despite Church opposition much of Catholic Switzerland soon cast off Papal and priestly domination.

Meanwhile the Protestant Reformation started by Martin Luther in Germany had found a champion in John Calvin in Geneva. To bring moral reform, he laid down a rigid system under which all luxuries, such as jewelry, all amusements including card playing, dancing, and gambling, were forbidden. Cursing, intemperance, vice, betrothing one's daughter to a Catholic, were made major offenses. Heresy was punishable by death. Yet Calvin did help to arrest Swiss moral decadence. Calvinism spread to France, Holland, and Scotland and made its way to the New World in the Puritanism of early settlers.

It was inevitable that these movements should clash. A Counter-Reformation led by Catholics brought civil wars in which Catholic forest cantons fought Protestant city cantons. Through this period of dissension, printing presses were active on both sides, pouring out floods of pamphlets, books, and propaganda sheets in a violent battle of creeds. The Swiss Federation came near to disintegration. It was not until the mid-sixteenth century that a compromise was reached which permitted each faith freedom in its own territories.

First Regular Newspapers

Despite these civil wars Switzerland's first regular newspaper, *Ordinari Zeitung*, appeared at Basle in 1610 as a weekly. It had the distinction of being the first regular newspaper published beyond the Alps and the third regular newspaper to appear in Europe. But authorities were not yet ready for a free press. Within a year the paper was suspended and the printer thrown into prison for commenting unfavorably on the government. In time, however, other weeklies were started. In 1633 *Wochenliche Ordinari* and *Extraordinari Zeitung* appeared in Zurich, and soon others were established in Berne and Schaffhausen. The first paper printed in French did not come till 1634 when *Le Mercure Suisse* was founded in Geneva.

Peace had not yet come to the Swiss, for in 1618 they became involved in the Thirty Years War, which began as a conflict between Catholics and Protestants and broadened into a series of political and dynastic wars embracing much of Europe. Unlike Germany, which was the chief battleground, Switzerland was not directly involved, though her mercenary armies fought on both sides and the Rhaetian cantons suffered thirty years of dreadful internecine warfare. As a result the first newspapers in Romansh and Italian did not appear until the eighteenth century. The 1648 Peace of Westphalia gave the Swiss Federation formal recognition of its independence. In the period of peace which followed, newspapers again raised their heads. But the oligarchy of wealthy families who dominated the government would permit no press freedom and for the next fifty years newspapers had to be gazettes and advertising sheets devoted only to public notices and small advertising.

The Swiss had prospered during the wars; but during peace, farmers found themselves hard up, and they resented the feudal tithes and taxes imposed by their oligarchic overlords. Two peasant revolts were put down; and in the end the Catholic nobles, in complete control, set up absolutist governments in every canton. They proceeded to stifle the press, permitting only their own official voices. Such papers as continued had to find safety in cultural discussion; toward the end of the century literary magazines modeled on English, French, and German lines bloomed and fostered a golden literary age.

The eighteenth century brought a remarkable economical and intellectual development. Growing industry and improved agriculture created wealth in the country. The population of many places doubled. The intelligentsia were filled with a great zeal for the education of the masses. They started periodicals for the people's instruction, to which historians, scientists, educators, philosophers, and essayists contributed. Printing offices were kept occupied in satisfying this intellectual craving. It was in this period that the oldest existing Swiss newspapers were founded, *Feuille d'Avis* at Neuchatel in 1738, *Feuille d'Avis* in Lausanne in 1763, and *Neue Zürcher Zeitung* at Zurich in 1780.

The Press a Battleground for Freedom

Resentment grew against the rule of the patrician families who governed their cantons with feudal tyranny. Intellectual leaders, led by Paul Usteri, editor of *Neue Zürcher Zeitung*, advocated changes in the constitution to bring a more democratic government and recognition of the rights of men. In the seventies and eighties revolts broke out in many cantons. These were suppressed with severity, but after the French Revolution had overthrown its autocracy there was no holding back the Swiss people. By 1798 the whole country was in flames. The French invaded, ostensibly to liberate the Swiss, but in a number of cantons the people had already overthrown their rulers. The old oligarchic federation fell. A new constitution approved by Napoleon established the Helvetic Republic with a central government modeled on that of France. Privileges of the nobility were abolished, and feudal burdens swept away. Every citizen was guaranteed liberty of conscience and religion, and the press at last was granted its freedom.

Immediately there came a flood of new politically free papers including the first dailies. Now there were a few papers serving the whole country instead of separate cantons. Important were *Schweizerischer Republikaner* and *Journal von und für Helvetien*. But the French made enemies for the new constitution by treating the Swiss as a conquered people, seizing their treasures, levying heavy contributions, and harassing the people. To many, deliverance seemed like subjugation. Two parties fought for a new constitution—the Centralists, led by Usteri, and the Federalists who urged return to the old federation system. The new free press became the battleground for this struggle till in 1802 a civil war broke out which Napoleon put down. He then drew up a new constitution which made Switzerland practically a dependancy of France. This time few popular rights were preserved; there was no mention of press freedom. This first period of press liberty had lasted only five years. From then on Napoleon's agents maintained strict supervision of all Swiss papers.

After the final defeat of Napoleon, the 1815 Congress of Vienna made Switzerland a buffer against the French in perpetual neutrality. Switzerland was returned to being a loose federation in which the twenty-two cantons enjoyed self-government and acted in concert only on foreign affairs and defense. The great powers, fearful of revolutionary agitation by their own refugees in Switzerland, forced the Swiss Diet to adopt a law binding cantonal governments to preventive control of the press. For the next few years the Swiss and their press were under the iron hand of their powerful neighbors. But the depths of subservience to which their nation had fallen roused the people to resistance. They began to yearn for their old liberties and their old free newspapers. Under the leadership of the dauntless Paul Usteri of *Neue Zürcher Zeitung*, Zurich was the first canton to remove press censorship in 1829.

The Paris revolution of 1830 had immediate repercussions in Switzerland and gave impetus to the constitutional reform movement. The press revived with vigor, attacked the Pact of 1815, and urged the establishment of representative democracy. People began to insist that government should exist only for the people and by the people. It was the press which chiefly contributed to this growing revolutionary spirit. Leading advocates were *Neue Zürcher Zeitung, Schweizerbote,* and *Appenselle Zeitung.* Finally in 1848, when Europe was swept by liberal revolts, the Swiss, in a short revolution, brought about the birth of a new and united Switzerland. These years of political discussion had led to press expansion. The four languages, the twenty-two cantons, the two religions, the separate valleys all had to have their organs of information. Whereas in 1833 there had been only thirty-three newspapers, by 1851 there were 180. Among some of the important papers of today founded in this period are *Journal de Genève* (1826), *Vaterland* of Lucerne (1833), *Basler National Zeitung* (1840), and *Basler Nachrichten* (1844). The new constitution guaranteed liberty of the press, subject to regulations against the abuse of that liberty, regulations which became similar to the libel laws of other countries.

The Modern Swiss Press Is Born

Now with years of peace and liberty the press made rapid strides. The second half of the century saw a tremendous growth of industrial and commercial activity. Daring tunneling made Switzerland the hub of Europe's transportation system. A free trade policy achieved a healthy surplus of exports over imports. Swiss bankers became creditors to all Europe. Rising prosperity and commercial activity brought a sound flow of advertising. By 1896 there were 418 papers, of which

105 were dailies. Today's important dailies founded in this period include *Der Bund* at Berne, *Tribune de Lausanne, La Tribune de Genève, Tages-Anzeiger* at Zurich, and *La Suisse* at Geneva. Technical improvements in typesetting machines and presses speeded production and permitted larger papers. The telephone and telegraph made possible quicker dissemination of news. Then in 1895 came the development of the Swiss Telegraph Agency owned by the papers themselves independently of federal or cantonal governments. This agency made itself responsible for gathering news cooperatively from all sections of Switzerland and exchanging it for reports from Reuters, Havas, and other countries. As a result Swiss papers were able to provide their readers with more foreign and domestic news.

The development of political institutions peculiar to Swiss democracy played an important part in shaping the character of the press. Although Switzerland had managed to maintain neutrality in the Franco–Prussian War, her dangers brought a popular demand for a federalization of the army. Then the growing industrial class of workers and the farmers, who had little voice in government, wanted improvement in their material conditions and in their school system. Agitation in the press and in many political clubs had resulted in a constitutional revision in 1874 which not only extended federal authority over the army but over labor, social, and economic legislation. This brought accident protection, regulation of the labor of women and children, alleviation of hours of labor, and compulsory workmen's insurance.

Even more interesting was the provision for "direct democracy." After the franchise had been extended, citizens were given the opportunity to participate directly in legislation and government decisions through the initiative, the referendum, and direct election of state and federal councilors. Under this plan, which is still in existence, any bill passed by both houses of the Federal Assembly is on probation for ninety days because if within that time 30,000 citizens of eight cantons demand a vote on the bill, a popular referendum must be ordered and final acceptance or rejection decided by this vote. As much as 88 per cent of the population take advantage of their right to vote on a referendum. Similarly any group which can get sufficient signatures can initiate legislation in the Federal Assembly or bring about the consideration of constitutional amendments by electors. Many a Sunday sees Swiss voters parading to the polls to vote for or against federal, cantonal, or local laws, credits, or decisions.

These innovations taught people to interest themselves in national as well as cantonal questions and to think of themselves as members of a nation. This made political news more important than ever, for newspapers now had not only to inform their readers on every sort of public question but inevitably to take stands on them. And even though most papers were independent of party subsidy, many became strong supporters of one party or the other, ranging through the Catholic Conservative, Liberal Conservative, Democratic, Farmer and Citizens, Social Democratic parties, to divisions of these which emerged. Hence the press began to take on a strongly political character.

Switzerland's strict adherence to neutrality also brought an interesting change. The founding of the International Red Cross at Geneva had placed Switzerland in a humanitarian relationship to other nations. It also became the natural intermediary between powers, the meeting ground of international congresses, and the seat of the International Arbitration Court. Curiously, the Swiss people began to think of foreign affairs as outside the concern of their nation and lost interest in foreign news. The press began devoting less space to foreign news and, for its opinion, leaning on the papers of surrounding countries. Thus the papers of French Switzerland looked to the papers of France, those of German Switzerland to the German press, those of Italian Switzerland to those of Italy. Most newspapers were still small, and with limited staffs it was easier for reporters to clip material from foreign papers than to write extended analyses of their own. Thus, when World War I broke in 1914, Switzerland as a nation was unprepared.

War Splits Press

When the Federal Council mobilized the army to guard frontiers, the consequent disruption of newspaper staffs and communications hurt Swiss newspapers; but this was as nothing compared to the differences that arose between sections of the country. The papers of German Switzerland, which had been fed German opinion, insisted that the origins of the war, the invasion of Belgium, and alleged atrocities were not sufficiently clear to warrant condemnation and that the country must remain strictly neutral. They were accused of being pro-German, but they countered by saying they were just being completely neutral. Italy decided that her allies, Germany and Austria, had provoked an aggressive war and declared her neutrality; hence the Italo-Swiss press was neutralist until Italy entered the war on the side of the Allies in May, 1915. The papers of French Switzerland were bitterly anti-German. The Romansh press staunchly took the side of the Allies, upbraiding the rest of the nation for being deceived by neutrality and for failing to see that the destruction of Belgium and a

German victory would leave no place for a free Switzerland. Despite the efforts of the government to curb the press through censorship, the war years were a period of great strain.

Economic neutrality also proved difficult. Switzerland had to import much of her food and could only live by importing raw materials and exporting manufactures. When the Allies threatened to cut off Swiss food supplies unless she ceased her trade with Germany, and when Germany threatened to cut off her coal supply, the situation became critical. But both sides needed to keep Swiss factories working, and in 1915 a *modus vivendi* was devised under which the Swiss guaranteed that raw materials sent into Switzerland by either side would not be exported as manufactured articles except to the nation which supplied them. While some manufacturers made fortunes, for most people these were years of rising living costs, privation, and constant regulation. During the war the Swiss won the gratitude of all Europeans for the establishment of their Bureau of Prisoners of War and for the efforts of their Red Cross which gave news of prisoners to their families and served as a clearing house for disabled prisoners and refugees who were repatriated.

Newspapers too had a difficult time. Newsprint rationing forced all to cut their size. Privations of the people brought reductions in circulation and a marked drop in advertising. Strict censorship was frustrating but most disturbing was the constant strain of division and agitation between the press of the different sections.

Postwar Years Bring Changes

There was much discussion in the press at the end of the war as to whether Switzerland could adhere to the League of Nations without deserting her neutrality, but the matter was settled by a popular vote in favor of adherence. Geneva became the seat of the League and a world capital for years. There were serious economic difficulties as Switzerland had to adjust her industrial production to the peacetime needs in an impoverished Europe, to find new markets behind new frontiers created as the map of Europe had been redrawn, and to meet new tariffs which had been set up all around her. There was much unemployment; newspapers lost circulation and advertising, causing the demise of some papers.

The war and postwar problems had roused the Swiss people from their indifference to international affairs, and the press now paid increasing attention to foreign news. There were few European countries where postwar international problems received more earnest consideration than in Switzerland. Papers changed their appearance with the use of more illustrations and slightly larger heads, but most retained their traditionally conservative makeup. More space was given to sports, film, and radio items, but the press as a whole maintained its century-old intellectual character.

Conditions improved in the last half of the twenties as Switzerland regained some measure of prosperity. Advertising and circulation picked up, and by 1928 there were 116 dailies. But the good years came quickly to an end as the world depression hit. Exports, upon which Switzerland was so dependent, dropped 50 per cent between 1929 and 1932. Unemployment soared. Losses in circulation and marked cuts in advertising forced many weeklies and some dailies to close.

World War II Problems

In the years immediately preceding World War II the Swiss press was among the first to realize that Hitler might plunge Europe into a new Armageddon. Switzerland took steps to strengthen her defenses. Her favorable mountain position and firm determination enabled her to maintain her neutrality in 1939 and in the ensuing years when the nations about her were engulfed in flames. Her strategic control of railways between Germany and Italy and her readiness to blow up her tunnels on a moment's notice, kept Hitler and Mussolini from attacking. But the war shook the Swiss economy to its foundation. Foreign trade declined to a fraction of what it had been and, ringed about by German-controlled territory, she was bled by the Nazis who raised their prices on coal 169 per cent, on steel 117 per cent, on oil 546 per cent. But at no time did Switzerland compromise her neutrality; and in 1943, at a great loss, she refused to renew her trade agreement with Germany.

At the same time this small country performed her usual humanitarian role, giving refuge to thousands of destitute war refugees, handling millions of letters and packages for war prisoners. She took over the diplomatic representation for twenty-three belligerent nations. Moreover, Switzerland came out of the war with labor and plant intact and enough reserves so that her people did not suffer the privation of the countries around her, all of which was to pave the way for her postwar prosperity.

While there were four pro-German papers supported by a small National Front fringe, the great majority were keenly aware of the dangers of Hitlerism and did not hesitate to warn against it. Strict military censorship had been imposed with the outbreak of the war, but once Switzerland came under the economic domination of Germany the Federal Council was forced to enact a law providing punishment for anyone publicly insulting a foreign state in the person of its ruling head or its diplomatic representatives. The Germans demanded action for anything they did not like in Swiss papers; but, with cunning, the Swiss had provided that the decision as to whether the limit had been transgressed lay not with administrative authorities but with the courts. Hence many cases dragged on in the courts without decision. Nevertheless, the press had to give up much of its former forthrightness in the interests of neutrality. The serious economic dislocation during the war hit newspapers hard. There was a great drop in advertising; papers became smaller and thinner and their numbers shrank.

The Postwar Years

Because of her neutrality Switzerland could not join the United Nations. She did, however, become a member of the Court of International Justice, and the old League of Nations buildings in Geneva became the headquarters for some specialized U.N. agencies and the meeting place for international conferences and summit talks. She accepted no Marshall Aid, preferring to achieve her own recovery. By 1947 Switzerland was the most prosperous nation in Europe. Through the fifties and into the sixties she expanded her industrial production and foreign trade till she became the most self-reliant of nations, with the most stable currency.

Press and parliament heatedly debated the government's rearmament program until the Russians suppressed the Hungarian Revolt in 1956. When that happened, the Swiss swung violently away from postwar pacifism. Soviet action was bitterly denounced in the press and large sums were subscribed for relief while thousands of Hungarian refugees were absorbed into Switzerland. In their first postwar referendum voters decisively defeated a Socialist attempt to strengthen the federal government and open the way for socialist nationalization. The Swiss want no powerful central government, for they fear it might be a menace to their liberties. Neither have they been interested in a welfare state. Their pension plans, health insurance, and unemployment compensation are handled by private organizations to which everyone contributes. There are no strikes; labor warfare makes no sense to them, and labor demands are met by negotiation. Prices have gone up, but so have wages till labor today is enjoying luxuries they could only dream about before. There is no unemployment; hundreds of thousands of foreign workers have been brought in to meet needs for labor.

This postwar prosperity with its growing purchasing power brought increased advertising and circulation to newspapers. In 1964 Switzerland reported 124 dailies and some 300 weeklies, semiweeklies, and triweeklies—a total of over 400 newspapers and an amazing number for so small a nation. But the many cities and towns that are cut off by the mountains must have their papers, and each political party wants its voice in every section. The Swiss press therefore is a very decentralized one; there is no journalistic capital. The five larger cities, Lausanne, Bern, Geneva, Basel, and Zurich, ranging in size from 130,000 to 441,000, each have five to eight dailies; but many smaller cities of 5,000 or more population, which in other countries would have a weekly, have two dailies. Hence circulations cannot be large. More than half of the dailies sell less than 10,000 copies; only two sell more than 100,000, both in Zurich. Yet Switzerland's 124 dailies had a total daily circulation of 2,042,574 in 1964, which means they sell 39.4 copies per 100 persons, the fourth highest index of readership in Europe.

Swiss newspapers are still largely political with 68 per cent representing "opinion" papers. Yet interestingly enough, there is a swing away from the old pattern, for thirty-nine dailies in 1964 listed themselves as independent or neutral, indicating an emphasis on information rather than politics. *Tages Anzeiger* at Zurich has the largest circulation, 160,459, in the country; but *Basler Tagblatt*, *La Tribune* and *La Suisse* at Geneva, and *Feuille d'Avis de Lausanne*, which have also become good information papers, have the largest circulations and the best advertising support in their areas. At Zurich a newcomer since 1959, *Der Blick*, has built a circulation of 132,923. A brash, sensational tabloid specializing in sex and crime, screaming heads and big pictures, it has offended many sedate Swiss. But some Swiss editors admit that if the German Swiss press had not been so dry and stodgy, *Der Blick* might not have succeeded.

Nevertheless, some of the political papers are among the best and most influential in the country. *Neue Zürcher Zeitung* (Radical Liberal) is the best-informed paper in the land. Although it has a circulation of only 80,065, it has earned the reputation of being one of the best papers in Europe. Among other strong political papers are *Der Bund* at Bern (Radical-Democrat), *Berner Tagwacht*, also at Bern (Socialist-Democrat), *Basler Nachrichten* (Liberal-Corservative), *Gazette de Lausanne* (Liberal-Democrat), *Vaterland* at Lucerne (Conservative-Catholic), and the famed old *Journal de Genève* (Liberal-Conservative). Though the *Journal*'s circulation is only 13,567, it is counted by the Swiss as one of their national papers, for it is read by leaders all over the country and in many European capitals. Actually few dailies are out-and-out party organs. Most are independent of party support but have definite party leanings. The one exception is *La*

Voix Ouvriere, the one Communist paper, which claims 8,000 circulation, probably less, has almost no advertising, and faithfully follows the Moscow line. It could not exist without party support.

Most dailies have fared well under Switzerland's booming economy. Stores are well-stocked, and advertising has increased greatly. The average Swiss daily gets 50 to 60 per cent of its revenue from advertising. Local retail advertising has not developed as it has in northern European countries, but there are much classified display and many ads from manufacturers. Some larger dailies are very profitable enterprises; some of the smaller ones are one-family operations. Swiss papers appear "wide open," for advertising is concentrated on solid ad-pages leaving other pages free for editorial matter. Most dailies are morning papers; only a few publish in the evenings. Some of the larger ones have morning and evening combinations. *Neue Zürcher Zeitung* puts out three editions a day, morning, noon, and afternoon, each entirely new; and each subscriber gets all three.

Since the German-speaking segment of the population is largest, it is not surprising to find that 72 per cent of all dailies are published in German, 23 per cent in French, and 5 per cent in Italian. None are published in Romansh.

Switzerland's good times got out of hand in 1965, and emergency restrictions on economic activity were put into effect. The government also ended its ten-year ban on commercial television, for it needed more income to expand its programing. This will mean increased advertising competition for the press.

Later in the year the country was much amused when *Blick* brought suit against the Action Committee on Trash Literature for circulating *Blick*'s advertisers. *Blick* lost its demand that the committee be restrained from future circulation and was compelled to pay its own court costs as well as those of the committee. It was awarded damages of one franc (23 cents).

Swiss Papers Are Different

Northern Europeans and Americans find Swiss papers totally unlike their own. So many are tabloid or semitabloid, set in four wide columns; even the few full-sized papers are set in six or seven wide columns. It is in content, however, that differences are most marked. The foreign visitor has difficulty at first in finding the news in the opinion papers, which are in the great majority. There is news, but in condensed form, serving only as springboards for interpretive articles, for these papers are most concerned with giving their readers the meaning of the news. Swiss journalists assert that their papers are easier to read than American papers because the latter are so filled with advertising and "trashy features" that one has difficulty finding the news.

Except for the very small local dailies under 5,000 circulation, most papers now run eight to sixteen pages or occasionally up to twenty-four, for this is the size traditional in Switzerland. Headline and picture display is exceedingly modest, so much so that except for an occasional cut on the cultural or sports page newspapers are brightened only by advertising illustrations. To the foreign journalist who questions this modesty, Swiss editors explain that their subscribers read their papers seriously, that because the papers are small they are read from end to end and there is no need to publicize individual articles or stories with large heads. Yet the success of *Der Blick* and some of the larger information papers would seem to indicate that Swiss readers might not be averse to having their papers more interesting in appearance.

The typical twelve-page opinion paper gives its front page to three or four leading articles. The second page begins with articles on Swiss affairs and news from other cantons, followed by two cultural pages. Next comes a solid page of advertising, opposite which is a page of comment on international affairs. Page seven contains more advertising and faces the economics and financial page. Pages nine and ten feature articles on local institutions, problems with sports, and small items of local news. Page eleven is then a solid page of advertising, and the back page carries late wire news and interpretive articles by foreign correspondents. The larger information papers are much more popular, providing more foreign, national, regional, and local news, more sports, and even staff-written women's features on fashions, foods, health, and home along with comic strips and much more advertising.

Except for *Der Blick* the Swiss press is a serious one. The crossword puzzle and the serial story are almost the only concessions to popular features. The single thing suggestive of "society" is a brief list of marriages and births. Crime and accidents are reported tersely in short items; suicide and divorce news is never printed. Swiss editors explain that both they and their readers have great respect for the rights of privacy and that Swiss readers would not like any paper which handles crime, sex, and scandal as do some papers in Paris and London.

Significant news alone is important, and in today's troubled world Swiss editors feel that their paramount duty is to bring to their readers an understanding of the major news developments of the day.

How Free Is This Press?

Except for the temporary restrictions placed upon them during the two world wars, Swiss newspapers have been free for more than a century, and any student of comparative journalism must admire their sturdy independence. This freedom is guaranteed in their constitution, subject to legal penalties for the abuse of that freedom; but the cautious and responsible Swiss press seldom gives reason for libel actions.

Swiss journalists, however, have two complaints. While doctors, lawyers, and clergymen are protected from having to reveal professional secrets, journalists are not; and courts have sometimes jailed them for refusing to reveal the sources of their information. And even though many decry *Der Blick*, they have questioned the right of the Federal Council to deny news to this paper.

Swiss papers have two strong organizations, the *Verein der Schweizer Presse* (VSP), which includes 8,000 working journalists, and the Union of Newspaper Publishers (SZV), both of which have been active in fighting for protection of press freedom. Both have urged a revision of the constitution which would spell out the rights and privileges of journalists and prevent courts from making them divulge the sources of their information. When a Communist paper was threatened with closure because a leading newsprint supplier refused to renew its contract, both organizations, even though they are very anti-Communist, stepped in and won a ruling which stated that the control of newsprint for political purposes was not up to private concerns.

And most of the Swiss people apparently feel strongly about any attempt by the government to interfere with their newspapers. They have seen too much of dictatorial governments in states around them, completely dominating the lives of the population. They want their own central government to interfere with their lives as little as possible. Well aware that newspapers helped them win their independence in the first place, as well as participated in their "direct democracy," the Swiss now rely on papers to keep them informed so that they can hold a checkrein on their government.

REPRESENTATIVE NEWSPAPERS

Neue Zürcher Zeitung (Zurich)—One of Switzerland's oldest papers. Under its great editor, Urs Schwartz, it has become one of the most respected in Europe. In addition to AFP, Reuters, and UPI connections, it has a great corps of correspondents and provides its subscribers in three editions a running story of each day's developments over the world. An additional foreign edition goes to many foreign nations, some three hundred copies to U.S.S.R. officials. Fat with advertising it is one of Switzerland's most prosperous papers. Appeals to upper class and intellectuals. Although it lists itself as Radical-Liberal, it is completely independent. Anti-Communist, generally friendly to the U.S., but criticizes it when it feels this is due. Its circulation is 80,065.

Tages-Anzeiger (Zurich)—Largest in Switzerland with a circulation of 161,212, most of it in its city and canton. An information rather than an opinion paper. Carries more local news and features than other Zurich papers but also fine coverage of world and national news. Leading advertising medium in German Switzerland. Popular morning paper appealing to middle class. Independent, but makes no attempt at political leadership.

Der Bund (Bern)—Leading paper in capital city, well-informed and one of best in German Switzerland. Generally conservative but has backed many social reforms. Pro-western and anti-Communist. Circulation 40,523.

Feuille d'Avis de Lausanne (Lausanne)—Switzerland's second oldest paper founded in 1862. With 81,975 it has the largest circulation in French Switzerland. A strong information paper with wide news coverage. Sells itself on news and features; no party affiliation.

La Tribune de Genève (Geneva)—Evening daily with 60,559, largest in Geneva. Full-sized paper with lively, interesting news display. Much local and sports news, a women's page, a literary page, and many special features. Covers world news with a back page of wire dispatches; independent of party affiliation.

Journal de Genève (Geneva)—Most influential in French Switzerland and respected in many foreign capitals. Strength lies in its backgrounding of foreign news. Very independent; circulation of 13,567 goes to intellectual leaders.

Vaterland (Lucerne)—Leading voice of Catholic Conservative party. Appeals to middle class and rural population. Circulation 36,035.

Volksrecht (Zurich)—Leading Socialist paper. Appeals to workers with news of labor unions and party activities, but also gives coverage of local and canton news and features. Anti-Communist but is sometimes reserved toward U.S. policies. Though it has only 15,649 circulation, it has considerable influence.

Part 3

The History Makers
of Southern Europe

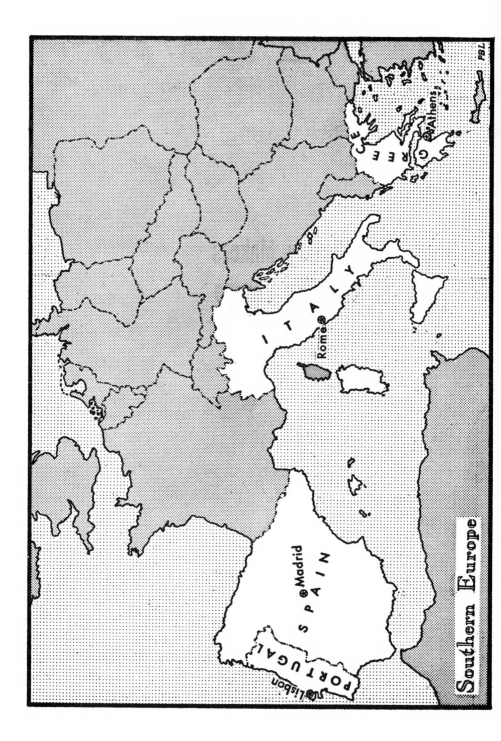

Southern Europe

Athens

GREECE

ITALY

Rome

SPAIN

Madrid

PORTUGAL

Lisbon

PBL

The Newspapers of Italy

It was curious that Benito Mussolini, who ruled everything else in Italy, could do nothing about the Vatican, that tiny city-
state of 105 acres within Rome which had been set up as a completely
independent realm through Il Duce's own initiative in the Lateran Pact
of 1929. Apparently trying to make peace with the Church and to gain
wider acceptance of his regime, he had settled the Roman Question,
that awkward problem which had existed since Pope Pius IV, deprived
of his Papal lands, had denounced the 1871 Pact of Papal guarantees
and made himself a voluntary prisoner in the Vatican. Every Pope
since had followed his example, and there was a deep schism between
the Church and the government. Now this small city-state was not
subject to any of Mussolini's decrees or to the laws of his government.
There was nothing he could do to silence *L'Osservatore Romano*,
official voice of the Vatican; and the new Pope Pius XII (1939–58),
who as Cardinal Pacelli had been papal secretary of state and had
denounced the Nazi superstition of race and blood, was not minded to
prevent his paper from telling the truth about what was going on in
the world and what the Fascist regime was doing to Italy. True,
Mussolini's "plug-uglies" could beat up news vendors who tried to sell
L'Osservatore Romano. But, so eager were the people for the truth,
which was being kept from them by a thoroughly fascistized press,
that dealers learned to ask "with or without?"; and since the answer
was usually "with," they would wrap the forbidden paper within a
"respectable Fascist paper." Circulation soared to 200,000 and it became Mussolini's greatest irritant. This was only one of the long series
of oppressions which were part of the history of Italian journalism. It
has, however, survived them all and is today represented by a vigorous
press.

Italian journalism emerged late, yet its precursors antedate those of
other countries. Julius Caesar in 60 B.C. established *Acta Diurna*, a daily

bulletin of government announcements posted in the Forum. After the fall of Rome to the barbarians, Italy for fourteen centuries had no organized existence as a nation. Instead there arose small states such as Venice, Lombardy, Tuscany, Milan, and Cremona, often fighting each other or being torn apart in wars between emperors and Popes. Despite the frequent ruination of their lands some rulers, by conquest or by maritime trade, acquired wealth which enabled them to encourage men of letters and art. This fostered a revival of learning which flowered into the Italian Renaissance in the fifteenth century.

From the Gazzettas to the First Weeklies

During the Renaissance there appeared men known as *mananti* in Rome, *gazzettanti* in Venice, *corrieri* in other states, who circulated handwritten newsletters telling of wars, extraordinary events, shipping news, travels, and customs in other lands. Venice and Genoa, great maritime powers, and Rome, center of the Catholic world, were the best news centers. The title *gazzetta* may have derived from the small coin, the price of a newsletter or the charge for admission to a group listening to its reading. All sheets which circulated publicly had to submit to strict state or Church censorship.

Printing came with the first German printers to cross the Alps, Arnold Panartz and Conrad Schweinheim, who set up a press at Subiaco near Rome in 1464. The art quickly spread to other cities, for the Italian Renaissance welcomed it with enthusiasm, and it developed here more than in any other country, gaining a new elegance and beauty. The roman types used everywhere in western countries were born in Italy under the hand of Nicholas Jenson; and the Bodoni types, which have become such favorites for newspaper headlines, were created by G. B. Bodoni, royal printer at Parma. The products of these presses were beautiful and costly reproductions of classics and religious works. In time some printers discovered a new and quicker income in printed newssheets. The earliest of record include one from Bologna in 1470, a second from Trieste in 1475, a third from Rome in 1493. The latter described the discovery of islands in the New World by Columbus. These small newssheets devoted to a single event, such as a battle, an earthquake, flood, comet, or unnatural birth appeared with increasing frequency but in time became most concerned with the wars against the Turks and the great religious conflicts which involved the whole Continent. These printed newssheets had no way of escaping the attention of authorities and therefore had to obtain licenses, submit to censorship, and carry on their title pages "con licenzia."

Amador Massi and Lorenzo Landi, Florentine printers, brought out

Italy's first weekly in 1636. Genoa had its first in 1639, then Rome in 1640, Milan and Turin in 1642, Venice in 1646. Best of these was *Sincero* of Genoa, published by Lukas Assarino in 1646, who gave readers better coverage of Italian and foreign news than any before him. But political conditions were not conducive to the development of Italian journalism. After Charles V of Spain had conquered the Italian peninsula, Italians entered a long period of servitude under Spanish governors who ruled the separate states. Fearful of the disruptive tendencies of the Reformation, Charles imposed, through the Spanish Inquisition, an era of darkness: Giordano Bruno, philosopher, was burned at the stake; Galileo was forced to recant his belief that the earth moved around the sun. Under this kind of repressive rule the first Italian weeklies were held under a tight curb. Nothing could be printed which might be interpreted as reflecting on the Church or on Spanish rule. In 1650 Peter Soconi of Turin was imprisoned for two years; Lukas Assarino in Genoa had his *Sincero* seized; and in Venice Ferrante Pallavicino was murdered for "disrespectful remarks" in his paper.

165 Years of Repression

The Italian press could do nothing but go into a literary phase. Italians resigned themselves to their servitude, but they still had to live and they turned to an interest in their classics. Literary journals, such as *Giornale di Letterati* in 1668, *Giornale Veneto di Letterati* in 1671, and *Galleria di Minerva* in 1696, through essays and treatises on art, music, literature, drama, and history, incited their readers to pride in being Italians and to a dream of future nationhood.

Then came the Wars of Succession (1701-58) which freed Italy from Spanish rule. Lombardy, Naples, and Sardinia were given to Austria; but Victor Amadeus, Duke of Savoy, because of his prowess against the Spaniards, emerged as an independent king, not only of Savoy but of the northern Italian territories and Sicily. Later Genoa was liberated and added to the kingdom. By his wise rule the King of Savoy laid the foundations of a future Italy. Even in the states attached to Austria, Queen Maria Theresa ushered in a long period of peace and reconstruction. But neither she nor the rulers of the independent states believed in press freedom. There was still rigid censorship, and in the Austrian states Italian papers were restricted to copying the official *Wiener Gazette*. Even the reformer, Joseph II, who succeeded Maria Theresa in 1780 and established press freedom in Austria, did not extend his leniency to the Italian states. Joseph's successor, Leopold II, fearful of growing revolutionary ideas, clamped down harder than ever on the press to prevent the printing of any news at all from revolutionary France.

Yet history was moving. Napoleon Bonaparte, having saved the French Revolution from royalist insurrection, had been made head of the Revolutionary armies and turned his ambitions toward Italy. In brilliant campaigns of 1796–99 he liberated most of Italy from Austria and set up republics on the French model. These did not last long, for after he had made himself Emperor of the French, he had himself crowned King of Italy as well. Most Italians had welcomed him as liberator; for the first time they had a sense of nationhood and a flag of their own. But the freedoms he promised proved illusory: thousands of Italian youths died in his battles; he despoiled the country to support his wars; and the press found it had a sterner master than ever before. In the end only one colorless paper was permitted in each state, and it had to echo carefully Napoleon's Paris mouthpiece, *Le Moniteur*. Napoleon's disastrous retreat from Moscow and his subsequent defeat and imprisonment ended an era. The 1815 Treaty of Vienna restored the autocratic reign of Austria and that of the rulers of the independent states. Fearful of what had happened as the result of "republicanism," they imposed most drastic controls on the press.

The Long Struggle for Independence

The dream of a free and united Italy would not die. Secret patriotic societies kept the ferment alive. The *Carbonari* instigated the unsuccessful revolts of 1820–21; the Young Italy Society, led by Joseph Mazzini, inspired thousands of Italian youths to an almost religious fervor for a new Italy. After Mazzini had had to escape to exile in Switzerland, his *Giovine Italia* (Young Italy), smuggled back into the homeland, became the bible of the younger generation. And Count Camillo Cavour, who looked on Mazzini as an unrealistic utopian, rallied the older generation through his National Society to the concept of an Italian constitutional monarchy. Again, because of repression, the press had to go into a literary phase but kept alive the desire for national independence.

The success of the 1848 popular revolts in France, Germany, and Austria roused Italians. Flames first broke out in Sicily and Naples. In Piedmont, where Cavour had brought out his daily *Risorgimento* in 1847, monster demonstrations forced the king to grant a constitution which guaranteed freedom of speech, press, and assembly. In Milan, Venice, Lombardy, and Tuscany the pent-up hate broke loose. Popular uprisings forced Austrians to withdraw for a time, but by mid-1849 the Austrian army had crushed the revolts. Austrian authoritarianism and that of the despots in the independent states were restored. Revolutionary papers which had sprung up all over Italy were suppressed. Yet the war had strengthened the feeling for unity, for Neapolitans had fought for Venice, Lombardians for Rome, Piedmontese for all Italy.

The next ten years were a decade of resistance. Victor Emmanuel, who had succeeded to the throne in Piedmont, and his prime minister Cavour, by participating in the Crimean War where Piedmontese troops distinguished themselves, had won England and France as allies. When in 1859 Austria attacked Piedmont, Napoleon III sent his army to help defeat the Austrians. Lombardy, Tuscany, Modina, and Parma joined Piedmont in 1860. Then Giuseppi Garibaldi, an old revolutionary fighter, returned from exile to head Victor Emmanuel's forces. In a month he had taken Sicily, then, crossing to the mainland, took Naples. Now the whole lower end of the boot was in the Italian kingdom. After Bismarck of Prussia had crushingly defeated Austria in 1866, Venice was able to join. Then when Bismarck had quickly vanquished France in the War of 1870, the Papal states no longer had a protector, and the Italian army took Rome. Its people overwhelmingly voted to join Victor Emmanuel's kingdom. After a struggle of 150 years, the unification of Italy was accomplished.

A New Press Emerges

The years of resistance and the wars of liberation had been hard on the press. Only in Piedmont, where Victor Emmanuel and Cavour had maintained press freedom, had newspapers been able to function. There in Turin *Gazzetta del Popolo* had come to be Italy's strongest voice for independence. Then came *Gazzetta Piedmontese*, which later, as *La Stampa*, grew to be one of Italy's great newspapers of today. Cavour, realizing the need his papers would have for foreign news, assisted Guglielmo Stefani in establishing Italy's first news agency, *Agenzia Stefani*, which made exchange agreements wth Reuters and Havas and continued for many years to function as a governmental agency.

In other states, papers had no opportunity till liberation. When Lombardy, east of Piedmont, was freed, Eduardo Sonzogno founded *Il Secolo* in Milan in 1865. It became the most influential paper in the north and by 1900 had a circulation of 200,000. After Garibaldi had liberated Sicily, Hieronymus Ardizzonne brought out in Palermo *Il Giornale di Sicilia*, today the island's leading daily. In Naples there rose *Il Popolo d'Italia* under Karl Mileti, whom Garibaldi called the greatest champion of freedom in South Italy. Venice had to wait till it was free in 1866 when *Gazzetta di Venezia* appeared. Rome had no free paper till 1870 when Giacomo Dina founded *L'Opinione Liberale* and made it the most serious paper in the country. In 1883 there was founded in Rome its first great liberal paper, *La Tribuna*, which by 1900 had become the leading paper in the capital with a circulation of 150,000. One by one in every state new free papers appeared. In all, twenty-one new papers were founded in this period.

The newly unified country faced many postwar problems, and dissension over their solution led to the development of warring political parties. Right-wing Conservatives governed well for fifteen years but were so intent on budget balancing that they forgot about needed social reforms and were defeated by the more leftist Progressives, who did initiate some reforms, including extension of the suffrage. But having tasted power, the premiers Agostino Depretis and Giovanni Giolitti built an electoral machine, which for graft and election manipulation was superior to anything ever developed in Chicago, and kept themselves in power for long years by a ruthless police system. They forgot about improving the conditions of the poor and thought only in terms of national prestige. They launched their country on years of colonial expansionist wars, won a foothold in Somaliland, took Libya from the Turks in 1912, and in so doing bankrupted their nation. Meanwhile the many poor, who wanted a better life and freedom from economic slavery, joined the Socialist party in great numbers. This party never achieved a majority in parliament but sometimes had the balance of power, and by fomenting strikes it managed to get laws providing nationalized insurance and old-age pensions. Then on the far right was the Papal party, extremely conservative and strongly active on any matters affecting the Church and education. In the trading and jockeying between parties there was often political chaos, and ministries changed an average of once a year.

All these parties had to have their press organs. The leading voice of the Conservatives was *La Liberta*, founded in Rome in 1870. *Popolo Romano*, started in 1873, was the chief organ of the Progressives. The Socialists had had to start with weeklies in the industrial north; but in 1896 Leonidas Rissolati brought out *Avanti*, still the leading Socialist paper in Italy. The Papal party had *Civilta Cattolica* in Rome in addition to the official Vatican organ *L'Osservatore Romano*, founded in 1861. There were soon too many papers for the poverty-stricken condition of the country, and many were short-lived. Those party papers which survived lived on party subsidy. There was also outright bribery under Depretis and Giolitti, who distributed secret funds to persuade papers to gloss over their scandals and to fan enthusiasm for their colonial wars.

There were, however, also honest and independent papers. Some of the industrially wealthy families in the north acquired newspapers. Thus in Milan, *Corriere della Sera*, founded in 1876 by Eugenio Torrell-Viollier, was acquired by the Crespi textile manufacturing family in 1885. It was given funds so it could be politically independent and provide exceptional news coverage; it became one of the best-informed papers in Europe, growing from a circulation of 9,000 to more than 100,000 in 1898. It took a neutral course in politics but did not hesitate to attack the corruption in the Depretis-Giolitti regimes. Similarly the Roux-Frassatti company in Turin acquired the old *Gazzetta Piedmontese* in 1895, changed its name to *La Stampa*, and built it into one of Italy's best papers. In Rome, Fedele Albanese started *Messaggero* in 1878. Given adequate backing and set on a neutral course of emphasis on news coverage, it became the outstanding paper in the capital. Such newsworthy papers stirred the Italian people to an interest in what was going on about them. By the end of the century such papers had achieved very substantial circulations, whereas party papers foundered between 10,000 and 20,000.

King Victor Emmanuel died in 1878 and was succeeded by King Humbert. Fortunately, the most powerful figure in the government at the time was Francisco Crispi, former journalist and revolutionary leader, whose strength and sagacity managed to effect a peaceful transition. In the years that followed, aided by increased industrialization, the financial position of the country and its government improved. King Humbert was assassinated by an anarchist in 1900 and was succeeded by King Victor Emmanuel III. Italy in 1882 had joined Austria and Germany in the Triple Alliance; now, to bring Italy out of its isolation, friendly relations were also established with England and France.

And Then Came World War I

The outbreak of World War I forced Italy to a grave decision. Under her treaty obligation she was bound to go to the aid of Germany and Austria; yet Italians felt their allies had launched a war of aggression, and they therefore chose neutrality. But popular opinion favored England and France. War spirit grew; the country was put on a war footing, and on May 23, 1915, Italy entered the war on the side of England, France, and Russia. During this period the great majority of papers supported the government. Socialist papers, however, opposed going to war; the Giolitti papers, still sympathetic with the

Triple Alliance, demanded continued neutrality; some Catholic papers were in sympathy with Catholic Austria. Yet nothing could stem the tide of opinion among the mass of Italians.

Italian armies scored initial successes against Austria; and, although their losses were fearful, during 1916–17 they pinned down Austria's best troops, preventing them from aiding Germany. Newspapers continued to publish without interference except for military security censorship. Socialist papers, opposing the war, were often in trouble with censors. The most vehement voice against the Socialists came from the militant editor of *Popolo d'Italia* who had been expelled from the party for his advocacy of war. His name was Benito Mussolini.

The heavy war costs, supported by bitter tax loads, the shortage of food, losses of manpower, scarcity of newsprint and other materials, skyrocketed newspaper production costs. Then, as industrial production fell off, advertising plummeted, and because of the poverty of the people circulations dropped. Weaker papers had to discontinue; all had to reduce their size.

The disastrous battle of Capporetta in October, 1917, dealt a stunning blow, and when Russian armies collapsed discouragement swept Italy. This was fanned by the Socialists and the defeatist campaigns of the Giolittians. Mussolini through his *Popolo d'Italia* charged the Socialists with being traitors and responsible for Capporetta. Italian armies were reorganized and in the final 1918 campaigns defeated the Austrians and contributed to their request for an armistice on November 3, followed a week later by one from Germany.

Postwar Changes

Once the war was over censorship was removed. The division of opinion over immediate postwar problems brought many new papers. By 1930 there were 157 dailies and 843 weeklies. Many did not last long. But strong national dailies forged ahead. In Milan, *Corriere della Sera*, under a new editor, Luigi Albertini—the best in its history—rose to 400,000 circulation by 1920. *La Stampa* in Turin was a close second. *Il Messaggero* in Rome had been acquired by the wealthy Perrone family and under Dr. Italo Falba became Italy's third great paper.

Italians were unhappy over the peace settlements which gave the Dalmatian coast and Fiume to Yugoslavia. Italy furthermore was in deep economic trouble, for her two best prewar customers, Austria and Germany, were flattened. Unemployment, rising prices, the inability of the government to solve these crises brought great unrest. Socialists fomented strikes, often violent. Communists, to solve all problems, urged a new revolutionary system in emulation of that in Russia.

Now Mussolini took leadership of the Right. In fiery editorials he attacked Socialists and Communists as traitors, promised a solution of the Fiume question, denounced the government for its inadequacy, said he would solve Italy's economic problems. Communists had seized many towns and installed their own town councils. Socialists promoted strikes, which threatened to paralyze the nation. Mussolini spearheaded the formation of a new party, the Fascisti, with a blackshirt army of dissatisfied war veterans who fought the Reds and in one city after the other installed their own rule with violence. In October, 1922, after Luigi Facta's government in Rome had almost broken down, Mussolini and his blackshirts marched on the capital, ousted the government, and forced the king to name Mussolini premier. To the latter's credit, although he clamped an iron vise of discipline on his country, he did bring in experts to help improve the domestic economy. Through friendly commercial treaties with neighboring nations he increased foreign trade and in continued negotiations with Yugoslavia was able to annex Fiume. In the 1935 elections Fascists received 65 per cent of the votes, although opponents accused them of using force to control balloting.

Il Duce Takes Over the Press

Mussolini's most outspoken opponent was a Socialist deputy, Giacomo Matteotti, who in a budget debate charged Fascists with having collected huge sums from an oil company seeking a concession. Four days later Matteotti was assassinated. All non-Fascist papers rose in protest, and many printed the confessions of two Fascist officials involved in the oil scandal. For a few days the Fascist regime seemed threatened with overthrow. Mussolini could not risk further press attacks and in January, 1925, decreed that newspapers could print nothing critical of the regime; he imposed strict censorship and authorized prefects to confiscate any issues containing objectionable material. *Avanti*, in that year, had one hundred issues confiscated.

When this type of persuasion was not sufficient, blackshirts resorted to the "castor oil" or "ice cake treatment" or severely beat up editors. A new law made it impossible for anyone to work on a newspaper without a Fascist party card. Thus great editors like Albertini of *Corriere della Sera*, Frassati of *La Stampa*, Bergamini of *Giornale d'Italia*, who refused to sign Fascist cards, were eliminated. Some papers were closed down. *Corriere della Sera* and *La Stampa* were closed for three months, then reopened with entirely Fascist staffs. Threats of confiscation forced many owners to sell to Fascists. Thus Milan's fine *Il Secolo* was taken over by Fascist Senator Bevione. The excellent *Il Mattino* at Naples was appropriated by a Fascist official,

Turatti. General Italo Balbo, one of the earliest blackshirt strong-arm men, took *Corriere Padona* in Ferrara. Bologna's respected *Il Resto del Carlino* suffered the same fate. All over Italy this process took place. *Corriere della Sera, La Stampa,* and *Messaggero* still provided the best news coverage, but they had to print the news and play it as the Fascists dictated. By the end of 1926 all newspapers had been completely fascistized. To better control information, the number of dailies had been reduced to fifty, a decrease of 65 per cent. *Popolo d'Italia* in Milan and *Giornale d'Italia* in Rome, run by Virginia Gayda, secretary of the Fascist party, were the principal organs of hate.

And the Fascists left nothing to chance. Through *Agenzia Stefani* they fed papers only what they wanted printed and through it gave daily instructions as to what stories should be given major heads, which should be ignored. When Il Duce's daughter bore a child, this news was suppressed for fear that becoming a grandfather might reduce Mussolini's popular image. The line to be followed in the daily leader articles was carefully outlined. And all workers were organized into syndicates till even printers became censors for fear they might be held liable for any dereliction. Long before Joseph Goebbels in Germany thought of it, Mussolini declared, "I consider Fascist journalism as my orchestra"; and he had a perfect conductor in his son-in-law, Galeazzo Ciano, who controlled all means of communication through his Ministry of Press and Propaganda, later called the "Bureau of Culture."

Under this system Mussolini had his people in a mental strait jacket. This did not mean that all Italians accepted this press without question. Many grew tired of the continuous glorification of Il Duce and Fascism in papers, which paid no attention to the hard facts of life. They wearied of seeing pictures of Mussolini on horseback, at the zoo, playing the violin, strutting in parades or on balconies. The fascistized press gave them only propaganda; but there was one paper, *L'Osservatore Romano,* voice of the Vatican, which he could not touch, as was explained earlier, and which provided the international news people were not getting and the stark truth of what the Fascists were doing to Italy. It was bought surreptitiously and passed from hand to hand till every copy was worn out, and its readership represented many times its press run of 200,000.

There were also clandestine papers, such as *La Rivoluzione Liberale* and *Non Molare,* which were eagerly passed from one person to another. As each editor was caught and disappeared, a brave new man took his place.

Yet all was not well in the Mussolini paradise. The world depression, which Il Duce blamed on the United States, dealt Italy a hard blow. Unemployment rose in the industrial north, and farmers too had a hard time. They could not raise enough food for a population growing by 450,000 a year; hence food prices soared. Austerity was prescribed; wages were cut; big public works were started including the draining of the Pontine swamps, which provided some employment. Then Mussolini began building his army and navy. He talked of his people's needing room—*i.e.*, colonies. Abyssinia appeared to be an easy prey. Il Duce had his eyes on the glory road and he was not to be outdone by Hitler, who was stealing world headlines. Furthermore, a nice easy war would rouse the enthusiasm of Italians and take their minds off their home problems. In the autumn of 1935 Italian forces struck. With a highly trained army, modernized equipment, complete mastery of the sky, and mustard gas, it was all over in seven months. Throughout this war the controlled press with hysterical headlines roused Italians to a fever pitch over this holy war to bring civilization to a country of slavery and barbarism. King Haile Selassie fled; Ethiopia with Eritrea and Somaliland were organized into Italian East Africa. In 1936 another adventure beckoned in Spain, where Franco had gone to war against the new leftist republic. Germany and Italy intervened to help Franco, and Russia sent assistance to the republic. Again the fascistized press was used to whip up enthusiasm. German and Italian ties now became close and the Rome–Berlin Axis was formed.

Involvement in World War II

When Hitler launched his war against Poland, France, and England, the Italian press became cautious, urging noninvolvement. Mussolini stalled on Hitler's demands; but when Hitler loosed his blitzkrieg and Germany seemed unstoppable, Italy on June 10, 1940, declared war on France and Britain. The Italian army was not effective, even against stricken France, and had advanced only a few miles when the armistice was signed. In North Africa they did more. Striking from Libya they drove well into Egypt until the British counterattacked and pushed them back to Tobruk, causing the loss of a third of this army. Hoping to get a good portion of the Balkans before Hitler got there, Mussolini attacked Greece through Albania; but the doughty Greeks not only drove him back but threatened to push him into the sea. However, Hitler was on the way, conquering one Balkan state after the other, till in April, 1941, he overran Greece. The Germans now went to the aid of Italians in North Africa. General Erwin Rommel took command and for a time the British were driven back; but Allied landings in North Africa coupled with General Bernard Montgomery's rapid sweep defeated the Axis and lost Italy the rest of its African army. When the Allies took Sicily, the Germans took over Italy.

Italians now were thoroughly discouraged. Successive defeats and the ineffectiveness of the government even aroused other Fascist leaders, and when the people demanded a voice in government the Grand Fascist Council ousted Mussolini. Milan mobs wrecked the offices of *Popolo d'Italia*, and the Italian press at last dared to raise its head. *Corriere della Sera* bannered "Mussolini is gone" and said: "We are finally free. It is difficult to bring out a newspaper today when for 20 years we have submitted to ministerial direction. The wonderful enthusiasm of the people wakes us from a drugged slumber." *La Stampa* gave front page display to a statement of the leaders of all nonfascist parties: "The painful nightmare of the past 20 years is ended, a nightmare which released bestial passions, shattered our national wealth, impoverished our consciences, dragged our nation into a war it did not want, which has left us in a tragic situation. But if we unite all our strength we can pave the new road we must follow. Henceforth our watchword will be 'Liberty.'"

But Marshal Pietro Badoglio, who had taken control of the government, was not inclined to grant the freedoms which papers had envisioned. By his second week he had the press muzzled again. All references to peace, liberty, and freedom were banned; and papers which tried to evade his dictum were confiscated. He did not want anyone rocking the boat. Yet the people wanted peace immediately—not the long drawn out negotiated peace Badoglio was trying to effect. There were strikes and riots. Defiant new papers tried to call for an immediate peace and the restoration of liberties, but confiscations kept them from speaking out. Military developments, however, were moving too fast for Badoglio, and on September 8 he accepted Eisenhower's unconditional surrender terms and called on Italians to fight the Germans.

The Germans had by now consolidated their position and held Rome and everything north; the great natural fortress of Cassini blocked all access to the capital. They rescued Mussolini and set him up as head of a Republican Fascist State in the north. Here tough Fascist controls over the press were now sterner than ever. American and British armies encountered some of the fiercest fighting of the war in that terrible winter. It was not till June 4, 1944, that they at last took Rome; and not until the spring of 1945 did the Germans finally yield all of Italy. In one of the last acts of this drama, a partisan band captured and executed Mussolini and his mistress.

A Postwar Press Rises

As Allied armies had advanced, the psychological warfare branch of the military government had closed all former Fascist papers and brought out Italian language newssheets in city after city as they were freed. In the north, where the Germans had held out longest and where partisan bands were hitting the enemy in guerrilla attacks, underground papers had circulated. Once Italy was free new papers appeared to replace suppressed Fascist sheets. Old, once-great independents were restored to their former owners; and to distinguish them from the prewar papers, which had a Fascist taint, the word "new" was added to their titles, as *Nuovo Corriere della Sera* and *La Nuova Stampa*. Everywhere men clamoured for the right to bring out papers. Some 15,000 applied to the military government; all were carefully screened to keep out Fascists. Eventually licenses were granted not only to independent individuals or groups but also to groups representing the six anti-Fascist parties, the Christian Democrats, Liberals, Democrats, Socialist Labor, and Communists.

People were slow in accepting the new press because of their disillusionment with all papers during the Mussolini regime. Within the press itself the reaction to the monolithic Fascist system made it inevitable for not only papers licensed to party groups but also those set up as independents to become party voices. More than 80 per cent of all were politically partisan. Among the leading party organs were *Il Popolo* (Christian Democrat), *Avanti* (Socialist), *Unita* (Communist), *Risorgimento Liberale* (Conservative), *Buon Senso* (Neo-Fascist), and *Italia Nuova* (Monarchist). Their complete devotion to political opinion gave an opportunity to some independents to gain larger followings through good news coverage, particularly of foreign and national news. Among these were *Messaggero* and *Il Tempo* in Rome, *La Nuova Stampa* in Turin, *Nuovo Corriere della Sera* in Milan, *Gazzettino* in Venice, and *Risorgimento* in Naples. A new arrival was the *Rome Daily American*, started by four former *Stars and Stripes* staffers. It made a place for itself as the only English language paper in the capital, nonpartisan, concentrating on news, particularly of America, till today it has become a godsend to tourists from Rome to Athens.

Many of the new flood of papers lived only a short time. There was almost no advertising; people were so poor that circulations fell off. Those which attracted enough readers could live on circulation income; the rest had to close or rely on party subsidy.

In January, 1945, a new agency to replace the discredited Stefani came into being as *Agenzia Nazionale Stampa Associata* (ANSA), a cooperative in which every daily owned a share and without any government control. With its main office in Rome and bureaus in other leading cities, it had by 1947 set up a teleprinter service providing 40,000 words daily, getting its foreign news principally from Reuters and the new French agency, AFP, but also having exchange agreements with smaller national agencies. Some seventy-five dailies were also getting service from AP, UP, or INS.

The first provisional governments had been headed by Socialists and Communists; but economic problems caused their downfall, and the Christian Democrats headed by Alcide Gaspari won the first postwar election in December, 1945. Gaspari was to prove the ablest man in the new Italy and, though he had to shuffle his cabinet several times, remained the head of government for seven years. Whether Italy should adhere to the monarchy became the major political question. In June, 1945, the people voted overwhelmingly to set up a republic. Massive aid from UNRRA helped relieve the food shortage, and in 1949 Marshall Aid from the United States began to revive the economy. By this time the newspaper situation had resolved itself to where there remained 114 dailies and some 700 weeklies. Some of the national papers of merit had regained considerable circulations. *Corriere della Sera* claimed 450,000 circulation plus 250,000 for its evening companion, *Corriere d'Informazione*. Turin's *La Stampa*, Rome's *Messaggero* and *Il Tempo*, Venice's *Gazzettino*, and Naples' *Risorgimento* each boasted 200,000 circulations. By this time the only control over the press was the practical one of shortage of newsprint. At first all dailies were limited to one sheet printed on both sides. By 1948 conditions had improved so that they were permitted four pagers, three or four times a week.

All papers were concerned with postwar settlements. The Soviet Union had been the first to recognize the new Italy; nevertheless under the leadership of Count Carlo Sforza, foreign minister, Italy took a pro-western orientation. Communist papers fought it bitterly, but most other papers supported the government in joining the Marshall Plan and the Atlantic Defense Pact. The disposition of Italy's prewar colonies was also a worry. In the end the United Nations took the trusteeship of Libya, which later won its independence in 1952. Though Italian Somaliland was placed under Italian trusteeship, it was stipulated that this country too should be granted its independence in ten years. But the source of greatest excitement was the warring between parties. The campaign of 1948 was even more bitter than that in 1945; and while the Christian Democrats won, the Communists came in a strong second. Extreme poverty among many and the agitation of Communist labor unions brought this about. The same thing happened in 1952 when the Christian Democrats, Liberals, and Republicans won 50 per cent of the votes and the Communists and the Nenni-Socialists gained 33 per cent. The rest were split among a half dozen minor parties. This fractionalism led not only to the instability of governments but to extreme partisanship in the press and the coming and going of party papers.

The total number of daily papers continued to drop until it reached 103; and even though the population increased to 47,000,000, total daily circulations in 1952 were still at their prewar average of 4,600,000. This was accounted for in part by the percentage of illiterates and semi-illiterates and also by the increase in newsstand price to 25 lire—the cost of two rolls of bread. It led to much sharing of papers and, though actual readership was probably higher than circulations indicated, revenue was not keeping pace with costs. The number of dailies would have been smaller had it not been for subsidy by parties and acquisition of some papers by important industrialists and financiers. Thus the Fiat auto company bought *La Stampa* in 1952, and *Mattino* and *Mezzogiorno* were acquired by the Bank of Naples.

A Decade of Startling Change

The next ten years saw great economic changes, but Italy and her press remained divided. From 1952 to 1963 there were eight different governments. The middle-of-the-road Christian Democrats consistently maintained control, but they never managed to get a parliamentary majority and had to govern in coalition. Sometimes they worked with the right, sometimes with the center, till in 1962 under Amintore Fanfani they undertook their "opening to the left" in a coalition with the Marxist-Nenni-Socialists who had broken with the Communists after the Russian suppression of the Hungarian Revolt. This event had brought sharp reaction, losing the Communists some 400,000 members and many fellow travelers. Italy continued her western orientation: she played an active part in the Western European Union, joined the coal and steel community and the United Nations, and accepted U.S. missile bases as part of her NATO commitment. These moves were generally supported by most papers with the exception of the Communist ones.

The miracle, however, occurred in the economic field. A modest beginning had been made in the breakup of large estates and distribution of land to peasants in southern Italy and in the establishment in 1955 of a ten-year program of industrialization; but the Common

Market, started in 1958, gave great impetus to both. By 1961 unemployment in northern Italy had disappeared. Industrial production had expanded at a rate faster than that in the United States and the Soviet Union. There were successive cost-of-living wage increases to workers; people now had money to spend, and they wanted the good things of life. Whereas in 1952 Italians had walked or ridden bicycles or motor scooters, by 1962 there were so many cars that many cities had serious traffic problems. Television aerials sprouted everywhere.

All this brought new life to the press. More people could now buy papers; circulations rose, advertisements for manufactured articles took more space. New grocery supermarkets brought the first burst of retail advertising. But classified ads showed the greatest increase, and "help wanted" ads had the largest linage. Southern Italy did not share in these advances to the same degree. While many workers had streamed to northern cities for jobs and some new industries had been started in the south, there were still many unemployed. And although the "Green Plan," calling for the expenditure of 500 billion lire over five years for agricultural development, had been adopted in 1961, it would take some years before the newspapers of southern Italy would profit. This was also the area of greatest illiteracy; hence newspapers of the south had been unable to keep up with the north in progress. There were fewer newspapers and their circulations were much smaller.

Italy's boom slowed markedly in 1963–64 owing to inflationary pressures of higher prices and wages, a decline in industrial production, a huge foreign debt deficit, and a flight of capital which threatened the stability of the lire. It was rescued only by help from the International Monetary Fund and extensive credit from the United States. Premier Aldo Moro's government was twice threatened with overthrow.

In 1965 Italy and her press suffered a setback; of all the Common Market countries, it was hardest hit by inflation. Newspapers saw advertising drop as well as circulation. Late in the year Pietro Nenni's left-wing Socialists, who had previously been in alliance with the Catholic Christian Democrats, voted overwhelmingly to merge with the Social Democrats. This may change the face of Italian politics and intensify the rivalry in political papers. It may also give Aldo Moro's government real trouble, plagued as it is by financial scandals involving cabinet and other high officials. The public is becoming completely cynical, convinced that the present government is only trying to line its own pockets.

Character of Press Changes

More and more dailies began calling themselves independent; even party organs, except for the Communist, could not be counted on to follow the party line consistently, for the mood of the people was changing. Italians love political argument, but they have no great love for politicians and are inclined to shrug off party propaganda. They no longer want to be told what to think; they had enough of that during the long Fascist regime. True, when times were bad they listened to the Communists and voted with them. Even in the November, 1964, elections they gave them 26 per cent of the votes, but voting Communist is just a handy device for putting pressure on the government. Actually the Communist party has been losing members and, most seriously, it has been losing the youth. In ten years Italy's Communist Youth Federation slipped from 500,000 to less than 160,000.

The people of Italy have become buyers of the good things of life, owners, doers, and enjoyers; and the old Communist propaganda no longer has much appeal. Luigi Longo, who succeeded the late Palmiri Togliato as party secretary, has had to sweeten the party propaganda. Whole pages of *Unita*, the party daily, do not mention the word "Communist." Instead they sponsor causes which appeal to everyone as, for instance, their opposition to the government's tax on new cars. Communist circulations have dropped, but so have those of other party voices. The hard core of party faithful may buy these papers, but most Italians prefer the papers which give them more objective news.

Unita, which in the early fifties claimed more than 300,000 circulation for its four daily editions in Milan, Turin, Genoa, and Rome and 1,000,000 on Sunday, was compelled to abandon its Turin and Genoa editions; and in 1964, while it claimed only 250,000 for its Milan and Rome editions, an honest audit would probably have shown much less than that. The Communist *Il Paese*, a sharply packaged, popular Rome paper, had to merge its morning and evening editions in 1963.

Of the eighty-eight dailies in 1964 which might have shown political tendencies, only twenty-five admitted party affiliation. The Catholics led with nine, the Democratic Christians had six, the Communists and Leftists four, the Social Democrats (former Monarchists) three, the Socialists two, and the Republicans one. By contrast thirty-two newspapers declared themselves independent and twenty-one showed no political affiliation—a great change from the day when 80 per cent were political.

In 1964 Italy counted eighty-eight dailies; but five were economic and financial, four were sports dailies, and three were foreign language papers in English, German, and Slavonian, leaving seventy-six regular Italian newspapers. Of the eighty-eight, fifty-three are published in north Italy, twenty-three in the central section, and twelve in southern Italy and the islands. Rome and Milan are the great journalistic centers with twenty-four dailies between them, including those with the largest circulations. Rome, even with a 2,278,000 population, could not support thirteen dailies unless some of them served other central and southern cities with regional or local editions. Thus *Messaggero* puts out twenty editions identical with the Rome edition except for one local page. Rome is also the seat of some of the principal party papers.

Total daily circulations have increased some 700,000 since 1961 to 5,702,427 in 1964; yet even these claimed figures represent only 11.2 copies per 100 persons, a lower ratio of readership than in any other nation in western Europe except Spain and Portugal. This is in part accounted for by the fact that, while the illiteracy rate for the country is 13 per cent, a great many of the older and middle-aged citizens never got beyond sixth grade. Furthermore, the growing costs of newspaper production have made things difficult for small newspapers, to the extent that sixty-two provincial capitals do not have their own dailies but rely on regional editions of larger papers. It must be remembered also that there are more than four hundred nondailies, publishing one or more times a week, dealing with local news and problems. Italy's geographic shape, moreover, makes it difficult for papers to circulate far out of their own region. The only morning dailies which can claim national or wide regional appeal are *Corriere della Sera* and the new popular *Il Giorno* in Milan, *La Stampa* in Turin, *Messaggero* and *Il Tempo* in Rome, *La Nazione* in Florence, and *Il Resto del Carlino* in Bologna. The economic situation of the people is also a determining factor. The established daily newspaper price is 40 lire, about seven cents. To the well-paid workers in the north this presents no problem, but to many in the south it does. Even though an Italian may look at papers in the *conditori*, wineshop, or barbershop, or read every page in glass-covered display cases at the local newspaper office, this adds nothing to circulation. The phenomenal growth of television and its news broadcasts and filmed presentations satisfies many in the provinces and less favored areas, as well as in the cities. Then the weekly news magazines and illustrated weeklies provide all the information that many people want. All these competing media operate to keep newspaper circulations down.

Unlike the American papers with their morning-afternoon and Sunday combinations, 78 per cent of Italy's dailies are morning papers, and they account for three-fourths of the total daily circulation. There are only seven Sunday papers, most attractive of which is *Corriere della Sera's La Domenica del Corriere* in Milian with more than 500,000 circulation. Its rival, *Il Giorno*, has some 360,000. *Messaggero* and *Il Tempo* in Rome claim 460,000 and 500,000, respectively. Dailies are limited to publishing six days a week; hence some put out Monday sports editions with *del lunedi* added to their titles to distinguish them from regular editions.

How Italian Papers Differ

Italian dailies, like their American counterparts, usually have full standard-sized pages, but some look larger because they employ nine columns. Their makeup with its many three- to six-column heavy black heads may seem confusing at first; but once one gets accustomed to them, he finds their news presentation not ineffective, with every page brightened with cuts, often large and well-reproduced. Smaller city dailies usually run eight pages, but larger independents appear with sixteen to twenty pages. The editorial article always leads the front page, often filling the two left-hand columns. In the larger independents the rest of the page plays the top foreign and national news. Party papers carry less foreign news and play national news interpreted from the party standpoint. Seldom do local stories make the front page except in small city dailies, which, like American non-metropolitan papers, pay more attention to local news. On the inside, however, sometimes on page two or four, a ribbon across the top such as *Cronaca di Roma* heads an entirely local page.

By long tradition page three is the cultural page, featuring signed articles on theater, films, art, music, literature, and sometimes history or the background of foreign news. Then follow pages providing news from other cities in Italy, more foreign and national news, a page with news of courts, government ministries, parliament; next is an entertainment page with movie ads and radio-TV schedules followed by news of business and finance. There is always a sports section of two or more pages and a final page of *Ultime Notizie* carrying the latest wire dispatches.

Italians feel their papers are more serious than American ones in that, except for the crossword puzzle and an occasional serial story, there are no entertainment features. *Il Paese, Il Giorno,* and a few Sunday papers have comic strips and panels; but otherwise there are no women's features, health columns, heart-advice columns, departments for teens or senior citizens. *La Domenica del Corriere,* however, has beautiful color illustrations of fashions for both women and men, home furnishing articles, personality features, comic panels, thriller short stories, astrology columns, and gardening and cooking departments. Its *Corriere del Piccolo* for youth has pages of colored comics, sports features, nature articles, jokes, puzzles, even doll cutouts.

Italian papers are anything but dull. The larger independents, it is true, are more conservative and objective in their news handling; but some others with their political charges and countercharges, their lack of objective factual reporting, their sensationalizing of the sordid details in crime and scandal stories sometimes merit the charge of irresponsibility, according to Italian newsmen. They ascribe this, in part, to a moral collapse during the war and, in part, to the sense of release after the fall of Fascism which had forbidden all sex and crime stories so that people had become morbidly curious about public and private scandals. A Press Council representing journalists in the National Press Federation and the Federation of Newspaper Publishers has established a court of honor to condemn press derelictions and to influence the press toward a greater sense of responsibility.

How Does the Press Fare Economically?

Since 1958 newspapers have been getting more advertising, particularly the larger independent information papers with sizeable circulations which may allocate 53–60 per cent of their space to advertising. Italian sources estimate that at least ten papers are profitable enterprises, including *Corriere della Sera* and its *Corriere d'Informazione*, as well as *Il Giorno*, all in Milan; *La Stampa* and *Stampa Sera* in Turin; *Messaggero*, *Il Tempo* and *Corriere della Sport* in Rome; *Il Resto del Carlino* in Bologna; and *La Nazione* in Florence. There are twenty-two which are political party organs and subsidized by parties. In addition to the profitable papers listed above, nine others are known to be supported by industries, and five are official voices of semistate organizations. This leaves almost 40 per cent of the Italian dailies which must be either marginal or unprofitable enterprises, and the latter probably are subsidized by someone.

The government itself provides some support for all papers on the ground that the press is a necessary public service. Thus papers are granted a subsidy of one-third the market price for newsprint up to 20,000 copies. If they qualify as having a political, cultural, or labor character they pay no general income taxes; and those who have no printing plants of their own get a tax reduction on the composition and printing costs. In addition, papers get lower freight rates for transportation of their newsprint on state railways and enjoy a reduction on telephone, telegraph, and leased-wire rates. Also there appear at intervals advertisments of government ministries.

All this does not mean the government wields any considerable influence on the press, for Italian editors have discovered that the surest recipe for success is to attack the government. Furthermore, the respect for by-lined writers, who express their own opinions, is so great that their copy is not edited. Strange though it may seem, despite widespread subsidization there is such a diversity of controlling interests and such a variety of opinion that Italians are kept fairly well-informed.

The day may come when Italy's papers become more viable. If the trend toward a smaller number of dailies continues, there may be fewer and better ones to divide the available circulation and advertising. Also, if papers learn to convert more of their readers to regular subscribers instead of relying so heavily on newsstand sales, their circulation revenue may be more stable. They may then be more willing to be honest with their advertisers, for there is now nothing like an Audit Bureau of Circulation. No advertiser knows what he is buying, and when a paper makes the same round-figured circulation claim year after year, advertisers are bound to suspect that it is actually far less. One day Italian dailies may find it more profitable to handle their own advertising solicitation, as do a few today, instead of permitting *concessionaires* to handle all their advertising at high commissions, thus robbing the papers of initiative and producing only the limited linage the *concessionaires* bring in.

Except for some of the better independents, the bias of Italian papers and their preoccupation with projecting their partisan position instead of the straight news is daily evident. One can read the same story of some parliamentary or other government event and get a half dozen versions of what actually took place. Stories are written in a verbose and involuted style; it may take a long time to get to what actually happened, and such details as what, where, when, and how are frequently omitted. A reporter's story is mixed with his personal commentary, and it is not unusual for an Italian correspondent's dispatch from abroad to be interlaced with the home editor's personal opinion. With such a diversity of opinion available, any Italian who takes the trouble to look can be fairly well informed of what is taking place at home and abroad.

One must admit that with all their individuality Italian newspapers today, after their centuries of struggle, are free. Some critics call them too free. Yet it is also true that in the sixties there have been journalists expelled from Italy or imprisoned for defamation of the Italian army or the Pope. This is a possible threat, like a sheathed claw, which might be extended to any criticism of government officials.

REPRESENTATIVE NEWSPAPERS

Corriere della Sera (Evening Courier)—Italy's best newspaper. Owned by Crespi textile interests which have permitted editors full independence. Has long maintained its tradition of being "A faithful mirror of the world."

Noted for its excellent foreign dispatches. Published in Milan; three editions distributed through Italy and abroad. Independent politically but generally leans toward the conservative side. Circulation 411,000; its evening companion *Corriere d'Informazione* distributes 175,000 in three editions.

Il Giorno (The Day)—The newcomer which brought a brisk new formula to Italian journalism with terse world, national, and local news, and a rich diet of popular features wrapped up in a brightly departmentalized package. Once, under Enrico Mattei, it was the brashest crusader in Italy; now it is much more tame. Calls itself independent but leans to the more liberal side of Christian Democratic party. Circulation 200,000 daily. Very popular in Milan and gaining outside.

La Stampa (The Press)—One of Italy's most highly regarded papers. Excellent coverage of foreign and national news. Published in Turin; circulation 329,000. Owned by Fiat auto company, which puts no checkrein on editors who have made it, with *Corriere della Sera*, one of two Italian dailies with not only national but international circulation. Its evening companion, *Stampa Sera*, is more popular with more pictures and more sports than any other regular Italian daily.

Il Messaggero (The Messenger)—Rome's most important independent paper and Italy's fourth largest. Publishes one national and twenty provincial editions covering central and southern Italy. Owned by the Perrone family which made its fortune in breweries; yet the Perrone brothers have taken an interest in making it an independent paper. Not highbrow but rather directed to the "lower intellectual" class. Sometimes accused of being a "sunshine paper," sparing its readers bad news. Circulation 187,000.

Il Tempo (The Times)—Founded in Rome in 1945 by Renato Angiolille, whom the author met when he was operating from a hole in the wall; from the start made it a vigorous anti-Communist paper; developed it into a well-balanced serious morning daily. In 1962 took in as partner a Genoese shipping magnate with no conflict in interest, for *Il Tempo* is considered the most influential spokesman for the right. Now second largest in Rome with 150,000 circulation.

La Nazione (The Nation)—What might have been considered just a provincial paper has become one of Italy's outstanding morning dailies with national prestige, putting out thirty-two editions for cities in Tuscany, Umbria, and Liguria. Owned by Eridana Sugar Combine which has given it independence. While it styles itself as independent, it generally leans to conservative. Circulation 175,000. Published in Florence.

Il Resto del Carlino (The Rest of the Carlino)—Derived its name from the change left from a small coin after buying a popular cigar. Of equal rank with *Nazione* but serving the provinces of Emilia, Romagna Marche, Vento, and Lombardia with a number of editions. Also owned by the Eridana Sugar Combine. Independent but leans conservative. Published in Bologna; circulation 168,000.

L'Osservatore Romano (Roman Observer)—Official daily of Vatican City. No longer as important as it was during Fascist and war periods yet its influence in Catholic Italy and throughout Catholic world is great. Its circulation, 70,000.

A Press Reborn

The Newspapers of Greece

Andro, with other newspaper friends, had gone underground when the Germans overran Greece in 1941. He dodged the Gestapo, putting out underground papers, bolstering the courage of his people and urging resistance; but in 1945 he was caught. For weeks he was interrogated, tortured, beaten, to make him divulge the names of others in his "ring." One night, to break him, he was taken out into the floodlit prison courtyard, made to stand against a wall, facing a firing squad, and told he had but five minutes to tell the names or he would be shot. This he knew was the end, but he could not bring himself to betray the others. Instead he prayed till the command "Fire!" rang out. Bullets sprayed all around him; he purposely was not hit. Then he was dumped back into his cell. His captors reasoned that, having so narrowly escaped death, he would submit. But death now held no terror; he never yielded. Not long after, British and American troops broke through German lines and opened his prison. Andro (the name is fictional] was but one of many Greek press heroes.

Greek journalism is one of the youngest in Europe. Greece may have been the birthplace of western civilization, but at the time when Gutenberg and his contemporaries were developing printing, the Turks captured Constantinople (Istanbul), the capital of the great Byzantine empire, and seat of Greek learning. They soon overran Greece and for four hundred years kept her in subjection, permitting no journalistic activity. Greek newspapermen like to think of Homer as the father of all war correspondents, and of ancient educated Athenians, who compiled written accounts of daily events, as the forerunners of their later newsletter writers. But two millennia were to elapse before true journalism came to Greece. Her great empire fell to the Romans, and for five centuries she was a neglected Roman province. Then came barbarian and Slavonic invasions, followed by Sicilians, Venetians, Normans, and Crusaders. Finally, under Turkish rule,

Europe forgot about Greece almost as completely as if she had sunk into the sea.

Greek Journalism Begins in Exile

When, toward the end of the eighteenth century, the Turkish empire showed signs of decline, Greeks rose in revolt but were ruthlessly suppressed. The stirring events in France, however, were like a clarion call and brought the first Greek newspaper. The Greek poet, Rigas Fereos, and two printers, the Pouliou brothers, brought out in Vienna on December 3, 1790, *Ephemeris* (Journal), carrying news from France, hymns, poems, and appeals to awaken their subject people. It appeared, when it could, every other week and was smuggled into Greece until the Turks protested to Austria and Fereos and the Pouliou brothers were deported. But exiles in Paris, London, and other European cities continued publication of literary and patriotic papers, also smuggled into Greece, where literary and patriotic organizations were started. Most important was *Hetari*, founded in 1815, with centers in Bucharest, Trieste, and Moscow and with secret branches in Greece itself. It collected arms and made preparations for revolt.

Greeks celebrate their Independence Day on March 25, for on this day in 1821 Archbishop Germanos, head of the *Hetari* in the Peleponnesus, raised a cross on a mountain as a signal for the rising of Christians. A press was needed as soon as the revolution broke, but there was no printing press in Greece, not even types cut in Greek. First papers had to be handwritten and of limited circulation, but they were eagerly passed from hand to hand. Then Prince Demetrios Ypsilantis arrived from Russia with a press which he set up in Kalavrita. Theoklitos Farmakides, a Greek publisher in Vienna who had come as a volunteer, was made editor; on August 1, 1821, *Salpinx* (Bugle) appeared as the first printed paper on Greek soil. But when Farmakides denounced Ypsilantis and other revolutionary leaders, *Salpinx* came to an end.

A Philhellenic committee in London under Colonel L. Stanhope, collecting arms for the insurgents, shipped four printing plants to Greece. One came to Messolonghi on the Gulf of Corinth, then under Turkish attack. Alexander Mavracordas, garrison commander, and Lord Byron, English poet, living in Messolonghi, were editors of *Ellenika Chronika;* and Byron also helped edit *Greek Telegraph* in English, French, German, and Italian as a propaganda medium for the revolution. After Byron's death from exposure these papers carried on till their plant was destroyed by Turkish shells. A second plant had gone to Athens where *Ephemeris Atheton* was published until Turks demolished the plant in 1826. A third went to Nauplion where *Genie Ephemeris Ellenikos* was put out as a revolutionary organ. The fourth was sent to the island of Hydra on which *O Filos tou Nomou* (Friend of the Law) was published. These were the firsts among Greek papers, but there is record of some sixty others appearing during the seven years of the revolutionary war.

Troubles Come with Freedom

The revolt went well for three years until Egypt, a Turkish vassal, came in to turn the tide. In 1827 Russia, France, and England intervened, annihilated the Turkish and Egyptian fleets, and exacted from Turkey a recognition of Greek independence. Greeks were now free, but thirty-seven years were to elapse before the Greek press won any measure of liberty.

Count Capo d'Istria, former Russian foreign minister, was made first president of the General Assembly but, with his Russian background, he quickly curbed the press. Editors who fought his autocratic methods and his refusal to establish constitutional government were jailed and had their plants wrecked. Revolutionaries assassinated Capo d'Istria in 1831. Anarchy followed till the powers made Greece an independent kingdom and placed Prince Otto of Bavaria on the throne. He proved just as despotic, just as arbitrary toward the press. The people still clamored for a constitution, but they could do little under his terroristic police system. Finally in 1862 they revolted, deposed Otto and brought Prince William George of Denmark to the throne as George I. His reign began auspiciously with a new constitution providing a democratic unicameral system and freedom for the expression of differing political views. This at once gave rise to political parties and strongly partisan papers, for leading journalists were outstanding personalities who used their papers to champion their differing views. By 1883 the number of papers had grown to 111, of which 28 were in Athens.

New Voices Rise

Greece produced her first daily in 1873 when Demetrios Koromilas founded *Ephemeris* at Athens as a new type of paper, independent of party and placing its emphasis on news. But it, too, soon became a political force as Koromilas attacked leaders of all parties. How active a political part this paper played is evidenced by the fact that from its staff eventually came eleven ministers and six premiers. Greek papers were often in a fever of excitement over national desires to bring

Greeks, in territories unredeemed from the Turks, into the kingdom. Greece became involved in three wars with Turkey. She won Thessaly in the first, but the last two ended disastrously. By the end of the century conditions in the country were deplorable, the people desperately poor, too poor to buy newspapers, the nation torn with dissension.

Meanwhile there had come a new and different paper, *Akropolis*, which started as a weekly and became a daily in 1884. Vlasios Gavrilidis, publisher, became the stormy petrel of Greek journalism. In violent editorials he fought for social reforms, individual liberty, reorganization of the army, and more productive methods for agriculture. He excoriated the leaders of the many parties for keeping the people divided. Completely changeable, he would laud the king one day and go to jail the next for blasphemous attacks against him. Yet he had an impact on Greek journalism, for he was the first to introduce modern reporting, interviews, special features, and departments for sports, agriculture, literature, and the theater, and the first to avail himself of telegraphic news. He soon outdistanced all his rivals and continued to publish this paper till 1920. *Akropolis* is today the oldest paper in Athens.

But politics still dominated the press. There were nearly a score of parties, and papers were fighting sheets for their candidates. So unstable were conditions that fourteen governments succeeded each other till in 1909 constitutional government was superseded by an attempted military dictatorship.

The Good Years under Venizelos

In the resulting chaos all parties agreed to call Eleftherios Venizelos from Crete to restore order. An old fighter against the Turks, he proved to be a statesman. He quickly brought security of life and property, overhauled the armed forces, and helped form a new constitution. Protection of the press against censorship or seizure, except for insult to the Christian religion or the king or for indecency, was defined. The king and the whole people, led by the press, rallied back of Venizelos and brought about greater unity than the country had had in some time. By 1912 Venizelos had whipped his country into shape to fight with its allies in the first and second Balkan Wars which gained large territories in the north and in the islands. This restored freedom to Greek newspapermen formerly under strict Turkish rule. Most important of the new papers was *Makedonia*, started in 1911 as Salonika's first daily, today the most important paper in northern Greece. New free papers began to spring up throughout former Turkish areas.

In the new Greece, doubled in population, multiplied in wealth, the press grew till Athens had fifteen dailies, many only two to four pages with flaring black and red heads, each like an extra heralding world-shaking news. Greeks read them with avidity to feed their never ending free-for-all political arguments in coffee shops. Since there was little advertising most papers had to be supported by politicians or parties.

King George was succeeded by his son Constantine in 1913. When World War I broke, the latter insisted on neutrality, for he was a brother-in-law of Kaiser Wilhelm. Venizelos, who favored the Allies, resigned, but returned when the Allies forced the abdication of Constantine. However, it was not until the last months of the war that Greeks fought alongside the Allies in taking Bulgaria. When peace came the people were weary of the state of war which had existed since 1912. In the 1920 election Venizelos was defeated and Constantine returned to the throne. For the next eight years Greece was in turmoil; yet two important papers were founded, *Kathimerini* (Daily) in 1919 and *To Vima* (Tribune) in 1922, two of the leading Athens papers today. A disastrous defeat in war with Turkey inspired the revolt of 1923 which deposed the king. A republic was established but strife continued; there were revolts and counterrevolts till General Theodore Pangalos set up a military dictatorship in 1926, suspended the constitution, closed all opposition papers, and imposed strict censorship. A coup overthrew the dictator, but unrest continued till 1928 when the country turned again to Venizelos.

The next four years brought peace and stability. Trade improved, industrial production and finances moved upward. Greek newspapermen look back on the years 1928–32 as among the best in their modern history, for with the restoration of freedom and an expanding economy the press grew till it embraced 50 dailies and 450 weeklies, magazines, and other periodicals. Most circulations remained small because of the difficulties of communication in this mountainous country and the poverty of the masses and their high illiteracy; weaker papers had to rely on party subsidy. Larger dailies were, however, able to install more modern printing equipment, and many were getting the telegraphic service of the Athens News Agency, privately owned but backed by the Foreign Ministry.

Metaxas Muzzles the Press

The world economic depression seriously affected Greece. The people were reduced to grinding poverty and frustration. The failure of traditional parties to find solutions to economic problems brought three years of instability and violence which paved the way for the return of Constantine's son as King George II in 1935. A few months later a new government was formed under General Joannes Metaxas, who dissolved parliament and set up a dictatorship.

Civil liberties and press freedom were suspended as Metaxas fastened on the country the iron grip of a fascistic state. In muzzling the press he borrowed techniques from both Italy and Germany. Theoloudus Nikoloudes, secretary for press and tourism, was given the task of selling the new ideology. Like Goebbels in Germany, he took control not only of newspapers and periodicals but radio, theater, and films. Communist sheets and many smaller papers were suppressed. Other papers were hounded into submission and placed under rigid censorship. Any criticism of the government or mention of labor organizations, the army, economic conditions, or the rising cost of living was prohibited. Through his control of Agence Athene (Athens News Agency), he supplied three-fourths of the contents of all papers and also used it to issue daily instructions. The face of the Greek press was changed completely and became so uniform and dull that circulations fell off 40 per cent. The people simply did not believe this regimented press, and 80 per cent regarded the dictatorship as anathema. But under a secret police reign of terror they could do nothing against a dictator supported by the king and the army.

World War II Engulfs Greece

Mussolini, seeking quick spoils, invaded Greece on October 28, 1940. When Metaxas defied his ultimatum, the whole people, despite their previous hatred of the dictator, rose in defense of Greece. Within three weeks intrepid Greek soldiers, although poorly armed, had driven Italian legions from Greek soil and in two months had them fighting in Albania to keep from being driven into the Adriatic. Mussolini's failure upset Hitler's plans, for it exposed his Balkan flank which he had to make secure before he could proceed with his invasion of Russia. Although overwhelmed by tremendous mechanized German forces, the Greeks fought to the Mount Olympus line, then to the Thermopylae line. Step by step they fought back to the southern ports, but by the end of April, 1941, Greece had been conquered.

The German military government, needing papers to communicate with Greeks in their own language, ordered seven of the larger Athens papers to continue under German direction. They seized the plants of *Makedonia* and *Phos* in Salonika. In Patras *Neologos* was ordered to continue, but its editors found ways to circumvent censors; they printed stories saying Goebbels denied such-and-such Allied advances, till the people began to understand that what Goebbels had denied, actually had happened. Most other provincial papers were suspended.

Many editors, publishers, and writers who refused to collaborate were sent to concentration camps; others escaped into the mountains. The Athens News Agency now supplied to official papers only German and Italian dispatches, but loyal Greeks on these papers learned to edit these dispatches so that people might read between the lines. They composed apparently innocuous poems so that the first letter of each line spelled messages such as "have courage" or "long live freedom."

The Greeks Fight Back

Hundreds of newspapermen, who had seemingly vanished, began putting out underground papers. Loyal Greeks, on German-controlled papers, managed to put out clandestine sheets in their own back shops. Some eighty-three underground papers and newssheets appeared during the occupation keeping up the morale of the people, informing them of war developments, exposing Greek collaborators and Axis cruelties, spurring people to resistance, recruiting men for guerrilla forces. They were avidly read and passed from hand to hand. Some were printed on small hand presses in church basements and belfries; others were mimeographed. Germans and Italians staged night raids and mass arrests, imprisoning or executing suspects. Always there were volunteers to take their places. Clandestine papers continued to appear, not without frequent casualties. But the people believed them and considered the official papers "lying sheets."

Because the Greeks never gave up and fought their conquerors as they could, Greece was made to suffer more than any other country in the war. Bands of guerrillas unceasingly harried enemy patrols, attacking their camps in large-scale nighttime battles, blowing up their communications. The enemy retaliated by killing ten Greeks for every one of their own lost. The world heard much of tragic Lidice in Czechoslovakia; but few heard of Kalavrita, Distoman, and other towns which suffered similar complete annihilation. When Greeks still resisted, the Axis requisitioned all local food supplies and livestock. Preposterous taxes were extorted to meet the cost of occupation. The reckless issue of paper money boosted food costs to a thousand times the normal prices. By August, 1944, the people faced acute starvation. All day long in Athens and Piraeus carts hauled away emaciated corpses. Only when the Allies through the Swiss and Swedish Red Cross were able to get some food supplies in, was the situation somewhat relieved.

Liberation and Then Civil War

The two strongest resistance forces were EDES (Greek Democratic Liberation Army) and ELAS (Communist Liberation Army). Fighting broke out between the two in 1943–44 but was halted by Allied arbitration. Then on September 24, 1944, an Anglo-American army landed in force and with the help of guerrilla bands liberated the country in forty days.

Papers published under German control ceased, and for a time only resistance papers appeared. Typical was *Eleftheria* (Liberty), started in the last year of the war, which now appeared as a daily and became one of the leading papers in Athens. Soon some of the older newspapers came out; and the people, realizing that these papers were no longer under enemy control, went back to them. Those which had been official papers found their plants intact, but many provincial papers discovered their printing equipment destroyed. Eight years later the author found some small dailies still being hand-set. Because of the extreme poverty everywhere, there was not room for the old papers and all the new resistance papers, and few of the latter lived long. There was complete press freedom, and papers reflected furious disagreement over postwar problems. Liberal and Communist papers opposed the return of the monarchy, suspicious of the "royal government in exile" which had had no part in the Greek resistance. Rightists and royalist papers were equally violent in their insistence on the return of King George.

The premiership was finally entrusted to George Papandreou, Social Democrat; and a conference of resistance leaders agreed to the formation of a new national government and army and the restoration of security and order as a prelude to a free choice of the form of government. But the Communists insisted on controlling five portfolios, including the Ministries of War and Interior, the method under which Communists took control of east European countries. When Papandreou refused these demands and attempted to dissolve the old guerrilla armies to set up a new national army, civil war broke out in December, 1944, between ELAS and the government. It was a bitter war, and for a time ELAS came close to taking over all Greece till British forces intervened, for Winston Churchill was unwilling to permit the establishment of a dictatorship in Greece. The new strength prevailed and the Communists reluctantly signed the Varitza peace agreement in February, 1945.

During this war all opposition papers in ELAS territory had been closed, and elsewhere papers had been handicapped under martial law. Once peace was declared, the new premier, Plastiras, decreed free circulation of papers of all political complexions. At once he was attacked by both the right and the left and had to give way to a succession of conservative ministries who suppressed all opposition papers. The demand grew for a national plebiscite to determine the form of government. Because of popular reaction against the Communists in the civil war, the Royalist party won the March, 1946, election; and in a national plebiscite six months later, 68 per cent of the Greeks voted for a restoration of the monarchy. King George returned to the throne.

This precipitated a second civil war as ELAS rose in protest. Fighting was particularly severe in northern Greece where guerrilla bands from Albania, Bulgaria, and Yugoslavia came over the hills in lightning raids, destroyed village after village, and carried off children to be reeducated in the Communist faith. England, beset by her own postwar problems, found herself unable to continue large-scale aid to Greece, and President Harry Truman announced that the United States would assume British responsibility. With American arms and retrained Greek units to fight a mobile offensive war, the tide began to turn; and by August, 1949, ELAS had been defeated after three years of terrible war. King George died of a heart attack during the fighting and was succeeded by his son, Paul I.

Greek Press Rebuilds

Nine years of war had left the country bankrupt. A sixth of its people had lost their lives. Except for the few who had enriched themselves, most lived in abject poverty. Of the 8,000,000 people left only 8,000 were well off; the rest were miserably poor. Despite American aid, the government's expenditures for its armies and for relief had been so great that it had financed its deficits by printing money. This led to spiraling inflation.

It was a poor base on which to build a new press; yet so great was the hunger of the people for news that newspapers succeeded in coming back, first in the south and the islands, later in the north. Severe damage to transportation as well as the difficulties of traveling the mountainous terrain tended to regionalize the press, for it was now difficult for even the larger papers to circulate over the country. Nevertheless, by 1950 there were 60 dailies, 13 appearing two or three times a week, and 136 weeklies and periodicals. Only *Kathimerini* in Athens and *Makedonia* in Salonika were getting much circulation outside their own cities. Newsprint shortage restricted even larger papers to four pages, most of the others to two.

The press went back to its old political disputativeness; there could have been few papers without support from politicians, parties, banks, or other business interests. Circulations were small and there was little advertising. Some papers were not careful of the facts and some were irresponsible. Many prewar journalists had died or had been incapacitated in concentration camps; their places were taken by young people with no journalistic experience. Some were not above playing a sensational story whether there were facts to back it or not. *Nea Demokratica* went too far in running a story allegedly exposing the sex life of the younger Venizelos, Liberal party leader, and was suppressed. Most other papers denounced the culprit paper editorially, some ran the story in full to show how bad it was but also to cash in on sales. The author recalls one morning in 1953 when some papers splashed, "A terrible accident between a train and a bus in which 44 have been killed." A quick check with police disclosed that reporters must have relied only on excited bystanders, for no one had been killed and only three had suffered slight injuries.

A succession of governments controlled Greece after the war; but under the system of proportional representation no party could ever get enough seats to take strong steps toward rehabilitating the country, and uneasy coalitions of Social Democrats, Liberals, and Populists or Royalists followed each other. Many editors became crusaders for social and governmental reform. Opposition crystallized under Marshall Alexander Papagos, a great war hero who had resigned from the army to form the Greek Rally party which promised abolition of proportional representation, reforms in government and taxation, and a program to get Greece on her feet. The new electoral law was passed; and in the November, 1952, election the Greek Rally won 239 out of the 300 parliament seats. For the first time in long years, Greece had a strong and responsible government.

New Programs Bring Problems

Most papers supported the government as it cut expenses, pared excessive bureaucracy, overhauled the tax system, and accelerated reconstruction. With American aid Greece, by 1953, was advancing her postwar recovery. Newspaper conditions improved with the easing of import restrictions till dailies could publish as many eight-page papers a week as they could afford and ten to twelve pages weekends. They expanded their foreign news and picture coverage. There were now only three effective parties, right, center, and left; hence there was no need for many party organs. A keener sense of responsibility developed; and strong papers emerged independent of the government, approving its worthwhile reforms and its efforts to balance the budget, yet alert to the welfare of the people. Thus when the government devalued the drachma from 15,000 to 30,000 to let Greek products compete abroad, papers warned that, while this moved out tobacco surpluses, food and consumer prices would skyrocket. Business did fall off; unemployment increased; there were waves of strikes. Newspapers became increasingly critical.

Threats to the Press

Devaluation also brought a newspaper crisis, for newsprint had to come from Scandinavia and its price shot up till most papers were forced back to four pages; other production costs rose 60 per cent. Advertising and circulation fell off badly. Publishers asked an increase in their sales prices, but this was refused. Instead they were granted temporary credits for newsprint purchases. Because of press criticism, the government enacted a bill providing fines for publication of matter which might undermine public confidence in the government, the army, or the currency. The greatest threat to Greek journalism was the provision that any paper convicted might be deprived of its duty-free newsprint, and this meant closure.

Another threat came in 1954 when the minister of information presented a bill for the control of all newspapermen, delegating to the minister the right to prevent "anyone not considered qualified" from working on any paper. It paralleled so closely the methods through which the Nazis and Fascists had muzzled their papers that the whole press rose in protest. The deputy premier and the minister of information were forced out of office, and the bill died with their departure.

Better Times Arrive

Papagos died in 1955 and was succeeded by Konstantinos Karamanlis, popular minister of public works. He initiated a period of stability and economic growth and an improved standard of living. This was disturbed by the Cyprus crisis where a majority of the Grecian population demanded *enosis* (union with Greece). There were no neutrals in the Greek press. Bitter fighting took place on Cyprus, mass demonstrations in Greek cities. There was much anti-British feeling in the press, and despite the massive aid provided Greece by the United States, some papers became bitter toward the Americans for not taking sides with Greece. But gradually the Karamanlis government and more sober newspapers began urging negotiations for a just settlement which brought the establishment of an independent Cypriot Republic with an equitable division of power between Greeks and Turks.

Greece settled down to normal life again. A great capital investment program was announced to provide jobs for 400,000. And when Greece had come to an agreement with foreign bondholders for a gradual settlement of her external debt, a consortium of western nations worked out a program for economic development. Lignite and bauxite mining became important; a great new aluminum plant was built; hydroelectric development gave a spur to other industries. Greece was admitted to an associate membership in the Common Market, and her foreign trade improved till she began to feel a little of the western European boom. To meet tourist needs, fine new hotels began to change the face of Athens and other cities. By July, 1962, American aid of $150,000,000 a year could be discontinued. But Greece was still a poor country, for a fourth of her people were unemployed or underemployed. In 1929 the per capita income for the whole country had been only $297 and for rural areas $175. It rose till in 1964 it was estimated at $373 for the country as a whole.

New Political Alignments Affect Press

Economic difficulties for the masses brought a new lineup both in the press and among voters. The Karamanlis National Democratic Union (ERE) was so strong that opposition groups joined a Union of the Democratic Left (EDA). But the Communists, though their own party was outlawed, sought to exploit distress among workers and farmers and soon became the hard core of EDA. Voters found themselves with only two choices. The author in 1959 visited a mountain village on the Bulgarian border which had suffered terribly from Communist raids in the civil war, yet had voted solidly for EDA candidates to shock Athens into doing something for their village, where people still lived in tents and still had no school ten years after the war. In 1960 the Democratic Center, the Liberals, and the Progressives left EDA to form the Union of the Center. In the bitterly fought 1961 election ERE won 176 seats, the Center 100, and the Communist dominated Agrarian Front, 24. There was now growing opposition in press and parliament to the Karamanlis administration, and Socialist leader Papandreou pursued in parliament an unrelenting campaign on every issue. Karamanlis resigned in 1963. During the last of his regime and the three caretaker governments which followed, war again broke out between Greeks and Turks on Cyprus. Again the Greek press was aflame. There was bitter fighting on the island till U.N. forces intervened and imposed a fragile truce, but no political settlement had been achieved by the end of 1965. Early in this crisis King Paul died and was succeeded by his twenty-three-year-old son as King Constantine.

In the 1964 election Papandreou and his United Center Party won a smashing victory, and this was to have an important effect on the press. True, prior to this time opposition papers had certainly exercised their freedom in attaching the rightist governments, in denouncing their abuses and mistakes; but this press had always been uneasy, for there was the risk that the government might crack down with fines or prison sentences, deny a paper duty-free newsprint, call its loans, or reduce its bank credit.

Now that that anxiety has disappeared, papers of all political views can speak as they wish. There is no censorship, and the press is much more free than radio, which is government-owned. The constitution provides freedom of the press, with due adherence to the laws of the state; and press laws do permit the government to punish papers for offending public decency, for insulting the royal family, for disclosing military information in times of danger, or for instigating treasonable acts. However, one cannot read the frank criticism in Greek papers without concluding that there is great freedom and that the government seldom uses the powers it possesses.

Many papers have become much more careful about checking facts and handling news responsibly. Reporting, editing, and display techniques have also improved so that papers are far more readable and interesting. This has brought larger circulations to the better papers. There are a few sensational papers which are uninhibited in reporting sex and crime stories, for in libel cases retraction and an apology are generally accepted as reparation for damages and exoneration of culpability. Strangely, the two most sensational are the small French language *Messager d'Athenes* and the English language *Athens News*.

In 1965 the press was torn by the bitter political battle between former premier Georges Papandreou and King Constantine, who dismissed the premier when he learned of a secret army leftist group organized with government connivance on Cyprus to force Greek withdrawal from NATO. There were massive leftist demonstrations and riots in Athens. The king named one premier after another; but none could win a parliament vote of confidence until September, when Stephen Stepanopoulos was appointed. Papandreou will probably call for elections in January, 1966; but the king can hardly agree, for a Papandreou victory might mean his own ouster. Newspaper surprise of the year was the tremendous growth of *To Vima* and *Ta Nea*, both strong supporters of Papandreou and his leftists.

The Greek Press Today

The Greek press reported ninety-nine daily papers in 1964, a gain of eleven over 1963. From this must be subtracted five foreign language papers in English, French, German, and Armenian, plus a plethora of eight financial papers and one sports daily, all in Athens, leaving eighty-five regular Greek daily newspapers. Because circulation figures are given only for the larger papers in Athens and those in Patras, Piraeus, Thessalonika, and Volos, no accurate circulation can be arrived at, but it is estimated that the total daily circulation is something in excess of 1,000,000. UNESCO in its 1964 World Communications estimated that for a population of 8,387,201 there was a daily distribution of but 12.5 copies per 100 persons. Because of the intense rivalry between political parties, there are a number of cities with populations of 18,000 to 30,000 with two, three, and even four dailies. The author in visiting many of these papers found some with only 1,000 to 2,500 circulation. Of the eighty-five regular daily newspapers twelve are in Crete and Rhodes, leaving seventy-three on the mainland. In addition there are 72 weeklies, 84 fortnightlies, and 155 monthly magazines and periodicals.

Athens, with 1,853,000 people, is the journalistic capital, for it has seventeen regular Greek dailies in addition to many periodicals. Thessalonika with 251,000 has five, and Patras with 95,364 has three. The rest are distributed in small cities, only nine of which are one-newspaper towns. The most important weeklies are *Embros* and *Tachydromos*, both serious Saturday journals, and *Romants*, the most popular woman's magazine, all in Athens. There are no large circulations; the largest paper, *Ta Nea*, had 86,500 in 1964. A circulation of 30,000 to 40,000 is considered good. There are reasons for this. Not only did nine years of war, occupation, and civil war leave the nation prostrate but there followed ten years of slow recovery. Even now that things are better, many cannot afford to buy a daily paper. Also, while literacy for the country as a whole is 82.3 per cent, it is much less in many rural areas. It must be remembered that for those who lived through the 1940–49 period, education stopped. However, low circulations are not a true measure of readership. In coffee shops and tavernas, papers are available for the price of a drink. On sunny days one can leave a small payment with the newsstand dealer and sit on a bench to peruse a paper for a half hour. Even in isolated mountain villages the author has seen a roomful of men eagerly listening to the local schoolmaster or priest reading a paper to those who cannot themselves read.

Despite the fact that Greece has a ratio of readership lower than that in any other western European nation except Italy, Spain, and Portugal, one cannot but admire the vitality of this Greek press which has survived great difficulties and maintains a surprisingly high intellectual level. It is still deeply political; but all papers, regardless of their political bent, try to keep their readers informed on international news and how it may affect them and of the political, social, and economic problems in their own country. All publish lively editorials and long commentaries on the news which are loved by readers, for they provide ammunition for the endless and often heated arguments in the squares and coffee houses.

Economic necessity limits most dailies to eight pages, but the larger ones sometimes run ten to fourteen in their weekend editions, occasionally as many as thirty. A typical eight-page daily appears in full standard page size in eight columns. Leading foreign and national news stories are played across the top and down the whole right side of the front page, often under heavy, many-decked heads with good picture display. The lower left is given to the lead editorial article and several shorter commentaries. Page two then presents a miscellany of local news, social items, deaths, marriages, movie, theater, and radio announcements, followed by a page of well-written background articles and more wire news. The fourth page is cultural with musical, theatrical, literary reviews and a serial story. Then follows a page of more local and wire news, particularly from other parts of Greece. Page six may be devoted largely to classified advertising except for a second serial story. The seventh page is given to business, finance, and sports. The back page is the "late news page," heavy with foreign and national news. This is read from top to bottom, for, while news elsewhere in the paper may be played according to the paper's political views, here the reader gets his news straight. The more popular papers are less solid with news, are given to playing sensational crime stories, beauty contests, pinup girls, and more pictures. Some of the larger papers are noted for their distinguished political cartoons.

But There Are Economic Problems

All pages except the first and last carry advertising. This has increased till in 1962 the total advertising bill was estimated at $8,500,-000, of which newspapers got 44 per cent. Some stronger dailies get 40 per cent or more of their income from advertising, but most get no more than 20 per cent and have to rely on circulation for the rest. Since this comes entirely from newsstand sales and fluctuates from day to day, depending on the news, many papers do not get enough from normal income sources. Most advertising is classified and general, the latter mainly from foreign manufacturers, particularly of electrical appliances. What local there is comes from movie houses, which advertise heavily on Monday and Tuesday, and from airlines, shipping firms, and banks There is little local retail advertising, for Greek merchants get most fun out of life bargaining with the customer over prices. Hence what local ads are run are usually only name ads without definite prices or any selling copy. The right kind of retail advertising could bring increased sales for local shops and increased linage, but no one has yet been able to effect this change. Papers also carry "wild advertising," publicity stories run at so much per line.

Many papers still suffer from economic anemia. There are stronger dailies whose operations are profitable enough so that they can stand on their own feet, but a number of dailies get help from political parties, banks, or industrial firms whose views they espouse.

Yet the press has earned the respect of the Greek people. Though it is politically oriented, this is what its readers want; it still keeps them well-informed. Most of its foreign news comes from *Agence Athene*, financed partly by the government, the rest by newspaper and radio subscriptions. It has exchange agreements with Reuters, AFP, and European national agencies. Some papers also subscribe to AP or UPI.

REPRESENTATIVE NEWSPAPERS

Kathimerini (Athens)—One of the quality papers published by Helen Vlachos, whose father made this the best and largest in Greece. Well-edited with wide news coverage. Generally Conservative. Like quality papers in other countries, does not have the largest circulation, but has a solid 62,000; and its evening companion, *Missimvrini*, has 25,000. Appeals to upper and middle classes.

To Vima (Athens)—Another quality paper published by Christos Lambrakis, who took over from his father and by 1964 had doubled circulation to 33,800. In 1965 circulation jumped to a claimed 135,629 because of strong support of Papandreou and his leftists. Provides good news and picture coverage. Appeals to lower middle and lower classes.

Ta Nea (Athens)— Afternoon companion of *To Vima;* in 1964, the largest paper in Greece with 86,500 daily circulation and 106,000 on Sunday. Much local news and popular features, but does not neglect foreign and national events. In 1965, because of its strong support of Papandreou, the paper claimed 225,052 daily circulation. It is the king-pin of the Lambrakis press, which also publishes *Tachydromos* (Courier), a weekly news magazine; *Economikos Tachydromos* (Financial Courier); *Omada*, a weekly sports magazine; *Epoxas*, a monthly literary magazine; and *Moda*, a monthly women's magazine.

Akropolis (Athens)—Second largest with 72,765 daily circulation. Popular, picture-minded paper inclined to sensation. Appeals to lower middle and lower class. Probably most nationalistic. Generally conservative and supporter of royalty. Has afternoon companion in *Apoyovmatini* with 46,564 circulation.

Eleftheria (Athens)—One of the few survivors of the underground press. A well-informed paper with no party ties but which generally favors liberal progressive ideas. Pro-western and strongly anti-Communist. Morning paper with 30,000 circulation. Appeals to middle and upper class.

Athinaiki (Athens)—Liberal paper with 42,000 circulation. Was most strongly opposed to Karamanlis government and king. Publishers spent seven months in prison for insulting royal family.

Vradyni (Athens)—Afternoon paper with 31,600 daily circulation and 40,000 Monday. Most strongly pro-rightist. Pro-western, anti-Communist, sometimes critical of U.S.

Avghi (Athens)—Disclaims Communist ties but is certainly a strong fellow traveler. Less concerned with news than with propaganda. Claims 20,000 circulation but probably has half of that. Could not exist without party support.

Makedonia (Salonika)—The foremost provincial daily in the most modern plant in Greece with 22,000 daily circulation and 46,999 Sunday. Covers all of northern Greece. A good, newsworthy paper; pro-Liberal.

The Press of Franco's Spain

Spain once ruled a great empire, but later Spaniards became a people apart, shut from the rest of Europe by the Pyrenees, and shut off from each other by their own interior mountains till being a Catalon, Basque, or Andalusian was as important as being Spanish. They were so proud of their own beliefs and institutions that they cared nothing for those of other nations. A people capable of deep mysticism, innately religious, respectful of authority yet independent and courageous, they are often amenable to a press controlled by state or church. Only for a few brief periods have they known a free press. From 1839 to 1962 their papers were the most completely controlled in Europe, except for those in the Communist states, but since then a faint breath of liberty has begun to blow.

The original Iberians, Phoenicians, Greeks, Carthaginians, Celts from the north, Visigoths from the east, and Moors from Africa, all played their part in the making of this nation. For seven hundred years it was ruled by the Moors who gave it a high civilization when the rest of Europe was in the dark ages; but as the Moorish Caliphate in Spain fell apart, Christian lords in the north began to assert themselves. In the Basque mountains they reconquered their territory and set up the kingdoms of Aragon and Navarre. In the east Castilian princes joined with those of León to set up the kingdoms of Castile and León. By the end of the thirteenth century most of Spain had thrown off the Moslem yoke.

The First Laws on Printing

In 1479 Ferdinand of Aragon and Isabella of Castile were married, joining these two states. After conquering Granada they became the undisputed rulers of the Christian kingdom of Spain and completed the reconquest of their country. Curiously, in 1474 when William Caxton published his first book at Bruges in Belgium, Queen Isabella of Castile issued her first decree on printing, specifying that there should be no taxes or duties on imported books which she termed "advantageous instruments for creating learning." Immigrant printers from Germany and Flanders were already crossing into Spain, and in 1474 the first Spanish book, "Verses in Praise of the Virgin Mary," appeared in Valencia. That was Catholic enough to arouse no fear, and neither did other religious books appearing in Madrid, Seville, Tortosa, Toledo, and Barcelona. But when printers branched out to publish secular classics, books of fable, and the romances of chivalry, the church became disturbed lest this freedom pose a threat to Catholic morals and "might warp the minds of men." Ferdinand and Isabella in 1480 had set up their Inquisition to promote the faith and to drive out Jews, Moslems, and other non-Catholics. Now in 1482 this was also made the chief instrument for controlling printing. Under royal decree every writer, printer, or bookseller had to obtain previous authorization; and ecclesiastical courts were charged with the responsibility of seeing that no unauthorized books appeared. Thus from the very beginning of the Spanish nation, printing came under strict control.

The Birth of an Empire

Glory was already beckoning their majesties when in 1492 they agreed to finance Christopher Columbus in his mad dream of finding a new route to the Indies by sailing westward across the Atlantic. He did find what he thought were the Indies and opened the way for the Conquistadors who ruthlessly conquered the native peoples and created a Spanish empire in the new world from which gold, other wealth, and trade flowed to Spain till she became one of the great powers of the world.

Ferdinand and Isabella were succeeded by their grandson, Charles of Austria, who in 1519 became Charles V, ruler of the Holy Roman Empire, sovereign over the greatest land area ever governed by one man. For the next 170 years Spain was made the tool of the Hapsburgs, sometimes the leader, later the paymaster, and then the dupe in their continual wars. After the Reformation she was made the sword and executioner of the Counter-Reformation, for Hapsburg power depended on religious unity in Europe. In spite of the flow of gold from her American possessions Spain did not profit, for this treasure was used to finance Hapsburg wars. Phillip II, who succeeded Charles, took personal control of Spain and devoted his reign to maintaining the supremacy of Spain in Europe and to upholding the Catholic Faith. His *Autos de Fe* (Articles of Faith) permitted the Inquisition to impose death penalties on printers for even minor infractions of the law.

Nevertheless his reign saw the beginnings of the Spanish Renaissance, later than that in the rest of Europe, and much preoccupied with religion and the themes of anguish and tragedy.

Letter Writers, Newssheets, and First Regular Papers

This intellectual awakening brought a considerable number of news-letter writers, but Pedro Martir de Angleria was the most prolific with 812 issues of his *Opus Epistolarium*. Then came *relaciones*, printed newssheets devoted to a single event. Queen Isabella had brought out the first, long before, when she had published Columbus' first report on his discoveries. But now came many more. Closely supervised, these printers had to avoid anything political and found it safer to report catastrophes, crimes, miracles, and the victories of Spanish armies. There is record of some 3,000 of these *relaciones*. Meanwhile Phillip II had become involved in the religious wars of Europe. Worst was the revolt of his Dutch subjects who, with English aid, won their inde-pendence. He determined to punish England. Once he became master of the British Isles he could insure the triumph of Catholicism there. But his Invincible Armada was ingloriously defeated in 1588, and Spanish pretensions to power began to fade. For the next 102 years this decline continued both in power abroad and in industry, commerce, and agriculture at home.

Nevertheless, the first regularly printed papers appeared in this period. In 1661 an annual appeared in Madrid whose title, trans-lated, was *Relation or Gazette of particular Occurrences such as Political and Military Events in most of the World till the end of December, 1660*. Its first two issues contained no news of Spain, only short dispatches from European capitals. It appeared irregularly for some time till in 1698 it was renamed *Gaceta de Madrid*, which continued monthly till 1809. Then its name appropriately was changed to *Gaceta del Gobierno* (Government Gazette), which lasted till 1936. For seventy-six years it was the only newspaper in Spain.

The sickly line of Spanish kings had about run out at the end of the seventeenth century; and when it became apparent that the imbecile Charles II could have no heir, Louis XIV of France, by a bit of offbeat chicanery, maneuvered his grandson, the Duke of Anjou, onto the Spanish throne as Phillip V. This precipitated the War of the Spanish Succession, which cost Spain Gibraltar and all her possessions in Italy. Phillip stayed on the throne, however, and this new line of Bourbon kings was at least healthy and brought some benefits to Spain and her journalism. Phillip was dissatisfied with the press he found in Spain; and, while he was fully as absolute a ruler and as strong a defender of the Catholic faith as his predecessors were, he did encourage the establishment of nonpolitical cultural journals. He, himself, financed *Diario de Los Literatos de Espagna* in 1737. He did not discourage Fray Joseph Alvarez who in 1732 brought out *Diario Historico, Canonico y Morale*. Interesting also was *El Mercurio Historico*, a translation from the French of events in European royal courts, published by Salvador Joseph Maner. Thus the Spanish press went into its first literary phase.

Tumultuous Years Bring Newspaper Advances and Retreats

Under Charles III (1759–88), an enlightened despot who greatly advanced material prosperity, Spain had her first daily, *Diario*, published by Don Francisco Mariano Nifo, considered the best of early Spanish journalists. It was to continue till the end of the nineteenth century. The reign of Charles IV (1788–1808) saw the first honest attempt to cover European news in *El Spirito de los Majores Diarios que se Publican en Europa*, which appeared three times a week from 1787 to 1790.

Spain now became involved in the Napoleonic wars in which she was rapidly invaded and had Napoleon's brother foisted upon her as King Joseph. An infuriated Spanish people rose in revolt in 1818 and, though often defeated, fought on as guerrillas. Cadiz became the capital of an independent Spain, and its *Cortes* (parliament) drew up the constitution of 1812 which provided for representative government, liberty of the press, suppression of the Inquisition, and curtailment of the privileges of the Church and nobility. With British aid the French were finally driven out of Spain.

These years had seen the press rise to leadership. Chief opponent of the French had been *Semanario Patriótico* (Patriotic Weekly), started by Quintana in Madrid in 1808. As Napoleon had advanced, it had retreated first to Seville and then to Cadiz. In the areas held by Napoleon, only his propaganda organs were permitted. Then, as French forces were driven out and Napoleon became involved in his disastrous campaign against Russia, Liberal papers arose everywhere. Among the most important in Madrid were *El Amigo de la Ley* (Friend of the Law) and *El Ciudadano Imparcial* (Impartial Citizen).

But press freedom was brief for when Napoleon was at last defeated by the allied coalition, he returned King Ferdinand VII whom he had held prisoner. Now, by a curious twist, independence was forgotten and Ferdinand was greeted with acclamation, not only by the Church and nobility but by a great proportion of the masses. He quickly put an end to all liberalism and abolished all Madrid papers except the government's *Gaceta* and *Diario*. In provincial cities there was ruthless censorship. Any criticism of the government meant closure. The press fared no better under Ferdinand's wife and successor, Cristina, regent for their daughter, until a Carlist revolution forced the queen to accept parliamentary institutions.

The Constitution of 1837 brought some liberal reforms, including a degree of press freedom. Now new papers appeared, most important of which was *Español*, founded by Don Andres Borrego, a former Paris and London newspaperman. He returned to Madrid to give Spain a better paper than it had had, better printed, more interesting in appearance, and providing much more foreign and local news as well as dispatches from provincial correspondents. But the journalist most remembered from this period was Manuel Maria de Santa Ana, who in 1848 founded *La Correspondencia de España* as a popular daily. He has been called the James Gordon Bennett of Spain for his innovations in local news reporting, features, the introduction of street salesmen, and other improvements. In 1848 Madrid had six morning and seven evening papers; but of the 210,000 people in the capital only 30,000 could read and less than half of these could afford to buy a newspaper. Total circulation of all Madrid papers was less than 10,000.

Under Cristina's successor, Isabella II, the people tired of despotic rule. There was a general revolution in 1869. An attempt to establish a limited monarchy was unsuccessful as was the First Republic declared in 1873. Anarchy reigned till General Francisco Serrano seized power as a military dictator and Isabella's seventeen-year-old son was proclaimed King Alfonso XII. Antonio Canovas del Castillo proved an able premier for the young king. The Carlist wars were brought to an end and the peninsula pacified. The new constitution of 1876 granted the right to publish ideas without previous censorship, but this proved a sham. For twenty years the Conservatives under Canovas and the Liberals under Práxedes Sagasta alternated in power, each governing with an inflexible hand. They did, however, bring recovery to the land.

Alfonso XII died in 1885 and was succeeded by his infant son with his mother Cristina as regent. Again Canovas and Sagasta alternated as premiers. The first *Cortes* under the regency restored trial by jury, the rights of association and public meeting while control of the press was liberalized. This gave the opportunity for new papers including *El Liberal* whose founder, Isidoro Fernandez Flores, is held in great esteem in Spain's history of journalism. Another was *Heraldo de Madrid*, whose Agosto Suarez de Figuero made it the best paper of its day. Yet newspapers still remained under official surveillance. With the new importance of the *Cortes*, parties came into existence. Liberals, Socialists, Carlists, Alfonsoists, and Conservatives each had their organs in different cities. There were also some independent papers, destined to survive long after their political counterparts disappeared.

As the nineteenth century was drawing to a close, Spain suffered a great loss. Her South and Central American colonies had won their independence by 1823. Now in the Spanish–American War she lost to the United States, the Philippines, Puerto Rico, and Cuba. Her overseas empire was gone.

World War 1 and Its Aftermath

The generation which entered the twentieth century did so in a chastened mood of introspection. Its pseudo-conservative-liberal representative government was blamed for the disaster of 1898, as were the navy and army. Intellectual leaders, however, realized that Spain's despotic-aristocratic-clerical-military government was an anachronism in a modern world, with its denial of rights and education to the people, swamped in mass ignorance and poverty. But powerful underground forces were rising which would brook no delay. Socialists and Anarcho-Syndicalists grew powerful; so did the Separatists, particularly in Catalonia and Asturia, who no longer wished to be run from Madrid, who demanded autonomy in their own affairs, and who precipitated civil wars when their demands were denied. In the cities people took to the streets in violent riots and bombings. One ministry followed another; premiers were assassinated. Major political parties disintegrated into splits of all kinds, and each party had its organs, some violent and incendiary.

The outbreak of World War I found the nation deeply divided. The army, Church, and Conservatives were sympathetic to Germany; the Liberal Republicans of various stripes and the leftists favored the Allies. Neutrality was the only solution, and Spain became rich supplying the needs of combatants on both sides. But the accumulated wealth at the top merely fed the discontent of workers whose wages were still kept down. The unrest came to a head, after the Communists had come to power in Russia in 1917, when general strikes were called in an attempt to create a republic on the Russian model. Then in 1921 a new crisis arose in Morocco, where a general uprising under Abdel Krim inflicted a serious defeat on the Spanish army. This was a last straw and General Miguel Primo de Rivera, in a 1923 coup, took power, saying it was necessary to liberate the country from the politicians who were responsible for all the country's ills since 1898. The new regime enjoyed initial goodwill, for it restored order, eliminated terrorists, brought material prosperity, and by 1926 had crushed the Moroccan revolt.

Political problems were less easy. Rivera imprisoned opposition leaders, drove parties and their organs underground. On papers which remained he imposed strict censorship, for 90 per cent of the papers had castigated the dictator. No blank spaces to indicate censor's deletions were permitted. A definite percentage of space had to be reserved for anything the administration wished published. *El Sol* of Madrid was suspended because it ran "obliged to be inserted" over government material. Editors and publishers might be fined or imprisoned, even though what they printed had passed the censor, if the issue contained anything to which Rivera objected. His clericalist-educational policy ranged universities against him, and the University of Madrid was closed for eighteen months. When he lost the support of the army in 1930, he left the country. His successor, General Dámaso Berenguer, did no better. Hunger strikes and riots broke out. In the 1931 election the rightists were overwhelmingly defeated. The king accepted the verdict and went into exile. Republican leaders came out of prisons and the Second Republic was born.

Prelude to Revolution

Republicans proceeded at once to take Church and army out of politics, to break up big estates and divide them among the starving peasantry, to make all men free and equal, to separate Church from state and provide better elementary education. Many properties of Church and religious orders were expropriated and sold. Reforms were long overdue, but they brought a bitter struggle between those who had everything to lose and those who had nothing. There were monarchist uprisings. The Republican constitution had proclaimed press liberty, but it soon became apparent that freedom was only for Republican papers. Opposition papers were suspended or had their offices sacked or burned. The 1933 election produced a sharp swing to the right.

Now the fascistic Falange party, started by José Antonio Primo de Rivera, son of the former dictator, took leadership and organized paramilitary organizations. A Madrid daily, *ABC*, now openly advocated a return to monarchy. *El Debate* and *Ya* became fascist mouthpieces and *Información*, an organ of the German Nazis. The left retaliated with strikes and riots. In the 1936 election the leftists won again and a Popular Front government set out to achieve the dissolution of the bourgeois society which was its enemy. Strikes and political assassinations paralyzed the country. In the first four months there were 269 murders; 170 churches, 69 political clubs, and 10 newspapers were burned; there were 135 strikes, and this violence came from both sides. The government seemed to have lost control. An army mutiny in Morocco led by General Francisco Franco broke out. In forty-eight hours the whole country was involved in civil war.

Civil wars are always the worst wars. This one was worse than most, fought with savagery and bitterness. Russia poured in help to the Loyalists, hoping that if they won a Communist state might emerge. Italy and Germany lavished help on the right and made their participation a prelude for World War II. In all it cost 1,000,000 lives and incalculable destruction. Loyalists not only burned churches but killed many priests and lay Catholics. Nationalists organized mass executions in towns they took. Loyalists took over all rightist papers in their areas. The Nationalists did likewise, or destroyed papers and executed captured Loyalist editors. Complete censorship was imposed by each side. No paper was permitted to print anything but the propaganda the Loyalist or Nationalist press officers wanted to get out. Except for some early military successes, the Loyalists were on the defensive through most of the three-year war. The conflict ended on April 1, 1939, when Franco took the last Loyalist holdout.

The Press Is Fascistized

The country now became a fascist state with Franco as the *caudillo* (leader) holding supreme power. His cabinet of ministers operated like generals of divisions, carrying on day-to-day operations under his orders. Later a legislature was added, largely appointive, with only advisory functions. The state was given complete control of newspapers, magazines, books, motion pictures, radio, and music.

One of Franco's first acts was the closing of Spain to the foreign press and the purging of Spanish journalists. Some 150 newspapers were shut down and their plants taken over by the Falange. Thus José Ortega y Gasset's *El Sol* plant was taken over by *Arriba*, central Falange organ; and *El Heraldo*, an old liberal paper, had its plant confiscated for *Madrid*. The Falange started twenty-nine papers; sixty-six others were founded by trusted individuals or the Church. *Agencia EFE* was created to distribute foreign news, replacing the French-owned prewar FABRA, and CIFRA was established as a domestic news service, both under Falange control. Thus the news available to papers was curtailed to what the government wanted to have printed.

As in the Nazi system, national delegations were set up to control all creative workers on all information media, all under the vice-secretary of national education, press, and propaganda, charged with censorship responsibility. A director was appointed for every paper, often a man with no journalistic experience, to make sure that nothing critical or subversive appeared. Anything offensive to government, Church, or army brought imprisonment or fines. The editor of a Malaga paper was arrested for a story about a bad orange crop; a Barcelona journalist was imprisoned for articles revealing faulty construction of workers' houses. Spanish papers soon had the boring aspect of propaganda sheets with little news except that dictated by the government.

Spain During World War II and After

Germany's attack on Catholic Poland shocked many Spaniards; but Franco, the Falange, and the army all favored the Axis. Franco, although he had signed a pact with the Axis, had to stay neutral, for the devastation from his own war was so great that he dared not attempt another one in six months. Yet he helped Germans and Italians by providing submarine and fueling ports, air bases for the Luftwaffe, and, through his radio stations, direct reports to Berlin of Spanish spying on allied shipping movements.

During the first part of the war, Spanish papers were decidedly pro-German. But Allied victories in North Africa and western Europe brought a change. Allied airmen who force landed in Spain were given refuge, and the Allies were allowed air bases. After Mussolini's fall the press changed its tune. Yet all this did little good, for at the end of the war Spain was ostracized by the United Nations. The United States, Britain, and France called for the overthrow of Franco; and the UN General Assembly urged member nations to withdraw their ambassadors from Madrid. France closed her frontiers to trade with Spain.

Now Spaniards were really a people apart, and these blows hurt their pride. They rallied back of Franco and said, "We are Spaniards; we will go our own way; we will not accept these insults; we will settle our own affairs." Then as the cold war developed, western nations began to have second thoughts, for Spain was the most staunchly anti-Communist nation in Europe. Franco made concessions by abandoning Spain's totalitarian label for "organic democracy"; the Falange was allowed to sink into the background, and a new *Cortes* was made to seem the watchdog over legislation. There was even talk of the eventual restoration of the monarchy. France and Britain reopened trade with Spain; by 1950 Spain had been admitted to the United Nations; and western nations had resumed diplomatic relations with Madrid. In 1953 the United States and Spain signed a pact permitting the building of American air bases in Spain. By 1960 this had brought the expenditure of $400,000,000 for military bases and more than a billion in economic aid. The International Monetary Fund, the World Bank, and the Organization for European Economic Cooperation moved in to sponsor a stabilization planned to transform the Spanish economy.

The Lid Remains on the Press

Franco emerged from all this still the one-man dictator, his regime stable, the country improving in economic well-being and civic peace. There were so many with a vested interest in Franco. The wealthy landowners, the industrialists, and the banks, who control two-thirds of Spanish industry, wanted no change. Neither did the bureaucrats nor the higher officers in the army, navy, and air force. The Church and all clergy were back of Franco. The common people did not worry so much about rights as long as Franco kept order, for what they feared most was civil strife. Hence there was tranquility and apathy.

Franco still controlled the press. There had been underground papers in the forties, circulated by hand or tucked within "legal" papers which the dissidents called *los tibios* (the comics). But all clandestine papers had been put down. The minister of press and tourism had censors in every newsroom exercising strict precensorship. Foreign publications were also subject to interferences. The international editions of *Time* and *Life*, for instance, by July, 1963, had suffered 112 punishments, usually confiscation of entire issues. Some correspondents of foreign papers were expelled.

A deadly uniformity had settled over the Spanish press, and a whole generation had grown up under severely restricted information. When in 1961 papers were permitted to carry stories of the Adolph Eichmann trial in Israel, it marked the first time Spaniards had heard of Nazi atrocities and shocked many who had been most sympathetic with the Germans during the war. People now read the papers, not for news, but for features, cultural articles, and entertainment. Some measure of their indifference to the press is indicated by the fact that in 1960 its 103 dailies had a total circulation of only 2,085,000 in a population of 30,128,000, which meant only 7 copies per 100 persons—the lowest distribution ratio of any country in western Europe.

A further control had been added with the creation of schools of journalism to which were admitted only those carefully screened to insure their conformity with the Franco regime. Three years of study in professional courses and political theory, which amounted to complete indoctrination, led not only to a diploma but to automatic inscription in the Official Register of Journalists. Without a press card no one could work in any form of journalism. All openings for newsmen had to be filled by selections from these graduates.

Despite its apparent disengagement from the government—to the point where Franco could announce that there was no Falangist in his cabinet and that the party no longer wielded any political power—the Falange was still the biggest newspaper publisher with thirty-three morning and five afternoon dailies well spotted over Spain, plus five weeklies and four magazines. It also controlled most radio, and the one TV network was likewise government-owned. The Falange controlled the news agencies EFE and CIFRA and while both of these and some newspapers had been permitted to use UPI, AP, Reuters, AFP, and Italian ANSA services, the news which papers could print from these was carefully selected. Thus the Falange, while ostensibly pushed into the background, remained the most effective channel for the transmission of government ideas to the people.

Finally a Breath of Freedom

There had been dissidents. Strangely, while the Church generally favored the regime, its publications began to take the lead in opposing censorship. *Ecclesia,* the weekly official organ of the Catholic hierarchy, had been exempted from precensorship; but in 1960 when it wished to publish a manifesto drawn up by 227 intellectuals against government censorship, it was not permitted to do so. Again when 339 priests signed a letter of protest against the excesses of dictatorship, a number of priests and Catholic writers were imprisoned as Communists. After the editor of *Ecclesia* wrote, "How can we consider our press regime as ideal when it obliges people to look elsewhere for news, which is the newspaper's 'raison d'etre?' " he was compelled to resign. But Catholic papers had one advantage in that they had been allowed to set up their own news agency, *Logos,* which managed to feed its papers stories of social reform in other countries that never got on EFE wires. Yet when Catholic papers went too far in this they were quickly suppressed. But others too were getting restive. Promonarchist papers suffered. *Informaciónes* in Madrid got a 50 per cent cut in newsprint for ultramonarchist articles. The National Congress of the Spanish Press had voted in 1953 for the creation of a National Press Council to defend journalists' freedom of expression. Franco did not sanction this council until 1959, and then it got nowhere.

Suddenly in July, 1962, the miracle happened. It is believed that Franco's desire for better relations with the west European Common Market persuaded him that some relaxation in his rigid system was necessary. At any rate he revamped his cabinet, replacing seven old ministers with younger men. Among those eased out was Arias Salgade, minister of information and tourism, indefatigable proponent of strict press control, who was replaced by Manuel de Fraga Iribane. He immediately brought a relaxation of censorship. Papers were now able to print news stories, articles, and pictures which previously would have been rejected. Censorship of foreign journalists and publications also was lifted. One Spanish editor in November, 1962, wrote, "The censor is still in our office, we must submit copy as usual, but not a single line has been pencilled out in weeks."

World press opinion, particularly the protests of the International Press Institute as well as those of dissidents within Spain, may well have contributed to the relaxation of control; but Franco's economic needs were probably the most important reasons for this change. To newspapers, however, this was a sensational development, for they had known no freedom in many years. Now they were able to publish much more foreign news. Previously, domestic news had been limited to official statements and accounts of the inauguration of new schools or highways, church ceremonies, bull fights, soccer, and the weather. At this time newspapers are able to discuss economic developments affecting their readers, even to print stories of murders and crimes which had previously been forbidden.

The old 1938 law, however, was still on the books. A new, more liberal law had been drafted by Minister de Fraga; but at the end of 1964 it was still "under study." That year saw the trial of many Spaniards for subversive activity and dissemination of propaganda. Many of those arrested were said to be Communists.

In 1965 the government approved a new press law, supposedly abolishing all press censorship and putting an end to the arbitrary measures in effect since 1921. There are, however, government safeguards: editors will be held responsible for the contents of their papers; and certain material, such as that prejudicial to morality, the constitution, national confidence, and security, or injurious to the personal reputation of certain government persons will still be subject to censorship. The new bill is expected to be made into law by the *Cortes* shortly.

The big development in 1965, however, was Spain's booming economy. Since the stabilization of currency and the throwing open of doors to foreign firms, new industries have sprung up all over the country, creating jobs for so many thousands of workers that farm production has fallen off. Tourism, too, has boomed. Some 36 million tourists have spent three and a half billion dollars in Spain in the past five years. Spain desperately hopes to be admitted to an associate membership in the Common Market but has twice been rejected. Despite improved economy, political liberalization will come more slowly.

The Spanish Press Today

In August, 1964, the Spanish Institute of Public Opinion issued its massive report on the Spanish press which listed 107 daily papers, a gain of five over 1960. Of these, ninety-five are on the Spanish peninsula, eleven in the islands, and one at Fernano Po in Spanish Guinea in Africa. Because of the improved economy and the new freedom which permitted papers to be more newsworthy and attractive, total daily circulations are claimed to have increased to 2,215,056. But for 31,000,000 people this still means a distribution of only 7 copies per 100 persons, one of the lowest distribution ratios in Europe. Beautiful Madrid with eight dailies and Barcelona, second largest city, are the journalistic capitals and together have 52 per cent of the total daily circulation.

Spanish papers get their wire news from three principal news agencies. *Agencia* EFE, the largest and most important, covers both domestic and foreign news extensively and has exchange agreements with Reuters, AFP, and UPI. *Agencia Mancheta* specializes in sports news but gives some domestic and foreign news. *Agencia Logos* distributes a more limited service of foreign and domestic news but in particular features any special items from the Vatican.

Spanish dailies are published Tuesday through Sunday for the larger papers, but only through Saturday for smaller dailies. This leaves Monday open for thirty-three *hoyas del lunes* (Monday papers), part of whose earnings go to provide pensions and medical care for newspaper workers. Three-fourths of all dailies are morning papers. In addition there are 97 weeklies, semi- and triweeklies and some 2,900 magazines, trade and technical publications.

Spanish papers are not much different in content from those of other western nations except that they are so carefully departmentalized. Some of the larger ones look different in that they are tabloid or semitabloid and at first glance appear to be picture magazines; but this is just a "wraparound" of from eight to thirty-six pages with news and feature pictures. Inside come the news sections, led by a front page of top foreign and national stories and followed by an editorial page. Next come perhaps eight pages of national and six of international news leading to four *paginas especialles* with features on aspects of Spanish life—then the cultural pages on theater, literature, music, film, radio, and TV. Now appear two pages of local news, a page of business and finance and a page of sports with final pages of solid advertising— all a nicely packaged product for the convenience of readers. While it is true that their typography and makeup are much more modest than that of other western European journals, these papers today are nevertheless more interesting than before and provide much more news than they ever did. Some smaller provincial dailies may run only eight pages; many of the larger papers will run up to forty-eight and, if tabloid, to as many as 120 on heavy advertising days.

Advertising has been increasing since 1957. In 1962 the nations advertising bill was estimated at only $900,000, of which newspapers and magazines got 40 per cent; but in 1964 this was apparently much higher. A Wednesday edition of *ABC*, an illustrated news tabloid, carried 47 pages of advertising out of its total of 120; and *La Vanguardia* of Barcelona, another nationally distributed paper, was equally heavy with advertising. Whereas movie advertising formerly constituted most of the local display, there is now considerable local retail store advertising, particularly in Madrid and Barcelona. Previously, classified was the largest category, and there are still pages of want ads, but there are now many advertisements from foreign advertisers or their Spanish distributors. There is also government advertising for the products of nationalized industries.

Thus, there are now some larger national papers which are clearly profitable enough to be independent financially. This is not believed to be true of many smaller papers of only local or group importance. The Falange is said to make up the deficits on its papers. Church groups, Monarchists, and others may do the same. Some observers feel that government advertising is used as an indirect subsidy.

How long the new breath of freedom may last is anyone's guess, but it has certainly brought improvement to the Spanish press and its people.

REPRESENTATIVE PAPERS

La Vanguardia Española (Barcelona)—Largest daily in Spain's second largest city, which has 1,664,000 inhabitants. Considered by many to be the best paper in Spain. Distributed nationally. Founded in 1881. Provides fine foreign and national news coverage, backed by its own correspondents in Europe, North and South America. Backed by Monarchists; loyal to Franco on domestic policies but independent on foreign affairs. Excellent cultural sections. Rotogravure employed for front and back provides fine picture display. Very heavily supported by advertisers. Circulation 187,000.

ABC (Madrid)—Largest daily in capital with 192,000 daily circulation and 242,196 Sunday. Small tabloid in size, it opens with picture magazine section in roto. Inside provides very complete news coverage carefully departmentalized. Very heavy with advertising. One of national papers and also publishes edition at Seville. Founded in 1905 by Bourbon Monarchists. For long considered the only big opposition paper tolerated, but now strong backer of Franco. Friendly to U.S.

Arriba (Madrid)—Literally, its title translates as "upstairs." Started by Primo de Rivera in 1935, it is the top voice of the Falange. Like others, has a roto "wraparound" picture section, but has few pictures inside. Reflects official opinion and gives good space to all government announcements. Has very little advertising. Because of its official character and less interesting contents, has circulation of 40,000.

Ya (Madrid)—Leading Catholic paper, nationally distributed, founded 1935. Provides well-balanced coverage of world, national, and local news. Probably most friendly to U.S. of all Madrid papers. Standard-sized morning paper, carries more advertising than most. Circulation 130,000.

Madrid (Madrid)—Popular evening paper. Heavy on sports and features, but has some good background by excellent writers. One of few papers in Spain operated as a strictly business venture. Politically independent. Circulation 67,000; heavily supported by advertising, hence financially independent.

Pueblo (Madrid)—Organ of national Syndicalists, Franco's union of workers, hence a child of government. Circulation 122,000. While Franco loudly proclaims his pro-U.S. attitude, this paper, perhaps to show his independence, is invariably critical of the U.S.

The Press of Portugal

This westernmost of European nations, where journalism was long delayed, has for thirty-two years been ruled by Dr. Antonio de Oliveira Salazar, a seemingly mild-mannered, ascetic professor who believes his country not ready for democracy and runs it under a moderate Mussolini-like system which has meant rigid press control. Portugal, just a bit larger than Maine but with a population of almost 9,000,000, has overseas holdings twenty-three times that of the mother country, the largest colonial empire left.

She shares her earlier history with Spain; yet in Portugal the amalgam of original Iberians and later conquerors produced a different people, generally easier going, more prone to enjoyment of living, not given to the heroic extremes of Spaniards, and speaking a different language. Her separate history began when King Alfonso VI of León and Castile, in gratitude for the help given him in his battles with the Moors by a French knight, Count Henry of Burgundy, gave him his illegitimate daughter Teresa in marriage, with a dowry of the lands south of the River Minho, set up as the County of Portugal. But this pair and their son spread their power southward and by 1263 had not only driven the Moors from the southern tip of their peninsula but also forced Spain to a recognition of their independence.

Portugal's days of glory came with King João and his son, Prince Henry the Navigator, who launched expedition after expedition into the unknown, following the west coast of Africa. The Azores, Madeira, and the Canary Islands were explored; by 1445 the Guinea coast and Senegal had been reached. By 1488 Bartolomeu Diaz had rounded the Cape of Good Hope, and in 1498 Vasco da Gama sailed around the Cape to India. Other explorers reached Java and Japan. Pedro Alvares Cabral, setting out for India, was borne so far west by storms, that quite by accident he discovered Brazil, and claimed it for Portugal. By 1515 Portugal was the greatest sea power in the world and wealth flowed to her from Brazil to Japan.

The new wealth and outside contacts brought to her a delayed and mild extension of the European Renaissance. It was in this period that printing came to Portugal. The first book printed in Portuguese, *Vita Christi* by Ludolphus, came from the Lisbon press of Fernandez and Saxonia in 1495. The latter is believed to have brought the new art from Germany. Other print shops were set up in Lisbon and in the university town of Coimbra in the next century, most of their products being religious works.

Portugal Falters and Is Conquered

Portugal's decline began in 1521, and by mid-century she was in difficulty: her Indian and far-eastern adventures had drained her of her lifeblood, and a languishing agriculture compelled a large scale import of African slaves. She grew poorer and poorer until by 1580 she fell to Philip II of Spain. His pledge to maintain the rights of the Portuguese were soon forgotten in his larger concerns as Holy Roman Emperor. He was particularly engaged with his battle for the souls of men and became the chief arm of the Counter-Reformation. His *Autos de Fe* for Portugal contained the same rules over printers that he had imposed in Spain and enabled the Inquisition to sentence printers to death for minor infractions. In possession of all Portuguese colonies, he not only robbed that country of her former revenues but permitted Dutch, British, and French to attack Portuguese ships. But Spain was also declining in power. Philip's final gamble in sending an armada to overwhelm England and to impose Catholicism on the English ended in complete catastrophe and Philip died a broken man.

His successors, Philip III and IV, were not interested in ruling and turned the government over to favorites who ministered to the king's extravagances, taxed the people unmercifully, and lined their own pockets while they ruled as dictators. Curiously, it was under the Count-Duke de Olivares, who controlled the country for two decades after 1621, that the first approach was made toward a newspaper. This was a hand-printed newsletter with a title which, translated, was "Universal Account of What Happened in Portugal from March 1625 to September 1626." Its fifty-two pages listed small items of military, political, foreign, colonial, religious, and society news in chronological order without any departmentalization. The author was Manuel Severim de Faria, a professor at the University of Evora. That it should have been permitted at all can only be attributed to the fact that it pleased the vanity of the king and his court. A second edition appeared in 1627; thus this first journalistic effort was an annual that lasted two years.

The First Printed Newssheets

The Portuguese were getting restive under Spanish captivity and when Olivares plunged Spain into the Thirty Years War, demanding Portuguese soldiers and money, nobles rose in revolt, proclaimed their independence of Spain in 1640, and made the Duke of Braganza their king as João IV. While the government remained despotic, independence did occasion the first printed newssheet, *Gazeta*, which appeared off and on till July, 1642, when it was suppressed for "being untruthful and in bad taste." Three months later it reappeared and continued its irregular publication till September, 1647. Like earlier European flysheets it carried brief items of foreign news, wars, battles, and such governmental reports as the rulers desired, but avoided the sensational and unnatural events which characterized northern European forerunners.

João IV gave his country two decades of peace and regained Angola and Brazil from the Dutch. Under his son, Pedro II, there came forty years of quiet and recuperation. Gold shipments from Brazil promised to make up for the loss of the eastern spice trade. During these years a second newssheet appeared in 1663 when Antonio de Sousa Macedo was permitted to bring out *Mercurio Portuguese*, which he soon made into a six-page monthly with more news of foreign affairs and wars. It survived till 1666 when an article, deemed to be a reflection on the Braganzas, caused its suppression and Macedo's exile.

The First Regular Newspapers

Pedro's son João V refused to be drawn into foreign wars and, aided by wealth flowing from the colonies, guided his nation's growth and prosperity. He was also an enlightened ruler, an enthusiast for learning and the arts. Jose Freire Monterroyo Mascarenhas was encouraged to bring out *Gazeta de Lisboa* in 1715 as Portugal's first weekly paper, a hundred years after weeklies had appeared in northern Europe. Monterroyo, considered the father of Portuguese journalism, was a learned and widely traveled man. From the beginning his paper enjoyed the favor of the state and became its semiofficial voice; in fact, he was paid for every story dealing with the crown. Outside of official news, the paper dealt mostly with foreign affairs. It succumbed not long after his death.

Such few papers as appeared in the next two decades were strictly censored and did not last long, without political news or comment. Literary criticism alone was safe; and the most prominent publication of the period was *Gazeta Literaria*, published by Francisco Bernardo de Lima in Oporto.

The brief reign of Queen Maria was marked by the revival of the *Gazeta de Lisboa* in 1788. In time it became a daily, the first in Portugal and the first to derive income from advertising although most of its revenue came from the government. This year also saw the birth of the first business and commercial paper, *Com Privilegio Real,* which was to survive till 1807.

When the French Revolution broke, Portugal allied herself with Spain against this threat; but Spain double-crossed her, leagued herself with France, and left Portugal to fight both. Napoleon required all continental states to close their ports to British ships, but Portugal refused and Napoleon overran the country in 1807. The British came to Portugal's aid, and in four years both the French and Spanish were driven out of the country. But during Napoleonic rule *Gazeta de Lisboa* had been taken over by the French, and other papers were started as French propaganda sheets. Patriotic Portuguese journalists, in their hatred for their oppressors, published underground sheets to expose the lies of the French and to inspire the people to resist. Passed from hand to hand, the sheets gained wide distribution and for the first time Portuguese papers had the respect of the people, which previous official papers had never had. Most important was *O Observador Portugues,* silenced many times, but finally appearing as *Diario Lisbonense,* under which name it lasted till 1813.

The Dam Finally Breaks

Some two hundred years had passed since Portuguese journalism had made its beginning; yet it had made little progress. But now there was a cause in which it could take a strong stand. The late Queen Maria's son, Don Juan, who had fled to Brazil during the Napoleonic period, refused to return home. The Portuguese resented his attempt to govern his nation from Brazil as if it were a province of the latter. They were infuriated when he invested British General William Carr Beresford with full powers to look after his interests. Liberal and Republican papers led by *Investigador Portugues* campaigned for a new form of government. The army, however, revolted and invited Don João to return as king provided he committed himself to a constitutional government. A popularly elected *Cortes* (parliament) in 1821 drew up a constitution which suppressed the Inquisition, stripped the Church and nobility of their privileges, and vested the sovereignty in the people. Alarmed, the king returned as João VI but was compelled to observe the new constitution. His departure gave Brazilian patriots opportunity to launch a war of independence which lost Portugal this colony.

These revolutionary changes at last brought a flood of publications. The official *Gazeta de Lisboa* became *Diario do Governo*. *Patriota* emerged as the leading voice of the Constitutionalists; the Liberals had *Correio Mariliense*, and the Absolutists *Correio do Porto*. There were papers representing every point of view, as well as women's magazines, scientific and literary publications. But this first burst of freedom did not last long, for after the death of the king the army, resenting the loss of Brazil, precipitated a civil war which brought a younger son Miguel to the throne as an absolute monarch. He annulled the constitution and the new press freedom. Under his terror-ridden rule the newspapers withered. The Constitutionalists rallied back of Maria, daughter of João VI, and in another civil war, with British help, restored Maria to the throne. The old 1822 constitution was reinstituted and press freedom guaranteed.

The Press Develops

For the next two decades papers enjoyed what Portuguese journalistic historians call the "Romantic Period" when the press had its greatest freedom. From 1800 to 1834 some two hundred papers had been born and quickly suppressed. Now the press began to bloom. Most newsworthy of the new papers were *O Nacional, Cronica, Constitucional de Oporto, Constitucional de Lisboa*, and the popular *Periodico dos Pobres* (Paper of the Poor). But most papers were political organs. There was a journal of fashion and literature for women; there was even a yellow paper, *O Interes Publico*, playing crime and low fiction. Many catered to special interests such as business, agriculture, law, medicine, and the Church, while anticlericals emerged in opposition.

Some papers discovered they could go only so far. Press hero of the period was Antonio Rodrigues Sampaio, who founded his daily *Revolucao de Setembro* in 1840 to support the Setembrists. They had first championed Maria but had become concerned over the influence of foreign interests which might endanger constitutional freedoms. Though educated for the priesthood, Sampaio had gone to work on liberal papers and was recognized as one of the most brilliant journalists of his day. Now he courageously attacked the queen's government. His paper was suppressed in 1844, but he continued it for some time as an underground sheet.

The Setembrists backed the 1822 constitution with its single chamber *Cortes* which could not be dissolved by the king. They were opposed by the Chartists who supported the 1826 charter with its two-chamber *Cortes*, the upper one the preserve of the hereditary nobles, and which gave the crown the right of veto and dissolution. These two parties alternated in power, no government lasting long. Finally the people grew tired of the instability, the riots and sanguinary street battles and badly defeated the Setembrists in the election. The queen acquiesced and entrusted power to Antônio da Costa Cabral, governor of Lisbon, who ruled as dictator, completely muzzling the press. He did quiet the country and brought some material progress, but his new tax laws brought such violent opposition that he fled to Spain. The queen revoked the tax laws, conceded universal suffrage, and restored press freedom. Yet the resurgence of newspapers brought such recrimination on the queen that she installed another strong man, Saldanha, a prominent Chartist, who imposed another five-year period of authoritarianism, marked by frequent civil strife.

Maria died in 1853 and was succeeded by her son, Pedro V, a conscientious and liberal ruler. The country settled down to a period of quiet and material advancement. Literature, after long lethargy, burgeoned and the press, with liberty restored, took on new life. The first labor papers appeared, idealistic rather than revolutionary. The press was now largely a political one.

The Last Days of the Monarchy

Leading thinkers and writers were beginning to reevaluate Portugal's position after the revolutionary events in France in 1870. Teófilo Braga dared attack the Catholic church for being inimical to tolerance and true education. When his temerity was stopped, the country had its first strike in 1872, serving notice that Socialism was now a new force. In 1876 a growing group, dissatisfied with even a liberal constitutional monarch, formed the Republican party. The two old major parties, the Setembrists, now called Progressives, and the Chartists, called Regenerators, while supposedly the chief protagonists, worked out a system of rotation in power to share prerogatives. Both shamefully falsified election returns and showed the same disregard for social problems. Republican, Socialist, Progressive, Regenerator, and Monarchist papers now fought each other.

But Portugal was riding for a fall. Extravagant building and management of state railroads brought a financial crisis. In 1902 Portugal could not pay the coupons of her foreign creditors. Panic ensued; banks and currency collapsed; foreign creditors demanded a voice in financial administration. Serious retrenchment followed in armed forces, civil service, and public undertakings. To meet the crisis King Carlos I established a *dictatura* under João Franco. All newspapers except government organs were suppressed. When Carlos, at Franco's request, signed a decree permitting Franco to deport his political enemies without trial, he signed his own death warrant, for the next day Carlos and his son, the crown prince, were assassinated.

A younger son, Manuel II, came to the throne wanting a program of conciliation but lacking leaders. Once the worst of Franco's decrees had been abrogated and liberty of association and press freedom restored, the old political game resumed in a rotation of do-nothing ministries. The old system could no longer govern; the Republicans grew in strength, and the election of 1910 gave them a smashing victory. On October 5, 1910, the Republic of Portugal was proclaimed.

The Press under the Republic

Portugal was not yet ready for democracy. A provisional government headed by Braga, the iconoclast of 1871, abolished the monarchy, decreed separation of Church and state, expelled religious orders, and secularized education, which alienated an essentially Catholic population. A new constitution guaranteed freedom of conscience, expression, and association and provided a parliament elected by all over the age of twenty-one. Labor was granted the right to strike, which it proceeded to use on a scale which created financial problems.

One would have expected that under the new press law and with the premier Dr. João Chaiga, a former editor who had fought for press freedom, that the press would now flower. But Republicans, beset by grave financial questions, clamped down on opposition papers. If they could not actually seize control of a paper, there were always hoodlums for hire. The liberal *Correio de Manha* and *Diario Illustrado* were demolished by mobs. And when the Republican editor of *Diario do Porto* protested against this suppression, his plant and home were destroyed. Catholic papers and all monarchist papers were either suppressed or wrecked by mobs. Even *O Liberal*, edited by the distinguished Alexandre de Albuquerque, was destroyed and its editor exiled. When it was revived next year by Antônio Cabral, its first and last issue told of the attack on its plant. Cabral had to flee the country. The press was now completely one-sided, for all opposition had been quashed. A few papers which steered clear of politics and concentrated on news were able to survive. Thus *A Ordem*, started in 1916, continued till 1927; and *Epoca*, begun in 1919, survived till 1931.

In 1910 Red Republicans (Communists) fomented thirty-six strikes, in 1911 forty-two—all marked by bombing and disorder. In 1912 there was a revolutionary strike to set up a Red Republic, which was only put down by martial law and the arrest of one thousand leaders. The remaining Republicans split into many factions, all jockeying for power. One ministry followed the other as financial conditions grew worse.

At the outbreak of World War I Portugal stayed neutral till 1916 when, on British urging, she seized seventy-two German ships interned in her ports and Germany declared war. Portugal played only a small part in the war, but involvement staved off financial debacle, for loans from England financed the war effort and the government. However, the cost of living and wartime shortages brought morale low. By 1921 there had been eleven different governments. Crisis followed crisis, characterized by ephemeral ministries, strikes, riots, and mutinies, till in 1926 an army revolt overthrew the Lisbon government. General Antonio Oscar de Fragoso Carmona emerged as the strong man and set up a dictatorship. Unfortunately, he knew little about government and less about finance. Portugal's debts grew greater than ever, and there was international talk of depriving her of her colonies.

Salazar and the New State

In 1928 Carmona called in Professor Antonio de Oliveira Salazar of the University of Coimbra and made him minister of finance and economic dictator. In a year he not only balanced the budget but produced a surplus. Carmona, having had himself elected president, made Salazar premier and political dictator as well in 1932. The budget has been balanced every year since then, and Portugal has achieved financial stability. In 1933 Portugal was proclaimed a "New State under a Corporative System" like Mussolini's fascist state. The premier was all-powerful, assisted only by a National Assembly, with advisory functions, and a Chamber of Corporations representing business, economic, and professional groups to advise on economic and social problems. Only one party, the National Union, was permitted; dissidents had no chance. The rights of freedom of speech, worship, teaching, association, and immunity from arbitrary arrest were mentioned in the new constitution but made subject to the government's interpretation of the "higher interests of society." This brought rigid control of the press; only the voices of the National Union could appear; only those completely subservient to the state remained.

Agriculture, industry, mining, and fishing were, however, greatly stimulated. Salazar began a campaign against illiteracy, for prior to 1910 four out of five persons could neither read nor write. Now with funds devoted to school improvement it was clamied by 1940 that illiteracy was down to 50 per cent. Since anyone who could write his name was counted literate this did not result in any great expansion of newspaper readership; in fact, with a dictatorial government taking care of everything, there developed an apathy toward government-controlled papers.

First Stirring of Discontent

Salazar kept Portugal neutral in World War II, and this resulted in great prosperity, for Portugal had the only free neutral ports on the Atlantic and profited from trade with both sides. When war ended, this boom collapsed. Poor people were caught by high prices; strikes, demonstrations, and riots increased. But Salazar had a solution. Carmona's third term was expiring; Salazar proclaimed a free election and for the first time gave the press some freedom. A straw man, General Norton de Mattos, was permitted to run against Carmona; and it was expected that his overwhelming defeat would give the regime a look of popularity. But de Mattos put on a surprising campaign, with slogans of "freedom and democracy." People rallied with enthusiasm to the new party. Salazar was shocked at the campaign of invective against him in newspapers, pamphlets, and newssheets. Only the government papers and a monarchist organ supported Carmona. Troops were called out, leaders of the de Mattos' party were arrested, and clamps again were put on the press. Three days before the election de Mattos withdrew, saying that every possible obstacle had been placed in the way of his election. Only one list of candidates appeared on the ballot. Carmona was reelected, but Salazar had had a scare and was not inclined to flirt again with press freedom.

Salazar's Press Theory

Portugal was admitted to the U.N. in 1955. She is very anti-Communist and has never recognized the Soviet Union nor any of its satellites. When her representatives were called to account by the U.N. Conference on Freedom of Information in 1948, they explained that they had a duty to protect public opinion against factors which might divert it from truth, justice, and good government. They insisted that anyone was free to found a periodical provided he had the required moral and intellectual qualifications (which made it possible to deny this right to dissidents). They declared that to prevent outrages against the rights of others or against internal or external peace, previous censorship had been imposed on publications dealing with political and social questions and that the National Secretariat for Information, Popular Culture, and Tourism had been created to co-ordinate press activities. Salazar in his engaging and benevolent manner had patiently made clear in an interview that censorship was the only legitimate defense against prevailing anarchy of thought, particularly international communism. This may explain why Portuguese papers are seldom permitted to print any news out of Communist states or any news of strikes in Britain, the United States, Italy, France, or other western nations.

Under Salazar, however, Portugal has advanced in well-being. Two six-year national developmental plans were launched in 1952 and 1958; but the average Portuguese still has a per capita income of $230 a year, the lowest in western Europe, and there is still discontent. When in 1958 General Humberto Delgado ran against Admiral Americo Deus Rodrigues Tomas, the National Union candidate for president, he openly criticized Salazar, charged corruption and favoritism in government, and promised, if elected, to dismiss Salazar. He received a surprisingly large vote but not enough to win. He was arrested, dismissed from the army, and took refuge in Brazil. Then in 1961 came the *Santa Maria* incident, when Captain Henrique Galvao and a crew of revolutionaries seized this luxury liner to call attention to Delgado's independence movement in Brazil. Hunted by a fleet of ships and aircraft, Galvao surrendered. He, Delgado, and thirty-two others were tried *in absentia* in Lisbon and sentenced to long prison terms, but they remained in Brazil.

News of African Troubles Manipulated

The above incident drew attention to Portugal's troubles in Angola and Mozambique where natives, inspired by other African independence movements, rose in revolt. Workers in Mozambique were getting an average daily wage of 12½¢; in Angola not even a hundred persons had a high school education. Forced labor was common, corporal punishment the rule. The fighting was particularly heavy in Angola. The U.N. General Assembly by a vote of 92–2 called on Portugal to cease its repressive measures, but Salazar did nothing. At home the people, through their controlled press, learned only the government's side of the story. They were persuaded that Portugal was in danger, that its good name had been defamed by the U.N., that they must rally back of Salazar. For a time all opposition to the regime was forgotten. There were great street demonstrations in Lisbon in fervent support of the dictator. The seizure of Goa and other small possessions by India in 1961 was used to heighten Salazar's popular support.

Thus Portugal's press remains the most tightly controlled and manipulated in western Europe. Portuguese papers belong to no international press organizations. Little news emerges, and one learns that *Time* magazine was kept out of Portugal for six years, that British papers entering Portugal have been censored for references to Portugal, that correspondents from other European countries have been turned back at the border. In October, 1963, a foremost author was arrested for expressing thoughts reflecting unfavorably on the regime; and in the next month Dr. Urbanos Rodrigues, a newspaperman and novelist, was arrested for signing a petition urging the release of writers arrested in Angola.

Yet at times some of the stronger papers like *Republica* in Lisbon and *O Primeiro de Janeiro, Journal de Noticias,* and *O Commercio* in Oporto have shown independence as they have learned that comment can be fairly free so long as it does not touch on the regime, that even the government's economic policy can be criticized as long as nothing is said about Dr. Salazar personally. *Republica* in particular has shown courage but is closely watched, sometimes has difficulty getting newsprint, and has occasionally been suspended or fined. Newspaper editors have several times appealed for the abolition of censorship and passage of a new press law.

Salazar held another of his mock free elections in late 1965, but most of the thirty-four opposition candidates were so harassed that they withdrew before the voting day. However, a group of 101 Catholic laymen took advantage of the pre-election freedom to publish in all the major dailies a bitter attack on "the totalitarian rule systematically offending and violating Christian conscience." It had no effect on the election; the Salazar regime counted the votes.

The Portuguese Press Today

In the official reports for 1964, Portugal claimed thirty-three dailies, the three new ones all being in the Azores and Madeira islands; but this is due to a change in the method of counting. Actually there are only four main dailies in these islands, publishing five local side editions for smaller islands from the same plants. On the mainland itself there are but twenty-one dailies, one of which is the official *Diario do Governo,* printing official announcements and laws which become effective on its publication; hence it cannot be considered a newspaper in the usual sense. Thus, with twenty on the mainland and four in the islands, Portugal has only twenty-four dailies, a drop of three from 1962. Round numbered circulation figures are reported only for a few of the larger papers, but it is estimated that total daily circulations do not exceed 800,000, which for a population of 9,123,000 means a sale of only 8.6 copies per 100 persons, second lowest index of readership in western Europe. This is in part accounted for by an illiteracy rate of 25 per cent, particularly among older citizens, but among the younger generation by an apathy toward their completely regimented press.

There are some thirty-five weekly or semiweekly papers in smaller towns, plus 377 periodicals.

Lisbon, with 802,000 population, is the largest publishing center with eleven dailies, one of which is the government gazette and another a commercial paper, which leaves but nine regular daily newspapers. It also has twenty-one weeklies and 164 periodicals. Oporto, second largest city with 303,000 inhabitants, has four dailies. The others are in smaller cities of only local or regional importance. Portugal is small enough so that dailies can quickly cover the country; but only three, *Diario de Noticias* in Lisbon, *Primeiro de Janeiro* and *Commercio do Porto* are national papers. The great bulk of circulation is by news-stand sale. Circulations are not large; the biggest, *Diario de Noticias*, claims 130,000. Smaller city dailies, having from four to eight pages, run from 1,000 to 7,000. Only the larger papers print as many as fourteen pages, and some of them publish seven days a week with their Sunday editions running to twenty pages.

Portuguese dailies are bolder in display than most European papers: red heads alternate with heavy black and often red bars separate major stories, contributing to a "circus" makeup. A typical ten-page issue presents a front page headed by a leader article at the left, the rest of the page playing top foreign, national, and sports stories, including whenever possible a picture and story about Salazar attending an exposition or dedication, but always at least three large pictures. The second and third pages carry front page jumps and news from other Portuguese cities. Then comes a solid page of advertising, mostly for movies, followed by a page of local news, deaths, organization meetings, and church news. Page six may then be devoted to cultural material. Now comes a page of additional wire and governmental news. Page eight is given to sports, with some advertising; page nine will be solid advertising, mostly classified and general; and page ten will be a mixture of late wire and local news with more advertising.

As Portugal has seen some increase in prosperity with a step-up in industrialization, advertising has increased and newspapers get about 32 per cent of the total. A number now have from two to three pages of advertising. But it must be remembered that two out of every five Portuguese workers earn their living from farming and that the per capita income for the whole nation is so low that only the wealthier ones can buy the products advertised. Yet a few of the larger papers are said to derive half their income from advertising. Smaller papers get much less and may have to be subsidized by other sources such as the National Union party, the Church, or private groups of backers. The government says it owns no papers except its official gazette.

However, the National Union party owns *Diario da Manha*, its official voice; and it is reliably reported that the government owns most of the shares in *O Seculo* and a considerable percentage of shares in *Diario de Noticias*. Several papers owned by groups of industrialists describe themselves as independent-conservative and independent-republican, but all of these might better be described as neutral for there is room for but one party. Only the palest shades of opinion are permitted even in the so-called independent papers.

In addition to printed media there are five main radio stations and five for television. These new media plus the newspapers are supplied news by two agencies, *Lusitania* and *Agencia de Noticias e de Informaçoes* (ANI). The latter is the most important, is supported by the Ministry of Interior, and provides all but a few Portuguese dailies with domestic and foreign news. *Lusitania* transmits a daily service of domestic and foreign news to Portuguese overseas territories. A few of the larger dailies use UPI, AP, or Reuters services, but all news distributed to papers is screened by the censor and no paper may appear without the censor's official stamp on the front page.

REPRESENTATIVE PAPERS

Diario de Noticias (Lisbon)—Largest national paper in Portugal with 130,000 circulation. One of the oldest, having first appeared in 1864 as a nonpolitical paper with emphasis on local news. Still carries much news, particularly foreign. Conservative in policy but sensational in makeup. Has been generally friendly to U.S.

Primeiro de Janeiro (Oporto)—Takes its name from January 1, 1868, when Lisbon and Oporto rose in protest against King Luis I for his excessive taxes and forced their withdrawal. The best of the provincial papers. Owned by an Oporto business group. General policy is liberal and friendly to U.S. Has dared to oppose some Salazar policies. Has a national circulation of 80,000.

Novidades (Lisbon)—The one Catholic paper which survived the Republican period. Today the daily organ of the Catholic church. Salazar likes it, for it ran his first articles on Portugal's economic problems. Deals largely with Church news; circulation, 35,000; important as a strong Salazar supporter in Catholic Portugal.

Republica (Lisbon)—Strongest opponent of Salazar, has occasional difficulties getting newsprint. Though once friendly to West, has moved steadily to support of U.S.S.R., which makes it doubly suspect. Has circulation of about 25,000.

A Voz (Lisbon)—The organ of the Monarchists, it completely supports the government. Staunch Catholic supporter and anti-Soviet. Circulation, about 20,000.

Part 4

The History Makers
of Eastern Europe

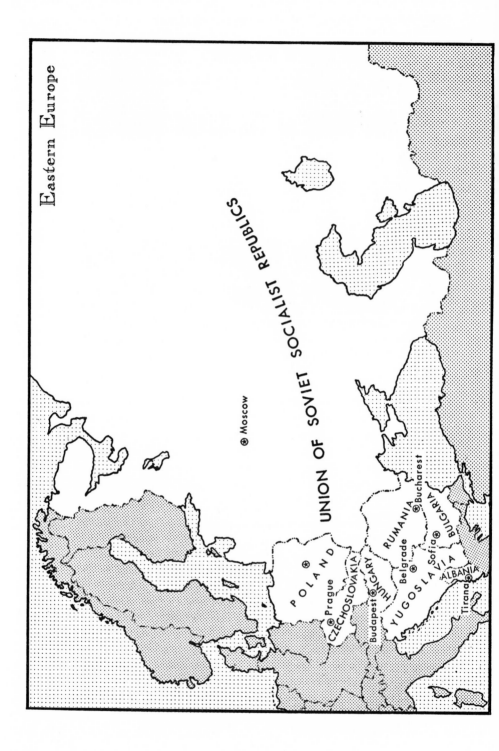

Eastern Europe

UNION OF SOVIET SOCIALIST REPUBLICS

⊕ Moscow

POLAND
⊕
Prague ⊕ CZECHOSLOVAKIA
HUNGARY
Budapest ⊕

RUMANIA
⊕ Bucharest

Belgrade ⊕ YUGOSLAVIA
Sofia ⊕ BULGARIA

ALBANIA
Tirana ⊕

The Press of the Soviet Union

In the spring of 1947 the American Society of Newspaper Editors was host to three Russian journalists, Ilya Ehrenburg,
Konstantin Simonov and Mikhail Galatkinov, the latter one of the
editors of *Pravda*. They were taken everywhere, visited newspapers,
met with press groups, were permitted to write as they wished and to
send home dispatches without censorship. In May Galatkinov was a
featured speaker at the Inland Daily Press Association in Chicago. The
question period turned into a debate with the author. At that time
there were only five American correspondents left in Moscow—men
who had married Russian women and were not allowed to leave. They
were practically restricted to Moscow, given no access to news, and
could get past the censors only quotes from *Pravda* and *Izvestia*. The
author contended that if American correspondents in Moscow were
given the same freedom accorded to Russians on this trip there might
ensue a better understanding between our two peoples. Galatkinov had
only one answer, "Impossible." But at the end of the session he asked
me to have dinner with him. We met in a private dining room,
Galatkinov seated at the head of the table, our State Department
interpreter at his left and I at his right, the rest of the entourage ranged
down a long table. When we had ordered Galatkinov said, "You
probably wonder why I wanted to talk with you. I want you to know
that I do not believe what I had to say this afternoon. You were right,
but there are two secret service men sitting at the end of this table who
take down every word I say and I do not dare depart from the official
line. But when I go back I am going to try to see what I can do to
bring about a freer exchange of information between our two
peoples."

In October of the same year there was a foreign ministers' meeting
in Moscow. The foreign editor of the Chicago *Sun-Times* called to ask
if there were anything he could do for me in Moscow. I asked him to

go over to *Pravda* and take my greetings to Galatkinov; not to ask him any questions which might embarrass him, but, if he volunteered any information, to bring it back to me. On his return in November he reported that he had gone to *Pravda* and found that no one had ever heard of Galatkinov. But, as a good newsman, he had kept boring in and had finally been given an address. He found it was an insane asylum. He rang the bell and after much argument Galatkinov was brought to the door, pale, obviously frightened, refusing to acknowledge that he had ever been in America. In January, 1948, *Editor and Publisher* carried a brief story to the effect that Galatkinov, one of the editors of *Pravda* who had been a guest of the American Society of Newspaper Editors the previous spring, had died. Galatkinov was probably a Russian press hero. He had tried to do something to ease the flow of information to the United States and was eliminated.

That was in Stalin's day. Things have changed, but the press of the U.S.S.R. is still one of the most controlled in the world. Its influence is not confined to the Soviet Federation, for its pattern of journalism, imposed on other Communist nations, now covers a third of the people of the world. This press must therefore occupy an important place in any study of press and world affairs because of its terrible importance to the peace of the world.

Early Beginnings

Muscovite princes had consolidated their holdings in north Russia and laid the foundations for the Russian state before printing came to the country. Ivan IV (the Terrible) was the first man strong enough to arrogate to himself the title of tsar (caesar), ushering in the autocratic rule under which Russians were to live for 350 years. In winning vast new territories, he had entered into commercial relations with England and, as a gesture of contact with western culture, set up the first printing press in Moscow in 1553. A half century later only a few religious books had been produced.

It was Peter the Great (1689–1725) who really opened for Russia a window on Europe, hoping to shock his sleeping giant of a nation into progress. From his press in Amsterdam came translations of European works on history, geography, arithmetic, and navigation, sent to Moscow for distribution. Then in 1703 he established in Moscow the first Russian newspaper, *Vedomosti* (Gazette). Previously, only the tsar and his circle had known what was happening abroad, and domestic news became so disfigured in telling that erroneous rumors spread everywhere. The first issue of *Vedomosti* published translations from foreign journals, reported the progress of the war with Sweden, and told of the cannon cast in Moscow and the progress of recruiting. Only one thousand four-page copies were printed; and because the paper was an official journal, only such news as the government permitted could be included.

But Peter's dream had not reckoned with the great illiteracy of his people. Only a few of the nobility and administrative staff could read. The only schools were in monasteries where education consisted mostly of perusing sacred books. He had to have schools but the only pupils with which he could start were the sons of the Diaks or administration employees, and their education had to begin with the alphabet. Yet Russian education began with Peter and in time came to include not only elementary schools but gymnasia. Russia's backwardness in learning was responsible for the fact that a newspaper did not appear in Russia till a hundred years after journalism had made its beginnings in western Europe. Peter was also the godfather of literature. Before him there had been no secular books. Previous centuries had been silent; there had been no age of Dante, Shakespeare, or Milton. In 1689 he brought from Amsterdam a compositor, a pressman, and a type founder to set up a press in Moscow, from which came a book on geometry and land survey, a "Complete Letter Writer," a history of the Trojan War, a history of Russia, and other cultural books. But then Peter became involved in wars, took Finland from Sweden, and made Russia a power of first rank. Nevertheless, he probably advanced Russia culturally by a century and a half over its previous evolution.

Under inferior successors there came no great advance till the advent of Catherine the Great (1762–96). A remarkable woman, she not only won great new territories but gave encouragement to education and literature: a university was founded in 1776, and she sponsored a magazine, *Vsiakaia-Vsiachina* (Every Little Thing, or Motley). Then she permitted the establishment of private printing houses from which came some 8,000 books. Younger intellectuals who had absorbed the ideas of Voltaire, Montesquieu, Rousseau, and the German philosophers were permitted to express their liberal views in magazines they founded.

But a bloody peasant revolt showed Catherine the dangerous forces which could be unleashed. Furthermore, the continued influx of revolutionary ideas from France changed her ideas on free expression. In her last years she developed such a fanatical hatred of liberal ideas that she did all she could to eradicate them. Under Paul I, her successor, came complete repudiation of anything that seemed liberal.

Foreign travel was restricted, and frontier posts were set up to prevent the importation of any literature from abroad. At home private printing houses were closed.

A Liberal Ruler Brings Change

Paul's son, Alexander I (1801–25), imbued with the ideas of his Swiss tutor, Frederic La Harpe, brought a complete turnabout. Education was encouraged; censorship was relaxed and there came a revival of newspapers and periodicals. Newspapers were restricted by censorship, but magazines were allowed considerable freedom. True, the first publications which gained wide acceptance were the romantic-idyllic type with sentimental novels and frivolous stories; but in 1805 progressives united around the *Magazine of Russian Letters*, which featured discussion articles, urged a free press and greater personal liberties, and argued the abnormalities of serfdom. However, Alexander, too, became involved in wars. The most serious was the one with Napoleon, who took Moscow but was then driven back by Alexander's forces through the disastrous winter retreat of 1812–13. Alexander's coalition of powers pursued Napoleon through France, took Paris, and forced his abdication. After Napoleon's final defeat at Waterloo, Alexander formed the Holy Alliance aimed at the pacification of Europe, which succeeded only in maintaining the dominance of conservatism for three decades.

The Napoleonic wars had an important effect on upper-class liberals, for many Russian officers who had been on the final drive into Paris had been deeply impressed with what they saw and came home with ideas for the abolition of serfdom and the establishment of a republic. But Alexander, occupied with his larger affairs, forgot about reforms at home and left administration to reactionary officials. By the end of his regime the press had been reduced to almost nothing. Resentment smouldered till on the accession of Nicholas I conspirators tried to seize the government in the Decembrist uprising of 1825. This was put down with great severity; 121 conspirators were either sent to Siberia or executed. The vindictiveness of Nicholas ushered in complete reaction. In the next twenty years there were 556 peasant uprisings, and the intellectual revolutionary movement began in earnest.

Yet, by curious paradox, Nicholas saw the need for education and, to get competent teachers, encouraged Russian students to study abroad. Many went to Germany and came back brimming with the ideas of Georg Hegel, Friedrich Schelling, and Johann Fichte. Groups of educated men interested in political and philosophic ideas began to emerge in Moscow and St. Petersburg, but because a political press was impossible to maintain, they put out semiliterary publications in which they could, by obscurantism in their writing, introduce challenging ideas.

The real revolutionary papers, however, rose in exile. Foremost among their editors was Alexander Herzen, leader of a reform circle at the University of Moscow until exiled. On his return he was persecuted again and fled to London where, in 1837, he founded *Kolokol* (The Bell), a weekly which was a clarion call to all who would end the regime of Nicholas.

Reaction Gives Way to Reform

After the French revolution of 1848 Nicholas began a determined fight against revolutionary ideas. Censorship raged mercilessly till all papers and magazines except those issued by the government were eliminated. But Nicholas died in 1855 in the midst of his ill-fated adventure in the Crimean War and was succeeded by his son Alexander II. Convinced, by the fundamental Russian weakness shown in this war, that essential reforms must be undertaken to preserve his country, Alexander accepted the Austrian ultimatum and ended the war. Censorship was stopped; restrictions against universities were abolished; and first steps were taken toward a consideration of the emancipation of 25,000,000 peasants who had become slaves to the state and the large landlords.

Newspapers and magazines gradually began to appear but, after thirty years of subjugation, dared take little initiative. Alexander moved slowly with studies as to how emancipation might be effected. He needed public support for his ideas, and from 1857 on newspapers and magazines were encouraged to discuss the serf problem. Finally in 1861, a year and a half before Lincoln freed America's slaves, Alexander emancipated millions of his people from bondage. Few, however, could get land of their own; most had to become members of rural communes collectively responsible for rent payments. Alexander proceeded with reforms in local government and courts and by encouraging industrialization tried to change Russia from a patriarchal to a more modern economic state.

Newspapers had begun to exert more influence, with greater freedom of discussion, but mass illiteracy limited their readership. Literate Russia, however, buzzed with political journalism. The reform program had brought suspicion to the whole of the old order. A Nihilistic movement sought liberation from old chains of family, society, and religion. Its chief organ was *Russ Koe Slovo* (Russian Word), founded in 1859 by Dimitri Pisarov, who attacked authorities mercilessly.

Savremennik (Contemporary), while more moderate, also moved left in its demands for further social reforms. Many termed Alexander's first steps but half measures. He was embarrassed by the boldness of the radical press, and although he believed the press should not be silenced, the revolts of 1862 and 1873 gave him pause. New rules embodying warnings and discontinuations were issued. Moscow and St. Petersburg papers still published without prior censorship; but, so long had they been held down, they did not dare discuss forbidden questions. At this time the intellectual life of the nation was almost confined to these two cities. In the silent solitudes of the provinces there were few oases. There were but two other dailies, one at Odessa, the other at Vilna—both official.

Press Repression Sets In

Alexander's reforms had not modified the rights of the autocracy, nor admitted any popular representation into government. The widespread desire for constitutional government was unsatisfied and revolutionary sentiment intensified. An attempt on Alexander's life in 1866 drove him into the arms of reactionaries. Reforms ended; preliminary censorship was restored; *Contemporary* and *Russian Word* were closed forever by imperial decree. Others were suspended for months and assessed heavy penalties. The official *Moskovski Vedomosti* (Moscow Gazette), relentlessly attacked the Nihilists; the liberal *Golos* (Voice), which dared expose administrative abuses, reached a top circulation of 30,000 before it was closed. The liberal *Novie Vremya* (New Times) was persuaded to become the weathercock of official policies and thus was able to survive till 1917. The tsar was still inclined to make concessions to moderate liberals, but three attempts on his life delayed his action. Finally in 1881 he announced a preliminary commission to study a plan for constitutional government. That afternoon he was killed by conspirators' bombs.

Alexander III was completely dominated by reactionary advisors. The move toward a constitution was ended. An attempt to murder the tsar in 1887 caused savage reprisals. One of those executed was the brother of Vladimir Ulyanov, later to be known as Nicolai Lenin. Surveillance of the press was tightened and heavy punishments were prescribed for mention of any forbidden topics. The minister of interior had a neat trick for punishing recalcitrant provincial papers. By appointing a special censor, residing at a great distance, he soon killed such papers. Yet courageous editors, often by double entendre, tried to get things over to their readers. One favorite device was to send a story to a foreign contemporary; then, when the story was printed, it would be quoted in full with the comment that of course it had no foundation in fact. By 1890 there were no papers of any consequence in the provinces and most liberal papers in the larger cities had been worried out of existence. In Moscow the leader was *Novie Vremya* with 25,000 circulation, which kept itself in favor by attacking Russia's enemies. The only other daily was the government mouthpiece, the *Moscow Gazette*. The *Journal of St. Petersburg* was a rose-colored affair published in French for perusal abroad and the edification of diplomats. It portrayed the Russians as living under the most paternal and benevolent government. There was never a hint of distress or poverty, no echo of the seething cauldron of discontent simmering under the smooth surface of society in the capital. This was the newspaper press of the period. Of the 107,000,000 people in Russia, 105,000,000 had to get along without any press at all.

The Rise of Revolutionary Parties and Papers

Nicholas II came to the throne in 1904 and started some liberal moves. Censorship was relaxed, taxes reduced, and the burdens of peasants lightened. But he did not understand the people and lacked the authority of his father; real power passed to the reactionary bureaucracy. His wanton flouting of deputations from the nobility, municipal councils, and universities who came to express their loyal felicitations and ask for needed reforms, helped revive movements against the dynasty. The rise of an industrial proletariat provided a fertile field for revolution. In 1883 George Plekhanov, the son of a nobleman who had embraced Marxism in Germany, organized the first Russian Marxist party at Geneva, Switzerland. He contended that, because of the mystic reverence of the peasants for the tsar, the hope for revolution lay not with them but with the rapidly growing urban workers. Through strikes, demonstrations, and illegal newspapers, Plekhanov's ideas spread. Soon underground groups of his followers began to form in principal Russian cities, calling themselves Social Democrats. For twenty years Plekhanov, through his terrorist section and underground papers, dominated the revolutionary movement.

One of his followers inside Russia was Nicolai Lenin. He was not Russian, but part German, part Swedish, and the rest Chuvash Mongolian. Son of an educator, he had been admitted to Kazan University to study law; but, when it was discovered that he was a brother of one of those executed after the 1887 attempt to murder Alexander III, he was expelled. This, and continued persecution of his family, embittered him. He was self-educated, a prodigious reader with a passion for economics, and he found in the writings of Sergey Nechayev and

Karl Marx his solution for Russia's ills—the destruction of the tsarist system and the establishment of a government under a proletariat of workers. He became the most energetic organizer of communist cells, investigator of conditions of the working class, and writer of propaganda pamphlets, till he was arrested and exiled to Siberia.

On his release in 1900, he joined Plekhanov at Geneva where they founded the first communist paper, *Iskra* (Spark). The two disagreed, and the fiery Lenin won control and became editor. His incendiary paper, printed first in Nuremberg, Germany, and later in London, was smuggled back into Russia. Meanwhile the peasants had organized their own Social Revolutionary party. Its *Revolutionary Russia* advocated the socialization of the land and its distribution to those who actually tilled it. The government, however, remained indifferent; and the people, in their misery and hopelessness, were goaded into outbreaks both in rural and urban areas.

Plekhanov and Lenin differed greatly on revolutionary methods. The former favored calling a national assembly in which Social Democrats would cooperate with other liberal groups; Lenin would have nothing to do with the bourgeoisie and felt that victory could be won only if the Social Democrats went their own way with strikes, uprisings, and terror. When the Assembly met in 1903, Lenin took advantage of the walkout of Jewish Bund delegates to win a majority of two, and his wing took the name Bolsheviks (Majority) while Plekhanov's wing became the Mensheviks (Minority). Lenin's victory was temporary; many of his supporters deserted him. He resigned from *Iskra*, which then reverted to the Mensheviks; and he devoted himself to trying to split the party.

The 1905 Revolution

The government, absorbed in foreign affairs, pursued an aggressive policy in the Far East which precipitated the Russo-Japanese War in which Russia was crushingly defeated. Naval forces mutinied; there were massive strikes and uprisings on the home front. Tragic was "bloody Sunday" in St. Petersburg when 200,000 men, women, and children marched to the winter palace singing "God Save the Tsar" to present a petition for an eight-hour day and a minimum wage of a ruble a day. Troops fired on them, killing several hundred and wounding more than 1,500. There followed a crescendo of strikes, street battles, and assassinations of hated government officials. It was Leon Trotsky, escaped from Siberia, who was the spark plug of this revolution. All Lenin did was to send frantic letters urging workers to fight, to use bombs, to assassinate officials, and to rob banks. Under Trotsky's dynamic leadership the revolution gained momentum; and after strikes had brought the country to an economic standstill the tsar finally yielded and granted Russians their first constitution, permitting a parliament or Duma. Outbreaks continued but in 1906 they were gradually suppressed. The Duma never was permitted to be more than a debating society. Laws still flowed, as an act of grace, from the sovereign and not from the people's representatives.

Press freedom was one of Nicholas' concessions. New papers appeared and Red revolutionary papers returned from exile to St. Petersburg and Moscow. They could not print enough to meet the demand, while government papers had to close, for the people would not read them and printers boycotted them. By August, 1905, there were 1,630 newspapers and periodicals. St. Petersburg had fifty papers and Moscow twenty-five; it seemed as if all the pent up speech of centuries had burst forth. But a year of attack was all the government could take, and 1906 saw the suppression of 563 papers and magazines and the punishment of 732 editors. Red papers had to go underground; but, while only 3 per cent of the people could read, the clandestine papers kept the ferment of freedom alive. Lenin had had to flee, and he spent the next years in frustration in France, Switzerland, and Austria. He had married Nedya Krupskaya in 1898 but he considered her more a clerk than a wife, and now he had a long affair with Inessa Armand, his favorite.

World War and Revolution

Through its intervention in the Balkans the government had saddled itself with the duty of protecting Serbia against Austria in 1914. Imperial Russia was totally incompetent to wage a modern war. The people gave the government loyal support till 1916; but their sufferings, the continued defeats, mounting losses, reports that men were being sent into battle without guns, rumors of treason, the ineffectiveness of the autocracy in prosecuting the war—all brought despair. A creeping paralysis spread as transportation broke down; food became scarce; strikes and major disturbances increased in violence. The tsar telegraphed orders to put down the revolt in St. Petersburg, but regiment after regiment refused to fire on the people and went over to them. When the tsar prorogued the Duma, it refused to be dismissed and organized a provisional government representing all parties except the Rightists and Marxists. By March 15, 1917, with the aid of mutinous troops, it had forced the abdication of the tsar.

Meanwhile in St. Petersburg, Marxists, leaders of workers, and strike committees had set up a Soviet (Council of Workers and Soldiers) which took over the food supply and organized the defense of the city. In its first orders March 28, in *Izvestia*, new organ of the Soviet, it assumed control of the armed forces. A network of soviets was set up in other cities and this became the real depository of power, issuing decrees, taking steps to prevent a counterrevolution, and placing the tsar and his family under arrest. At the same time *Pravda* was made the organ of the Bolshevist party.

The provisional government now under the leadership of Alexander Kerensky, a youthful Social Revolutionary, announced sweeping reforms and immediate convocation of a Constituent Assembly. But this government faced insoluble problems—hunger, war, a country in chaos. The people were getting impatient; and when Foreign Minister Pavel Milyukov declared that the Russians were determined to continue fighting side by side with the Allies until victory over Germany was won, serious riots occurred, for the masses had no interest in war or international relations.

And where was Lenin? Still watching history pass him by from Geneva, for he had no way of getting to the capital, now called Petrograd. Finally Geneva Marxist exiles made a deal with the Germans who agreed to return them in a sealed car to Russia to start a counterrevolution and take Russia out of the war. Lenin's group had had no part in the March revolution. Lenin arrived three weeks late, but he immediately launched a virulent attack on Petrograd Bolshevists, accusing them of being laggards and traitors to the revolutionary cause. The existing republic must be destroyed at once so that all power could pass to the Soviets. For a time Lenin appeared about to win, but sober minds began to see that what he advocated was a negation of Social Democratic doctrine, even of Marxism, that would lead only to a Lenin dictatorship. People began to ask whether the civil war he advocated was not serving the German cause alone. Was he in fact a traitor? Kerensky ordered his arrest and he fled to Vyborg, Finland, where he was a fugitive for ten weeks. Then he came back and beat down the objections of his opponents. First he would end the war and the army would come over to him. Then he would take the lands of the aristocrats and give them to the peasants who would join him. The factories would be taken from the capitalists and given to the workers. He demanded an immediate uprising. It was voted and Trotsky was entrusted with military preparations. During the night of October 24, 1917, Petrograd was taken with little fighting, as was true in many other cities. All resistance was over by November 11. Lenin now proclaimed that the provisional government had been overthrown. A new government was announced with Lenin as chairman and Trotsky as commissar of foreign affairs. Last on the cabinet list was Joseph Stalin, Georgian terrorist and bank robber, who was named commissar of nationalities.

How Bolshevists Took Over the Press

When the tsarist regime had fallen, Bolsheviks, Mensheviks, and Social Revolutionaries seized the plants of government papers. Soon there ensued a terrific battle for public opinion. Bolshevik papers became so violent that Kerensky tried to silence those most outspoken against continuing the war; but his suppressions were ineffective, for the Soviets controlled the police and the troops. For a time there was unbridled press freedom.

When the Bolsheviks seized power the picture changed. On October 28, 1917, the Council of Peoples Commissars placed all non-Bolshevik publications under precensorship and forbade them to carry advertising. There was violent opposition; but the new government replied that, at the moment when the power of the people was being consolidated, it would be madness to leave this weapon, more powerful than machine guns, in the hands of the enemy. A press tribunal was established with jurisdiction over "crimes committed against the people by the press," and the Cheka (Secret Police) was empowered to arrest editors and bring their cases to the press tribunal. One paper after another was suppressed. When they refused to die, and reappeared under new titles, their editors were hunted down, the plants confiscated. By June, 1918, all non-Bolshevik publications had been closed and their plants nationalized.

Meanwhile the government had proceeded to reconstruct a new "socialist order." Private ownership of land was abolished, banks and industry nationalized. The stock market was swept away, as were the rights of inheritance. Old traditions and institutions were uprooted. Even civil marriages took the place of church ceremonies, and divorce could be obtained by merely asking for it.

Communists Fight Off Dissidents

But the Bolsheviks were not yet secure. Railway, postal, and telegraph workers declared themselves opposed to the Communist coup and demanded a coalition government of all socialist parties. Kerensky had gone to the front and rallied Menshevist forces to march on the capital. Moreover, there was no surety that the millions in the rest of the country would submit to the orders of 240,000 Bolsheviks. In the south, in the Don River area, General Kornilov was raising an army to fight Communists. Bolshevik forces, however, quickly defeated Kerensky's meager army and soon shelled out the last resistance forces in Moscow's Kremlin. Lenin now refused any coalition. But he quickly learned that his control was impossible without terror. He had not hesitated to order the execution of the tsar and his family in July, 1918; now he began liquidating "traitors among Mensheviks and Social Revolutionaries" without trial. Surprisingly, when the November 25 elections for the Constituent Assembly were held, the Communists got only 9,800,000 out of the 41,600,000 votes cast; but when elected deputies came for the assembly, Bolshevik forces fired on non-Bolsheviks. Many managed to get through, but when they tried to organize the assembly they were shouted down by a house packed with Bolshevik members and soldiers and were finally routed, never to meet again, for Lenin had decided that the assembly was a mistake in his plan and would only be an obstacle to his one-man rule.

Lenin and Trotsky now sued for peace with Germany, but enemy demands were so exorbitant that they stalled for time till German forces began a general advance into Russia. Then they signed the Brest-Litovsk Treaty, which lost Russia one-third of her population and croplands and half of her industry. To make a complete break for his dictatorship, Lenin now moved his capital to the Kremlin in Moscow. The civil war between the Reds and the Whites was bitterly fought for three years. For a time armies of General Anton Denikin, Admiral Aleksander Kolchak, and General Nikolai Yudenich occupied nine-tenths of the country; but despite the help given the Whites by the United States and Britain, the revolt was put down by 1921 and the Marxist regime was secure.

Press Is Expanded

With all opposition papers blotted out, the Bolsheviks had to fill the vacuum and start papers in new areas. To make good their victory, they had to sell the new order to the people. Many persons were mobilized who had little education or aptitude for journalism, and most of the first new papers were poor, dull propaganda sheets of the small despotic group. But despite mechanical difficulties and newsprint shortages many papers were established. In 1919 all governmental publishing agencies were united in Gozizdat, part of the commissariat of education. This controlled everything from paper supply and machinery to the actual publishing and distribution of all papers, magazines, and every other form of printed matter. Only Gozizdat-approved papers could be published and only where the government wanted circulation.

Illiteracy was the great hindrance. In the Communist concept the press was to be the agitation and propaganda arm of the party, its basic purpose to build a new society and to mold the kind of citizen desired. Once the civil war was over, the government started trying to wipe out the illiteracy left by the tsarist regime. Schools were begun everywhere but there were not enough teachers. Millions of adults had to be taught to read. In factories, in farm villages, in classes held at night or on rest days, literates were drafted to teach others to read. Slowly the veil of illiteracy began to lift. Newspapers were distributed free to all who could read, and party members held reading groups at night to impart the gospel to those still illiterate.

The 1918 Constitution had stipulated: "In order to secure for the laboring classes real freedom to express their own opinions the R.S.F.S.R. destroys the dependence of the press on capital and transfers it into the hands of the laboring classes and the poor peasantry, together with all technical and material resources for publication of all newspapers, pamphlets, books and all other printed matter, and guarantees their free circulation throughout the country."

Lenin had said, "Liberty of the press serves as one of the main battle cries of pure democracy. Nevertheless, workers know, and socialists of all countries have admitted that this serves as a deception as long as the best presses and the largest reserves of paper remain in the hands of capitalists."

The flaw in this idealistic statement was that under the Communist system the power of the press was not transferred to the people but to the small group of Communist party leaders who presumed to think and speak for all and who used the press to keep themselves in power. The dictatorship of the proletariat had become a dictatorship of the few over the proletariat.

NEP Sets Press Back

Three years of world war, then two revolutions, followed by three years of civil war, had demoralized economic life. Furthermore, workers who had seized factories in 1917 had been unable to run them efficiently, and by 1921 industrial production was down to 20 per cent of the prewar level. Peasants had gone back to primitive methods; food production had declined seriously; and the government forcibly requisitioned food stocks from all peasants. By 1921 all reserves had been used and a drought brought serious famine. Lenin decided to call a halt in the pace of socialization. In the New Economic Policy the peasant was allowed to keep his surplus, after paying a tax in kind, and private trading was permitted to encourage him to produce more. Industries were combined in groups under state trusts, and foreigners were brought in to reorganize production.

As part of NEP the press was thrown on its own. State subsidies for free distribution were withdrawn and all publications were put on an individual subscription basis. The result was drastic. The dullness and crudeness of Soviet papers did not attract subscribers. It was one thing to get a paper free, but to have to buy a colorless propaganda sheet was another. *Pravda* excoriated provincial papers by saying, "They are as like as two drops of water, uniform, gray and dull." Circulations fell, and whereas at the beginning of 1922 there had been 803 newspapers, by August the number had been reduced to 299 with a total circulation of only 933,000.

The government, however, recognized too well the value of the press as a powerful party weapon to abandon it. By compelling all party members to subscribe, by assisting papers with some state advertising, and by providing outright subsidy for others, the government helped the press move ahead. Workers' and farmers' cooperatives were encouraged to set up their own papers; and through peasant and worker correspondents, writing of the life and sentiment in their own factories and farm villages, the press sought to make itself not only one for the masses, but of the masses. By 1925 there were 498 papers with 2,500,000 circulation.

At the same time a new pattern was stamped on papers. In 1921 editors were informed that their basic task was uniting workers and peasants in building a new economic life. Instructions one day in 1922 specified a lead article of eighty to one hundred lines, dealing with a practical discussion of local reconstruction. The remaining space was to be distributed as follows: life of the nation, 120–150 lines; foreign affairs, 80–100 lines; agriculture, 100–150 lines; and so on. Lenin declared that after the revolution too much space had been given to political news and personalities. He dictated "less politics and more economics"; and he made it clear that he did not mean "highbrow theoretical twaddle" but the workaday aspects of farm, factory, village, and military life. Thus the Soviet press took on a character different from any in the western world with a totally different set of news values. Foreign news was printed only to show the machinations of capitalistic powers or to portray the success of communism in other parts of the world. Play was given to stories of production, records of sowing and harvests, and the achievements in factories, mines, and forests of Stakhanovites—workers who set the production pace and whose efforts were held up for emulation.

A new supercensorship board, Glavlit, was established with branches everywhere in the country. Gozizdat now became merely the state publishing agency. Glavlit supervised not only all papers but theater, films, music, and books; and its police not only controlled censorship but began arresting violators of regulations, confiscating editions, cutting down on circulations, even closing some publishing enterprises. Thus the Russian press came to be regulated down to the last en quad. By 1927, Russia was claiming 1,105 papers with a circulation of 7,600,000. Two years earlier *The Moscow Journalist* had reported that the government had found it necessary to subsidize forty-one peasant and sixty-eight non-Russian language papers, the implication being that most others were now beginning to pay their way.

Stalin Comes to Power

Lenin had become ill with overwork and had had two strokes. To ease his load, he had picked Joseph Stalin, a hardworking, ruthless official "who would get things done" as secretary of the Central Committee. While recuperating, Lenin apparently began to be troubled by his conscience. The state which had been wrung from so much blood to bring a paradise for workers had not lived up to expectations. The peasants had not been given land but had been made hired hands on state farms. And after Stalin, by means of a blood bath, forced Georgia into union with the R.S.F.S.R., Lenin turned against him. He made a remarkable recovery in 1923 and had expected to return to office, but on January 21 he died very suddenly. Robert Payne in his "Life and Death of Lenin" insists that Stalin poisoned him. This might have happened, but the contention has not been sufficiently authenticated.

Stalin now quickly made himself the dictator of all Russians. In sensational treason trials many "Old Bolsheviks" were purged; some fifty were executed, others sent to labor camps or banished. Trotsky was exiled, then pursued to Mexico and murdered. Stalin's power was now absolute. His first years were devoted to reconstruction, the reorganization of industry, and the development of trade relations abroad. To the outside world it seemed that Russia had now settled down to be a peaceful neighbor. Britain and all great powers, except the United States, established diplomatic relations with her, and Russia's foreign trade began to rise. Even the press expanded and in 1928 claimed 1,179 publications with a circulation of 9,400,000.

Stalin had engineered a new governmental federation incorporating all the separate nationalities into the new Union of Soviet Socialist Republics (U.S.S.R.) with all power concentrated in the central government, not only in defense and foreign affairs, but in the economic aspects of the entire nation. In 1928 he announced the first Five-Year Plan designed (1) to transform an agrarian nation into one possessing its own industries and producing finished commodities from its own raw materials; (2) to reorganize agriculture on the basis of collective farms to increase production; (3) to reorganize the distributive system using cooperatives instead of middlemen; (4) to reorganize the entire transportation system; (5) to develop the technical and economic resources to defend against foreign aggression; and (6) to promote education and literacy. It was a monumental plan to remodel the life of a still relatively primitive people, numbering 170,000,000, and to outpace in a few years the century-old achievement of western nations. Definite goals in each category were set by the state planning commission, Gosplan.

Plans for the Press

This plan included a precise design for the growth of the press, for it was a necessary instrument in mobilizing workers and peasants to the gigantic effort needed to achieve these goals. Papers were developed to reach every segment of the people. The tsarist government had profited by the ignorance of what it considered inferior colonial people. Despite the fact that the empire embraced 175 ethnic groups, no language but Russian had been permitted, and there were no schools for other language groups. Thus while the national illiteracy rate was 79 per cent, in great areas of Asia it was almost 100 per cent. The Soviet government now began promoting the languages and cultures of its many peoples. It was essential that a press be set up for each language group. Alphabets had to be created for those who had had only primitive ideographs; written languages had to be developed; then people had to be taught to read and write their language. It was a monumental task. Through outright subsidy a press had to be imposed on every part of the Union. The Tanjug republic, on the borders of Afghanistan, which had had no papers, by 1937 had forty; Uzbekistan, the legendary land of Samarkand, by 1935 had 118 papers in five languages. This was a tremendous accomplishment. By the outbreak of World War II the Soviet press was publishing in so many different languages that it reached into the forests, mountains, towns, and factories because everyone had access to a paper he could read. Even remote villages had their wall newspapers. The first Five-Year Plan was succeeded by a second in 1933 and a third in 1938. By 1939 Russians were claiming 8,789 publications with a circulation of 38,000,000.

Despite the relative success of these plans, their accomplishment had come at the expense of the people. Excessive development of heavy industry and heavy exports to pay for industrial equipment sharply depressed living standards; ruthless compulsion of peasants into collective farms, equally heartless extraction of their crops, and sharp limitations of food stuffs for domestic consumption caused great suffering. There were series of crises of which the world learned nothing from the Soviet press, which concentrated only on drives for economic goals. It was a completely standardized press. If one had made an extended tour of the Soviet Union one would have found not only the same ideas but the same inflections of thought hammered home from European Russia to the pioneer stretches of Siberia. During these years communism had become Stalinism. One-party dictatorship became the personal tyrannical rule of one man. The last pretenses that "the state would wither away to make room for more human freedom" had faded out and a rigid police state took shape. Press and radio came to reflect only the ideas of the dictator. Lenin's trade unions now had become only a technical branch of the government to wring the most labor from workers for the least money. The peasants, for whom Alexander had abolished serfdom, were again little more than serfs, but under socialist labels.

During the twenties and thirties the Soviet press swung through sharp changes. At first it was deeply distrustful of the West, always fearful of aggression. Because both had been defeated nations and had economic need of each other, Russia and Germany drew together and entered into close commercial and military relations. Russia's press was very friendly to Germany; but when Hitler and his Nazism with its outspoken anti-communism rose to power, the Soviet press turned bitter against the menace of Fascism, particularly after Germany and Russia had taken opposite sides in the Spanish Civil War. When Russia, in a complete about-face, joined the League of Nations and her foreign minister, Litvinov, took the lead in trying to prevent the dismemberment of Czechoslovakia, the press became strong for collective security. Reaction to the Munich Agreement was immediate. The press turned with fury on Prime Minister Neville Chamberlain and England for having given in to Germany. Yet, when in 1939 Stalin callously concluded a pact with Hitler, newspapers changed their tune again. And when Hitler, without declaration of war, invaded Russia on June 22, 1941, the press once more had to reverse its stand. In a nation where all information was completely controlled and manipulated, such sudden shifts were more easily explainable to readers than were the handsprings by New York's *Daily Worker*.

German Invasion Hits Press

The German attack not only brought tremendous devastation but a severe setback to the press. In six months Germany, attacking along a one thousand-mile front, drove to the outskirts of Moscow and Leningrad. Fronts lost themselves in rapid pincer movements. Huge populations were swallowed up in the flood of battle. But while Russians retreated, they exacted a heavy price in German lives, and the areas they abandoned were put to the torch before they fell into enemy hands. Long years of Communist repression now revealed one of the shortcomings of the system. Despite twenty-two years of indoctrination, many people greeted the German invaders as deliverers. By 1943 a well-organized anti-Bolshevik revolution was under way in the Ukraine. But Nazi terrorism was more than any of these Russians could take, and the powerful force of Russian patriotism switched to all-out defense of the motherland. While Anglo-American forces kept the vital sea-lanes open, poured in supplies, and contained German, Italian, and Japanese forces in North Africa and the Far East, the Russians through 1942 carried on an implacable battle against the Axis.

The press suffered along with the people. More than 2,700 papers disappeared as plants were wrecked in the battle zones and newspaper personnel were lost. The largest paper-producing areas had been overrun. In other regions newspapers continued to rally the people to all-out defense efforts. Even larger papers were now down to four pages, many provincial papers to two. The year 1943 saw the tide turn, and by early 1944 the Germans were in full retreat. Reconstruction was begun as soon as occupied areas were retaken, and attention was given to the restoration of the press system.

This was the time when American and British air armadas in blazing attacks, often with great losses, were smashing Nazi industrial and transportation centers, not only in central Europe but in the Balkans to help the Russians. In North Africa the Allies had routed Axis forces and opened the second front the Russians had demanded. Now they were fighting their way up through Italy and France. Yet the Russian people were told almost nothing of Allied advances, and they learned even less of the $11,000,000,000 in war material supplied to Russia by the United States. Not till the Normandy landing did the press change its tune. No wonder the Russian people emerged from the war thinking they had won it almost single-handedly.

Postwar Press Revival

As soon as fighting ended the Soviet government turned to reconstruction. Seven million Russians had lost their lives, twenty million more were homeless, and Russia had lost a quarter of her prewar wealth. A new Five-Year Plan was inaugurated in 1946, again with emphasis on heavy industry. Territories conquered by Russians were stripped of industrial plants, and all the states of eastern Europe as well as the Soviet Zone of Germany were organized under Russian economic hegemony so that considerable trade developed with east-bloc countries in which Stalin had engineered a Communist take-over in order to provide a ring of friendly states.

Special efforts were made to reestablish papers lost during the war. But there were many consolidations, and in numerous cases district papers were set up to replace several smaller local papers. Foreign correspondents revealed that many former newspapermen, now considered unreliable, were purged and their papers eliminated. *Pravda*, in its Press Day issue of May 5, 1950, claimed that the Soviet Union had 7,700 papers with a total circulation of 33,500,000; but it must be remembered that the number included dailies, weeklies, bimonthlies, and monthlies. There was no relaxation in press control. Stalin and his troubleshooter, Andrei Vishinsky, frequently reiterated that there could be no freedom for "enemies of socialism" and that any criticism of the Soviet regime or party decisions might be punishable by from five to twenty-five years in labor or reeducation camps. In spite of their number, Soviet papers were spread much more thinly than in western Europe. But when a state can plan the structure of its press to eliminate what Communists call "useless commercial competition of a capitalistic economy," it can reach and influence every section of the population—and this press was planned with great exactitude.

Press Is Made Cold War Instrument

It had been hoped that wartime cooperation between the West and the Soviet Union might bring closer relations after the war. But these years had revealed that many people were still not sold on the communistic system. Farmers had enjoyed private production during the war when almost any practice was permitted that would produce more crops. Workers had enjoyed the ascendency of industrial managers over party supervisors. Millions of Russian soldiers had found that even in war-torn Western Europe, people were better off than at home. To Stalin, world conciliation seemed the shortest road to self-destruction. The only means to hold power was to proclaim an emergency, surround the Soviet Union with rapacious enemies, and call on the people to give their all as an alternative to destruction by capitalistic wolves. Despite the wartime friendship between Roosevelt and Stalin, the latter now turned on the United States.

Now the press became filled with denunciations of "capitalistic encirclement" and "imperialist aggressors" as the people were taught, by every means of propaganda, to hate and fear the West, and the United States in particular. With the creation of the Comintern, Communist parties in other countries were encouraged to participate in governments to weaken them from within; and Soviet papers, reporting their successes in France and Italy, led people to believe that communism would soon take over Europe. In the United Nations Security Council the Soviet Union used its veto power to prevent the West from interfering in areas in which Russia was interested, and the General Assembly was made a propaganda forum to assail the motives of non-Communist states and keep them divided. These long speeches were often run serially for days in Soviet papers to get the whole propaganda effect over to the people. The outbreak of the Korean War gave the press an opportunity to assail "American aggression" and to air unfounded charges of "germ warfare."

Stalin's Death Brings Changes

Stalin's death on March 5, 1953, brought to Greece, where the author was working at the time, the largest sale of newspapers in the history of Greek journalism, for Greeks blamed Stalin for the two civil wars they had had to fight with their Communists. Sales zoomed in every country; and in the Soviet Union papers could not print enough copies to meet the demand, for Stalin's dictatorship had been dominant for thirty years and had remained virtually unchallenged till his death. A small Council of Ministers headed by Georgi Malenkov took over the government. There ensued a jockeying for power till in 1956 Nikita Khrushchev, as first secretary of the Communist party, emerged dominant. At the twentieth Communist Party Congress he delivered a six-hour speech denouncing Stalinism. This now became the subject of propaganda campaigns throughout the press.

The new regime brought some relaxation of restrictions for the press. Khrushchev, speaking to newspaper editors in late 1953, criticized the stereotyped character of newspapers, their dullness, superficiality, and failure to meet reader interests. The party magazine, *Kommunist*, and *Sovetskaya Pechat*, organ of the Journalists' Union, hammered at the provincial papers for copying Moscow papers and for being more concerned with making an impression on officialdom than in serving readers. As a result papers began to look more lively and to provide a more varied content. Stories of everyday life in different parts of the Union became more numerous. Reprinting *Pravda*'s editorials was no longer a must, and provincial papers printed their own. Serial stories and light humorous pieces appeared. More space was given to pictures and to sports, particularly in evening and youth papers. Newspapers enjoyed more freedom in "self criticism" of economic progress, even to differing with each other, which had never been permitted under Stalin. Even foreign news came to be handled a little more objectively. During the 1955 Geneva Summit Conference the speeches of President Dwight D. Eisenhower and other western statesmen were printed. All this, however, was designed to make papers more readable and more effective instruments for mass persuasion and did not diminish party control.

In 1956 the Soviet Union ran into difficulty when revolts erupted in East Berlin and Poland in June and in Hungary in October. Khrushchev could not afford to let these satellites move out of the Soviet orbit and put down the revolts with Soviet tanks and armored divisions. The Soviet press treated all the same. East Berlin strikers were described as "hordes of pillagers and fascist incendiaries, which had to be dispersed, to save the German Peoples Republic." No Soviet reader learned that German workers had risen against the Soviet regime. Hungarian rebels were described as reactionaries trying to restore the dictatorship of Admiral Miklós Horthy. Readers were told that Russian troops had intervened on the appeal of the Hungarian working class.

In 1957 Khrushchev encountered a personal threat when Vyacheslav Molotov, Georgi Malenkov, and Lazar Kaganovich attempted to oust him. Khrushchev summoned the full Central Committee, expelled the dissidents, and sent them to minor posts far distant from Moscow. In March, 1955, he was made chairman of the Presidium of the Soviet Union, the undisputed top man in the U.S.S.R.

Press Control Is Carefully Planned

With Khrushchev's recognition of the press as a most important instrument of agitation and propaganda, its previous careful plotting was perfected. The circulation of each paper, its format, size, and the segment of the public to which it was to go, was regulated by the party.

The organization of this press might be pictured as a pyramid. At the apex is the Central or All-Union Press, emanating from Moscow and composed of the national newspapers which speak with the authority of the Presidium, the party, and the principal ministries and public organizations. They carry the word of authority down the line to all the lesser divisions of the country. Few of these papers are sold on kiosks. Most go to party members, party leaders, and administrative and economic heads in every section of the country. Private citizens do not generally subscribe to these newspapers because other special papers are published for them. However, they may occasionally see Moscow papers in reading rooms. The last official report on the press of the Soviet Union listed twenty-two papers in this All-Union group, nine of which were dailies. Applying the UNESCO classification, of this twenty-two there were only six dailies, one triweekly, and one biweekly with sufficient news to qualify as national general interest papers; the rest were definitely for special audiences.

First place in the hierarchy is occupied by *Pravda* (Truth), which celebrated its fiftieth anniversary in 1964. It had started as an underground paper in 1912 and for the first five years was often suppressed, reappearing under different titles till in 1917 it was made the chief voice of the party. With 6,296,000 circulation *Pravda* is the largest paper in the U.S.S.R.; it is printed in twenty-eight different cities and has two-thirds of its circulation outside Moscow. This is the power in the throne room of communism, the mentor of the entire press. It sets the line to be followed on national and international developments and acts as the pacemaker for economic drives. Its journalists are probably the best in the country. Foreign news used to be found mainly on the back page, but more recently it is placed also on page one. Always it is carefully selected to show the peacefulness of the eastern bloc and the aggressive imperialism of the west. It averages six pages, though often it has only four.

Next is *Izvestia* (News of Soviet and Workers Deputies), the voice of the Kremlin, less concerned with theoretical communism and more with practical government problems, the business of the Supreme Soviet, the work of national planning. It carries more foreign news than *Pravda* and speaks for the government on foreign policy. It took on new life when in 1958 Khrushchev's son-in-law, Alexei Adzhubei, an able journalist, became editor. He transformed the paper and gave it better makeup and heads, more pictures, more human interest stories, and actual on-the-spot reporting. As an evening paper it became much more popular and even ran women's features. By 1964 Adzhubei had raised the circulation from 1,000,000 to 6,000,000 It, too, averages six pages and goes all over the country. It puts out a separate Sunday tabloid, *Nedelya* (The Week), averaging twenty-four pages.

Behind these leaders come first the organs of the ministries. The defense ministry publishes *Krasnaya Zvezda* (Red Star) for the armed forces; the transportation ministry puts out *Gudok* (Whistle) for railway workers; the agricultural ministry has its *Selskaya Zhizn* (Rural Life). The ministries of trade, heavy industry, timber, and others put out papers for their workers.

Then come the organs of public organizations. One of the most important is *Trud* (Labor), organ of the Central Council of Trade Unions with 1,600,000 circulation, heavy with union affairs but also including some general news. Other unions have their papers, such as the Union of Soviet Writers with its triweekly *Liternaya Gazeta* and the All-Union Committee on Physical Culture, which publishes the triweekly *Sovetsky Sport*. A third category is made up of the papers for the Communist youth. Most important is *Komsomolskaya Pravda* (Young Communist League's Truth) for those over 17, with a circulation of 4,200,000. Then there is *Pionerskaya Pravda*, for younger children, with 6,500,000 triweekly. Both set the pattern for nearly a hundred similar publications in other parts of the union.

The Regional and Local Press
In the middle of the Soviet press pyramid stand the papers of the fifteen republics and various small autonomous territories, created to provide nominal autonomy for important ethnic groups. This press includes also some papers in larger cities. Thus *Leningradskaya Pravda* with 275,000 circulation is considered part of the middle press because of the large territory it serves, even though it is published by the City Communist party and Soviet.

This middle press follows the same party, government, and public organization hierarchy. Each republic, for instance, has its equivalent of *Pravda*, usually printed in Russian, and its equivalent of *Izvestia* in the language of the republic. Thus at Kiev in the Ukraine, the party organ is *Pravda Ukraina*, while the organ of the Ukraine Soviet is *Radyanska Ukraina* in Ukrainian. At Tashkent in Uzbek the party organ is *Pravda Vostoka* in Russian, the Soviet organ *Kzyl Uzbekistan* in its own language. Not all chief party organs are called *Pravda;* in Georgia it is *Zarya Vostoka* (Dawn of the East), in Latvia *Cina* (Struggle). The pattern on the republic level provides in most cases only two dailies, one for the party, one for the government. All the rest run from weeklies to triweeklies.

Behind these leaders come the organs of the regional branches of the various ministries, the public and youth organizations. Thus the Ukraine has its army paper in *Chernovy Armia*, its agricultural paper in *Selskaya Ukraina*, its equivalent of *Trud* in *Robochaya Gazeta* (Workers Gazette), and its youth paper in *Komsomal Ukrainy*, each directed to its own interest group. These middle sector papers are intended to serve their republic or autonomous regions, not only in carrying the decisions of the national government to their readers but also in dealing concretely and specifically with the administrative and economic problems of their areas. Moscow's *Pravda* has frequently criticized regional papers for their superficial treatment of their own economic and political problems.

The third stratum, at the base of the soviet press pyramid, includes the district, small city, and town papers. There are some small city dailies, a few with circulations of 5,000 or more. Most are weeklies or biweeklies, published for rural communities, which range from a few hundred to 2,000 circulation. This small town press is defined as having special responsibility "in teaching and educating the masses in the resolution of the tasks standing before the district." It is expected to concentrate on practical local problems such as increasing farm or factory production, improving local sanitation, and insuring the Communist order in accomplishing set tasks. Its importance in drives for economic goals is not to be underestimated.

Supervised by the party and directed by the state in conformity with its careful plan, which leaves no room for the unforeseeable, the Soviet press has evolved a schematic framework so that there may be an organ of indoctrination for everyone, no matter what his work or special interests may be.

Revision of Soviet Claims Necessary

Soviet 1964 figures, showing 7,771 newspapers with a total circulation of 88,000,000, need discounting. Circulation figures are provided only for some of the Moscow All-Union and a few of the republic papers. Except for a few of the chief papers, no others are allowed to circulate outside the Soviet Union. The author has access regularly to only *Pravda* and *Izvestia*.

Leo Grullow, editor of "The Current Digest of the Soviet Press" and an expert on this press, reported in 1964 not more than 7,771 so-called newspaper titles of which 3,000 were not newspapers but factory and collective farm house-organs. That left 4,771 newspapers, of which not more than 440 were dailies. If one applies the UNESCO criterion of general interest papers, it is apparent that in 1964 the entire Soviet Union with a population of 225,000,000 had only 270 dailies providing some general news along with propaganda and that the other 170 were all directed to special audiences with little if any general news.

Soviet methods of reporting newspaper circulations, moreover, are completely misleading. The total circulation claimed in 1964 was arrived at by adding up all daily, triweekly, biweekly, weekly, and monthly circulations as if they were published all on one day, which produced the fantastic total of 88,000,000. It is likely that the 270 dailies which can be counted as "news-papers" have a circulation of only about 27,000,000 which would mean a distribution of but 12.1 copies per 100 persons. In the same year the 1,763 U.S. dailies reported audited circulations topping 64,000,000. Yet the entire Russian press structure is devised to reach every family in the U.S.S.R. Daily circulation could not accomplish this end; but with all the nondaily publications and house organs, every family may possibly see some publication once a week, all feeding the people only such information as the government desires and regimenting the whole people to achieve the desired economic, political, and diplomatic goals. And while the membership of the Communist party in 1964 was reported at 10,863,-000, this was only 4.3 per cent of the entire population and it in turn was ruled by a small group of powerful party and governmental leaders at the top.

The Soviet press therefore has developed a form of journalism totally different from anything in the western world. News is incidental, for the chief function of papers is to serve as a collective propagandizer, agitator, and organizer for the Communist cause. Stalin spoke of the press as "the transmission belt between the party and the masses," and Khrushchev said, "Just as an army cannot fight without arms so the party cannot carry on its ideologic missions without the efficient and powerful weapon, the press. We cannot put it in unreliable hands; only the most faithful, most trustworthy and politically steadfast people, devoted to our cause."

Is the Communist Press Free?

Soviet journalists insist they have the freest press in the world because it is free from capitalistic controls. Freedom of the press means something totally different. The individual Russian journalist is not concerned with the right to say what he pleases, for he places his responsibility to Communist society first and readily accepts the party's dictum, believing that party leaders, in their wisdom, know what is best for the people. He makes much of "freedom of access to expression" which he claims is denied to most people in the United States, whereas in the Soviet Union a million people a year write letters to the editor voicing their complaints and criticisms. He does not realize that many more than a million letters from Americans are printed every year in its 1,763 dailies and some 30,000 nondailies—letters attacking the government, its foreign and domestic policies, its president and other government officials, even the newspaper itself. While Russian letter writers may criticize local officials for failing to carry forward the plans of their socialist system, they may not criticize the system nor question the party line.

There is no precensorship; yet party control is no less effective, for every editor and writer has been carefully selected and chief editors are on the executive committee of the party organization at whatever level they may work. Whether a man has come into journalism through faithful party work or has graduated from one of the twenty five-year schools of journalism, he has been so carefully indoctrinated that the government can be sure of his unquestioned loyalty and certain that he will accurately interpret and present the party line in every editorial activity. The plainest proof that this press does not enjoy the freedom permitted in the West is that in all the vast expanse of the Soviet Union there is not a single independent newspaper, whereas in many western countries there are Communist publications which operate freely. Soviet newsmen, moreover, are constantly watched; and although there is a continuous flow of directives and instructions, there is always a danger that these may be misunderstood and that an editor may find himself accused of deviationism and removed as "unreliable."

It follows that there is seldom objectivity in the Soviet press. Authorities have often criticized editors, writers, and broadcasters for any such manifestation. Editorializing in the handling of the news is a must. In the Soviet press, people and events are not newsworthy except as they may be identified with the continuing building of the Communist society. It is the social process which is news. And, in all fairness, the story of the building of this vast nation, which has literally lifted itself by the bootstraps into a modern industrial state since 1917 is one of the great stories of all times; to a people who had nothing before, the development of their nation has been a tale of absorbing interest.

How Truth Is Twisted

Soviet reporting of international tensions is nothing less than unusual, and more often disingenuous. Take, for example, the Berlin crisis in 1961. According to Leo Grullow, Soviet readers were told nothing of the mass exodus of 103,000 East Germans in the first six months, which often rose to 3,000 a day. The departure of so many people hurt the East German economy, already desperately short of manpower. Not till a month after the Berlin Wall had gone up did Russian readers learn that cement blocks and barbed wire had been used to seal off the two parts of the city. Nor were they told of any hindrance to the crossing by persons with relatives on the other side. They were informed that the border was closed only to "revanchists," (seekers for revenge), spies, and speculators. They were given no hint that

Russian tanks had been deployed. They were not told of the dramatic escapes over or under the wall or of the shooting of many who attempted it. Pages were filled with declarations of support for the Soviet stand by individuals and organizations at home and by other Communist papers around the world.

In another instance the U.S.S.R. on August 31, 1961, (while test ban negotiations were in progress), announced its intention to resume nuclear tests with new massive explosions. Soviet readers were not informed that fifteen tremendous detonations were set off in September. Britain and the United States protested and pointed out fallout dangers, but their statements were practically ignored. In fact TASS managed to report the White House statement without once mentioning "fallout." Again, when Dag Hammarskjöld, who had defied Khrushchev, died on September 18, 1961, *Pravda* and *Izvestia* editorialized on U.N. proceedings that day without mentioning the secretary general's death except in a short news item on the back page.

Then in 1962, when it was learned that the Soviet Union was erecting missile bases in Cuba, with a strike range covering most of North America, President John F. Kennedy summarily announced a naval quarantine of Cuba and notified Khrushchev that any nuclear missile launched from Cuba toward the United States would be regarded as an attack by the Soviet Union and would bring full retaliatory response. Immediate Russian press reaction was one of covering up by explaining that Cuba had been continually in danger of attack since the Bay of Pigs invasion. The naval quarantine was presented as an attempt to starve Cuba's women and children by cutting off supplies. Soviet readers were never told that U.S. ships were turning back no Soviet vessels with peaceful cargoes; American aerial photos of missile sites were derided as "farcical fakes." For three days Soviet papers were filled with accounts of public demonstrations against America's quarantine with one recurring headline: "We are with you, Cuba."

Khrushchev's accedence to Kennedy's demands was so sudden that some papers were caught with denunciatory articles on page one and the story of "Peace and the Triumph of Reason" on the next. But the Soviet press never did explain how "inoffensive" weapons turned out to be offensive, not Cuban but Russian. Their installation one week and their removal the next were made to seem "statesmanship" by the great peacemaker Khrushchev. When Red China and Albania accused Khrushchev of appeasement, the campaign turned against these two "who would risk World War III which might destroy the world."

And Then Came Great Changes

In 1963 there came a succession of economic crises. Food production declined and food prices rose. Steel priorities were cut and a new emphasis placed on the chemical industry, partly to provide large-scale land fertilization. It became necessary to make heavy purchases of grain from western countries. The split with Red China widened. All through 1963 and 1964 the other satellites in eastern Europe moved away from total dependence on Moscow and toward new relations with the West. Increased industrialization had opened the path of a new way of life, and Czechoslovakia—even the formerly loyal Bulgaria, Hungary, Poland, and Rumania—joined Yugoslavia in seeking at least a national economic independence of Moscow. There was no longer a Moscow-dominated Communist monolith.

Early in October, 1964, while Khrushchev was vacationing at his Black Sea villa, a secret meeting of the Communist party Central Committee was called. In a nonstop session it was decided that Khrushchev had outlived his usefulness. He was sent for and, on October 14, subjected to a biting attack, denounced for his agricultural fiascos, accused of trying to start a new "cult of personality," cited for his inability to control himself which had lowered the reputation of the Soviet Union throughout the world, and reprimanded for his provocative attitude toward the Chinese. Not only the Presidium but the full Central Committee voted against him. Khrushchev resigned and was stripped of all party positions. Leonid Brezhnev succeeded to his position as new head of the Communist party and Aleksei Kosygin to the premiership. There was immediate reaction from French and Italian Communist parties which sent fact-finding missions to Moscow. A few of the east-bloc nations also expressed some doubt concerning Khrushchev's summary ouster; but after Brezhnev and Kosygin had assured everyone that Khrushchev's basic foreign and domestic policies would be continued, the new regime was generally accepted.

Inevitably there were some changes in the press. Adzhubei, Khrushchev's son-in-law, was ousted as editor of *Izvestia;* so was the editor of *Pravda* and the head of radio and television. *Izvestia* still retained its livelier style, its cartoons and even comic panels. *Pravda* maintained its more sober mien; but both, in their editorials, stressed the importance of discussion of public issues, and the range of their topics did not narrow. Collective leadership became the slogan of the regime and of the press. It is curious that after all the publicity given to Khrushchev, the publicity for the new regime was muted. After Kosygin's visit to Peking and North Viet Nam, the line against the United States was hardened.

Soviet Newspaper Economics Is Different

Because from the beginning of the Communist regime the state had owned all industry and the entire distributive system, earlier Marxists saw no need for advertising. They insisted that newspaper advertising in western nations foisted on people shoddy and shopworn merchandise with shameless lies and false claims. Hence, during the Lenin and Stalin regimes there was little advertising beyond small listings of surplus goods in state stores, movie and theater listings, small advertisements for books, and occasionally a few want ads. Most direct income came from subscriptions and kiosk sales; and it must be remembered that all party members had to subscribe to their proper papers and that press dues were assessed against all union members. Some papers, with larger circulations, were able to pay their way, but for most, deficits had to be made up by the government.

Under Khrushchev's increased production of consumer goods, it was found that advertising was needed to facilitate the sales of merchandise, particularly after the discovery that factory warehouses were piled high with surplus shoes, watches, bicycles, electric appliances, and other consumer goods. City trade administrations, under local soviets, organized some 120 city-wide advertising agencies; and some of the larger *univermags* or department stores set up their own advertising departments. While *Izvestia* carried no advertising and *Pravda* only a two-column by eight-inch listing of movies and theaters, most larger city dailies began carrying not only local retail but some product advertising for state factories. More papers began to pay their way, but there were still many whose deficits had to be absorbed by government subsidy.

Now under Kosygin, an able economist who recognized that the Soviet economy had grown too complex to be dictated by Moscow bureaucratic planners, some four hundred clothing and shoe factories and seventy-eight of their raw material suppliers were removed from control by party bureaucrats who were responsible for the great surpluses of goods which people would not buy. They were placed under a market-oriented economy where consumer demand would dictate product design and quantity and profits would be made the indicator of factory performance. In 1965 one-third of all consumer goods plants effected this changeover. This will inevitably increase the need for advertising and bring more profitable operations to some papers.

The Brezhnev-Kosygin leadership remained firmly in control through 1965. Because industrial growth, national income, and farm production were lagging, Premier Kosygin announced a new economic policy which would relieve factory managers from central bureaucratic planning and place direction in the hands of factory managers who would be judged by what they were able to sell. Profit will be the criterion of a manager's effectiveness, and a portion of it may be kept for improving production through new tools and research. The remaining profits will go to the government, however, not to the plant manager.

A change came in the editorship of *Pravda* when Alexei Rumantsev was replaced by Mikhail Zimyanin, Soviet deputy foreign minister, apparently to implement a new, harder line toward the United States over Viet Nam. In late 1965 the new Soviet team, having had enough of Red Chinese insults, denounced China's leaders as "impossible" and called them threats to world peace. At the same time the Russians began rearming more vigorously than they had in years, perhaps as a safeguard against a possible war with China.

Other Differences in the Soviet Papers

An American who defected to Russia would find himself missing many things to which he had become accustomed in his home papers, most of all the news of people and events which he had always found interesting. Instead he would be subjected to papers which read like "preachy editorials" from beginning to end. And of course there would be no comic strips or syndicate features, and little sports except in *Izvestia*, in other more popular papers, and in *Sovetski Sport*.

Scandal and divorce news never appears, for extracurricular activities are held to be private affairs. There is no society news even though an upper class has developed because its comings and goings are not considered news. Even weddings and deaths are held to be the personal concern of the families affected. A film star is important for her art, not her sex life. For long years nothing like a "pinup" picture appeared; but with the popularity of seaside resorts, beach pictures inevitably show bikini-clad bathing beauties. Similarly, for long, there was no crime news except when spectacle trials were capitalized for political purposes. But recent troubles with juvenile delinquents and more serious criminals have brought reports of penalties to show that crime does not pay. Accidents likewise get little space unless they can be connected with suspected sabotage or breakdowns which can then be criticized as imperfections in the Communist system to be corrected.

Murders, catastrophes, race riots, strike violence, and scandals in the United States, however, are reported to show the decadence of life in America. Most disturbing to any man from the outside would be sense of isolation through an inability to get much straight news of what was going on in the rest of the world. John Gunther said that in a remote city he felt as apart from the world as if he had been on Mars.

Although there have been some moves toward using human interest stories, this press on the whole is serious. Its papers are published not to entertain but for the political and economic education of the people. Moreover, since the process of social reconstruction is a continuing one, there is no urgency about getting a news development into the paper the day it happens. If an editor must devote major space for a few days to a government pronouncement or program he can hold other news developments until he has cleared his decks and then pick them up as if they had just happened.

What About Foreign News?

In 1917 the Bolsheviks had seized the old tsarist agency Viestnik, moved it to Moscow, and renamed it Rosta. Then in 1925, when many more papers needed telegraphic service, TASS was established as a new superagency and given monopoly over all foreign news distributed in the Soviet Union. During the Stalin period, TASS became the perfect instrument through which the Communist leadership carried on its propaganda and agitation, keeping the people in ignorance of the news of the outside world and distorting what it did provide to suit its masters. Moreover, the very large staffs maintained by TASS in foreign capitals and the involvement of some TASS correspondents in spy cases indicated that the agency was being used as a cover for espionage.

In the more liberal post-Stalin era, TASS became more factual and objective in its news handling. Then in 1961 a new agency, APN, was created to provide foreign news organizations truthful information about the Soviet Union and to give Soviet readers an acquaintance with foreign peoples as an aid to mutual understanding. APN is still a minor agency, but its purposes are laudable. Now that foreign correspondents in Russia have been relieved of censorship of their dispatches, it would seem that some of what Galatkinov tried to suggest may be closer to realization. Yet every so often some foreign correspondent is expelled as an enemy of the Soviet Union. In 1964, Peter Johns, chief Moscow correspondent for Reuters, was expelled for his dispatch on the demonstration of African students in Moscow, which the government considered a slander on Soviet life and policy.

Still a Tool of State and Party

Thus the Soviet press, while it has increased its thaw in its relations with the West, remains a faithful servant of the state and party. Yet the system is an unusual one which every citizen of western nations should understand. Press control covers not only all newspapers but some 4,000 magazines and other periodicals and all radio and television as well. With all means of communication in its hands, the party can determine what the people shall know and lead them as it wishes them to go.

The new regime, like that of Khrushchev, is probably as afraid of atomic war as are Americans. It wants "coexistence" and increased trade relations with other nations. It shies away from getting into war itself, but this has not prevented the Soviet Union from egging others on to brush-fire wars in southeast Asia, in South America, in Africa, capitalizing on the national aspirations of former colonial peoples and trying to make the world forget that the Soviet Union has been the greatest of colonial exploiters.

The Soviet press is certainly better than it was. One striking difference is that there are no longer the venomous personal attacts on foreign statesmen. These have come to be considered "uncultured and undignified."

Increasing cultural contacts, the visits of many Americans to the Soviet Union and of many Russians to the United States have persuaded them that Americans are friendly people who do not want war. When "misunderstandings" arise, press attacks are not against the American people but only against "plutocratic and governmental warmongers."

The Soviet Union's is a touchy and often suspicious press, yet more relaxed than formerly. But, while it supports economic and to an extent diplomatic coexistence, the support does not extend to ideology. It may not win the whole world to communism but it will not give up its communistic system and its sacrosanct ideology.

The Press of Albania

Long a forgotten and unknown land, Albania has made news since her break with Moscow and her alliance with Red China. Her press, which did not rise till 1913, barely had a chance to try its wings before the nation was engulfed in wars and then swallowed in the maw of Communist expansion.

Albania is a small, poor, peanut-shaped country, about the size of Vermont, with 1,760,000 people. Rugged mountains divide her territory into a patchwork of isolated districts. She went from the oxcart to the airplane without an intermediate railroad period. Even today she has only 107 miles of railroad, 1,937 miles of motorable roads, and only 2,000 passenger cars, few of which are privately owned.

Albanians are the oldest Balkan people. In 1000 B.C. they ruled Illyria, which encompassed much of Yugoslavia and part of Greece. These native peoples, who called themselves the *Shkypeters* (sons of the eagle), fought invading Greeks and Romans, then Goths and Slavs, and finally the Turks in 1412. The Albanian hero, Scanderbeg fought off the Turks for years and organized all the tribes into an independent kingdom. On his deathbed he bequeathed his realm to his ally, the Venetian Republic, for he knew his people could not fight the enemy alone.

It was under the Venetians that printing first came when Stefan of Scutari, who had learned the art in Venice, returned to set up a press in his native city in 1563. But by 1571 the Turks had conquered the entire country and put an end to printing, for Albanian nationalism had to be stamped out; even teaching in Albanian was forbidden. For more than three hundred years this servitude continued; but when the Congress of Berlin in 1878 threatened to partition Albania among its neighbors, a wave of indignation swept the country. To capitalize on this, and to prevent the loss of his territory, the Sultan lifted the ban on Albanian schools and printing. The embers of patriotism burst into flame, but the movement was handicapped by almost complete illiteracy among the people and the fact that the language had not been reduced to a form practical for writing and printing.

An Albanian patriot, Constantin Christophorides, translated the Four Gospels into Latin characters. His new alphabet was adopted, schools started teaching the people how to read, and for the first time primitive newssheets began to appear. The Sultan, alarmed at the spread of Albanian nationalism, again in 1886 banned the use of the Albanian language, closed schools and forced the printers of the newssheets to flee into exile. In Bulgaria, Egypt, Greece, Italy, Rumania, Switzerland, Belgium, England, and the United States, exiled Albanians published some thirty newspapers to be smuggled back into their own country, but also to plead the cause of their people before the world. Even after young Turks overthrew the Sultan, complete Ottomanization of Albanians continued.

Finally a general rising of all Albanian tribes in 1912 won Albania the right of autonomy within the Turkish empire. But in the Balkan wars she was overrun by her neighbors, all seeking a slice of her territory. Britain, Italy, and Austria-Hungary intervened and brought Albania recognition as an independent sovereign state in 1913. Ismail Kemal Bey, an old editor in exile and an acknowledged leader of the Albanians, became provisional president. Now that Albania was free, weekly newspapers appeared in the principal cities; and on September 26, 1913, *Taraboshi*, the first daily paper, was born at Scutari. But 90 per cent of the people were poor, illiterate farmers, scattered over wide areas. Lacking the cohesive force of a national press, the country fell apart. Then, when World War I broke, the young press was swallowed up in the country's disaster as Italian, French, Greek, Serbian, and Montenegrin armies invaded. Austria-Hungary held much of the country from 1916 on. During the occupation Albanian patriots carried on from abroad.

In the United States the Free Albanian movement grew most rapidly. From Boston, New York, Chicago, and Denver papers pleaded the cause of the Albanian people. Others appeared at Rome and Lausanne. In Albania itself underground papers published off and on as they could. When the war ended Albanians stood firm against partition, and President Woodrow Wilson was adamantly against it. At last in 1920 Albanians were able to set up their own national government with Tirana as their capital. Newspapers had already appeared; some sixty were founded in the years up to 1925.

The liberals, who hoped to establish a progressive and democratic government, were led by Bishop Fan Noli of Boston. They were opposed by the landowning beys, led by Ahmed Bey Zogu, who feared democratic tendencies might interfere with their traditional exploitation of the peasantry. In the revolt of 1924 Liberals drove out Zogu and made Fan Noli president. Six months later Zogu returned with Yugoslav forces, and Fan Noli and other democratic leaders had to flee. Zogu now assumed the presidency and proceeded to reconstruct the country. For the first time in years Albania enjoyed peace. A new constitution guaranteed press freedom, for Zogu favored the establishment of papers to help impose the authority of the central government on tribal peoples who lived by the law of vendetta. There were soon papers in all principal towns. In 1929 the Constituent Assembly changed the republic into a monarchy with Zogu as King Zog I, and it became a one-man dictatorship under his military and police system. Yet Albania began to take on modern ways; law and order acquired meaning. Agrarian reforms laid the foundation for peasant land ownership, and progress was made in education.

The Press Is Subjugated

Zog became impatient with press criticism; his 1931 law not only required heavy caution-money deposits, which could be confiscated for any dereliction, but also gave courts the right to impose excessive fines or suppress a paper for any liberal expression. Soon all opposition papers had been stilled. Tirana now had three pro-government dailies. These plus a few local weeklies comprised the press. High illiteracy kept circulations small; *Arbenia*, the largest, had only 2,800. None of Zog's critics found it wise to live in Albania.

Then the face of the Albanian press was changed again by World War II. Mussolini attacked on April 7, 1939; and though Albanians fought valiantly, they were soon overpowered. King Zog and his queen fled the country. Now Mussolini, intent on using Albania as a base from which to attack Greece, thoroughly fascistized it. But the Greeks outfought the Italians till Hitler's armored divisions forced them back. For the next two years Albania and her press were under Fascist rule. Zog's papers had been suppressed; Tirana was allowed one daily, *Fashizma;* three weeklies were permitted in the provinces. Albanian papers had to chorus the Italian press in virulent denunciation of the Greeks; after that they were only the tool of Il Duce's propaganda.

Albanian patriots had not given up, and their guerrilla raids harried Italians throughout the occupation. First among the resistance groups was the National Front (*Balli Kombtar*) headed by Midhat Frisheri, veteran Albanian nationalist and a well-known writer. Then Marshal Tito sent Enver Hoxha from Yugoslavia, who not only organized an Albanian Communist party but also developed the most militant of the resistance forces. Both fronts had their underground papers; but despite their pretense at collaboration, the clandestine Communist papers began to undermine the National Front by every propaganda means available, charging that it was not fighting the enemy, that it was seeking compromises to avoid the destruction of the country, and that only their Liberation Front was pressing strong action against the foe.

The Communist Take-over

It soon became apparent that the Reds were intent on their own civil revolution under the guise of liberation. Tito's forces grew stronger, and the victorious Russian armies were advancing. When Italy collapsed and the Germans entered Albania, the British decided the Communists would kill more Germans than the Nationalists and threw their support to the Liberation Front just as they had backed Tito over Draja Mikhailovitch in Yugoslavia. Now with Allied arms, the Communists set out to liquidate their rivals. More Albanians died from Communist bullets than from German. Caught in the crossfire and with the Allied radio calling on Albanians to support the Liberation Front, the Democratic front disintegrated. After German withdrawal Hoxha, with Tito's aid, set up a provisional government at Tirana and proceeded to try as war criminals all his opponents he could round up. Some 7,000 were executed and 27,000 imprisoned. Then to give his government the stamp of legitimacy he staged an election on December 2, 1945. With all opposition held down by police terror, only Hoxha candidates appeared on the ballot; he won unanimously. A constitutional assembly now proclaimed the new Peoples Democratic Republic with Hoxha as its chief.

Few Albanians knew about Karl Marx. The Albanian Communist party numbered only 2,800, but this ruthless group now set out to sovietize a puzzled people. Professor Sefjula Maleshova, who had left Albania in 1924 and spent twenty years in Moscow becoming a trusted tool of Stalin, was sent home to be Hoxha's minister of popular culture and propaganda. There were, of course, no opposition papers for Maleshova to harry to death, but a soviet-style press was needed. First *Bashkimi* was set up at Tirana as the central daily organ of the Communist party. Then *Gazeta Zyrtare* was established as the biweekly official voice of the government, carrying its orders and decrees. Some weeklies were published in other cities. Together this press proceeded to glorify Stalin and Tito's Yugoslavia as examples of the true democracy to be established in Albania. Schools were started and youth organizations set up to regiment young minds: *Rinia* appeared as a biweekly organ of the Peoples Youth of Albania.

In the meantime Hoxha had nationalized Albania's few industries, banks, mines, and oil wells, driven out all merchants as "parasites," taken over all printing plants, and made all newspaper workers civil servants. The huge estates of the beys and the church were broken up and distributed among peasants in 12.5-acre plots; but the state retained ownership, and peasants were allowed to keep only such produce as the state did not requisition. Albania, never self-sufficient, needed a patron and a meal ticket. Tito supplied both with his economic aid, and all through this period Albanian papers lauded him.

But Stalin became concerned over Tito's "different path to socialism": Albania was too important in his plans for him to take any chance of losing this sub-satellite should the chief satellite leave the orbit. Early in 1948 Russian military and civilian missions established themselves in Albanian army units and ministries so that when Stalin expelled Yugoslavia from the Cominform in June, 1948, he had Albania well in hand. Hoxha, to save his own skin, quickly jumped to support Stalin and executed his anti-Stalinist aides. He cut all ties with Yugoslavia, expelled all Tito agents, and removed Tito's pictures from building walls. Albanian papers immediately fell in line, decrying Tito's "brutal, hostile, unlawful, and arbitrary interference in Albania" and his "capitalistic, colonial exploitation." Russians took over Radio Tirana and Russian overseers were placed on the ministry of popular culture and propaganda. Editors and writers who had taken Hoxha's previous predilection for Yugoslavia literally and had written too enthusiastically of what Tito was doing for Albania were rooted out; some were executed; others, sent to prison.

Stalin's plans for Albania soon became apparent. For a year she served as the base from which Albanian Communist guerrillas launched attacks on Greece to aid the Communist ELAS, now engaged in the second civil war to take over Greece. When this failed, Stalin turned to his more important purpose. Ten good airfields were readied. The island of Saseno was cleared of local population, heavily fortified, and provided with submarine pens from which he could strike at Italy or Yugoslavia and harass all Mediterranean shipping. Albania was cut off so completely that she became the most inaccessible country in Europe, a nation stricken with desperate hunger and disease, her people forgotten in Stalin's larger plans. Yet the controlled Albanian press continued mouthing its praises of Stalin.

Hoxha Breaks with Moscow

Stalin died in 1953. After Nikita Khrushchev had come to power and in 1956 denounced Stalin's brutal rule and ushered in "de-Staliniza-tion," Hoxha, ruling his people with the same ruthlessness, refused to follow the other satellite states. No statues of Stalin were pulled down in Albania. For his own safety he could not follow Khrushchev's revisionist dogma, and the latter's growing friendship with Tito raised his fears of the partition of his country. Khrushchev's advice that Albania forget about industrialization and concentrate on becoming a supplier of food, raw material, and Adriatic resorts for the rest of the Communist bloc, infuriated him. Albanian U.N. delegates now sided with Red China in her dispute with Moscow. Khrushchev withdrew his economic aid; Peking moved in quickly, sending Canadian wheat. Then in 1961 Khrushchev denounced Albanian pro-Stalinism and severed all relations. Consequently, Hoxha's press became violent in its denunciation of the Soviet Union and more laudatory than ever of Red China, whose ideology, it maintained, represented the only true communism.

Chinese help did stave off starvation; but despite the fact that 86 per cent of the farms had been collectivized, lack of machinery, shortage of parts, and reversion to age-old methods kept production low. Food prices rose in the state-owned MAPO stores where there were serious shortages. In cities and towns life remained backward; Tirana still had many mud huts. Not till 1963, when some twenty-five industrial projects were started, did Chinese help begin to boost the economy. But China, beset with her own grave problems, could not supply Albanians with many things they needed. Radios, even simple household tools, became unattainable luxuries. Albania remained not only the poorest of all European nations but the most tightly controlled police state. The rift with Russia continued in 1964; Soviet embassy buildings in Tirana were seized. After Khrushchev's downfall in October, Zeri i Poppulit criticized the new Russian leaders for continuing Khrushchev's policies.

Red China, lacking a voice in the United Nations and protesting in 1965 that she wanted no part in it, nevertheless found Albania a convenient mouthpiece and Hoxha more than willing to play China's tool. Thus in February, 1965, when Albania's delegate demanded a roll call vote to deprive the Soviet Union, France, and ten other nations, who were more than two years delinquent in their U.N.

payments, of their votes in the Assembly, it was an apparent attempt to embarrass the Soviet Union and the United States and to wreck the United Nations. It was overwhelmingly defeated, and the Assembly adjourned till September 1 with the problem to be settled by negotiation.

The Albanian Press Today

What press there is in Albania today follows the Communist pattern; but, unlike the papers of other east-bloc countries where there has been considerable thaw, Albanian newspapers remain as tightly frozen in complete regimentation as the Soviet press was in the Stalin era. It is extremely difficult to get accurate information about Albanian papers. The ministry of propaganda and popular culture in its 1950 report to UNESCO claimed twelve dailies, but careful checking of that year with recently arrived Albanian refugee editors in the United States revealed that there were only two dailies. The 1964 report lists only two dailies with a total circulation of 87,000, which would mean a distribution of only 4.9 copies per 100 persons, the lowest distribution ratio in all Europe.

The leading paper is *Zeri i Poppulit* (Peoples Voice), the mouthpiece of the Communist party, the *Pravda* of Albania claiming 57,000 circulation. The other daily is *Bashkimi* (Unity), the voice of the government, claiming 30,000. But these are the same claims that have been made for these two papers for years, and an audited circulation would probably reveal less than this. There are separate nondaily publications for different segments of the people. Thus *Puma* (Labor) is published Tuesdays and Fridays by the Communist Trade Union Federation, and *Zeri i Rinig* (Youth's Voice) is published Wednesdays and Saturdays. *Luftetar*, organ of the army, and *Hosteni* (Goad), published by the Communist Writer's Union, are also available. Weekly or biweekly local papers also appear in Elbasan, Koritza, Durrazo, Argyrocastro, and two smaller towns. As far as can be ascertained this is the extent of this completely regimented press. The sole source of foreign and domestic news is ATA (Albanian Telegraphic Agency) with head offices in Tirana and correspondents in principal towns. Formerly ATA obtained its foreign news from TASS, but now the China News Agency has taken its place with news transmitted by shortwave radio.

Because of newsprint shortage, the two dailies are limited to four tabloid pages; the smaller local papers may appear with only one sheet printed on both sides.

Postscript

Just as in the days of earlier repressions, an exile press carries on work in Boston, New York, Paris, Rome, and Belgrade. In the latter city 30,000 refugees wait for the day when they can strike a blow for the liberation of their country. Forbidden papers are smuggled into Albania. Reports seeping out indicate that many Albanians are not nearly as interested in the quarrel between the two brands of communism as they are in getting rid of all Communists. There are reports of guerrilla bands in the mountains being swelled by army deserters.

But until the ruthless dictator who controls the army and the police gives way, there may be little chance of deliverance. Exiled groups have dropped leaflets over their imprisoned homeland, but much more precision bombing comes from clandestine sheets inside. Descendants of the old *Shkypeters* still hope to bring freedom to their land.

The Press of a Loyal Satellite

The Newspapers of Bulgaria

Bulgarian journalism was very late in developing, for this nation did not win her independence from Turkey till 1908. Long after other Danubian peoples had been liberated, she remained an almost forgotten province under Turkish oppression.

Much earlier there had been a great Bulgarian nation. The original Bulgars, a nomadic people akin to the Tartars of Ghengis Khan, had overcome the peaceful, agricultural Slavs and formed a Slavo-Bulgar state which, by the ninth century, under Boris I ruled a realm embracing what is now Yugoslavia, Rumania, Bulgaria, Albania, and northern Greece. Boris made Christianity the official religion, but he wanted a church independent of both Rome and Constantinople. To that end he encouraged two priests, Cyril and Methodius, who created the Slavic or Cyrillic alphabet and began translating important church books into this language. Thus Bulgaria was the cradle of Slavonic written culture, and her language became the literary language of Russia. By the eleventh century the Byzantine Empire at Constantinople had beaten Bulgaria into submission. A century later the Bulgarians freed themselves and set up a Second Empire which lasted two hundred years and at its zenith achieved a renaissance a hundred years before the rest of Europe. But it was torn apart by warring, ambitious nobles; and when the Turks advanced, the people had no strength to stand against them. By 1396 all of Bulgaria had passed under the Turkish yoke.

Bulgaria's two periods of greatness came before the invention of printing. The literary works produced were handwritten and laboriously copied by scribes in monasteries. Long before printers might have come from Italy, France, or Germany, the Turks had subjugated the Bulgarians and permitted nothing as revolutionary as printing presses. Hence printing did not come to Bulgaria till in the nineteenth century, four hundred years after it had risen in western Europe.

Under Turkish Oppression

The Turks did establish much-needed order, but they introduced a tough feudal system which reduced all Christians to a miserable level of existence. Persons who refused to embrace Islamism were classed as *raya*, a subject population. Renegade Christians who became Moslems moved at once into the privileged class and rose to high positions in the administration and the army; but they were hated as traitors by the great mass of Bulgarians. For 478 years most Bulgarians suffered national degradation and persecution: many were taken into slavery, and girls and women were carried away to Turkish harems.

Yet the Bulgarian culture did not die; in remote monasteries old manuscripts were copied and recopied. Some monasteries even had secret schools which taught reading and writing with church manuscripts as texts. Many of Bulgaria's literary men escaped to other countries and produced the first Bulgarian printed books in exile. The first, a liturgy, appeared in Targoviste in Rumania in 1508. A Psalter was printed in Venice in 1560. Among the great awakeners was Paisi, a monk at Mount Athos (now in Greece), who in 1762 completed his *History of the Bulgarian and Slavonic People* to make his countrymen proud they were Bulgars, conscious of their glorious traditions and of the fact that they were a people in their own right. Nearly fifty manuscript copies of this book have been preserved, but it was not printed until 1845 at Budapest.

By now Turkish power had begun to decline under the crippling military expenditures necessary to hold together an empire stretching into three continents. When Austria, Poland, and Venice formed a Holy Alliance against Turkey, Bulgarians rose to fight with their allies. The Turks in retaliation unleashed a reign of terror against the *raya*, but Bulgarians took to the mountains where their guerrilla bands continued the fight. Russia undertook the protection of her Slavic brothers; and, while her efforts brought no improvement for Bulgarians, Turkey's two unsuccessful wars against Russia spurred revolts throughout the Balkans and persuaded the sultan to undertake a series of reforms. By 1845 there were fifty Bulgarian schools and five Bulgarian printing presses.

Steps Toward Revolution

Bulgarian papers had to make their beginnings in exile. Some thirty papers were put out by *émigrés* from 1844 to 1876. Georgi Sava Rakovsky's *Bulgarski Dnevnitsa* (Bulgarian Journal) from Novisad, in what is now Yugoslavia, fought for Bulgarian liberation and joint action by Serbs and Bulgarians. In Brăila, Rumania, C. Vladicoff through his *Bulgarska Ptchela* (Bulgarian Bee) assailed Turkish economic mismanagement. In Leipzig, D. J. A. Bogoroff launched *L'Aigle Bulgare* (Bulgarian Eagle) in 1876 which attempted to provide news from all Bulgarian provinces and neighboring Slavic countries to rouse people to their common cause. But it was Vasil Levski and his collaborator Lyuben Karavelov who started in 1869 *Svaboda* (Freedom) at Budapest, calling for revolution as the only salvation, and who organized a network of revolutionary committees in Bulgaria which put out their own underground papers.

In 1873, however, the Turks caught Levski and other revolutionaries and executed them. *Svaboda* was quashed. When uprisings took place all over Bulgaria, the Turks instituted a reign of terror in which 30,000 Bulgarians were massacred, some 10,000 imprisoned, 80 villages utterly destroyed, and 200 others sacked. These atrocities brought sharp reaction from Italy, France, England, and Russia. The latter declared war on Turkey, and Bulgarians fought with Russians to decisively defeat their enemy. The Congress of Berlin in 1878 set up Bulgaria as an independent Turkish principality. A constituent assembly met at Turnovo and enacted a democratic constitution. The first Bulgarian assembly elected Prince Alexander of Battenburg, nephew of the Russian tsar, as king.

Almost free of Turkish rule, a native Bulgarian press began to emerge. The first journals were literary reviews. Assembly discussions caused a split between Conservatives and Liberals; hence the first regular papers were party organs—*Vitocha* was the voice of the Conservatives and *Nezavisimost,* the voice of the Liberals. Soon there were others till by 1881 there were nineteen Bulgarian papers, all weeklies.

Alexander became a problem, for he considered himself less a Bulgarian than a representative of Russia and he was high-handed and dictatorial. Twice he suspended the constitution and ruled as a dictator. He was finally forced to abdicate and a new prince, Ferdinand of Saxe-Coburg-Gotha, was elected in 1887. Threatened by Russian-inspired revolts, the Bulgarians allowed the Liberal leader, Stefan Stambolov, to take power as dictator for a time.

These tumultuous events had their effect on the press. Under the period of Russian domination and the Stambolov dictatorship, strict censorship had been imposed. After Stambolov ended his rule by resignation in 1894, the press grew again till there were 192 Bulgarian journals, 61 in the capital Sofia and 131 in the provinces. Most of the latter were small weekly sheets of merely local interest, supported by parties or wealthy candidates running for office. Even the larger Sofia papers were mostly political, appearing two to three times a week, none with circulations of more than 3,000 to 4,000, hence dependent on party support. During the Stambolov regime, *Svaboda* was revived as a government organ and became Bulgaria's first daily. It was also the first paper in Bulgaria to take on the appearance of a European paper.

Freedom Brings Changes to Bulgaria and Its Press

The danger of war with Turkey caused King Ferdinand, a diplomat, to seek the friendship of Austria-Hungary. Backed by an understanding with Emperor Francis Joseph, Bulgaria proclaimed her complete independence of Turkey on October 5, 1908; this was confirmed by the other European powers the following April.

In peace and stability, Bulgaria began an economic revival. Farm production increased; industry, almost nonexistent under the Turks, began to expand. Towns grew as workers found jobs in factories; stores sprang up. Roads and railroads were built; trade and commerce progressed. Elementary schools were enlarged and supplemented by secondary schools. New political forces made themselves felt as farmers began to organize in opposition to the bourgeoisie classes in the cities, as did the growing class of industrial workers. This brought a great burst of party newspapers. Among the leaders were *Preporetz* (Banner) of the Democratic party, *Mir* (Peace) of the Populists, *Nov Vek* (New Century) of the National Liberals, *Robotnitcheski Vestnik* (Workers Paper) of the Social Democrats, and *Zemedelsko Zname* (Farmers Flag) of the Agrarians. Improved economic conditions soon enabled parties to bring out dailies like *Dene* (The Day) for the Progressives; *Kambana* (Clock), Socialist; *Balkanska Tribouna*, Populist; and *Narodne Glas* (Voice of the People), Liberal.

Most important was the emergence of nonpolitical information papers providing broad news coverage. The pioneer was M. S. Changhoff who, following the example of Girardan's *La Presse* in Paris, brought out *Vetcherna Poschta* (Evening Courier) in 1900 at a price within the reach of the masses. It proved so popular that it was followed in 1903 by *Dnevnik* (Journal). Very shortly both had circulations of 15,000, unheard of in Bulgaria prior to that time. Their success forced political papers to lower their prices, to improve their news coverage, and to reach out for new readers with popular features and cultural articles. The development of commerce and industry brought more advertising; and papers became aggressive in circulation promotion, adopting display heads to sell their news and placing posters in public places that announced hours ahead of time the sensational developments to be presented. By 1911 Bulgaria counted 239 newspapers, 116 in Sofia and 123 in the provinces, most of them weeklies. In Sofia, Plovdiv, and Varna good dailies were developing, the better ones reaching toward 30,000 circulation.

And Then Came Wars

In 1912 Bulgaria was involved in the First Balkan War, winning much of Macedonia; but in the Second Balkan War, she was badly defeated by Serbia and Rumania and lost all she had gained and more. When World War I broke in 1914, Ferdinand was certain that Germany was invincible and that only through its aid could Macedonia be regained. Despite the opposition of most of the people he brought Bulgaria into the war against Serbia, England, France, and Italy. Bulgarian armies reconquered Macedonia and Dobruja; but when the war was pressed against Rumania and Bucharest was taken, the people and the opposition press raised a clamor against conquering foreign territories. National objectives had been obtained and the opposition urged retirement from the war. There were army mutinies. Pillaging of the land by Germans, food shortages, and exhaustion had by late 1917 brought much of the country into revolt against the government. Then, as Germans were driven back, Bulgarians were left to stand alone; and French and British troops quickly occupied the country. The peace settlement was disastrous. Bulgaria was disarmed, assessed staggering reparations, shorn of a third of her territory and her people. Six years of war had left the country completely impoverished.

The war years had also been hard on the press. Most provincial papers had disappeared. Those in Sofia, which survived, had to reduce their size and increase their prices. Nevertheless, the great interest in war news had swelled the circulation of remaining dailies to from 30,000 to 50,000. All were subject to military censorship, but opposition papers had been able to operate with considerable freedom till the Germans took over the country. Then no news of German defeats, nor anything suggesting Bulgaria's withdrawal from the war could be printed.

Conditions were appalling at the end of the war. Starvation stalked the cities, prices skyrocketed, and there were serious strikes. Alexander Stamboliski, strongest opponent of the war policy, became premier and, allying himself with the Communists, imposed virtual dictatorship till 1923 when he was overthrown in an army coup. He was executed and his ministers imprisoned. Then came attempts by Yugoslav Communists, encouraged by Russia, to bring about revolution. These were put down with great severity. One short-lived government followed the other. However, in the late twenties and early thirties conditions improved materially and some calm returned.

One by one prewar papers had tried to reappear, but the people were too poor to buy them and there was no advertising. Thus, they came and went. The one exception was the Communist press, subsidized from abroad. After 1935 not only Conservative but Democratic, Liberal, and Radical papers began to publish with more freedom. Encouraging was the revival of the old independent information papers. As conditions improved, the press made considerable progress and, in newsworthiness, improved appearance, and appeal, began to resemble papers of the rest of Europe.

Totaliarianism, War, and Communist Take-over

The world depression staggered Bulgaria, and the trend in other Balkan countries was reflected when in 1934 militarists upset the government and instituted a dictatorship under King Boris III. All former political parties and their newspapers were suppressed. At the onset of World War II in 1939, the Boris dictatorship saw the possibility of restoring prewar frontiers with German help. Germans occupied the country and for three years the Bulgarian press was under stringent Nazi control. Underground papers emerged, and the Communists won considerable prestige through the resistance of their Partisan bands. Bulgaria had declared war on Britain and the United States, and Bulgarian troops helped Germans occupy Greek and Yugoslav territories. However, when the victorious Russian armies advanced into the Balkans in 1944, Bulgaria renounced her pact with the Axis and declared war on Germany, after which the Soviets granted an armistice and occupied the country.

The Communists lost no time in taking control of the government. An uprising of Communists, left-wing Agrarians, and Social Democrats on September 9, 1944, seized power and installed Kimon Georgiev as premier of a Fatherland Front government, with a cabinet acceptable to the Soviet Union. Large-scale purges of alleged collaborators with the Germans were organized; thousands were executed or imprisoned, many for merely being anti-Communist. The Fatherland Front announced an election, but it submitted only a single list of candidates. The United States and Britain protested and secured a postponement. But now Georgi Dimitrov, formerly a power in the Bulgarian Communist party, and Vasil Kolarov, who had been party secretary, returned from Moscow to organize the take-over. In the November, 1945, election the Fatherland Front won a decisive victory and the following March under the personal intervention of Vishinsky, Soviet foreign minister, Georgiev was installed as premier with an all-Communist cabinet. There remained only the liquidation of resistance elements. Nikola Petkov, secretary, and other leading members of the old Agrarian party, in dramatized trials, were convicted and hanged. In December, 1946, the assembly adopted a constitution closely modeled on the Soviet pattern, and the Peoples Republic of Bulgaria was born. But the U.S.S.R. kept a careful eye on its new satellite. Georgi Dimitrov had now moved into the premiership and Kolarov was president, but when Dimitrov concluded an economic agreement with Tito, just at the time Stalin was breaking with him, Dimitrov was summoned to Moscow where he disappeared. It was reported in 1949 that he had died in a sanitarium. He was succeeded by Vulko Chervenkov, and the Soviet control of Bulgaria was complete.

The Press Is Communized

Step by step the Communists closed down the papers of all other parties; even the independent information papers were suppressed. Newspaper plants became the property of the state, and all newspapers were owned by the Communist party and its Peoples Republic. Now *Rabotnichesko Delo* (Workers Cause) became the voice of the party Central Committee, the *Pravda* of Bulgaria, while *Otechestven Front* (Fatherland Front) became the organ of the government, the *Izvestia* of the country. After 1946 there were no free papers in Bulgaria; instead the press was made the instrument for manipulating news and propagandizing the people.

With complete control and regimented information, the Communists marshaled the people into economic progress with considerable aid from the Soviet Union. Where before the war there had been little industry, now in many cities factory stacks were silhouetted against ancient mosques. Twenty million persons moved from farms to cities and became accustomed to electric lights, radios, and even television. A 10 per cent increase in industrial production in 1963 followed a series of goal achievements. But producing enough food for the growing population was a problem. Bulgaria had moved faster than any other eastern state in collectivizing its farmers, yet 1962 government figures showed that agricultural production was little ahead of 1960. To provide greater incentive to farmers, the government raised minimum wages and increased old-age pension benefits; it relieved farmers of compulsory deliveries on certain crops and introduced a new system of contractual purchases at higher prices. But since better prices for farmers meant higher prices for consumers, the new system caused great discontent in the cities.

The Communists did, however, revolutionize education, not only to provide proper indoctrination of the young but also to increase its availability. Before the war few young Bulgars had learned to read and write. Now, except in the more remote areas, almost every child can go to school; and in the last decade the number of primary and secondary school students has risen 30 per cent and the number of college students doubled. This has meant higher literacy and should have brought a commensurate increase in newspaper circulations, but the circulation figures of the five leading dailies over the past decade have grown only 12 per cent. After twenty years of indoctrination many Bulgarians are apparently still unconvinced of communism's desirability, and they hear too many foreign broadcasts to swallow all the propaganda in their papers. Even die-hard, old-line Bulgarian Communists admit that 60 per cent of the people are opposed to their regime. And, as is true in other countries where the press is completely controlled by government, the people have grown apathetic to their newspapers.

Loyal Bulgarian Press Follows Russian Line

The successive Bulgarian governments have run one of the most tightly controlled Communist systems in the eastern bloc. No criticism of the government or its policies is permitted. When in 1956 a number of Communist intellectuals called for greater press freedom and a revision of party policies in industry and agriculture, punitive measures were taken against them with the explanation that under no circumstances could hostile criticism be tolerated because it was directed against the state. Bulgaria has been most loyal to the U.S.S.R. While Stalin lived, she followed his dictates slavishly. After he broke with Tito her press mounted a violent hate campaign against Yugoslavia. But after Stalin died and Khrushchev made peace with Tito, the press switched to praise of this "friendly neighbor." Khrushchev then launched his de-Stalinization campaign, and the Bulgarian party followed right along, even, to ousting Premier Chervenkov and other officials for "devotion to the cult of personality." When Khrushchev put down the Polish and Hungarian revolts with Russian tanks, the press gave the story little space and told only the Soviet version. As Khrushchev began trying to ameliorate conditions for his people, the Bulgarian government diminished its own police terror and tried to improve the lot of the peasants. It supported Russia's foreign policy completely: after Khrushchev began making friendly overtures to the United States, the Bulgarian press relaxed its diatribes, even though for two decades it had, next to Albania, been the most anti-American of all satellites.

Among Bulgarian Communists there soon rose a feeling that Bulgaria had too long been exploited by the Soviet Union. So dangerous did this anti-party group become that in 1962 a number of high officials on the Central Committee were dismissed; Todor Zhivkov, first secretary of the party and Khrushchev's hand-picked candidate, was made premier. But many engineers, technicians, plant managers, doctors, lawyers, and intellectuals on whom the success or failure of the Communist regime depended were eager to see their country more independent of the Soviet Union, for the bulk of Bulgaria's trade was still with Russia and they wanted more friendly relations with the West. Although there was a latent gratitude to Russia for their liberation from the Turks, many disliked being the tail wagged by the Russian dog.

Bulgarian trade expanded in 1964 as agreements were made with other countries and West Germany and Italy became her chief customers. The arrest of a Bulgarian for "spying" for the U.S. Central Intelligence Agency brought anti-U.S. propaganda in the press for a time. When Khrushchev was ousted in October, 1964, Zhivkov, to avoid trouble with the new Kremlin rulers, refrained from speaking up for his erstwhile protector and busied himself with promising greater democratization and a streamlining of the Bulgarian economy. In April, 1965, the government put down an attempted revolt against Zhivkov. At first it was ascribed to a pro-Peking plot, but reports out of Vienna indicated that it was a pro-Tito attempt at making Bulgaria another neutral like Yugoslavia. Significant was the appearance on Sofia walls of inscriptions reading "Za Levski," a reference to the journalist and nationalist leader who was hanged by the Turks in 1873.

The Press Today

This beautiful country of majestic mountains, tablelands, and deep valleys is a bit larger than Ohio but has only four-fifths its population. Its friendly people do not have much enthusiasm for their government, and it must be remembered that of 8,000,000 people only 506,000 belong to the Communist party. As one journalist put it in American slang, "Only the squares belong to the party." The majority of people have no tendency to revolt and feel rather a massive indifference—a strong factor in the attitude of the people toward their press. Yet they take a certain pride in having built a new Bulgaria from scratch though many think they could have done better under a different system.

Bulgaria in 1964 reported eleven dailies, seven serving as central or national dailies. All were published in Sofia the capital, a modern city of 725,000 people. There are also four district dailies in Burgas, Plovdiv, Russe, and Varna, published by provincial party committees. In addition there are eight weekly and fifteen biweekly district papers and seven published for minority groups—Turks, Greeks, Armenians, gypsies, and Jews. Magazines are popular and there are about three hundred. Five radio stations and one television station broadcast to the Bulgarian people, all under the control of the government.

The leading central daily is *Rabotnichesko Delo* (Workers Cause), organ of the party, a descendant of the first workers' paper started in 1897. A morning daily, it is the voice for the party faithful and claims a circulation of 558,000, little more than the membership of the party. Second is *Otechestven Front* (Fatherland Front), the mouthpiece of the government, which began as an underground paper in 1942. It appears every morning except Monday and has been claiming 300,000 circulation for years. Next is *Zemedelsko Zname* (Agricultural Banner), the only prewar paper dating back to 1902. Once the Communists had liquidated Agrarian party leaders they took over this paper as the chief organ for regimenting peasants into collective farms. It appears mornings except Monday and claims 150,000 circulation. Then there is *Narodna Mladezh* (Peoples Youth), which claims to reach 278,000 persons. Important also are *Trud* (Labor), organ of the trade unions claiming 114,000 circulation, and *Narodna Armia* published by the defense ministry. Finally there is *Vecherni Novini*, the only evening paper in Sofia and the only paper carrying as much as a half-page of advertisements; it is supposed to be more popular and newsier but claims a circulation of only 150,000.

This system of eleven dailies and supporting nondailies is designed to carry the Communist truth to every segment of the Bulgarian people. How well it does cover the country is open to question, for even if one takes at face value the total daily claimed circulation of 1,558,000, this represents only ten copies for every 100 persons. Since the same round-figured circulations have been claimed year after year, they are probably subject to discount. In view of the indifference of the people, it is probable that the actual distribution is much less. This press is the manipulated instrument of one of the most reactionary regimes in eastern Europe. All dailies as a rule have four pages but at the time of important events or pronouncements may carry six to eight. Aside from the fact that their mastheads are printed in red, they look much like Soviet papers.

Bulgarski Telegrafischeka Agentzie (BTA), government-owned, is the sole source for both foreign and domestic news. Most of its foreign news is drawn from TASS although it has exchange agreements with

Reuters and AFP, from which it selects what may fit best into its propaganda pattern.

There are about 2,000 journalists, all trusted Communists. A department of Journalism at Sofia University offers a four-and-one-half-year course, during the last twenty-five weeks of which students do practical internship on Sofia newspapers. The Bulgarian Journalists Union also holds seminars during the year for working journalists in various sections of the country.

The Press of Czechoslovakia

Czechoslovakia did not come into existence till 1918, yet, in the twenty years before she was dismembered by Hitler, she made herself one of the most progressive of the democracies and was the one eastern European country which enjoyed continuous press freedom after World War I. Yet after the Communist coup in February, 1948, she became the toughest of the satellite states, her press the instrument of the Communist party.

This country's people come from Slavic tribes who migrated from the Vistula watershed southwestward into the fair lands of central Europe. Most powerful were the Cechova (Czechs) who settled Bohemia. Others who located in the Morava River valley became known as Moravians, the first to be Christianized. Still other clans settled eastward and were called Slovaks. They fought Avars, Magyars, Huns, and other Germanic peoples till in the tenth century, under the leadership of the Czechs, the tribes were unified and under their Premyslide princes ruled a large domain. Days of glory came when their King Charles I became head of the Holy Roman Empire and Prague, its capital. Known as "the Father of his country," Charles consolidated administration, suppressed brigandage, founded the University of Prague, and made Bohemia a power in Europe. His reign was also a period of cultural development. This was carried forward by King Poděbrad who ascended the throne in 1458 and who helped his people attain not only prosperity but intellectual progress as well.

First Printing Followed by Newssheets

Toward the end of Poděbrad's reign in 1468 the first printing press was set up at Pilsen, and a second at Prague in 1486. A number of Czechs had learned the printing trade in nearby Germany; even Gutenberg claimed to be of Bohemian origin. Other German printers came and obtained royal privileges to set up presses. The name of the first Pilsen printer is unknown, but the one first mentioned was Mikula Bakalar (Nicholas the Bachelor), a graduate of Cracow University who printed from 1498 to 1510.

The next 110 years saw a great proliferation of presses in the country. These master printers were men of learning and prestige who contributed much to the cultural development of the people. Most of their products were religious works, classics, and a few histories. The rise of the Hussite Protestant movement, in opposition to the Catholics, led to the development of rival presses of the two faiths. The first newssheets, however, came as a result of the Turkish conquest of Hungary in 1526 which was of tremendous news interest to the people, for it brought the Turk almost to their doors. In the meantime, Martin Luther had started his Reformation in Germany, and the Lutheran doctrines won many converts among the Czechs. First handwritten, then printed sheets carried the battle for men's souls on behalf of both Protestants and Catholics.

Censorship and Germanization under Hapsburgs

After Charles V had been crowned Holy Roman Emperor, things changed for the Czechs, Moravians, and Slovaks. Charles made his brother Ferdinand lieutenant of the Empire to govern all Austrian possessions. In 1526 Austria, the Slavic states, and what was left of Hungary were joined in what was to be the beginning of the Austro–Hungarian Empire under the almost four hundred-year rule of the Hapsburgs. Ferdinand, an ardent Catholic, began a systematic repression of Protestant sects and set up censorship of the press which seriously affected the printing of Protestant books. There were no newspapers, but every newssheet had to have the approval of the censor before it could be published. What galled the Slavic peoples most was the suppression of their language and the attempt to completely Germanize them. Since most of the people were Protestant, religious antagonism was added to racial feeling. This policy persisted throughout the reigns of Maximilian II and Leopold II till in 1609 the nobles and the Diet threatened civil war and forced Leopold to grant full religious liberty to Protestants. When he sent troops to take Bohemia, he was driven out and forced to abdicate.

Mathias and Ferdinand II, his successors, were equally despotic, and again the Protestant nobles went to war in what was to be the prelude to the Thirty Years' War. This time they declared their independence, but after their decisive defeat in the Battle of White Mountain in 1620, independent Bohemia ceased to exist. For the next three hundred years the kingdom was reduced to three provinces in the Hapsburg monarchy—Bohemia, Moravia, and Silesia. Meanwhile Protestant rulers in North Europe had joined the crusade against Austrian aggression and Catholicism. Bohemia became one of the chief battle grounds of the Thirty Years' War and her population was reduced from 3,000,000 to 900,000. The estates and wealth of the Protestant nobility and the bourgeoise were confiscated and handed over to the Catholics. The Jesuits forcibly proceeded to reconvert the population to Catholicism and did everything possible to destroy the Czech language and literature.

But Czech patriots kept up their fight. After Joseph II came to the Austrian throne in 1780 there rose a Czech renaissance, for though this monarch did his best to Germanize his new subjects, he also abolished censorship so that Czech authors found it possible to publish books extolling their language and literature and urging people not to forget their heritage. Francis I, who was crowned in 1792, lived in fear of the French Revolution and brought complete reaction. Once the Napoleonic wars were over, Metternich, as Austrian foreign minister, in order to prop up the old order, established an absolute police state. Yet Czech nationalism managed to grow. The publication of books by Matice Ceska after 1831 came to be considered a national enterprise; the History of the Czech Nation by Fratisek Palacky, a rising young historian, became a bible awakening the people. Prominent Czechs and the Diet asked the monarchy to restore the ancient rights of the kingdom of Bohemia, but the Emperor and Metternich were adamantly against such a move. While Austria had had newspapers since 1620, no Czech paper had as yet been permitted. True, there were German language papers, but they were for the German minority. There was no paper around which the Czech people could rally.

The Advent of the First Newspaper

The Paris Revolution of 1848 brought revolts in Vienna, Venice, Pesht, and Prague. Early in 1948 Karel Havliček, one of the leaders of the national movement, had ventured to start the first Czech newspaper, *Narodni Noviny*, in which he roused his countrymen to a desire for national unity and, with Palacky's help, outlined a political program for them. He is honored as the founder of Czech journalism. The Prague revolt broke out on June 12 when the Slav Congress was meeting, but within three days Prince Windischgratz, Austrian military commander, had bombarded Prague into surrender. The Slav Congress was dissolved, the plans for a Diet abandoned. The only gain from the revolt was the freeing of the serfs; and as these new property owners developed into a middle class, profiting from free education, they not only paved the way for a future Czecho-Slovak state but greatly expanded the base for newspaper readership.

With the accession of Emperor Francis Joseph, absolutism returned. *Narodni Noviny* was suppressed in 1850, and when Havliček in 1850 became editor of *Slovan*, he was imprisoned for inflaming Czech nationalism. The next six decades were years of political frustration but also of great material gains, for Bohemia became the center of Austrian industry and, with her prosperous agriculture, the richest possession of the Hapsburgs. The Czechs refused to be terrorized by the regime and until 1879 continued their passive resistance by refusing to send representatives to either the parliament in Vienna or their own Diet in Prague. However, the rise of a new Czech bourgeoise, growing out of the industrial revolution, developed the Young Czech party, which after the 1873 elections entered the Diet and later the Vienna parliament. At first they "won only crumbs" but in time acquired a majority in their Diet and put through legislation giving the Czech language official equality with German and making the University of Prague both a Czech and a German university.

The last twenty years of the century brought considerable liberalization till by 1905 Bohemia had fifty daily papers. The first had been *Narodni Listy* (National Journal), founded in 1860, which by 1905 was the best and most widely circulated paper among the Czechs, a strong supporter of the Young Czech party; another leader was *Revnost*, organ of the Social Democrats.

Among the professors called to teach at the University of Prague was Thomas Mazaryk, a social philosopher who came to be the intellectual and spiritual leader of the Czechs. In 1886 he aided Jan Herben in establishing the daily, *Cas*, a determined voice of the new liberal movement. There were of course many German papers, such as *Bohemia* and *Prager Tagblatt*, which supported existing relations with Austria. Thus from the very beginning of this modern period the press was strongly political. Growing literacy saw its reflection in increased space in newspapers for literary and cultural materials. Slovaks in other parts of the empire, in their submerged state, were attracted to the dynamic development among the Czechs and sent their young people to the University of Prague.

World War I and the Press

Despite their differences with the Vienna government, few Czechs or Slovaks thought of setting up a state separate from Austria-Hungary. They had won considerable independence and equality, and the Czechs in particular had profited from industrialization and the wider market provided under the empire. Palacky had written of the empire, "If it did not exist we would have to invent it." Even Mazaryk had voiced his fear that if the empire were broken up, Czechs would be integrated into Germany; and Eduard Beneš, his disciple, in his doctoral dissertation had said he did not believe in the dismemberment of the empire.

But as the European conflagration drew nearer, the fear of Germany grew. When World War I erupted in 1914, Czechs and Slovaks felt that they were forced into it against their will since Austria was an ally of Germany, and that the war was being fought only for pan-Germanism. Czech soldiers refused to fight against their kinsmen, the Serbs and Russians. Austria broke up those regiments which did not desert, and at home she imprisoned and executed a number of Czech leaders. The principal Czech papers were suppressed. Those permitted to continue were dragooned into supporting the government. When they were forced to urge their people to support war loans, one paper printed as a top ribbon, "Austrians, Subscribe to the War Loans," which Czechs understood to mean they did not need to do so. When papers appeared with blank spaces left by the censors, newsboys, if the police were not around, cried, "That which is white is true; the black is a lie." An underground Czech Mafia-type group was organized to carry on the fight and to keep the people informed through clandestine papers.

By 1917 a national Czechoslovak army was fighting on three fronts with the Allies. Mazaryk and Beneš, in Paris, London, Moscow, and Washington, won the support of allies, who included in their war aims the liberation of Czechoslovakia. On October 28 national independence was proclaimed and two days later Slovakia pronounced itself in favor of unity with the Czechs. The Paris and Prague national councils met in Geneva October 28–31 and set up a provisional government with Mazaryk as president, Dr. Karel Kramer, Slovak leader, as vice-president, and Beneš as foreign minister, which was quickly recognized by the Allies. The 1919 peace conference gave the new nation the Czech regions of Austria, the Slovak district of Hungary, and sub-Carpathian Ruthenia. This created a state in which 34 per cent of the population was non-Czecho-Slovak, including 3,500,000 Germans living on the outer rim of Bohemia, an element that was to bring grave crises after 1933.

The new nation faced many problems. Lying at the crossroads of European trade routes, it had often been coveted by European rulers. Now it was just as vulnerable with Germany and Poland to the north, the Soviet Union, Austria, and Hungary to the south. Here was a little landlocked country, a bit smaller than Illinois, with 13,000,000 people. Its new constitution provided for a democratic government with a bicameral parliament, elected by universal suffrage; but, fearing dissident elements might tear it apart, the government was from the first highly centralized. The Germans refused to be reconciled and would not participate in the government. Autonomy for Ruthenia, a backward section, was postponed time and time again. Four years of war and the disintegration of Austria-Hungary spelled economic collapse and the country came near to starvation till the United States brought relief. Hard times indicated a swing toward socialist solutions. There came danger, too, from the Communist Béla Kun regime in Hungary; and the government signed a mutual assistance pact with France, allying itself with Rumania and Yugoslavia in the Little Entente designed to curb German, Austrian, and Hungarian revisionism.

Internally it proceeded with needed reforms, including the breakup of patrician estates, tax reforms, extension of insurance, and an amicable separation of church and state. Commercial treaties with neighboring countries increased trade. Manufacturing was encouraged, and intensive farming by new small landowners improved the food supply. By 1925 industrial production was almost back to normal, and the Czech food surplus was the largest on the Continent.

The Press Expands

The new constitution guaranteed "full freedom of the press." Old prewar papers revived and new ones appeared. The Czechs proved a nation of avid readers, interested in world affairs and domestic politics, eager to learn the mechanics of democracy, and proud of their successes. It was a serious press, avoiding sensationalism and giving readers foreign and domestic news, editorials, backgrounding articles, and much cultural material. Journalists came to enjoy a special status, highly respected and well-paid. Prague had nine dailies, and Brno, the second largest city and capital of Moravia, had five. There were dailies in all larger cities and weeklies in many small towns. A news agency, *Ceteka*, had been founded in 1918 to supply both foreign and domestic news to papers all over the country.

Because independence had brought a reorientation of politics and conflicting ideas as to the path the nation should take, new parties developed and the press again became largely political. Mazaryk and Beneš were associated with the Czech National Socialists, who published seven papers led by *Cesko Slovo*. The National Democrats, successors to the Young Czechs, were intensely nationalistic, opposed any rapprochement with Germany, and attacked Beneš' foreign policy as too weak. They had seven papers, led by *Narodny List*. The Agrarian party also had several dailies of which *Venkov* was outstanding. Among the German Socialist papers, *Deutsche Zeitung Bohemia* was the leader. The Peoples Catholic party, strongest in Slovakia, had several papers. The Sudeten German party had nine, led by *Rundschau* and *Die Zeit*. There were in addition seven minor parties, each with its press supporters. Destined to be disturbing was the split in the Socialist party that created the Czech Communist party. It soon had eight papers led by *Rude Pravo* at Prague and *Pravda* at Brno. In the larger cities there were also nonpolitical independent papers such as *Lidove Noviny*, which Czechs called their New York *Times* because of its broad news coverage. Papers were running twelve to twenty pages, and some had considerable circulations. The evening edition of *Cesko Slovo* claimed 208,000, and *Lidevy Denik*, an Agrarian paper, was close behind with 200,000.

For the first five years the press operated with great freedom; but both internal and external dangers brought in 1923 the "Law for Protection of the Republic," which prohibited insults to the president, agitation against the republican form of government, incitement of hatred against individual groups, and the founding of secret organizations undermining the constitutional structure of the state. This law in time came to be used to censor and even confiscate papers in the German and Slovak areas as well as to control the Communist organs.

World Depression Brings Crisis

The world depression, coming to a climax in Czechoslovakia in 1931, brought disaster. The Sudeten Germans, highly industrialized, were hard hit and clamored that Prague was not doing enough to alleviate unemployment. Konrad Henlein, Sudeten leader, demanded local autonomy. Hitler came to power in Germany in 1933, and many Sudeten extremists formed Nazi-type organizations. In the 1935 elections Henlein's party won forty-four seats in the parliament, only one seat less than the formerly dominant Agrarian party.

President Mazaryk retired in 1935 at the age of eighty-six and was succeeded by Beneš; Dr. Milan Hodza, Slovak, became premier. Hitler demanded justice for oppressed Germans in Czechoslovakia. Despite Hodza's efforts to make concessions, the Sudeten papers constantly grew more violent. To protect itself, the government gave the president the right to suppress papers, to suspend opposition parties, and to proscribe parties hostile to the state. Henlein's *Die Zeit* was censored as were others; but as the Nazi press attacks in Germany mounted in 1937, even pro-government papers were restained and not allowed to print reports which might provoke foreign press attacks. Tension mounted till Hitler suddenly took Austria in March, 1938, which really left Czechoslovakia under German guns. The Czechs mobilized but England and France, concerned about the possibility of a general war, intervened; after their Munich meeting with Hitler, the two countries notified Czechoslovakia that, if she rejected their plan, they would not support her and would hold her responsible for the ensuing war and her own destruction.

Thus, the Czechs were forced to accept their dismemberment. They lost 28,680 squares miles to Germany, 11,380 to Hungary, 1,086 to Poland and 5,000,000 of their people. Beneš resigned, went into exile, and was succeeded by Elim Hacha, a respected judge and nonparty man. On March 15 Hacha was called to Berlin and forced to sign a document creating the protectorate of Bohemia and Moravia. German troops had already started their occupation. Free Czechoslovakia was no more.

Nazis Take over Nation and Press

Hacha continued to hold office, and a fiction of a separate government was maintained; but control swiftly passed into Nazi hands. On the very first day of the occupation the Jewish publishers of *Prager Tagblatt* were ousted. *Narodni Osvobezeni*, one of the most respected Czech papers, dared to defend Beneš and was summarily suppressed. Many others were closed; still more voluntarily suspended rather than be obliged to damn what they had formerly praised. More than 1,000 periodicals ceased publication in the first eighteen months of the occupation. *Ceteka* was made an adjunct of *Deutsches Nachrichten Buro*, a mere translating service for DNB dispatches. Nearly 1,000 new Nazi sheets and magazines appeared, run by German officers and staffs. Censors sat in the offices of what few Czech papers were permitted to remain in business, and all papers read as if they had been put out by Nazis. The only outside papers sanctioned were *Volkischer Beobachter* and *Angriff*. Czechs were practically shut off from the rest of the world and read only what the Germans wanted them to know. Nazis supervised content, headlines, and placement of stories and dictated suggested phrasings. It was a completely regimented press.

But the spark of freedom still flickered. Underground papers emerged to provide forbidden news from the BBC (British Broadcasting Company) and to encourage the people to hope for liberation. Best loved of the newspapers was *V-Boy* (To Arms), put out by Joseph Skalda who in the first week of occupation was distributing his little mimeographed sheet through collaborators to many towns and villages.

It provided encouragement, supplied news from Allied fronts, warned of Nazi plans for new restrictions, urged resistance and sabotage. In 1941 Skalda and fifteen others were caught and executed, but *V-Boy* continued to appear. It was never silenced during the occupation. Many other pre-occupation papers had gone underground after they were suppressed. Among the more important were *Narodni Osvobezeni, Ceska Slovenska Republica,* and *Pravda.*

Accommodation with Russia

Beneš, meanwhile, had organized a Czech government in exile in London; and Czech journalists who had fled there put out a daily, two weeklies, two monthlies, and a literary quarterly for their exiles and troops, and also to keep the image of Czechoslovakia alive in the minds of Allied peoples.

At home the hand of the Gestapo grew heavier. In 1942 Reinhard Heydrich, deputy protector, was assassinated and brutal reprisals followed. One of the worst was the total destruction of the village of Lidice and the massacre of all its men and boys. Nazi efforts were directed particularly against Czech cultural life. Universities were barred to Czechs; learned societies were dissolved; great numbers of Czech schools were closed; clergymen were arrested; church properties were confiscated; and some 70,000 intellectuals were sent to concentration camps. When underground forces initiated widespread sabotage, some 250,000 persons died at the hands of the Gestapo. But by the spring of 1945 Czech underground forces were in full revolt.

Russian armies, thundering in from the east, drove to Prague on May 9, 1945, and were greeted as deliverers by the Czechs. Beneš had visited Moscow in March and had agreed to form a liberation government, including Slovaks and Communists. It must be remembered that when Czechoslovakia's other allies deserted her in 1938, the Russians alone tried to prevent her dismemberment; and there was a natural sympathy between the two Slav peoples. The Russians, furthermore, had signed a twenty-year mutual-aid pact with them. Now Beneš and Jan Mazaryk, son of the founder of the republic, believed they could build their country as a bridge between East and West. Ruthenia was ceded to Russia without argument. The Beneš government proceeded to break up the last of the great estates, nationalized banks and industries. A purge was instituted against all pro-Nazi collaborators, and a beginning was made in the expulsion of the 3,000,000 Sudeten Germans and 650,000 Magyars to the occupied zones of Germany. In the 1946 election the Communists polled 38 per cent of the vote. Beneš was elected president; Klement Gottwald, the Communist leader, premier.

Jan Mazaryk became foreign minister. Though Communists were appointed to only eight of twenty-three cabinet posts, control of the important ministry of the interior, and consequently control of the police force, went to a Communist.

The Press Is Sovietized

At first there was no censorship. All Nazi papers had been suppressed, but soon permission to publish newspapers was given only to authorized parties forming the National Front and official corporations such as trade unions, rural cooperatives, the army, the National Youth organization, certain ministries, and learned societies. Private persons were denied this right. Beneš justified this by saying: "Journalism is a public service. Unbridled freedom to publish newspapers should not be reestablished. We all know what the yellow press meant before the war. The public interest must come first."

What Beneš apparently forgot was that newspapers in private hands, before the war, had not put public interest in the background; that the great majority were sober, serious papers serving the nation well; that there had been only a handful of sensational papers—the very ones which had collaborated with the Germans and had been suppressed after the war.

For a time newspapers operated by non-Communist Czechs were free to print the news and comment upon it, even to take a line in opposition to the government; but gradually controls tightened, starting with a purge of "unreliable journalists." Then a single Union of Journalists was established to which all journalists had to belong if they were to exercise their profession, which meant that no man could work on a paper without the approval of the Communist party. What little freedom was left was further restricted by party control of the means of publication and supplies of newsprint. The ministries of interior and information now had the press in absolute control.

The Red Coup of 1948

During this period Stalin, through Communist parties in eastern European countries, had set up a ring of friendly states on his borders to balance his economic system by taking Russian exports and supplying his import raw-material needs. But Czechoslovakia's economy had been greatly weakened since her close ties with the West had been curtailed. When the Czechs decided to accept Marshall aid for their economic revival, Gottwald was summoned to Moscow and reprimanded. Therefore his country was not represented in the Marshall program but signed a five-year trade agreement with Russia instead.

Many Czechs who had joined the Communist party, hoping its solutions might cure their problems, became disillusioned, and non-Communist parties began to coalesce in defiance of the Communists. Gottwald decided to move in. Red papers launched a violent attack on "enemies of the people." Communist-inspired strikes in nationalized factories made it appear that the government could no longer maintain order; a faked plot to assassinate Beneš was "discovered" to heighten the crisis. Nosek, minister of the interior, dismissed eight non-Communist police chiefs and replaced them with Communists. Twelve non-Communist ministers resigned, demanding that the police chiefs be reinstated, for they saw Nosek's move as a step toward a complete police state. Nosek refused and the Czech Communist party called for the support of all workers and the organization of action committees to seize press and radio. On February 21, the Communist militia occupied Prague and Bratislava. The Red press announced that Soviet troops in Austria and East Germany were within easy call. Student and other civilian protest marches were repressed. By February 25 the coup was complete: Gottwald and Vaclav Nosek had taken over the government for the Communists.

Now began a wholesale purge of journalists, army officers, university professors, former non-Communist government employees, and any others who might be a threat to the new order. Jan Mazaryk remained the one non-Communist in the cabinet, but on March 10 he was reported to have "committed suicide" by throwing himself from a foreign ministry window. It has now been established that he was killed and thrown out the window by Soviet agents.

The Press Is Reorganized

The Communist masters soon muzzled all opposition papers. Some had their newsprint supplies cut off; others found production impossible because printers were unwilling to work for them. On Communist orders the printers of *Svobodne Noviny*, organ of the federation of cultural organizations, refused to work so long as Ferdinand Peroutka remained editor. He was one of the most eminent figures in Czech journalism, had been a victim of the Nazis, but since liberation had not hesitated to oppose Russian interference with his country's internal affairs. He was arrested and condemned to hard labor but managed to escape abroad. Half of the editors of Prague dailies were forced to resign; some fifty were expelled from the journalists union. Whereas Czechoslovakia had had forty-four dailies at the beginning of 1948, there were now only twenty-two left; and the number of political weeklies had been cut by three-fourths.

Before long the Czech press had been completely remolded on the Soviet pattern. A new constitution banned precensorship; but none was needed, for all editors were chosen by the party and received daily instructions as to what might be published and what line to take on every question. The duty of the press was outlined as "to assist in the constructive efforts and the struggle for peace of the Czechoslovak people and to contribute to their education toward Socialism." Control of radio and *Ceteka* was established. The latter was given monopoly of news distribution, and as it was served by TASS it brought a tremendous flow of copy from Moscow. On internal news only items from official sources could be published. The Czechs had now lost all their liberties, and the press was completely Stalinized, following Moscow's orders to the letter.

The new regime moved more quickly and drastically to consolidate its authority than that in any other east-bloc country. New laws made it a crime to criticize the government. Special labor camps were set up to reeducate those who had not completely accepted communism. A five-year plan adopted in 1949 set greatly increased production goals. Peasants were herded into collective farms; workers, farmers, and managers who failed in their duties were denounced. Difficulties in meeting the quotas led to the hunt for scapegoats. Most sensational was the arrest of Rudolph Slansky, who had been secretary of the Communist party and premier from 1948 to 1951. He and ten others in a 1951 show trial were condemned to death. Czechoslovakia became one of the toughest of Communist states.

New Masters Tighten Screws

Gottwald died in 1953 and was succeeded by Antonin Zapotocky, who as premier was fully as stern a taskmaster. Then in 1955 Antonin Novotny became secretary of the Czech Communist party; and, just as Stalin and Khrushchev had used this position to achieve supreme power, so did Novotny employ it to become the master. He too was an old-line Stalinist, and Khrushchev's denunciation of Stalinism in 1956 had little effect in Czechoslovakia except that it did bring a bit more toleration of criticism. *Pravda* of Pilsen admitted that the newspapers had become organs of unsurpassable boredom and that Czech journalists slavishly imitated Soviet methods. At the April Congress of Czech Writers, speakers attacked Communist methods so bitterly that the government administered a severe rebuke. In June the country remained calm during the East German and Polish revolts, for the papers never let the people know that these were uprisings against communism; instead, every medium declared the nation's unshakable allegiance to the Soviet Union. Now Novotny issued a strict warning to the press, and it became as rigidly conformist as ever.

In 1957 Zapotocky died and Novotny had himself declared president. Immediately he announced a grandiose scheme to raise industrial production 90 per cent and agricultural production 40 per cent by 1965. The prime function of the press was to be agitation to force all workers and farmers to greater efforts.

Next Novotny turned on the critics of his regime. He was particularly concerned over incipient nationalism in Slovakia. Stephen Sebasta, a high official, and twenty-six others were arraigned in another show trial. Five were condemned to death and twenty-one to long prison sentences. The Catholic Church was assailed for its tendencies; there were many trials of priests and other critics of the regime. The writers union reaffirmed political control of creative workers; and two literary journals, *Novy Zivot* and *Kveten*, which had shown signs of independence, were suppressed. Doctors were nationalized and private practice forbidden.

While industrial production had been increasing, farm production still lagged despite the fact that 86 per cent of the land had been collectivized by 1960. Radical measures were undertaken, such as the abolition of private farm plots, the amalgamation of 5,216 collectives into 1,746 state farms, and the payment of guaranteed wages to farm workers. Novotny led his delegation to the twenty-second Communist Party Congress and there declared in strongest terms Czech loyalty to the Soviet Union and acceptance of Soviet leadership.

Discontent Rises and Press Gains Some Freedom

But high government officials were not all happy with Novotny's rule, for the Czech economy was in trouble. Farm production worsened, and even industrial production in 1962 was falling far behind. There was mounting discontent as food prices rose; and on May Day, 1963, protest marches were staged against the regime. The government made concessions. Vilem Siroky, the premier, and other ministers were removed. Archbishop Beran of Prague was released after fourteen years imprisonment, and soon other clericals were set free. The third five-year plan was cancelled; the free market for farm surpluses was partially restored.

Papers began to take the bit in their teeth. Because of the failure of Communist planners and the hardships imposed on the people, journalists, writers, and scholars became a vocal opposition. When serious strikes occurred in 1963 even *Praca* (Labor), the government's trade-union paper, printed details of the strike and the workers' complaints, the first time since 1948 that even the existence of a strike had been admitted in the press. Resentment increased; people began to murmur that Novotny did not understand the people nor what to do about the major depression facing the nation. In November, 1964, when the Communist parliament convened to elect a new president, great crowds gathered, hoping to witness the fall of their Communist boss; but Novotny apparently persuaded his tame parliament that this was no time for a Communist shake-up and was reelected for a five-year term. The crowds outside Hradcany Castle faced Novotny in grim silence, for under his inept rule potentially rich Czechoslovakia had suffered a continuous economic crisis and that week *Ceteka* had admitted that Czechoslovakia would be compelled to buy 2,200,000 tons of grain abroad because of a disastrous domestic harvest.

The regime was in grave trouble. Young Communists, economists, and technocrats persuaded the party Central Committee to accept the profit motive as an incentive to greater production and to announce a new elastic price policy which would operate partly by supply and demand. Factories were encouraged to show a profit and to reward workers with pay increases and bonuses, but this was a very mild approach to the kind of industrial revolution which other east-bloc nations had enthusiastically embraced in order to achieve economic independence of Moscow. Novotny did announce, as a first step toward modernizing industry, that by the end of the year, 162 hopelessly inefficient factories, employing 60,000 workers, would be closed and some 30,000 bureaucrats dismissed.

Czechoslovakia has been the slowest of the east-bloc nations to change; and since the power structure has not altered, this new liberalized economic program will be difficult to implement as long as Novotny remains in power, for he will be reluctant to oust old party hacks who run most of Czechoslovakia's economy.

Prague in late 1965 was a drab, gray city, its people living poorly, afraid of saying anything to strangers because of informers in this tough police state. The Soviet Union, building its armament faster than ever before, made Czechoslovakia boost its arms production and increase its armed forces to be ready for a Moscow Pact call. Whether this was done to attack West Germany or in fear of war with Red China was anyone's guess.

What Is the Czech Press Like Today?

Like the press of the Soviet Union, the Czechoslovakian press is organized on the same hierarchical system, subject to the same party controls. If it shows a bit more independence today, it is only because of the dissatisfaction within the party itself.

It is difficult to get out of Czechoslovakia any accurate information on the extent of its press. The latest report for 1964 lists twenty-four dailies, but circulations are given for only the twelve larger papers. These figures are practically the same as those claimed by the papers for several years and probably should be discounted as in the case of the Soviet Union. As nearly as can be ascertained, total claimed circulations amount to only 3,500,000; but an audited report might show a much lower readership and indicate a distribution among the 13,745,000 population of only 15 copies per 100 persons, a low ratio for a nation with an illiteracy rate of less than 3 per cent. For information about other publications there is only the 1961 report showing 471 nondailies and 725 magazines, but in view of the country's economic difficulties these numbers may have been reduced. While most dailies are published in the Czech language, four are printed in the Slovak language and one in Hungarian.

As in the Soviet Union, the national or central press is centered in the capital, Prague, a city of 1,003,000 people. This is headed by *Rude Pravo* (Red Justice), organ of the Czech Communist party, with a claimed circulation of 1,100,000. It is even made up to look like Moscow's *Pravda* and, like it, is the chief mentor and carries the word of the party all over the nation. It appears to fulfill the functions of both *Pravda* and *Izvestia*. There are organs of the government ministries, largest of which is *Zemedelske Noviny* (Agricultural News), published by the ministry of agriculture with a claimed 100,000 circulation. A labor paper, *Praca*, organ of the trade unions with a claimed 250,000 circulation, and a youth paper, *Mlada Fronta*, with a claimed 175,000 circulation, appear daily. There is even an equivalent of Moscow's *Evening News* in *Vecerni Praha* with a claimed 85,000 circulation. One variant on the Soviet pattern is the pretense of allowing papers of other parties to appear. Thus *Lidova Demokracie* (Peoples Democracy) represents the Peoples Party, and *Svobodne Slovo* (Free Word) speaks for the Socialist party; but both are captives and as communistic in their appeal as any others.

On the middle level, since the ministries serve the whole country, their publications are not repeated. There are, however, papers representing regional divisions of the party. Thus at Bratislava, a city of 247,000, *Pravda* represents the Communist party of Slovakia; *Praca*, the Slovak trade union; *Uj Szo* the Hungarian trade union; and *Lud* (People), the Slovak Rebirth party. All are thoroughly communistic.

The lower stratum consists of weeklies and semiweeklies which have the same function as those in the Soviet Union—carrying on agitation and propaganda for the fulfillment of party programs on their level.

What about Wire News?

Two cousinly news agencies serve the two major geographical areas of Czechoslovakia. The old *Ceteka*, which is an abbreviation for *Ceska Teskova Kancelot* (CTK), collects and distributes news in Bohemia and Moravia. Slovakia is served by the Slovak News Agency (ZAS), but the relationship between the two is very close. CTK is the major agency with headquarters in Prague, branch offices around the country, and some bureaus abroad. ZAS is headquartered in Bratislava and gathers news of Slovakia which it feeds to CTK. The latter has an exchange agreement with TASS, AFP, AP, and Reuters as well as east-bloc agencies, but selects only that news which will have the best propaganda value for the Communist cause. Except for purely local items, it supplies most of the news which appears in Czech dailies. It is owned by the state, controlled by the ministry of information, and gets its revenue from state subsidy and subscriptions from newspapers, radio, and four television stations. It is as much a creature of the state as are the newspapers, radio, and television which use its services.

What Are Newspapers Like?

Prague dailies are not impressive in appearance; they are dull and gray, poorly printed, their pictures badly reproduced. They carry little straight news, mostly party propaganda and continued campaigns to the people to sacrifice and work harder. It is not surprising that the older generation, who remember their good papers prior to 1938, find these uninteresting, and even the younger generation considers them boring except for the sports page. *Rude Pravo*, the largest, is standard-sized, made up in six wide columns, and averages four pages with little news except party business, government pronouncements and appeals, and background pieces interpreting the news according to the Communist line. Regional papers are more interesting, usually averaging eight semitabloid pages. The front page of *Pravda* at Bratislava, while it features a leader article, devotes three-fifths of its space to national and local news. Inside there is much wire news, carefully slanted background pieces, cultural material, illustrated feature stories, even a serial story and special things for the young. The back page, the most interesting, is given to sports. But like all others, this paper is a creature of the state, its contents manipulated to serve the interests of the Communist party.

There is little advertising in Czech papers. *Rude Pravo* may break even on its circulation income, but many others must inevitably be subsidized by the government. This, however, is considered a legitimate expense by the party leaders who maintain that the press their sharpest weapon in keeping the people in line and persuading them to support their political, social, and economic programs.

If an audited circulation of Czech dailies were available, it probably would represent in large part the 1,624,000 party members and the members of trade unions who must subscribe whether they read the papers or not. This testifies to the indifference of the great part of the Czech people to their party-controlled press.

The Newspapers of Hungary

When Khrushchev in 1956 put down the Hungarian Revolution with Russian tanks and picked Janos Kadar as Red boss, he left a nation of rebellious prisoners, all the fight knocked out of them, working with gloomy resignation under Russian guns. Yet Kadar was to prove the most progressive of East European rulers. The country recovered till Budapest became the showplace of satellite capitals. Even the press, while Communist controlled, dares voice criticism.

Hungary is a bit smaller than Indiana but has twice its population. It is surrounded by east-bloc nations—Czechoslovakia, the Soviet Union, Rumania, and Yugoslavia—only Austria to the west is free. Hungary's history began in 896 A.D. when fierce Magyar horsemen ravaged their way through the Balkans and Italy and into Germany. There the Germans finally stopped them, and they settled down in the middle Danube valleys to become a stable agricultural people.

Under their first great king, Stephen I, they accepted Christianity and, as they came in contact with European civilization, they made tremendous progress. They are proud of the fact that the English Magna Carta is only seven years older than their Golden Bull. Hungary became one of the mighty medieval powers and for two hundred years was the chief bastion of Christian Europe against Turkish onslaughts. Her most brilliant early period came under Mathias Corvinus (1462–90), who not only defeated the Hapsburgs and made Vienna his capital but time and again drove back the Turks. He was also a great humanist, who made his palace a renaissance court, fostered education, and established a university. Three years before Caxton set up the first press in England, Corvinus invited Andreas Hesse from Italy to establish a press at Buda, the first product of which was "Chronica Hungarorum" in 1472.

Corvinus in time grew jealous of the press, and his successors were even more suspicious. Although most press products were religious works, there were long periods when no printing was permitted. Warring, ambitious nobles tore the country apart in civil wars, but the worst were the terrible rebellions of the peasants who rose with savagery against their lords. Hungary's enemies saw their opportunity: the Hapsburgs attacked from the west, the Turks from the east. By 1541 most of Hungary had been conquered by the Turks. Parts of the country were emptied of population, long lines being driven as slaves to Asia Minor. While the press was making its beginnings in western Europe no printing was allowed in Hungary, and newssheets were considered too dangerous to the regime.

Over 150 years of darkness followed. Only whispered words kept national dreams alive. There remained only traumatic memories. It was not till in 1699 that the Austrians, aided by Poles and thousands of Hungarians, drove out the Turks; but since liberation had been accomplished by Austrians, Emperor Leopold I claimed Hungary by right of conquest. She was now a province of conquered people, sullen and embittered, till the emperor became involved in the War of the Spanish Succession and had to withdraw most of his troops. Led by Prince Francis Rákózcy, the people rose in revolt and in 1707 declared their independence, an insurrection which was put down four years later by imperial troops.

First Newspapers Appear

The new emperor, Charles III, was, however, a humanitarian who granted religious freedom and amnesty to all who laid down their arms. His reign (1711–40) and that of his daughter Maria Theresa (1740–80) were years of reconstruction. Both were trying to hold together a vast ethnic and geographic crazy quilt of their possessions and attempted to ward off rebellions by granting concessions. In 1721 the first regular Hungarian publication, *Nova Poseoniensis* (Poseony News), a Latin weekly, was founded by Matyas Bel, an evangelist minister. It was followed in 1763 by a second weekly, this time in German, the *Pressburger Zeitung*. Because of the Hapsburg policy of Germanization, the first Hungarian language paper did not appear till 1780 when Ferenc Agostin Packo brought out *Magyar Hirmondo*. But the Hapsburgs tolerated no political opinion; and the first Hungarian papers were published under severe censorship till in 1780 the reform-minded Joseph II came to the throne, abolished censorship, and established press freedom. Whereas in Austria this gave rise to many newspapers, in Hungary his attempts to tax the nobles and curb their privileges turned them against any of his reforms. Moreover, his attempt to make all Hungarians use the German language infuriated them. Thus the Hungarian press enjoyed no freedom.

Francis I, whose reign spanned the period of the French Revolution and the Napoleonic Wars, was a complete reactionary. The wars hardly touched Hungarian territory, but the nobles made great profits supplying the competing armies. The country settled down to a period of calm beneath which seethed the discontent of the masses. When Napoleon went down in defeat and Prince Metternich, Austrian foreign minister, reorganized the European system at the Congress of Vienna, the control of Hungary became even more complete. Under Metternich's Karlsbad Resolutions, press restriction was made absolute and the publication of any subversive ideas was followed by swift and harsh retribution. By 1830 there were some thirty papers and magazines being published in Hungary, all under strict control.

New Ideas Bring Revolution

The ideas of the American and French Revolutions could not, however, be kept out of Hungary. Young Hungarians, who had studied in west European universities, came back to preach reform. They were led by Lajos Kossuth, a young noble who had been employed by a wealthy magnate, frequently absent from his seat in the Diet, to write up the proceedings; and he gave his employer both sides. Up until this time newspapers had been unable to print anything about Diet proceedings except what presented the Hapsburg point of view. Others heard about Kossuth's letters and persuaded him to make them public under the title, *Diet Bulletin*. For this he was imprisoned; but after his release in 1841, he founded *Pesti Hirlap* (Pesti News), which roused the wrath of the people against their feudalistic lords and Austria; Kossuth also became the leader in their struggle for human and national liberty. *Pesti Hirlap* was suppressed in 1845, but it reappeared later to become one of Hungary's great papers.

The revolutions of 1848, which swept France, the German states, and Austria, frightened the weak emperor, Ferdinand V, into acceding to the demands of Kossuth and his Liberal party. A new constitution changed Hungary from a feudal into a democratic state with an elected parliament and a responsible ministry, provided for broadened suffrage, and guaranteed liberty of the press. Quickly the press expanded till by the end of 1848 there were eighty papers and magazines, all debating freely the problems of the new state.

The die-hard absolutists in Vienna saw in all this a threat of secession from the empire and organized a counterrevolution among Croats, Serbs, and Rumanians in Hungary, who had long hated the Magyars.

Then Francis Joseph I came to the throne, abolished Hungary's new constitution, and made her a second-rate province of the empire. Kossuth launched a war for Hungary's freedom and defeated Austrian and Slav forces till Russia came to their aid with a large army which crushed the Hungarians. Again they lived under dictatorship, and the press promptly felt it. Of the eighty publications in 1848 there soon were only three left. German papers now came to the fore, and the famous *Pesti Lloyd* was founded in 1849 as a government organ. But in 1850 Joseph Svenveny dared bring out *Pesti Naplo,* which in fire-eating editorials attacked Austrian occupation authorities. Police hounded him, broke his health, ruined him financially, and forced him to flee to England. Successors carried on his fight, each persecuted in turn; although its first years were precarious, *Naplo* was later to become one of Hungary's foremost papers. In 1852 came a new press law which made censorship more arduous and exacted large sums of caution money from every paper. Independent journalism virtually died, and Hungarian patriots had to resort to underground papers.

Independence and Divisiveness

Austria's international problems began to give her pause. The Crimean War had isolated her in Europe, and her bitter defeats in the wars with France and the Italian states threatened the dismemberment of the empire. Francis Joseph, to placate his dissident peoples, began a series of reforms in 1860. Hungary was offered a shadow of autonomy; even newspapers were given a bit more freedom. Francis Deak, a journalist who had become Hungary's leading statesman, through his *Pesti Naplo* advised against accepting the unsatisfactory constitution which had been offered, and the Diet agreed. Francis Joseph thereupon dissolved the Diet, and a period of police rule followed while Hungarian resistance continued. Deak realized that to gain freedom, Hungary had to resolve her quarrel with Austria; and at Easter in 1865, in a front-page editorial in *Pesti Naplo,* he outlined Hungary's terms. He stated that Hungary was ready to harmonize herself with the security of the empire, acknowledged that common affairs, such as defense, finance, and foreign policy, should be negotiated by common agreement, and proposed a dual monarchy. Austria's defeats in the Seven Weeks War with Prussia had made her ready to compromise with the Magyars, and in 1866 Deak's plan was adopted. After eighteen years of helplessness, Hungary, thanks to the leadership of a great statesman-journalist, was at last a legal state on her own. With the new constitution the old 1848 press law came into force. Again the press was free. It expanded with remarkable vigor till by 1890 there were 368 newspapers and periodicals. Under the leadership of the press and its great statesmen, Hungary made economic strides, exploiting her natural resources, starting mines and factories. Education was expanded, cities and towns grew, and a new middle class emerged.

The new political freedom gave rise to parties, and the press now entered a phase of political divisiveness. The Liberal party, which had won independence and stayed in control for some time, feared that the masses might upset their power and turned conservative. The old *Pesti Hirlap*, *Pesti Naplo*, and *Az Ujzag* (The News) lost their revolutionary independence and became the organs of the ruling party. Kossuth, who had refused amnesty and stayed in exile, still had influence; and his followers founded the Kossuth Independence party which through *Magyarorszag* (Hungary), *Egyetertis* (Understanding), and *Fuggetlenseg* (Independence) demanded more social reforms. They were strongly supported by peasants and workers. To these major protagonists there was added the Radical party, led by Oscar Jaszi, which advocated the adoption of western European social reforms and political institutions, and won wide acceptance among the middle class and intellectuals. But the Rumanians, Croatians, and Slavs, resisting Hungarianization, started papers promoting their own independence. When they became troublesome, new laws were used to curb this press. With so many political voices and with increased prosperity Hungary by 1904 had fifty dailies, fifteen of them in Budapest, and some two hundred political weeklies.

Sowing the Wind

But neither the government nor the divided press were serving the people well. Count Stephen Tisza, leader of the government party which ruled most of the time from 1875 to 1914, was entirely reactionary. He opposed extension of suffrage, for he held that only the aristocracy knew how to govern and feared that any relaxation of his strong hand would bring appalling social unrest. Even by 1914 only 6.4 per cent of the people could vote. Industrial workers were considered too dangerous a force, peasants equally so, and although serfdom had supposedly been abolished, many people were little more than serfs working from dawn till dark for the equivalent of 10 cents a day. Great numbers emigrated, many to the United States, till almost a tenth of the population had gone. The press, while allegedly free, was actually free only to support the government; and it concerned itself solely with the complications of Austro-Hungarian relations, taking no interest in social problems.

In addition to the major parties there now developed a rightist

National party, Catholic and Protestant parties, a new Socialist party of workers, and a new Agrarian Socialist party. All had to have their organs, but any who tried to take leadership in solving Hungary's problems were promptly punished for their "incendiarism." Many editors were haled into court for treason or lèse majesté and given months of imprisonment. Censorship and suppression of Rumanian and Slovak papers were particularly severe till, in the years before World War I, there were more Slovak papers in the United States than in Slovakia and only two Rumanian papers in Transylvania.

War and Revolution Take Their Toll

The assassination of Austrian Crown Prince Ferdinand by south Slavs precipitated World War I, and Hungary went in on the side of Austria and the Central Powers. But Hungarian troops fought on the Russian and Serbian fronts only to defend their territory. In the Diet there had arisen an anti-war group, headed by the distinguished Count Mihály Károlyi, who felt that medieval Hungary was an anachronism in the twentieth century. Károlyi's Socialists and Jaszi's Radicals joined forces in a democratic bloc which tried unsuccessfully to separate Hungary from Austria and her misfortunes, and to make contact with the Allies. The war settled down into a stalemate of trench warfare, and for the people at home it was an appalling period of attrition and starvation. The press now had considerable freedom, and the war issues and the proposals to convert Hungary into a federation of autonomous nationalities were debated without restraint.

After the collapse of the dual monarchy, a revolution broke out on October 21, 1918; and Hungary was proclaimed an independent republic with Károlyi as provisional president. The new constitution, which safeguarded press freedom, lasted less than six months, for in March, 1919, Communists under Béla Kun set up a soviet-style government and proclaimed a dictatorship of the proletariat. In five months of terror many anti-Communists were executed and the press totally suppressed except for Béla Kun's own mouthpieces. But by August a counterrevolution, aided by Rumania, swept aside the Communist regime. Rumanian troops finally withdrew in November and Hungarian forces, under the command of Admiral Miklós Horthy, advanced to Budapest to establish a new government which Horthy soon made a fascist regime, the first of this system in Europe. All ties with Austria were dissolved. Then in 1920 the Allies took Transylvania, west Hungary, Slovakia, Croatia, and Slovenia from Hungary in the Trianon Treaty. The nation of 20,000,000 inhabitants was reduced to a small landlocked state of only 8,000,000; and some 3,000,000 Magyars found themselves living outside Hungary.

Wars, revolutions, Bolshevik purges and peace treaty reductions had likewise taken their toll of the press. While some old prewar papers reappeared after 1920, there were now less than a third of the number of dailies, weeklies, and periodicals that had flourished in 1914.

Restoration of order did not bring press freedom. As Mussolini was to do in Italy, Horthy set up controls so that the press might mold a new order. Every paper now had to get a government permit and police kept editors in line. Communists were eliminated in Horthy's own "white terror," but editors of all papers had to be cautious. War losses and heavy reparations payments brought an ecomomic crisis and widespread impoverishment. Circulations were sharply reduced and advertising dried up. Many papers had to be subsidized by big capital or the government in order to continue. The latter soon acquired ownership of the leading papers in the capital. But the provincial press was gravely stricken and was long in recovering. In 1921 Stephen Bethlen succeeded in merging the strongest parties into a Party of Unity. For ten years this coalition of large proprietors, small land-owners, and commercial interests governed the country; and while it made some progress in reconstruction, it held the nation under tight control.

Although the regime claimed there was no precensorship, it was risky to write anything critical of the government; hence, on domestic issues Hungary had a hesitant press. Papers with courage to speak for the people were reduced to impotence by prosecutions, heavy fines, and imprisonment of staff members. Offending editions were con-fiscated, and on those days the paper had to pay a fine equal to what its receipts for the day would have been. Unable to speak on domestic affairs, papers turned to external problems and agitated for the revision of what they considered their unfair peace treaty. Revisionism became almost a national obsession of the press.

Nazis Lead Nation into World War II

Economically crippled, Hungary was shattered by the world de-pression. Unemployment spread in the cities, and in the countryside peasants became desperate. A fourth of the journalists found them-selves without jobs as their papers closed. As in Germany, the discon-tented joined extreme rightist pro-Nazis groups. General Julius Gom-bos, Nazi leader, became premier in 1932 and started a progressive Nazification of Hungarian life. German-subsidized papers attacked the government for its failure to take a stronger anti-Semitic line. Following Hitler's example, Gombos appointed a Goebbels of his own, M. Antal. By constant coercion and daily instructions he set the tone for the whole press. He took over *Fuggetlenseg* as his own organ, and as soon as any so-called opposition papers got into financial trouble Antal took them over also.

Gombos' death brought no change, for his successors carried on his policies. Béla Imredy founded a press chamber on the German model. and most Jewish and Socialist journalists were expelled from their profession. Once Germany had taken Austria and thus became a direct neighbor, it was dangerous for any Hungarian to oppose friendship with Germany. Imredy seized all publications which showed any sign of liberalism. But Imredy overreached himself in his anti-Semitism; and when Horthy learned that Imredy himself had Jewish ancestry, he exposed him and forced his resignation. Count Paul Teleki, who now became premier, was not pro-Nazi but realized that Hungary must walk with caution. When, however, he won a strong majority in the 1939 elections he gave newspapers more freedom and permitted them to apply the brakes to Nazi orientation. He and Horthy were averse to involvement in Hitler's war plans and dared to refuse the latter's demand that Hungary attack Poland. They did not even permit German troops to go through Hungary for that purpose. Non-Nazi papers also reflected popular aversion to Germany's attack on Poland.

Hungary maintained her neutrality through the first year of the war; and despite increasing economic pressure, Teleki tried to avoid involvement. His last act of defiance was the conclusion of a peace treaty with Yugoslavia. When Hitler demanded immediate cooperation in the attack on Yugovlavia and marched into Hungary, Teleki, in protest, committed suicide. Pro-German Laszlo Bardossy, who succeeded him, had no difficulty leading his country into war against Yugoslavia, for this led to the reconquest of territories lost in 1918. Hungary followed Germany into the war against Russia.

Papers now gave vent to their old hatreds against their ancient Russian enemy and Bolshevism. But after the German defeat at Stalingrad and Allied landings in North Africa Hungarians began to be more independent. Non-Nazi papers ventured to print news monitored from London's BBC to give their readers some idea of what was going on in the world. Nicholas Kallay, a liberal who succeeded Bardossy, made secret proposals to the Allies that Hungary withdraw from the war at an opportune time without sacrificing the old territories she had won; but the invariable reply was "unconditional surrender." Kallay, aware of his nation's predicament, allowed somewhat greater press freedom, but it was a cautious laxity, for while Hungarians knew they were in the wrong camp they feared disengagement might mean annihilation. Nevertheless, Hungary was the only east European nation which permitted her papers to print Allied news and to carry the full texts of Roosevelt's speeches.

Nazi Occupation, Then Communist Take-over

In March, 1944, Germany occupied the entire country and put in power a puppet Nazi government. A reign of terror was initiated against Jews and anti-Nazis. Some 43,000 Jews, including many journalists, were sent to Auschwitz to be gassed. Nazis took over all newspapers, and lies and distortions filled the German-controlled press. But Germany's game was up. Victorious Russian armies swept into Hungary, and by March, 1945, the Germans had been driven out and all Hungary occupied by the Russian army.

As the country was liberated, a a coalition of Smallholders, Social Democrats, National Peasant, and Communist parties set up a provisional government under General John Miklos. All parties joined at first in publishing one paper *Szabadsag* (Freedom). Near the war's end the Allies agreed that each ally should supervise political developments in the areas its armies had taken from the Germans. Thus Hungary fell into the Soviet orbit, and Marshal Klementy Efremovitch Voroshilov ruled without any western participation. Trying hard to win over the common people, the Communists pushed through the Miklos government a bill confiscating 14,000,000 acres from great estates and church lands for distribution to 700,000 farm laborers, but there was deep resentment when many were forced into collective farms. Hungary never was permitted the right, guaranteed by the Yalta agreement, to create democratic institutions of her own choice. Red troops controlled the country.

Reds did not overlook the press. A national committee was created to license newspapers. The Red army daily, *Ujszo* (New World), was the first to appear. Still on their good behavior, Communists allowed parties of the coalition government to use the plants of defunct Nazi papers. But somehow the Russians, who controlled the newsprint supply, always had difficulty finding paper for non-Communist sheets. In the months before the 1945 election the Communists, with the best presses, ample paper, and complete control over radio, were able to blanket the country. Yet, in this last free election in Hungary, the Communists won only 17 per cent of the vote while the Smallholders got 57 per cent, the Social Democrats 17 per cent, and the National Peasants 7 per cent.

This shocked the Communists into action. The other parties were pressured into a new coalition, "more broadly representative" in which the Communists took over the ministry of interior, which controlled the police, and the ministries of finance and communication. Quickly all industries were nationalized till the Communists had a strangle hold on the economy. The National Assembly on February 1, 1946, declared Hungary a republic. Still playing in a low key, the Reds permitted Zoldan Tildy and Ferenc Nagy from the Smallholders party to be president and premier; but the real power was soon in the hands of Matyas Rakosi, captured by the Russians in World War I and taken to Moscow where he had become a fanatical Communist and secretary of the Communist Internationale. Now he returned to Budapest as secretary general of the Hungarian Communist party and was installed as deputy premier. With power in their hands, the Communists demanded the suppression of Catholic youth organizations and the Boy Scouts, the exclusion of certain non-Communist journalists from their profession, and the discharge of several officials. Nagy yielded, fearing that refusal might mean complete take-over, but now the attack turned against non-Communist members of parliament who were accused of "plotting with western nations for the overthrow of the People's Republic." Accusations in the Communist press rose to a scream against reactionary deputies while opposition papers had their issues seized or were suspended. One by one non-Communist deputies were expelled.

The Hungarian Press Is Reorganized

The Communist minister of interior immediately clamped strict censorship on the press, threatening severe measures for the publishing of any news about the purges of deputies. Desya Sulyok, one of those expelled, risked his neck by declaring in his *Holnap:* "The wildest and most obnoxious terror rages in Hungary. No paper may be published which tells the truth. We have become a police state." *Holnap* was suppressed, and Sulyok had to flee the country. In the 1948 decrees the last vestiges of press freedom were wiped out, and the ownership of all printing plants was "transferred to the people," which meant to the Communist hierarchy, headed by Rakosi, the little Stalin of Hungary.

The press was soon reorganized on the Soviet model with *Szavad Nep* (Free People), official organ of the Communist party, as the dominant daily. Under it was the usual subhierarchy of papers directed to workers, peasants, the army, and the youth. The Hungarian Telegraph Agency (MIT) was then made part of the Central Information office, getting most of its news from TASS and funneling to all papers properly slanted news and propaganda. The Hungarian people, who had known only brief periods of press freedom, now had none. All those who had dared stand for democratic rights had been eliminated as "Fascists"; tens of thousands had disappeared. The rest dwelt in a harsh police state, served by a press that fogged their understanding with misinformation. Peasants were ruthlessly forced into collectives. When the Church was offered what Cardinal Mindszenty knew meant state control, he refused and was sentenced to life imprisonment.

Rakosi, following the Moscow line, started his first three-year plan with emphasis on heavy industry, manufacturing armaments for the U.S.S.R. and completely neglecting agriculture. By 1953 there were food shortages and great discontent over the pressures being applied to all groups. Waves of strikes swept the land. After Stalin's death in 1953 Rakosi was evicted from premiership and Imre Nagy took his place. He at once started sensational changes, reducing the pace of economic development, turning the emphasis on agriculture and light industry. Peasants were permitted to leave collectives and half of them departed in a year. Food and clothing prices were cut and wages raised to improve the standard of living. The press was even permitted to print criticism of Rakosi's dictatorship. Rakosi returned after Malenkov had fallen in the U.S.S.R. and by 1955 had undone Nagy's reforms; but in July, 1956, Khrushchev dismissed him and put in his place Erno Gero, equally as fanatic a Muscovite. Dissatisfaction and despair continued to grow.

Revolution and the Press

On October 23, 1956, all the hopelessness exploded when Budapest university students demonstrated in sympathy with the Polish rebels in Posnan. Huge crowds formed around them; and when Gero's police and Russian troops fired on them, they were all turned into revolutionaries. The crowds called for Imre Nagy. He replaced Gero and promised reforms, but by that time all Hungary was aflame and armed resistance organized. The Communist party began to disintegrate, and on November 1 a democratic government was formed. Free papers appeared hailing the rebirth of Hungarian independence. Khrushchev could not afford to let this satellite divorce itself from his rule and sent Russian tanks. There was heavy fighting for a fortnight before the revolt was crushed. Some 180,000 fled the country. Cardinal Mindszenty found asylum in the U.S. Legation.

The role played by the press in the revolution was noteworthy. Since 1954 *Irodalmi Ujsag* (Literary Gazette) had been protesting censorship. Communists had tried to control this agitation by requiring editors to attend ideological courses and pass examinations, but even

Communist newsmen resented this and openly declared that the nationalization of the press was responsible for its decline and its incredibly low standards. During the revolution, when free papers bloomed everywhere and were eagerly bought by a news-hungry people, journalists played an heroic role. But once the revolution had been put down, all non-Communist papers were suppressed and only party papers could be published. The people, however, refused to buy them and up to the end of 1957 Communist papers were frequently burned in Budapest streets.

Kadar Ushers in New Regime

Janos Kadar, picked by Khrushchev to sit on the lid as premier, had himself been a Rakosi victim, had spent years in prison, and had been cruelly treated. He entered office, hated by the people, but gradually won their respect. Surprisingly, he did not disavow the revolution; in fact, he called it a praise-worthy struggle for liberty. The press was encouraged to criticize Rakosi and Gero as agents of Stalinism. In late 1957, however, those responsible for the revolution were publicly tried. Many leaders were executed; 30,000 persons were deported to the Soviet Union. Thereafter, Kadar pursued a more liberal policy. Peasants were forced back into collectives, but they were given their own private plots of land and awarded bonuses for production. In time food became more plentiful, and by 1963 the people of Budapest were better fed than those in any other Communist capital. Since 1956 some 700,000 persons have moved into the capital till it has become a city of 2,000,000; and its shop windows display more and better goods than those in any other eastern capital except possibly Belgrade.

Kadar, the most liberal of east-bloc rulers, is considered a true Hungarian trying to sugarcoat the Communist pill and to stay independent of Moscow. He sees increased production and the raising of living standards as the best path for his party, and he has embraced the profit motive for industry. Communist bureaucrats have been replaced by a new managerial class which in both 1963 and 1964 achieved substantial gains in industrial production; farm production too showed marked gains, largely from household plots. Kadar cares nothing about a man's ideology so long as he produces. The party still rules but stays in the background; there are no big pictures of Kadar on display. People no longer fear the secret police, and they can find good jobs even if they are not party members.

Newspapers are still owned and operated by the party, but more open debate on national shortcomings is permitted; letter writers no longer fear to sign their names. City papers have been encouraged to discuss the housing shortage. There are few restrictions on writers providing they do not criticize what Kadar calls his "Humanist Social- ism." Yet a highly popular state television program, received by some 424,000 home sets, is entitled "This Does Not Please" and airs frank criticism of government programs. Despite this greater liberality, all papers must toe the line and follow the government's bitter denuncia- tion of the United States for its escalated war in Viet Nam in 1965.

And what of the people? Despite years of incessant propaganda, they have not been sold on communism. They do not talk about 1956, for they say it hurts too much to think about it. They know they cannot win another revolt because of the Russian and Hungarian troops which sit over them. Thus they have decided to live with their government and force as many changes as they can. Most persons still hate the Russians and are proud of their increasing independence and their expansion of trade with the West. They have been willing to go along with their government's anti-Chinese policy, for they see Peking as a greater threat to peace than Moscow. They are more financially solvent than they have been in a long time, and their children have a better chance for education. With more freedom to travel, tens of thousands each year take vacations in western Europe. They know they cannot have free elections and have therefore become apathetic toward Communist politicians and their pronouncements. The Com- munist party, which in 1954 had 864,607 members, in 1956 saw 45 per cent of them tear up their party cards. Membership has increased since then; but in 1964 it totalled only 512,000, a tiny minority in a nation of 10,116,000.

The Hungarian Press Today

Hungary in 1964 had thirty-one dailies, an increase of three over 1963, but considerably less than the fifty-three in 1929 and the seventy- three before World War I. The smaller number is easier to control. Budapest is the journalistic capital with six dailies representing the national press and accounting for 80 per cent of the total daily circula- tion. The others appear in provincial cities, organs of Communist party county committees.

It is difficult to evaluate Hungarian circulations, for they are all claimed figures; yet they are not the same round figures claimed for years, as is true in other east-bloc countries. The chief daily, *Nepsza- badsag* (Peoples Freedom), is the Hungarian *Pravda*, boasting 750,000 circulation which is probably the total of the enforced subscriptions of party and labor union members. Other principal capital papers include *Magyar Nemzet* (Hungarian Nation), organ of the People's Patriotic

Front and the voice of the government, claiming 95,000; *Nepszava* (People's Voice), organ of the Trade Union Council, claiming 250,000; the more popular *Esti Hirlap* (Evening Herald), claiming 157,000; and *Nepsport* (People's Sport), published by the Hungarian Council for Physical Training, claiming 110,000. None of these dailies are large, for they are semitabloid, running ten to twelve pages daily and up to twenty pages in weekend editions. In addition there are weeklies for special groups such as *Magyar Ifjusag* (Hungarian Youth) and *Irdalmi Ujsag* (Literary Gazette). The twenty-five provincial dailies, most of small circulation, are tabloids of six to eight pages. The total daily circulation of 1,357,000 shows a small increase over 1963; yet for a population of 10,116,000 it means a distribution of only 13.4 copies per 100 persons, thin coverage in a nation with an illiteracy rate of less than 10 per cent. The meager distribution further testifies to the indifference of the great majority of Hungarians to their press. It must be said, however, that in addition to this daily press, there are weeklies in smaller towns, several religious publications, and a number of popular magazines. With all industry and most retail outlets nationalized, there is little need for competitive advertising. The recent increase in foreign trade has caused some manufacturers to advertise their products, but most advertising is classified. Large papers may have a whole page of small ads set in nine narrow columns. Most papers are state subsidized.

Hungarian papers look different from their Russian counterparts, for they use Roman letters instead of Cyrillic. There are few pictures except in weekend editions. Makeup is modest but not unattractive in five wide columns. The front page of a typical ten-page Budapest daily leads with a two-column editorial article setting the propaganda line for the day. The remaining three columns are given to comment on foreign and national news. Then follow two pages of foreign and national news, the latter placing its emphasis on economic planning and goals. A page of local and county news, one devoted to cultural affairs, a page of radio and TV programs, a solid page of advertising, and a back page given to sports comprise the rest of the paper. Weekend papers are the most popular, presenting more cultural articles, even women's pages and comic panels. Most dailies are published every day except Monday. All are served by *Magyar Tavirati Iroda* (MIT), a government-owned agency which has the monopoly on all news dissemination. Formerly most of its foreign news came from TASS, but now more is used from Reuters, AFP, and AP, for whom it has exclusive distribution rights. All wire copy is carefully screened by the party. MIT also has exchange agreements with other east-bloc countries.

The Hungarian press must be accepted for what it is—a Communist organ presenting only such news as the government wishes, carefully interpreted from the party standpoint, heavily overlaid with propaganda to which the great majority of the people are indifferent.

The Newspapers of Poland

The Poles, who have known periods of national greatness, have suffered more than other Slavic peoples from rapacious neighbors who for long periods subjugated them and silenced their press. Yet until 1963 their papers, even though they were behind the Iron Curtain, were among the most independent and westernized in the Communist world.

Part of the great Slavic migrations from the Ukraine, the Poles did not appear in history till in the tenth century when Mieszko I united the tribes, set up a powerful kingdom, and accepted Christianity for himself and his people. Then under Casimir the Great (1333–79) the country began a rule of such influence that by the sixteenth century Poland controlled a territory extending from the Baltic in the north to the Black Sea and the Adriatic in the south. Her civilization reached a new splendor; towns prospered, and the University of Cracow attracted scholars from all Europe. Poland became the home of Italian Renaissance art; prose and poetry flourished. Her people had the greatest civil and intellectual liberty in Europe. In an age of religious persecution she offered asylum to the oppressed from many lands, including Jews, Germans, Czechs, Magyars, Armenians, and Russians.

In this atmosphere Poland's press flourished earlier than those in other Slavic countries. Monks in their monasteries, who had kept learning alive by copying classics and religious works, were her first chroniclers, producing Annual Chronicles, which listed the year's happenings in the world and commented on them. These were hand-copied in Latin and distributed to wealthy patrons, often selling for 200 ducats to the few who could afford them.

First Presses and Newspapers

Printing came to Poland within twenty years of its invention in Germany, and the first printed book appeared in Cracow in 1474.

384

Nicholas Sharftenberg, the most famous Polish printer, ranked with Koburger of Germany and Aldus in Italy in the quality of books produced. Other important printing centers developed at Lemberg, Warsaw, and Lublin. Printers had to obtain a royal privilege which was often held by some noble or bishop under whose protection the printer worked.

Printing was not placed at the service of journalism till 1661 when *Merkurjusz Polski* (Polish Mercury) appeared at Cracow as a weekly. It was short-lived as were others which appeared sporadically, called *Relacze* (Reports), *Noviny* (News), or *Poisania* (Description). Priests and monks were the outstanding journalists of the period; but, while they provided some foreign news, they selected items of particular interest to the Church and seldom dared deal with Polish problems because of the suspicions of powerful nobles. The military landowning gentry had organized the country for their own benefit. Townsmen, a rising middle class, were denied the franchise or the right to own land outside city walls. Peasants were reduced to serfdom. Sixteen great families maintained luxurious courts and lived like sovereign princes while waging wars with each other.

Under such circumstances Poland's fledgling press received no encouragement. It was constantly under suspicion; any dereliction was followed by immediate suppression. Yet two well-founded papers, *Kurjer Polski* at Cracow and *Kurjer Warsawski*, began publishing in 1729, providing better news coverage, mostly of foreign news, and keeping themselves out of trouble by eschewing political comment.

War Bleeds Nation

The Hundred Years War, starting in 1654, was another press deterrent, for many of the battles between the great powers were fought on Poland's soil. Polish heroism rose to its greatest heights when her armies under John Sobieski halted the Turks in 1683 at the very gates of Vienna. But only Russia and Austria profited while Poland paid with the loss of many of her best sons and further impoverishment. Her strength diminished as Russia and Prussia became more powerful. Lacking a forthright press, the people were not aware of their dangers as their rulers dallied, trying to effect understandings with these two great powers. The government became increasingly ineffective under the custom of *liberum veto*, under which any deputy in the Diet could adjourn it by imposing his veto. Forty-five Diets between 1652 and 1772 were thus exploded; the country as a result fell into economic stagnation and political anarchy while the gentry led lives of reckless gaiety on their princely estates. Poland came to vie with Turkey for the questionable honor of being "the sick man of Europe."

Through French influence a reform movement arose, led by the Czartoryski family and its adherents, demanding the abolition of the *liberum veto* and the adoption of other political reforms. Some newspapers dared to interpret these events, to back these reforms, and to warn the people; but their efforts came too late. The leading paper of this period was *Monitora*, started in 1765.

Poland Is Partitioned

Neither Russia nor Prussia was interested in Poland's regeneration; and in 1772 Russia, Prussia, and Austria joined in the first partition of Poland on the grounds of its "continued anarchy and refusal to cooperate with [its] neighbors in restoring order." Poland lost a third of her territory and population. In the Russian area, Catherine, preoccupied with her eastern wars, withdrew her troops; and Poland was given an opportunity to institute reforms. Towns shook off their decadence; administration was improved; an educational system was established. The new 1791 constitution made the country a constitutional monarchy, controlled by a responsible bicameral parliament. The *liberum veto* was abolished, townsmen were given representation in the Diet, and peasants were allowed the protection of the law. The new freedoms gave some encouragement to the press, and one of Poland's best newspapers, *Gazeta Warszawski*, was started in 1774; it was to last till 1939.

Shorn of their privileges by the new constitution, the Polish aristocracy denounced it for "spreading the contagion of democratic ideas" and asked Catherine to intervene in their behalf. Prussia joined Catherine, "in view of the imminent danger threatened from the revolution in France," in the second partition of Poland in 1793, which took away half of Poland's remaining territory and population and reduced her to a narrow corridor from Courland to Cracow. The Poles fought off their invaders for three months but had to yield at last. The 1791 constitution was abolished as a "dangerous novelty."

But the Poles did not give up. Led by Thaddeus Kosciuszko, they proclaimed a national insurrection in 1794. Kosciuszko called the peasants to arms, and they responded eagerly to his promise of freedom from serfdom; but overwhelming Russian forces defeated them, and he himself was wounded and captured. A violent massacre marked the taking of Warsaw. The powers who had engaged in the first partition now staged a third—which wiped Poland off the map of Europe for one hundred years.

The Poles in Captivity

The Poles settled down under the grim rule of the occupying forces. Napoleon and his conquering armies gave them hope, and Polish legions fought for him all over Europe. Napoleon himself, however, set up the same Draconian rule he had installed in other conquered territories and allowed only one paper to publish—under French control. After Napoleon was defeated, the powers at the Congress of Vienna in 1815 confirmed the Polish partition. Most of old Poland went to Russia; Germany got the northeastern section, and Austria was given the southeastern province of Galicia.

The lives of the people and the freedoms accorded the press varied with the zones of occupation. Conditions were best under the Russians, for by then the liberal-minded Alexander I had come to the throne. He gave the Poles a constitution which granted them freedoms still denied the Russians and permitted them a Diet. Individual freedom and the right to use their language was ensured. Even liberty of the press was promised. A number of Polish papers revived, particularly in Warsaw. They operated with considerable freedom until 1804 when Alexander, disturbed by the attacks of his own press at home, instituted pre-censorship for both Russian and Polish papers.

In the Austrian zone Francis II, fearful of revolutionary ideas, gave no encouragement to Polish papers in Galicia and subjected them to severe censorship. Nevertheless one good paper, *Gazeta Lwowski*, appeared at Lwow in 1811. After Metternich, that arch foe of liberalism, became premier, devastating press restrictions were put into effect, and *Gazeta* had to close. Conditions were most difficult in the Prussian zone where the conquerors set out to denationalize the Poles. There was no room for even the existence of Poles, and no Polish papers were allowed.

Attempts at Revolt

Triggered by the oppressive rule of Nicholas I and the French 1830 revolution, Poles in the Russian zone rose and fought for a year till vanquished. Now Russians also turned to the destruction of Polish nationalism. No Polish papers were permitted; even the universities were closed. Polish leaders fled, mostly to Paris, and issued papers in exile which were smuggled back into their country. Within Poland itself some one hundred underground papers appeared. In 1855 the liberal Alexander II succeeded to the throne and gave Poles their own administration under a Polish Council of State. The university was reopened and "Polenized" as were high schools. Polish peasants benefited from the abolition of serfdom in 1861. But Russia's attempt to draft politically suspect youths into Russian regiments sparked another insurrection in 1863 which went on for two years before it was crushed. There were wholesale executions and deportations, and a thorough policy of Russification was instituted. From then on what few Polish papers were permitted had to go literary. They nevertheless played an important part, for in stimulating the pride of the people in their art, literature, music, and history, they inspired a deep sense of patriotism. The Russians did, however, lay the foundations for industrial expansion in their Polish province. As a result there developed a class of industrial workers who later were to recognize a common cause with the Russian Social Democrats.

In the Austrian zone the rulers of a multinational monarchy regarded the Poles as but another of their many provinces, and Galicia was granted a constitution with a Diet of its own and a measure of autonomy; even press freedom was affirmed and newspapers had a better opportunity here than in any other part of old Poland. With fifty-seven votes in the Austrian parliament the Poles often held the balance of power and a number of them held cabinet offices in Vienna.

Now that Bismarck had created a unified German empire the Germanization of Poles in the German zone was intensified. Poles were dispossessed of their land and Germans settled in their places. The press remained completely impotent. The Poles in this zone became the most bitter enemies of the Germans.

Russia's Defeat Brings Changes

Russia's disastrous war with Japan and the subsequent Russian Revolution of 1905 raised Polish hopes, and one of the concessions to which Nicholas II had to agree was the lifting of censorship. In this freedom old papers revived and new ones rose. Best was *Kurier Warsawski*, independent politically, emphasizing news, and edited with a high literary touch. In Lodz the chief daily was *Gonie Lodzki* (Lodz Messenger), conservative and pro-Russian. Cracow had a Socialist daily *Naprzod*, reliable and influential among workers. The Polish Communist press, born in exile in Switzerland, now moved to Poland. *Czerwony Sztandar* (Red Banner) moved from Zurich to Cracow and then to Warsaw. Unfortunately, the new freedom lasted only a year, for by that time the tsar had taken all the criticism he could stand and clamped down on the press once more. Many papers were forced to suspend operations.

In the Duma, Russia's first parliament, Polish delegates had twenty-six seats. They won there the right to establish many new schools.

Russia propagandized the idea of uniting all Poles, with autonomy within the Russian empire, and this became the program of the National Democratic party led by Roman Dmowski, head of the Polish Duma delegation. Opposed were the irreconcilable revolutionaries led by Joseph Pilsudski. Both movements were stifled by Russian autocratic reaction. Pilsudski had to flee to Galicia; Dmowski's delegation was reduced to ten; and all liberties gained in 1915 disappeared.

The ensuing years were bitter ones. Poets and political leaders began to dream of a world war which might give Poland independence. But when the war broke in 1914 there seemed no possibility for revolt, for the western democracies, intent on maintaining their alliance with Russia, would give no help. And the Poles themselves were divided. Dmowski's party was in favor of accepting Russia's promises and tried to raise a Polish legion to fight for Russia. But in Galicia Pilsudski recruited armies to fight for Austria, for he had no faith in Russian promises. By the summer of 1915 Germany and Austria-Hungary had conquered much of Poland. After the Austrian armies collapsed Germans took control of the entire "liberated area"—and they had no love for Poles.

Independence Brings Press Revival

After the Russian Revolution of 1917 the new Russian government recognized Poland's right to self-determination. Polish leaders now transferred their activities to Allied capitals, Dmowski in Europe and Ignace Jan Paderewski in the United States. President Wilson announced his support for a free and united Poland; and late in 1917 the United States, France, Britain, and Italy recognized the Polish National Committee. The collapse of Germany in 1918 led the Poles to declare their independence on October 6 and on November 3 the Polish Republic was established. Pilsudski as first president proceeded to restore order, to evacuate German troops, and form a new government. Poland did not get all she asked for at the peace conference, but she was given the areas in which the majority of inhabitants were Poles—a total of 90,000 square miles embracing 28,000,000 people and including a corridor to Danzig separating East Prussia from Germany proper.

The new nation faced tremendous tasks of reconstruction, for, with the exception of Belgium, Poland had suffered greater devastation than any other nation. There were political problems, too, because the government had proclaimed universal suffrage and proportional representation in the chamber of deputies or *Sejm*. In the first parliament fourteen parties were represented, all passionate and disparate groups.

Each, of course, had to have its newspaper. The new constitution guaranteed press freedom; hence, there was an immediate flowering of the press. But because of difficult economic conditions no papers could be independent; all had to be supported by parties. Actually there was little freedom, for the minister of interior, province governors, and police could censor papers, even confiscate editions. With the *Sejm* so divided, no party could achieve a majority; coalitions came and went; one ministry succeeded the other. Thus the first postwar press proved exceedingly ephemeral, for newspapers rose and fell with changes in government.

Conditions went from bad to worse. Pilsudski, completely hamstrung by his parliament, retired to private life. But in 1926, fearing the country was drifting into anarchy, he seized control by means of a military coup. He reformed the constitution, limiting the powers of parliament and strengthening the executive, but stopped short of the kind of dictatorship later set up by Mussolini. Nevertheless he governed by decree. Freedom of political discussion was limited by a decree under which the printing of news that might lead to public demonstrations or that ridiculed or criticized the government could bring imprisonment and fines. He hated Communists and Socialists and did everything to harry their papers out of existence. Despite this dictatorial control, 165 newspapers managed to continue publishing, though they were kept rigidly in line.

Pilsudski died in 1935 and was succeeded by a group of colonels who had fought in his legions. Most prominent was Colonel Joseph Beck. Pilsudski's "authoritarian democracy" continued; but the colonels exercised their power in a conciliatory spirit, for national unity was now demanded in the face of dangers from Hitler's Germany. A freer press was tolerated; and by 1938 there were 620 newspapers, 208 of them dailies, 99 of them with Sunday editions. Most had circulations ranging from 3,000 to 10,000. Some outstanding papers did even better, notably *Kurier Warsawski*, independently owned but representing the Conservative Catholic viewpoint. It provided the best news coverage and became the best advertising medium, often giving half its space to ads. Although it had a certified circulation of only 70,000 it was the most respected paper in the country. More popular was *Maly Dziennik* (Little Journal), a penny paper designed for the masses, which achieved a 200,000 circulation. Close behind was *Illustrawany Kurier Codzienny*, a tabloid picture paper with 190,000.

Polish papers resembled their European counterparts with modest, carefully balanced makeup. Many were tabloids, and all were meticulously departmentalized. Political, economic, and intellectual matter predominated while local news was given little space. Polish journalists were persons of distinction who inspired respect. Each paper depended upon its staff for commentaries, backgrounding, and cultural articles. Dailies relied upon Polish news agencies, largest of which was PAT (Polish Telegraph Agency), the official government service, for local, national, and world news. Others included KAT (Catholic Press Agency), ZAT (Jewish Telegraph Agency), ATE (Express Telegraphic Agency), ISKRA (Transcontinental), and PAP (Polish Press Agency), the last four being independent.

In this period, while government control was less rigid than in Germany, Italy, or Spain, censorship was strict and there were frequent confiscations. The government felt it had to protect the country from internal dissensions which might undermine Poland's precarious position and from any expressions which might give offense to the dangerous powers around her.

Crises Lead to Nazi Invasion

Germany considered the Polish frontier one of the "injustices of Versailles" and had never accepted Poland as more than a temporary state. Pilsudski, recognizing Hitler's rising power and fearing that neither Britain nor France could be counted on to maintain treaty provisions, had concluded a nonaggression pact with him. After Hitler had taken Austria and Czechoslovakia, Poland was left dangerously isolated. When she concluded a pact with Britain, Hitler renounced his agreement with Poland. He tried to provoke Poland with Danzig incidents and started a press propaganda campaign against alleged ill treatment of German minorities in Poland. Then, after Stalin and Hitler had concluded their callous pact, Hitler was free to carve up Poland. He invaded her on September 1, 1939, hideously bombing Warsaw. Polish forces fought against overwhelming odds till September 27, when Russia invaded from the east, on the ground that Poland no longer existed. Russia took all the eastern provinces, Germany all of the western ones. Five years of subjugation followed.

Hitler turned on Russia in June, 1941, and all the eastern Polish provinces were seized by Germans as the Nazis advanced. Poland was reduced to a slave nation. All Polish papers were suppressed. Since there were no Poles who would collaborate, the Nazis brought in Germans to operate their papers, published only in larger cities and in German, for Polish was considered an inferior language. The two exceptions were *Nowy Kurier Warsawski* (New Warsaw Courier) and *Gazeta Zydowska* (Jewish Journal). The latter lasted only till most of the 3,000,000 Polish Jews had been exterminated at Auschwitz.

Polish newspapers and the government had gone underground. One day after the Germans had occupied Warsaw, the first clandestine paper appeared; a month later there were sixty. There are records of several hundred illicit papers; but no accurate count could ever be made, for if the Gestapo caught up with a publication and executed its staff, it might appear a few days later in a different place with a different title. When the Germans discovered the secret office of one Warsaw paper, the five men and three women, surprised in their hideaway, bolted their steel doors and fought for three days till their ammunition was gone and their building a shambles. All eight were executed. Three days later the paper reappeared with a black bordered announcement of the death of the eight heroes and heroines and informed readers that the paper would continue as before.

These underground papers gave news of Poles who had disappeared, reported German atrocities. To gainsay German claims of continued victory, they printed news, monitored from London radio stations, of Allied victories and setbacks. They reported the success of their sabotage and told of Poles fighting with the Allies on many fronts. Their whole purpose was to keep alive the morale of the Polish people and their hopes of eventual liberation.

Germans tried every possible means to stamp out this press. The penalty for even possession of a clandestine sheet was death. When the Gestapo caught up with *Dziennik Polska*, 170 were arrested, 120 of them shot. To spread the risk, as many as 150 to 200 persons were used by a single underground paper, each one responsible for only a small part of the operation, not knowing the others in the chain. Thus thousands of Poles regularly risked their lives that their nation might survive despite Nazi attempts to destroy them. Distributors were often street urchins. Hurried purchasers did not stop for change, but the boys turned in everything to finance the papers. Other money came from private persons or from London. There had to be money to pay for paper and ink. Most of the paper came from not so loyal Nazis in Germany who accepted bribes to sell needed supplies.

End of War Brings Communist Take-over

Russia's desperate war with Germany had brought betterment in Russo-Polish relations and ended the state of war between them. By 1943 the tide had turned against Germany; but, as Russian troops began occupying Polish territory, Soviet authorities grew more anti-Polish, renewing their claims to the eastern provinces and throwing their support to the Polish Communists known as the Lublin Committee. The crisis was heightened when Germans discovered the bodies of 8,000 Polish officers in a mass grave in Katyn Wood near Smolensk. When the Poles raised questions, the Soviets refused investigation by the International Red Cross, broke relations with the Polish government, and began a propaganda campaign to discredit the legal government in exile in London.

However, the real treachery occurred when Soviet generals appealed to the Poles for help in reconquering Poland from the Nazis. The people were willing, and the Polish home army on August 1, 1944, rose against the Germans in Warsaw. Other allies tried to get arms and supplies to them, but the Soviet generals not only stopped that but did nothing to help the Poles. The battle lasted sixty-three days and ended with the virtual decimation of the Polish underground army. The advancing Russians disarmed and deported those who escaped death. The Lublin administration declared itself the sole legal authority in Poland and early in 1945 made itself the provisional government of the Polish Peoples Republic. At Malta, Roosevelt and Churchill were persuaded by Stalin to recognize the Lublin government, though they did require it to reorganize and include other democratic leaders from Poland and abroad. In the final territorial settlements Poland lost her eastern provinces to Russia but was compensated by being given the same amount of territory in eastern Germany as far as the Oder-Niese river line. Some 8,500,000 Germans were forced out of this area and about 5,000,000 Poles moved in.

Under British and American pressure elections were finally held January 9, 1947. Official results, announced by the government, gave Communists 382 seats of the 444 in parliament. It was officially stated in both the United States and Britain that the election had been neither free nor fair, but the Communists were now in control of postwar Poland.

And What Happened to the Press?

As soon as German armies had been pushed out, old prewar papers appeared as well as underground papers, now publishing openly. For a time there was relative freedom as Communist pro-Russian and Democratic anti-Russian papers blasted each other. Soon the Communists, having nationalized all industry and business, took over the press and organized it on the Soviet model. All dissident papers were suppressed; private ownership was abolished; only workers' cooperatives and the Communist party could put out newspapers or periodicals. Only trusted Communists were permitted to work in journalism and at once the press began slavishly following the Moscow line. The government controlled all newsprint. A 1947 UNESCO survey revealed there were but 51 Polish dailies as compared with 208 in 1938.

The new press began under severe handicaps. The country was in pitiable condition: it had been fought over, bombed, and plundered by two great armies. Six million Poles had died. A large percentage of industry had been destroyed or looted. The people were terribly poor. Many newspaper plants had been wrecked or robbed of their equipment by marauding armies. Yet Communist leaders had to have papers to sell their new order to the people. There was almost no advertising, so all papers had to be subsidized. The Communists readily accepted this necessity because the press was to be an important arm of the government. Papers were small; there were few pictures; yet this Red press did develop. By 1950, while the number of dailies had dropped to 32, there were 76 weeklies and 550 magazines and other official periodicals. All dailies were now getting *Polska Ajencia Prasowa* (PAP), the official state news service supplying 25,000 words a day, 28 per cent of it foreign news derived from TASS.

During the early fifties the press continued its subservience to Moscow and, at Stalin's behest, became concerned over the danger of aggressive war threatened by the United States. The rearming of Germany was cited as a preliminary to such a war, in which Poland would be the first victim. There was great alarm over spies and enemies of the Peoples Republic. The press even turned on Wladyslaw Gomulka, secretary of the Communist party, when he was denounced by Stalin for "deviationism." He was arrested and spent three years in prison.

Things Change with Stalin's Death

Stalin died in 1953. Almost at once there were signs of independence, first in literary magazines which dared question "social realism" and servile imitation of Russian writers. Newspapers followed suit. Most surprising was the publication by *Zycie Warszawy* in late 1955 of criticisms by its readers, who complained about their one-sided papers, the lack of international news from western Europe and America, the failure to print internal news because of government taboos. The press began improving its reporting of national and foreign news. Internal news, even of previously prohibited subjects, began to be reported with fewer delays and omissions. In parliamentary debates a Catholic deputy declared, "Our press should not be a pro-government press—it is a popular press and its role should be to serve the people."

In June, 1956, came the Posnan revolt, in which industrial workers staged a general strike and demanded "bread, freedom, free elections and the departure of the Russians." Riots which followed were put down by army tanks. Then ensued a struggle in the Communist Central Committee between the pro-Stalin group and those who wanted democratization to continue. In the end all agreed that the only man who could restore order and unity was Gomulka and he was thereupon officially rehabilitated. On October 19, when the new *politburo* was to be elected, Khrushchev, Molotov, Kaganovich, and Anastas Mikoyan arrived in Warsaw accompanied by Russian generals; and it was learned that Soviet divisions were poised to move. But the independent Poles were not to be denied. There were tremendous demonstrations for Gomulka. Khrushchev realized that Gomulka had to be the man or there would be great bloodshed. In a stormy session Gomulka persuaded the Soviet visitors that Poland must be an equal, independent, and sovereign state. The Soviet visitors returned to Moscow. Gomulka was elected first secretary of the party and immediately announced a program of industrial and agricultural reorganization. No Stalinists remained in the government and Russian officers in command of Polish armed forces were dismissed and replaced by Poles.

Polish papers reported the Posnan riots and the events which followed with great freedom. They denied Moscow's attribution of them to foreign agents and ascribed them instead to the miserable conditions of the proletariat. When the Hungarian revolution broke in late 1956, most Polish papers reported it with sympathy for the insurgents. Meanwhile, there was much discussion about censorship; and the Polish Journalists Association decried the unjustifiable interference of the Press Control Office. Censorship regulations were eased, and papers were permitted greater freedom of discussion. Furthermore, some papers declared their independence of the official organizations which published them, such as the Workers Publishing Coop (Praca). Some became financially independent, and this factor led to competition which brought in western techniques and the abandonment of space previously devoted to political orientation in favor of greater space for news. *Express Wieczorny* saw its circulation grow by 80,000 in a few months, whereas the purely Communist pary organs saw their circulations shrink by 50 per cent between December, 1956, and May, 1957.

Setbacks Balanced by Gains

In their new freedom some papers ventured to question the fundamental tenets of Marxism and proposed liquidation of the Polish Communist party. This provoked strong reactions not only from Warsaw authorities but from Moscow. *Pravda* published violent diatribes against the Polish press for "sapping the foundations of the People's regime, for shaking the pillars of their system, sowing distrust and polluting readers' minds with the imported poison of an ideology alien to the workers." The tragic end of the Hungarian revolt brought realization of the need for prudence. Gomulka began calling on papers to obey party instructions. The threat of economic sanctions was effective, for, since the government abolition of subsidies, papers had become vulnerable. They had had to double their prices and some had had to suspend operations. Gomulka's organ, *Polityka*, began to urge journalists to moderate their tone and limit themselves to constructive criticism. Some editors were dismissed and some papers closed. By 1958 papers found their freedom shrinking. For reasons of state, Gomulka, who had been responsible for many press concessions, could not afford to allow complete emancipation. Nevertheless, Polish journalists had shown they wanted this freedom, and even though they might be Communists, they were to continue their struggle for more independence.

Yet there were also gains as the Gomulka government continued its progress on Poland's separate road to socialism. Greatest gain for the people was being freed from the political police. Far-reaching reforms were undertaken in education. Most surprising was the freeing of peasants from compulsory inclusion in collectives. In foreign affairs Poland maintained a close alliance with the U.S.S.R. but increasingly insisted on independence in concluding trade agreements with west European nations.

At the end of the fifties press censorship was stricter, but the Polish press was still relatively freer than its counterparts in most east-bloc countries. Censorship rules forbade any criticism of the Soviet Union or opposition to Marxism though suggestions for reforms were permitted. But the government was sensitive; editors began to be suspended or jailed and fined for evading censorship when what they printed somehow offended the sensibilities of the government. The president of the Polish Authors Association wrote *Trybuna Ludu* of the alarm of Polish authors who found themselves defenseless against the misuse of censorship, but no relief was forthcoming. Foreign correspondents also had difficulties. Rosenthal, Warsaw correspondent of the New York *Times*, was expelled in 1959 for "having interested himself too much in Poland's internal affairs." *The Times* was banned for two years and not permitted to replace Rosenthal. In addition, one of his Polish assistants was imprisoned.

In the sixties the press situation deteriorated. By 1962 Poland's economy was in difficulty both in industry and agriculture. In 1963 Gomulka decided that Polish society was not yet socialist because it had not rid itself of the remnants of bourgeois ideology and announced an intensive effort at "improving the education of the people." Step by step Poles began losing freedoms they had won in 1956. Writers and commentators with independent views were damned as "revisionists" and dismissed from newspapers, magazines, radio, and television. Two of the prominent cultural weeklies were closed and replaced by one hewing close to the party line. Claiming paper shortage, authorities began choking off any dissent. Earlier, Dan Larrimore, UPI Warsaw correspondent, had been at his post less than a month when authorities notified UPI that they would prefer another correspondent: *Izvestia* had attacked him as an agent of the American Intelligence Agency. Screws were steadily tightened on intellectuals. In 1964 seventy-two-year-old Melchior Wankewitz, a Polish-American writer whose return to Poland in 1960 had been hailed as a propaganda victory and evidence of Poland's intellectual freedom, was sentenced to eighteen months imprisonment for "false and slanderous writing against the government both at home and abroad." He was one of thirty-three intellectuals who had issued a sharp protest against growing intellectal repression. His conviction was supposed to be a sharp warning to the Polish intelligentsia to stop their criticism, but he was released after one month, as if it had all been a mistake.

Government control of the press, however, was once more based on the old hard Communist line, and Gomulka became one of the east-bloc rulers most anxious to please Russia. When Khrushchev was ousted in October, 1964, Gomulka was quickly talked out of his misgivings and endorsed the Kosygin-Brezhnev regime. In early 1965 Poland played host to the Warsaw Pact leaders to discuss relations with China. The Polish people feared that any *detente* with China might encourage Stalinist elements within the Polish Communist party.

While 1964 had been a good year, 1965 saw the economy decline. Prices rose and consumer goods became hard to come by, causing great popular discontent. Up to the end of 1965, authoritarian press control stiffened. Because of Gomulka's cooperation with the U.S.S.R., all papers bitterly denounced America's war in Viet Nam. Yet among the Polish people there is a reservoir of good will for the United States as was evidenced by the enthusiastic welcome given John A. Gronouski, the grandson of a Polish immigrant, when he arrived as the new American ambassador. Young Poles are particularly dissident and have become unpolitical. They want to be left alone to live a fuller life. However efficient Gomulka may be in consolidating orthodox Communists, he will have to reckon increasingly with this younger generation.

The Polish Press Today

Poland in 1964 reported the existence of forty-one dailies, apparently a sharp drop from the sixty-eight in 1955. But a Warsaw editor explained that in 1955 the report included branch editions of regional dailies in which there was one local page, the rest the same as the main edition. The entire press is controlled by the Polish Communist party, which with 1,475,000 members represents only 4.7 per cent of the entire population.

The Polish press is organized like that of the Soviet Union. At the top of the order is the national press emanating from Warsaw. This is headed by *Trybuna Ludu* (Workers Tribune), the voice of the Central Committee of the Communist party. It combines the tasks of *Pravda* and *Izvestia* in the Soviet Union and claims a circulation of 205,000, less than a sixth of the party membership. Then there are the organs of the various ministries and public organizations. The ministry of defense publishes *Zolnierz Wolnosci* (Soldier of Freedom), which claims 57,000 circulation; the Trade Union Federation puts out *Glos Pracy* (Workers Voice) and claims 120,000; the Socialist Youth Union has *Sztandar Mlodych* (Youth Banner), claiming 93,000; the ministry of agriculture issues *Chupska Droga* (Peasants Way) twice weekly with a circulation of 300,000; the committee for physical culture has *Prz Eglad Sportowy*, a small daily.

The middle press grouping consists of eight dailies in larger provincial cities, each with a number of regional editions plotted with interlocking circles to cover wide areas. Largest is *Trybuna Robotnicza* with a claimed 450,000 coverage of most of western Poland; second is *Zycie Warszawy* (Warsaw's Life) with a 220,000 circulation reaching, with its side editions, a large circle in northeast Poland. These papers are published by provincial party committees and are more popular than the national papers.

The lower press consists first of all of the twenty-eight local dailies spread over the country. Although a city may be served by a branch edition of a regional daily, it may also have its own local daily. Thus at Gdansk (Danzig) the local *Dziennik Baltycki* (Baltic Daily) outstrips the regional daily by 103,000 circulation to 70,000. With more local news and features and local advertising these papers have more of a western look. Largest is *Express Wieczorny* (Evening Express) at Warsaw, which claims to sell 550,000 copies. Many of the small local dailies range from 35,000 to 65,000. This local press also includes some two hundred weeklies and biweeklies in smaller towns. Poland claims to have 1,047 magazines and other periodicals; some of the women's magazines have circulations of more than 1,000,000. Warsaw is the publishing capital with ten dailies and eight hundred other publications.

As in East Germany a pretense is made of permitting the existence of other party papers. Thus the pro-regime Democratic party publishes *Kurier Polski* (Polish Courier) in Warsaw, and the pro-regime Catholic party issues *Slowo Powszechne* (Universal Word). Both are run by trusted Communists.

Circulation reports for the forty-one dailies totaled 4,216,000 in 1964, which meant distribution of 13.6 copies per 100 persons in a country with a literacy rate of 95 per cent. It must be remembered that these are all claimed circulations, and the same round-numbered figures have been used for the last four years; hence they are probably incorrect. If audited circulations were available, the distribution rate would probably be lower and illustrate graphically the indifference of a great many Polish people to their completely controlled and propagandistic press.

Character of Papers

Polish newspapers are not large. Before the war Poland was an important newsprint producer, but Nazi armies cut down huge areas of timber and it will take fifty years to replace them. Therefore most newsprint has to be imported from Scandinavian countries. Only larger papers like *Zycie Warszawy* can have eight pages. Even *Trybuna Ludu* has only six; many smaller dailies have only four. The larger papers are standard-sized; many smaller ones are semitabloid. In appearance today's Polish dailies are attractive and interesting. A typical eight-page paper devotes the first two pages to wire news, all carefully interpreted according to the party line. Then follows a cultural page, one of editorial articles, and one of local events. Pages six and seven are given to advertising, and at the back is a lively sports page.

Wire news comes from *Polska Ajencia Prasowa* (PAP), owned and subsidized by the government. Much of its foreign news is gleaned from TASS, though it maintains twenty-nine correspondents abroad. At home it gathers domestic news through bureaus in eighteen principal cities, funneling their reports to headquarters in Warsaw which supplies dailies with some 36,000 words a day. All reports are carefully screened to provide only such news as the government desires. It serves not only the forty-one dailies but Polski Radio and Polski Television as well.

Editors in the early sixties insisted that Polish papers had more freedom than those in any other east-bloc country except perhaps Yugoslavia and that they had a good deal of freedom of discussion so long as it was exercised within the bounds of constructive criticism. But since 1963 they have lost most of that liberty. With Gomulka's return to the hard Communist line they probably have less today than papers in any other east-bloc countries except Albania, Bulgaria, Czechoslovakia, and East Germany.

The Press of Rumania

Rumania is different from other Communist states in that she is a Latin island in a sea of Slavs and Magyars. Her people are an amalgam of the ancient Dacians and their Roman conquerors. In the mountains they survived the invasions of Goths, Huns, Tartars, Slavs, and Magyars, retained their Latinity, and still use a language akin to Vulgate Latin. Rumania is a little smaller than Oregon, a beautiful land of splendid mountains and wide plains rich in resources. Like the peoples of the other east-bloc countries, her 19,000,000 population was taken over by the Communists after World War II. Until 1953 Rumania was a docile Russian satellite; since that time she has become one of the most independent of eastern European nations.

Rumanians fought for their liberty against Hungarians, Poles, and Turks; but in the early sixteenth century they were conquered by Turkey and stayed captive for 350 years. Still they tried to keep alive their own culture and in the period from 1507 to 1565 set up printing presses in monasteries where they produced religious works and histories. But then the Turks silenced all presses and made Rumanians mere slaves.

To wring more money out of the country, the Sultan farmed out Rumanian administrative duties to rich Greeks known as Phanariotes. Usurious and tyrannical as they were, they did bring the leavening influence of French culture and began to encourage education. The sleeping Latin spirit of younger Rumanians was aroused, and many managed to get to Paris for an education. A cultural renaissance combined with the influence of the French Revolution inspired Rumanians to revolt in 1821. Though they were defeated, their struggle brought the first precursors of the press, at first mere pamphlets, then newssheets urging the people to resist their oppressors. Russia stepped in to make a protectorate of Rumania and in 1829 gave the country virtual autonomy. However, the Russians continued their occupation and imposed a harsh reactionary constitution.

First Newspapers Appear

In 1829 Ion Eliade Radulescu, a Rumanian revolutionary, founded Rumania's first newspaper, *Curierul Romanesc* (Rumanian Courier), assailing the new constitution and urging the unification of an independent Rumania. His attacks on Turkey were permitted, but any criticism of Russia was suppressed. At Brasov in Transylvania Johann Gott brought out in 1831 *Gazeta Transilvaniei*, the first Rumanian paper in this province. In universities and political clubs the unionist movement grew. Authorities tried to smother it, and even went so far as to close the universities. When the revolutions of 1848 swept through Europe, Rumanians again revolted; but their attempt was put down by the Turks, Russians, and Austrians, who maintained a joint military occupation till 1851.

Exiled patriots were forced to carry on their fight from Paris by smuggling pamphlets and newssheets back into their country. Surprisingly, Alexander Chika, the Russian-appointed governor of Moldavia, backed the nationalists and, after foreign forces were withdrawn, granted press freedom. For a brief period several nationalistic papers appeared, but in 1854 Russia put a stop to this when she again occupied the Rumanian provinces as a preliminary to her drive into the Balkans. This precipitated the Crimean War in which Russia was defeated and had to grant autonomy to Wallachia and Moldavia, representing much of southern and eastern Rumania. The assemblies of both provinces declared that they wanted union as a single state. Constantin Rosetti, editor of *Romanul* (The Rumanian), was the leading champion of their cause. When the powers would not permit the union, the nationalists circumvented them by electing Colonel Alexander Ion Cuza as prince of both principalities. He did try to break up some of the great estates, a maneuver so violently opposed by the wealthy landowners that he assumed dictatorial powers in 1864.

Like any dictator, Cuza could not stand criticism. He disciplined Rosetti, imposed strict censorship on papers, and silenced the new press completely. When Cuza was deposed during a palace revolt and exiled in 1866, the national assembly, with the consent of the powers, chose Prince Charles of Hohenzollern-Sigmaringen to rule Rumania. He was smuggled into the country by Ion Bratianu, a young revolutionary.

A Modern Press Is Born

Charles proved a wise and energetic ruler. He reorganized the army, put through administrative reforms, interested foreign capital in developing industries, expanded the school system, and built railroads and roads. He helped his country pass from the middle ages to modern times.

Opposing parties had buried their differences and formed a coalition government; but soon strife broke out between the Liberals, headed by Rosetti and Bratianu, and the conservative landed interests, who opposed all reforms. When the Franco-German War broke in 1870, feeling ran high against the German prince. The people, most of whom were sympathetic to France, started revolutionary outbreaks; and the Conservatives used the opportunity to take control of the government. They restored order; but for the next six years, newspapers were given little encouragement. They were few and poor and followed the easy path of translating news from Vienna and Budapest papers.

It was not till the Liberals came to power that modern journalism began and better papers appeared. The two most important were *Romania Libera* and Rosetti's now revived *Romanul*, both battling for a new constitution and universal suffrage. The outbreak of the Russo-Turkish War heightened an interest in newspapers. Prince Charles broke relations with Constantinople and allied himself with Russia. After two defeats the tsar called on Charles who took command of both armies and decisively defeated the Turks, finally winning for Rumania her independence in 1878. In 1881 the country raised itself to the status of a kingdom and Charles was crowned Carol I.

Under the liberal Bratianu government, the press was given real freedom; and new papers emerged—most of them political organs. One outstanding exception was the daily *Universul*, founded in Bucharest in 1882 by an Italian, Luigi Cazzavillan, who set a new pattern with a paper impartial in politics and placing its main emphasis on news. It gained popularity rapidly, made itself the best paper in Rumania, and was the first to achieve general circulation throughout the country. Another popular daily was *Adeverul* (Truth), founded by A. V. Beldimanu in 1888. It was also an information paper but much more aggressive. Under its editor, Constantin Mille, it fought administrative abuses and crusaded for distribution of land to peasants, naturalization of native Jews, and better schools. That most of these reforms were realized was due in no small part to *Adeverul*. In 1904 it added a morning companion, *Dimineata*, which provided such a wide coverage of news that people began to call it the New York *Times* of Rumania.

Among the political papers, the leading Conservative organs were *Epoca* at Bucharest and *Lupta* (Fight) at Iasi, both born in 1885. The strongest Liberal papers were *Romanul* and *L'Independance Roumaine*, the latter dating from 1875. The Socialists had started with a biweekly at Iasi in 1879 and in 1894 established their first daily, *Lumea*

Nuoa, in Bucharest. Many of the new party papers were small in circulation, showed marked political bias in their news treatment, and devoted much space to polemics.

Press Expands and Divides in World War I

Rumania entered the twentieth century after a decade of material advance. Liberal and Conservative governments alternated in power as the country progressed in the development of industry, railroads, shipping, and trade. Moreover, the school system, started in 1866, was now bearing fruit; a generation of literates had grown up. Even in 1905 an American writer spoke of Rumania as "the Balkan country whose people read most and where most people read." It was a country that supported several hundred periodicals and papers.

But all was not peace. The peasants had not shared in the ecomomic advance. Although they had been freed from serfdom in 1864, few had been able to acquire land; and most still lived as vassals. Liberal papers repeatedly warned of the "volcano trembling beneath our feet" and urged the government to undertake reforms. The volcano erupted in 1907 in a bloody peasant revolution which was brutally put down; and though a new land law was passed, peasants were destined to get little relief till after World War I. The press was also disturbed over the millions of Rumanians living under the rule of Austria-Hungary, Russia, and Turkey and kept calling for their liberation. Rumania remained neutral in the First Balkan War; but when it appeared that Bulgaria might dominate the Balkans, Rumania joined Serbia and Greece in the Second Balkan War, which brought the defeat of Bulgaria and the redemption of Dobrudja on the Black Sea coast. This was in compensation for Russia's seizure of the rich southern province of Bessarabia.

Rumanians were completely divided as World War I approached. Many papers attacked their ally, Austria-Hungary, for her denial of the rights of subject Rumanians. Both sides tried to bribe Rumania. Germany offered Bessarabia; Russia promised Transylvania. King Carol felt a natural pro-German sympathy, but the Crown Council decided for neutrality. Carol died in late 1914 and was succeeded by his nephew, King Ferdinand, who faced a press and people torn in their sympathies by two years of neutrality. The Conservatives, because of business dealings with Germans, were pro-German; but Nicolae Filipescu and his *Epoca* and Take Ionescu with his *La Roumanie* practically seceded from the Conservative party to attack Conservative Germanophiles. The Liberals favored neutrality but were sympathetic to the Allies. *Universul,* among the independents, opposed entry into the war on the side of the Central powers, while *Adeverul* favored military support of the Triple Entente as the best guarantee of union for all Rumanians in one country.

The trend of opinion in favor of the Allies continued; and on August 18, 1916, Rumania entered the war on the side of France, England, and Russia. Her armies invaded Transylvania but failed to get the expected support from the Allies when Germany attacked. By December most of the country had been conquered. For sixteen months enemy forces ruled and despoiled the country. All papers except those of the Germanophiles were suppressed. But then the tide of the war began to turn; and when in November, 1918, Germany was forced to surrender, the Allies made good their pledge to Rumania. In the 1919 peace treaty Rumania not only regained her prewar territory but was given Transylvania, Bucovina, and Bessarabia, doubling her area and population. Thus the Rumanians, after being divided for a thousand years, were finally brought together; and King Ferdinand and Queen Marie were crowned sovereigns of Greater Rumania.

Postwar Press Takes New Political Orientation

The nation had, however, suffered great war losses and was economically crippled. In the new provinces millions found no satisfaction in the old prewar parties. The Transylvanian party led by Iuliu Maniu and a Peasant party led by Ion Mihalache joined forces in the National Peasant party which won the first election and proceeded to put land reform and universal suffrage into effect. Great estates of the *boyars* (wealthy landowners) were broken up and 14,000,000 acres distributed to landless peasants. With the loss of their lands and because of their Germanophile tendencies the *boyar* Conservative party disappeared. The Liberal party, now led by a younger Bratianu, Vintila, had come to represent banking and business interests. General Alexandru Averescu, war hero, organized a new rightist Peoples party. Further left were the Socialist and Radical parties, and there were still other minority parties. Each had to have its voices; hence, there developed a proliferation of party organs, and the postwar press became one of bitter political partisanship.

The Liberal party came to power in 1922 and initiated a reconstruction program, including the building of schools in country villages and the establishment of a farm bank. But more important, it brought the adoption of a new constitution in 1923. This provided a parliamentary government on a western model and guaranteed to everyone the right to publish his ideas without censorship or previous authorization. It prohibited suspension or suppression of papers or preventative arrests of editors and publishers. By the end of 1926 Rumania had a fairly large and diversified press enjoying great freedom.

Universul was now the leading information paper, approaching 100,000 circulation. *Adeverul* and *Dimineata* were close behind and supported the democratic parties against the Liberals, whose leading paper was *Viitorul* (Future). The Peoples party had *Indreptaria* (Guidance); the National Peasant party had *Patria* and *Dreptatea* (Justice); the Socialists published *Elore* (Forward). There were many other political organs throughout the country.

Prince Carol Brings Royal Dictatorship

Iuliu Maniu's Peasant party came to power in 1928. Maniu was a man of great integrity and his administration from 1929 to 1930 marked the peak of good government and civil rights. The economic depression, however, brought clamor from hard-hit farmers and business interests, and everyone objected to his tax program. To circumvent opposition, Maniu consented to a bold stroke. Prince Carol, who had married Princess Helen of Greece, had renounced his rights to the throne in 1925 and gone into exile with his red-haired mistress, Magda Lupescu. On King Ferdinand's death in 1927 Carol's son, still a minor, took the throne under a regency which did not work out successfully. Maniu now agreed to Carol's return, provided he broke off his affair with Lupescu, for Carol had been popular with millions of Rumanians. Once he returned, however, Carol ensconced Lupescu in Bucharest, dismissed Maniu and ushered in a new, hard rule, for he had visions of becoming another Mussolini.

Now papers of a new stripe appeared, such as *Curentul*, aggressively militaristic, and *Tara Noastra* (Mother Country), not only nationalist but anti-Semitic. The nation was soon torn apart: one cabinet crisis followed another, and there were eight different governments between 1930 and 1933. This gave Ion Codreau an opportunity to build up his Iron Guards, who could be paid to break up political meetings or strikes. Nevertheless, by 1935 Rumania counted 299 papers—104 of them dailies. *Universul*, appearing seven mornings a week, was the largest with 140,000 circulation and had now developed strong nationalistic tendencies. *Adeverul* with 100,000 circulation vigorously supported the Peasant party. *Dimineata* with 90,000 circulation was the most important information paper, printing sixteen to twenty-four pages daily. Carol began tightening his reins on the press, suspending any papers that ventured to raise voices against Rumanian Fascism and introducing press laws similar to those in Germany. All democratic papers, including *Adeverul* and *Dimineata,* were muzzled. Jews were deprived of their citizenship and driven out of journalism. A new Fascist constitution made government control of the press complete.

In the next two years Rumania's position deteriorated. The Iron Guard, prodded by Hitler, prepared to take control. Carol struck back, arresting hundreds of Iron Guardsmen and executing many. When World War II erupted, Rumania remained neutral; but after Germany and Russia had become allies, and after France had fallen, Carol was powerless. Hitler forced him to release imprisoned Iron Guards and to reorganize his government with the Guards as a nucleus of a new totalitarian state. Russia, too, stepped in and forced Carol to give up Bessarabia and northern Bucovina. Similarly, Germany and Italy compelled him to cede northern Transylvania to Hungary and southern Dobrudja to Bulgaria. Thus, Rumania lost 40,000 square miles and 6,000,000 of her people. The Iron Guard then forced Carol to abdicate and vested real power in General Ion Antonescu, who set up a new dictatorship under German overlordship. In a reign of terror many former high officials, publishers, and editors were assassinated. As riots and revolts broke out Hitler's legions moved in and occupied the entire country "to help Antonescu restore peace." All newspapers were suppressed except those willing to follow the German line. Recalcitrant editors and publishers were sent to prison or concentration camps. The free journalism of which Rumania had been so proud from 1923 to 1935 was buried.

The Soviet seizure of Bessarabia and Bucovina still rankled deeply. When Hitler attacked Russia in June, 1942, there was great popular enthusiasm as Antonescu led Rumania into war to recover the lost provinces. These were quickly reconquered, but Rumanian armies continued the drive into the Ukraine and on to Stalingrad where Rumanian casualties were particularly heavy. Discontent rose at home where Germany held the country in an unshakeable grip.

In spite of the iron Nazi rule, strong opposition began rallying around Iuliu Maniu's Peasant party. After the reconquest of Bessarabia that party had urged Antonescu to get out of the war, for it did not want to be tied up with German totalitarianism. When, after Pearl Harbor, Antonescu declared war on the United States, Maniu secretly made contact with the British, hoping to devise a way to get Rumania out of Hitler's camp. Maniu was not alone. Through underground papers, opposition forces rallied democratic elements to resistance. As in other Nazi-occupied countries, underground editors and workers were relentlessly hunted by the Gestapo, shot, or placed in concentration camps; yet the resistance movement went on.

By the end of 1944 Russian armies were approaching Rumania, and she saw herself faced with a revengeful enemy. But the Russians, after retaking Bessarabia, stopped at the Rumanian border and pledged themselves to respect Rumania's sovereignty and territory. For a time the Soviet army kept its pledge. Antonescu's regime was tottering. Young King Michael, who had succeeded his father and had been kept a German puppet, now with the aid of Maniu and loyal generals arrested Antonescu and his cabinet and ordered Rumanian armies to cease fire against Allied forces and to fight on the side of the Russians against the common enemy, Germany. Within a short time Rumanian and Russian troops had cleared the country of German soldiers and had retaken Transylvania from Hungary.

Communists Take Over Press

A new government representing the Peasant, Liberal, and Communist parties restored the former democratic constitution, opened concentration camps, and proclaimed liberty of the press. For a few months there was complete freedom and old friends appeared on newsstands. The Nazi and the fascist papers were gone. The most popular now was *Curierul*, published by Maniu's Peasant party, which was soon selling 350,000 daily. *Universul, Adeverul,* and *Dimineata* were back with their old independence. The Liberals had their *Viitorul* and a new *Liberalul*. The Communists had *Graiul Nou* (New Language) and *Scanteia* (Spark). The people, who had seen nothing but distorted Nazi reports, were now delighted to get straight news once more. Editions were quickly sold out; news and editorials were eagerly discussed, and there was intimate contact between press and public.

Maniu's plans for a democratic government were foiled by an Allied agreement allocating Rumanian affairs to Russian control. Under armistice terms dictated by Russia, Rumania was required to permit Russia free troop movements within her territory, to pay Russia's expense in her defense and $300,000,000 in reparations, to disband all fascist organizations, and to place all publications, plays, films, post, telegraph, and telephone under the Soviet high command. Rumania's freedoms began to disappear as she was bound hand and foot to the Soviet Union.

The Peasant, Liberal, and Socialist parties tried to form a new government under General Nicholas Radescu. At once Communist papers turned on him. The Communist Democratic front headed by Peter Groza, organized violent street demonstrations, commandeered police and radio stations, and attacked opposition newspaper plants. The Liberal *Democratul* was suppressed and its editor arrested.

Curierul's plant was seized for use by *Scanteia* and *Graiul Nou*. *Universul*'s plant was expropriated and the paper transformed into a Communist propaganda sheet. *Viitorul* was silenced. By the time Stalin was ready to take over, Radescu had no newspaper supporters, and democratic forces had nothing but clanderstine mimeographed sheets. Then Andrei Vishinsky, Russian vice-commissar for foreign affairs, arrived to restore order in what was made to appear a popular civil war against oppressors of the people.

King Michael was compelled to dismiss Radescu and to appoint a new cabinet headed by Groza. A new press regime was inaugurated far more drastic than that of the Nazis. Under increasing pressure King Michael abdicated on December 30, 1947.

The western Allies demanded Groza's promise to respect civil rights, to restore press freedom, and to include Peasant and Liberal party representatives in his cabinet. As a gesture he allowed *Dreptatea*, *Patria*, and *Liberalul* to reappear. But once his regime was secure, Groza started repression anew. *Patria* succumbed to violence after a few weeks of heroic resistance. *Dreptatea* and *Liberalul*, trying to carry on for the next fifteen months, wrote a most heroic chapter in the history of Rumanian journalism. Harassed by Communist censors, deprived of adequate newsprint so that they could print only a limited number of copies each day, attacked by mobs attempting to wreck their plants, they still carried on their fight for Rumanian liberties. Newsstand men were beaten till they dared not display these papers. Communist union printers refused to set type for what they did not like. Publishing a paper was a daily adventure.

Groza had promised a free parliamentary election; but as the day approached Communist violence increased, and every Red paper called for "Death for Maniu." Russian soldiers broke up democratic meetings. The men on *Dreptatea* and *Liberalul* risked their lives by supporting opposition candidates. Not one opposing voice was permitted on radio. Peasant and Liberal leaders who should have watched the counting of ballots were jailed. Rumanians marched to the polls with flags flying; and the Groza government, after a five-day delay, announced an overwhelming victory despite the fact that the Peasant and Liberal parties represented 75 per cent of the people. Now all opposition parties were outlawed, and *Dreptatea* and *Liberalul* were suppressed. Maniu was arrested and condemned to life imprisonment. A new 1948 constitution, modeled after that of the Soviet Union, was adopted. It guaranteed press freedom by placing all means of printing at the disposal of the workers, but making clear that freedom was only for the Communists. Rumania became the most closely held satellite for exploitation by the Soviet Union.

By 1950 Stalin was tired of his Rumanian stooges. Groza was made a mere figurehead president; and Moscow-trained Communists, headed by Gheorghiu-Dej, Ana Pauker, and Vasile Luca were placed in power. In 1949 a decree legalized the government's control of information and the right to regulate newspapers and all other publications. Serious food shortages brought trouble; and in 1952 Pauker, Luca, and seven other ministers were dismissed for "poor planning" while Gheorghiu-Dej emerged with the real power. Until Stalin's death in 1953 Rumania continued to be the most docile of Russian satellites.

Rumania Breaks Soviet Hold

Gheorghiu-Dej was a Rumanian nationalist, and once Stalin's fierce grip was removed he began to assert his independence. Amnesty was proclaimed for many political prisoners; taxes and prices were cut. In 1954 the joint Soviet-Rumanian companies which had been set up to exploit Rumanian resources were dissolved; and new trade agreements were made with West Germany, Denmark, Turkey, and Greece. After the Austrian peace treaty had been signed in 1955 Gheorghiu-Dej began questioning the continued presence of Russian troops, whose purpose had been to keep open the supply lines between Russia and Austria. He made a trade agreement with Yugoslavia and in complete defiance of Soviet policy removed peasants' compulsory deliveries to the state, except for meat and wool.

All this made no difference to the press, for it was now the servant of Gheorghiu-Dej. He used it for continual propaganda to inveigle farmers into collectives. Quickly Rumania changed from a quiescent to a defiant member of the Soviet bloc. She refused to be just a primary producer for the U.S.S.R. and, despite Soviet objection, continued her six-year program of industrialization. She made substantial trade agreements with Italy, France, even Albania and China, and sought some form of association with the Common Market.

Khrushchev had threatened reprisals against Rumania after she threw his bloc-wide economic scheme out of kilter. Hence, Gheorghiu-Dej was delighted with Khrushchev's fall, and Rumanian papers were quick to print China's twenty-five-point attack on the Soviet, for Rumania's Red boss preferred an amorphous Communist commonwealth in which Peking would provide steady opposition to Moscow and thus permit Rumania more freedom to maneuver outside the bloc. Jamming of western broadcasts ceased, and trade agreements were made with Britain and the United States.

Gheorghiu-Dej did not embrace as many capitalistic ideas as had other eastern leaders, but he did more business with capitalistic nations. He preferred to buy western plants and skills and to use western technicians to make Rumania an outstanding industrial producer. Yet all this was accomplished at high cost to the people, for wages of both industrial workers and farmers are today very low and the prices of foods and other necessities are high. There is a lack of even passable consumer goods and a great shortage of housing. Farmers endure the worst hardships, for even though some have been allowed to till private plots, the plots are only eight-tenths of an acre in size and the total number amounts to 8 per cent of the arable land. They hate having to march to work each morning for low wages on collectives. There has been no free press to plead their cause. While industrial production increased 12.5 per cent in 1963 and again exceeded goals in 1964, farm production lagged far behind.

For eighteen months Gheorghiu-Dej did not confer with Russian leaders. When he finally did go to Poland to talk with Kosygin, Brezhnev, and other Warsaw Pact leaders, he was the prime dissident of the lot.

Gheorghiu-Dej died in March, 1965, and was succeeded by Nicolae Ceausescu, who has gone even farther in his independence. When in July delegates from fifty-six Communist parties from around the world met in Bucharest, Ceausescu, asserted in an astounding declaration that Rumania was developing economic relations with other countries irrespective of their social systems and on the basis of mutual advantage. Earlier, Rumania had practically withdrawn from the Moscow Pact by reserving the right to decide whether to declare war in defense of the other pact countries. Late in 1965 Rumanian papers made much of their government's attempt to bring about peace negotiations between the United States and North Viet Nam; but Hanoi proved to be adamantly against any negotiation, and Washington reported that nothing had come of this attempt at peace-making.

The Press Today

Rumanians may be freer of Soviet control, but their press is still as enchained as ever. The only difference is that now it is run by Rumanian Communists who follow their own line instead of Moscow's. Newspapers are directed by the council of minsters through its General Administration of Publishing. This monolithic organization not only determines editorial content but operates all printing plants, ink and supply manufacturing, and controls newsprint supply and distribution of publications. Each paper is organized into a collective made up of the entire personnel of all departments. There is an "editorial collegium" headed by the chief editor, and a daily editorial conference plans the material to be printed. Newspapermen are but functionaries with no latitude in their work. They have to be careful, for a slip might mean punishment under a harsh legal code. A five-year school of journalism at Bucharest University turns out properly indoctrinated workers. All newspaper workers must belong to their Communist unions if they wish to work. The General Administration does not concern itself with what might interest the people. It gives them only that information it thinks they should have. All party and union members must subscribe to their papers. The tone of uniformity in all papers is striking: every editorial sounds as if it had been written by the same person. Papers even look alike. Most dailies have only four pages.

Dailies get their news from *Agerpress*, established in 1949, responsible to the council of ministers. It has exclusive right to the collection and distribution of all news and pictures. Until 1960 it received its foreign news from TASS. Now it has exchange agreements also with AFP, Reuters, AP, and UPI as well as the agencies of other east-bloc countries. Headquarters are in Bucharest, to which bureaus in sixteen other principal towns report. It also has correspondents in Moscow, Warsaw, Prague, Budapest, Peking, Berlin, Paris, and Rome. All news is carefully screened before distribution to make sure that nothing dangerous to the regime appears. Its service goes to all dailies, forty-one other newspapers, and the two radio and one television stations.

The number of dailies has decreased markedly from 141 before the war to 33 in 1962 and only 14 in 1964. As in other Communist countries, the press is organized in the usual hierarchy. At the top is *Scanteia*, the chief organ of the Rumanian Workers (Communist party), the mentor, propagandist, and exhorter of the people, corresponding to *Pravda* in the Soviet Union. It claims 1,000,000 circulation, but this would be little more than the enforced subscriptions of party and union members. No circulation figures are available for other dailies in 1964. The only clues are the last claimed figures in 1961. In second place is *Romania Libera*, official organ of the government, similar to *Izvestia* in the Soviet Union, which claimed 200,000. Counted important, also, is *Scanteia Tineretului* (Spark of Youth), which last claimed 300,000. There are five other party and governmental dailies including a sports daily for which no circulations are available. These eight constitute the All-Union or central press supposed to circulate throughout the country.

Only five dailies are listed in provincial cities, all organs of regional party committees. There are weeklies such as *Scanteia Satelor* for farmers; *Contemporanul,* organ of the ministry of culture; *Gazeta Literara* of the writers union; and *Gazeta Invatamantuliu* of the teachers union. House organs are provided for workers in industrial plants and oil fields. In the smaller towns are weekly organs of the district or local party committees. All together the party claims 80 nondaily publications and 276 magazines and other periodicals.

In its 1964 issue of World Communications, UNESCO credited Rumania with thirty-three dailies and a total circulation of 2,986,000, indicating a distribution of 16.1 copies per 100 people. But these figures are four years old and were based on more than twice as many dailies as there are today. It is significant that *Scanteia*'s circulation, despite the diminished number of dailies, is the same 1,000,000 that was claimed in 1960. In addition, it should be remembered that available circulation figures are based on claims and should be discounted along with the round numbers reported from other Communist countries. In an honest audit the ratio of readership would probably be a good deal less than that reported by UNESCO in 1961.

One should also bear in mind that, with high prices, taxes, and average real incomes scarcely above subsistence levels, many Rumanians cannot afford to buy newspapers. Moreover, despite twenty years of propaganda a large part of the population is unhappy about communism and the present existence. These people dare not criticize the system openly, for theirs is one of the most ruthless police states in Europe. Economics, they believe, must provide the guiding force for their country. They have been encouraged by their government's defiance of the Soviet Union, for they feel the latter system is an experiment that has failed. Rumanians have hopes that their leaders might move away from traditional communism to bring them a higher standard of living and more freedoms. The concessions Gheorghiu-Dej had to give to win more popular support were evidence of this discontent. But with the press totally controlled and constantly beating them with propaganda to achieve governmental goals, there is not much they can do but conform. In prewar days Rumanian dailies had considerable advertising, both classified and display; but now that the government owns all business, including retail outlets, there is very little. Most papers have to be subsidized, but that is what the propaganda budget is for.

Rumanians in the United States have pointed out the anomaly of papers titled Free Rumania or Liberty, which the average citizen knows stands for neither freedom nor truth. There is an old Rumanian saying that the stalk which bends does not feel the knife. In the past Rumanians had to bend to Turks, Russians, and Austro-Hungarians. Now for two decades they have had to bend to the Communists, but the author has been told that there are millions in that unhappy land who pray for the day when they can raise their heads as independent Rumanians.

Gheorghiu-Dej died in March, 1965, presumably from penumonia; but for the last two years he had been suffering from cancer. In his last few months he became less truculent toward Russia and tried to mediate Sino-Soviet differences. His death is likely to mean little change, for the party strong men who succeeded him had been fellow architects in his national planning. It certainly meant no change for the press.

The Press of Yugoslavia

Led by Marshal Tito, who dared defy Stalin in 1947, the Yugoslavs have become the front runners in building their own separate road to socialism, and their press has developed a pattern different from that in other east European nations.

Established as a nation in 1918, Yugoslavia is a land of beautiful mountains and valleys, embracing the same area as Illinois and Wisconsin, with a population of 19,292,000. The people who make up this nation, through accidents of geography, religious diversity, and separate fates at the hands of conquerors, developed into dissimilar elements whose hatreds made the Balkans one of the most explosive areas of Europe.

These Slavs from beyond the Dniester River early began migrating into central Europe, not in military campaigns but rather by gradual infiltration into comparatively unoccupied regions. In 400 A.D. Slavs dwelt in the area of present day Poland. In the sixth century fierce Avars, akin to Tartars, pushed them south. Then in the ninth century Magyar hordes crowded them down into the Balkans. Intervening mountains caused them to settle in different valleys separate from each other. Since they could not unite to repel Turkish, Greek, Bulgarian, Hungarian, and Germanic invaders, they crystalized into separate peoples. The Slovenes and Croats eventually fell to the Hapsburgs and accepted the religion and culture of the West. The Serbs, who fought for centuries against Byzantium, nevertheless accepted the Greek Orthodox religion. The Bosnians, Montenegrins, and Macedonians fell under the Turkish yoke for centuries and many adopted the Moslem faith. Only the Montenegrins in their mountains managed to maintain some independence and kept alive the flame of political freedom after it was extinguished in the rest of the Balkans.

First Printing Presses and Papers

In view of this troubled history it is surprising that printing came to the Balkan Slavs within a half century of its birth in western Europe.

Venice, desiring to spread the Catholic faith eastward, in 1492–93 set up presses in Montenegro. Later, between 1548 and 1690, presses appeared in Serbia, Slovenia, and Croatia. Although the products of these presses were only religious works, the Turkish, Austrian, and Hungarian conquerors disapproved of any medium which might unite the peoples or keep alive their culture; and presses were frequently silenced.

But no matter who their conquerors were, there burned in the hearts of the south Slavs a longing for freedom that found its expression in poetry and song, first in Montenegro, where alone this flame could be given expression. However, because the Serbs were so bitterly oppressed by the Turks, their patriotism was the first to find voice in an exile journal, *Slaveno Serpski Magazin,* established by Zaharija Orefelin in Venice in 1768. The journal sought safety in literature, but it also provided Serbian writers an opportunity to communicate their yearnings between the lines. By 1791 Austria, Hungary, and the Italian states, bitterly opposed to the Turks, permitted the publication of small weeklies to agitate for Serbian independence from Turkey. The first was *Serpskija Povsednevnija Novini* edited by Markides Pulja. The Croats and Slovenes were the next to have papers, for they benefited from the rule of the reformer, Emperor Joseph II of Austria, who had lifted censorship in all his dominions. But, intent on completely Germanizing his provinces he insisted that the first Croat paper, *Kroatischer Korrespondent,* had to be printed in German. Croat resentment against Germanization kept this paper small and of little influence. Slovenia had its first paper in 1797 in *Ljubljanska Novize.* In both provinces Austrian censorship, imposed after Joseph's death, forced these papers to be literary. In other south Slav states under the Turks no native papers were permitted.

Serbs Lead Next Advance

Resentment over Turkish misrule, religious persecution, and the brutal massacre of prominent Serbs brought a revolt in 1804 led by George Petrovic, who became famous as Karageorge or Black George. Aided by a simultaneous Russian war against the Sultan, the Serbs by 1807 had driven the Turks out of their province. They were later reconquered but in 1815 a second rising broke out under Milos Obrenovic, a great fighter and diplomat. With the help of Russia and Britain, he won concessions toward self-government; but it was not till after the Russo-Turkish War of 1828–29 that Turkey recognized Serbia's autonomous status under Milos, who ruled with high-handed tyranny till 1838. Yet under his rule the first real Serbian newspaper was founded on Serbian soil. Dimitrije Davidovic, who had published a paper in exile in Vienna, revived his *Novini Srpske* at Kragujevic south of Belgrade. But Milos soon found it "dangerous," and the paper led a harried existence under the censorship of Milos and his successors until it became the official government gazette in 1882. Conditions were not yet propitious for the development of journalism. The intelligentsia were few; most people were illiterate. Still, a beginning was made, a few schools were started, and the sons of the well-to-do went abroad to study and absorb the revolutionary ideas of western Europe.

Croatia had its first paper in its own language when Ljuevit Gaj founded his weekly *Narodne Novini* (The People's Paper) at Agram (now Zagreb) in 1835. It was important because Gaj advocated that the names Croat, Serb, and Slovene be dropped and that all south Slavs call themselves Illyrians. He also advocated the abandonment of sectional dialects and the acceptance of the Serb literary language. Elsewhere in the south Slav states journalism was given no opportunity.

Although he was a ruthless despot, Milos made Serbia independent in all but name, the one state around which other south Slavs might rally in their desire for a united Slav nation. Reaction to the July, 1830, Paris Revolution brought an armed rising in 1834 which forced Milos to agree to a constitution giving considerable powers to an elected assembly. When he suspended it, he was forced to abdicate. One prince followed the other; some were assassinated; others were ousted in military coups. The country was often in chaos. Yet the revolution against Hungary in 1848 and the efforts of the Serbs to help their kinsmen caused an upsurge of national feeling. Danilo Medakovic started a revolutionary paper in Novi Sad in northwest Serbia. Then in 1852 he founded Serbia's first daily, *Srpski Dvenik* (Daily Servian), which for twelve years was the leading Serb paper.

In Croatia and Slovenia the revolution at first promised to bring press liberty. Several papers appeared in 1849 and 1850; but once the Austrians had put down the revolt and restored order, there followed ten years of pitiless reaction and oppression. By the end of the 1850's the press of all the south Slav states had been reduced to eight papers.

The Tumultuous Last Half of the Century

The accession of Milos' son Michael, a more enlightened ruler, brought respite in Serbia, for he introduced western methods in government, broadened the power of the peoples' assembly (the *Skipstuna*), and reorganized the army. He even encouraged the press, and papers representing the growing Liberal and Radical parties came into being. But he became so engrossed in his plans for alliances against the

Turks that he neglected domestic reforms, grew impatient with the *Skipstuna*, reduced it to a mere advisory capacity, and imposed rigid censorship. His plans collapsed with his assassination in 1868.

Meanwhile in Montenegro, Prince Nicholas, to modernize his state and to raise its cultural level, started schools and made education compulsory. In 1867 newspapers were allowed to appear, and soon he gave his people a constitution. But he sought his orientation with Austria, whereas the people wanted union with Serbia. The leading paper at Cetinje, *Glas Kronogaza* (Montenegrin Spokesmen), was completely pro-Serbian. Constitutional government and press freedom irked Nicholas, and in the rest of his reign he ruled as a dictator and suppressed all opposition leaders and papers.

Journalism fared better in Croatia and Slovenia, for the new dual monarchy, Austria-Hungary, granted them considerable autonomy; and the people shared in the cultural advantages of this exposure to the West. The first daily in Croatia, *Obzor* (Survey), appeared in 1860; and in 1867 Slovenia had its first political paper, *Slovenski Narod* (Slavonia People). Soon there were political party organs in several cities, all urging the formation under the Hapsburgs of an autonomous Slavic state. *Serbobran* (Serbian Defender) was especially influential in the formation of a Croat-Serbian coalition. In Bosnia, Herzegovina, and Macedonia journalism was still given no opportunity under the harsh rule of the Turks.

At this point outside events intervened. Turkey was soundly defeated in the Russo-Turkish War of 1877–78, but the great powers of Europe under the "honest brokerage" of Bismarck were fearful of Russian intentions in the Balkans and redrew the map of Europe without consulting the people involved. Serbia and Montenegro were recognized as independent states with some additions to their territories. Austria was allowed to occupy Bosnia and Herzegovina, thus cutting off the Serbs from their kinsmen in other Slav territories. Prince Milan, who had come to power in Serbia in 1868, had proved a harsh and dissolute ruler. He sought safety in complete cooperation with Austria; but his people, and the Radical party in particular, hated Austria. Belgrade became the center of Serbian life and journalism, and the papers continued a courageous agitation for a new constitution. In 1889, after his disastrous invasion of Bulgaria, Milan was forced to grant a constitution which extended the franchise, gave more power to the *Skipstuna*, and, amazingly, guaranteed press freedom. But that liberty was short-lived, for his successor, Alexander, set up a completely reactionary regime which demoralized the press. His tyrannical rule and his scandalous personal life so alienated the army that both the king and the queen were assassinated in a conspiracy that brought to the throne Peter Karageorgevic, grandson of the original Karageorge.

Journalism Rises in Serbia

The new king proved a good monarch who in the years after 1903 gave his country its highest period of constructive development. The constitution of 1889 was restored; tampering with courts, press, or the right of assembly was checked; and Peter set about giving his people a democratic government.

The Serbian press began to flower. In 1903 there appeared a new independent information paper, *Politika*, which was to become Yugoslavia's best all-round newspaper. Soon there were papers publishing in all parts of Serbia with considerable freedom, and by 1905 there were twenty dailies in Belgrade alone, most of them organs of political parties. Of all the Slav states, only Serbia had a free press; and it developed as ultra-political, jingoistic, and chauvinistic, carrying little news, devoting most space to polemics, and promoting the idea of a Greater Serbia with the union of all south Slavs. The one exception was *Politika*, published by the Ribnaker brothers. To get more news they had encouraged the organization of a telegraphic agency under the foreign ministry which made exchange agreements with Reuters. It lent itself to no party and devoted itself to providing complete and impartial news coverage.

Peter's Serbia was obsessed with the plan to liberate all south Slavs. In alliance with Bulgaria, Montenegro, and Greece, Serbia attacked the rapidly disintegrating Turkish empire in the Balkan wars of 1912–13. This enabled her not only to double her territory and population but also, because of her military prowess, to emerge as the political and military leader of all south Slavs.

Russia encouraged Serbian ambitions while, understandably, Austria opposed them. Despite the latter's effort to bar any political comment in the papers of Slovenia and Croatia and despite the complete suppression of papers in Bosnia, nationalistic feeling grew, fed by underground papers. The same thing took place in Montenegro where Nicholas permitted no criticism of Austria.

The Tragedy of World War I

To Austria-Hungary the rising Pan-Slav feeling in her provinces made Serbia a menace. In 1908 she had annexed Bosnia and Herzegovina on the pretext of protecting herself from the Greater Serbian propaganda. In the years that followed, the agitation in the Serbian press heightened her fears. On June 18, 1914, when Crown Prince

Francis Ferdinand was assassinated at Sarajevo by a Bosnian student, Austria had the excuse it needed to crush Serbia. After Serbia's rejection of an unusually severe ultimatum, Austria declared war on the Slavic nation and precipitated World War I.

Austrians quickly captured Belgrade; but the Serbians rallied, drove out the Austrians, and even invaded Bosnia. Late in 1915 the German machine crushed Serbia and drove what remained of her army with King Peter into Albania, whence they were finally evacuated to Corfu. At home the people began a three-year martyrdom.

German-Austrian troops were ruthless in their oppression. All Serbian papers were suppressed; many editors and publishers were shot; the Cyrillic alphabet was prohibited; and only the official papers of the conquerors appeared. Even in Croatia and Slovenia, thousands of political suspects were imprisoned, and many executed. Here all papers were placed under severe censorship. In Bosnia and Herzegovina where the Sarajevo assassination had occurred, oppressions amounted to a terror. Montenegro was under the strict control of the Austrian occupation army. Macedonia lay under the brutal dominion of Bulgaria. The very fury of oppression united all south Slavs, and underground papers kept alive the hopes of the people. By the summer of 1916 the Serbian army, rearmed by the Allies, joined Anglo-French forces before Salonika. In the next year they fought their way back to Serbian soil and finally spearheaded the attack on the Bulgarians as they and the French broke through and pursued Austrians and Germans till on November 1, 1918, they took Belgrade.

The Allies meanwhile had come to look with favor on a south Slav state, and President Woodrow Wilson approved self-determination for the subject nationalities of the old monarchy. The peace treaty created a new state which King Peter proclaimed the kingdom of Serbs, Croats, and Slovenes on December 1, 1918. Other south Slav peoples soon joined. King Peter, who had been incapacitated by illness from wartime hardships, died in 1921 and was succeeded by his son Alexander.

The Postwar Press

The new state was now one of the largest small countries of Europe, with a population of more than 12,000,000 persons as diverse in religion and race as could be brought together. Most were south Slavs but there were many Germans, Italians, Albanians, Greeks, Turks, Rumanians, and Magyars. While there was a desire for union, the many different elements could not pull together. Serbian centralism had won out in the 1921 constitution, but Serbs showed no understanding of other peoples. The nation was split into many political parties fighting each other. In the first ten years there were twenty cabinet crises. Seldom did the Serbs have majorities in the assembly and kept themselves in power by coalitions. Belgrade misrule and interference with the rights of minorities kept the country in turmoil.

This intense partisanship was reflected in the press. The new constitution had guaranteed press freedom, and papers burgeoned throughout the country. Each nationalistic group developed its own press, united at times in defense against foreign nations, as in the four-year dispute with Italy over the Fiume, but usually representing bitterly opposed ideas on domestic questions. By the late twenties the kingdom had 163 political papers, 33 of them dailies. The Croats particularly resented Serbian interference with their affairs; and when Stjepan Radic, leader of the Croat Peasant party, was assassinated during an Assembly debate, the Croats withdrew from parliament and set up their own *Skipstuna* at Zagreb. To prevent dissolution of the state, Alexander proposed its reorganization into seven federal units. When the proposal was not accepted, he suspended the constitution in January, 1929, to restore order, set up a royal dictatorship, and changed the name of the country to Yugoslavia.

The press was reduced to a frightened and often false recorder of events. All parties were abolished and many party organs ceased publication. The remaining newspapers were rigidly censored. With no history of press freedom behind them, editors were coerced into an agreement to print nothing against the king or his regime. The government took over the distribution of papers and made Avala the official agency, feeding papers only what it wanted printed. Yugoslavia was now a tough police state in which most civil liberties disappeared. With no press to defend the people's rights, underground organizations came into being. Police terror was met by underground terrorists till in 1934 Alexander was assassinated by a Macedonian revolutionary at Marseilles.

Alexander's twelve-year-old son was crowned King Peter II, and the late king's brother, Paul, became regent. Paul had been educated in England and set out to create a parliamentary democracy. For a short time in 1935 even censorship was ended. Jubilant editors became so loud in their criticism of the government that they were warned to exercise control or face censorship. Guarded comment on domestic affairs was permitted; but because of the threatening international situation, nothing could be printed which might offend the Axis powers.

Despite its difficulties the press grew till by 1937 there were fifty dailies printed in six different languages. Its character had changed; and because of restrictions the papers had become less political, more informational, and more cultural. Foremost at Belgrade was *Politika* with 165,000 circulation; second was *Vreme* (Times) with 65,000, more popular, presenting condensed news and many pictures. How illiteracy held back the press is indicated by the fact that, despite a population of 13,000,000, total daily circulations were only 760,000.

The Nazis Move In

Hitler had been on the march since 1933, and he had his eyes on the Balkans. Milan Stojadinovic, pro-Nazi premier from 1936 to 1939, considered himself the Führer of Yugoslavia. More than half of Yugo- slav trade was with Germany. Nazi agents overran the country, and German language papers spread the Axis propaganda that there would be no war. Even after Poland had fallen in 1939 the Nazi Minister at Belgrade dictated the line that Yugoslavia would not be attacked. The government tried to keep neutral but on March 31, 1941, it signed a pact with the Axis.

Popular resentment was so great that two days later a coup led by General Dusan Simovitch overthrew Prince Paul's regime and installed an anti-Axis government. The people felt defiled, and they defied Hitler even though they knew they stood alone and could expect no Allied help. Nazi reaction was swift. On April 16 Belgrade was terribly bombed; German armies invaded; Bulgaria, Hungary, and Italy at- tacked. In two weeks Yugoslavia was crushed. Five days later Ger- many, Italy, Bulgaria, and Hungary divided up prostrate Yugoslavia. The Germans, first on the scene, quickly took control of press and radio. All former Yugoslav papers were closed. Four German language dailies and forty weeklies which had previously carried Nazi propa- ganda now became the important papers. The Italians, Bulgarians, and Hungarians followed the same pattern in their areas.

The indominable Yugoslavs did not give up. From well-concealed hideouts in caves and forests, underground newssheets called on the people to rally against their aggressors. Peasants, through their farm cooperatives, covered the country-side; in cities waiters, workmen, housewives, and children joined in the distribution. Guerrillas rallied around Colonel Draja Mihailovich, whose peasant *Chetniks* harried German communications and patrols. As Germany moved her divi- sions to the Russian front, *Chetniks* struck in force; and by August, 1941, they dominated most of Serbia. Once Russia was under attack, south Slav Communists also rose. They were led by Josip Broz, known as Tito, a Croatian metal worker and labor leader who had several times visited Stalin and had kept the Communist underground move- ment alive during the dictatorship. His Partisans proved fanatical fighters. Germans and Italians turned on both *Chetniks* and Partisans, mauled them severely, and took savage measures against the civilian population. Some half million Yugoslavs were killed, but resistance forces fought on.

Mihailovich and Tito could not agree. The former, who had been made war minister by King Peter's government in exile in London, wanted Tito's forces to become part of the Yugoslav army. When Tito refused, Mihailovich charged that the latter was most interested in fighting for Russia and in paving the way for a Communist revolution. Tito would have nothing to do with the old order and accused Mihailovich, because of his lack of aggressiveness, of cooperating with the Axis. Partisans and *Chetniks* slaughtered each other. Both sides had their underground papers, the *Chetniks* their *Ravna Gora*, the Partisans their *Borba*. Both sides, through sympathizers in London, brought to the people broadcasts giving reports of the fighting on many fronts and the progress of their own forces. The leading Slovene underground paper was *Svoboda Ali Smrt* (Freedom or Death).

Tito's Star Rises

Whatever the truth may have been in the Mihailovich-Tito controversy, the British, under pressure from Russia, and because the Partisans seemed more aggressive in fighting Germans, threw their support to Tito and sent him supplies and arms. In December, 1943, Tito set up a provisional government in opposition to Peter's. Russian and Yugoslav forces combined in taking Belgrade and by the end of 1944, with British help, liberated much of the country. Tito announced his plans for a federation of the six south Slav peoples. This solution to the nationality problem appealed to many; and to the multitudes, fed up with the old dictatorial prewar order, Communist promises of a new type of state in which everything would belong to the people made a great impression. Many journalists, too, saw hope in the new Yugoslavia.

Within a week after liberation Belgrade papers were again appearing from bombed out shops. *Politika* was back on the streets selling 120,000 copies, looking much as it did before the war. But there was a difference, for Edvard Ribnaker and many of his staff had fought with the Partisans. By January, 1945, thirty papers were being published in the federated states, many of them former Partisan papers. The old Peasant, Democratic, and Republican parties rose in opposition; but their papers were rigidly censored, for the government was impatient with any opposition to the new National Front that supposedly represented all parties.

In April Tito signed a twenty-year pact with Stalin, after which Yugoslav policy was perfectly coordinated with the Soviet Union's.

Under the Yalta agreement a coalition government was supposed to have been set up representing not only the Partisans but Peter's London government and other party groups. However, all non-Communists were soon forced out; and Tito, backed by the secret police who were responsible for "maintaining order and the right spirit" among the people, had complete control. Prior to the November 11 election all opposing candidates, and the papers which supported them, were persecuted by the police. They refused to participate in the election since it had become apparent that it would be neither free nor fair. As a result the government counted 6,500,000 votes for its candidates, only 700,000 against. Tito declared this proved conclusively that the Yugoslav people rejected any return to the old state of affairs. On November 28, 1945, Tito's Federal Peoples Republic was officially established and the monarchy was abolished. In a single day a docile constituent assembly adopted a new constitution patterned after the Soviet constitution of 1936.

Press Is Made Arm of Communist Party

In keeping with the precept that everything belonged to the people, not only banks, mines, transportation, and industries but also the press were nationalized. This did not mean the people had anything to say about their papers; rather, newspapers were made a propaganda weapon of the party leadership, which set up its own publishing enterprises and a news agency, *Tanjug*, which drew foreign news largely from TASS so that all dailies might be fed proper information. The press was organized on the Soviet model with a national press represented by such papers as *Borba* (Struggle), chief organ of the party in the same position as *Pravda* in Moscow; *Rad* (Labor), trade union organ similar to *Trud* in Russia; *Narodna Armia*, organ of the ministry of national defense; and *Omlandia* for Communist youth. In the same pattern a middle press was organized with organs of the Peoples Front in each of the federal subdivisions, and a lower press was set up in smaller cities and towns. By issuing editions in both Cyrillic and Roman type, the national papers were able to reach persons all over the country; and by 1947 Yugoslavia's dailies were claiming 1,000,000 circulation.

During this period Yugoslavia's press constantly railed against capitalistic imperialism in the United States and Britain. At home the press was used in a gigantic propaganda effort to support reconstruction. The country had suffered tremendous damage in the war. Housing was terribly scarce, railroads were crippled, and many industries were bombed out. Great numbers of young Slavs were rallied; and with UNRRA help, a start was made on rebuilding railroads, motor transportation systems, and factories and enrolling small farmers in collectives. At the time a determined effort was made to root out enemies of the new regime. Many prewar leaders were imprisoned; Draja Mihailovich was found guilty of treason and executed.

Break with Stalin Brings Change

In 1948 Tito rebelled against Stalin's attempt to set up joint trading companies which would have meant complete economic subordination. To Stalin this was heresy. Furthermore he recognized that, unlike other satellite states, Yugoslavia's regime had not been set up by Moscow emissaries but by Tito and his Partisans, whom Stalin considered unreliable. He not only denounced Tito but in June, 1948, expelled Yugoslavia from the Cominform; all other satellite states joined in a complete boycott. By the end of the year Yugoslavia was in deep economic trouble, and Tito turned to Britain and the United States for help.

The Yugoslav press at first reflected shock and worry, then turned to bitterness and anger against the Soviet Union for imposing Russian imperialism on other neighbor states, trying to exploit them for its own interests, and interfering in their internal affairs. At the same time the press began giving a fairer picture of the West, particularly of the United States. During the Korean War Communist aggression was decried in Yugoslav papers.

Led by Tito, Yugoslavia began to devise a new type of socialism that was far less rigid than the old Stalinism and more concerned with the people's problems. The new 1953 constitution gave greater power to local governments and more self-government to factories through workers' councils. The councils spread through industry and brought increased production. They were also set up on newspapers and gave workers more independence. Significant was the change in agriculture where collectivization was practically abandoned and most peasants became independent farmers, participating in general cooperatives only for the buying of equipment, seed and for the sale of farm products.

Stalin died in 1953 and Khrushchev, after two years of continuing the hard line toward Yugoslavia, came to Belgrade to improve relations and affirmed a new understanding of co-existence.

Reaction Sets In

The new independence of writers worried party leaders and brought a reimposition of party discipline. In 1955 Milovan Djilas, a close friend of Tito, president of the National Assembly, and a leading

writer, revolted against this tightening of controls. In *Borba* he attacked Communist bureaucracy as more dangerous than capitalism and
declared the Leninist type of party and state as outdated. He and
Vladimir Dedijer, the editor of *Borba*, who defended him, were
arrested and Dedijer was ousted from the newspaper. After Djilas, in
statements to American newspapers and magazines, had advocated the
formation of a new party in Yugoslavia and had praised the Hungarian
Revolution he was sentenced to three years imprisonment. When his
book *New Class* appeared in New York, he was retried and sentenced
to an additional seven years.

The new 1960 press law enumerated in detail the obligations of the
press to the state and made printing stories or articles injurious to the
honor and reputation of Yugoslavia, the president of the republic, and
other public officials criminal offenses. Some foreign correspondents
were expelled for insulting Tito and their papers banned.

In the following years Tito continued his careful balancing act
between East and West. He was bitterly attacked by Red China,
Albania, and Bulgaria for siding with the U.S.S.R. in the Sino-Soviet
split. In a friendly gesture he visited the United States, but he also won
closer friendship with Khrushchev. Growing trade with both East and
West brought prosperity, and the economic condition of the people
improved. But in 1962 there came a marked drop in both farm and
industrial production. Tito, through his press, blamed conditions on
too much liberalism. During the good years there had been hope of
greater freedom; and Edvard Kardelj, vice president, had spoken of the
hope that the state controls would wither away. At the same time he
pointed out that as long as anti-socialist forces persisted, the rights of
Yugoslavs would have to be restricted. Therefore, much tighter
controls were instituted in 1963, and greater power was concentrated
in the central government. Industrial production rose during 1963 and
1964, but inflation brought higher prices and labor unrest. Tito spoke
of his recognition of the inadequacy of wages in many industries.
When Khrushchev was deposed in 1964, Tito accepted Brezhnev's
explanation but followed with praise of the former Russian leader.
Nevertheless a trade agreement was arranged calling for a 35 per cent
increase each way in Yugoslav-Soviet commerce.

The people of Yugoslavia in 1965 were enjoying a better life than
those in most other east European nations. Stores in cities were well
stocked with a wide variety of consumer goods. But the people were
beginning to be concerned that the government's devaluation of the
dinar, to attract more tourist trade, might increase prices. Tito tightened his press controls during the year, but Yugoslav papers still gave

their readers more news of the world and of east and west Europe than even the papers of the Soviet Union. Following Tito's lead, newspapers in late 1965 bitterly attacked the United States for its stepped up war in Viet Nam, insisting that this conflict could be settled only by negotiation.

What Is Yugoslav Press Like Today?

In 1964 Yugoslavia reported 18 dailies, three less than the previous year, 12 papers published two or three times a week, 184 weeklies, plus 1,571 magazines and other periodicals. Total daily circulation was 1,392,000, which amounted to 7.2 copies per 100 persons, a lower ratio of readership than in any western European nation and lower than some other east-bloc countries. Some other Communist states make large round-figured claims for their principal dailies and report no circulations for all other papers. Yugoslavia, however, gives circulations for all her dailies; and these appear to be reasonably accurate. Yet, it is evident that a little less than one-third of Yugoslavian families in a population of 19,292,000 buys a daily paper. Does this represent a certain indifference to a party propaganda press, since only 1,035,003 persons belong to the party? It cannot be poverty, for Yugoslavs are relatively well-paid. Her 23 per cent illiteracy, as reported in 1961, may be a factor though her widespread educational system is reducing this steadily. Some men may see dailies in their coffee shops, but most families apparently read only the local weeklies which almost every town has. It is possible also that many rely on their forty-four radio and three television stations which were made very powerful to drown out broadcasts from other nations.

Yet the Yugoslav daily press is the most independent in Eastern Europe; it provides its readers more news of the world and the nation than do any other Communist dailies, and reports it rather accurately. There are no privately owned papers. Those in Belgrade are owned outright by the Socialist Alliance of the Working People of Yugoslavia; those in other cities are owned by the local branches of the Socialist Alliance. Papers are printed in Serbo-Croat, Croatian, Slovenian, Macedonian, and other languages to meet the needs of the people in the different republics and also in Albanian, Bulgarian, Czech, Italian, Hungarian, and Turkish for minorities. Unlike some other east-European nations, Yugoslavia is almost self-sufficient in newsprint; hence, her dailies run larger than those in the Soviet Union, often sixteen or more pages. They are lively in content and more interesting in appearance than other Communist papers.

One thing different about this press is its management by workers' councils made up of editorial, mechanical, and administrative representatives. The council names managers, decides editorial and financial policy, divides profits between capital improvements and bonuses for workers. It was the author's impression, from talking with Yugoslav editors, that they have more freedom in putting out their papers and are less subject to government instruction than any other similar group in east Europe. Only stories involving critical government policy or fast-breaking international events are likely to be held up till the line can be determined. Criticism is permitted, but limited to the functioning of the system, the errors and mismanagement of bureaucrats; it is never directed against Yugoslavia's special brand of socialism or against Tito.

Another difference is the unusual financial setup. Because the government owns all distributive organizations, there is little advertising except classified advertising, some display ads from state stores, and other public announcements. A few larger papers fill from 13 to 17 per cent of their space to such matter. The advertising income is not large; and since most papers are sold on newsstands and circulations are small, the usual sources of newspaper income would be insufficient to meet costs. But under the Yugoslav system of state publishing enterprises, eight large publishing firms, located in the principal cities, print not only their own papers but others for their areas in addition to magazines, reviews, and other periodicals. The profits from these operations, plus what circulation and advertising income they get, enables the eight firms to meet costs as well as make profits. This system has apparently freed the Yugoslav press from the financial tutelage of the state characteristic of other Communist nations.

Financial independence has resulted in intensification of competition between papers. While the rest of the Communist press is still rigid and monotonous, Yugoslav papers compete for readers by means of lively makeup, cartoons, comic strips, detective serials, spicy love stories, and even crime reporting, unless a murder involves a government official. Because the purpose of this press is the social and economic education of the people, good space is given to foreign news and to commentaries and articles on home affairs. *Tanjug* today depends on TASS for only a small percentage of its news; much more comes from Reuters, Associated Press, AFP, twenty-one other agencies, and from *Tanjug*'s correspondents in fourteen world capitals. Yugoslavs are very sports-minded; hence, papers carry good sports pages. There is always a local page and a page or two of cultural material. To attract readers there are entertainment features, columns for women, departments for children, elaborately illustrated feature articles and even competitions for prizes. Yugoslav newspapermen insist that their press is free, though they admit this freedom has limitations. Certainly it is much freer than that in other Communist countries; yet neither press, radio nor television are actually free, for they represent the propaganda arm of the party which rules the nation.

Only a small percentage of the people belong to the party; but to the great masses who had so little under prewar regimes, the accomplishments since 1945—the growing industrialization, the new housing, the workers' councils in factories, the freeing of farmers from collectives—all have given them a feeling that theirs is a nation of boundless energy which has pulled itself up by the bootstraps. They may grumble but they go along with Tito because of what he has done for his country. Propaganda dins at them through newspapers, radio, and television. That these controlled voices have sometimes been defiant of the Soviet Union does not make them any less the mouthpieces of a totalitarian state. Although their masters represent separatists within the Communist family, they nevertheless follow the same pattern of authoritarian regulation.

REPRESENTATIVE PAPERS

Borba (Struggle)—Published in the capital, Belgrade. Chief organ of the Socialist Alliance of Working People of Yugoslavia (Communist party). Morning daily except Thursday; publishes one edition in capital, one in Zagreb. Combined circulation 362,000.

Politika—Published in Belgrade. Formerly an independent paper; now an official organ. Follows its old tradition and places greatest emphasis on news. A morning paper with 290,000 daily and 280,000 Sunday. Largest circulation in Yugoslavia.

Vecernji Novosti (Evening News)—A more popular paper. Published in Belgrade every day except Sunday. Circulation 155,000.

Kommunist—Most influential of political weeklies and the ideological mentor of all papers. Publishes Thursdays in Belgrade in Serb-Croat in both Cyrillic and Latin alphabets; printed Thursdays at Ljubljana in Slovenian; printed Fridays at Skoplje in Macedonian. Claims combined circulation of 234,000.

Delo—The party organ for Slovenia, the little *Pravda* of this republic. Morning daily except Thursday. Claims 75,000 circulation. Published at Ljubljana.

Oslobodjenje (Liberation)—Chief party organ for Bosnia-Herzegovina. Sarajevo morning paper with 140,000 circulation daily and 90,000 Sunday.

Nova Makedonija—Chief organ for Macedonia; morning daily with 45,000 circulation. Published at Skoplje.

Vjesnik (Messenger)—Party organ for Croatia. Published mornings at Zagreb except Tuesday. Printed in Latin type; circulation 98,000 daily, 105,000 Sunday. For Yugoslavia, rather sensational makeup: many pictures, much entertainment material, many comic strips.

Bibliography

These bibliographies are included to aid those persons who wish to pursue further, different aspects of the press problems presented in this history of the press in Europe.

A general bibliography is presented suggesting sources covering the entire area to provide background for understanding the historical, political, economic, and international factors which have shaped the press or have been shaped by the press. Then there are listed the books, periodical articles, and other sources which apply to the particular country.

GENERAL

Black, C. E., and E. C. Helmreich. *Twentieth Century Europe.* New York, 1950.

Chamberlain, Harris, Bayley. *This Age of Conflict.* New York, 1950.

Cook, Don. *Floodtide in Europe.* New York, 1965.

Desmond, Robert. *The Press and World Affairs.* New York, 1937.

Dunn, Watson. *International Yearbook of Advertising.* New York, 1964.

Ergang, Robert. *Europe from Renaissance to Waterloo.* New York, 1939.

Graham, M. W. *New Governments of Europe.* New York, 1924.

Gunther, John. *Inside Europe Today.* New York, 1936, 1938, 1961.

Hughes, Henry S. *Contemporary Europe.* Englewood Cliffs, N.J., 1961.

International Press Institute. *Improvement in Information.* Zurich, 1952.

———. *Government Pressures on the Press.* Zurich, 1955.

———. *The Press in Authoritarian Countries.* Zurich, 1959.

Library of Congress. *European Press Today.* Washington, D.C., 1949.

Lichtheim, George. *The New Europe.* New York, 1963.

Merrill, John C., C. R. Bryan, and Marvin Alisky. *The Foreign Press.* Baton Rouge, 1964.

Nafziger, Ralph. *International News and the Press: an Annotated Bibliography.* New York, 1950.

Peddie, R. A. *Printing, A Short History.* London, 1927.

Shotwell, James T., *et al. Governments of Continental Europe.* New York, 1940.

UNESCO. *Statistics of Newspapers and Other Periodicals*. Paris, 1959.
————. *Technical Needs of Press, Film, Radio*. Paris, 1947–56–57–58.
————. *World Communications*. Paris and New York, 1950–51, 56, 64.
Other Sources. Files of Britannica books of the year. *Editor and Publisher* and its International Yearbooks, New York *Times*, London *Times*, Chicago *Daily News* and Chicago *Tribune*, International Press Institute Reports. Also files of *Cahiers de la Presse, Gazette, Journalism Quarterly, World's Press News* and *Zeitungswissenschaft*. Press directories available from many of these countries. Much of the information about Europe and the conditions of the European press today was gathered on a number of trips to the Continent since World War II. Interviews with newspapermen, editors, and publishers—some living in their own countries and some in exile—have also proved very valuable. *Atlantic* reports, *Newsweek*, *Time*, and *U.S. News and World Report* are useful for current updating.

BY COUNTRY

Great Britain

BOOKS

Andrews, Alexander. *History of British Journalism*. London, 1859.
Andrews, W. E. *The British Newspapers*. London, 1952.
Belloc, Hilaire. *The Free Press*. London, 1949.
Blake, George. *The Press and the Public*. London, 1930.
Bleyer, W. G. *Main Currents in American Journalism*. Boston, 1927.
Blumenfeld, R. D. *The Press in My Time*. London, 1933.
Bourne, H. R. Fox. *English Newspapers*. London, 1887.
Bowman, W. D. *The Story of the Times*. New York, 1931.
Camrose, W. B. *British Newspapers and Their Controllers*. London, 1947.
Clark, Tom. *Northcliffe in History*. London, 1950.
Cranfield, G. A. *Development of Provincial Newspapers*. London, 1962.
Cronin, A. J. *The Northern Light*. New York, 1958.
Cudlip, Hugh. *Publish and Be Damned*. London, 1953.
Emery, Edwin. *The Press and America*. New York, 1962.
Frank, Joseph. *Beginnings of English Newspapers*. Boston, 1961.
Fyfe, Hamilton. *Sixty Years of Fleet Street*. London, 1949.
Gerald, J. E. *British Press Under Economic Controls*. Minneapolis, 1956.
Gibbs, Philip. *The Journalist's London*. London, 1952.
Grant, James. *The Newspaper Press*. London, 1871.
Hall, W. P., and R. G. Albion. *History of England and the British Empire*. New York, 1953.
Harris, Wilson. *The Daily Press*. Cambridge, 1943.
Herd, Harold. *The March of Journalism*. London, 1952.
Hindle, Wilfrid. *The Morning Post*. London, 1937.
Hudson, Derek. *British Journalists and Newspapers*. London, 1945.
Hunt, F. Knight. *The Fourth Estate*. London, 1850.

Innes, H. A. *Press a Neglected Factor in 20th Century History*. London, 1949.
Kingsley, Martin. *The Press the Public Wants*. London, 1947.
Morrison, Stanley. *The English Newspaper from 1622*. Cambridge, 1932.
Mott, Frank L. *American Journalism*. New York, 1962.
Pemberton, Max. *Lord Northcliffe*. London, 1923.
Political and Economic Planning. *Report on British Press*. London, 1938.
Robbins, Allen P. *The Newspaper Today*. London, 1956.
Royal Commission on the Press. *1947–49 Report*. London.
Schaeber, Matthias. *Some Forerunners of the Newspaper*. Philadelphia, 1929.
Scott-James, R. A. *The Influence of the Press*. London, 1926.
Siebert, F. S. *Freedom of the Press in England*. Champaign-Urbana, Ill., 1952.
Symon, James. *The Press and Its Story*. London, 1914.
Taylor, H. A. *The British Press, A Critical Survey*. London, 1961.
Williams, Frances. *Dangerous Estate, The Anatomy of Newspapers*. London, 1957.
Williamson, J. A. *The Evolution of England*. London, 1945.
Wilson, McNair. *Lord Northcliffe, A Study*. Philadelphia, 1927.

PERIODICALS

Bakeless, John. "Christopher Marlowe and the Newsbooks," *Journalism Quarterly*, XIV (1937).
Bleyer, W. G. "The Beginnings of English Journalism," *Journalism Quarterly*, VIII (1931).
Casey, Ralph. "The British Press," *Journalism Quarterly*, XIV (1937).
Desmond, Robert. "Journalism in England in 1933," *Journalism Quarterly*, X (1933).
Fraser, Peter. "The British Government's Use of Parliamentary Publicity in the Past," *Gazette*, XI, No. 2-3 (1965).
Gerald, J. E. "The British Press Council," *Journalism Quarterly*, XXXVI (1959).
Levin, Rene. "Advertising Media in Britain," *Gazette*, XI (1965).
Noah, James E. "Oliver Cromwell, Protector, and the English Press," *Journalism Quarterly*, XXXIX (1962).
Robson, Norman. "Official Secrets Act and the British Press," *Journalism Quarterly*, XV (1938).
Rosenberg, Marvin. "Rise of England's First Daily Newspaper," *Journalism Quarterly*, XXX (1953).
Schlack, Harry G. "Fleet Street in the 1880's," *Journalism Quarterly*, XLI (1964).
Siebert, Frederick. "Regulation of the Press in the 17th Century," *Journalism Quarterly*, XIII (1936).
Siebert, Frederick. "Taxes on Publications in England in the 18th Century," *Journalism Quarterly*, XXI (1944).
Taylor, H. A. "The British Concept of Freedom of the Press," *Gazette*, XI (1965).
Warr, Peter, and Knapper, Chris. "A Content Analysis of the English National Daily Press," *Gazette*, XI (1965).

OTHER SOURCES

Press Sections of *New Statesman*, London.
Institute of Journalists Journal.
British Press Directories.

Sweden

BOOKS

Ander, Oscar. *The Building of Modern Sweden.* Rock Island, Ill., 1958.
Anderson, Ingvar. *Newspapers in Sweden.* London, 1956.
Anderson, Nils. *Dagspressen i Sverige.* Stockholm, 1948.
Bjurman, Gunnar. *Den Svenska Pressen Förr och Nu.* Stockholm, 1929.
Childs, Marquis. *Sweden, The Middle Way.* New York, 1948.
———. *Democracy, Collective Bargaining in Sweden.* New Haven, Conn., 1930.
Ekman, Ernst. *Svenska Tidningskungar.* Uppsala, Sweden, 1924.
Fleisher, Wilfred. *Sweden, the Welfare State.* New York, 1956.
Göranson, Jean. *Aftonbladet.* Uppsala, Sweden, 1937.
Grimberg, C. *History of Sweden.* Stockholm, 1935.
Hedin, Naboth. *Sweden, the Dilemma of a Neutral Foreign Policy Association.* New York, 1943.
Herlitz, N. *Sweden, Modern Democracy on Ancient Foundations.* Minneapolis, 1939.
Hinshaw, David. *Sweden, Champion of Peace.* New York, 1949.
Joesten, Joachim. *Stalwart Sweden.* Garden City, N.Y., 1943.
Kenney, R. *Northern Tangle, Scandinavia in the War.* London, 1946.
Key, Emil. *Svenska Tidningspressens Historia.* Stockholm, 1883.
Pers, Anders Y. *Newspapers in Sweden.* Stockholm, 1954.
———. *The Swedish Press.* Stockholm, 1963.
Ronblom, H. K. *Tryckfriheten i Sverige.* Stockholm, 1940.
Sylwan, Otto. *Svenska Pressens Historia.* Lund, Sweden, 1896.
———. *Tidnings Pressens Historia.* Stockholm, 1902.
Svanstrom, Ragnar, and C. F. Palmstierna. *History of Sweden.* London, 1934.
Wieselgren, Harald. *Lars Johan Hierta.* Stockholm, 1881.

PERIODICALS

Bellquist, Eric. "Emergency Regulations and the Press in Sweden," *Journalism Quarterly* (March, 1938).
Benson, Ivan. "Neutrality and Swedish Press Freedom," *Journalism Quarterly* (March, 1940).
Bjurman, Gunnar. "Press Is Modern Yet 300 Years Old," *World's Press News* (October 2, 1947).
Dahlgren, Sten. "Legislation Governing Swedish Press," *Journalism Quarterly* (September, 1943).
"Guide to Foreign Press—Sweden," *New Europe* (May 16, 1918).
Hoyt, Stuart. "Swedish Press Laws," *Journalism Quarterly* (September, 1948).

Oiseth, Howard. "News Agency Practices in Scandinavia," *Journalism Quarterly* (March, 1938).
Walz, Jay. "Peace Is No Fun for Sweden," *Saturday Evening Post* (February 5, 1944).

OTHER SOURCES

The libraries of the Universities of Stockholm, Uppsala, and Göteborg. The author is particularly grateful to Mr. Ivar Hallvig, president of the Swedish Newspaper Publishers Association, for his many helpful suggestions on this chapter.

Denmark

BOOKS

Andrews, John. *History of Revolutions in Denmark*. London, 1874.
Bain, R. N. *Scandinavia, 1513 to 1800*. Cambridge, Eng., 1905.
Birch, John H. *Denmark in History*. London, 1938.
Cavling, Henrik. *Journalist Liv*. Copenhagen, 1930.
Dahl, Svend. *Avisen i Dag*. Copenhagen, 1956.
Danstrup, John. *History of Denmark*. Copenhagen, 1948.
Eliassen, Peter. *Ritzaus Bureau 1866–1916*. Copenhagen, 1916.
Hansen, A. P. *International Nyhedsformidling*. Copenhagen, 1953.
Hjelje, Bernt. *Dagspressen og Samfundet*. Copenhagen, 1951.
Joesten, Joachim. *Rats in the Larder*. New York, 1939.
Jones, Hugh. *Modern Denmark*. London, 1927.
Kjaer-Hansen, Ulf. *Danske Dagspressens Udvikling*. Copenhagen, 1946.
———. *Avisalaget i Kobenhavn*. Copenhagen, 1955.
Lauring, Palle. *History of the Kingdom of Denmark*. Copenhagen, 1960.
Palmer, Paul. *Denmark*. London, 1945.
Pedersen, Oluf. *Den Politiske Modstand under Besaettelsen*. Copenhagen, 1946.
Pedersen, Martin. *Dagspressen under Debat*. Copenhagen, 1950.
Rasting, Carl. *Presseretten*. Copenhagen, 1951.
Rothary, Agnes E. *Denmark, Kingdom of Reason*. New York, 1931.
Starke, Viggo. *Denmark in World History*. Philadelphia, 1963.
Stangerup, Hakon. *Presse Frihed og Arbejdefrihed*. Copenhagen, 1951.
Stangerup, Hakon, et al. *Storre Danske Journalister*. Copenhagen, 1956.
Steinmetz, Eigil. *Pressen og Censuren*. Copenhagen, 1952.
Thorsen, Svend. *Newspapers in Denmark*. Copenhagen, 1953.
Von Jessen, Franz. *200 Years of Berlingske Tidende*. Copenhagen, 1949.

PERIODICALS

Agerstop, Torben. "The Daily Press in Denmark," *Gazette*, II, No. 4 (1957).
Andersen, Martin. "The Danish Press," *Gazette*, IX, No. 2 (1963).
Buschardt, Leo, and Helge Tonneson. "Illegal Press in Denmark Under Occupation," *Gazette*, IX, No. 2 (1963).
Dodge, Daniel. "Great Newspapers of Continental Europe," *Bookman* (July, 1900).
Redlich, Monica. "Denmark and Its Papers," *Spectator* (May 5, 1939).

Norway

BOOKS

Baden, Gustav, and Andreas Feldborg. *History of Norway.* London, 1917.
Beyer, Harald. *History of Norwegian Literature.* New York, 1957.
Bourneuf, Alice. *Norway, the Planned Revival.* Boston, 1958.
Braekstad, O. *Constitution of Norway.* London, 1905.
Broehm, Herman. *History of German Occupation.* Lippilsberg, Norway, 1957.
Eide, Richard. *Norway's Press, 1940–1945.* Stillwater, Okla., 1948.
Gjerset, Knut. *History of the Norwegian People.* New York, 1915.
Johnsen, Gunnlak. *Den Illegala Press.* Oslo, 1945.
Johnson, A. *Norway, Her Invasion and Occupation.* Decatur, Ga., 1948.
Keilhan, W. C. *Norway in World History.* London, 1945.
Kirkvaag, Ole. *Arbeiderpressen i Norge.* Oslo, 1935.
Larson, Karen. *A History of Norway.* Princeton, N.J., 1948.
Luihn, Hans. *De Illegale Avisene.* Oslo, 1960.
Nielsen, Ynvar. *Norge's Historia efter 1814.* Oslo, 1892.
Oisang, Per. *The Press of Norway.* Unpublished Medill Research Report by a former underground editor. 1946.
Oslo University. *Norske Avisor 1763 to 1920.* Oslo Library, 1924.
Petersen, K. *Den Konservativa Pressforening.* Oslo, 1917.
Winsnes, Fredrik. *Omrids av Norsk Presserett.* Oslo, 1930.
Worm, Muller. *Norway Revolts Against the Nazis.* London, 1941.

PERIODICALS

Brunvand, Olav. "The Underground Press in Norway," *Gazette,* IX, No. 2 (1963).
Christensen, A. R. "The Norwegian Press," *Gazette,* IX, No. 2 (1963).
Grassman, Paul. "Die Anfange der Norwegischen Presse," *Zeitungswissenschaft* (Jan. 1, 1936).
Hallen, Burgit. "Norway's Underground Press," *Journalism Quarterly,* XXIV (1947).
Oiseth, Howard. "News Agency Practices in Scandinavia," *Journalism Quarterly,* XXIV (1947).

OTHER SOURCES

Facts about Norway from *Aftonposten,* 1948 on; from Norway Yearbooks, 1948 on; from Norske Annonsers Forening Avisernas Opplagoppgaver.

Finland

BOOKS

Enckell, Arvid. *Democratic Finland.* London, 1948.
Hannula, J. O. *Finland's Wars of Independence.* London, 1939.
Hinshaw, David. *Heroic Finland.* New York, 1952.
Hornborg, Eirick. *Det Fria Finland.* Stockholm, 1957.
Jackson, John H. *Finland.* New York, 1940.
Jutikkala, Eino. *History of Finland.* New York, 1962.
Langdon, Davis J. *Finland: First Total War.* London, 1948.

Lundin, C. L. *Finland in Second World War*. Bloomington, Ind., 1957.
Mazour, A. G. *Finland Between East and West*. Princeton, N.J., 1956.
Shearman, Hugh. *Finland: Adventures of a Small Power*. New York, 1950.
Toivola, Urhu. *Introduction to Finland*. Helsinki, 1960.
Wuorinen, John H. *Nationalism in Modern Finland*. New York, 1931.
———. *Finland and World War II*. New York, 1948.

PERIODICALS

Bess, Demaree. "Valiant Is the Word for Finland," *Saturday Evening Post* (October 12, 1946).
———. "Finland Has Not Surrendered to Russia," *Saturday Evening Post* (June 6, 1948).
"Finland," *Time* (July 21, 1952).
Finnish Foreign Ministry. "The Finnish Press," Pamphlet (1947).
Gronvick, Axel. "The Press of Finland," *World's Press News* (December 8, 1949).
Gruenbeck, Max. "Die Presse Finlands," *Zeitungswissenschaft* (May 15, 1930).
Hamburger, Ernst. "La Presse Finlandaise," *Cahiers de la Presse* (April–June, 1938).
Lauren, George. "Finland's Daily and Periodical Press," *World's Press News* (December 24, 1935).
Pederson, A. E. "Kekkonen and the Finish Press," *Journalism Review* (1962).
Tornudd, Allan. "The Press of Finland," *World's Press News* (July 11, 1936).
Waldrop, Gayle. "The Daily Newspaper in Finland," *Journalism Quarterly*, XXXIV (Spring, 1957).

OTHER SOURCES

"The Character of the Finnish Press," Mimeographed survey supplied by Finnish Foreign Office.
Bulletins and Information, supplied by Joshua Powers, International Press Representative, New York.
Data supplied by P. Hankkula, Oy Nainos Advertising Agency, Helsinki.
Data from Finnish Information Office, New York.
Files of *Finn Facts*, Finnish-American Chamber of Commerce, N.Y.
By-laws and Reports of Finnish Union of Journalists; Finnish Yearbooks.
Correspondence with Prof. John Wuorinen.

Germany

BOOKS

Brunhaber, Joseph. *Das Deutsche Zeitungswesen*. Leipzig, 1908.
Bullock, Alan. *Hitler, A Study in Tyranny*. London, 1954.
Busch, Moritz. *Bismarck, Secret Pages in His History*. New York, 1902.
Deuel, Wallace. *People Under Hitler*. New York, 1942.
Erler, Kurt. *Von der Macht der Presse in Deutschland*. Berlin, 1911.
Ettlinger, Harold. *The Axis on the Air*. New York, 1943.
Hale, Oron J. *The Captive Press in the Third Reich*. Princeton, N.J., 1964.
Halperin, S. W. *Germany Tried Democracy*. New York, 1946.
Henderson, E. P. *History of Germany*. New York, 1902.

Jarman, T. L. *The Rise and Fall of Nazi Germany.* New York, 1964.
Kirchner, Joachim. *Die Deutschen Zeitschriften.* Wiesbaden, 1958.
Koszyk, Kurt. *Zwischen Kaiserreich und Dictatur.* Heidelberg, 1958.
Lochner, Louis. *The Goebbels Diaries.* New York, 1948.
Mendelssohn, Peter. *Zeitungstadt, Berlin.* Berlin, 1959.
Mowrer, Edgar A. *Germany Turns the Clock Back.* New York, 1933.
Prutz, Robert E. *Geschichten des Deutschen Journalismus.* Hanover, 1845.
Rennert, Georg. *Die Ersten Postzeitungen.* Berlin, 1940.
Roberts, Stephen. *The House That Hitler Built.* New York, 1938.
Schottenloher, Carl. *Flugblatt und Zeitung.* Berlin, 1922.
Schulze, Heinz. *Die Presse im Urteil Bismarcks.* Leipzig, 1930.
Scott, Jonathan. *Five Weeks.* New York, 1927.
Shirer, William. *Rise and Fall of the Third Reich.* New York, 1960.
Sington-Weidenfelt, Derrick. *The Goebbels Experiment.* New Haven, Conn., 1943.
Solomon, Ludwig. *Geschichte des Deutschen Zeitungswesen.* Leipzig, 1906.
Verlag, Archiv und Kartie. *Presse in Fesseln.* Berlin, 1947.

PERIODICALS

Blücher, Viggo G. "Content Analysis—East German Press," *Gazette,* V, No. 1 (1959).
Brandt, Joseph A. "Testing Time for West German Press," *Journalism Quarterly,* XXXIV (Spring, 1957).
Brooks, Robert C. "Lese Majesty in Germany," *Bookman* (June, 1904).
Collier, Price. "German Political Parties and the Press," *Scribners* (December, 1912).
Dovifat, Emil. "The German Press Council," *Gazette,* V, No. 1, (1959).
Fischer, Henry. "Great Papers of Continental Europe," *Bookman* (January, 1900).
Hirsch, Felix. "German Press Yesterday and Tomorrow," *Current History* (August, 1945).
Hofmann, Josef. "CDU Press in Federal Republic," *Gazette,* V, No. 1 (1959).
Koszyk, Kurt. "German Papers with Socialist Tendency," *Gazette,* V, No. 1 (1959).
Löffler, Martin. "Legal Position of West German Press," *Gazette,* V, No. 1 (1959).
Lowe, Charles. "German Press in 19th Century," *Fortnightly Review* (December, 1891).
Newman, E. "Regimentation of German Thought," *Living Age* (December, 1939).
Victor, Walter. "German Press Must Start from Scratch," *Quill* (November–December, 1945).
Williams, J. Emlyn. "Journalism in Germany 1933," *Journalism Quarterly,* X (December, 1933).

OTHER SOURCES

Correspondence with German editors, UNESCO officials, and U.S. High Commissioners Office.

Wayne Jordan's mimeographed report on German Press, 1953.
Schafer and Wittgen Internationaler Press Katalog, 1961–62.
Files of Leitfaden, German press directories for eighteen years.

Belgium

BOOKS

Cammerts, Emile. *Belgium*. London, 1921.
de Meeus, Adrian. *History of the Belgians*. New York, 1962.
Eppstein, John. *Belgium*. Cambridge, 1944.
Gores, John Albert. *Belgium Under Occupation*. Berkeley, Calif., 1945.
Massart, Jean. *The Secret Press of Belgium*. New York, 1918.
Omond, C. W. T. *Belgium and Luxembourg*. London, 1923.
Press Ass'n of Belgium. *Livre Commemorativ*. Brussels, 1949.
Reed, T. H. *Government and Politics of Belgium*. New York, 1924.
Stigns, Marcel. *De Pers en de Internationale Betrekkingen de Vlaamse Gids*. Brussels, 1948.
Vander Essen, Leon. *A Short History of Belgium*. Chicago, 1920.
Vander Linden, H. *Belgium, The Making of a Nation*. London, 1920.
Whitlock, Brand. *Belgium, A Personal Narrative*. New York, 1919.

PERIODICALS

"Before You Advertise in Belgium," *World's Press News* (March 4, 1937).
"Belgium's Clandestine Journalism," *Literary Digest* (March 10, 1917).
"Die Politische Presse Belgiens," *Zeitungswissenschaft* (January 15, 1929).
Dons, Herman. "La Liberté de la Presse en Belgique," *Cahiers de la Presse* (January–March, 1939).
"How Libre Belgique Defied Death and Kaiser," *Literary Digest* (March 1, 1919).
Kobler, J. "Needle in the Nazis," *Saturday Evening Post*, CCXV, No. 12.
"La Libre Belgique," *Outlook* (May 31, 1916).
"Press of Brussels," *Literary Digest* (September 14, 1918).
"Secret Journalism in Belgium," *Current History* (April, 1917).
Sint-Jan, R. van. "Die Altesten Zeitungen in Flandern," *Zeitungswissenschaft* (May 15, 1928).
Stigns, Marcel. "The Flemish Press," *Gazette*, III, No. 4 (1957).
Vienne, Antony. "La Presse Politique en Belgique," *Presse Publicité* (March 7, 1938).

OTHER SOURCES

Files of Belgian newspapers.

Holland

BOOKS

Barnouw, A. J. *A Portrait Study of the People of Holland*. New York, 1940.
———. *The Making of Modern Holland*. New York, 1944.
Boolens, J. J., and J. C. Van der Does. *Five Years of Occupation*. Amsterdam, 1945.
Clark, George. *Holland and the War*. London, 1941.
Clatlin, W. H. *Holland and Belgium*. New York, 1936.

Dahl, Folke. *Amsterdam, Early Newspaper Center of Europe*. The Hague, 1939.
Edmundson, George. *History of Holland*. Cambridge, Eng., 1922.
Gehl, Pieter. *The Netherlands in the 17th Century*. New York, 1961.
Goedhait, H. A. *De Pers in Nederland*. Amsterdam, 1943.
Hatin, Louis Eugene. *Les Gazettes de Hollande*. Paris, 1865.
Renier, Gustav. *The Dutch Nation*. London, 1944.
Schneider, Maarten. *The Netherlands Press Today*. Leiden, 1951.
Stolp, Annie. *De Erste Couranten in Holland*. Amsterdam, 1938.
Van Duiveland, Plemp. *Journalistiek in Nederland*. The Hague, 1924.
Van Velkenburg, Sam. *The Netherlands*. Also chapters by Bernhard Vlekke, David Friedman, Reimans, and De Haas. Berkeley, Calif., 1943.
Van Kleffens, E. H. *Juggernaut over Holland*. New York, 1945.
Vankrijker, A. C. J. *Het Wervende Woord*. Amsterdam, 1950.
Warmbrun, Werner. *The Dutch Under German Occupation*. Palo Alto, Calif., 1963.

PERIODICALS

Blokzijl, Max. "Die Presse in Holland," *Wirtschaftsdienst* (September 27, October 4, 1929).
Boskamp, M. A. J. "Faire Serieux des Journaux Hollandaise," *Presse Publicite* (February 21, 1938).
"Financial Setup of Dutch Dailies," *World's Press News* (March 23, 1950).
Klinkert, Jan R. "Postwar Influences Transform Papers of Holland," *Journalism Quarterly* (December, 1947).
"Ninety Dailies Reach 2,000,000 Dutch Homes," *World's Press News* (January 23, 1936).
Schneider, Maarten. "Some Aspects of Netherlands Daily Press," *Journalism Quarterly*, XXXIV (Winter, 1957).
———. "Dutch Press Reflects Political and Religious Groups," *International Press Institute Report* (December, 1954).
"What People Read in Holland," *Review of Reviews* (August, 1905).

France

BOOKS

Avenel, Henri. *La Presse Française au Vingtième Siècle*. Paris, 1901.
Bellanger, Claude. *La Presse Clandestine (1940–44)*. Paris, 1961.
Billy, André. *La Guerre des Journaux (1917–18)*. Paris, 1919.
Bret, Paul. *Au Feu des Evenements 1929–44*. Paris, 1959.
Brisson, Pierre. *Vingt Ans de Figaro*. Paris, 1959.
Calvet, Henri. *La Presse Contemporaine*. Paris, 1958.
Dahl, Folke. *Les Debuts de la Presse Française*. Göteborg, Sweden, 1951.
Gagniere, A. *La Presse Sous la Commune*. Paris, 1872.
Hatin, L. Eugene. *Histoire de la Presse en France*. Paris, 1859.
Hisard, Claude. *Histoire de la Spoliation de la Presse*. Paris, 1956.
Lazareff, Pierre. *Deadline*. New York, 1942.
Ledre, Charles. *Histoire de la Presse*. Paris, 1958.
Mazadier, René. *Histoire de la Presse Parisienne*. Paris, 1945.
Mitton, Fernand. *La Presse sous la Revolution—L'Empire*. Paris, 1945.
Morenval, Jean. *Les Createurs de la Grande Presse*. Paris, 1938.

Mottin, Jean. *Histoire Politique de la Presse.* Paris, 1949.
Raffalovitch, A. *L'Abominable Venalité de la Presse.* Paris, 1931.
Reclus, Maurice. *Emile Girardin.* Paris, 1934.

PERIODICALS

Archambault, Pierre. "Soaring Growth of French Provincial Press," *Gazette,* VIII, No. 2 (1962).
Bellanger, Claude. "L'Agence France Presse since Reorganization," *Gazette,* VIII, No. 2 (1962).
Boris, Georges. "The French Press," *Foreign Affairs* (January, 1935).
Dell, Robert. "Corruption of French Press," *Current History* (November, 1931).
Eide, Richard. "How French Patriots Fought Nazis," *Quill* (January, 1946).
Hauser, Ernest. "France Starts Over," *Saturday Evening Post* (November 15, 1958).
Kaskeline, Egan. "French Fifth Column Newspapers," *Christian Science Monitor* (March 7, 1942).
Levy, Raphael. "The Daily Press in France," *Modern Language Journal* (January, 1929).
Massot, Henri. "Distribution of French Press," *Gazette,* VIII, No. 2 (1962).
Stoneman, William. "Nobody Is Bored with French Newspapers," *A.S.N.E. Bulletin* (October, 1959).
Terrou, Fernand. "La Presse de la Cinquième Republique," *Gazette,* VIII, No. 2 (1962).
Weigle, Clifford. "The Paris Press from 1920 to 1940," *Journalism Quarterly* (December, 1941).
———. "The Rise and Fall of Havas," *Journalism Quarterly,* (September, 1942).

Austria

BOOKS

Gedge, G. E. R. *Betrayal in Central Europe.* New York, 1939.
McCartney, C. A. *Social Revolution in Austria.* Cambridge, Eng., 1926.
MacDonald, Mary. *The Republic of Austria, 1918 to 1934.* London, 1946.
Roucek, J. S. *Central Eastern Europe: Crucible of Wars.* New York, 1946.
Seton-Watson, Hugh. *Eastern Europe Between Wars 1918–1941.* Cambridge, Eng., 1946.
Strong, David F. *Austria, October 1918–March 1919.* New York, 1939.
Taylor, Allen J. P. *The Hapsburg Monarchy.* London, 1948.
Taylor, Edmund. *The Fall of the Dynasties.* Garden City, N.Y., 1963.
For much of the earlier press history of Austria, the author is indebted to Dr. Franz Rokl of the University of Vienna for translations of pertinent data from the following sources:
Brugel, Ludwig. "Geschichte der Österreichischen Sozialdemokratie."
Ergert, Vikor. "Wiener Pressegeschichte durch 5 Jahrhunderte."
Friedjung, Heinrich. "Ein Stück Zeitungsgeschichte."
Liszt, Franz. "Lehrbuch des Österreichischen Presserechtes."
Pollak, Henri. "30 Jahre aus dem Leben eines Journalisten."
Von Helfert, Freiherr. "Die Wiener Journalistik."
Winkler, Johann. "Die Periodische Presse Oesterreichs."

Weisner, Adolph. "Denkwurdigkeiten der Österreichischen Zensur."
Zenker, Victor. "Zur Geschichte der kaiserlichen Zeitungen."
Additional sources include the USIA report on this press.

Switzerland

BOOKS

Arcis, Max d'. *The Diplomatic Position of Switzerland.* Geneva, 1949.
Bonjour, Edgar. *History of Switzerland.* Oxford, 1952.
Bonjour, Felix. *Real Democracy in Operation.* New York, 1920.
Brooks, R. C. *Switzerland, A Study of Democratic Life.* Chicago, 1930.
Dandliker, Charles. *History of Switzerland.* New York, 1935.
Gossin, Albert. *La Presse Suisse.* Neuchatel, Switz., 1936.
Herold, J. C. *The Swiss Without Halos.* New York, 1948.
Hughes, Christopher. *The Parliament of Switzerland.* London, 1962.
Lloyd, W. B. *Waging Peace, the Swiss Experience.* Washington, D.C., 1958.
Martin, William. *Histoire de la Suisse.* London, 1931.
Rappard, W. E. *Cinq Siècles de Securité Collective.* Geneva, 1945.
———. *Government of Switzerland.* New York, 1936.
Uebelhör, Max. *Die Zürchische Presse 1802–1921.* Zurich, 1908.
Weber, Karl. *The Swiss Press.* Bern, 1948.
———. *Die Schweiz im Nervenkrieg.* Bern, 1948.
Wettstein, Otto. *Die Schweizerische Presse.* Zurich, 1902.

PERIODICALS

Bess, Demaree. "Truman Could Have Learned from the Swiss," *Saturday Evening Post* (June 24, 1950).
Chapuisat, Edouard. "Coup d'Oeil sur la Presse Suisse," *Cahiers de la Presse* (January–March, 1938).
"A Lesson in Swiss," *Time* (October 18, 1963).
Tijnstra and Gaspard. "La Diffusion des Opinions dans la Presse Suisse," *Gazette,* IV, No. 2 (1958).
"Von der Presse der Schweiz," *Zeitungswissenschaft* (June 1, 1935).
"What People Read in Holland, Belgium, and Switzerland," *Review of Reviews* (August, 1905).

OTHER SOURCES

Files of representative Swiss newspapers.

Italy

BOOKS

Bernardina, Nikolas. *La Stampa Periodica.* Turin, 1890.
Bolitho, William. *Italy Under Mussolini.* New York, 1926.
Buchan, John. *Italy. London,* 1929.
Bustico, Guido. *Del Giornalismo del Risorgimento.* Florence, 1925.
Dresler, Adolf. *Geschichte der Italienische Presse.* Munich, 1933.
Fattorello, F. *L'origini del giornalismo moderno in Italia.* Udine, Italy, 1937.
Finer, Herman. *Mussolini's Italy.* Hampden, Conn., 1935.
Giacchi, Giovanni. *Il Giornalismo in Italia.* Rome, 1919.

Harris, C. R. S. *Italy, History of Allied Occupation*. London, 1957.
Hearder, Harry. *Short History of Italy*. Cambridge, 1963.
Information Service, Republic of Italy. *Italy Today*. Rome, 1965.
Levine, Irving. *Main Street, Italy*. New York, 1963.
Matthews, Herbert. *Fruits of Fascism*. New York, 1953.
Packard, Reynolds, and Eleanor Packard. *Balcony Empire*. New York, 1942.
Piccioni, Leone. *Il Giornalismo Letterario*. Turin, 1949.
Schneider, Herbert. *Making of a Fascist State*. New York, 1928.
Seldes, George. *You Can't Print That*. New York, 1929.
Smith, Denis Mac. *Italy, a Modern History*. Ann Arbor, 1959.
Steel, Ronald. *Italy*. New York, 1963.
Sturzo, Luigi. *Italy and Fascismo*. New York, 1926.
Trevelyan, George. *Garibaldi and the Making of Modern Italy*. London, 1924.

PERIODICALS

"Albertini Gave Italy First Modern Daily," *Editor and Publisher* (December 26, 1925).
Arbib-Costa, Alfonso. "Journalism in Italy 1933," *Journalism Quarterly* (December, 1933).
Bruto, Frank. "In Italy the World Is 'Complicated,'" *Montana Journalism Review* (Spring, 1962).
Caldwell, William. "Press and Propaganda in 1948 Election," *Journalism Quarterly* (Spring, 1963).
Cole, Taylor. "Italian Ministry of Popular Culture," *Public Opinion Quarterly* (July, 1938).
"Communism in Italy," *Atlantic Monthly* (February, 1965).
Cornetta, Anna. "Italy's Disappearing Dailies," *Nieman Reports* (July–October, 1962).
"The Daily Press in Italy," *Nation* (February 13, 1958).
Di Robilant, Irene. "Catholic Press in Italy," *Foreign Affairs* (April, 1930).
"Early Italian Papers," *Review of Reviews* (March, 1914).
"Instructions to Italian Press," *Current History* (July, 1937).
"Italian Newspapers," *Bookman* (June, 1900).
"Italy's New Liberty of the Press," *Literary Digest* (September 8, 1923).
"Italy's Press Helpless in Grip of Dictator," *Editor and Publisher* (May 11, 1929).
MacLean, Malcolm, and Luca Pina. "Mass Media in Scarperia," *Gazette*, IV, No. 3 (1958).
Murphy, James. "The Italian Newspaper Press," *Fortnightly Review* (February 1, 1925).
"Mussolini Chokes Press," *Nation* (June 11, 1927).
Porter, William. "Influence of Italy's Communist Dailies," *Journalism Quarterly* (Fall, 1954).
Seldes, George. "The Truth About Fascist Censorship," *Harper's* (November, 1927).
Weiss, Ignazio. "Distribution of Advertising Media in Italy," *Gazette*, VI, No. 4 (1961).
———. "The Daily Press in Italy," *Gazette*, IV, No. 3 (1958).

OTHER SOURCES

"The Italian Scene." *Annuario della Stampa Italiano.*

Greece

BOOKS

Cassavati, M. K. *Hellas and Balkan Wars.* New York, 1940.
Casson, Stanley. *Greece.* London, 1942.
Daskalis, A. P. *La Presse Hellenique.* Paris, 1930.
Eppstein, John. *Greece.* Cambridge, 1944.
Foster, Edward. *History of Modern Greece.* London, 1941.
Gibberd, Kathleen. *Greek History.* Cambridge, 1944.
Gibbons, H. A. *Venizelos.* New York, 1920.
Kousoulas, Dimitrious. *Price of Freedom, 1939–53.* Athens, 1954.
McNeil, W. H. *Greek Dilemma—War and Aftermath.* New York, 1947.
Martin, Percy. *Greece in the Twentieth Century.* London, 1913.
Mears, E. G. *Greece Today.* London, 1929.
Miller, W. A. *History of the Greek People.* London, 1922.
Ministere de la Presse. *La Presse Grecque.* Athens, 1933.
Papalexandro, K. *The Greek Press—Great Greek Encyclopedia.* Athens, 1934.
Phillips, Walter. *The War of Greek Independence.* London, 1897.
Queris, de Saint. *La Presse dans la Grece Moderne.* Paris, 1871.
Sellnas, Spiros. *Greece and the War.* Athens, 1946.
Stanhope, L. *Greece in 1823–1824.* London, 1825.
Stavrianos, L. S. *Greece, American Dilemma and Opportunity.* Chicago, 1952.
Yalentis, John K. *A Treatise on Press Freedom.* Athens, 1883.

PERIODICALS

Bach, Julian. "The Mailed Fist in Greece." *Nation* (August 21, 1937).
"Embattled Democracy," *Life* (May 9, 1960).
Gaedicke, Herbert. "Statistik der Griechischen Presse," *Zeitungswissenschaft* (March, 1932).
Graves, Wallace. "Journalism in the First Democracy," *Journalism Quarterly* (Spring, 1959).
"The Great Abduction—2800 Greek Children," *American Mercury*, March, 1958.
Heizler, Rudolph. "Neues Griechisches Pressgesetz," *Zeitungswissenschaft* (January 1, 1939).
"The Hungry Ones," *Time* (January 30, 1956).
Joanides, John V. "The Underground Press." *Romanzi* (February, 1946).
Liebling, A. J. "Reporter at Large," *New Yorker* (August 9, 1958).
Marceau, Marc. "With Full Freedom, Greek Press Is Making Steady Progress," *International Press Institute Report* (December, 1964).
McGhee, G. C. "Fifteen Years of Greek–U.S. Partnership," *State Department Bulletin* (July, 1962).
Mirkine Guetsevitch, B. "Recent Developments in Press Laws," *Political Quarterly* (October, 1932).

"Storms Threaten an Ancient Nation," *Saturday Evening Post* (June 15, 1963).

OTHER SOURCES

Files of Greek newspapers.

Spain

BOOKS

Altimera y Creves, Rafael. *History of Spain to Present Day*. New York, 1948.

Arias, Saldago, Gabrial. *Doctrina Española de la Informacion*. Madrid, 1954.

Atkinson, William C. *History of Spain and Portugal*. London, 1960.

Benjamin, Robert Spiers. *Eye Witness*. New York, 1940.

Bertrand, Louis, and Charles Petrie. *The History of Spain*. London, 1934.

Brenan, Gerald. *The Spanish Labyrinth*. Cambridge, 1943.

Bowers, Claude G. *My Mission to Spain*. New York, 1954.

Clark, Clyde. *Evolution of Franco Regime*. Madrid, 1939.

Cleugh, James. *Spain in the Modern World*. New York, 1953.

Criado y Dominiques, Juan. *Importancia del Periodismo Español*. Madrid, 1892.

Del Vayo, Julio. *Freedom's Battle*. New York, 1940.

De Madariaga, Salvador. *Spain, A Modern History*. New York, 1958.

Emmet, John H. *Report from Spain*. New York, 1947.

Foss, William, and Cecil Gerahty. *The Spanish Arena*. London, 1938.

Gardiner, Harold, S.J. *Catholic Viewpoint on Censorship*. New York, 1956.

Hamilton, Thomas. *Appeasement's Child—Franco Regime*. New York, 1943.

Instituto de la Opinion Publica. *Estudio sobre los Medios de Communicacion de Masas en España*. Madrid, 1964.

McSorley, Joseph. *The Church by Centuries*. London, 1949.

Matthews, Herbert L. *The Yoke and the Arrows*. New York, 1961.

Ortega y Gasset, Jose. *Invertebrate Spain*. New York, 1937.

Palencia, Isabel. *I Must Have Liberty*. New York, 1940.

Pattee, Richard. *This is Spain*. Milwaukee, 1951.

Peers, E. Allison. *The Spanish Tragedy*. London, 1936.

Pitcairn, Frank. *Reporter in Spain*. London, 1936.

Quesada, Vincente. *Legislation on Printing in Old Spain*. New York, 1938.

Ratcliff, Dillwyn F. *Prelude to Franco*. New York, 1957.

Ruis, Nicolas Gonzales. *El Periodismo*. Barcelona, 1960.

Rumia de Arnas, Antonio. *Historia de la Censure Literari Gubernative en España*. Madrid, 1940.

Sencourt, Robert. *Spain's Ordeal, Documented History of Civil War*. New York, 1940.

PERIODICALS

Alisky, Marvin. "Spain's Press and Broadcasting," *Journalism Quarterly* (Winter, 1962).

Barth, Heinz. "Die Spanischen Zeitschriften," *Gazette*, IV, No. 3 (1958).

Brewer, Sam. "Under Cover Press," *N.Y. Times Magazine* (August 24, 1947).

Brown, Robert U. "Smuggling Undoes Spanish Censors," *Editor and Publisher* (August 29, 1936).

Fernsworth, L. A. "Spanish Gag under Republic," *Editor and Publisher* (April 30, 1932).

Johnson, Albin. "Spain's Muzzled Press," *Editor and Publisher* (June 1, 1920).

Littel, Robert. "Spain Crosses the Pyrenees," *Readers' Digest* (November, 1962).

Riegel, O. W. "Press, Radio and Spanish Civil War," *Public Opinion Quarterly* (January, 1937).

"What People Read in Spain and Portugal," *Review of Reviews* (January–June, 1905).

OTHER SOURCES

"Annuario de la Prensa Española, 1960–61." *Ministerio de Informacion y Turismo*.

"Textos Legales, Prensa." *Ministerio de Informacion y Turismo*.

Catholic Encyclopedia. Volumes VIII, XII, and XIV.

Files of Spanish News Letter, Communications Affiliates, New York, for 1962.

Files of Gaceta de la Prensa Española for 1962.

Portugal

BOOKS

Ameal, J. *Historia de Portugal*. Oporto, Portugal, 1942.

Atkinson, W. C. *A History of Spain and Portugal*. London, 1960.

Cunha, V. Braganca. *Revolutionary Portugal*. London, 1927.

Derrek, Michael. *The Portugal of Salazar*. London, 1938.

Edgerton, F. C. C. *Salazar, Rebuilder of Portugal*. London, 1949.

Ferra, Antonio. *Salazar: Portugal and her Leader*. London, 1939.

———. *Salazar, Doctrine and Action*. London, 1939.

Jayne, K. G. *Vasco da Gama and His Successors*. London, 1910.

Livermore, H. V. *History of Portugal*. Cambridge, 1953.

Martins, Oliveira. *History of Iberian Civilization*. Oxford, 1930.

Martins, Rocha. *Pequeña Historia da Imprensa Portuguese*. Lisbon, 1941.

Nowell, Charles. *History of Portugal*. New York, 1952.

Sanseau, Elaine. *Henry the Navigator*. London, 1947.

Stephens, H. Morse. *Portugal*. London, 1891.

Young, George. *Portugal Young and Old*. Oxford, 1917.

PERIODICALS

Bayles, W. D. "Present Situation in Portugal," *Life* (April 28, 1941).

"Causes of Portugal's Revolutions," *Current History* (October, 1926).

Costa, Alfonso. "L'Ancienne Influence des Parties Politiques sur les Journaux," *Cahiers de la Presse* (December, 1930).

"Declining Freedom of the Press," *Literary Digest* (April 14, 1934).

Dillon, E. J. "Republican Portugal," *Contemporary Review* (November, 1910).
"How Bad Is the Best?" *Time* (July 22, 1946).
McCullagh, Francis. "Freedom in Portugal," *Living Age* (March 11, 1911).
Nowell, Charles. "Portugal and Partition of Africa," *Journal of Modern History*, XIX (1947).
"What People Read in Spain and Portugal," *Review of Reviews* (May, 1905).

OTHER SOURCES

Imprensa Nacional. "Imprensa, Laws Affecting Press," Lisbon, 1950.
Journais. "No Tricentenario da Gaceta," Lisbon and Oporto Papers, 1941.
United Nations. Reply of Portuguese government to United Nations Conference on Freedom of Information. Columbia, 1940.
Bulletins on political, economic, and cultural affairs. Lisbon.
Files of Portuguese Newspapers.

Russia

BOOKS

Abramovitch, Raphael. *The Soviet Revolution*. New York, 1962.
Allen, Robert L. *Soviet Economic Warfare*. Washington, 1960.
Chamberlin, William H. *The Russian Revolution*. New York, 1935.
———. *Russia's Iron Age*. Boston, 1934.
Cranshaw, Edward. *Khrushchev's Russia*. Baltimore, 1959.
Duranty, Walter, *U.S.S.R., The Story of Soviet Russia*. New York, 1944.
Ellison, Herbert J. *History of Russia*. New York, 1964.
Fischer, Louis. *Life and Death of Stalin*. New York, 1953.
Graham, Stephen. *Peter the Great*. London, 1929.
———. *Tsar of Freedom: Alexander II*. New Haven, Conn., 1935.
Gunther, John. *Inside Russia Today*. New York, 1957.
Hill, Christopher. *Lenin and the Russian Revolution*. London, 1953.
Inkeles, Alex. *Public Opinion in Soviet Russia*. Boston, 1950.
Kennan, George. *Russia and the West under Lenin and Stalin*. Boston, 1961.
Kornilov, Alexander. *Modern Russian History*. New York, 1943.
Lamont, Corliss. *People of the Soviet Union*. New York, 1946.
MacNeal, Robert H. *The Russian Revolution: Why Did Bolshevists Win?* New York, 1960.
Magidoff, Robert. *In Anger and in Pity*. Garden City, N.Y., 1949.
Miller, Wright W. *The U.S.S.R.* London, 1963.
Pares, Bernard. *History of Russia*. New York, 1944.
Payne, Robert. *Life and Death of Lenin*. New York, 1964.
Pipes, Richard. *The Formation of the Soviet Union*. Boston, 1954.
Schwartz, Harry. *Russia's Soviet Economy*. New York, 1950.
Seton-Watson, Hugh. *Decline of Imperial Russia*. New York, 1964.
Spector, Ivar. *Soviet Strength and Strategy in Asia*. Seattle, 1950.
Stevens, Edmund, *This Is Russia Uncensored*. New York, 1950.
Sulzberger, Cyrus. *The Big Thaw*. New York, 1956.

Taracouzio, T. A. *War and Peace in Soviet Diplomacy*. New York, 1939.
Tompkins, Stuart R. *Russia Through the Ages*. New York, 1940.
Treadgold, D. W. *Twentieth Century Russia*. Chicago, 1959.
Trotsky, Leon. *History of the Russian Revolution*. New York, 1932.
Vernadsky, George. *History of Russia*. New Haven, Conn., 1943.

PERIODICALS

Tsarist Period

Edwards, Albert. "Death and Resurrection of Russian Press," *Harpers Weekly* (March 24, 1906).
"Fourth Estate in Russia," *Nation*, March 25, 1909.
"Press, Main Political School of Russian People," *Review of Reviews* (July, 1913).
"Russian Newspapers and Magazines," *Nation* (July 9, 1868) and under same title (February 14, 1914).
"Russian Press Censorship," *Outlook* (February 27, 1904).
Schierbrand, Wolf von. "Conducting a Russian Newspaper," *World's Work* (January, 1903).
Stone, Melville. "Removal of Russian Censorship," *Century* (May, 1905).
Trench, General F. C. "Russian Newspapers," *Blackwood's Magazine* (July, 1890).
"What the People Read in Russia," *Review of Reviews* (April, 1904).
Yarros, Victor. "Russian Newspapers," *Bookman* (May, 1900).

Lenin Period

"Bolshevik Way with the Press," *Literary Digest* (January 31, 1920).
Bruck, Richard. "Press of Soviet Russia," *Living Age*, April 14, 1923.
Ellis, William T. "How Lenin and Trotsky Established an Advertising Monopoly," *Editor and Publisher* (January 5, 1918).
Faraut, Leon. "The Press Under the Soviets," *Living Age* (September 29, 1923).
Harris, F. T. "Russian Press Slowly Stifling Under Soviet Control," *Editor and Publisher* (October 27, 1923).
Kazarine, S. M. "The Soviet Press." *New Statesman* (June 9, 1923).
Pasvolsky, Leo. "The Soviet Newspapers," *Forum* (September, 1922).
"Rise of the Soviet Press," *Literary Digest* (October 25, 1919).
"Russian Newspapers Since Revolution," *New Statesman and Nation* (May 26, 1917).
"Russian Papers Red but not Read," *Literary Digest* (July 7, 1923).
"Soviet Newspapers," *Living Age* (September 8, 1923).
Talmy, L. "The Soviet Press." *The Nation* (November 7, 1923).

Stalin Period

Chamberlin, W. H. "The Soviet Press," *Asia* (May, 1937).
———. "Soviet Taboos," *Foreign Affairs* (April, 1935).
———. "According to the Press," *Christian Science Monitor* (July 15, 1936).
Durant, Kenneth. "Growth of the Soviet Press," *Journalism Quarterly* (March, 1937).

Duranty, Walter. "Russian News and Soviet Censors," *Spectator* (February 13, 1932).

Geta, Josef. "The Soviet Press," *Contemporary Review* (February, 1950).

Jaryc, Marc. "Press in Soviet Union," *Slavonic Review* (July, 1933).

Jenson, Jay, and Richard Bailey. "Highlights in Russian Journalism, 1553–1917," *Journalism Quarterly* (Summer, 1964).

Johnson, Albin. "Russian Newspapermen Privileged," *Editor and Publisher* (November 23, 1929).

Krassov, Vladimir. "Journalism in Russia," *Journalism Quarterly* (December, 1933).

Martin, Lawrence. "Soviet Press," *Current History* (October, 1937).

Martin, Kingsley. "The Russian Press," *Political Quarterly* (January, 1933).

McGill, Ralph. "Free News and Russia," *Atlantic Monthly* (April, 1946).

Romm, Vladimir. "The Free Press in the USSR," *Journalism Quarterly* (March, 1935).

"Soviet Lifts Censorship," *World's Press News* (May 11, 1939).

Stein, Gunther. "What Moscow Reads," *Living Age* (February, 1932).

Strachey, J. S. "The Russian Press," *Spectator* (April 7, 1928).

Since Stalin

Grullow, Leo. "After Khrushchev," *International Press Institute Report* (December, 1964).

———. "Berlin, Nuclear Testing and the Soviet Press," *Ibid.* (October, 1961).

———. "What Soviet Readers Never Knew," *Ibid.* (December, 1961).

Grunwald, H. A. "Quality of Life Behind Russian Statistics," *Fortune* (March, 1964).

Krankshaw, E. "Case History of an Unfree Press," *New York Times Magazine* (December 2, 1962).

"Misfire at Ole Miss., Embarrassment for Pravda," *America* (October 27, 1962).

Nixon, R. M. "Khrushchev's Hidden Weakness: Captive Nations," *Saturday Evening Post* (October 12, 1963).

Rostow, W. W. "Third Round," *Foreign Affairs* (October, 1963).

Schwartz, H. "How the Russians Get the News," *New York Times Magazine* (February 13, 1955).

Tatu, Maurice. "Reporting Russia Is Easier Now," *International Press Institute Report* (November, 1961).

"What Ivan Knows About Cuba," *Newsweek* (November 12, 1962).

OTHER SOURCES

Files of *Pravda* and *Izvestia* and scattered issues of such other papers and magazines as could be gotten out of Russia.

Files of *Current Digest of the Soviet Press*, Leo Grullow, editor, published at Columbia University by the Joint Committee of the American Council of Learned Societies and the Social Science Research Council.

Files of the Soviet press in translation by the School of Journalism at the University of Wisconsin.

Albania

BOOKS

Bishop, Robert, and E. S. Crayfield. *Russia Astride the Balkans.* New York, 1948.
Chekresi, Constantin. *Albania Past and Present.* New York, 1919.
Roucek, Joseph. *Politics in the Balkans.* New York, 1939.
Swire, Joseph. *Albania's Rise as a Kingdom.* London, 1930.
Wadham, Peacock. *Albania, Foundling State of Europe.* New York, 1914.
Federal Writers Project. *Albanian Struggle in Old World and New.* Boston, 1939.

PERIODICALS

"Albania a Balkan Bridgehead," *World Today* (February, 1950).
"Albania Kicks Out Russians," *U.S. News and World Report* (June 19, 1961).
Bogdan, Radista. "Battleground in Stalin-Tito Feud," *Saturday Evening Post* (December 17, 1944).
Cameron, James. "Albania, Last Marxist Paradise," *Atlantic* (October 24, 1963).
"D.P.'s at U.N.," *Reporter* (October 24, 1963).
"Fortress on Adriatic," *Newsweek* (June 17, 1919).
"Progress Enters Albania," *Fortune* (February, 1950).
Ravry, Andre. "La Presse Albanaise," *Cahiers de la Presse* (July, 1939).
"Tiniest Thorn in Axis Side," *Saturday Evening Post* (October 24, 1948).
Stavro, Skendi. "Albania within Soviet Orbit," *Political Science Quarterly* (June, 1940).
"Why All the Fuss Over Little Albania?" *U.S. News and World Report* (June 19, 1961).

OTHER SOURCES

Such few issues of the two main dailies as the author could get out of Albania.

Bulgaria

BOOKS

Andreeff, Boris. *Die Bulgarischen Zeitschriften, 1845–1925.* Sofia, 1927.
Bartlett, Vernon. *East of the Iron Curtain.* New York, 1950.
Black, C. E. *Establishment of Constitutional Government in Bulgaria.* London, 1943.
Bishop, Robert, and E. S. Crayfield. *Russia Astride the Balkans.* New York, 1948.
Chandan, K. S. *La Presse Bulgare.* Paris, 1933.
Evans, Stanley. *Short History of Bulgaria.* London, 1960.
Genov, G. P. *Bulgaria and Treaty of Neuilly.* Sofia, 1935.
Logio, George C. *Bulgaria Past and Present.* London, 1936.
McDermott, Mercia. *History of Bulgaria, 1303–1885.* London, 1962.
Roucek, J. S. *The Politics of the Balkans.* New York, 1939.

Royal Institute of International Affairs. *Southeast Europe, a Political and Economic Survey.* London, 1939.
Runciman, Steven. *History of First Bulgarian Empire.* London, 1930.
Saxene, H. L. *Bulgaria Under the Red Star.* New Delhi, 1957.

PERIODICALS

"Das Eingreifen der Konstantinopler Bulgarischen Presse in die Bulgarische Freiheitsbewegung 1860–1879," *Zeitungswissenschaft* (March 15, 1929).
Germann, John. "Zur Entwicklung der Balkanpresse," *Zeitungswissenschaft* (March 15, 1932).
"Internationale Pressegesetzbegung," *Zeitungswissenschaft* (November 11, 1927).
Levenson, Heinrich. "*Stand und Bedeutung der Bulgarischen Presse von Heute,*" *Zeitungswissenschaft* (February 15, 1926).
Prichit, V. S. "Bulgaria Today," *Holiday* (December, 1960).
Todorov, Dafin. "The Press in Bulgaria," *Gazette,* III, No. 3 (1962).
Vichinich, W. S. "Economic Development in Bulgaria," *Current History* (July, 1957).
Wallisch, Friedrich. "Bulgarien und seine Zeitungen," *Zeitungswissenschaft* (April, 1934).

OTHER SOURCES

Files of Bulgarian newspapers supplied by Bulgarian Embassy in Washington plus statistical and economic data.

Czechoslovakia

BOOKS

Bartlett, Vernon. *East of the Iron Curtain.* New York, 1950.
Fischer, Louis. *The Soviets in World Affairs.* Princeton, N.J., 1951.
Fodor, M. W. *South of Hitler.* London, 1938.
Gedge, G. E. P. *Betrayal in Central Europe.* New York, 1939.
Glazer, Kurt. *Czechoslovakia, A Critical History.* Caldwell, Idaho, 1961
Graham, M. W. *New Governments of Europe.* New York, 1924.
Hanc, J. *Tornado Across Eastern Europe.* New York, 1942.
Josten, J. *Oh, My Country.* London, 1949.
Kerner, R. J. *Czechoslovakia–Twenty Years of Independence.* Berkeley, Calif., 1940.
Ripka, Hubert. *Czechoslovakia Enslaved.* London, 1950.
Roucek, Joseph. *Central Eastern Europe, Crucible of Wars.* New York, 1946.
Seton-Watson, Hugh. *Eastern Europe Between Wars.* New York, 1962.
Seton-Watson, R. W. *History of Czechs and Slovaks.* Cambridge, 1943.
Taylor, Edmund. *Fall of the Dynasties.* New York, 1963.
Wiskemann, Eliz. *Czechs and Germans.* London, 1938.
Zurcher, A. K. *Experiment with Democracy in Central Europe.* New York, 1933.

PERIODICALS

"AFP Closes Prague Office," *Editor and Publisher* (June 21, 1948).
Bass, Eduard. "Czech Reads His Papers in Cafes," *World's Press News* (July 21, 1938).

Black, Robert. "Leftists' Distorted Press Laws Capture Czech Papers," *Journalism Quarterly* (June, 1949).

"Communists Take Over," *New York Times* (February 24, 1948).

"Complete Nationalization of Czech Press," *World's Press News* (October 28, 1948).

Crha, V. "Czechs Are the Biggest Readers in Europe," *World's Press News* (July 21, 1938).

"Czechs Decree Rigid Control of Advertising," *Editor and Publisher* (June 26, 1948).

"Czechoslovakia Warns Foreign Journalists," *Newspaper World* (March 26, 1938).

"Die Umschichtung in der Presse der Tschecho-Slowakei," *Zeitungswissenschaft* (March 1, 1939).

Dresler, Adolf. "Die Anfänge der Zeitungspresse in Böhmen," *Zeitungswissenschaft* (November, 1938).

"Economic and Racial Divisions Affect Czech Press," *World's Press News* (July 21, 1938).

"Editorial Hammer and Sickle," *New York Times* (July 27, 1951).

"Foreign Newsmen Denied Entry," *Editor and Publisher* (May 7, 1948).

"Free Press Suppressed," *New York Times* (February 24, 1948).

"German Propaganda Against Czechoslovakia," *Living Age* (April, 1937).

Heide, Walter. "Der Pressekampf um das Sudetendeutschtum," *Zeitungswissenschaft* (November, 1938).

Hendvichova, Eliska. "History of Czech Communist Press," *Novinarsky Sbornik* (July, 1956).

"Importation of Four U.S. Czech Weeklies Banned," *New York Times* (October 11, 1946).

"Is Russia Losing East Europe?" *U.S. News and World Report* (April 20, 1964).

Johnson, Albin. "Czech Journalism Encouraged by Government Expenditures," *Editor and Publisher* (August 17, 1929).

Kocourek, Franta. "Die Tagespresse in der Tzchechoslowakei," *Nord und Sud* (September, 1930).

Krejci, Milan. "New Czech Press Influenced by Soviet Press," *Novinarsky Sbornik*, II, No. 4 (1956).

Lesko, John. "Press Censorship in Czechoslovakia," *Editor and Publisher* (July 14, 1934).

Machi, Ladislov. "How Sober Communist Makeup Had To Be Brightened in 1953," *Novinarsky Sbornik*, II, No. 1 (July, 1957).

Osusky, Stefan. "T. G. Masaryk, Journaliste," *Cahiers de la Presse* (January–March, 1938).

Panofsky, Walter. "Der Pressekampf um Böhmen," *Zeitungswissenschaft* (July 1, 1938).

"Prague A.P. Chief Arrested," *Editor and Publisher* (April 26, 1948).

Rossipaul, Lother. "Die Haltung der Tschechischen Presse zur Errichtung des Protektorats," *Zeitungswissenschaft* (May, 1939).

"A Trip Through Eastern Europe," *Newsweek* (October 28, 1963).

"Underground Press Grows," *New York Times* (July 19, 1948).

Volf, Joseph. "Zur Geschichte des Zeitungswesen in der Tschecho-Slowakei," *Zeitungswissenschaft* (May, 1939).

"What People Read in Austria and Bohemia," *Review of Reviews* (January, 1905).

OTHER SOURCES

International Encyclopedia and its Books of the Year.
Copies of papers and statistics from Czech Information Ministry, Prague.

Hungary

BOOKS

Bain, Leslie B. *The Reluctant Satellite.* New York, 1962.
Bartlett, Vernon. *East of the Iron Curtain.* New York, 1950.
Birinya, L. K. *The Tragedy of Hungary.* Cleveland, 1924.
Eckhart, Ferenc. *History of the Hungarian People.* London, 1931.
Fejto, François. *Behind the Rape of Hungary.* New York, 1957.
Gunther, John. *Behind the Iron Curtain.* New York, 1949.
Headley, Phinneas. *The Life of Louis Kossuth.* New York, 1952.
Kosary, Domokosg. *History of Hungary.* New York, 1941.
Lengyel, Emil. *100 Years of Hungary.* New York, 1958.
Montgomery, J. F. *Hungary, the Unwilling Satellite.* New York, 1947.
Nagy, Ferenc. *The Struggle Behind the Iron Curtain.* New York, 1947.
Pesti Hirlap. *Justice for Hungary.* Budapest, 1930.
Radisics, M. E., and A. Kun. *Hungary Yesterday and Today.* London, 1936.
Teleki, Paul. *Evolution of Hungary.* New York, 1923.
Zinner, Paul E. *Revolution in Hungary.* New York, 1962.

PERIODICALS

Griffiths, Eldon. "A Trip Through Eastern Europe," *Newsweek* (October 28, 1963).
"Inside Hungary Seven Years After Uprising," *U.S. News and World Report* (December 30, 1963).
"Is Russia Losing East Europe?" *Ibid.* (April 10, 1964).
Johnson, Albin. "Hard-won Rights of Hungarian Newsmen Scrapped," *Editor and Publisher* (October 26, 1929).
Larson, L. "Twenty Months After," *New York Times Magazine* (June 22, 1958).
Limedorfer, Eugene. "Great Newspapers of Continental Europe," *Bookman* (April, 1900).
Major, Robert. "The Hungarian Press, 1914–1918," *Journalism Quarterly* (March, 1949).
Nagy, Ferenc. "How Russians Grabbed My Government," *Saturday Evening Post* (August 30, 1947).
Skottny, John. "What People Read in Hungary," *Review of Reviews* (November, 1904).
"Statistisches uber das Zeitungswesen in Ungarn," *Zeitungswissenschaft* (April 15, 1927).
Ternay, Kalman. "Hungarian Journalism 1900 to 1943," *Gazette*, III No. 1 (1957).

Vali, F. S. "Hungary Faces the Future," *Current History* (May, 1963).
Wachsburg, J. "Letter from Budapest," *New Yorker* (March 14, 1964).

OTHER SOURCES

"The Hungarian Newspaper" an unpublished Medill Research Report by Susan Fodor, a former Hungarian newspaperwoman.

Poland

BOOKS

Bartlett, Vernon. *East of the Iron Curtain.* New York, 1950.
Brant, Irving. *The New Poland.* New York, 1946.
Buell, Raymond. *Poland, Key to Europe.* New York, 1939.
Cary, William. *Poland Struggles Forward.* New York, 1949.
Frankel, Henryk. *Poland, The Struggle for Power, 1772–1939.* London, 1946.
Gluckstein, Ygael. *Stalin's Satellites in Europe.* Boston, 1952.
Gunther, John. *Behind the Iron Curtain.* New York, 1945.
Halecki, O. *History of Poland.* New York, 1943.
Korbel, Joseph. *Poland Between East and West.* Princeton, 1963.
Lane, A. B. *I Saw Poland Betrayed.* New York, 1948.
Machray, Robert. *The Poland of Pilsudski.* London, 1936.
Reddaway, W. F., *et al.,* (eds.). *Cambridge History of Poland.* Cambridge, 1941.
Rose, W. J. *Poland Old and New.* London, 1948.
Segal, Simon. *The New Order in Poland.* New York, 1942.
Zweig, Ferdynand. *Poland Between Wars.* London, 1944.

PERIODICALS

Baskerville, B. C. "Present Condition in Poland." *Fortnightly Review* (October, 1906).
"Course in Despotism," *Editor and Publisher* (November 20, 1926).
"Das Polnische Zeitungswesen," *Zeitungswissenschaft* (April 15, 1927).
Dunbar, Ernest. "Poland 1963—Retreat to Stalinism," *Look* (August 27, 1963).
"German Rule in Poland," *Current History* (May, 1921).
"Getting Democracy in Poland," *Atlantic* (October, 1925).
Harsch, Joseph. "Curtain Isn't Iron," *Harper's* (October, 1949).
How to Exterminate a Nation," *Saturday Review of Literature* (April 5, 1944).
"In Free Poland," *Literary Digest* (March 3, 1917).
Jarkowski, Stan. "Die Polnische Presse in Vergangenheit und Gegenwart," *Zeitungswissenschaft* (August 1, 1937).
Lane, A. B. "How Russia Rules Poland," *Life* (July 14, 1947).
Leiser, E. "Poland Gets New Russian Boss," *Saturday Evening Post* (December 19, 1950).
"Muzzle Is Clamped on Polish Press," *Editor and Publisher* (November 20, 1926).
Olszyk, Edmund. "Poland," *Journalism Quarterly* (December, 1928; March, 1939).
Paderewski, Ignace. "Independent Poland," *World's Work* (December, 1916).

"Pilsudski's Steamroller," *Newsweek* (March 30, 1935).

"Poland," *Atlantic* (November, 1951).

"Poland," *Ibid.* (December, 1962).

"Poland After Pilsudski," *Current History* (January, 1936).

"Poland's Fate," *Ibid.* (June, 1949).

"Poles Fight Suppression," *Editor and Publisher* (January 1, 1927).

"Presse im Ersten Jahreszeit des Neuen Selbstandigen Staates," *Zeitungswissenschaft* (December, 1938).

"Profiles of Poland," *Current History* (May, 1963).

"Recent Developments in Poland," *New Statesman* (March 24, 1917).

Rojek, M. E. "Press Freedom Being Destroyed in Poland," *World's Press News* (October 3, 1942).

Tyrowicz, Marian. "Journalism in Poland," *Journalism Quarterly*, (March, 1933).

"What People Read in Poland," *Review of Reviews* (July, 1904).

Wionczech, M. "Postwar Press in Poland," *Foreign Press News* (March, 1948).

Wrzos, Konrad. "Poland's Press," *Independent Journal* (February, 1939).

OTHER SOURCES

300 Lat Prasy Polskiej (300th anniversary of Polish press). Warsaw, 1961.

"Poland, 1944 to 1964," Polonia Publishing House, Warsaw, 1964.

Concise Statistical Yearbook of Poland. Warsaw, 1963.

Sowa, Walter, "Postwar Press of Poland," Unpublished Medill Research Report by former Polish journalist, 1949.

Roepken, Henry. "The Press of Poland," Unpublished Medill Research Report, 1953.

Copies of papers and statistics from Polish General Consulate, Chicago.

Rumania

BOOKS

Bishop, Robert, and E. S. Crayfield. *Russia Astride the Balkans.* New York, 1948.

Bohmer, Karl. *Handbuch der Welt Presse.* Leipzig, 1937.

Byrnes, James. *Speaking Frankly.* New York, 1947.

Clark, Charles Upson. *United Rumania.* New York, 1932.

Cretzianu, Alexandre. *Captive Rumania.* New York, 1956.

Department of State. *Violation of Rights, Rumanian Press and Publications.* Washington, D.C., 1951.

Georgesco, Jean. *La Presse Periodique en Roumanie.* Rumania, 1936.

Iorga, N. *History of Rumania.* London, 1925.

Kormos, C. *Rumania.* Cambridge, 1944.

Markham, Reuben. *Rumania Under Soviet Yoke.* Boston, 1949.

Mitrany, David. *The Land and the Peasant in Rumania.* Cambridge, 1930.

Riker, T. W. *The Making of Rumania.* London, 1931.

Roucek, J. S. *Contemporary Rumania.* Stanford, Calif., 1932.

Samuelson, James. *Rumania Past and Present.* London, 1882.

Seton-Watson, R. W. *History of Roumanians.* Cambridge, 1934.

PERIODICALS

Ben, P. "Another Split in Communist Ranks," *New Republic* (October 19, 1963).

Fein, Leonard J., and Bonell, Victoria E., "Press and Radio in Rumania, Recent Developments," *Journalism Quarterly*, Summer, 1965.

Griffiths, Eldon. "A Trip Through Eastern Europe," *Newsweek* (October 28, 1963).

"Is Russia Losing East Europe?" *U.S. News and World Report* (April 20, 1964).

"Just Beyond the Curtain," *Fortune* (July, 1958).

Kruglak, T. E. "Agerpress, Rumanian News Agency," *Journalism Quarterly* (Summer, 1958).

Leonard, O. "What People Read in the Balkans," *Review of Reviews* (March, 1905).

Lindley, E. K. "Friendly but Cautious," *Newsweek* (October 20, 1958).

Nano, Frederick. "First Soviet Doublecross," *Journal of Central European Affairs* (1952).

Pritchit, V. S. "Rumania Today," *Holiday* (February, 1961).

"Stalinist Rumania," *Current History* (July, 1957).

"U.S., Rumania Agree to Cultural and Other Exchanges," *State Department Bulletin* (December 26, 1960).

Vuchinich, W. S. "Rumania's Foreign Policy Evaluated," *Current History* (April, 1959).

Wachsburg, J. "Reporter at Large," *New Yorker* (November 14, 1953).

"Want Amid Plenty," *Time* (June 8, 1962).

OTHER SOURCES

Rumanian editors, who supplied copies of their papers; copies of other Rumanian papers found on the newsstands in Vienna.

Yugoslavia

BOOKS

Adamic, Louis. *My Land and People.* New York, 1943.

Anastosoff, C. *The Tragic Peninsula, Macedonia.* St. Louis, 1938.

Bishop, Robert, and E. S. Crayfield. *Russia Astride the Balkans.* New York, 1948.

Buchan, John. *Yugoslavia.* London, 1923.

Farrell, Robert B. *Yugoslavia and the Soviet Union.* Hamden, Conn., 1956.

Gewehr, W. M. *Rise of Nationalism in the Balkans.* New York, 1931.

Heppel, Muriel, and F. B. Singleton. *Yugo Slavia.* London, 1961.

Hoffman, George W. *Jugoslavia and the New Communism.* New York, 1962.

Hoptner, Jacob. *Yugoslavia in Crisis.* New York, 1962.

Kerner, Robert, *et al. Yugoslavia.* Berkeley, Calif., 1949.

Markham, R. H. *Tito's Imperial Communism.* Chapel Hill, N.C., 1947.

Micheles, Vera. *Yugoslavia's New Form of Communism.* New York, 1950.

Mitrany, David. *Effect of War on Southeastern Europe.* New Haven, Conn., 1936.

Newman, Bernard. *Tito's Yugoslavia.* London, 1952.

Pribicevic, Stoyan. *World Without End, Saga of Southeast Europe.* New York, 1940.

Roucek, Joseph. *Politics in the Balkans.* London, 1939.

Schevill, F. *History of the Balkan Peninsula.* New York, 1922.

Sforza, Carlo. *Fifty Years of War and Diplomacy in Balkans.* New York, 1940.

St. John, Robert. *The Silent People Speak.* Garden City, N.Y., 1948.

Stavrianos, L. S. *Balkan Federation for Unity.* Northampton, Mass., 1944.

Temperley, H. W. *History of Serbia.* London, 1917.

PERIODICALS

Brome, Vincent. "Europe's Underground Press," *Quill* (November-December, 1943).

Campbell, J. C. "Yugoslavia: Crisis and Choice," *Foreign Affairs* (January, 1963).

Chumarevich, S. "La Presse Yugoslav," Historical brochure, Belgrade (1937).

"Foreign Press Curbed," *Editor and Publisher* (August 6, 1932).

"The German Invasion Press," *World's Press News* (November 26, 1942).

Johnson, Albin. "Yugoslav Government Safe from Press Censure," *Editor and Publisher* (September 7, 1921).

Leonard, O. "What People Read in the Balkans," *Review of Reviews* (March, 1905).

Neal, W. M. "Our Communist Ally," *Saturday Evening Post* (March 3, 1951).

———. "Titoism in Flux," *Current History* (May, 1963).

Petrovitch, Mihailo. "La Presse Yugoslav," *Cahiers de la Presse* (July–September, 1939).

Raditsa, Bogan. "Sovietization of Satellites," *Annals of American Academy of Political Science* (September, 1950).

Rubinstein, A. Z. "Tito's Home-made Communism," *Reporter* (January 19, 1961).

"Slavic Darkness," *Editor and Publisher* (September 10, 1932).

"The Underground Press," *World's Press News* (February 5 and May 7, 1942; also November 2, 1944).

"Yugoslavs' Shackled Press," *Literary Digest* (January 31, 1931).

OTHER SOURCES

Files of *Yugoslav Life.*

"Press, Radio and Television in Yugoslavia" from Yugoslav Institute of Journalism.

"Law of the Press," by the Yugoslav Jurists Association.

Photo Credits

For permission to reproduce some of the photographs in this book, the author is grateful to:

Dr. L. Reichert, Verlagsleiter, Otto Harrassowitz Verlag, Wiesbaden, West Germany (Frontispiece and front page of *Avisa Relation oder Zeitung*, from Walter Schöne's *Die Deutsche Zeitung im Ersten Jahrhundert*)

Folmer Wisti, director-general, *Det Danske Selskab*, Copenhagen, arranged by Terkel M. Terkelsen, editor-in-chief, *Berlingske Tidende*, Copenhagen (Photos of Christian Gulmann, Henrik Cavling, and Viggo Horup, from Svend Thorsen's *Newspapers in Denmark*)

E. P. Dutton, Inc., New York, and Allen and Unwin, Ltd., London (Front page of *La Libre Belgique* from Jean Massart's *The Secret Press in Belgium*)

Folke Dahl, author, University of Lund, Sweden (Front page of *Nouvelles Ordinairies* from Folke Dahl's *Les Debuts de la Presse Française*)

The author also acknowledges with gratitude the assistance of the following who provided photographs:

E. V. Matthewman, managing editor, *Daily Mail* (London *Daily Mail* leader page attacking Lord Kitchener and photo of Alfred Harmsworth)

Folke Anderberg, executive vice-president, *Stockholms Tidningen* and *Aftonbladet* (Lars Hierta and Hjalmar Branting)

Eilis Andreasson, *Handels och Sjofarts Tidning*, Göteborg (Torgny Segerstedt)

Sven Gerentz, president of *Svenska Dagbladet*, Stockholm (C. G. Tengwall)

457

For great assistance in obtaining pictures of Swedish history makers the author is indebted to Ivar Hallvig, president, and Arne Nygren, assistant director of the Swedish Newspaper Publishers Association, Stockholm.

Aatos Erkko, publisher of *Helsingin Sanomat*, Helsinki (Eljas Erkko)

Marcel Stijns, editor, *Het Laatste Nieuws*, Brussels, and honorary president of International Federation of Journalists (Victor Jourdain)

M. Louis Gabriel-Robinet, editor, *Figaro*, Paris (Pierre Brisson)

International Press Institute Report (Oskar Pollak)

Urs Schwarz, editor, *Neue Zürcher Zeitung* (Paul Usteri)

Alfio Russo, editor, *Corriere della Sera*, Milan (Luigi Albertini)

Mme. H. Loundra, his daughter, publisher of *Kathimerini*, Athens (George Vlachos)

Joaquín Lumbreras, Minister of Information, Madrid (Manuel de Fraga Iribane)

The front pages of *Pravda* and *Borba Trybuna Ludu* and the front page of *Völkischer Beobachter*, Hitler's paper, were reproduced from originals in the files of the author or of the Northwestern University Library.

Index